MODERNIST CUISINE
The Art and Science of Cooking

Nathan Myhrvold
with Chris Young
and Maxime Bilet

Photography by
Ryan Matthew Smith
and Nathan Myhrvold

Modernist Cuisine
The Art and Science of Cooking

Volume 6
Kitchen Manual

The Cooking Lab

Copyright © 2011 by The Cooking Lab, LLC

All rights reserved. Except as permitted under the U.S. Copyright Act of 1976, no part of this publication may be reproduced, distributed, or transmitted in any form or by any means, or stored in a database or retrieval system, without the prior written permission of the publisher. All trademarks used are property of their respective owners.

The Cooking Lab
3150 139th Ave SE
Bellevue, WA 98005
www.modernistcuisine.com

ISBN: 978-0-9827610-0-7
First edition, 2011

Library of Congress Cataloging-in-Publication Data available upon request

Printed in China

TABLE OF CONTENTS

CHAPTER 8: COOKING IN MODERN OVENS — 2
- How to Make Bacon and Eggs in a Combi Oven ... 2
- Cantonese Fried Rice ... 2
- How to Roast a Chicken in a Combi Oven ... 3
- Combi Oven Roast Chicken ... 3
- Combi Oven Rib Eye ... 4
- Roast Pigeon Crown ... 4
- Combi Oven–Steamed Broccoli ... 5

CHAPTER 10: THE MODERNIST KITCHEN — 6
- Best Bets for Stocks ... 6
- Best Bets for Stock Aromatics ... 8
- Spiced Shellfish Stock ... 9
- Paella Stock ... 9
- Triple Dungeness Crab and Pork Stock Infusion ... 10
- Brown Beef Stock ... 10
- Brown Veal Stock ... 11
- Pressure-Cooked White Chicken Stock ... 11
- Onion Stock ... 11
- How to Make Stock Sous Vide ... 12
- Sous Vide Fish Stock ... 12
- Sous Vide Vegetable Stock ... 13
- Best Bets for Broths ... 14
- Borscht Broth ... 14
- Hon Dashi ... 15
- Ham Broth ... 16
- Oxtail Pho Broth ... 16
- Duck Broth with Vanilla and Bay Leaf ... 16
- Laksa Broth ... 17
- Bouillabaisse Broth ... 17
- Bacon Dashi ... 18
- Tom Yum Broth ... 18
- Cured Ham Broth ... 18
- Baked Potato Broth ... 19
- Goulash Broth ... 19
- Mushroom Broth ... 19
- Best Bets for Infused Liquids ... 20
- Seasoning with Salt and Other Flavor Enhancers ... 21
- Sous Vide Ponzu ... 22
- Best Bets for Lowering pH ... 22
- Typical Acid Concentrations ... 23
- Seaweed Vinegar ... 23
- Elder Flower Vinegar ... 23
- Passion Fruit–White Soy Sauce Vinaigrette ... 23
- Constructed Red Wine Glaze ... 24
- Best Bets for Adding Flavor with Alcohol ... 24
- Clove Oil ... 25
- Cinnamon-Scented Pea Juice ... 25
- Condrieu Butter ... 25
- Glazed Carrot ... 25
- Marinated Spaghetti Squash ... 26
- How to Wash Citrus Oil ... 26
- Extracting Flavor with Alcohol ... 26
- Brown Butter Fumet ... 26
- Hazelnut Oil Extract ... 26
- Best Bets for Extracts ... 27
- House Bitters ... 27
- Fines Herbs Extract ... 27
- Best Bets for Infused Fats ... 28
- Shellfish Butter ... 29
- Sous Vide Lemon Herb Oil ... 29
- Spiced Chili Oil ... 29
- Molasses Butter ... 29
- Curry Oil ... 30
- Crab Oil ... 30
- Malaysian Aromatic Oil ... 30
- Additives to Preserve the Color and Flavor of Fresh Juice ... 31
- Meyer Lemonade ... 31
- Melon Water ... 31
- Pen Shell Clam, Pluot, Myoga, Scallop Mochi ... 32
- Sous Vide Berry Juice ... 32
- Strawberry Consommé ... 32
- Green Asparagus and Morels with Asparagus Jus ... 33
- Strawberry Gazpacho ... 33
- Best Bets for Jus ... 34
- Jus de la Presse ... 34
- Root Vegetable Jus ... 36
- Sous Vide Vegetable Jus ... 36
- Clam Juice ... 36
- Lamb Garlic Jus in a Jar ... 37
- Mushroom Jus ... 37
- Sous Vide Mussel Juice ... 37
- Toasted Oat Jus ... 38
- Banyuls Glaze ... 38
- Tagine Base ... 39
- Squash Glaze ... 39
- Sous Vide Prawn Jus ... 39
- Sous Vide Rare Beef Jus ... 40
- Sous Vide Beef Juice ... 40
- Centrifuged Carotene Butter ... 40
- Tomato Water ... 40
- Centrifuged Pea Juice ... 41
- Centrifuged Roasted-Hazelnut Oil ... 41
- Banana Yogurt ... 41
- Best Bets for Consommé ... 42
- Oyster Consommé ... 42
- Clarifying a Consommé ... 43
- Apple Cider Consommé ... 43
- Spring Garlic Consommé ... 44
- Bagna Càuda Consommé ... 44
- Pistachio Consommé ... 44
- Pot-au-Feu Consommé ... 45
- Oxtail Consommé ... 46
- Red Coleslaw ... 46
- How to Distill with a Rotavap ... 47
- Buddha's Hand Vodka ... 47
- Vacuum-Concentrated Apple and Cabbage Juice ... 47
- Mock Turtle Soup ... 48
- Indies Spice Blend ... 48
- Quatre Épices ... 48
- Chili Tomato Spice Blend ... 49

Page references of the form 4·381 refer to volume 4, page 381. Selected component recipes from the plated-dish recipes in volume 5 have been reprinted here. Each appears in the chapter for which it is most relevant.

MODERNIST CUISINE

- Memphis Rub 49
- Kansas Rub 49
- Chaat Masala 50
- Sweet Spice Blend 50
- Passion Fruit Granita 50
- Fish Spice Mix 51
- Pain d'Épices Powder 51
- Citrus Spice 52
- Licorice Powder 52
- Ras el Hanout 52
- Exotic Spice Mixture 53
- Pacojet Pea Soup 53
- Mozzarella Powder 53
- Frozen Cheddar-Cheese Powder 53
- How to Mill a Creamy Nut Butter 54
- Frozen Crème-Fraîche and Pine-Nut Cream 54
- Sour Rhubarb Sorbet 54
- Romesco Sauce 54
- Best Bets for Vegetable and Fruit Purees 55
- Broccoli and Hazelnut-Oil Puree 56
- Creamed Watercress 56
- Pistachio Puree 57
- Black Truffle Concentrate 57
- Celery Root Mousseline 57
- Best Bets for Freeze-Drying 58
- How to Use a Spray Dryer 59
- Spray-Dried Buttermilk 59
- Spray-Dried Blood Orange Juice 59
- Prefreezing Temperatures for Freeze-Dried Foods 59
- Freeze-Dried Beef Gravy Granules 60
- Salted, Freeze-Dried Lobster 60
- Ramen Vegetables 61
- Ramen Stock Powder 61
- How to Carbonate Fruit with Dry Ice 62
- Strawberry Milk Shake 62
- Orange Soda 62
- Carbonated Golden Raisins 63
- Shigoku Oyster with Fizzy Grapes, Fresh Wasabi, and Miso Powder 63

CHAPTER 11: MEAT AND SEAFOOD   64

- Best Bets for Tartares 64
- Hanger Steak Tartare 65
- Beef and Oyster Tartare 65
- Scallop Tartare 66
- Salmon Tartare Cornets 67
- Best Bets for Cooking Tender Meats Sous Vide 68
- Rack of Lamb 68
- Pork Tenderloin with Juniper 69
- Venison Loin Rossini 69
- Rib Eye with Cherry Mustard Marmalade and Porcini 70
- Sous Vide Rabbit Loin 70
- Best Bets for Cooking Tender Red Poultry Sous Vide 71
- Best Bets for Cooking Tender White Poultry Sous Vide 71
- Poulet au Feu d'Enfer 72
- Pigeon with Shellfish Butter 72
- Quail with Apple-Vinegar Emulsion and Water Chestnuts 73
- Best Bets for Cooking Fish Sous Vide 74
- Ling Cod with Bergamot-Infused Milk 75
- Escolar with Red Wine Butter 75
- Turbot with Onion and Marrow Broth 76
- Black Cod 76
- Steelhead Trout Confit with Fennel Salad 77
- Sous Vide Monkfish Pavé 77
- Sous Vide Snapper 78
- Sous Vide Salmon 78
- Skate Pavé with Bread Crust 78
- Best Bets for Cooking Tender Shellfish Sous Vide 79
- Sous Vide Mussels 79
- 19th-Century-Style Lobster with Sherry and Cocoa 80
- Shrimp Cocktail 80
- Oyster Escabeche 81
- Steamed Live Spot Prawn 81
- Poached Lobster Tail 81
- Best Bets for Cooking Tough Poultry 82
- Sous Vide Duck Confit Pavé 82
- Sous Vide Guinea Hen 83
- Best Bets for Cooking Tough Shellfish 83
- Sous Vide Braised Snails 83
- Squid Sicilian Lifeguard-Style 84
- Abalone and Foie Gras Shabu-Shabu with Yuba and Enoki 84
- Razor Clam with Sauce Verte 85
- Sous Vide Octopus 85
- Best Bets for Cooking Tough Cuts 86
- Suckling Pig Shoulder with Shallot and Orange Sauce 87
- Crispy Duck Tongues 87
- Beef Shank Rillette 87
- Sous Vide Pork Belly 88
- Braised Lamb Shoulder 88
- Beef Brisket 88
- Pork Ribs 88
- Pulled Pork Shoulder 89
- Braised Veal Foreshank 89
- American Wagyu Beef Cheek 89
- Rare Flatiron Steak 89
- Braised Short Ribs 90
- Sous Vide Veal Tongue 90
- Beef Short Ribs 90
- Glazed Oxtail 90
- How to Pressure-Cook Tough Cuts for Quick Results 91
- Sous Vide and Pressure-Cooked Veal Breast with Bulbous Vegetables 91
- Pressure-Cooked Carnitas 92
- Microwaved Tilapia with Scallions and Ginger 92
- How to Puff the Skin on a Pork Roast 93
- Ultracrisp Chicken Crown 93
- Pork Loin Roast 94
- Puffed Cockscomb 94
- Monkfish with Constructed Skin 95
- Puffed Salmon Skin Pillows 95
- Puffed Chicken Feet 95
- Best Bets for Cooking Tough Offal Sous Vide 96
- Best Bets for Cooking Tender Organ Meats Sous Vide 96
- Sous Vide Foie Gras 96
- Ankimo Torchon 97
- Sweetbreads with Sour Mango Powder and Shiitake 97

Foie Gras and Button Mushroom Tart	98
Sous Vide Pigeon Offal	98
Foie Gras Soup with Bomba Rice and Sea Lettuce	99
Sous Vide Veal Sweetbreads	99
Crispy Sweetbreads	100
Best Bets for Brines	101
Best Bets for Wet Cures	102
Best Bets for Dry Rubs	102
Best Bets for Brining	103
Best Bets for Curing	103
Foie Gras Torchon	104
Foie Gras Parfait	104
Bacon Chip	104
Shaved Foie Gras	105
Duck Leg Confit with Pommes Sarladaises	105
Confit Cure Mix	106
Miso-Cured Black Cod	106
Grapefruit-Cured Salmon	107
House-Cured Bacon	107
Microwaved Beef Jerky	108
Crispy Beef Strands	108
Crispy Beef and Shallot Salad	108
Juniper Brine	109
Sous Vide Duck Ham	109
Foie Gras and Hazelnut Ganache	109
Fluke Cured in Kombu	110
Blackstrap Molasses Country Ham	110
Cured Beef Tenderloin "Bresaola Style"	111
Sea Urchin Bottarga	111
Salted Halibut	112
Halibut Brandade	112
Seafood Paper	113
Bacon Chips with Butterscotch, Apple, and Thyme	113
Kalbi Flank Steak	114
Lutefisk	114
Yakitori	115
Tuna Ribbons with Ginger Marinade	116
Fluke Ceviche	117
Chicken Tikka Masala	118
Gong Bao Chicken	119
Beet Juice–Fed Oysters	119
Best Bets for Smoking Meats	120
Russian Smoked Salmon	121
Beef Cheek Pastrami	121
Hay-Smoked Chicken Crown	122
Smoked Pork Cheek	122
Heather-Smoked Sturgeon	122
Smoked Octopus	123
Best Bets for Burgers	123
Best Bets for Coarse-Ground Sausages	124
Farce Royale	126
Toulousain Garlic Sausage	126
Green Garlic and Pork Sausage	127
Best Bets for Emulsion-Style Sausages	128
Italian Sausage	130
Frankfurter	130
Boudin Blanc	131
Best Bets for Fermented Sausages	132

Saucisson Sec	134
Fermented Shrimp Sheets	134
Fast-Cured Pepperoni	135
Coarse Fat-Gel Sausage	136
Emulsified Sausage with Fat Gel	136
Low-Fat Chicken Sausage	136
Rare Beef Sausage	137
Fried Chicken Sausage	137

CHAPTER 12: PLANT FOODS 138

Best Bets for Cooking Fruits Sous Vide Until Tender	138
Sous Vide Baby Beet Salad	138
Sous Vide Glazed Pearl Onion	138
Best Bets for Cooking Vegetables Sous Vide Until Tender	139
Sous Vide Turnip	139
Glazed White Carrot	139
Braised Turnips with Saffron	140
Glazed Pearl Onion	140
Potato Salad	140
Fresh Bean Salad	141
Sweet-and-Sour Cipolline Onion	141
Carrot and Dill Fricassee	141
Sous Vide Lentils	142
Sous Vide Green Asparagus	142
Sous Vide Artichoke	142
Best Bets for Cooking Vegetables Sous Vide with Fat Until Tender	143
Chestnut Confit	143
Salsify Fondant	143
Sweet Potato Fondant	144
Lobster Mushroom Confit	144
Best Bets for Cooking Fruits or Vegetables Sous Vide for Purees	144
Salted Caramel Apple Puree	145
Tamarind Paste	145
Date Puree	145
Best Bets for Cooking Fruits Sous Vide in Sugar Syrup Until Tender	146
Pink Grapefruit Confit	146
Best Bets for Warming Vegetables Sous Vide	147
Red Wine Cabbage	147
Best Bets for Potato Purees	148
Potato Puree	148
Best Bets for Pressure-Cooking Plant Foods	149
Baked Beans	149
Pressure-Cooked Tarbais Beans	149
Caramelized Carrot Soup	150
Autoclaved Onion Soup	150
Crispy Boiled Peanuts	151
Pressure-Cooked Sesame Seeds	151
Potato Puree	151
Best Bets for Risotto	152
Steamed Sticky Rice	152
Risotto Milanese	153
Paella Rice	153
Sous Vide Clam and Oat Risotto	154
Pressure-Cooked Vegetable Risotto	154

Braised Pine Nuts with Winter Squash	155
Ragout of Grains	156
Root Vegetable Risotto	156
Best Bets for Microwaving Vegetables	157
Microwave-Fried Parsley	157
Tomato Powder	157
Artichoke and Potato Chaat	158
Sichuan Bok Choy	158
Best Bets for Naked Frying	159
Toasted Garlic Chips	159
Deep-Fried Brussels Sprouts	159
Pommes Pont-Neuf	160
Pectinase-Steeped Fries	160
Stir-Fried Fiddlehead Ferns	160
Starch-Infused Fries	161
Ultrasonic Fries	161
Starch-Infused Ultrasonic Fries	161
Best Bets for Fried Fruit and Vegetable Chips	162
Watermelon Chips	162
Restructured Potato Chips	162
Best Bets for Batters	163
Spot Prawn and Lotus Root Tempura with Smoked White Soy Sauce	164
Fried Pickles	164
Crispy Halibut Cheek	165
The Colonel's Fried Chicken	165
Modernist Fried Chicken	166
Oyster Beignet	166
Breading	167
Crispy Okra	167
Cromesquis	168
Fried Green Tomatoes	168
Corn Croquetta	169
Pork Trotter Beignet	169
Onion Rings	170
Razor Clam "Takoyaki"	171
Crispy Corn Pudding	172
Salting, Pickling, and Fermenting	173
Preserved Pear in Mustard Oil	173
Preserved Lemons	174
Pickled Garlic	174
Pickled Tapioca Pearl	174
Kimchi	175
Watermelon Rind Kimchi	175
Nukazuke	175
Sous Vide Cucumber Pickles	176
Garlic Confit	176
Aromatic Alsatian Mustard	176
Sauerkraut	177
Braised Sauerkraut	177
Pickled Figs	177
Compressed Dill-Pickled Vegetables	178
Pickled Jerusalem Artichokes	178
Pickled Ramps	178
Pickled Lemon	179
Pickled Celery Root	179
Tomato Confit	179
Pickled Bing Cherry	180

Green Papaya Pickle	180
Pickled Butternut Squash	180
Crispy Dosa	181
Yuzu and Kumquat Marmalade	181
Enzyme-Treated Pink Grapefruit	182
Best Bets for Preservation	182
Best Bets for Heat-Treated Fruit	183
Best Bets for Smoked Plant Foods	183
Smoked Potatoes with Vin Jaune Sabayon	184
Smoked Potato Confit	184
Best Bets for Dehydration	185
Garlic Nougatine	185
Formulas for Dehydrating Produce	186
Green Pea Wafer	186
Crystallized Rose Petals	187
Spinach Paper	187
Mandarin Leather	187
Pineapple Glass	187
Best Bets for Freeze-Drying Plant Foods	188
Onion Sablé	188
Seared Strawberry	189
Caesar Salad	189
Freeze-Dried Onion Powder	189
Shrimp and Grits	190
Best Bets for Pasta Doughs	191
Herb-Embedded Pasta Veil	191
Spaghetti Carbonara	192
Mac and Cheese	192
Pad Thai	193
Pasta Marinara	193
Cocoa Tajarin	194
Ramen Noodles	194
Buckwheat Dough	194
Semolina Pasta	195
Best Bets for Compressing or Impregnating Produce	195
Smoked Lettuce	195
Curry-Impregnated Apple	196
Compressed Muscat Grapes	196
Compressed Melon Terrine	196
Watermelon Meat	197
Vegetable Coals	197
Pulled Mushroom	197
Squid-Ink Bean-Sprout Risotto	198
Frozen White "Truffle"	198
Clay Potatoes	199
Fossilized Salsify Branch	199

CHAPTER 13: THICKENERS — 200

Best Bets for Thickening with Natural Starch	200
Pregelatinized Starch Paste	200
Best Bets for Thickening with Modified Starch	201
Avocado Puree	201
Modernist Béchamel	202
Jerusalem Artichoke Pudding	202
Steamed Cod with Cod Roe Velouté	203
Smoked Pepper Puree	203
Caramelized Crème Fraîche	203
Pomegranate and Garum Jus	204

Turkey Wing	204
Thanksgiving Turkey Gravy	204
Heather-Smoked Sturgeon Rillettes	205
Crispy Goat's Milk Ricotta Dumpling	205
Marcona Almond Butter Paste	205
Malt Vinegar Powder	206
Bacon Powder Squares	206
Parmesan Nuggets	206
Spiced Ash	206
Vanilla Olive Oil Powder	207
Cashew Halvah	207
Almond Polenta	207
Edible Earth	208
Corn Pebbles	209
Best Bets for Thickening Hot Liquids	210
Best Bets for Thickening Cold Liquids	211
Ham Consommé with Melon Beads	211
Tomato Whey Broth	212
Truffle Jus	212
Beef Tenderloin with Jus de Roti	212
Olive Oil Spread	213
White Grape Syrup	213
XO Sauce	213
Caramelized Coconut Cream	214
Pressure-Cooked Polenta with Strawberry Marinara	214
Creamed Spinach	215
Warm Potato and Pistachio Pesto Salad	215
Aged Rare Beef Jus	216
Shiitake Marmalade	216
Maple Vinegar Gastrique	216
Mushroom Ketchup	217
Apricot and Jasmine Puree	217
Seaweed Tapenade	218
Tamarind Puree	218
South Carolina Barbecue Sauce	219
Kentucky Barbecue Sauce	219
North Carolina (Lexington-Style) Barbecue Sauce	219
House Barbecue Sauce	220
Kansas City Barbecue Sauce	220
Memphis Barbecue Sauce	221
North Carolina (Eastern Region) Barbecue Sauce	221
East Texas Barbecue Sauce	221
Mughal Curry Sauce	222
Pea Vine Salad	222
Muslim Curry Sauce	223
Green Mango and Cashew Salad	223
Goan Curry Sauce	224
Kerala Curry Sauce	224
Masala Curry Sauce	225
Red-Eye Gravy	225
Best Bets for Making Milks and Creams	226
Low-Fat "Cream"	226
Instant Crème Fraîche	227
Herbed Cheese Spread	227
Soy Milk	227
Toasted Rice Milk	228

Toasted Almond Milk	228
Horchata (Chufa Milk)	228
Lemon Strips	228
Best Bets for Edible Films	229
Crispy Cream Cheese	229
Spiced Honey Glass	230
Dried Cherry and Hazelnut Nougatine	230
Edible Wrappers	230
Onion Arlette	231
BBQ Caramels	231

CHAPTER 14: GELS   **232**

Best Bets for Cooking Whole Eggs	232
Liquid Center Duck Egg	232
Egg Blossom	232
Deviled Eggs	233
Custard Textures	233
Best Bets for Pickled and Preserved Eggs	234
Century Egg	234
Pickled Quail Eggs	234
Best Bets for Separated Egg Gels	235
Cauliflower Crème Anglaise	235
Eggs Benedict	236
Miso-Cured Egg Sheets	236
Parmesan Crème Brûlée	237
Sauce Allemande	237
Egg Salad Sandwich	238
Best Bets for Blended Egg Gels	239
Boudin Noir Custard	239
French Scrambled Eggs	240
Ham and Cheese Omelet	240
Asparagus Royale	241
Dashimaki Tamago	241
Pressure-Cooked Egg Toast	241
Chawanmushi	242
Boudin Noir Bread Pudding	242
Chorizo French Toast	243
Olive Marmalade	243
Omelet Base	243
Best Bets for Smoking Dairy and Eggs	244
Smoked Egg Crème Caramel	244
Pecorino with Truffle Honey on Cedar	244
Best Bets for Protein Curds	245
Cocoa Nib Curd	246
Goat Cheese Dumplings	246
Silken Tofu	246
Fresh Cheese Curds	247
Modernist Burrata	247
Goat Milk Ricotta	248
Firm Tofu	248
Mozzarella Balloons	249
Green Pea Yuba	249
Milk Skin with Grilled Salsify and Truffle Puree	250
Best Bets for Gelling with Transglutaminase (Activa)	252
Sour Cream Spaetzle	252
Salmon Custard	253
Edamame Sheets, King Crab, Cinnamon Dashi	254
Flourless Gnocchi	254

Deep-Fried Custard 255
Burmese Chickpea Tofu Laksa 255
Corn Bread 256
Corn Custard 256
Peanut "Tofu" 257
Idiazábal Gnocchi 258
Everything Bagel Broth 258
Dill Spheres 259
Squid Ink Fluid Gel 259
Best Bets for Cold Gels 260
Salt Gel 261
Two-Meter Parmesan Spaghetto 262
Long Island Iced Tea Gel Shot 262
Spiced Walnut Vinegar Gel 262
Cauliflower Panna Cotta 263
Knot Foie 264
Madeira Gelée 264
Chili Pearls 265
Guinness "Pâte de Fruit" 265
Olive Oil Noodles 266
Sea Urchin Tofu, Tokyo Negi, Sesame, Ponzu 266
Olive Oil Gummy Worms 267
Sherry Gel Cube 267
Sunny-Side Up "Eggs" 268
Best Bets for Firm Coating Gels 269
Foie Gras Parfait Spheres 270
Foie Gras Cherries 270
Halibut Cheek Gel Base 270
Crimini in Amber 271
Salmon Poached in Licorice 272
Foie Gras Torchon with Beet and Hibiscus Glaze 272
Halibut in Verbena Bubble 273
Best Bets for Hot Gels 274
Agar Carbonara 275
Gruyère Custard 275
Shellfish Custard 276
Bone Marrow Custard 276
Boeuf en Gelée 277
Fruit and Vegetable Acidities 278
Best Bets for Hot Fruit Gels 279
Hot Orange Gel 279
Hot Banana Gel 280
Hot Green Apple Gel 280
Hot Quince Gel 280
Quinoa and Idiazábal with Bonito Stock Veil 281
Dungeness Crab and Apple Roulade 281
Best Bets for Methylcellulose Gels 282
Properties and Applications of Cellulose Gums 282
Instant Tofu Noodles 283
Potato Beignets with Caviar 283
Sweet Pea Clusters 284
Mackerel with Spicy Tomato Skin 284
Best Bets for Fluid Gels 285
Passion Fruit Brown Butter Fluid Gel 286
Hot and Cold Tea 286
Passion Fruit Jelly 287
Popcorn Pudding 287
Lemon Egg-Yolk Fluid Gel 287
Parmesan "Polenta" 288
Onion Fluid Gel 288

Confit Egg Yolk Puree 288
Umami Seasoning Fluid Gel 289
Fizzy Grape Fluid Gel 289
Best Bets for Spherification 290
Carbonated Mojito Spheres 291
Melon Caviar 291
"Poached" Egg 292
Tomato Spheres with Basil Oil 292
Gruyère Spheres 293
Caper Droplets 293
Mussels in Mussel Juice Spheres 294
Liquid Pimento Olive 294
Prosciutto and Melon "Raw Egg" 295

CHAPTER 15: EMULSIONS 296
Ultrastable Beurre Blanc 296
Poached Lobster 296
Beet Flexicurd 296
Sea Urchin Butter 297
Oyster Butter Emulsion 297
Black Butter Emulsion 297
Broiled Tuna Belly with Montpellier Butter 298
Blood Pudding Custard 298
Best Bets for Constructed Cheeses 299
Constructed Veal Cream 300
The American Cheese Slice 300
Cheese in a Tube 300
Cheesy Whip 301
Cheddar Soup 301
Rémoulade Sauce 302
White Coleslaw 302
Sea Urchin Tartar Sauce 303
Basic Mayonnaise 303
Hot Egg Mayonnaise 303
Soft-Boiled Egg and Garlic Emulsion 304
Sous Vide Lemon Curd 304
Bacon Jam 304
Deep-Fried Hollandaise 305
Sous Vide Instant Hollandaise 305
Black Olive Puree 306
Thickened Oil 306
Invincible Vinaigrette 306
Spot Prawns with Foie Gras Nage 307
Eggless Citrus Curd 307
Mustard Vinaigrette 308
Sauce Vin Jaune 308
Eggless Mayonnaise 309
Spice Mix Emulsion 309
Olive Oil "Margarine" 309
Pistachio Gelato 310
Hazelnut "Cream" 310
Jus Gras 310
Chilled Chicken-Noodle Soup 311
Ginger Cola 311

CHAPTER 16: FOAMS 312
Best Bets for Airs, Bubbles, and Froths 312
Citrus Air 312
Oysters with Mignonette Air 313
Parsley Foam 313

Kanpachi Sashimi with Citrus Foam	313
Geoduck with Seawater Foam	314
Edible Soap Bar with Honey Bubbles	314
Saffron Honey Foam	314
Lychee and Lime Soda	315
Tomato Vinegar Foam	315
Cappuccino Foam	315
Best Bets for Light Foams	316
Horchata Foam	316
Whipped Cheese	317
Blood Orange Foam	317
Milk Foam	317
Lemon Verbena and Peach Froth	318
Corn Foam	318
Blood Orange Sabayon	318
Sous Vide Sole with Bergamot Sabayon	319
Coconut-Lobster Emulsion	319
Mushroom and Bacon Cappuccino	320
Poached Apple with Pecorino Foam	320
Grapefruit and Black Pepper	321
Best Bets for Thick, Fine-Textured Foams	322
Chocolate Chantilly	322
Instant Swiss Meringue	323
Eggplant Foam	324
Baked Potato Foam	324
Hot Butter Foam	324
Coconut Chutney Foam	325
Suet Mousseline (Thick)	325
Dairy-Free Whipped Cream	326
Cauliflower Foam	326
Fried Egg Foam	326
Horseradish Foam	327
Oysters with Cava Foam	327
Barbecued Eel with Whipped Caramel	327
Uni with Whipped Tofu and Tapioca	328
Chestnut Cream	328
Whipped Butter	329
Yogurt Foam and Sweet Potato Chips	329
Best Bets for Set Foams	330
Passion Fruit Marshmallow with Chorizo Powder	332
Cryopoached Green Tea Sour	332
Whipped Yogurt Crisps	333
Green Tea Cake	333
Microwaved Pistachio Sponge Cake	333
Hot Apricot Marshmallow	334
Hamburger Bun	334
Beet Meringue	335
Steamed Blancmange	335
Chestnut Puffs	336
Buttermilk Biscuits	336
Rye Bread	337
Moroccan Batbout Flatbread	338
Siphoned Soufflé à la Lorraine	338
Green Olive Meringue	339
Soy Sauce Cloud	339
Freeze-Dried Carrot Foam	340
Gruyère Soufflé	340
Zucchini Blossom Beignets	341
Pâte à Choux	341
Best Bets for Puffed Snacks	342

Pommes Soufflées	342
Tapioca Starch Cracker	343
Black Sesame Rice Crisps	343
Rice Crisp	343
Puffed Chickpeas	344
Puffed Crab Cracker	344
Cheese Puffs	344
Socarrat Tuile	345
Candied Puffed Oats	345
Scallop Mochi	345
Gremolata Crisp	346
Aerated Mango Sorbet	347
Edible Prune Coals	347
Aerated Foie Gras	348
Aerated Gruyère	348
Aerated Coffee Ice Cream	349
Aerated Chocolate	349

CHAPTER 18: COFFEE   **350**

Coffee Butter	350
Stable Latte Foam	350

REFERENCE TABLES   **352**

Converting Temperature	352
Converting Grams to Volume for Common Ingredients	354
Converting Weights	354
Common Conversion Factors	356
Converting Volume Measures	357
Water Content of Typical Foods	358
Fat Content of Typical Foods	361
Volumetric Equivalents for Amounts of Typical Foods	362

HOW TO MAKE BACON AND EGGS IN A COMBI OVEN

FOR THE BACON:

① Assemble two sheet trays and two silicone mats for each batch of bacon.

② Slice the bacon to 1½ mm / ⅝ in thick. Partially freezing the bacon before slicing may make this step easier and more precise.

③ Arrange the sliced bacon on the trays in an even layer. Place a second silicon mat on top of the bacon and top it with a second baking sheet to hold the slices flat.

④ Cook in a combi oven at 160 °C / 320 °F and 0% humidity until the bacon is brown and crisp, 20–30 min. If you prefer really dry bacon, remove the top tray and silicon mat, reduce the heat to 79 °C / 174 °F, and then dehydrate for another 20–30 min. The exact cooking time depends on the moisture content of the bacon. A sugar-based bacon cure browns quicker and needs a lower temperature.

FOR THE EGGS:

① Butter several 10 cm / 4 in baking rings and place them on a very flat baking sheet lined with a silicon mat. Alternatively, use the Rational baking tray designed for cooking eggs (see page 2·166).

② Place one egg white in each buttered ring, reserving yolks.

③ Cook the egg whites in a preheated combi oven at 79 °C / 174 °F and 90% humidity for 15 min.

④ Reduce the oven temperature to 63 °C / 145 °F. You may need to leave the door open a bit to cool the oven down. Check oven temperature (via temperature probe or by pressing the temperature-control button) to verify that it is at the proper temperature before going on to the next step.

⑤ Place a single egg yolk in the center of each egg white and cook for 25 min.

⑥ Unmold the "fried" eggs and serve.

CANTONESE FRIED RICE

Yields 1.2 kg

INGREDIENT	QUANTITY	SCALING	PROCEDURE
Chicken fat, rendered, see page 3·116	56 g	7%	① Preheat oven to 245 °C / 475 °F.
			② Add fat to nonstick roasting pan, and let heat.
Shiitake mushroom, thinly sliced	80 g	10%	③ Add mushrooms, followed by sausage, and oven-fry until mushrooms soften and sausages blister, about 5 min.
Chinese sausage, thinly sliced	80 g	10%	
Jasmine rice, cooked and cooled	800 g	100%	④ Add, stir to evenly distribute other ingredients into rice.
			⑤ Oven-fry for 3 min.
Garlic chives, cut into 5 cm / 2 in lengths	80 g	10%	⑥ Add, stir to distribute evenly, and oven-fry for about 30 s.
Scallions, white only, fine julienne	40 g	5%	
Red Thai chili, seeded and cut in fine julienne	2 g	0.25%	
English peas, shucked and blanched (frozen peas work)	80 g	10%	⑦ Fold into rice and oven-fry for about 2 min.
			⑧ Remove rice mixture from oven, leaving heat on.
Duck egg, beaten	160 g (four eggs)	20%	⑨ Make a well in the middle of the fried rice.
			⑩ Return rice mixture to 245 °C / 475 °F oven to heat.
			⑪ Add egg, and allow to cook until just coagulated, about 1½ min.
			⑫ Remove fried rice from oven.
White soy sauce	32 g	4%	⑬ Combine liquids and stir into fried rice evenly to season.
			⑭ Check seasoning and serve.
Dark soy sauce	24 g	3%	
Mushroom soy sauce	12 g	1.5%	
Toasted sesame oil	1.5 g	0.4%	

from page 2·176

Note that this recipe can be made in a CVap oven just as well. Be sure to vent heat from the oven in step 4, and wait until the temperature stabilizes, about 5–10 min.

HOW TO ROAST A CHICKEN IN A COMBI OVEN

① Make brines. Whisk together 200 g of water with 16 g of salt until dissolved to make 8% brine. Repeat with 200 g of water and 10 g of salt to make a 5% brine. Reserve.

② Separate the skin from the meat. Wearing gloves, work your fingers under the skin to detach it from the surface of the meat over the entire body of the chicken. Be very careful not to tear the skin.

③ Inject the breast meat with an 8% salt brine.

④ Fill the syringe with brine equal to 10% of the weight of the bird. For a 1 kg bird, for example, use 100 g of brine.

⑤ Hang the chicken by its legs in the refrigerator for 48 h. The brine will diffuse fully, and the skin will dry out. Just before cooking, inject the breast again, this time with the 5% salt brine. Use an amount of brine equal to 5% of the weight of the bird.

⑥ Cook at 62 °C / 144 °F and 0% humidity until the core temperature of the breast meat is 60 °C / 140 °F, about 4 h. Cook the bird hanging in the oven above a drip tray.

⑦ Remove from the oven, and hang at room temperature for 45 min. Resting will help the meat retain its juices when it is cut (for details, see page 3·84).

⑧ Brush chicken evenly with clarified butter or neutral frying oil.

⑨ Cook at 285 °C / 550 °F and 0% humidity until the skin is brown and crisp, about 7 min.

⑩ As an alternative to air-drying in a refrigerator for three days, put the chicken in a blast chiller for 2–4 h on the chill (not freeze) setting. The air-drying step can also be omitted—the first cooking step may take a bit longer, and the skin will not be quite as crispy, but it will still be much crispier than when roasted conventionally.

⑪ Holding the core temperature of the bird at 55–60 °C / 130–140 °F for about 2 h effectively pasteurizes the meat. For more on pasteurization times for poultry, see page 1·181.

COMBI OVEN ROAST CHICKEN

Yields 650 g

INGREDIENT	QUANTITY	SCALING
Whole chicken	2.0 kg	100%
Water	200 g	10%
Salt	16 g	0.8%
Water	200 g	10%
Salt	10 g	0.5%
Frying oil or clarified unsalted butter	as needed	

from page 2·178

PROGRAM

STAGE	TEMPERATURE	HUMIDITY	COMMAND
1			① Preheat oven to 62 °C / 144 °F.
2	62 °C / 144 °F	0%	② Roast to core temperature of 60 °C / 140 °F, about 4 h.
3			③ Remove chicken, and let rest 45 min.
4	285 °C / 550 °F	0%	④ Brush chicken with oil.
			⑤ When oven has reached temperature, place chicken in oven, and sear for 7 min.

COMBI OVEN RIB EYE

Yields 900 g

INGREDIENT	QUANTITY	SCALING	PROCEDURE
Beef rib eye, bone in	900 g	100%	① Brush rib eye with butter.
Unsalted butter, melted	as needed		② Place meat on perforated rack, and begin program.
Salt	to taste		③ After stage 5, brush with more butter.

from page 2·180

PROGRAM

STAGE	TEMP	HUMIDITY	COMMAND
1	55 °C / 131 °F	100%	④ Preheat oven to 55 °C / 131 °F in steam mode.
2	55 °C / 131 °F	100%	⑤ Steam until core temperature reaches 54 °C / 129 °F, about 1 h.
3	55 °C / 131 °F	0%	⑥ Dry for 5 min.
4	58 °C / 136 °F	0%	⑦ Dry for 5 min.
5	61 °C / 142 °F	0%	⑧ Dry for 15 min.
6			⑨ Remove steak from oven.
7	300 °C / 575 °F	0%	⑩ Preheat oven until it reaches temperature, about 10 min.
8	300 °C / 575 °F	0%	⑪ Sear for 2 min.
			⑫ Turn and sear another 2 min.

This cooking program uses 25 min of drying to prepare the surface for searing. During the drying steps, the temperature is increased, but the humidity is decreased so that the wet-bulb temperature does not exceed the cooking temperature. The temperature is increased in stages to give the oven time to get rid of the extra humidity.

The temperatures at left are for what we judge to be a medium-rare steak. The temperatures can be adjusted for other levels of doneness by using the table below.

STAGE	RARE	MEDIUM RARE	MEDIUM
1	51 °C / 124 °F with 100% humidity to core of 50 °C / 122 °F	55 °C / 131 °F with 100% humidity to core of 54 °C / 129 °F	60 °C / 140 °F with 100% humidity to core of 58 °C / 136 °F
2	51 °C / 124 °F with 0% humidity for 5 min	55 °C / 131 °F with 0% humidity for 5 min	60 °C / 140 °F with 0% humidity for 5 min
3	53 °C / 127 °F with 0% humidity for 5 min	58 °C / 136 °F with 0% humidity for 5 min	63 °C / 145 °F with 0% humidity for 5 min
4	56 °C / 133 °F with 0% humidity for 15 min	61 °C / 142 °F with 0% humidity for 15 min	66 °C / 151 °F with 0% humidity for 15 min

ROAST PIGEON CROWN

Yields 800 g

INGREDIENT	QUANTITY	SCALING	PROCEDURE
Pigeon crown	600 g	100%	① Remove skin in one piece, making sure to remove skin around arm and shoulder.
			② Cut out shape from still-cold skin to fit over crown, using actual crown as template.
Farce royale see page 126	200 g	33%	③ Dust farce sheet with Activa, and place over crown.
			④ Pull skin over crown.
Activa RM or GS	as needed		⑤ Wrap crown tightly in plastic wrap, and vacuum seal.
			⑥ Place on small baking sheet in vacuum machine, and pull full vacuum to collapse any residual air pockets.
			⑦ Refrigerate for 6 h to allow enzyme to bind proteins.
Duck fat	as needed		⑧ Sear prepared pigeon crown in dry, hot nonstick pan, rotating and applying pressure to brown evenly, about 5 min.
Salt	to taste		⑨ Brush with duck fat, and season with salt.
			⑩ Bake in 65 °C / 150 °F oven for 40 min.
			⑪ Carve breasts off crown, and cut into slices 1 cm / ⅜ in thick.
Toasted oat jus, warmed see page 38	200 g	27%	⑫ Serve with jus.

from page 5·132

COMBI OVEN–STEAMED BROCCOLI

Yields 1.5 kg

INGREDIENT	QUANTITY	SCALING	PROCEDURE
Rice vinegar	100 g	10%	① Whisk together to make pickling brine.
Sherry vinegar	100 g	10%	② Bring to simmer.
Water	64 g	6.4%	③ Reserve.
Sugar	28 g	2.8%	
Salt	3 g	0.3%	
Broccoli stems, peeled and thinly sliced	40 g	4%	④ Combine.
			⑤ Pour warm brine over broccoli-stem mixture to pickle.
Shallots, thinly sliced	28 g	2.8%	⑥ Cool completely.
Currants	18 g	1.8%	⑦ Reserve.
Broccoli florets	1 kg	100%	⑧ Arrange florets in one layer in combi oven steam basket.
			⑨ Steam at 90 °C / 195 °F and 100% humidity for 8 min, or until desired texture is achieved.
Broccoli, small florets	200 g	20%	⑩ Toss small florets in oil, and place on baking sheet.
Frying oil	50 g	5%	⑪ Oven-fry in combi oven at 270 °C / 520 °F and 0% humidity for 4 min.
			⑫ Drain.
Salt	to taste		⑬ Season steamed and fried broccoli.
Pickling brine, from above	to taste		⑭ Strain reserved pickled mixture, reserving brine.
			⑮ Toss steamed and fried broccoli with pickles, brine, pumpkin seeds, and chili oil.
Toasted pumpkin seeds	50 g	5%	
Chili oil see page 29	30 g	3%	
Salted lardo, frozen and very thinly sliced	100 g	10%	⑯ Drape over warm broccoli mix, and serve.

from page 2·181

STOCKS

① Weigh cold water. Scale all other ingredients relative to the water weight. For every 1 kg of water, for example, use 200 g of chicken wings and 750 g of ground chicken meat for chicken stock. Although the amount of water used is the biggest factor in the yield, the moisture of the ingredients used, the cooking time, and the cooking method all affect the yield.

② Mix vegetables and aromatics. See Best Bets for Stock Aromatics on page 8 for our recommendations.

③ Add stock ingredients and water. See the Best Bets for Stocks table below for our recommendations. You can use more or less water than indicated depending on the purpose of your stock.

④ Cook. The table lists suggested cooking methods, times, and temperatures. If pressure-cooking, set the pressure shown on the gauge to 1 bar / 15 psi. Vacuum seal ingredients before cooking sous vide.

⑤ Rest until pressure cooker has depressurized, about 20 min. Strain.

VARIATION: WHITE STOCK

① Follow steps 1 and 2 at left.
② Blanch bones. Cover the bones in cold water, and bring to a boil.
③ Sweat stock ingredients and aromatics in fat. See the Best Bets for Stocks table below for recommended ingredients.
④ Follow steps 3–5 at left.

Best Bets for Stocks

Stock	Fat	(scaling)	Bone	(scaling)	Meat	(scaling)	Liquid	(scaling)
chicken, duck, or pigeon	frying oil	8%	wings	40%	ground chicken	75%	water	100%
beef	suet	5%	calf's foot, split	20%	ground beef	80%	water	100%
							red wine (for brown stock only)	10%
veal	frying oil	5%	veal knuckle	50%	ground veal	25%	water	100%
							Madeira	15%
lamb	frying oil	5%	lamb shoulder and neck	35%	ground lamb	100%	water	100%
pork	frying oil	7.5%	pork ribs	50%	ground pork	50%	water	100%
							white port (dry)	8%
shellfish	clarified unsalted butter	5%	lobster, shrimp, or crab shells and heads	65%	squid or scallop meat (optional)	20%	water	100%
							dry vermouth	15%
vegetable	vegetable oil	5%	n/a		n/a		water	100%
fish	olive oil	10%	fish bones	100%	n/a		water	100%
							white wine	10%
Chinese banquet			pork ribs	20%	cured ham, thinly sliced	10%	water	100%
			duck wings	20%			Shaoxing wine	5%
			chicken wings	15%				
Chinese everyday			chicken carcass	30%	ground pork	40%	water	100%
Japanese			chicken carcass	24%	ground pork shoulder	8%	water	100%
			chicken feet	6%				
			pork trotter	12%				
Thai			chicken wings	20%	ground pork	35%	water	100%
			pork ribs	12%			coconut water	40%

from page 2·296

VARIATION: SHELLFISH STOCK

① Follow steps 1 and 2 in Stocks, previous page.
② Sauté shellfish, aromatics, and tomato paste in fat on stove top. See the table below for recommended ingredients.
③ Follow steps 3–5 in Stocks.

VARIATION: RICH BROWN STOCK

① Weigh water.
② Roast meat, bones, and vegetables. Cook at 190 °C / 375 °F for the time indicated in the table at left. Add tomato paste if desired.
③ Deglaze roasting pan. Use wine or water.
④ Combine aromatics with roasted ingredients.
⑤ Follow steps 3–5 in Stocks, previous page.

Preparation (brown stock only)	(h)	Cook	(h)	(°C)	(°F)
roast meat and bones	½	pressure-cook	1½	n/a	n/a
roast meat and bones	1	pressure-cook	2½	n/a	n/a
roast meat	¾	pressure-cook	2½	n/a	n/a
roast meat	1	pressure-cook	1½	n/a	n/a
roast meat and bones	1	pressure-cook	2	n/a	n/a
fry shells with tomato paste until golden brown	10 min	cook sous vide	¾	88	190
sauté sliced vegetables until golden brown	1	cook sous vide	3	85	185
roast bones	20 min	cook sous vide	1¼	88	190
		pressure-cook	2	n/a	n/a
		pressure-cook	1¼	n/a	n/a
		cook sous vide	1¼	90	194
		pressure-cook	1½	n/a	n/a

Best Bets for Stock Aromatics

Stock	Vegetable	(scaling)*	Herb	(scaling)*	Spice	(scaling)*
vegetable	onion	33%	parsley	0.75%	black peppercorns	0.1%
	carrot	25%	bay leaf	0.01%	coriander seed	0.2%
	leek	8%	thyme	0.10%	star anise	0.2%
	tomato, peeled and seeded	8%	chive	1.00%		
	celery	5%				
	mushroom	5%				
poultry	onion	6%	parsley	0.50%	black peppercorns	0.1%
	carrot	5%			garlic	1%
	leek	5%				
meat, beef	onion	10%	thyme	0.8%	star anise	0.05%
	carrot	10%	rosemary	0.15%	garlic	1%
	celery	2%				
	tomato paste (for brown stock)	5%				
game, lamb	onion	7%	bay leaf	0.01%	star anise	1.5%
	carrot	7%	thyme	1.00%	garlic	2%
	celery	2%	sage	0.20%	black peppercorns	0.2%
shellfish	carrot	5%	parsley	0.25%	fennel seed	0.01%
	onion	5%	thyme	0.10%	saffron	0.005%
	leek	2%	basil	0.20%		
	fennel	2%				
	button mushroom	2%				
	tomato paste (for brown stock)	5%				
fish	carrot	33%	n/a		garlic	2%
	onion	26%			coriander seed	0.3%
	leek	13%			star anise	0.2%
	fennel	13%				
	tomato paste (for brown stock)	5%				
Chinese banquet	scallion	0.2%	n/a		ginger	0.4%
					white peppercorns	0.01%
					cinnamon sticks	0.05%
Chinese everyday	scallion	1.2%	n/a		ginger	1%
Japanese	onion	3.5%	n/a		ginger	0.4%
	carrot	3.5%			garlic	0.75%
	scallion	1%			kombu	0.1%
					bonito flakes	5%
Thai	scallion	1%	cilantro stalks	0.20%	ginger	0.4%
	cabbage	1%	Thai basil	0.30%	garlic	0.5%
	fried shallot	4%	makrud lime leaf	0.40%		

from page 2·298 *(set weight of water to 100%)*

SPICED SHELLFISH STOCK

Yields 800 g

INGREDIENT	QUANTITY	SCALING	PROCEDURE
Chicken wings, chopped	500 g	33%	① Roast together in 230 °C / 450 °F oven until uniformly golden brown, about 25 min, and reserve.
Ground pork	500 g	33%	
Dungeness crab (whole)	1.5 kg (about three medium)	100%	② Crush crab shells and meat into smaller pieces.
			③ Fry in bottom of pressure cooker in oils until golden, about 8 min.
Grapeseed oil	150 g	10%	④ Remove crab pieces from oil, and reserve crab pieces and imbued oil.
Coconut oil	25 g	1.7%	
Leeks, thinly sliced	250 g	17%	⑤ Fry prepared vegetables together with reserved crab oil in pressure cooker until golden.
Carrots, peeled and thinly sliced	200 g	13.5%	
			⑥ Add tomato paste.
Green onions, thinly sliced	150 g	10%	⑦ Continue frying until mixture is amber and cooked tomato flavor develops, about 3 min.
Shallots, thinly sliced	150 g	10%	
Tomato paste	50 g	3.5%	
Water	1.5 kg	100%	⑧ Deglaze pressure cooker.
Carrot juice	100 g (from 250 g carrots)	7%	
Shaoxing wine	82.5 g	5.5%	
Star anise	1.8 g	0.12%	⑨ Combine, and place in sachet.
Black peppercorns	0.8 g	0.05%	⑩ Combine reserved pork and chicken mixture, vegetable mixture, and crab pieces in pressure cooker.
Grains of paradise	0.6 g	0.04%	
Coriander seeds	0.4 g	0.03%	
Cardamom pod	0.3 g	0.02%	⑪ Add sachet, and pressure-cook at gauge pressure of 1 bar / 15 psi for 1 h.
			⑫ Strain, and refrigerate until use.

from page 5·186

PAELLA STOCK

Yields 750 g

INGREDIENT	QUANTITY	SCALING	PROCEDURE
Rabbit trimmings	350 g	35%	① Brown in 190 °C / 375 °F oven until golden, about 25 min.
Rabbit carcass	335 g	34%	
Yellow onions, thinly sliced	125 g	12%	② Sweat onions until translucent, about 5 min.
Grapeseed oil	100 g	10%	
Tomatoes, peeled and seeded	100 g	10%	③ Add to onions, and sauté vegetable mixture until golden, about 7 min.
Carrots, thinly sliced	75 g	7.5%	
Leeks, thinly sliced	60 g	6%	
Fennel, thinly sliced	55 g	5.5%	
Piquillo peppers, thinly sliced	40 g	4%	
Pimentón de la Vera (sweet)	6 g	0.6%	
Thyme	2.25 g	0.2%	
Water	1 kg	100%	④ Combine in pressure cooker with browned rabbit pieces and vegetable mixture.
White chicken stock see page 11	550 g	55%	
			⑤ Pressure-cook at gauge pressure of 1 bar / 15 psi for 1 h.
			⑥ Cool.
			⑦ Strain through fine sieve.
			⑧ Refrigerate until use.

from page 5·240

TRIPLE DUNGENESS CRAB AND PORK STOCK INFUSION

Yields 850 g

INGREDIENT	QUANTITY	SCALING	PROCEDURE
Dungeness crab, chopped	1.35 kg	135%	① Panfry until golden brown, about 15 min.
Chicken wings, finely chopped	1 kg	100%	② Remove from pan, and reserve.
Ground pork	650 g	65%	
Grapeseed oil	315 g	31.5%	
Scallions, thinly sliced	400 g	40%	③ Add to pan used for meat, and sauté vegetables until lightly browned.
Carrots, peeled and thinly sliced	280 g	28%	
Leeks, thinly sliced	280 g	28%	
Fennel, thinly sliced	246 g	24.6%	
Shallots, thinly sliced	135 g	13.5%	
Tomato paste	50 g	5%	④ Add to vegetables, and continue to sauté until mixture is golden brown, about 4 min.
Sake	10 g	1%	⑤ Deglaze pan of vegetable mixture with sake.
Water	1 kg	100%	⑥ Add water and reserved browned crab, chicken, and pork mixture.
			⑦ Pressure-cook mixture at gauge pressure of 1 bar / 15 psi for 1 h.
			⑧ Cool, and then strain through fine sieve, yielding about 850 g of stock.
Star anise, lightly crushed	1 g	0.1%	⑨ Bring stock to boil, and remove from heat.
Cinnamon stick	0.4 g	0.04%	⑩ Add spices, and steep for 1 min.
Black peppercorns	0.3 g	0.03%	⑪ Strain through fine sieve.
Sugar	3 g	0.3%	⑫ Whisk sugar into stock infusion until dissolved.
			⑬ Cool, vacuum seal, and refrigerate until use.

from page 5·254

BROWN BEEF STOCK

Yields 650 g

INGREDIENT	QUANTITY	SCALING	PROCEDURE
Beef chuck, finely ground	200 g	40%	① Vacuum seal.
			② Cook sous vide in 90 °C / 194 °F bath until juices are released, about 1 h.
			③ Strain, reserving juice; discard meat.
			④ Cool beef juice, and reserve.
Oxtail, thinly sliced on a band saw	500 g	100%	⑤ Roast oxtail with suet in 190 °C / 375 °F oven until oxtail is brown, about 30 min.
Rendered beef suet	75 g	15%	⑥ Discard excess fat.
			⑦ Cool and reserve.
Water	500 g	100%	⑧ Combine in pressure cooker with beef juice and oxtail.
Red wine (full-bodied)	100 g	10%	⑨ Pressure-cook at gauge pressure of 1 bar / 15 psi for 2½ h.
Carrots, peeled and thinly sliced	50 g	10%	⑩ Strain.
Yellow onions, peeled and thinly sliced	50 g	10%	⑪ Cool.
Celery, peeled and thinly sliced	20 g	4%	⑫ Vacuum seal, and refrigerate until use.
Leeks, whites only, thinly sliced	20 g	4%	
Red port (dry)	20 g	4%	
Parsley leaves	10 g	2%	
Thyme	1 g	0.2%	
Bay leaf	0.5 g	0.1%	

from page 2·301

BROWN VEAL STOCK

Yields 650 g

INGREDIENT	QUANTITY	SCALING	PROCEDURE
Veal knuckle and neck bones, sawed into 5 cm / 2 in pieces, if possible	500 g	50%	① Cover with water. ② Bring to boil, skimming often. ③ Drain, discarding water.
Neutral oil	75 g	7.5%	④ Coat bones with oil. ⑤ Roast in 190 °C / 375 °F oven until golden brown, about 30 min. ⑥ Reserve bones, and discard excess oil.
Veal trimmings, finely ground	500 g	50%	⑦ Combine on nonstick baking sheet.
Neutral oil	50 g	5%	⑧ Roast in 190 °C / 375 °F oven until evenly brown, about 20 min. ⑨ Strain, and reserve meat.
Unsalted butter	15 g	1.5%	⑩ Melt butter in pressure cooker.
Sweet onions, peeled and thinly sliced	50 g	5%	⑪ Add vegetables to pressure cooker.
Carrots, peeled and thinly sliced	25 g	2.5%	⑫ Cook uncovered, stirring frequently, until moisture has evaporated and vegetables are tender, about 7 min.
Leek, thinly sliced	25 g	2.5%	
Tomato confit see page 179	40 g	4%	⑬ Add to pressure cooker, and increase heat to high. ⑭ Sauté vegetables and confit uncovered, stirring constantly until brown, about 4 min.
Water	1 kg	100%	⑮ Add to pressure cooker with bones and meat.
Vodka	20 g	2%	⑯ Pressure-cook mixture at gauge pressure of 1 bar / 15 psi for 2½ h.
Parsley leaves	3 g	0.3%	⑰ Cool.
Black peppercorns, crushed	1 g	0.1%	⑱ Strain. ⑲ Vacuum seal and refrigerate until use.

from page 2·300

PRESSURE-COOKED WHITE CHICKEN STOCK

Yields 400 g

INGREDIENT	QUANTITY	SCALING	PROCEDURE
Chicken wing meat and bones, chopped	350 g	70%	① Cover with cold water. ② Bring to boil, and then drain chicken immediately. Alternatively, for brown stock, roast wings and bones, and fry ground chicken until golden brown.
Water	500 g	100%	③ Combine with blanched chicken in pressure cooker.
Chicken thigh meat, finely ground	350 g	70%	
Sweet onions, peeled and thinly sliced	50 g	10%	④ Pressure-cook at gauge pressure of 1 bar / 15 psi for 1½ h.
Carrots, peeled and thinly sliced	25 g	5%	⑤ Strain through fine sieve.
Leeks, thinly sliced	25 g	5%	⑥ Cool.
Garlic, thinly sliced	5 g	1%	⑦ Vacuum seal, and refrigerate until use.
Parsley leaves and stems	1 g	0.2%	
Black peppercorns	0.5 g	0.1%	

from page 2·301

ONION STOCK

Yields 650 g

INGREDIENT	QUANTITY	SCALING	PROCEDURE
Sweet onions, thinly sliced	400 g	100%	① Sauté onions over medium-high heat, stirring frequently until golden, about 15 min.
Clarified unsalted butter	50 g	12.5%	
Water	500 g	125%	② Simmer with sautéed onions for 1 h.
Vermouth (dry)	30 g	7.5%	③ Strain. ④ Cool, and refrigerate until use.

from page 5·264

HOW TO MAKE STOCK SOUS VIDE

① Prepare ingredients. Grind meat finely, and slice vegetables thinly. Use ratios recommended in the table of Best Bets for Stocks on page 6. Roast bones.
② Vacuum seal ingredients together.
③ Cook sous vide in 85 °C / 185 °F bath for 3 h.
④ Cavitate in ultrasonic cleaning bath for 30 min (optional). If the ultrasonic bath has a temperature setting, put it at the highest degree available, typically 60 °C / 140 °F.
⑤ Refrigerate for 12 h, and then strain.
⑥ Vacuum seal again, and refrigerate or freeze until needed.

SOUS VIDE FISH STOCK

Yields 1.5 kg

INGREDIENT	QUANTITY	SCALING	PROCEDURE
Fish bones, cleaned and rinsed	2 kg	133%	① Panfry bones until golden.
Neutral oil	50 g	3%	
Vermouth	350 g	23%	② Deglaze bones.
White wine (dry)	200 g	13%	③ Cool mixture completely, and reserve.
Carrots, peeled and thinly sliced	500 g	33%	④ Prepare vegetables as noted.
Onions, peeled and thinly sliced	400 g	27%	⑤ Combine, and cook until soft.
Fennel, thinly sliced	200 g	13%	⑥ Cool completely.
Leeks, thinly sliced	200 g	13%	
Garlic cloves, thinly sliced	30 g	2%	
Neutral oil	20 g	1.5%	
Water	1.5 kg	100%	⑦ Combine with bones and vegetables.
Coriander seeds	5 g	0.3%	⑧ Vacuum seal.
Star anise	2.5 g	0.17%	⑨ Cook sous vide in 80 °C / 176 °F bath for 1¼ h.
			⑩ Strain.
			⑪ Cool.
			⑫ Vacuum seal, and refrigerate until use.

from page 2·303

SOUS VIDE VEGETABLE STOCK

Yields 350 g

INGREDIENT	QUANTITY	SCALING	PROCEDURE
Water	500 g	100%	① Prepare vegetables as noted.
Onions, peeled and thinly sliced	280 g	56%	② Combine.
Carrots, peeled and thinly sliced	200 g	40%	③ Vacuum seal.
Celery, peeled and thinly sliced	100 g	20%	④ Cook sous vide in 85 °C / 185 °F bath for 3 h.
Leeks, whites only, thinly sliced	100 g	20%	⑤ Transfer to ultrasonic cleaning bath, and cavitate for 30 min to improve extraction. If unavailable, proceed with remaining steps.
Button mushrooms, thinly sliced	50 g	10%	⑥ Cool, and refrigerate for 12 h.
Tomatoes, peeled, seeded, and chopped	50 g	10%	⑦ Strain.
Chives	10 g	2%	⑧ Vacuum seal, and refrigerate until use.
Parsley	10 g	2%	
Coriander seeds	1.5 g	0.3%	
Black peppercorns	1 g	0.2%	
Thyme	1 g	0.2%	
Bay leaf	0.5 g	0.1%	
Star anise	0.5 g	0.1%	

from page 2·303

BROTH

① Select a broth from the table.

② Prepare and scale the liquid, meat, vegetables, and aromatics. Weights in the table are proportional to the liquid scaled to 100%. For example, to make dashi, for every 100 g of water used, add 5.2 g of bonito flakes and 2.5 g of kombu.

③ Pressure-cook at a gauge pressure of 1 bar / 15 psi, or vacuum seal and cook sous vide. Recommended cooking methods, temperatures, and times are given in the table.

④ Sieve.

When making dashi, the bonito flakes are added only after the kombu has been cooked sous vide.

Best Bets for Broths

Broth	Stock	(scaling)	Meat	(scaling)
pot-au-feu	white beef stock*	100%	oxtail, chopped	30%
	vegetable stock*	50%	short rib meat, ground	20%
	madeira	4%		
ham broth	water	100%	prosciutto, thinly sliced	62.5%
	madeira	25%	ham, thinly sliced	25%
	fino sherry	19%	Ibérico ham, thinly sliced	25%
game broth	brown chicken stock*	100%	venison, ground, roasted	50%
	gin	10%	pigeon wings, roasted	12%
	red wine	10%	pheasant trimmings, blanched	10%
capon broth	white chicken stock*	100%	capon meat, ground	30%
	white wine (dry)	25%		
salt cod broth	water	100%	salt cod skins, soaked for 12 h in cold water	20%
dashi	water	100%	bonito flakes	5.2%
pho broth	water	100%	beef knuckles, roasted	44%
			oxtail, jointed and seared	18%
Chinese ginger soy fish broth	Chinese fish stock**	100%	n/a	n/a
	Shaoxing wine	1.5%		
	light soy sauce	1.5%		
"Marmite broth" adapted from Heston Blumenthal	red wine	750%**	n/a	n/a
	water	100%		

from page 2·304   *(see page 6)   **(reduced to 250%)

BORSCHT BROTH

Yields 400 g

INGREDIENT	QUANTITY	SCALING	PROCEDURE
Red beet juice	200 g	100%	① Vacuum seal together.
Water	110 g	55%	② Cook sous vide in 85 °C / 185 °F bath for 30 min.
White fish stock see page 6	90 g	45%	③ Pass through fine sieve.
Rhubarb juice	16 g	8%	
Red wine vinegar	8 g	4%	
Caraway seeds, finely ground	to taste		④ Warm borscht broth, and season.
Salt	to taste		

from page 5·235

				Cook				
Vegetable	(scaling)	Aromatic	(scaling)	Method	(h)	(°C)	(°F)	See page
carrot	10%	clove	0.01%	pressure-cook	2	n/a	n/a	
turnip, thinly sliced	10%	bay leaf	0.05%					
onion, thinly sliced	8%							
shallot, thinly sliced	25%	black pepper	2.50%	pressure-cook	1½	n/a	n/a	next page
garlic, thinly sliced	12.5%	sherry vinegar	to taste					
whole onion	5%	juniper berries, crushed	0.2%	pressure-cook	1	n/a	n/a	72
carrot, thinly sliced	5%							
celery, thinly sliced	2%	sage, thinly sliced	0.1%					
shallot, thinly sliced	15%	Parmesan, grated	10%	cook sous vide	2	88	192	27
		cinnamon extract	3%					
		sage, thinly sliced	0.15%					
onion, thinly sliced	20%	thyme	0.2%	cook sous vide	3	90	196	
garlic, thinly sliced	10%							
kombu	2.5%	n/a		cook sous vide	1	60	140	below, 241
whole onion, charred	24%	black pepper	0.04%	pressure-cook	1½	n/a	n/a	next page
ginger, charred	5%	star anise	0.02%					
		cinnamon	0.02%					
		allspice	0.01%					
scallion	3%	Szechuan pepper	0.05%	cook sous vide	35 min	80	176	
ginger	2%	rice vinegar	to taste					
chili	0.05%	honey	to taste					
leek, thinly sliced	1,000%	black pepper	to taste	cook sous vide	45 min	80	176	
carrot, thinly sliced	500%	Marmite	to taste					
onion, thinly sliced	1,000%	sherry vinegar	to taste					

HON DASHI ADAPTED FROM YOSHIHIRO MURATA

Yields 360 g

INGREDIENT	QUANTITY	SCALING	PROCEDURE
Water	475 g	100%	① Vacuum seal together.
Rishiri kombu, or best quality seaweed available (brown kelp)	12 g	2.5%	② Cook sous vide in 60 °C / 140 °F bath for 1 h.
			③ Cool, and refrigerate for 2 h.
			④ Strain.
Bonito flakes (katsuobushi)	25 g	5.3%	⑤ Heat broth to 85 °C / 185 °F.
			⑥ Add bonito flakes, and steep for 10 s.
			⑦ Strain.
			⑧ Cool.
			⑨ Vacuum seal, and refrigerate until needed.

The kombu flavor can be increased by extending the refrigerator time from 2 h to as long as 12 h. The longer the time, the stronger the flavor.

from page 2·306

HAM BROTH

Yields 535 g

INGREDIENT	QUANTITY	SCALING	PROCEDURE
Water	500 g	100%	① Prepare ingredients as noted.
Prosciutto ends, thinly sliced	250 g	50%	② Combine in pressure cooker.
Cooked white ham, thinly sliced	100 g	20%	③ Pressure-cook at gauge pressure of 1 bar / 15 psi for 1½ h.
Jamón Ibérico, thinly sliced	100 g	20%	④ Strain.
Madeira	100 g	20%	⑤ Cool completely.
Shallots, thinly sliced	100 g	20%	⑥ Measure 500 g.
Fino sherry	75 g	15%	
Garlic, thinly sliced	50 g	10%	
Black peppercorns, crushed	10 g	2%	
Ham broth, from above	500 g	100%	⑦ Disperse gelatin and gum in cold broth.
160 Bloom gelatin	4 g	0.8%	⑧ Heat broth just enough to dissolve gelatin.
Xanthan gum (Keltrol T, CP Kelco brand)	0.75 g	0.15%	
Salt	to taste		⑨ Season and cool.
Sherry vinegar	to taste		⑩ Vacuum seal, and refrigerate until needed.

from page 2·306

Any cured meat can be used here instead of ham.

OXTAIL PHO BROTH

Yields 4.75 kg

INGREDIENT	QUANTITY	SCALING	PROCEDURE
Black peppercorns	2 g	0.04%	① Combine.
Cinnamon stick	1 g	0.02%	② Toast spice mix.
Star anise, ground	1 g	0.02%	③ Place in sachet made of cheesecloth.
Allspice	0.5 g	0.01%	
Water	5 kg	100%	④ Combine in pressure cooker.
Beef knuckles, blanched	2.2 kg	44%	⑤ Add sachet.
White onions, whole, unpeeled, and charred	1.2 kg	24%	⑥ Pressure-cook broth at gauge pressure of 1 bar / 15 psi for 1½ h.
Oxtail, jointed and seared	900 g	18%	⑦ Discard sachet.
Ginger, halved and charred	250 g	5%	
Fish sauce	to taste		⑧ Season and cool.
Salt	to taste		⑨ Vacuum seal, and refrigerate until needed.
Sugar	to taste		

from page 2·307

The sachet is a pouch made of cheesecloth that keeps the spice mixture together in much the same way that a tea bag holds tea leaves. The broth can be made without the sachet, but then you will have to filter out the loose spice mix to get a perfectly clear broth.

DUCK BROTH WITH VANILLA AND BAY LEAF

Yields 500 g

INGREDIENT	QUANTITY	SCALING	PROCEDURE
Duck meat, finely ground	400 g	400%	① Brown together lightly in pressure cooker, about 10 min.
Duck wings, chopped	100 g	100%	
Duck fat	30 g	30%	
Shallots, thinly sliced	125 g	125%	② Add to duck parts, and cook until translucent.
Leeks, thinly sliced	75 g	75%	
White port (dry)	150 g	150%	③ Add to duck parts, and reduce to 225 g.
White wine	150 g	150%	
Water	700 g	700%	④ Place with duck reduction in pressure cooker, and pressure-cook at gauge pressure of 1 bar / 15 psi for 1½ h.
Vanilla bean seeds	1.5 g	1.5%	
Bay leaf	0.5 g	0.5%	
			⑤ Strain through fine sieve.
Lime juice	to taste		⑥ Season and serve broth, or cool and refrigerate until use.
Salt	to taste		

from page 5·110

LAKSA BROTH

Yields 500 g

INGREDIENT	QUANTITY	SCALING	PROCEDURE
Onions, peeled and chopped	100 g	28%	① Prepare ingredients as noted.
Lemongrass, finely minced	40 g	11%	② Blend together in food processor.
Candlenuts, roasted and grated	30 g	8.3%	③ Measure 28 g of paste, reserving the rest.
Shrimp paste	20 g	5.5%	
Dried chili	5 g	1.4%	
Galangal, peeled and chopped	5 g	1.4%	
Turmeric (fresh), peeled and chopped	0.7 g	0.2%	
Laksa paste, from above	28 g	7.8%	④ Sauté until golden and very fragrant, about 3 min.
Neutral oil	20 g	5.5%	
White fish stock see page 6	360 g	100%	⑤ Transfer paste to large pot, and whisk in stock and cream.
Caramelized coconut cream see page 214	100 g	28%	⑥ Simmer broth for 5 min.
Fish sauce	to taste		⑦ Season and cool.
Lime juice	to taste		⑧ Vacuum seal, and refrigerate until needed.

from page 2·307

Laksa is one of the great dishes of the Peranakan culture that merges Chinese and Malay traditions. Many feel that the best laksa is found in the food-hawking centers of Singapore.

BOUILLABAISSE BROTH

Yields 750 g

INGREDIENT	QUANTITY	SCALING	PROCEDURE
Tomatoes, peeled, seeded, and diced	120 g	13%	① Prepare vegetables as noted.
White onions, thinly sliced	115 g	13%	② Combine.
Fennel, thinly sliced	100 g	11%	③ Cook over low heat until tender and golden, about 25 min.
Shallots, thinly sliced	85 g	9.5%	
Leeks, thinly sliced	80 g	9%	
Carrots, thinly sliced	75 g	8%	
Olive oil	50 g	5.5%	
Garlic, thinly sliced	25 g	3%	
Tomato confit, pureed (or tomato paste) see page 179	60 g	7%	④ Add, and increase heat to medium high.
			⑤ Sauté until browned, about 5 min, and reserve.
Fish bones and head	800 g	89%	⑥ Coat bones in oil.
Neutral oil	75 g	8%	⑦ Bake in 180 °C / 325 °F oven until golden, about 45 min.
			⑧ Cool.
Water	900 g	100%	⑨ Combine with vegetable mixture and fish parts.
White wine (dry)	200 g	22%	
Pastis	50 g	5.5%	⑩ Vacuum seal.
Thyme	3 g	0.33%	⑪ Cook sous vide in 80 °C / 175 °F bath for 1¼ h.
Black peppercorns, crushed	1 g	0.1%	
Bay leaf	0.6 g	0.06%	⑫ Strain.
Saffron threads	0.3 g	0.003%	⑬ Cool.
			⑭ Skim fat from surface.
Blood orange juice	17 g	2%	⑮ Season.
Red miso paste	13 g	1.4%	⑯ Cool.
Blood orange zest, finely grated	1 g	0.1%	⑰ Vacuum seal, and refrigerate until needed.
Salt	to taste		

from page 2·308

THE MODERNIST KITCHEN

BACON DASHI INSPIRED BY DAVID CHANG

Yields 800 g

INGREDIENT	QUANTITY	SCALING	PROCEDURE
Water	1 kg	100%	① Vacuum seal together.
Kombu	25 g	2.5%	② Cook sous vide in 60 °C / 140 °F bath for 1 h.
			③ Strain out kombu.
Bacon, thinly sliced	250 g	25%	④ Vacuum seal with kombu-infused water.
Sake (dry), flamed off	30 g	3%	⑤ Cook sous vide in 85 °C / 185 °F bath for 1 h 30 min.
			⑥ Strain out bacon.
Mirin	10 g	1%	⑦ Combine.
Soy sauce	10 g	1%	⑧ Adjust seasoning as needed.
Sake	6 g	0.6%	
Sugar	1.4 g	0.14%	

The quality of the bacon used determines the quality of the final dashi.

from page 2·308

TOM YUM BROTH

Yields 750 g

INGREDIENT	QUANTITY	SCALING	PROCEDURE
Shallots, chopped	160 g	32%	① Prepare ingredients as noted.
Lemongrass, bruised and sliced thinly	78 g	15.6%	② Combine in blender.
			③ Puree.
Palm sugar	60 g	12%	④ Measure 100 g of paste.
Tamarind paste	60 g	12%	
Garlic, chopped	50 g	10%	
Ginger, peeled and cut into coin shapes	45 g	9%	
Cilantro stems, washed and chopped	40 g	8%	
Galangal, peeled and chopped	40 g	8%	
Belacan shrimp paste	10 g	2%	
Makrud (kaffir) lime leaf, bruised	8 g	1.6%	
Bird's Thai chili, chopped	5 g	1%	
Neutral oil	as needed		⑤ Sauté paste until dry and very fragrant, about 5 min.
Shrimp stock (or vegetable stock) see page 6	500 g	100%	⑥ Whisk into sautéed paste in large pot, and bring to simmer.
Palm sugar	20 g	4%	⑦ Season.
Fish sauce	7 g	1.4%	⑧ Cool.
Salt	2 g	0.4%	⑨ Vacuum seal, and refrigerate until needed.
Lime juice	to taste		

from page 2·309

CURED HAM BROTH

Yields 350 g

INGREDIENT	QUANTITY	SCALING	PROCEDURE
Sweet onions, thinly sliced	50 g	16.7%	① Sauté onions and leeks in oil until translucent.
Olive oil	25 g	8.3%	
Leeks, thinly sliced	21 g	7%	
Dry-cured ham, thinly sliced	50 g	16.7%	② Add to onion and leek mixture, and sauté for 5 min.
Garlic, thinly sliced	5.5 g	1.8%	
Brown pork stock see page 6	300 g	100%	③ Combine with sautéed mixture.
			④ Pressure-cook at gauge pressure of 1 bar / 15 psi for 1 h.
Salt	1.2 g	0.4%	⑤ Strain through fine sieve, and cool.
Thyme	0.3 g	0.1%	⑥ Season, and serve or refrigerate until use.

from page 5·84

BAKED POTATO BROTH

Yields 300 g

INGREDIENT	QUANTITY	SCALING	PROCEDURE
Russet potato skins	100 g	100%	① Coat skins with oil.
Frying oil	20 g	20%	② Bake in 95 °C / 200 °F oven for 7 h, until golden and completely desiccated.
			③ Cool.
Russet potatoes, peeled and thinly sliced	75 g	75%	④ Panfry over medium-high heat until deep golden, about 15 min on each side.
Clarified unsalted butter	15 g	15%	⑤ Cool.
Potato juice, decanted from starch residue	300 g (from 700 g of potatoes)	300%	⑥ Vacuum seal with cooked potato skins and slices.
			⑦ Cook sous vide in 80 °C / 176 °F bath for 1½ h.
			⑧ Strain.
Water	300 g	300%	
Salt	to taste		⑨ Season and cool.
			⑩ Vacuum seal, and refrigerate until needed.

from page 2·309

GOULASH BROTH

Yields 1 kg

INGREDIENT	QUANTITY	SCALING	PROCEDURE
Tomato confit see page 179	100 g	17%	① Panfry confit with oil, stirring constantly to prevent burning, until dark, about 10 min.
Grapeseed oil	50 g	8.5%	
Red bell pepper juice	120 g (from 300 g red bell peppers)	20%	② Deglaze pan.
			③ Measure 250 g of mixture, and reserve.
Red onions, thinly sliced	600 g	100%	④ Cook onions slowly in suet until deep amber and dry, about 45 min. If pan becomes too dry, add small amount of water to prevent onions from becoming too dark.
Rendered suet	100 g	17%	
Brown beef stock see page 10	800 g	133%	⑤ Combine all ingredients with both reserved tomato confit mixture and reduced onions.
Caraway seeds, toasted	3.5 g	0.6%	⑥ Cook sous vide in 85 °C / 185 °F bath for 2½ h.
Black peppercorns, toasted	3 g	0.5%	⑦ Strain through fine sieve.
Sweet paprika	2 g	0.3%	⑩ Clarify with centrifuge at 27,500g for 1 h.
Hot paprika	1.25 g	0.2%	⑪ Refrigerate until chilled.
Black cumin seeds, toasted	0.5 g	0.08%	⑫ Measure 25 g of fat from surface of broth; reserve fat and broth separately.
Cumin seeds, toasted	0.5 g	0.08%	
Sherry vinegar	45 g	7.5%	⑬ Season broth.
Sugar	6 g	1%	
Salt	to taste		

from page 5·56

MUSHROOM BROTH

Yields 250 g

INGREDIENT	QUANTITY	SCALING	PROCEDURE
Shallots, thinly sliced	37 g	25%	① Sauté until golden, about 15 min.
Olive oil	8.5 g	6%	
Water	250 g	180%	② Pressure-cook with shallots at gauge pressure of 1 bar / 15 psi for 45 min.
Crimini mushrooms, thinly sliced	140 g	100%	③ Strain and cool.

from page 5·14

THE MODERNIST KITCHEN

INFUSING FLAVOR INTO A LIQUID

① Combine ingredient with cold liquid. Quantities in the table Best Bets for Infused Liquids below are proportional to the weight of the liquid. For example, to infuse rice vinegar with lemongrass, add 50 g of thinly sliced lemongrass for every 100 g of vinegar.

② Vacuum seal (optional), and cook. Recommended cooking methods, temperatures, and times are given in the table. Sieve.

Best Bets for Infused Liquids

Ingredient	(scaling)*	Method	Infusion (°C)	(°F)	(h)	Example use	See page
cured bacon, thinly sliced	30%	cook sous vide	85	185	2	bacon water	
black pepper, crushed	0.50%	infuse sous vide	3	37	12		
chili, dried	2%	infuse sous vide	3	37	12	Chinese broth	
cinnamon, finely crushed	3%	infuse sous vide	3	37	12	cinnamon dashi	254
coffee, ground	7%	infuse sous vide	3	37	12	beef jus	
ginger, thinly sliced	120%	blend, infuse	3	37	12	Chinese broth	
juniper, crushed	7%	cook sous vide	70	148	15 min	game broth	
lemon zest, grated	10%	infuse sous vide	3	37	12	broth for pasta	
lemongrass, thinly sliced	50%	cook sous vide	85	185	20 min	Thai or Vietnamese broth	
lemon verbena	30%	infuse sous vide	3	37	12	lemon verbena sponge	318
licorice root, grated	5%	infuse sous vide	3	37	12	broth for foie gras	
mushroom, dried	6%	cook sous vide	60	140	20 min	mushroom cappuccino	320
nutmeg, grated	0.2%	infuse sous vide	3	37	12		
Parmesan cheese, grated	80%	cook sous vide	85	185	12	Parmesan water	
prosciutto, thinly sliced	30%	cook sous vide	80	176	2	prosciutto water	
saffron threads	1.5%	infuse sous vide	3	37	24	tomato vinegar	315
star anise, crushed	3%	infuse sous vide	3	37	12		
tarragon	20%	infuse sous vide	3	37	12	beurre blanc, fish broth	
tea, black	3%	ultrasonic bath	85	185	5 min	bergamot sabayon	319
tea, green	2%	infuse sous vide	3	37	12		
tea, white	4%	cook sous vide	70	158	7 min		
paprika, finely ground	2%	infuse sous vide	3	37	3	goulash	
young pine buds	8%	boil and refrigerate	3	37	12	citrus seafood broth	
vanilla	1.5%	infuse sous vide	3	37	24	broth for foie gras	5·109

from page 2·310   *(set weight of liquid to 100%)

Seasoning with Salt and Other Flavor Enhancers

When cooks judge the flavor balance and seasoning of a dish, salt is typically checked first. Get the salt level wrong, and diners will quickly be distracted from their enjoyment of the food. Table salt enhances our perception of flavor, and so do nucleotides and monosodium glutamate (MSG), which are savory salts that trigger different taste receptors than salt does. You can enhance flavor in many ways besides sprinkling salt crystals over your food: anchovies, dried scallops, and shrimp paste all layer on tastes of the sea and the shore. Ingredients such as bacons, hams, and cheeses carry hints of the country, barnyard, and sometimes smoke. Soy sauce, fish sauce, miso, and natto are all fermented seasoning agents, and each has a certain tanginess and vegetal quality.

Salts	Taste	Aroma	(scaling)*	Note
salt	defines salty	none	0.5%–2.0%	most useful flavor enhancer in the kitchen; most people find 0.75–1% best for savory foods
monosodium glutamate	defines umami (also called savory)	none	0.1%–2.0%	found naturally in all high-protein foods; some people find >1% harsh and metallic-tasting
5' ribonucleotides	savory	none	0.02%	found naturally in most foods; boosts existing savory flavors
Seasonings				
aged cheese	salty, sharp, acidic, strongly savory	varies greatly	3%–10%	hard cheeses like Parmesan contain both salt and glutamate
anchovy	salty and oily	fishy; roasted scent when cooked	0.2%–0.8%	used as a seasoning since the time of Imperial Rome
bacon	salty	smoky, fried, meaty	3%–15%	can quickly overwhelm a dish
capers (salt-packed)	salty, slightly bitter and astringent	mustard oil, hint of thyme	2%	add at the last moment; high heat degrades aromas
cured meats	salty, strongly savory, slightly sweet	varies greatly; often nutty, fruity, and floral	5%–15%	use with moderation; combination of salt, sugar, fat, and Maillard flavors with smoke aromas is powerful
dried scallops	slightly sweet	pungent, slightly fishy, cured	3%–5%	used primarily in Asian cooking
fish sauce	salty, strongly savory, slightly sweet	pungent, slightly fishy	2%–10%	adds depth and savory flavor; tastes better than it smells; a favorite in ancient Rome
garlic	pungent, slightly sweet, enhances savory	sulfurous	1%–7%	when garlic is crushed and raw or lightly cooked, its allicin compounds trigger pain and temperature receptors in the mouth, thereby enhancing flavors
Marmite or Vegemite	salty, strongly savory	yeasty, meaty, malted	0.3%–1.5%	adds meat-like flavors to vegetarian dishes
miso, red	slightly sweet, savory	strong, roasted, hint of cocoa	1%–8%	includes all three primary salts listed above; pungency varies with degree of fermentation
miso, white		mild, caramel, toasty	1%–8%	
natto	salty, savory	pungent, fermented, roasted, cheesy	1%	
shallots	pungent, slightly sweet, enhances savory	sulfurous	5%–30%	similar to garlic but does not cause onion breath because sulfurous compounds do not enter bloodstream
shrimp paste	salty, slightly sweet, savory	pungent, slightly fishy, cured	1%–3%	used primarily in Southeast Asian cooking
soy, dark	salty, slightly sweet, mildly astringent	strong, fermented, roasted, molasses	2%–5%	tastes and aromas vary greatly among styles and brands
soy, white		mellow, slightly sweet, floral	2%–5%	
tomato	sweet, acidic, savory	fruity, musky, sometimes floral	5%–9%	rich source of sugars, acids, and salts when ripe; enhances roasted aromas when browned with meats
Worcestershire sauce	salty, sweet, savory, acidic, slightly spicy	fermented, roasted, molasses, spicy, vinegary	2%–5%	has many applications; underused as a seasoning; a distant relative of Roman fish sauce (*garum*)

from page 2·312

*(set weight of food being seasoned to 100%)

SOUS VIDE PONZU ADAPTED FROM KYLE CONNAUGHTON

Yields 1.95 kg

INGREDIENT	QUANTITY	SCALING	PROCEDURE
Yuzu	120 g (about four whole)	17%	① Grate zest, and juice flesh.
Sudachi (optional)	35 g	5%	
Mirin	700 g	100%	② Combine in pan, and simmer until reduced to about 80% of original volume.
Sake	65 g	9.5%	
Kombu (Rishiri if available)	15 g	2%	③ Toast over open flame on all sides.
Tamari soy sauce	550 g	79%	④ Combine with citrus zest and juice, kombu, and reduced mirin–sake mixture.
Red rice vinegar (yusen)	525 g	75%	
Shoyu soy sauce (usu-kuchi shoyu)	110 g	16%	⑤ Vacuum seal.
			⑥ Refrigerate for 3 weeks.
Bonito flakes (katsuobushi)	10 g	1.4%	⑦ Strain.
			⑧ Use immediately, or vacuum seal and refrigerate until needed.

As it does for vegetable stocks, putting a broth in an ultrasonic bath for 30 minutes improves flavor extraction. This should be done after the sous vide cooking step.

from page 2·313

Best Bets for Lowering pH

Ingredient	Typical pH	Flavor profile	Example uses
Vinegar (pH 2.4–3.4)			
cider vinegar	2.4	sharp, apple	salad dressing, marinade, coagulation
malt vinegar	2.4	bittersweet, hops, caramel	sauce, marinade
red wine vinegar	2.4	currant, tannic	dressing
rice vinegar	2.8	sweet, subtle, toasty	salad dressing, marinade, coagulation
sherry vinegar	3.4	sweet, oak, cherry, earthy	salad dressing, finishing meat sauce
white wine vinegar	2.8	clean, bright, green grape	salad dressing, fish broth, butter sauce
Citrus (pH 1.8–3.9)			
grapefruit juice	3.7	floral, light citrus, coffee	finishing sauces, seasoning seafood dishes
lemon juice	2.3	bright, perfumed	dressing, sauce, balancing oil
lime juice	1.8–2	sharp, coconut, pine	sour broth, finishing fruit and vegetable water
orange juice	3.9	sweet, neroli	mellows other acids
Pure acids (diluted 1:10 with water; pH 2.4–2.9)			
acetic acid (vinegar)	2.9	pungent	wine sauce, dressing
ascorbic acid (vitamin C)	2.9	crisp	color preservative
citric acid (citrus)	2.4	sharp, citrus	fruity sauce for fish
lactic acid (dairy)	2.6	buttermilk, sour cream	dairy applications, enhancing fermented flavors for quick kimchi and sauerkraut
malic acid (apple, cherry)	2.4	tangy with light fruit notes	finishing glaze, sauce, raw fruit sauce, and water
tartaric acid (grape)	2.4	heavy acidity, light flavor	reduction, wine sauce, fruit sauce
Tart fruit (pH 2.5–4.2)			
red currant	3.1	tannic, bitter, berry	glaze or sauce for red meat, game
rhubarb juice	3.4	astringent, herbal, mellows when cooked	sauce or broth for fish, foie gras
tamarind paste	3.7	sour, caramel, pungent	sauce, sweets, dressing, broth
tomato juice	4.2	earthy, complex, vegetable	vegetable broth, dressing
verjus	2.7	tannic, grape must	finishing sauce (best used raw)
gooseberry juice	2.6	bitter, sour, floral	dressing for shellfish and oysters

from page 2·314

Typical Acid Concentrations

Acid type	For seasoning (pH 5.5–6.5)	For souring (pH 4.0–4.5)	For vinaigrettes (pH 3.0–3.8)	For pickles (pH 2.3–3.0)
kitchen acids	0.2%–0.5%	1%–3%	3%–6%	5%–10%
citrus juice	1%–3%	5%–15%	10%–100%	65%–100%
astringent fruit	3%–10%	10%–50%	10%–60%	65%–100%
vinegar	1%–5%	25%–75%	30%–100%	50%–100%

from page 2·315

Kitchen acids include ascorbic, acetic, citric, lactic, malic, and tartaric acids. Note that the wide ranges in this table are due to variations in the initial pH and in the buffering capacity of the food.

SEAWEED VINEGAR

Yields 250 g

INGREDIENT	QUANTITY	SCALING	PROCEDURE
Cider vinegar	200 g	100%	① Combine.
Muscovado sugar	26 g	13%	② Bring to simmer.
Palm sugar	16 g	8%	③ Stir mixture until sugar is dissolved, and reserve warm.
Coriander seeds, toasted and crushed	2 g	1%	
Kombu, shredded, soaked for 45 min in warm water, and drained	30 g	15%	④ Combine, and add to vinegar mixture.
			⑤ Vacuum seal and steep at room temperature for 12 h.
Ginger, grated	3 g	1.5%	⑥ Strain.
Whiskey	10 g	5%	⑦ Whisk into strained vinegar.
Salt	to taste		⑧ Season.

from page 2·315

Japanese flavor combinations often include multiple variations on the umami flavor theme. In this recipe, different soy sauces and kombu provide umami notes, which are balanced by the bright yuzu citrus flavors.

ELDER FLOWER VINEGAR

Yields 700 g

INGREDIENT	QUANTITY	SCALING	PROCEDURE
White wine vinegar	500 g	100%	① Whisk together.
Elder blossoms, thoroughly washed	170 g	34%	② Vacuum seal.
			③ Infuse refrigerated for at least 1 week.
Malt vinegar	100 g	20%	④ Strain.
Rice vinegar	100 g	20%	⑤ Use to dress salads or as condiment for raw shellfish.
Sugar	65 g	13%	
Malic acid	2 g	0.4%	

from page 2·315

Many foods have compounds in them that will react with any acid you add, which tends to neutralize the acid. Chemists call this property buffering. A food with a high buffering capacity requires more acid to be added to reach a given level of final acidity than one with a low buffering capacity. Because this capacity varies from food to food, it is hard to give precise numbers on how much acid to add. A pH meter is the best way to achieve consistency.

PASSION FRUIT–WHITE SOY SAUCE VINAIGRETTE

Yields 70 g

INGREDIENT	QUANTITY	SCALING	PROCEDURE
Passion fruit juice	55 g	100%	① Mix together until malic acid is fully dissolved.
White soy sauce	10.5 g	19%	② Refrigerate until use.
Lime juice	7 g	13%	
Jalapeño, brunoise	3 g	5.5%	
Malic acid	1 g	1.8%	

from page 5·183

CONSTRUCTED RED WINE GLAZE

Yields 65 g

INGREDIENT	QUANTITY	SCALING	PROCEDURE
Blackberries (fresh)	100 g	100%	① Vacuum seal.
Blueberries (fresh)	50 g	50%	② Cook sous vide in 65 °C / 149 °F bath for 1 h.
			③ Cool and puree.
			④ Pass through fine sieve.
Verjuice (store-bought)	50 g	50%	⑤ Blend well with 50 g of berry puree.
Kalamata olive brine (from store-bought olives)	2 g	2.0%	⑥ Vacuum seal, and refrigerate.
Tannin powder (Obipektin brand Enocianin-A)	1.5 g	1.5%	
Tartaric acid	1 g	1.0%	
Fructose	0.5 g	0.5%	
Oak chips, grated	0.25 g	0.25%	
Malic acid	0.2 g	0.2%	
Unsalted butter, cold	5 g	5%	⑦ Warm wine glaze, and whisk in cold butter until fully emulsified. Check salt and acidity; add salt if needed.
Salt	to taste		

from page 5·221

Best Bets for Adding Flavor with Alcohol

Ingredient	Broth (scaling)*	Sauce (scaling)*	Characteristic aromas	Alcohol content	Example uses	See page
aquavit	2%–7%	10%–30%	caraway, fennel	high	finishing raw, cold items	
Armagnac	1%–5%	10%–30%	smoke, oak	high	glaze, sauce, adding body and subtle flavors	347
beer or ale	10%–20%	15%–40%	malt, barley, bitter	low	meat sauce, glaze, adding grain flavors and bitterness	42
Cognac	2%–6%	10%–30%	smoke, oak, tobacco	high	glaze, sauce, adding body and subtle flavors	109
gin	1%–5%	10%–30%	juniper, pine, cassia	high	marinade and game sauce, adding spice	109
Madeira	5%–10%	20%	pepper, plum	low to moderate	sauce with dairy or mushrooms, adding sweetness and fruit flavors	
pastis	1%–5%	1%–5%	anise, licorice, sugar	moderate	seafood broth, soup	
port, red	10%–20%	15%–40%	cherry, berry, oak	low to moderate	broth and sauce	212
port, white	15%–40%	15%–100%	pear, sour grape	low to moderate	broth, sauce, adding sweetness	16
sake	5%–16%	25%–75%	light pepper, honeydew	low	fish broth, adding sweetness and a little spice	5·197
Shaoxing	3%–15%	10%–30%	sweet rice, floral	low to moderate	pork, fish sauce, adding acidity and sweetness	5·167
sherry, dry	3%–8%	15%–40%	almond, hazelnut	low to moderate	shellfish broth, adding body and tannins	5·31
sherry, sweet	5%–10%	5%–20%	cherry, currant	moderate	glaze broth, adding sweetness and complexity	
vermouth	5%–20%	15%–40%	chamomile, cardamom	moderate to high	fish broth, sauce, enhancing flavors	5·233
vin jaune	2%–20%	25%–74%	walnut, almond, melon	low to moderate	broth, sauce, adding acidity and body	5·113
whiskey	7%–10%	20%–60%	smoke, leather, vanilla, char, peat	high	glaze, adding sweet and smoky flavors	5·66
wine, red	7%–15%	25%–100%	tannin, berry, oak	low to moderate	glaze, meat sauce, adding complexity and fruit flavors	34
wine, white	7%–15%	25%–100%	apple, pear, floral	low to moderate	broth and sauce, adding acidity and complexity	76

from page 2·317   *(set weight of broth or sauce to 100%)

CLOVE OIL

Yields 100 g

INGREDIENT	QUANTITY	SCALING	PROCEDURE
Grapeseed oil	100 g	100%	① Combine and reserve.
Clove essential oil	0.5 g	0.5%	

from page 5·52

CINNAMON-SCENTED PEA JUICE

Yields 210 g

INGREDIENT	QUANTITY	SCALING	PROCEDURE
Sweet peas, frozen and juiced	200 g	100%	① Whisk together.
Cinnamon essential oil (optional)	0.05 g	0.025%	② Centrifuge at 27,500g for 1 h.
			③ Strain.
Lime juice	to taste		④ Season broth.
Salt	to taste		⑤ Refrigerate until use.

from page 5·275

CONDRIEU BUTTER

Yields 340 g

INGREDIENT	QUANTITY	SCALING	PROCEDURE
Condrieu wine	750 g	500%	① Vacuum reduce to 150 g, and reserve.
Shallots, thinly sliced	60 g	40%	② Sauté until tender, about 10 min.
Clarified unsalted butter	50 g	33%	
Lychee juice (fresh)	100 g	67%	③ Deglaze shallots.
			④ Remove from heat.
			⑤ Strain.
Condrieu reduction, from above	150 g	100%	⑥ Whisk into deglazed shallots.
Unsalted butter, cold and cubed	75 g	50%	⑦ Warm Condrieu butter base, and blend in cold butter until fully emulsified.
Osmanthus vinegar	15 g	10%	⑧ Season.
Orange blossom essential oil	0.05 g	0.03%	
Rose essential oil	0.05 g	0.03%	
Salt	to taste		

from page 5·172

GLAZED CARROT

Yields 120 g

INGREDIENT	QUANTITY	SCALING	PROCEDURE
Young carrots (preferably Thumbelina), peeled	100 g	100%	① Vacuum seal together.
			② Cook sous vide in 85 °C / 185 °F bath for 40 min.
Carotene butter (or regular butter) see page 40	20 g	20%	③ Cool, remove carrots from bag, and reserve.
Mandarin juice	48 g	48%	④ Vacuum reduce (or reduce over heat) to glaze, about 7 min.
Valencia orange juice	45 g	45%	
Honey	5 g	5%	
Mandarin essential oil	0.1 g	0.1%	⑤ Season glaze.
Salt	to taste		⑥ Stir in carrots and warm through.

from page 5·186

MARINATED SPAGHETTI SQUASH

Yields 150 g

INGREDIENT	QUANTITY	SCALING	PROCEDURE
Spaghetti squash	130 g	100%	① Steam until tender, about 15 min.
			② Shred strands while still hot.
			③ Cool and reserve refrigerated.
Orange juice	24 g	18.5%	④ Combine to make dressing.
Honey vinegar	11 g	8.5%	⑤ Marinate squash in dressing for 10 min.
Extra virgin olive oil	8 g	6.2%	
Sichuan peppercorns, coarsely ground	2 g	1.5%	
Orange zest, finely grated	0.5 g	0.4%	
Acetaldehyde	0.015 g	0.01%	
Salt	to taste		

from page 5·149

HOW TO WASH CITRUS OIL

① Combine the ingredients in a separatory funnel with the stopcock closed. Use 10 parts essential oil, 40 parts distilled water, and 50 parts pure alcohol (either ethanol or Everclear), or use a high-proof vodka that has been run through a water filter a few times in place of both the water and the ethanol.

② Stopper the funnel and shake until the mixture becomes cloudy.

③ Let stand undisturbed until the mixture separates. The oil rises to the top. When the liquid is clear—after a day or even a week of resting—the essence is ready. Longer time will yield a more intense extraction.

④ Remove the stopper, open the stopcock, and drain the flavored water through a coffee filter. The filter will remove any waxes and impurities. Close the stopcock just before the oil starts to emerge.

EXTRACTING FLAVOR WITH ALCOHOL

① Select and prepare ingredient. The table Best Bets for Extracts on the next page suggests a number of good options.

② Vacuum seal ingredient with neutral vodka. Quantities indicated in the table are proportional to the weight of the vodka. For example, use 25 g of chili for every 100 g of alcohol.

③ Infuse. Recommended infusing temperatures and times are listed in the table. Some preparations benefit from cooking; for others, infusion at refrigerator temperatures does a better job of capturing their delicate flavors.

④ Sieve. Reseal, and refrigerate until needed.

⑤ Add recommended concentration of alcohol extract to broth or sauce. For example, add 4 g of brown butter extract for every 100 g of broth or sauce. Adding more than 5% will make the alcohol flavor perceptible.

BROWN BUTTER FUMET

Yields 200 g

INGREDIENT	QUANTITY	SCALING	PROCEDURE
Brown fish stock see page 6	200 g	100%	① Simmer together until reduced to 200 g.
			② Cool.
Sake	150 g	75%	
Vermouth (dry)	50 g	25%	
Rice vinegar	10 g	5%	
Brown butter extract see page 4·213	8 g	4%	③ Whisk in.
Xanthan gum (Keltrol T, CP Kelco brand)	0.3 g	0.15%	
Salt	to taste		④ Season and serve, or refrigerate until use.

from page 5·158

HAZELNUT OIL EXTRACT

Yields 300 g

INGREDIENT	QUANTITY	SCALING	PROCEDURE
Roasted hazelnut oil see page 41 (or store-bought)	300 g	100%	① Combine in separatory funnel.
			② Shake vigorously for 2 min.
Vodka	300 g	100%	③ Allow oil and alcohol to separate overnight.
			④ Decant alcohol from bottom of funnel.
			⑤ Use hazelnut oil–infused alcohol to season broths or sauces without adding fat.

from page 2·321

Best Bets for Extracts

Ingredient	(scaling)*	Infuse (°C)	(°F)	(h)	Example concentration**	Example use	See page
bay leaf, fresh	1%	60	140	4	5%	fish sauce, broth	46
brown butter, melted	100%	65	149	5	4%	vegetable broth	42, 297
butter, melted	100%	65	149	3	4%	popcorn broth	
chili (dry), crushed	25%	refrigerate		24	2%	Sichuan-style broth	
cinnamon stick, crushed	5%	60	140	4	3%–4%	meat sauce	14
citrus zest, finely grated	27%	50	122	3	3%	fish sauce, broth	
coffee bean, ground	20%	refrigerate		12	3%	meat sauce, red-eye gravy	5·101
coriander seed, crushed	20%	60	140	3	5%	seafood sauce	
fennel seed	5%	3	37	24	3%–4%	pork broth, Parmesan jus	
ginger, thinly sliced	25%	60	140	4	3%	Chinese broth	
roasted hazelnut oil	100%	65	149	3	8%	root vegetable broth	
nutmeg, grated	7%	refrigerate		24	2%–3%	guinea fowl consommé	
rosemary	10%	refrigerate		24	1.5%–2.5%	lamb broth, lamb jus	
saffron threads	1%	refrigerate		24	0.6%	cream sauce	
star anise, crushed	5%	60	140	4	4%	oxtail consommé	46
thyme leaf	10%	60	140	4	3%–4%	beurre blanc	
vanilla bean, split	5%	refrigerate		24	3%	sauce or broth of foie gras or lean fish	

from page 2·326 *(set weight of vodka to 100%)* **(set weight of broth or sauce to 100%)*

HOUSE BITTERS

Yields 500 g

INGREDIENT	QUANTITY	SCALING	PROCEDURE
Vodka	500 g	100%	① Combine.
Kumquat, thinly sliced	40 g	8%	② Seal in glass bottle with airtight lid.
Burdock root	12 g	2.4%	③ Shake bottle twice a week for 4 wk.
Vanilla beans, halved	12 g	2.4%	④ Pour mixture through fine sieve into sterilized bottle.
Orange zest	10 g	2%	
Gentian flowers	6 g	1.2%	
Cinnamon	5 g	1%	
Cloves	3 g	0.6%	
Heather tips	2 g	0.4%	
Anise seeds	1.5 g	0.3%	

from page 2·327

FINES HERBS EXTRACT

Yields 100 g

INGREDIENT	QUANTITY	SCALING	PROCEDURE
Vodka	100 g	100%	① Combine and vacuum seal.
Chervil, thinly sliced	33 g	33%	② Refrigerate for 24 h to steep.
Chives	33 g	33%	③ Strain through fine filter.
Parsley leaves, whole	33 g	33%	④ Add 2%–5% of extract to season broth or sauce, or reseal and refrigerate until use.
Tarragon, crushed	15 g	15%	

from page 2·327

INFUSING FLAVOR INTO A FAT

① Wash and dry all produce thoroughly to prevent contamination of the fat.

② Vacuum seal ingredient with fat. The table Best Bets for Infused Fats below lists many good combinations. Quantities are proportional to the weight of the fat. When making coffee butter, for example, add 55 g of coffee beans for every 100 g of butter.

③ Cook sous vide to infuse the fat. Recommended temperatures and times are given in the table.

④ Place food in bag into an ultrasonic bath for 15 min to 1 h (optional). Ultrasonic treatment enhances extraction and should be done while the food is still hot. Use the same bath temperature used for infusion or the highest setting possible. Or use a sous vide bath that has ultrasonic capability to do the infusion.

⑤ Sieve, and then refrigerate. Do not sieve truffle or other infusions in which the flavorful flecks are desirable.

This recipe works with crab, crawfish, shrimp, prawn, and lobster of all varieties. It is a culinary classic that dates to traditional French cuisine.

Best Bets for Infused Fats

Ingredient	(scaling)*	Fat	Cook sous vide, or infuse cold (°C)	(°F)	(h)	Example use	See page
cured ham, thinly sliced	40%	peanut oil	70	158	8	add to XO sauce, season fresh melon	
dried chili, crushed	3%	sunflower oil	70	158	24	poach fish, season sauteed broccoli	next page
cocoa nib, crushed	40%	sunflower oil	65	149	6	garnish sashimi	
coffee beans, whole	55%	unsalted butter	70	158	12	garnish sea urchin, shellfish, lemon risotto	350
garlic, thinly sliced	50%	olive oil	90	194	4	garnish pizza, roasted potatoes	5·211
fresh ginger, thinly sliced	45%	sunflower oil	puree until smooth 70	158	3	garnish steamed fish	
Ibérico ham fat, thinly sliced	75%	olive oil	90	194	20 min	serve warm, blend into ham broth, garnish grilled peaches or watermelon	
langoustine (or other shellfish) shell, crushed to a fine paste and roasted	125%	unsalted butter	88	154	5	poach shellfish, blend into shellfish sauces	next page
thyme leaves	20%	grapeseed oil	55	131	45 min	season cooked fish and shellfish, finish lemon risotto	
lemon zest, finely grated	45%	grapeseed oil	60	140	2	garnish salads and fish	
makrud (kaffir) lime leaf, sliced	15%	grapeseed oil	3	37	24	drizzle over grilled fish, brush on pork cutlets	next page
fresh mint, thinly sliced	16%	olive oil	80	176	1	mix into vinaigrette	
molasses adapted from Michel Bras	50%	unsalted butter	80	176	20 min refrigerate for 4 d after cooking	fry sweetbreads or foie gras	next page
dry porcini	50%	sunflower oil	70	158	1	blend into game broth	
rosemary	10%	olive oil	80	176	1	drizzle over roast lamb	
rose petal, untreated	80%	sweet apricot oil	55	131	1¼	make salad dressing, beurre blanc for fish	
truffle, minced	30%	unsalted butter	55 ultrasonic bath	131	1 15 min	garnish poached scallops or artichokes	

from page 2·329

(set weight of fat to 100%)

SHELLFISH BUTTER

Yields 400 g

INGREDIENT	QUANTITY	SCALING	PROCEDURE
Crustacean heads, bodies, and shells, finely crushed or ground	500 g	100%	① Vacuum seal together.
			② Cook sous vide in 88 °C / 190 °F bath for 5 h.
Clarified unsalted butter	400 g	80%	③ Remove from bag, and cool at room temperature.
			④ Refrigerate for 12 h.
			⑤ Heat mixture to melt.
			⑥ Strain; discard heads.
			⑦ Decant butter.
			⑧ Vacuum seal, and refrigerate until use.

from page 2·329

SOUS VIDE LEMON HERB OIL

Yields 400 g

INGREDIENT	QUANTITY	SCALING	PROCEDURE
Grapeseed oil	400 g	100%	① Combine.
Lemongrass, thinly sliced	80 g	20%	② Vacuum seal.
Lemon thyme leaves	50 g	12.5%	③ Cook sous vide in 60 °C / 140 °F bath for 1½ h.
Lemon balm leaves	20 g	5%	④ Chill and refrigerate for 12 h.
Makrud (kaffir) lime leaves	20 g	5%	⑤ Strain.
			⑥ Refrigerate until use.

from page 2·330

SPICED CHILI OIL ADAPTED FROM JEAN-GEORGES VONGERICHTEN

Yields 1 kg

INGREDIENT	QUANTITY	SCALING	PROCEDURE
Grapeseed oil or other neutral oil	1 kg	100%	① Vacuum seal together.
Chipotle chilies, thinly sliced	180 g	18%	② Cook sous vide in 70 °C / 158 °F bath for 24 h.
Coriander seeds, toasted and crushed	30 g	3%	③ Cool and refrigerate for 12 h.
Mace, crushed	30 g	3%	④ Strain.
Dry red chilies, crushed	30 g	3%	⑤ Vacuum seal and refrigerate until use.
Star anise, crushed	30 g	3%	
Cinnamon sticks, toasted and crushed	20 g	2%	
Fennel seeds, toasted and crushed	12 g	1.2%	

from page 2·330

MOLASSES BUTTER ADAPTED FROM MICHEL BRAS

Yields 200 g

INGREDIENT	QUANTITY	SCALING	PROCEDURE
Unsalted butter, melted	200 g	200%	① Blend together.
Molasses	100 g	100%	② Transfer mixture to mason jar, and seal.
			③ Place sealed Mason jar in 85 °C / 185 °F bath for 30 min.
			④ Remove jar from bath, and take off lid.
			⑤ Rest in jar at room temperature for 30 min to allow butter and molasses to separate.
			⑥ Pour butter into sealable container, and discard molasses.
			⑦ Seal, and refrigerate infused butter for 4 d.
			⑧ Decant butter, and refrigerate for use.

from page 2·331

CURRY OIL ADAPTED FROM THOMAS KELLER

Yields 1 kg

INGREDIENT	QUANTITY	SCALING	PROCEDURE
Coriander seeds, toasted and crushed	90 g	9%	① Toast separately in small pans until just fragrant.
Cinnamon stick, crushed	35 g	3.5%	② Remove from heat.
Canola oil or other neutral oil	1 kg	100%	③ Blend fully with toasted spices.
			④ Vacuum seal.
Chaat masala see page 50	140 g	14%	⑤ Cook sous vide in 90 °C / 194 °F bath for 1 h.
Cayenne pepper	30 g	3%	⑥ Refrigerate for 12 h.
Mace	15 g	1.5%	⑦ Strain.
			⑧ Repackage, and refrigerate until use.

from page 2·331

CRAB OIL

Yields 400 g

INGREDIENT	QUANTITY	SCALING	PROCEDURE
Frying oil	400 g	200%	① Deep-fry crab parts in 175 °C / 350 °F oil for 1 h to infuse.
Crab shell and liver	200 g	100%	② Strain through fine sieve.
			③ Cool, and reserve in dry place.

from page 5·190

MALAYSIAN AROMATIC OIL

Yields 350 g

INGREDIENT	QUANTITY	SCALING	PROCEDURE
Grapeseed oil	350 g	100%	① Combine, and simmer until oil is deep red and heavily saturated with aromatics, about 45 min.
Tomatoes, peeled and seeded	140 g	40%	② Cool.
Red shallots, thinly sliced	75 g	21.5%	③ Vacuum seal.
Sweet onions, sliced	65 g	19%	④ Refrigerate for 12 h to finish infusion.
Sichuan chilies, seeded and crushed	40 g	11.5%	⑤ Strain through fine sieve.
Garlic, pounded to paste	10 g	3%	
Shrimp paste (belacan)	10 g	3%	
Ginger, grated	7.5 g	2%	
Red bird's eye chili, thinly sliced	2.5 g	0.7%	

from page 5·168

Additives to Preserve the Color and Flavor of Fresh Juice

Function	Ingredient	(scaling)	Note
inhibits browning, preserves color	ascorbic acid (vitamin C)	0.1%–0.3%	works best with citric acid
	citric acid	0.5%–2.0%	these fruit acids interfere with browning enzymes directly and by lowering pH; they work best in conjunction with ascorbic acid
	malic acid		
	tartaric acid		
	oxalic acid		
	honey	10% or more	high concentrations have preservative effects
	sodium benzoate	0.05%–0.1%	use only for foods with a pH ≤ 4.5; maximum permitted quantity is 0.1%; slows both browning and bacterial and fungal growth
	sodium metabisulfite (Campden tablets)	0.01%–0.05%	most effective at 0.03%; unpleasant flavor above 0.05%
restores or preserves flavor	fresh juice	5%–10%	add just-squeezed juice before serving to produce fresh volatile aromatics that refresh the flavor in some juices
	essential oil	0.001%–1%	add a few drops of the appropriate citrus essential oil just before serving to replenish natural oils from the peel and restore fresh flavor
	alpha tocopherol (vitamin E)	0.025%–0.05%	antioxidants such as vitamin C and vitamin E help protect aromas from the ravages of oxidation

from page 2·339

MEYER LEMONADE

Yields 325 g

INGREDIENT	QUANTITY	SCALING	PROCEDURE
Meyer lemon juice	300 g	100%	① Centrifuge at 27,500g for 1 h.
			② Decant juice and strain through fine sieve.
Fructose	30 g	10%	③ Whisk into clarified juice until dissolved and reserve.
Citric acid	1.5 g	0.5%	
Gum arabic	5 g	1.7%	④ Blend together until fully emulsified.
Water	2 g	0.7%	⑤ Add 1.5 g of emulsion to sweetened juice.
Lemon essential oil	0.12 g (seven drops)	0.04%	⑥ Hand-blend until smooth.
			⑦ Strain through fine sieve.
			⑧ Chill before serving.

Always add the essential oil just before serving. The acidity of the juice will destroy the essence. This is why the best quality citrus oils are made by removing the peel before cold pressing so there is no chance for the acidic fruit juice to damage the peel oil.

from page 2·340

MELON WATER

Yields 100 g

INGREDIENT	QUANTITY	SCALING	PROCEDURE
Melon juice	100 g (from 200 g of melon)	100%	① Whisk together and season to taste.
			② Centrifuge at 27,500g for 1 h.
			③ Decant only clear juice.
Fructose	5 g	5%	④ Vacuum seal, and refrigerate until use.
Lime juice	2.5 g	2.5%	
Tartaric acid	0.5 g	0.5%	
Salt	to taste		

The flavor of melon is created by enzymatic reactions during juicing. The fresh flavor can be reinvigorated by adding a small amount of fresh melon juice to the batch just before serving.

from page 2·340

PEN SHELL CLAM, PLUOT, MYOGA, SCALLOP MOCHI

Yields 650 g

INGREDIENT	QUANTITY	SCALING	PROCEDURE
Pluots (or red plums)	400 g	200%	① Juice.
			② Clarify juice using preferred method.
			③ Measure 200 g.
Malic acid	2 g	1%	④ Season juice.
White soy sauce	to taste		⑤ Refrigerate.
Pen shell clams, shucked	200 g	100%	⑥ Measure and refrigerate.
Scallop mochi see page 345	60 g (four pieces, 15 g each)	30%	⑦ Measure and reserve individually.
Freeze-dried scallop powder (optional, see page 58)	28 g	14%	
Frying oil	as needed		
Ginger oil see page 20	20 g	10%	⑧ Dust pen shell clams with scallop powder, if using, and then sear in oil over high heat for 1 min.
			⑨ Season, and allow to rest at room temperature.
Salt	to taste		⑩ Deep-fry scallop mochi in 190 °C / 375 °F oil until puffed, about 2 min, and then optionally, season with scallop powder.
Dinosaur Pluot (or red plum), thinly sliced	20 g	10%	⑪ Toss pluot and myoga with small amount of seasoned pluot juice.
			⑫ Arrange pen shell clams and pluot slices on each plate.
Myoga, fine julienne	12 g	6%	⑬ Garnish with scallop mochi.
			⑭ Pour additional pluot juice at table.

from page 5·202

SOUS VIDE BERRY JUICE

Yields 50 g

INGREDIENT	QUANTITY	SCALING	PROCEDURE
Blackberries (fresh)	100 g	100%	① Combine.
Sugar	7 g	7%	② Vacuum seal sweetened berry mixture.
Isomalt	5 g	5%	③ Cook sous vide in 65 °C / 149 °F bath for 1 h.
			④ Remove from bag, and cool at room temperature.
			⑤ Strain through fine sieve; discard pulp.
			⑥ Chill before serving.

This process works equally well for blueberries, raspberries, and strawberries.

from page 2·340

STRAWBERRY CONSOMMÉ

Yields 265 g

INGREDIENT	QUANTITY	SCALING	PROCEDURE
Strawberry juice	250 g (from about 400 g strawberries)	100%	① Centrifuge at 27,500g for 1 h.
Fructose	15.5 g	6%	② Season, and refrigerate until use.
Malic acid	1.25 g	0.5%	

from page 5·278

GREEN ASPARAGUS AND MORELS WITH ASPARAGUS JUS

ADAPTED FROM JEAN-GEORGES VONGERICHTEN

Yields 650 g (four portions)

INGREDIENT	QUANTITY	SCALING	PROCEDURE
Pencil green asparagus, unpeeled	200 g	80%	① Juice with Champion-style juicer.
			② Measure 50 g for recipe.
Asparagus juice, from above	50 g	20%	③ Whisk ascorbic acid immediately into fresh juice to prevent browning.
Ascorbic acid	0.4 g	0.16% (0.8%)*	④ Vacuum seal.
			⑤ Refrigerate.
Jumbo green asparagus, stalks peeled	250 g (eight stalks)	100%	⑥ Sauté for 3 min on all sides until just tender and golden.
			⑦ Remove from heat, and reserve.
Clarified unsalted butter see page 4·213	25 g	10%	
Jumbo green asparagus, stalks peeled	250 g (eight stalks)	100%	⑧ Vacuum seal.
			⑨ Cook sous vide in 85 °C / 185 °F bath for 12 min, immediately remove from bag, and reserve.
Clarified unsalted butter	25 g	10%	
Morels, thoroughly washed	120 g	48%	⑩ Meanwhile, sweat together for 5 min until tender and just cooked through.
Unsalted butter	50 g	20%	
Shallot, finely minced	30 g	12%	
Vin jaune (or Fino sherry)	25 g	10%	⑪ Add to morels, and cook for 3 min.
Heavy cream	15 g	6%	
Instant hollandaise see page 305	80 g	32%	⑫ Warm to 65 °C / 149 °F.
			⑬ Dispense from siphon, and fold into morels.
			⑭ Set aside, and keep warm.
Asparagus puree see page 55	50 g	20%	⑮ Warm prepared asparagus juice over medium heat.
			⑯ Whisk in puree.
Unsalted butter	10 g	4%	⑰ Whisk into warm thickened jus until fully emulsified.
Lime juice	to taste		⑱ Season jus.
Salt	to taste		
Flaky sea salt	to taste		⑲ Reheat reserved asparagus stalks.
			⑳ Season.
			㉑ Place two sous vide cooked stalks and two panfried stalks in center.
Chive blossoms (or finely minced chives)	10 g	4%	㉒ Garnish with warm morels and blossoms.
			㉓ Pour jus around plates at table.

from page 2·341

*(% of total weight of asparagus juice)

STRAWBERRY GAZPACHO

Yields 850 g

INGREDIENT	QUANTITY	SCALING	PROCEDURE
Strawberries, sliced	560 g	100%	① Prepare ingredients as noted, blanching onions if needed, to remove sulfurous notes.
Cucumber, peeled, seeded, and sliced	140 g	25%	② Vacuum seal together.
Red bell pepper, steamed for 10 min, peeled, and thinly sliced	115 g	20.5%	③ Macerate in refrigerator for 12 h.
Sweet onions, thinly sliced	115 g	20.5%	④ Blend to fine puree.
Extra virgin olive oil	50 g	9%	⑤ Pass gazpacho through fine sieve.
White balsamic vinegar	20 g	3.5%	
Balsamic vinegar	13 g	2.5%	
Garlic clove, crushed	2 g	0.5%	
Strawberry consommé see page 32	65 g	12%	⑥ Add to gazpacho.
			⑦ Serve, or vacuum seal and refrigerate until use.
Lime juice	15 g	2.7%	
White balsamic vinegar	4 g	0.7%	
Malic acid	2 g	0.4%	
Black pepper	to taste		
Salt	to taste		

from page 5·278

Preparing gazpacho in advance? Create *à la minute* flavor with this trick from Heston Blumenthal. At the last minute, juice a small amount of the principal ingredient—whether red cabbage, tomatoes, or strawberries—then add it to the existing gazpacho. Enzymes already present in the soup attack components of the added juice and rapidly regenerate some of the aromas lost over time. The fresh flavor comes right back.

MAKING JUS

Best Bets for Jus

Recipe	Liquid	(scaling)	Protein	(scaling)	Aromatic	(scaling)
beef juice	not applicable		ground beef	100%	not applicable	
beef jus	brown beef stock	100%	ground beef	35%	carrot, thinly sliced	12%
	red wine	30%	oxtail, jointed	15%	onion, thinly sliced	10%
chicken juice	not applicable		ground chicken	100%	not applicable	
brown chicken jus	brown chicken stock	100%	ground chicken wing	15%	shallot, thinly sliced	20%
	chicken juice (from above)	40%	chicken foot	8%	dried morel	5.0%
	fino sherry	20%			thyme	0.1%
mushroom jus	mushroom stock	100%	not applicable		crimini mushroom, thinly sliced	75%
	fino sherry	20%			shallot, thinly sliced	20%
	white port	10%			white miso	7.0%
	tamari	1%			thyme	0.1%
mussel jus	white wine	10%	mussels	100%	shallot	10%
					bay leaf	0.01%
pork and Banyuls roasting jus	brown pork stock	100%	ground pork shoulder	75%	sweet onion, thinly sliced	8%
	Banyuls wine	25%	ground pork trotter skin and meat	10%	carrot, thinly sliced	7%
rare beef jus	water	5%	beef, cubed	100%	not applicable	
rare salmon jus	water	5%	salmon fillet, cubed	100%	not applicable	
shellfish jus	shellfish stock	40%	shellfish heads	100%	tarragon extract	1.5%
	white wine	38%			white pepper	to taste
	vermouth	13%				
vegetable jus	onion juice, clarified	100%	not applicable		not applicable	
	carrot juice, clarified	80%				
	celery juice, clarified	55%				
	leek juice, clarified	30%				

from page 2·344

JUS DE LA PRESSE INSPIRED BY ALAIN DUCASSE

Yields 350 g

INGREDIENT	QUANTITY	SCALING	PROCEDURE
Lobster heads	600 g (about four heads)	100%	① Sauté until shells are golden and very aromatic, about 10 min.
			② Baste constantly with butter to cook through.
Clarified unsalted butter	60 g	10%	③ Place heads in basket of wine press.
			④ Extract juices by crushing shells completely with wine press.
White wine (dry)	200 g	33%	⑤ Combine with extracted lobster juices.
Lobster stock see page 6	120 g	20%	⑥ Reduce lobster juice by half.
Cognac	30 g	5%	
Lobster roe	80 g	13%	⑦ Blend with warm reduction until fully emulsified.
Unsalted butter	80 g	13%	
Olive oil	35 g	6%	
Lemon juice	to taste		⑧ Season.
Salt	to taste		

from page 2·347

Method	Cook (bar)	(psi)	(°C)	(°F)	(h)	See page
cook sous vide			90	194	1½	40
pressure cook	1	15			1½	
cook sous vide			90	194	1	
brown meat and bones, pressure cook	1	15			1	
pressure cook	1	15			25 min	37
cook sous vide			100	212	4 min	294
brown meat and bones, pressure cook	1	15			1½	5·17
cook sous vide			53	127	4	40
cook sous vide			50	122	1	5·161
cook sous vide			88	190	1½	
cook sous vide			85	185	3	

① Select a recipe from Best Bets for Jus.

② If cooking sous vide, vacuum seal the liquids, proteins, and aromatics together. Otherwise combine ingredients in a pressure cooker. Quantities are proportional to whichever ingredient (usually the protein or the stock) is set to 100%. For example, use 38 g of wine and 13 g of vermouth for every 100 g of heads when making shellfish jus.

③ Cook. Recommended cooking methods, temperatures, and times are indicated in the table. Pressures given are gauge pressures.

④ Press, strain, or sieve.

⑤ Season. For seasoning options, see Best Bets for Lowering pH on page 22, Seasoning with Salt and Other Flavor Enhancers on page 21, and Best Bets for Adding Flavor with Alcohol on page 24.

ROOT VEGETABLE JUS

Yields 350 g

INGREDIENT	QUANTITY	SCALING	PROCEDURE
Salmon belly, trimmed	200 g	200%	① Vacuum seal.
			② Cook sous vide in 43 °C / 109 °F bath for 1 h.
			③ Strain through fine sieve, and measure 100 g of salmon juice.
			④ Refrigerate.
Turnip juice	270 g (from 400 g turnips)	270%	⑤ Vacuum seal together.
			⑥ Cook sous vide in 85 °C / 185 °F bath for 3 h.
Rutabaga juice	115 g (from 300 g rutabagas)	115%	⑦ Strain through fine sieve.
			⑧ Reduce to 200 g.
Celery root juice	75 g (from 150 g celery root)	75%	
Sweet onion juice	50 g (from 120 g onions)	50%	
Leek juice	30 g (from 90 g leeks)	30%	
Parsnip juice	15 g (from 65 g parsnips)	15%	
Strained salmon juice, from above	100 g	100%	⑨ Stir into vegetable juice reduction.
Cold-smoked butter *see page 244*	70 g	70%	⑩ Blend in smoked butter until fully emulsified.
			⑪ Season with lime juice and salt.
Lime juice	to taste		
Salt	to taste		

from page 5·163

SOUS VIDE VEGETABLE JUS

Yields 750 g

INGREDIENT	QUANTITY	SCALING	PROCEDURE
Yellow onions, thinly sliced	400 g	100%	① Prepare vegetables as noted.
Carrot, peeled and thinly sliced	270 g	67.5%	② Combine, and vacuum seal.
			③ Cook sous vide in 85 °C / 185 °F bath for 3 h.
Water	160 g	40%	④ Strain through fine sieve, and cool.
Celery, peeled and thinly sliced	120 g	30%	
Leek, white only, thinly sliced	120 g (from 275 g peeled leeks)	30%	
Unsalted butter, cubed	45 g	11%	⑤ To serve, heat stock to 85 °C / 185 °F.
			⑥ Blend in butter until fully emulsified.
Lemon juice	to taste		⑦ Season.
Salt	to taste		

from page 2·347

CLAM JUICE

Yields 175 g

INGREDIENT	QUANTITY	SCALING	PROCEDURE
Clams, rinsed and soaked to remove sand	475 g	100%	① Combine.
			② Vacuum seal.
Shallots, minced	10 g	2%	③ Steam or boil for 3 min until clams have just released their juices.
Thyme	0.3 g	0.06%	
Bay leaf	0.1 g	0.02%	④ Cool.
			⑤ Strain juices and reserve. Solids can also be reserved for another use.

from page 5·230

LAMB GARLIC JUS IN A JAR

Yields 300 g

INGREDIENT	QUANTITY	SCALING	PROCEDURE
Lamb trim, ground	1 kg	100%	① Panfry ground lamb until golden.
Frying oil	90 g	9%	② Reserve meat and 10 g of rendered fat.
Carrots, peeled and thinly sliced	300 g	30%	③ Prepare vegetables as noted.
Shallots, thinly sliced	200 g	20%	④ Sauté together in saucepan with reserved lamb fat, until tender.
Sweet onions, thinly sliced	150 g	15%	
Fennel, thinly sliced	125 g	12.5%	
Garlic, peeled and thinly sliced	50 g	5%	
Red bell pepper, thinly sliced	50 g	5%	
Tomato paste	25 g	2.5%	⑤ Add to vegetables, and increase heat to high.
Star anise, crushed	3 g	0.3%	⑥ Stir mixture continuously until golden brown and fragrant, about 3 min.
Water	500 g	50%	⑦ Deglaze pot, and stir in browned meat.
White wine	200 g	20%	⑧ Remove from heat.
Thyme	5 g	0.5%	⑨ Divide mixture equally between two Mason jars.
Bay leaf	2 g	0.2%	⑩ Seal jars, and place on rack in pressure cooker.
			⑪ Fill cooker with water to cover bottom 2.5 cm / 1 in of jars.
			⑫ Pressure-cook at gauge pressure of 1 bar / 15 psi for 1½ h.
			⑬ Remove jars from cooker, remove lids, and cool jus to room temperature.
Lemon juice	to taste		⑭ Strain stock.
Salt	to taste		⑮ Reduce strained stock until thickened, about 12 min, and season.

from page 2·348

MUSHROOM JUS

Yields 270 g

INGREDIENT	QUANTITY	SCALING	PROCEDURE
Crimini mushrooms, thinly sliced	150 g	60%	① Sauté mushrooms and shallots together in butter until deep golden brown, about 12 min.
Shallots, thinly sliced	40 g	16%	
Clarified unsalted butter	25 g	10%	
Mushroom stock see page 6	200 g	80%	② Combine with cooked mushroom mixture in pressure cooker.
Fino sherry	40 g	16%	③ Pressure-cook at gauge pressure of 1 bar / 15 psi for 25 min.
White port (dry)	20 g	8%	④ Strain through fine sieve, and discard solids.
			⑤ Measure 250 g of mushroom jus.
Mushroom jus, from above	250 g	100%	⑥ Blend together until dissolved.
White miso	14 g	5.6%	⑦ Strain.
Tamari soy sauce	2 g	0.8%	
Thyme	2 g	0.8%	
Konjac gum	0.75 g	0.3%	
Salt	to taste		⑧ Season.
Sherry vinegar	to taste		

from page 2·348

SOUS VIDE MUSSEL JUICE

Yields 100 g

INGREDIENT	QUANTITY	SCALING	PROCEDURE
Mussels, rinsed thoroughly with beards removed	1 kg	100%	① Vacuum seal in one even layer.
			② Cook in 100 °C / 212 °F steam or boiling water for 4 min.
			③ Shock in ice-water bath.
			④ Shuck, and reserve meat for another use.
			⑤ Strain rendered mussel juices from bag and shells.
			⑥ Vacuum seal and refrigerate until use.

Mussel juice is classically used to accentuate the flavor of seafood broths and sauces. This sous vide method extracts the juices from the mussels without overcooking them so the meat can be used as a garnish for cooked fish (see page 5·151). Inspect mussels carefully and discard any dead or sandy shellfish. These can spoil the juice.

from page 2·346

TOASTED OAT JUS

Yields 250 g

INGREDIENT	QUANTITY	SCALING	PROCEDURE
Pigeon carcass	650 g	260%	① Roast in 175 °C / 350 °F oven until golden, about 35 min.
Pigeon wings	200 g	80%	
Sweet onions, thinly sliced	300 g	120%	② Sauté onions until translucent.
Grapeseed oil	45 g	19.2%	③ Add garlic, and sauté for 5 min.
Garlic, thinly sliced	10 g	4%	
Brown pigeon stock see page 6	750 g	300%	④ Combine with roasted carcass, wings, and onion mixture.
Red wine (dry)	300 g	120%	⑤ Bring mixture to simmer.
Rendered foie gras fat	65 g	26%	⑥ Skim surface.
Cognac	50 g	20%	⑦ Pressure-cook at gauge pressure of 1 bar / 15 psi for 1½ h.
Steel-cut oats, rinsed to remove surface starch	30 g	12%	⑧ Strain, and reduce to 250 g.
Sherry vinegar	20 g	8%	
Sugar	13 g	5.2%	
Black peppercorns	2 g	0.8%	
Reduced oat jus, from above	250 g	100%	⑨ Combine.
			⑩ Simmer for 25 min.
Pancetta	25 g	10%	⑪ Season.
Cognac	7.5 g	3%	⑫ Strain through fine sieve, and serve or refrigerate until use.
Sherry vinegar	5 g	2%	
Salt	2.5 g	1%	
Black peppercorns	0.25 g	0.1%	

from page 5·133

BANYULS GLAZE

Yields 300 g

INGREDIENT	QUANTITY	SCALING	PROCEDURE
Ground pork	2.25 kg	100%	① Coat meats with oil.
Pork trotter, bone in, finely ground	500 g	22%	② Roast in 190 °C / 375 °F oven until golden brown, stirring frequently to ensure even browning.
			③ Remove browned meat from pan, reserving fat.
Frying oil	225 g	10%	
Sweet onions, peeled and thinly sliced	500 g	22%	④ Sweat vegetables in pressure cooker with reserved fat until tender.
Carrots peeled, thinly sliced	450 g	20%	
Water	1.2 kg	50%	⑤ Deglaze vegetables.
Brown pork stock see page 6	400 g	18%	
Banyuls wine (or other semisweet red wine)	350 g	16%	
Bay leaf (fresh)	4.5 g	0.2%	⑥ Add with browned meat to vegetables in cooker.
			⑦ Pressure-cook at gauge pressure of 1 bar / 15 psi for 1½ h.
			⑧ Cool and strain.
			⑨ Reduce to glaze.
Banyuls vinegar (or other semisweet red vinegar)	50 g	2%	⑩ Blend in butter and vinegar until fully emulsified.
Unsalted butter	50 g	2%	⑪ Season.
Salt	to taste		

from page 5·19

TAGINE BASE

Yields 150 g

INGREDIENT	QUANTITY	SCALING	PROCEDURE
Sweet onions, thinly sliced	100 g	100%	① Sauté onions until translucent.
Neutral oil	25 g	25%	
Brown chicken stock see page 6	325 g	325%	② Add to onions, and bring mixture to simmer.
Ginger juice	21 g	21%	③ Reduce by half, about 20 min.
Water	10 g	10%	
Garlic, thinly sliced	9 g	9%	
Lemon juice	9 g	9%	
Clear honey	5 g	5%	
Salt	3.5 g	3.5%	
Cinnamon, freshly ground	1 g	1%	
Preserved lemon peel, brunoise see page 174	8.5 g	8.5%	④ Whisk into reduction and adjust seasoning. ⑤ Serve or cool, vacuum seal, and refrigerate until use.
Pickled fig, small dice see page 177	6 g	6%	
Saffron threads	1 g	1%	

from page 5·137

SQUASH GLAZE

Yields 150 g

INGREDIENT	QUANTITY	SCALING	PROCEDURE
Butternut squash juice	100 g (from 400 g squash)	17%	① Combine. ② Bring to simmer, and remove from heat. ③ Strain through fine sieve to clarify.
Sweet onion juice	100 g (from 200 g onions)	17%	
Carrot juice	50 g (from 200 g carrots)	8.5%	
White veal stock see page 6	600 g	100%	④ Combine with strained vegetable juice, and blend until smooth.
Shank cooking juices see page 276	100 g	17%	⑤ Reduce to 150 g.
Tomato confit see page 179	7 g	1.2%	
Unsalted butter, cubed	25 g	4%	⑥ Blend in butter and oil until fully emulsified.
Extra virgin olive oil	15 g	2.5%	
Lemon juice	to taste		⑦ Season glaze.
Salt	to taste		

from page 5·63

SOUS VIDE PRAWN JUS

Yields 250 g

INGREDIENT	QUANTITY	SCALING	PROCEDURE
Prawn heads	400 g	100%	① Combine.
Shellfish stock see page 6	160 g	40%	② Grind coarsely in food processor. ③ Vacuum seal.
Vermouth (dry)	80 g	20%	④ Cook sous vide in 88 °C / 190 °F bath for 1½ h. ⑤ Strain through fine sieve.
Tarragon extract see page 27	6 g	1.5%	⑥ Whisk in.
Salt	to taste		⑦ Season.
White pepper	to taste		

from page 2·347

SOUS VIDE RARE BEEF JUS

Yields 350 g

INGREDIENT	QUANTITY	SCALING	PROCEDURE
Beef (preferably a tough cut)	1 kg	100%	① Cut into 1 cm / ½ in cubes.
Bromelain powder (optional, NOW brand)	2 g	0.2%	② Combine meat and bromelain (optional).
			③ Cook sous vide in 53 °C / 128 °F bath for 4 h.
			④ Strain rendered juices through fine sieve, and measure 300 g of juice.
Water	50 g	5%	⑤ Combine with juice.
Salt	to taste		⑥ Season.
Sherry vinegar	to taste		⑦ Vacuum seal, and refrigerate. Do not reheat above 53 °C / 127 °F, or jus will coagulate.

from page 2·349

Rare beef jus created this way can be used for many purposes. Tougher meats may require more time to release their juice.

SOUS VIDE BEEF JUICE

Yields 300 g

INGREDIENT	QUANTITY	SCALING	PROCEDURE
Ground lean beef	1 kg	100%	① Vacuum seal.
			② Cook sous vide in 90 °C / 194 °F **bath** for 1½ h.
			③ Strain juice, and discard meat.
			④ Cool juice completely.
			⑤ Vacuum seal, and refrigerate until use.

from page 2·349

This process can be applied to all types of meats. Using the resulting juice, although more costly than water, is a more flavorful alternative than using water to make broths and sauces.

CENTRIFUGED CAROTENE BUTTER

Yields 1.4 kg

INGREDIENT	QUANTITY	SCALING	PROCEDURE
Carrot juice see page 2·336	2.2 kg (from 3.5 kg of carrots)	100%	① Bring 1.4 kg of carrot juice to simmer.
			② Blend in butter, and simmer for 30 min.
			③ Blend in remaining 800 g of carrot juice.
Unsalted butter, cubed	1.4 kg	64%	④ Divide mixture equally (check weight) among centrifuge bottles.
			⑤ Centrifuge bottles at 27,500g for 1 h.
			⑥ Refrigerate bottles until butterfat has solidified, about 2 h.
			⑦ Pierce congealed butterfat on top of each bottle.
			⑧ Pour out clarified carrot juice, and set aside for another use.
			⑨ Warm bottles in water bath, or microwave to melt butter.
			⑩ Decant clear, melted butter, and discard accumulated solids from bottoms of bottles.
			⑪ Vacuum seal and refrigerate until use.

from page 2·365

TOMATO WATER

Yields 1.2 kg

INGREDIENT	QUANTITY	SCALING	PROCEDURE
Tomatoes, peeled, seeded, and chopped	2 kg	100%	① Process with Champion-style juicer.
			② Measure evenly among centrifuge bottles.
			③ Centrifuge at 27,500g for 1 h, and decant.
Salt	to taste		④ Season juice, and refrigerate until use.

from page 2·366

Vacuum filters, wine filters, and enzyme clarification are good alternatives to centrifuging when making tomato water.

CENTRIFUGED PEA JUICE

Yields 325 g

INGREDIENT	QUANTITY	SCALING	PROCEDURE
Frozen sweet peas, thawed	700 g	100%	① Blend to fine puree.
Water	70 g	10%	② Divide evenly among centrifuge bottles, ensuring filled bottles are of equal weight.
			③ Centrifuge bottles at 27,500g for 1 h.
			④ Decant juice, and filter, to obtain about 325 g.
			⑤ Skim off and reserve thin, middle layer of pea butter—about 50 g—to spread on bread or blend into sauces.

from page 2·367

CENTRIFUGED ROASTED-HAZELNUT OIL

Yields 150 g

INSPIRED BY NILS NORÉN AND DAVE ARNOLD

INGREDIENT	QUANTITY	SCALING	PROCEDURE
Hazelnuts	400 g	100%	① Roast in 160 °C / 325 °F oven for 25 min.
			② Transfer while warm to food processor.
			③ Blend to form smooth butter.
Sugar	40 g	10%	④ Combine, and bring to boil to make syrup.
Water	40 g	10%	⑤ Remove from heat.
			⑥ Blend syrup with hazelnut butter.
			⑦ Divide mixture evenly among centrifuge bottles.
			⑧ Centrifuge at 27,500g for 1 h.
			⑨ Decant oil on top, and refrigerate until use.

The sugar syrup dramatically improves the yield of the product by helping to force a cleaner separation between the layers. It also sweetens the result, however. Use plain water to boost yield without adding sweetness.

from page 2·367

BANANA YOGURT

Yields 150 g

INGREDIENT	QUANTITY	SCALING	PROCEDURE
Bananas, unpeeled	500 g	500%	① Cook sous vide in 88 °C / 190 °F bath for 12 min.
			② Peel, puree, and measure 100 g.
			③ Centrifuge 400 g of puree at 27,500g for 1 h.
			④ Decant juice, and reserve 40 g.
Banana puree, from above	100 g	100%	⑤ Puree until smooth.
Banana juice, from above	40 g	40%	
Crème fraîche	30 g	30%	
Salt	to taste		⑥ Season yogurt.
			⑦ Refrigerate until use.

Adding 0.2% of Pectinex Smash XXL enzyme to fruit and vegetable purees and juices before centrifuging can both speed the separation process and increase the yield by up to a factor of two—see page 43.

from page 5·98

Best Bets for Consommé

Recipe	Liquid	(scaling)	Flavoring	(scaling)	Aromatics	(scaling)
bacon consommé	white pork stock	100%	bacon, thinly sliced	50%	sweet onions, thinly sliced	25.0%
	lager	8%			black pepper	3.5%
					maple syrup	5.0%
brown butter consommé	white chicken stock	100%	brown butter extract see page 4·213	5%	star anise	0.3%
	butternut squash juice	20%			saffron	0.1%
	vodka	5%				
chocolate water adapted from Sam Mason	water	100%	dark chocolate (80% cocoa)	24%	cocoa nib	10.5%
					cocoa powder	10.0%
consommé madrilène	white chicken stock	100%	ground chicken, browned	30%	coriander seed	0.5%
	tomato water see page 40	100%	tomato, peeled and seeded	15%	star anise	0.1%
	vermouth	5%				
kimchi consommé	ramen stock	100%	kimchi, pureed	6%	fish sauce	to taste
					lime juice	to taste
Parmesan water	water	100%	Parmesan cheese, grated	100%		
pea consommé	pea juice	100%	cinnamon essential oil (optional)	to taste	lime juice	0.01%
rhubarb water	rhubarb juice	100%	white soy sauce	12%	lime juice	2.5%
					fructose	to taste
shellfish consommé	shellfish stock	100%	lobster bodies	30%	onion, thinly sliced	4%
			crab knuckles	20%	carrot, thinly sliced	4%
			shrimp shells	12%	tomato paste	1%

from page 2·374

OYSTER CONSOMMÉ

Yields 300 g

INGREDIENT	QUANTITY	SCALING	PROCEDURE
Clarified unsalted butter	95 g	95%	① Sauté prepared vegetables together until fragrant and scallions are translucent, about 7 min.
Scallions, thinly sliced	20 g	20%	
Ginger, peeled and thinly sliced	11 g	11%	
Galangal, peeled and thinly sliced	9 g	9%	
White vegetable stock see page 6	425 g	425%	② Add to scallion mixture, and mix together.
			③ Reduce to 300 g, about 15 min.
Roasted coconut juice (store-bought)	100 g	100%	④ Strain.
			⑤ Cool.
Clam juice see page 36	150 g	150%	
Sake (dry)	110 g	110%	
Lemongrass, thinly sliced	20 g	20%	
Cilantro leaves and stems	5 g	5%	⑥ Add to strained liquid.
Makrud (kaffir) lime leaf	2 g	2%	⑦ Steep in refrigerator for 2 h.
Oyster juice	50 g	50%	⑧ Strain infused liquid, and season.
Lime juice	to taste		⑨ Clarify with vacuum filter.
Salt	to taste		⑩ Refrigerate until use.

from page 5·206

Method	Cook (°C)	(°F)	(h)	Clarify
cook sous vide	88	190	2	freeze filtration
cook sous vide	80	176	1	vacuum filtration
cook on stove top	90	194	10 min	centrifugation
cook sous vide	80	176	1	methylcellulose fining
infuse sous vide	refrigerated		24	agar filtration
cook sous vide	88	190	1½	freeze filtration
	n/a			centrifugation
	n/a			Buon Vino wine filter or Büchner funnel with Whatman 597 paper
fry shells, cool, cook sous vide	88	190	1	centrifuge

CLARIFYING A CONSOMMÉ

① Select a recipe. See the table at left for suggestions.

② Combine the liquids, flavoring agents, and aromatics. Quantities given in the table are proportional to the weight of the principal liquid. For example, use 8 g of lager for every 100 g of stock when making bacon consommé.

③ Cook (if applicable). Recommended cooking methods, temperatures, and times are indicated in the table. If cooking sous vide, vacuum seal all ingredients together.

④ Clarify. See Strategies for Filtering Liquids and Clarifying Consommés on page 2·352 for more details on the clarification methods suggested in the table; alternative strategies may work as well.

⑤ Season. For seasoning options, see Best Bets for Lowering pH on page 22, Seasoning with Salt and Other Flavor Enhancers on page 21, and Best Bets for Adding Flavor with Alcohol on page 24.

APPLE CIDER CONSOMMÉ

Yields 850 g

INGREDIENT	QUANTITY	SCALING	PROCEDURE
Sugar	40 g	8%	① Cook over high heat; allow caramel to become dark.
Water	20 g	4%	
White miso paste	10 g	2%	
Water	40 g	8%	② Deglaze caramel.
			③ Whisk until dissolved.
			④ Cool.
Apple cider	500 g	100%	⑤ Combine with caramel water.
Green apple juice	250 g	50%	⑥ Vacuum seal.
Cider vinegar	10 g	2%	⑦ Refrigerate for 4 h to infuse.
Malic acid	6 g	1.2%	⑧ Strain.
Salt	6 g	1.2%	
Thyme leaves	6 g	1.2%	
Pectinex Smash XXL (Novozymes)	1.6 g	0.32% (0.2%)*	⑨ Whisk into juice.
			⑩ Pour into tall, clear container, and refrigerate for 24 h to clarify.
			⑪ Decant clarified liquid without disturbing solids settled at bottom.
			⑫ Check seasoning.
			⑬ Serve with grilled mackerel or raw foie gras dressed in walnut oil.

from page 2·377   *(% of total combined weight of apple cider, green apple juice, and cider vinegar)

During the clarification process, the enzyme will force solids to the bottom of the container. See page 2·352 for more clarification methods.

SPRING GARLIC CONSOMMÉ

Yields 250 g

INGREDIENT	QUANTITY	SCALING	PROCEDURE
Carrots, thinly sliced	80 g	40%	① Sauté together until onions are translucent.
White onions, thinly sliced	80 g	40%	
Unsalted butter	25 g	12.5%	
Duck meat, ground	350 g	175%	② Combine with carrots and onions.
Water	200 g	100%	③ Pressure-cook at gauge pressure of 1 bar / 15 psi for 1 h.
Black peppercorns	0.2 g	0.1%	④ Strain through fine sieve.
			⑤ Centrifuge at 27,500g for 1 h.
			⑥ Strain, measure 100 g of consommé, and reserve.
Green garlic spears	200 g	100%	⑦ Blanch for 3 min.
			⑧ Puree.
			⑨ Centrifuge at 27,500g for 1 h.
			⑩ Measure 20 g of resulting clear juice, and whisk into consommé.
Lime juice	to taste		⑪ Season and serve, or vacuum seal and refrigerate until use.
Salt	to taste		

from page 5·86

BAGNA CÀUDA CONSOMMÉ

Yields 200 g

INGREDIENT	QUANTITY	SCALING	PROCEDURE
Garlic cloves, green removed and thinly sliced	80 g	52%	① Sauté garlic in oil until golden, and reserve.
Grapeseed oil	80 g	52%	
Sweet onions, sliced	75 g	48%	② Sauté onions in butter and oil until translucent.
Unsalted butter	50 g	32%	
Olive oil	25 g	16%	
Clam juice see page 36	155 g	100%	③ Add reserved garlic and remaining ingredients to onions, and simmer for 20 min.
Water	155 g	100%	④ Cool.
White wine (dry)	50 g	32%	⑤ Process in centrifuge at 27,500g for 1 h, or use alternative clarification method.
Garlic confit see page 176	27 g	17.5%	⑥ Refrigerate until use. Serve hot or cold.
Anchovy, chopped	25 g	16%	
Chives, minced	2 g	1.3%	
Thyme, minced	1 g	0.6%	

from page 5·230

PISTACHIO CONSOMMÉ

Yields 80 g

INGREDIENT	QUANTITY	SCALING	PROCEDURE
Raw pistachios, shelled	100 g	33%	① Combine.
Sugar	15 g	5%	② Roast in 190 °C / 375 °F oven until very dark and sugar has caramelized, about 20 min.
Grapeseed oil	10 g	3.3%	
Water	300 g	100%	③ Puree with roasted pistachios until smooth.
Pistachio oil	20 g	6.6%	④ Vacuum seal.
			⑤ Refrigerate for 12 h.
			⑥ Centrifuge at 27,500g for 1 h.
			⑦ Decant clear liquid through fine sieve, and discard remaining solids.
Salt	to taste		⑧ Season.
			⑨ Vacuum seal, and refrigerate until needed.

The remaining nut solids in the centrifuge bottles are not used for anything in this recipe or these volumes, but they're a delicious snack for the chef.

from page 2·376

POT-AU-FEU CONSOMMÉ

Yields 200 g

INGREDIENT	QUANTITY	SCALING	PROCEDURE
Oxtail	300 g	40%	① Cut through center of bone and joints to release marrow.
Ground beef shank	750 g	100%	② Coat oxtail and ground beef shank with oil.
Neutral oil	75 g	10%	③ Roast in 190 °C / 375 °F oven, stirring often to ensure even browning, until golden brown, about 15 min.
Sweet onions, cut in half	280 g	37.3%	④ Prepare vegetables as noted.
Turnips, peeled and thinly sliced	200 g	26.6%	⑤ Sear onions, cut side down, until dark brown.
Leeks, thinly sliced	170 g	22.6%	⑥ Sweat vegetables and garlic in suet until tender.
Celery root, peeled and thinly sliced	100 g	13.3%	
Garlic head, halved	70 g	9.3%	
Rendered beef suet	50 g	6.6%	
White beef stock *see page 6*	800 g	106.6%	⑦ Combine with roasted meats and vegetables.
			⑧ Pressure-cook at gauge pressure of 1 bar / 15 psi for 2 h.
Carrot juice	350 g (from about 550 g carrots)	46.6%	⑨ Strain, discarding solids.
			⑩ Clarify liquid with preferred method.
Parsnip juice	180 g (from about 650 g parsnips)	24%	⑪ Reduce to 200 g.
Black peppercorns	1.1 g	0.15%	⑫ Add to consommé.
Cloves, whole	1 g	0.13%	⑬ Infuse at room temperature to desired flavor, about 5–7 min.
Allspice berries	0.55 g	0.07%	
Salt	to taste		⑭ Season.
Sherry vinegar	to taste		

from page 5·52

OXTAIL CONSOMMÉ INSPIRED BY DAVID BOULEY

Yields 2.5 kg

INGREDIENT	QUANTITY	SCALING	PROCEDURE
Spanish onions, peeled and halved	500 g (two large onions)	25%	① Sear cut side down until light golden, about 8 min. ② Cool.
Water	50 g	2.5%	③ Vacuum seal with seared onions. ④ Cook sous vide in 85 °C / 185 °F bath for 7 h. ⑤ Transfer mixture from bag to bowl, and cool. ⑥ Strain, discarding onion solids. ⑦ Measure 250 g of onion jus, and reserve.
Oxtail, jointed	1.5 kg	75%	⑧ Brown oxtail over high heat on all sides until golden, about 15 min.
Neutral oil	30 g	1.5%	
Brown beef stock see page 10	2 kg	100%	⑨ Combine with browned oxtail in pressure cooker. ⑩ Pressure-cook at gauge pressure of 1 bar / 15 psi for 2 h. ⑪ Strain, discarding solids. ⑫ Measure 2 kg of oxtail broth.
Onion jus, from above	250 g	12.5%	
Gin	250 g	12.5%	
Veal marrow	250 g	12.5%	
Button mushrooms, thinly sliced	150 g	7.5%	
Carrots, peeled and thinly sliced	100 g	5%	
Celery stalk, peeled and thinly sliced	30 g	1.5%	
Oxtail broth, from above	2 kg	100%	⑬ Mix 200 g of broth with super methylcellulose.
Ground beef	300 g	15%	⑭ Whisk into ground beef to make paste.
Super methylcellulose SGA 150 (Dow brand)	2 g	0.1%	⑮ Mix paste into remaining oxtail broth for consommé. ⑯ Simmer consommé on low until clarified, about 45 min. ⑰ Strain.
Bay leaf extract see page 27	to taste		⑱ Season.
Lovage leaves, fine julienne	to taste		
Salt	to taste		
Star anise extract see page 27	to taste		

For photos of the steps involving methylcellulose, see page 2·359.

from page 2·376

RED COLESLAW

Yields 300 g

INGREDIENT	QUANTITY	SCALING	PROCEDURE
Green apple juice, clarified	400 g	267%	① Combine. ② Vacuum concentrate, using vacuum reduction equipment, to 150 g, about 2 h.
Red cabbage juice, clarified	400 g	267%	
Red wine vinegar	400 g	267%	
Honey	30 g	20%	③ Season juice reduction.
Black peppercorns, finely crushed	0.4 g	0.27%	
Salt	to taste		
Red cabbage, julienne	150 g	100%	④ Mix with juice reduction, and serve immediately.
Pickled mustard seeds see page 3·348	10 g	6.5%	

from page 5·72

HOW TO DISTILL WITH A ROTAVAP

① Prepare the liquid to be evaporated. If you are using citrus, remove the outer skin (zest) without including the white pith or the acidic juice. Mix with vodka (or, optionally, higher concentrations of ethanol); run the mixture through a homogenizer or blender to completely blend its components. Optionally, seal the zest-vodka mixture in a sous vide bag, and place the bag in an ultrasonic bath for 1 h (see page 2·415).

② Place the zest-vodka mixture in the evaporation flask of a rotary evaporator.

③ Set the target vacuum to 50 mbar / 38 torr and the bath temperature to 35 °C / 95 °F. Set the condenser chilling water temperature to 1 °C / 34 °F if you are using a helical condenser. If you are using a cold-trap-style condenser, fill it with ice water, and prepare a salt brine (see page 2·260). You may have to use a higher bath temperature if the rate of distillation is too slow.

④ Distill. The time required depends on the size of the batch and many other factors. Check the condensation coil periodically; if the condensation line rises more than three-quarters of the way up the coil, or if you can smell what is being distilled, too many volatiles are escaping. There are several ways to correct this problem. You can decrease the condenser chilling water temperature, increase the flow, or do both. Or you can decrease the bath temperature, but in that case, you must also decrease the vacuum. Release the vacuum when distillation is complete.

⑤ Separate the oil from the solvent. Pipette the thin layer of oil floating on top of the receiving flask into a separatory funnel. Allow the oil to separate overnight, or use a centrifuge (see page 2·360) to separate the components more quickly.

⑥ Drain any solvent from the funnel, and then drain the essential oils into a separate vessel.

⑦ Keep the essential oil refrigerated in an airtight container.

Boiling Point vs Vacuum Pressure

To set your rotary evaporator, choose a temperature appropriate for the boiling point of the solvent or material you want to distill, and then adjust vacuum pressure accordingly.

Boiling point		Water		Ethanol	
(°C)	(°F)	(mbar)	(torr)	(mbar)	(torr)
20	68	23	17	58	44
30	86	42	32	102	77
40	104	72	54	167	125
50	122	120	90	289	217
60	140	194	145	463	347

Because we start this recipe with vodka and end up diluting the result to 40% (80 proof) alcohol, no concentration of alcohol occurs. We are simply using alcohol as a solvent for the citrus essential oils.

One can also extract citrus essential oil mechanically, instead of distilling it. Commercially, this is done by pressing; the result is called a pressed essential oil. You can make your own by homogenizing citrus zest and alcohol as in step 1 (preferably by treating the mixture in an ultrasonic bath). Then use a centrifuge to separate the oil. It will have a different aromatic quality than the oil produced by distillation.

> We do not recommend distilling materials that are not obviously food-grade. A safer approach is to collaborate with a perfumer to recreate the scent with food-grade essences.

BUDDHA'S HAND VODKA

Yields 1.5 kg

INGREDIENT	QUANTITY	SCALING	PROCEDURE
Vodka	1.5 kg	100%	① Blend together for 3 min. Optionally, infuse in sous vide bag or jar placed in an ultrasonic bath for 1 h (see page 2·302).
Buddha's hand citron zest	400 g	27%	② Place liquid in rotary vacuum distiller for 3 h with vacuum pressure at 50 mbar / 38 torr and bath temperature at 35 °C / 95 °F. Set condenser chilling water to 1 °C / 34 °F.
			③ Distill.
Distilled water	as needed		④ Dilute distillate to 40% alcohol. Use hydrometer to measure ethanol concentration.

from page 2·389

VACUUM-CONCENTRATED APPLE AND CABBAGE JUICE

Yields 180 g

INGREDIENT	QUANTITY	SCALING	PROCEDURE
Green apple juice, centrifuged	400 g	267%	① Combine.
Red cabbage juice, centrifuged	400 g	267%	② Set bath temperature to 50 °C / 122 °F, condenser chilling water to 5 °C / 41 °F, and target pressure to 50 mbar / 38 torr.
Red wine vinegar	400 g	267%	③ Distill.
			④ Reserve concentrated source liquid.
Juice concentrate, from above	150 g	100%	⑤ Season.
Honey	30 g	20%	Because we discard the solvent, the concentration can be done by using a vacuum evaporator instead of a rotary evaporator.
Black peppercorns, finely crushed	0.4 g	0.27%	
Salt	to taste		

from page 2·389

MOCK TURTLE SOUP ADAPTED FROM HESTON BLUMENTHAL

Yields 4 kg (about 90 servings)

INGREDIENT	QUANTITY	SCALING	PROCEDURE
Brown beef stock see page 10	1 kg	200%	① Gently warm stock until no longer gelled but still cool.
Cherry tomatoes, quartered	120 g	24%	② Add cherry tomatoes, and infuse at room temperature for 20 min. Strain, and reserve infused stock.
Mushroom jus see page 37	290 g	58%	③ Combine, and mix with infused stock. Vacuum seal, and freeze.
Fino sherry	165 g	32%	④ When frozen, remove from bag, and place on perforated tray lined with double layer of cheesecloth.
White soy sauce	133 g	26%	⑤ Refrigerate, while freeze-filtering for 72 h (see page 2·370).
			⑥ Vacuum seal filtered stock, and freeze.
			⑦ Transfer frozen stock to food processor; pulse until coarsely crushed.
			⑧ Drain crushed, frozen stock over fine sieve lined with double layer of cheesecloth.
			⑨ Collect thawed, concentrated stock, and discard remaining ice.
			⑩ Transfer concentrated stock to Genevac Rocket bottles, and reduce by half at 8 mbar / 6 torr, heating temperature of 50 °C / 122 °F, and condenser at 1 °C / 34 °F.
			⑪ Reserve 500 g of reduced stock.
Freeze-concentrated stock, from above	500 g	100%	⑫ Combine, and vacuum seal.
			⑬ Cook in 60 °C / 140 °F bath until all gelatin dissolves, about 5 min.
Gelatin, 160 Bloom	60 g	12%	⑭ Transfer to depositing funnel, and dispense 6 g into each pocket-watch silicone mold.
			⑮ Refrigerate, and allow to set completely, about 4 h.
Gold leaf sheets	as needed		⑯ Remove gelled stock from molds, and place flat side down on corner of gold leaf sheet. Use tweezers to gently fold gold leaf over top of each gelled stock portion; use fine brush to tuck gold leaf under bottom edges.
			⑰ Refrigerate until needed.
			⑱ To serve, place each stock portion in bottom of teacup; pour 40 g of hot water over stock. Stir until gelled stock dissolves.

from page 2·394

Most Indian recipes start with toasting spices in a dry frying pan to develop the flavor. A better way to toast spices is to put them in a shallow pan in a combi oven or convection oven at 170 °C / 338 °F until fragrant. This avoids scorching the spices.

INDIES SPICE BLEND ADAPTED FROM OLIVIER ROELLINGER

Yields 20 g

INGREDIENT	QUANTITY	SCALING	PROCEDURE
Coriander seeds	2.1 g	28%	① Combine and toast in frying pan until fragrant.
Black peppercorns	1.7 g	22.7%	② Remove from heat, and cool.
Caraway seeds	1.5 g	20%	
Cinnamon stick, grated	1 g	13.3%	
Mace	1 g	13.3%	
Sichuan peppercorns	1 g	13.3%	
Star anise	0.4 g	5.3%	
Clove	0.2 g	2.7%	
Turmeric powder	7.5 g	100%	③ Combine in coffee grinder with toasted spice blend.
Orange peel, grated	2.5 g	33.3%	
Vanilla seeds and pulp	1.5 g	20%	④ Grind to fine powder.
Cayenne pepper	0.5 g	6.7%	⑤ Store in airtight container until needed.

from page 2·403

To make the vanilla seedpod scrapings, split a vanilla bean lengthwise with a knife then scrape the seeds and the residue surrounding them from the seedpod.

QUATRE ÉPICES

Yields 420 g

INGREDIENT	QUANTITY	SCALING	PROCEDURE
Black peppercorns	200 g	100%	① Toast spices in dry skillet until fragrant.
Cinnamon, ground	100 g	50%	② Combine in coffee grinder and grind to fine powder.
Nutmeg	80 g	40%	
Cloves	40 g	20%	③ Store in airtight container until needed.

from page 2·403

CHILI TOMATO SPICE BLEND

Yields 70 g

INGREDIENT	QUANTITY	SCALING	PROCEDURE
Freeze-dried tomatoes see page 188	30 g	100%	① Grind together to fine powder.
Freeze-dried piquillo pepper see page 188	25 g	83%	② Store in airtight container until needed.
Coriander seeds, toasted and ground	5 g	16.7%	
Sweet paprika powder	5 g	16.7%	
Controne hot pepper, finely ground	2 g	6.7%	
Hot-smoked paprika powder	1 g	3.3%	
Saffron threads	1 g	3.3%	
Fennel seeds, toasted and ground	0.6 g	2%	
Ajowan seeds, toasted and ground	0.5 g	1.7%	

from page 2·403

MEMPHIS RUB

Yields 32.5 g

INGREDIENT	QUANTITY	SCALING	PROCEDURE
Sweet Hungarian paprika	12.5 g	100%	① Grind finely, and sieve.
Salt	7.5 g	60%	
Garlic powder	3 g	24%	
Chili powder (McCormick brand)	2.5 g	20%	
Onion powder	2.5 g	20%	
Sweet paprika	2.5 g	20%	
Black peppercorns	2 g	16%	

from page 5·68

For our friends who think barbecuing is throwing a piece of meat on a flaming-hot grill: it's not. That's grilling. Barbecuing is done low and slow, with lots of smoke (see Smoking, page 2·132). In some places, you'd be laughed out of town or worse for suggesting otherwise.

KANSAS RUB

Yields 60 g

INGREDIENT	QUANTITY	SCALING	PROCEDURE
Brown sugar	50 g	100%	① Grind finely, and sieve.
Salt	4 g	8%	
Black pepper, ground	3.5 g	7%	
Chili powder (McCormick brand)	2.5 g	5%	
Sweet paprika	2.5 g	5%	
Garlic powder	1.5 g	3%	
Onion powder	1 g	2%	
Red chili, minced	1 g	2%	

from page 5·68

Dry rubs are usually put on 12 hours before cooking. However, we also use them as a spice mix added at the end.

CHAAT MASALA

Yields 70 g

INGREDIENT	QUANTITY	SCALING	PROCEDURE
Coriander seeds	19 g	76%	① Combine, and roast in 175 °C / 350 °F oven until golden, about 7 min.
Cumin seeds	15 g	60%	
Ajowan	3 g	12%	
Black peppercorns	3 g	12%	
Dried chilies	1 g	4%	
Salt	25 g	100%	② Combine roasted spice mix with remaining ingredients.
Dried green mango powder (amchoor)	8 g	32%	③ Grind mixture to powder.
Dry pomegranate seeds (anardana)	4 g	16%	④ Pass through fine sieve, and vacuum seal and refrigerate until use.

from page 5·282

SWEET SPICE BLEND

Yields 25 g

INGREDIENT	QUANTITY	SCALING	PROCEDURE
Star anise, toasted and ground	10 g	100%	① Mix together.
Dried ginger, ground	4 g	40%	② Vacuum seal and reserve until use.
Vanilla bean seeds and pulp	4 g	40%	
Black pepper, ground	3 g	30%	
Cinnamon, toasted and ground	3 g	30%	
Nutmeg, ground	1.5 g	15%	

from page 5·212

PASSION FRUIT GRANITA

Yields 180 g

INGREDIENT	QUANTITY	SCALING	PROCEDURE
Passion fruit juice	150 g	100%	① Combine.
Sugar	20 g	13.5%	② Transfer to Pacojet beaker, and freeze. Alternatively, freeze mixture in container, and break it up with fork into flakes periodically as it freezes. Reserve frozen.
Lime juice	10 g	6.5%	
Salt	1.5 g	1%	③ Pacotize once to serve.

from page 5·177

FISH SPICE MIX

Yields 450 g

INGREDIENT	QUANTITY	SCALING	PROCEDURE
Hazelnuts, peeled, roasted, and coarsely ground	24 g	100%	① Prepare ingredients as noted.
Sesame seeds, toasted	22 g	92%	② Combine in food processor or mortar.
Coriander seeds, toasted	6 g	25%	③ Grind to coarse powder.
White poppy seeds, toasted	5 g	22%	④ Vacuum seal to preserve aroma.
Dried ginger, ground	2 g	8.5%	⑤ Refrigerate until use.
Salt	1.6 g	6.5%	
Dried chamomile, ground	1.2 g	0.05%	

from page 5·154

This spice mixture is incredibly versatile. We highly recommend it for sole, turbot, or any similar fish simply panfried in butter.

PAIN D'ÉPICES POWDER

Yields 300 g

INGREDIENT	QUANTITY	SCALING	PROCEDURE
Cinnamon stick	8 g	3.3%	① Toast spices together in 170 °C / 340 °F oven.
Star anise	3.2 g	1.3%	② Grind spices to fine powder.
Cloves	2.5 g	1%	
Aniseeds	2 g	0.8%	
Coriander seeds	2 g	0.8%	
Spray-dried honey powder (store-bought)	240 g	100%	③ Blend into toasted spice powder.
Salt	12 g	5%	
Ginger powder	3 g	1.3%	
Nutmeg, grated	3 g	1.3%	
Mace blade	1.5 g	0.6%	
Orange zest, grated	1.2 g	0.5%	

from page 5·22

CITRUS SPICE ADAPTED FROM HESTON BLUMENTHAL

Yields 30 g

INGREDIENT	QUANTITY	SCALING	PROCEDURE
Orange zest, finely grated	11 g (from two oranges)	100%	① Combine.
Lemon zest, finely grated	9 g (from two lemons)	82%	② Spread on silicone baking mat.
			③ Dehydrate at 50 °C / 120 °F until completely dried, about 35 min.
Lime zest, finely grated	3 g (from two limes)	27%	
Licorice root, finely ground	3 g	27%	④ Combine with dried zest and grind to fine powder.
Vanilla seeds and pulp	1.5 g	13.6%	⑤ Vacuum seal and refrigerate until use.
Coffee beans, roasted and finely ground	1 g	9%	
Coriander seeds, deeply toasted and finely ground	1 g	9%	
Mint leaves, freeze-dried see page 188	1 g (20 leaves)	9%	

from page 2·404

LICORICE POWDER ADAPTED FROM MICHEL BRAS

Yields 280 g

INGREDIENT	QUANTITY	SCALING	PROCEDURE
Black olives, pitted	400 g	250%	① Arrange on nonstick baking sheet in one even layer.
			② Dehydrate in 80 °C / 175 °F oven for 8–12 h until completely dried.
			③ Measure 160 g of dried olives.
Dried black olives, from above	160 g	100%	④ Grind together to fine powder (N-Zorbit M will prevent powder from turning into paste), and reserve.
N-Zorbit M (National Starch brand)	20 g	12.5%	
Almond powder (meal)	80 g	50%	⑤ Mix together, and spread on nonstick baking sheet.
Demerara sugar	10 g	6.25%	⑥ Bake in 135 °C / 275 °F oven until light golden, about 35 min, and cool.
			⑦ Blend into olive powder.
Licorice root, finely ground	5 g	3.1%	⑧ Stir into powder.
Salt	5 g	3.1%	
Tonka beans, finely ground	1 g	0.625%	

from page 2·405

RAS EL HANOUT

Yields 155 g

INGREDIENT	QUANTITY	SCALING	PROCEDURE
Ginger powder	40 g	100%	① Dry-blend together.
Turmeric powder	30 g	75%	② Vacuum seal, and refrigerate until use.
Black peppercorns, finely ground	25 g	62.5%	
Coriander seeds, finely ground, toasted	15 g	37.5%	
Grains of paradise, finely ground, toasted	12 g	30%	
Cinnamon stick, finely ground	5.5 g	13.75%	
Star anise, finely ground, toasted	5.5 g	13.75%	
Dried chili, finely ground	5.4 g	13.5%	
Dried rosebuds, finely ground	5 g	12.5%	
Allspice, finely ground	4 g	10%	
Cubeb pepper, finely ground, toasted	3.6 g	9%	
Clove, finely ground	2 g	5%	
Nutmeg, finely ground	2 g	5%	

from page 2·405

EXOTIC SPICE MIXTURE INSPIRED BY OLIVIER ROELLINGER

Yields 90 g

INGREDIENT	QUANTITY	SCALING	PROCEDURE
Sesame seeds	50 g	100%	① Combine, and toast in frying pan until golden.
Cumin seeds	8.2 g	16.4%	② Cool completely, and reserve.
Sumac	18 g	36%	③ Grind together in spice grinder.
Ajowan seeds	6.5 g	13%	④ Add sesame and cumin blend, and grind to fine powder.
Dried oregano	2.9 g	5.8%	⑤ Store in airtight container until needed.
Cardamom seeds	2 g	4%	
Ground cinnamon	2 g	4%	
Nutmeg, freshly ground	1.5 g	3%	

from page 2·405

PACOJET PEA SOUP

Yields 660 g

INGREDIENT	QUANTITY	SCALING	PROCEDURE
Green peas, frozen	300 g	100%	① Combine and transfer to Pacojet beaker.
Heavy cream	200 g	67%	② Freeze to at least –20 °C / –4 °F.
Pea juice see page 41 (or white vegetable stock, page 6)	150 g (from 500 g of peas)	50%	③ Pacotize once. ④ Optionally, freeze and Pacotize once more for smoother texture. ⑤ Transfer soup to pot, and warm until just melted and velvety.
Salt	6 g	2%	⑥ Season.
Mint leaves, fine julienne	3 g	1%	

This soup is best served when at or below 60 °C / 140 °F, so that it retains its sweetness. At higher temperatures, the peas will taste cooked and less sweet.

from page 2·410

MOZZARELLA POWDER

Yields 450 g

INGREDIENT	QUANTITY	SCALING	PROCEDURE
Buffalo mozzarella	250 g	100%	① Cut into 2.5 cm / 1 in cubes.
Buffalo mozzarella brine	100 g	40%	② Dissolve glucose into whey.
Glucose syrup DE 40	100 g	40%	③ Blend whey mixture with mozzarella cubes until smooth.
			④ Transfer mixture to Pacojet beaker and freeze to at least –20 °C / –4 °F.
			⑤ Pacotize once without venting.
			⑥ Serve powder immediately, or store frozen for up to 1 h.

from page 2·411

FROZEN CHEDDAR-CHEESE POWDER

Yields 400 g

INGREDIENT	QUANTITY	SCALING	PROCEDURE
Water, cold	250 g	100%	① Combine.
Agar	2 g	0.8%	② Bring to boil, and hold for 1 min to fully hydrate.
			③ Blend over ice-water bath to create fluid gel.
Sodium citrate	8 g	3.2%	④ Disperse into fluid gel.
			⑤ Bring mixture to simmer.
Cheddar cheese, finely grated	150 g	60%	⑥ Incorporate slowly into simmering mixture until fully melted.
Salt	2.5 g	1%	⑦ Transfer mixture to Pacojet beaker, and freeze to –30 °C / –22 °F.
			⑧ Pacotize once, and refreeze to –60 °C / –76 °F.
			⑨ Pacotize again once more to make very fine powder.
			⑩ Serve immediately or store frozen for up to 1 h.

from page 2·411

HOW TO MILL A CREAMY NUT BUTTER

① Place the nuts in the feed funnel of the mill. Any tree nuts or peanuts will work.
② Run nuts through the machine. Repeat as many times as necessary to achieve the desired texture, tightening the collar for each successive pass. In using our machine, we have found that four passes yields a silky-smooth butter.

FROZEN CRÈME-FRAÎCHE AND PINE-NUT CREAM

Yields 1 kg

INGREDIENT	QUANTITY	SCALING	PROCEDURE
Water	500 g	500%	① Blend together.
Glucose syrup DE 40	135 g	135%	② Place in Pacojet beaker, and freeze to at least –20 °C / –4 °F.
Crème fraîche	100 g	100%	③ Pacotize once.
Pine-nut butter *see above*	100 g	100%	④ Serve frozen cream immediately, or freeze.
Skim milk powder	79 g	79%	
Isomalt	60 g	60%	
Salt	10 g	10%	
Sugar	10 g	10%	
Guar gum	2 g	2%	

from page 2·411

SOUR RHUBARB SORBET

Yields 780 g

INGREDIENT	QUANTITY	SCALING	PROCEDURE
Rhubarb, thinly sliced	500 g	100%	① Vacuum seal.
Glucose syrup DE 40	130 g	26%	② Cook sous vide in 90 °C / 194 °F bath for 2 h.
Sugar	30 g	6%	③ Pass through fine sieve.
Rhubarb juice	200 g (from 350 g rhubarb)	40%	④ Blend with cooked rhubarb.
			⑤ Adjust acidity to taste.
			⑥ Freeze in Pacojet container. Alternatively, churn in ice cream machine, and store in freezer.
White balsamic vinegar (or other semisweet white vinegar)	9 g	1.8%	⑦ To serve, Pacotize or temper churned sorbet.
Malic acid	3 g	0.6%	

from page 5·279

ROMESCO SAUCE

Yields 950 g

INGREDIENT	QUANTITY	SCALING	PROCEDURE
Water	150 g	60%	① Soak peppers at room temperature for 2 h.
Smoked Hungarian paprika peppers, dried	20 g	8%	② Remove peppers from water, and blend into paste.
			③ Press through fine sieve.
Olive oil	250 g	100%	④ Combine with paste.
Pine nuts, toasted	250 g	100%	⑤ Process mixture 3–4 times through colloid mill, using increasingly fine settings until desired texture is achieved.
Hazelnuts, peeled and toasted	150 g	60%	
Piquillo peppers (store-bought in jar, seeded)	150 g	60%	
Red wine vinegar	90 g	36%	
Garlic cloves, blanched	19.5 g	7.8%	
Paprika	9.5 g	3.8%	
Pomegranate molasses (store-bought)	8 g	3.2%	
Salt	to taste		⑥ Season.

from page 2·419

MAKING A SMOOTH PUREE

① Prepare the vegetables by cutting into evenly shaped, small pieces, as indicated in the table below.

② Cook as indicated. Suggested methods, temperatures, and times are listed in the table.

③ Combine vegetable with the liquid or seasoning indicated in the table. Set the weight of the produce to 100%. For example, use 12 g of butter for every 100 g of mushrooms.

④ Puree by using the tool indicated, and pass through a fine sieve. Optionally, process with rotor-stator homogenizer, ultrahigh-pressure homogenizer, or ultrasonic homogenizer for finer texture. For large quantities, a colloid mill is an ideal tool.

Best Bets for Vegetable and Fruit Purees

Ingredient	Prep	Method	(°C)	(°F)	(min)	Liquid	(scaling)*	Tool	See page
apple	peeled, quartered	sous vide	90	194	2½ h			commercial blender	5·17
asparagus	thinly sliced	sauté	high heat		10	vegetable stock	25%	commercial blender	33
						unsalted butter	15%		
artichoke	hearts, thinly sliced	sous vide	90	194	45	vegetable stock	50%	commercial blender	
						olive oil	5%		
beet	peeled, thinly sliced	sous vide	90	194	1 h	cooked beet juice	50%	commercial blender	
						unsalted butter	15%		
broccoli	stems, peeled and sliced	sauté	medium heat		12	neutral oil	3%	commercial blender	next page
	florets, sliced	boil	high heat		4	hazelnut oil	10%		
carrot	peeled, thinly sliced	sauté	medium-low heat		30	carrot juice	50%	commercial blender	150
						carotene butter	15%		
cauliflower	florets, sliced	sauté	medium-low heat		1½ h	vegetable stock	50%	commercial blender	5·281
						unsalted butter	15%		
corn	kernels	sous vide	85	185	1 h	corn juice	25%	commercial blender	5·101
						unsalted butter	15%		
celery root	peeled, thinly sliced	sous vide	90	194	1½ h	skim milk	34%	commercial blender	57
						unsalted butter	15%		
Jerusalem artichoke	thinly sliced	sauté	medium heat		45	whole milk	25%	commercial blender	
						unsalted butter	15%		
mushroom	thinly sliced	sauté	medium-high heat		30	water	50%	commercial blender	57
						unsalted butter	12%		
onion	peeled	oven roast	175	345	35	whole milk	12.5%	commercial blender	next
parsley	leaves	sous vide	90	194	7	water	to cover	Pacojet	
parsnip	peeled, thinly sliced	sous vide	90	194	45	unsalted butter	25%	commercial blender	
pea	whole	freeze and thaw	n/a			pea juice	50%	Pacojet	53
						heavy cream	10%		
potato	peeled, thinly sliced	sous vide	100	212	35	unsalted butter	50%	food mill or ricer	144, 148, 151
						heavy cream	30%		
shallot	peeled, thinly sliced	sauté	medium heat		30	unsalted butter	25%	commercial blender	
spinach	leaves	blanch	90	194	7	water	15%	Pacojet	
winter squash	peeled, thinly sliced	sous vide	90	194	45			commercial blender	5·60

from page 2·425

(set weight of prepared vegetable to 100%)

BROCCOLI AND HAZELNUT-OIL PUREE INSPIRED BY JACQUES MAXIMIN

Yields 400 g

INGREDIENT	QUANTITY	SCALING	PROCEDURE
Broccoli florets	300 g	100%	① Blanch florets in 2% saline water for 3 min.
			② Rinse in ice water.
Broccoli stalks, peeled and sliced	220 g	73%	③ Sauté stalks until golden and tender, about 4 min. Cool.
Neutral oil	10 g	3%	
Roasted hazelnut oil (Walnut oil or other nut oils can also be used for this recipe)	30 g	10%	④ Combine with florets and stalks.
			⑤ Puree in blender on high power until smooth.
			⑥ Transfer puree to beaker.
			⑦ Process with rotor-stator homogenizer at 4,000 rpm until extremely silky, about 3 min.
Salt	to taste		⑧ Season and drizzle with more hazelnut oil if desired.
			⑨ Warm through or refrigerate until use.

from page 2·426

CREAMED WATERCRESS

Yields 700 g

INGREDIENT	QUANTITY	SCALING	PROCEDURE
Watercress, large branches removed	450 g	150%	① Cook sous vide in 90 °C / 194 °F bath for 7 min.
			② Shock in ice water, and then remove from bag.
			③ Puree.
			④ Pass through fine sieve.
			⑤ Measure 300 g of puree for recipe, and reserve.
Water	125 g	42%	⑥ Dry-blend gellan and sodium citrate, and disperse in water.
Low-acyl gellan (Kelcogel F, CP Kelco brand)	7 g	2.3% (1.2%)*	⑦ Vacuum seal solution.
			⑧ Hydrate sous vide in 85 °C / 185 °F bath for 5 min.
Sodium citrate	2 g	0.7% (0.35%)*	⑨ Refrigerate gel stock until set.
Watercress puree, from above	300 g	100%	⑩ Combine with gel stock.
			⑪ Puree.
Glucose syrup DE 40	60 g	20%	
White onion, thinly sliced and blanched	51 g	17%	
Water	21 g	7%	
Olive oil	51 g	17%	⑫ Combine with puree.
Maltodextrin DE 19	27 g	9%	⑬ Pour into Pacojet beaker.
Egg white	24 g	8%	⑭ Freeze to at least −20 °C / −4 °F.
Garlic, thinly sliced and blanched once	20 g	7%	⑮ To serve, Pacotize once and serve cold as garnish for roast beef, or warm and use as sauce for roasted fish.
Capers	15 g	5%	
Salt	9 g	3%	

from page 2·426

*(% of total combined weight of the puree and subsequent ingredients)

PISTACHIO PUREE ADAPTED FROM ALEX STUPAK

Yields 445 g

INGREDIENT	QUANTITY	SCALING	PROCEDURE
Sicilian pistachios, shelled	200 g	100%	① Soak pistachios in water for 12 h, refrigerated.
Water	125 g	62.5%	
Pistachio oil	75 g	37.5%	② Puree together pistachios and soaking water, oil, and glucose.
Glucose syrup DE 40	40 g	20%	
Salt	4 g	2%	③ Pass through fine sieve.
			④ Season with salt.
N-Zorbit M (National Starch brand)	2.5 g	1.25% (0.6%)*	⑤ Whisk into puree to thicken.
			⑥ Vacuum seal and refrigerate until use.

from page 2·427

*(% of total combined weight of first four ingredients)

A colloid mill works superbly for making pistachio puree, as shown on page 54. A blender or Pacojet also works.

BLACK TRUFFLE CONCENTRATE

Yields 325 g

INGREDIENT	QUANTITY	SCALING	PROCEDURE
Black winter truffles, scrubbed thoroughly and thinly sliced	100 g	100%	① Combine and puree in blender or with rotor-stator homogenizer.
Brown chicken jus see page 34	25 g	25%	② Vacuum seal puree.
Red wine (dry)	15 g	15%	③ Cook sous vide in 80 °C / 176 °F bath for 1 h.
Portobello mushroom gills	10 g	10%	④ Transfer sealed puree to ultrasonic bath if available (see page 2·415), and process for 30 min. If bath is unavailable, proceed with remaining steps.
Tawny port (medium dry)	10 g	10%	
			⑤ Refrigerate sealed puree for later use, or prepare to serve.
			⑥ To serve, warm sealed puree in 80 °C / 176 °F bath for 10 min.
			⑦ Remove from bag, and blend until completely smooth.
Black truffle oil (store-bought)	7 g	3.5%	⑧ Season, and serve immediately.
Champagne vinegar	to taste		
Salt	to taste		

from page 2·427

This puree is quite expensive and a small amount can go a long way. Use it sparingly as a seasoning for sauces and dressings. To make a more diluted puree that can be served as a garnish, use more liquid, and then thicken with a fluid gel (see page 4·176) or blend into a mushroom puree (see page 5·216).

European summer and autumn truffles, Oregon truffles, and Australian truffles are all acceptable substitutes.

CELERY ROOT MOUSSELINE

Yields 500 g

INGREDIENT	QUANTITY	SCALING	PROCEDURE
Sugar	30 g	10%	① Heat to 190 °C / 375 °F to make caramel.
			② Cool completely.
			③ Break into small pieces.
Celery roots, peeled and thinly sliced	300 g	100%	④ Vacuum seal with caramel.
			⑤ Cook sous vide in 90 °C / 195 °F bath for 1½ h.
Skim milk	100 g	33%	⑥ Combine, and bring to simmer.
Unsalted butter	45 g	15%	⑦ Add celery roots, and puree to fine consistency.
			⑧ Pass through fine sieve.
Roasted peanut oil	30 g	10%	⑨ Whisk in oil, and season.
Salt	to taste		⑩ Serve or cool and refrigerate until use.

from page 2·427

FREEZE-DRYING

① Prepare the ingredients. Cut the food into bite-size pieces or thin slices to greatly reduce drying times. Arrange the food in a single layer on conductive trays that fit in your dryer. Aerate liquids and purees before freezing or grind them into small pieces after freezing.

② Prefreeze the food to below the critical temperature. See the table Prefreezing Temperatures for Freeze-Dried Foods on the next page for suggested temperatures. Faster freezing will yield better texture but will slow sublimation. Some foods have critical temperatures so low that liquid nitrogen or a laboratory freezer is needed to reach them.

③ Set the freeze dryer temperatures. Set the shelf temperature to 20 °C / 36 °F above the critical temperature of the prefrozen food. Set the condenser to 20 °C / 36 °F below the critical temperature.

④ Freeze-dry the food. Insert a fine temperature probe into the core of the frozen food. Engage the vacuum pump, and run it until the core temperature of the food is within 1 °C / 2 °F of the shelf temperature. Because of the physics of freeze-drying, the core temperature of the food may fall at first. This is not unusual. But if the core temperature of the food fails to increase within a few hours, increase the shelf temperature by 5 °C / 10 °F to supply more energy.

⑤ Increase the shelf temperature to 5 °C / 40 °F. When the core temperature of the food exceeds 0 °C / 32 °F, preliminary drying is complete.

⑥ Begin secondary drying. Set the condenser to the coldest temperature available and increase the shelf temperature to the temperature recommended in the table on the next page, or 20–60 °C / 70–140 °F (as warm as the food will tolerate without damage). When the core temperature of the food reaches the shelf temperature, freeze-drying is complete.

Best Bets for Freeze-Drying

Ingredient	Prep	Dimension (cm)	Dimension (in)	Primary Shelf (°C)	Primary Shelf (°F)	Primary Condenser (°C)	Primary Condenser (°F)	Secondary Shelf (°C)	Secondary Shelf (°F)	Total drying time (h)	Example use
beef	raw, sliced	1	⅜	−20	−4	−45	−49	30	86	8	grind to a fine powder, and use to form a meaty crust on steaks and hamburgers
beef tenderloin	raw, pounded paper-thin			−20	−4	−45	−49	30	86	4	break into "carpaccio chips," and dust with olive oil, grated Parmesan, and arugula powder
eggs	cooked, peeled	sliced or quartered		−35	−31	−60	−76	60	140	12	Astronaut Ramen
fruits	sliced	0.1	1/32	−40	−40	−65	−85	30	86	4	enjoy whole; use in cereal or as a garnish or seasoning
	pureed	1	⅜							8	
	chunks	2	¾							64	
ice cream	sliced	2.5	1	−30	−22	−55	−67	40	104	96	sold commercially as astronaut ice cream
lettuce and tender greens	leaves	whole		−25	−13	−50	−58	40	104	12	Caesar Salad (see page 189)
lobster	raw, whole, shelled			−10	14	−35	−31	20	68	120	reconstitute in melted butter; grind to a powder, and use as a seasoning
noodles	cooked	0.1	1/32	−15	5	−40	−40	70	158	12	Astronaut Ramen
pork belly	cooked or raw, thinly sliced	0.5	¼	−20	−4	−45	−49	30	86	6	
pork shoulder	cooked tender, shredded			−20	−4	−45	−49	30	86	12	
scallops	raw, pureed			−10	14	−35	−31	20	68	8	grind to a fine powder, and use as a seasoning
	whole									48	break into panko-like slivers, and use as a breading or garnish
stocks, broths, and sauces	cubed	2	¾	−15	5	−40	−40	70	158	36	instant bouillon, breading; use to enrich soups and sauces
	ground	1	⅜							8	
vegetables	fine julienne			−25	−13	−50	−58	40	104	4	Astronaut Ramen, breading, onion tart, instant potato flakes
	minced									4	
	sliced	0.1	1/32							4	
	mushroom caps	whole								24	
	pureed	1	⅜							8	

from page 2·451

HOW TO USE A SPRAY DRYER

① Prepare the liquid. Add a bulking agent and any flavoring as needed. Place the liquid into the intake system of the spray dryer.

② Set the temperature of the liquid spray. Use the dial at the top of the machine to set the spray or inlet-control temperature. We have found 70 °C / 160 °F to be a good starting point for kitchen-scale machines.

③ Set the air temperature or outlet temperature. The control is at the base of the machine. Start at 50 °C / 120 °F.

④ Begin spray-drying. The powder will collect in a receptacle at the bottom of the machine. If the liquid is too wet and sticky, or if it clumps, increase the amount of bulking agent, and set the inlet and outlet temperatures 5–10 °C / 10–20 °F higher.

Evaporative cooling keeps the juice much cooler as it dries than the outlet temperature would suggest.

SPRAY-DRIED BUTTERMILK

Yields 200 g

INGREDIENT	QUANTITY	SCALING	PROCEDURE
Buttermilk	2 kg	100%	① Blend together thoroughly.
Dextrose DE 36	20 g	1%	② Set spray dryer's inlet temperature to 90 °C / 194 °F. The outlet temperature should read about 57 °C / 135 °F.
Microcrystalline cellulose (Avicel CG 200, FMC Biopolymer brand)	20 g	1%	③ Spray-dry at full pressure until liquid is fully processed, about 2 h.
Lactic acid	0.4 g	0.02%	④ Store powder in airtight container.

from page 2·443

SPRAY-DRIED BLOOD ORANGE JUICE

Yields 250 g

INGREDIENT	QUANTITY	SCALING	PROCEDURE
Blood orange juice, clarified	2 kg	100%	① Blend together thoroughly.
Maltodextrin DE 9	100 g	5%	② Set spray dryer's inlet temperature to 100 °C / 212 °F. The outlet temperature should read approximately 65 °C / 149 °F.
Citric acid	20 g	1%	③ Spray-dry at full pressure until liquid is fully processed, about 2 h.
			④ Allow spray-dried juice to cool completely. If powder clumps, grind in coffee grinder, and try adding more maltodextrin and using higher drying temperature for the next batch.
			⑤ Store powder in an airtight container.

from page 2·443

Prefreezing Temperatures for Freeze-Dried Foods

Ingredient	Freeze to below (°C)	(°F)
fruit	−45	−49
eggs	−40	−40
ice cream	−35	−31
vegetables	−30	−22
meat	−25	−13
pastas, grains, and legumes	−20	−4
stocks, broths, and sauces	−20	−4
seafood	−15	5

When freeze-drying liquids such as stocks, grind the frozen liquid before spreading it out as a thin layer for much faster drying. A Pacojet does a good job on the grinding.

FREEZE-DRIED BEEF GRAVY GRANULES

Yields 200 g

INGREDIENT	QUANTITY	SCALING	PROCEDURE
Beef shank, ground	1.2 kg	160%	① Panfry; brown until dark.
Neutral oil	100 g	13.3%	② Remove beef from pan, and reserve.
			③ Measure 50 g of rendered suet and reserve.
Carrots, thinly sliced	150 g	20%	④ Prepare vegetables as noted.
Button mushrooms, thinly sliced	100 g	13.3%	⑤ Brown vegetables together in suet until deep amber.
Leeks, thinly sliced	100 g	13.3%	
Sweet onions, thinly sliced	100 g	13.3%	
Turnips, thinly sliced	100 g	13.3%	
Garlic heads, split	75 g	10%	
Rendered suet, from above	50 g	6.7%	
Red wine	150 g	20%	⑥ Deglaze vegetables.
Brandy	50 g	6.7%	⑦ Add browned beef.
White beef stock see page 6	1 kg	133%	⑧ Transfer beef and vegetable mixture to pressure cooker.
			⑨ Add stock, and pressure-cook at 1 bar / 15 psi for 1 h.
			⑩ Strain through fine sieve.
			⑪ Pour strained stock into centrifuge bottles.
			⑫ Centrifuge at 27,500g for 1 h, and strain through fine sieve.
			⑬ Measure 750 g of stock, and cool.
Centrifuged beef stock, from above	750 g	100%	⑭ Disperse gelatin into cold stock, and warm to dissolve gelatin.
160 Bloom gelatin	7.5 g	1%	⑮ Pour stock into 30.5 cm by 20 cm / 12 in by 8 in hotel pan, and freeze completely.
			⑯ Wrap frozen stock sheet in cheesecloth.
			⑰ Place perforated hotel pan (30.5 cm by 20 cm / 12 in by 8 in) onto another hotel pan that is same size but deeper.
			⑱ Lay wrapped frozen stock sheet flat on perforated pan; allow thawing stock to drip down into deeper pan below it.
			⑲ Freeze-dry clarified broth for 12 h, by using table on page 58.
For rehydration:			
Freeze-dried beef gravy granules	12 g	1.6%	⑳ Mix together.
Ultra-Sperse A	8 g	1.1%	
Salt	2 g	0.3%	
Water, boiling	120 g	16%	㉑ Whisk into dry blend.
			㉒ Divide gravy into four servings.

from page 2·454

SALTED, FREEZE-DRIED LOBSTER

Yields 20 g

INGREDIENT	QUANTITY	SCALING	PROCEDURE
Water	100 g	167%	① Mix until dissolved.
Salt	7 g	12%	
Lobster tail	60 g	100%	② Brine, refrigerated, for 12 h. Cook sous vide in 57 °C / 135 °F bath for 20 min.
			③ Freeze-dry for 12 h, by using the table on page 58.
			④ To use as seasoning, grate the dried lobster over food.

from page 2·454

RAMEN VEGETABLES

Yields 50 g

INGREDIENT	QUANTITY	SCALING	PROCEDURE
Mirin	205 g	205%	① Combine, vacuum seal, and cook sous vide in 80 °C / 176 °F bath for 2 h.
Water	205 g	205%	② Cool.
Soy sauce	105 g	105%	③ Strain; discard liquid.
Bamboo shoots	100 g	100%	④ Slice bamboo shoots 1 mm / 1/16 in thin.
Sugar	50 g	50%	⑤ Freeze-dry by using the table on page 58.
Carrots, fine julienne	100 g	100%	⑥ Blanch for 30 s.
			⑦ Shock in ice-water bath.
			⑧ Freeze-dry as above.
Young ginger, minced	40 g	40%	⑨ Vacuum seal and cook sous vide in 90 °C / 194 °F bath for 1 h.
			⑩ Freeze-dry as above.
Hon-shimeji mushrooms, tops	100 g	100%	⑪ Freeze-dry as above.
Scallions, greens only, fine julienne	100 g	100%	

from page 2·455

RAMEN STOCK POWDER

Yields 38 g

INGREDIENT	QUANTITY	SCALING	PROCEDURE
Japanese stock see page 6	300 g	100%	① Combine and vacuum seal.
Chinese everyday stock see page 6	250 g	83%	② Cook sous vide in 60 °C / 140 °F bath for 1 h.
			③ Strain.
Scallions, whites only, thinly sliced	10 g	3.3%	④ Heat broth to 85 °C / 185 °F.
Kombu	6 g	2%	
Smithfield ham, thinly sliced	6 g	2%	
Garlic, finely minced	5 g	1.7%	
Dried scallop (store-bought)	4 g	1.3%	⑤ Add to simmering broth.
Bonito flakes (katsuobushi)	2 g	0.7%	⑥ Steep for 10 s.
White soy sauce	to taste		⑦ Strain.
			⑧ Season.
			⑨ Freeze-dry by using the table on page 58.
			⑩ Grind into powder.

For more on how to assemble these components to make Astronaut Ramen, see page 5·247.

from page 2·455

HOW TO CARBONATE FRUIT WITH DRY ICE

① Put a layer of crushed dry ice in the bottom of a plastic, sealable container. Remember to use all safety procedures when handling dry ice.

② Place an insulating layer of paper towels or a clean, dry tea towel on the ice layer. This protects the fruit from the extreme temperature of the dry ice.

③ Put the cold fruit on the insulating layer. Let the dry ice and fruit settle a few minutes so that the "steam" pushes out the oxygen in the container.

④ Seal container. The lid may pop off a couple of times due to a buildup of air pressure. That's fine. Just put the lid back on.

⑤ Let the fruit carbonate. This will take only 30 min for small fruits like grapes and overnight for larger, whole fruits like apples and oranges. Longer carbonation times require refrigeration.

STRAWBERRY MILK SHAKE ADAPTED FROM JUAN MARI ARZAK

Yields 1.2 kg

INGREDIENT	QUANTITY	SCALING	PROCEDURE
Strawberries, washed and trimmed	1 kg	167%	① Arrange in one layer, and dust with fructose.
Fructose	400 g	67%	② Freeze.
			③ Thaw at room temperature.
			④ Puree.
			⑤ Strain through fine sieve and reserve 600 g of strawberry juice.
Skim milk	600 g	100%	⑥ Disperse powders in milk.
Sweet whey powder	12 g	2% *(1%)**	⑦ Bring to simmer, and remove from heat.
Locust bean gum (Tic Gums brand)	1.2 g	0.2% *(0.1%)**	⑧ Cool.
Strawberry juice, from above	600 g	100%	⑨ Blend cooled milk into reserved juice.
Dry ice	100 g	16.7%	⑩ Crush dry ice in blender to fine powder.
			⑪ Divide evenly among four glasses.
			⑫ Pour 200 g of milk shake into each glass. Wait 10 s; milk shakes will bubble over.
			⑬ Serve alongside our Mushroom Swiss Burger (see page 5·11).

from page 2·473   *(% of the total weight of the strawberry juice and milk)

ORANGE SODA

Yields 340 g

INGREDIENT	QUANTITY	SCALING	PROCEDURE
Navel orange juice* see page 2·352	300 g (from 700 g of oranges)	100%	① Centrifuge at 27,500g for 1 h.
			② Strain through fine sieve.
Fructose	30 g	10%	③ Combine with juice, and reserve.
Phosphoric acid	2 g	0.67%	
Gum arabic	5 g	1.67%	④ Blend together until smooth.
Water	2 g	0.67%	⑤ Add 1.5 g of emulsion to sweetened juice, and refrigerate remaining emulsion for later use.
Orange essential oil	0.12 g (about seven drops)	0.04%	⑥ Hand-blend juice until smooth.
			⑦ Strain through fine sieve.
			⑧ Transfer to soda siphon, and charge with two carbon dioxide cartridges.
			⑨ Refrigerate soda in siphons for at least 2 h before serving.

For other methods of clarifying juice, see page 2·352.

from page 2·472

CARBONATED GOLDEN RAISINS

Yields 100 g

INGREDIENT	QUANTITY	SCALING	PROCEDURE
Verjuice (store-bought)	125 g	250%	① Combine.
Golden raisins	50 g	100%	② Refrigerate for 2 h to hydrate.
Water	10 g	20%	③ Transfer to carbonating siphon, and charge with three carbon dioxide cartridges for 1½ h before serving.

from page 5·159

SHIGOKU OYSTER WITH FIZZY GRAPES, FRESH WASABI, AND MISO POWDER

Yields 300 g

INGREDIENT	QUANTITY	SCALING	PROCEDURE
Shiro miso	150 g	125%	① Dehydrate at 45 °C / 113 °F for 12 h.
			② Grind to fine powder, and reserve.
Shigoku oysters (or Kumamoto)	120 g (12 oysters)	100%	③ Shuck, reserving juice.
			④ Clean thoroughly.
			⑤ Refrigerate oysters.
			⑥ Strain juice, and measure 40 g.
Muscat grapes	120 g	100%	⑦ Blanch for 10 s.
			⑧ Shock in ice water.
			⑨ Peel, and halve through stem end.
Verjuice (store-bought)	50 g	42%	⑩ Combine.
Rice wine vinegar	5 g	4%	⑪ Pour over peeled grapes.
Salt	1 g	0.8%	⑫ Place grapes and juice into siphon.
			⑬ Charge with two cartridges of carbon dioxide for at least 5 h before service, and refrigerate.
Wasabi (fresh)	8 g	6%	⑭ Grate finely, and reserve.
Oyster juice, from above	40 g	33%	⑮ Combine.
Verjuice	30 g	25%	⑯ Blend until smooth.
Sucrose esters (Sucro, Texturas brand)	0.7 g	0.58% (1%)*	⑰ Remove carbonated grapes from siphon, and place 5½ pieces at bottom of each bowl.
			⑱ Top each bowl with one shucked oyster.
			⑲ Garnish with miso powder and wasabi.
			⑳ Whip foam until frothy with handheld foaming wand.
			㉑ Dress bowls with oyster-Verjuice foam.

from page 5·200   *(% of total weight of oyster juice and sour grape juice)

THE MODERNIST KITCHEN

63

Best Bets for Tartares

Meat	Recipe	Texture	Seasoning	Note
beef	traditional French steak tartare	coarse	raw shallot, raw egg yolk, ketchup, capers, parsley, mustard, Worcestershire, Tabasco sauce	the classic tartare
	Syrian kafta nayyeh	fine	mint, hot mustard, allspice, raw onion, olive oil	
	Ethiopian kitfo	fine	chili powder, niter kibbeh	traditionally served with injera or kocho
	Wylie Dufresne's hanger steak tartare	coarse	Béarnaise ice cream, scallion, pickled Asian pear, amaro	hanger steak is tenderized sous vide (see page 2·244)
lamb	Lebanese kibbeh	fine	bulgur wheat, raw garlic, cinnamon	young lamb is best
langoustine	Pierre Gagnaire's langoustine and poppy seed tartare	fine	green mango, thyme nougatine	use only extremely fresh langoustines
mackerel	horse mackerel (aji) tartare with ginger	moderately coarse	young ginger, shiso, sansho pepper	
musk ox	René Redzepi's musk ox tartare with oxalis and tarragon cream	fine paste	oxalis, juniper, tarragon	musk ox is dry-aged for 48 days
oyster	David Kinch's oyster and beef tartare	fine	mustard, horseradish, hot sauce	
salmon	salmon tartare with citrus	coarse	makrud lime, sesame oil, chili, yuzu	do not add citrus until just before serving; otherwise, it will cook surface of fish
scallop	Alain Passard's scallop and truffle tartare	small cubes	truffle, artichoke, hazelnut oil, lemon, tarragon	sear quickly over high heat before chopping to develop sweetness
	Heston Blumenthal's scallop and white chocolate tartare	fine	preserved lemon, white chocolate, caviar	
tuna belly	Nobu Matsuhisa's toro and caviar tartare	fine paste	soy sauce, caviar	
tuna loin	Hawaiian poke	medium cubes	ogo, candlenut, sweet onion, toasted-sesame oil	
venison	cured venison tartare with coffee	small cubes	blackberry, fennel, coffee, smoked salt	

from page 3·63

HANGER STEAK TARTARE ADAPTED FROM WYLIE DUFRESNE

Yields 650 g (four portions)

INGREDIENT	QUANTITY	SCALING	PROCEDURE
Champagne vinegar	500 g	125%	① Combine, and reduce until syrupy.
White wine	400 g	100%	② Strain.
Shallots, diced	290 g	72.5%	③ Measure 45 g, and reserve.
Tarragon stems	five stems		
Water	260 g	65%	④ Combine in small pot.
Sugar	140 g	35%	⑤ Heat while whisking until sugar has dissolved completely.
Glucose	60 g	15%	⑥ Remove from heat, and cool syrup slightly.
Egg yolks	625 g	155%	⑦ Temper with warm syrup.
			⑧ Hand-blend.
Béarnaise reduction, from above	45 g	11.25%	⑨ Add to egg mixture, to taste.
			⑩ Blend mixture.
Salt	5 g	1.25%	⑪ Freeze in Pacojet containers, or churn in ice-cream maker.
Hanger steak	400 g	100%	⑫ Vacuum seal, and cook sous vide in 50 °C / 122 °F bath for 3 h.
			⑬ Cool quickly in ice-water bath, and refrigerate.
Extra-virgin olive oil	6 g	1.5%	⑭ Sear one side of steak.
			⑮ Cool completely, and dice finely.
Salt	4 g	1%	⑯ Season steak tartare.
Tarragon, minced	3 g	0.8%	⑰ Pacotize ice cream, if using Pacojet.
Tabasco sauce	1.5 g	0.4%	⑱ Spoon steak onto plates, and garnish with spoonful of ice cream.
Black pepper	0.75 g	0.2%	

from page 3·65

BEEF AND OYSTER TARTARE ADAPTED FROM DAVID KINCH

Yields 680 g (four to eight portions)

INGREDIENT	QUANTITY	SCALING	PROCEDURE
American Wagyu beef bavette or rib eye	400 g	100%	① Trim off fat.
			② Dice finely.
Pemaquid oysters	80 g	20%	③ Shuck, reserving juices.
			④ Keep refrigerated.
Ketchup (Heinz brand)	60 g	15%	⑤ Combine.
Extra-virgin olive oil	40 g	10%	⑥ Adjust ketchup mixture to taste.
Orleans mustard	18 g	4.5%	
Hot sauce (Crystal brand)	8 g	2%	
Worcestershire sauce	5 g	1.25%	
Lemon juice	3 g	0.75%	
Whipping cream	120 g	30%	⑦ Whip to stiff peaks.
			⑧ Refrigerate.
Cream cheese (Philadelphia brand)	100 g	25%	⑨ Soften with paddle mixer until silky.
Horseradish root, finely grated	40 g	10%	⑩ Fold into cream cheese.
			⑪ Fold cream cheese mixture carefully into cold whipped cream.
Rice vinegar	to taste		⑫ Season whipped horseradish cream carefully to taste; chill.
Lime juice	to taste		⑬ Mince raw oysters, and combine with reserved oyster juices.
Salt	to taste		⑭ Fold oysters into diced raw beef, and season with ketchup mixture as desired.
			⑮ Place spoonful of beef and oyster tartare on each plate, and garnish with spoonful of horseradish cream.

from page 3·66

SCALLOP TARTARE INSPIRED BY ALAIN PASSARD

Yields 300 g

INGREDIENT	QUANTITY	SCALING	PROCEDURE
Mayonnaise (Kewpie or other good quality brand)	30 g	15%	① Whisk to form truffle mayonnaise.
Black truffle concentrate see page 57	20 g	10%	
Black truffle, minced	10 g	5%	
Lime juice	3 g	1.5%	
Roasted-hazelnut oil	3 g	1.5%	
Lime zest	1 g	0.5%	
Sea scallop (sushi quality), minced	200 g	100%	② Fold into truffle mayonnaise.
Fuji apple, peeled and minced	40 g	20%	
Chives, minced	0.75 g	0.4%	
Lime juice	to taste		③ Season scallop mixture generously.
Salt	to taste		④ Chill.
Brioche, frozen and sliced 2 mm / 1/16 in thick	10 g	5%	⑤ Dust brioche slices with powder.
Freeze-dried scallop powder see page 58	8 g	4%	
Clarified unsalted butter	25 g	12.5%	⑥ Panfry brioche until golden.
			⑦ Drain on paper towels.
			⑧ Cut into desired shapes.
Chive blossoms	as desired		⑨ Spoon scallop tartare into serving bowls.
			⑩ Garnish with brioche and chive blossoms.

from page 3·67

SALMON TARTARE CORNETS ADAPTED FROM THOMAS KELLER

Yields 400 g (24 cornets)

INGREDIENT	QUANTITY	SCALING	PROCEDURE
For the cornets:			
All-purpose flour	65 g	45%	① Combine and reserve.
Sugar	20 g	13.5%	
Salt	4 g	2.5%	
Unsalted butter, softened but still cool to touch	115 g	77%	② Whisk until completely smooth and texture resembles mayonnaise.
Egg whites, cold	90 g	60%	③ Beat egg whites into flour mixture until smooth.
			④ Whisk in softened butter by thirds until batter is creamy.
			⑤ Place circular stencil, 10 cm / 4 in. in diameter, on silicone mat.
			⑥ Spread some batter evenly inside stencil.
			⑦ Lift stencil off sheet, and repeat process to make 24 circles.
Black sesame seeds	20 g	13.5%	⑧ Sprinkle over each batter circle.
			⑨ Bake in 205 °C / 400 °F oven until batter is set and rippling, 4–6 min.
			⑩ Transfer sheet with circles to open oven door to keep warm.
			⑪ Flip one circle over, sesame seed side down; place an 11.5 cm / 4½ in cornet mold (size #35) at bottom of circle.
			⑫ If you are right-handed, place pointed end of mold to your left and open end to your right. Tip of mold should touch lower left edge of circle. Reverse if left-handed.
			⑬ Fold bottom of circle up and around mold.
			⑭ Roll carefully upward and to left to wrap circle tightly around mold. Leave circle wrapped around its mold.
			⑮ Repeat cornet molding process for remaining circles.
			⑯ Arrange cornets seam side down and leaning against each other.
			⑰ Bake in 205 °C / 400 °F oven until golden brown, another 3–4 min, to set seams.
			⑱ Take out of oven, and cool slightly for 30 s. Remove from molds.
			⑲ Store in airtight container for 48 h maximum.
For the salmon tartare:			
Salmon fillet, preferably belly	150 g	100%	⑳ Remove skin and pin bones.
			㉑ Mince finely.
Shallot, finely minced	7 g	4.5%	㉒ Add to minced salmon.
Chives, finely minced	5 g	3.5%	㉓ Fold in to combine.
Extra-virgin olive oil	2 g	1.5%	㉔ Adjust for seasoning, if necessary.
Kosher salt	2 g	1.5%	㉕ Cover salmon tartare, and refrigerate for at least 30 min.
Lemon zest	1.6 g	1%	
White pepper, freshly ground	to taste		
For the red-onion cream:			
Red onion, finely minced	9 g	6%	㉖ Rinse onion in strainer under cold water, and dry.
Crème fraîche	115 g	77%	㉗ Whisk until soft peaks form.
			㉘ Fold onions in.
Salt	to taste		㉙ Season.
White pepper, freshly ground	to taste		㉚ Transfer onion cream to pastry bag.
			㉛ Refrigerate for at least 1 h to firm up.
Chive tips, 2½ cm / 1 in long	24 tips		㉜ Pipe onion cream into each cornet.
			㉝ Spoon 3 g of salmon tartare over cream.
			㉞ Garnish with single chive tip.

from page 3·68

TENDER MEATS SOUS VIDE

① Select an ingredient and target temperature. The table below provides final core temperatures for many popular tender cuts; our preferences are highlighted in bold.
② Set sous vide bath to 1 °C / 1.8 °F above the target temperature selected.
③ Vacuum seal the meat with any flavorings, fats, or liquids desired.
④ Cook sous vide until the core temperature of the meat reaches the target. Use a digital probe thermometer, as described on page 2·243.
⑤ Optionally, sear the meat by using whichever method you prefer. For options, see page 2·270.
⑥ Season as desired.

Best Bets for Cooking Tender Meats Sous Vide

Ingredient	Rare (°C)	Rare (°F)	Medium rare (°C)	Medium rare (°F)	Pink (°C)	Pink (°F)	Medium (°C)	Medium (°F)	Note	See page
beef, filet mignon	**50**	**122**	53	127	56	133	62	144		
beef, flank	54	129	**56**	**133**	59	138	62	144	cut thinly against the grain for maximum tenderness, or use kalbi marinade	114
beef, hanger	51	124	54	129	**58**	**136**	60	140		
beef loin (rib eye)	54	129	**56**	**133**	58	136	60	140		5·5
beef, strip steak	52	126	**54**	**129**	58	136	62	144	dry aged is ideal	287
lamb, leg	54	129	57	135	**60**	**140**	65	149		
lamb loin (rack)	54	129	**57**	**135**	59	138	62	144		68
veal loin	**52**	**126**	54	129	56	133	60	140		
venison loin	**50**	**122**	53	127	58	136	60	140	high enzymatic activity can cause mushiness; cooking to a hotter-than-core temperature is recommended; use the same temperatures for similar game	69
pork loin	n/a		58	136	**60**	**140**	62	144		94
pork tenderloin	n/a		56	133	**59**	**138**	61	142		69
pork, shoulder blade	n/a		58	136	**60**	**140**	64	147	see page 3·48 for specific cuts	89
rabbit loin	n/a		56	133	**59**	**138**	62	144	cook in 72 °C / 162 °F bath to core temperatures to prevent mushiness	70
suckling pig loin	n/a		56	133	**58**	**136**	60	140		

from page 3·96   (temperatures in **bold** are those that we prefer)

RACK OF LAMB

Yields 400 g

INGREDIENT	QUANTITY	SCALING	PROCEDURE
Rack of lamb, eight ribs, frenched to loin	600 g	100%	① Wrap rosemary sprigs around bone to prevent them from being pressed into meat.
Rosemary sprigs	10 g	1.65%	
Olive oil	100 g	16.5%	② Vacuum seal rack with oil.
Neutral oil	as needed		③ Cook lamb sous vide in 62 °C / 144 °F bath to core temperature of 57 °C / 135 °F, about 40 min, and then rest at room temperature for 10 min.
Salt	to taste		④ Sear lamb, fat side down, until golden. Slice between ribs into individual chops.
			⑤ Season with salt.

from page 5·29

PORK TENDERLOIN WITH JUNIPER

Yields 500 g

INGREDIENT	QUANTITY	SCALING	PROCEDURE
Pork tenderloin, tendon and silverskin removed	500 g	100%	① Vacuum seal together.
			② Refrigerate for 12 h.
Juniper brine see page 109	200 g	40%	③ Drain, and refrigerate for 24 h.
Water, cold	100 g	20%	④ Disperse gelatin in water, and warm until fully dissolved.
160 Bloom gelatin	10 g	2% (0.9%)*	⑤ Reserve.
Leeks	300 g	60%	⑥ Peel away first layer, and discard.
			⑦ Peel away next four layers, and cut into large sheets.
			⑧ Vacuum seal leek sheets with gelatin mixture.
			⑨ Steam for 4 min, shock in ice-water bath, and pat dry.
Activa RM	5 g	1%	⑩ Arrange sheets on plastic wrap to make single large sheet, overlapping sheets every 1 cm / ⅜ in.
			⑪ Dust sheets evenly with Activa.
			⑫ Roll brined pork in leek sheets, twisting ends of plastic wrap tightly to form roll.
			⑬ Vacuum seal.
			⑭ Refrigerate for 12 h to ensure leek wrapper adheres to pork.
			⑮ Cook pork tenderloin sous vide in 60 °C / 140 °F bath to core temperature of 59 °C / 138 °F, about 50 min.
			⑯ Slice to desired thickness, and serve with mushroom jus or red-eye gravy (see pages 37 or 225).

from page 5·36

*(% of total weight of tenderloin, juniper brine, water, and leeks)

VENISON LOIN ROSSINI ADAPTED FROM YANNICK ALLÉNO

Yields 1.1 kg (four portions)

INGREDIENT	QUANTITY	SCALING	PROCEDURE
Venison rack (first four ribs only), bones frenched	600 g	100%	① Vacuum seal together.
			② Cook sous vide in 65 °C / 149 °F bath to core temperature of 56 °C / 133 °F, about 25 min.
Olive oil	45 g	7.5%	③ Let rest at room temperature for 10 min.
			④ Reserve.
Duck foie gras, sliced 2.5 cm / 1 in thick	200 g	33%	⑤ Vacuum seal.
			⑥ Cook sous vide in 55 °C / 131 °F bath to core temperature of 54 °C / 129 °F, about 20 min.
			⑦ Hold for further 20 min at temperature to pasteurize (optional).
Truffle jus see page 212	150 g	25%	⑧ Heat jus until just warmed.
Game broth or brown chicken stock see page 14 or page 6	100 g	16.5%	⑨ Simmer pasta shells in game broth and mushroom jus until al dente.
Semolina pasta shells	50 g	8.5%	
Mushroom jus see page 37	30 g	5%	
Heavy cream, warmed and whipped	25 g	4%	⑩ Fold into pasta.
Salt	to taste		⑪ Slice venison into individual rib chops.
Summer truffle, peeled, thinly sliced and ring cut into 1.25 cm / ½ in circles (optional)	as desired		⑫ Cover top of each loin portion with truffle slices, if using.
			⑬ Slice foie gras into sections 1 cm / ⅜ in thick.
			⑭ Season venison, foie gras, and pasta.
			⑮ Arrange evenly among plates, and garnish with truffle jus.

from page 3·98

Flaky sea salt is a great way to finish a cooked piece of meat or fish. It adds crunchy bursts of saltiness. The only problem is that the salt tends to dissolve into the natural juices by the time the dish reaches the table. Hervé This came up with a solution: toss the salt crystals with oil or fat. A thin layer of oil then separates the flakes from the cooking juices and prevents the salt from dissolving.

RIB EYE WITH CHERRY MUSTARD MARMALADE AND PORCINI
ADAPTED FROM ALAIN DUCASSE

Yields 1 kg (four portions)

INGREDIENT	QUANTITY	SCALING	PROCEDURE
Beef rib eye, bone in, 5 cm / 2 in thick	800 g	100%	① Vacuum seal together.
Unsalted butter	40 g	5%	② Cook sous vide in 54 °C / 129 °F bath to core temperature of 53 °C / 127 °F, about 1¼ h.
			③ Sear surfaces with blowtorch.
Shallots, finely minced	50 g	6%	④ Sweat until shallots are tender but not browned.
Fennel, finely minced	25 g	3%	
Neutral oil	12.5 g	1.5%	
Pickled cherry brine see page 180	150 g	19%	⑤ Add to shallot mixture.
Red wine vinegar	50 g	6%	⑥ Reduce to 100 g to form cherry marmalade.
Red wine (Pinot Noir)	40 g	5%	
Quatre épices see page 48	0.5 g	0.06%	
Black peppercorns, crushed	0.4 g	0.05%	
Juniper berries, finely ground	0.4 g	0.05%	
Coriander seeds, finely ground	0.15 g	0.02%	
Pickled cherries, finely minced see page 180	100 g	12.5%	⑦ Whisk into marmalade.
Grain mustard	40 g	5%	
Morello cherry puree	35 g	4.5%	
Pressure-cooked mustard seeds see page 151	8 g	1%	
Porcini (fresh)	100 g	12.5%	⑧ Slice porcini very thinly, and quickly sauté until golden and cooked through.
Neutral oil	as needed		
Salt	to taste		⑨ Slice meat to desired thickness.
			⑩ Season meat, marmalade, and mushrooms, and arrange on plates.

from page 3·97

SOUS VIDE RABBIT LOIN

Yields 450 g

INGREDIENT	QUANTITY	SCALING	PROCEDURE
Rabbit loins, trimmed and silver skin removed	450 g	100%	① Dust rabbit loins evenly with Activa.
Activa RM or GS	10 g	2.2%	② Position opposing loins, tapered sides together, to form even cylinders 3 cm / 1¼ in. in diameter.
			③ Wrap each pair of loins tightly in plastic wrap, and vacuum seal.
			④ Refrigerate for at least 6 h to allow enzyme to bind loins.
Extra virgin olive oil	50 g	11%	⑤ Vacuum seal loins with oil.
			⑥ Cook sous vide in 57 °C / 135 °F bath to core temperature of 56 °C / 133 °F, about 25 min.
Freeze-dried piquillo pepper powder see page 188	10 g	2.2%	⑦ Dust rabbit loin with piquillo pepper powder, and then slice on bias, 1 cm / ⅜ in thick.
Salt	to taste		⑧ Season.

from page 5·242

TENDER POULTRY SOUS VIDE

① Select an ingredient and target temperature. The table below provides final core temperatures for many kinds of poultry, both red (top table) and white (bottom table). We prefer the temperatures in bold.
② Set sous vide bath to 1 °C / 1.8 °F above the target core temperature.
③ Vacuum seal the poultry with any flavorings, fats, or liquids.
④ Cook sous vide until the core temperature of the meat reaches the target. Use a digital probe thermometer, as described on pages 2·202 and 2·243.
⑤ Pasteurize (optional). Hold at cooking temperature for the amount of time indicated in the table to achieve full pasteurization.
⑥ Optionally, sear the meat. See page 2·270 for searing methods.
⑦ Season as desired.

"Time to pasteurize" is the amount of time to hold *after* the core reaches the specified temperature, if the bath is 1 °C / 1.8 °F above core temperature.

Best Bets for Cooking Tender Red Poultry Sous Vide

	Rare		Hold to pasteurize	Medium rare		Hold to pasteurize	Pink		Hold to pasteurize	
Ingredient	(°C)	(°F)	(h)	(°C)	(°F)	(h)	(°C)	(°F)	(min)	See page
duck breast	52	126	5 h 15 min	**54**	**129**	2 h 17 min	58	136	30	5·121
goose breast	50	122	n/a	**52**	**126**	5 h 15 min	55	131	40	
grouse breast	**50**	**122**	n/a	52	126	5 h 15 min	58	136	30	
ostrich fillet	**50**	**122**	n/a	54	129	2 h 17 min	58	136	30	
pigeon breast	52	126	5 h 15 min	**54**	**129**	2 h 17 min	58	136	30	5·125

from page 3·99 (*temperatures in **bold** are those that we prefer*)

Best Bets for Cooking Tender White Poultry Sous Vide

	Medium rare (slightly pink)		Hold to pasteurize	Medium		Hold to pasteurize	Medium well		Hold to pasteurize		
Ingredient	(°C)	(°F)	(min)	(°C)	(°F)	(min)	(°C)	(°F)	(min)	Note	See page
chicken breast	**58**	**136**	30	61	142	13	65	149	2		5·113
chicken "oyster"	61	142	15	**65**	**149**	2	68	154	½		
guinea hen breast	52	126	5 h 15 min	**54**	**129**	2 h 17 min	58	136	30	best tenderized with a yogurt- or enzyme-enriched marinade	5·135
pheasant breast	54	133	35	**56**	**129**	2 h 17 min	58	136	30		
quail breast	50	122	12 h	**52**	**126**	5 h 15 min	54	129	2 h 17 min		73
turkey breast	54	129	2 h 17 min	**56**	**133**	35	58	136	30	brine	101

from page 3·99 (*temperatures in **bold** are those that we prefer*)

POULET AU FEU D'ENFER ADAPTED FROM FERNAND POINT

Yields 1.1 kg (four to eight portions)

INGREDIENT	QUANTITY	SCALING	PROCEDURE
Chicken breasts, skin on	500 g	100%	① Season chicken pieces.
Chicken thighs, bone in and skin on	500 g	100%	② Vacuum seal individually.
Salt	to taste		③ Cook breasts sous vide in 59 °C / 138 °F bath to core temperature of 58 °C / 136 °F, about 35 min.
			④ Hold for additional 30 min to pasteurize (optional).
			⑤ Cook thighs sous vide in 65 °C / 149 °F bath for 1½ h.
Chicken wings, whole, finely chopped	250 g	50%	⑥ Sauté until golden, about 12 min.
Shallots, thinly sliced	100 g	20%	
Unsalted butter	30 g	6%	
Garlic, thinly sliced	20 g	4%	
Brown chicken stock see page 6	200 g	40%	⑦ Deglaze wings.
			⑧ Reduce liquid by two-thirds until syrupy, about 10 min.
White wine (dry)	90 g	18%	⑨ Strain sauce.
Red wine vinegar	80 g	16%	
Heavy cream	50 g	10%	
Black pepper, coarsely ground	to taste		⑩ Season vinegar sauce.
Salt	to taste		
Clarified unsalted butter	as needed		⑪ Heat thin film of butter over high heat in two separate pans.
Chanterelles, washed thoroughly	200 g	40%	⑫ Sauté chanterelles until just cooked through, and season with salt.
			⑬ Sear cooked chicken pieces, skin side down only, until skin is just crisped, about 2 min.
			⑭ Slice, and divide evenly among plates.
Chives, finely minced (or chive blossoms)	30 g	6%	⑮ Garnish with vinegar sauce, chanterelles, and chives.

from page 3·100

PIGEON WITH SHELLFISH BUTTER ADAPTED FROM ALAIN CHAPEL

Yields 550 g (four portions)

INGREDIENT	QUANTITY	SCALING	PROCEDURE
Pigeon breast roulade see page 3·254	240 g (two roulades)	100%	① Vacuum seal together.
			② Cook sous vide in 55 °C / 131 °F bath to core temperature of 54 °C / 129 °F, about 25 min.
Shellfish butter see page 29	80 g	33%	③ Hold for additional 2½ h to pasteurize (optional).
			④ Remove roulades from bag, and let rest for 5 min.
			⑤ Reserve infused shellfish butter in warm place.
Spot prawn tails, peeled	180 g (12 tails, 15 g each)	75%	⑥ Vacuum seal tails.
			⑦ Cook sous vide in 50 °C / 122 °F bath to core temperature of 49 °C / 120 °F, about 12 min.
Oyster mushrooms, small	80 g	33%	⑧ Sauté mushrooms until just cooked through.
Unsalted butter	12 g	5%	
Salt	to taste		⑨ Season mushrooms, pigeon, and prawns.
Crystallized ginger, small dice	10 g	4%	⑩ Slice each roulade into six pieces, discard ends, and divide among four plates.
			⑪ Garnish evenly with prawn tails, shellfish butter, mushrooms, and candied ginger.

from page 3·100

QUAIL WITH APPLE-VINEGAR EMULSION AND WATER CHESTNUTS

ADAPTED FROM CHARLIE TROTTER

Yields 350 g

INGREDIENT	QUANTITY	SCALING	PROCEDURE
Quail, whole, semi-boneless	400 g (four whole)	100%	① Pack cure evenly onto quails.
Confit cure mix see page 106	60 g	15%	② Vacuum seal together.
			③ Refrigerate for 2 h.
			④ Rinse off cure, and vacuum seal quails individually.
			⑤ Cook sous vide in 55 °C / 131 °F bath to core temperature of 54 °C / 129 °F, about 25 min.
			⑥ Hold at 54 °C / 129 °F for another 2 h 17 min to pasteurize (optional).
			⑦ Remove from bags, and allow to rest for 15 min.
Brown chicken stock see page 6	200 g	50%	⑧ Reduce over high heat to 100 g, and strain.
Apple cider (fresh)	125 g	31%	
Apple cider vinegar	50 g	12.5%	
Shallots, thinly sliced	50 g	12.5%	
Unsalted butter	30 g	7.5%	⑨ Blend into reduction until fully emulsified.
Salt	to taste		⑩ Season.
Chervil	5 g	1.25%	⑪ Whisk into apple-vinegar emulsion, and reserve warm.
Unsalted butter, cubed	40 g	10%	⑫ Sauté water chestnuts and pickled apples in butter until just warmed through, about 2 min, to make topping.
Water chestnuts, peeled, finely diced, and blanched in boiling water for 2 min	40 g	10%	
Sweet pickled apples, brunoise see page 3·348	30 g	7.5%	
Salt	to taste		⑬ Season topping.
Tarragon, thinly sliced	2 g	0.5%	⑭ Fold into pickled apple and water chestnut topping, and reserve.
Crisp Coat UC or potato starch (National Starch brand)	100 g	25%	⑮ Dry blend powders.
			⑯ Dredge cooked quails, and shake off excess coating.
Quatre épices see page 48	20 g	5%	
Frying oil	as needed		⑰ Deep-fry quails in 230 °C / 450 °F oil for 35 s.
Quatre épices see page 48	as needed		⑱ Place in center of plates.
			⑲ Garnish with apple and water chestnut topping, and apple-vinegar emulsion.
			⑳ Dust with additional quatre épices, if desired.

from page 3·101

FISH AND SHELLFISH SOUS VIDE

① Select an ingredient and target temperature. The table below provides final core temperatures for many kinds of fish. We prefer the temperatures in bold.
② Vacuum seal the fish or shellfish with any flavorings, fats, or liquids.
③ Cook sous vide until the core temperature of the food reaches the target. Use a digital probe thermometer, as described on page 2·243.
④ Optionally, sear the food by using whichever method you prefer. See page 2·270 for searing options.
⑤ Season as desired.

The times and temperatures given for "barely cooked" and "tender," and some of those for "firm," will not pasteurize the fish. See page 1·190 for more food safety information.

Best Bets for Cooking Fish Sous Vide

Ingredient	Barely cooked (°C)	Barely cooked (°F)	Tender (°C)	Tender (°F)	Firm (°C)	Firm (°F)	Flaky (°C)	Flaky (°F)	Note	See page
black cod	40	104	**45**	**113**	48	118	52	126		76
cod*	38	100	**41**	**106**	45	113	49	120	use same temperatures for cooking ling cod	next
eel	n/a		n/a		54	129	**59**	**138**		
escolar	38	100	41	106	**46**	**115**	50	122		next
hake*	n/a		**44**	**111**	50	122	54	129		
halibut	40	104	**42**	**108**	45	113	50	122		112
halibut cheek	n/a		45	113	**48**	**118**	52	126	use same temperatures for monkfish and cod cheeks	165
hamachi	34	93	**38**	**100**	40	104	46	115		5·147
John Dory	n/a		45	113	**48**	**118**	50	122		
mackerel	40	104	**42**	**108**	46	115	48	118	if cooking to less than 46 °C / 115 °F, brine before cooking	284
monkfish*	42	108	45	113	**48**	**118**	50	122		77
rockfish	n/a		44	111	48	118	**52**	**126**		
salmon*	38	100	41	106	**43**	**109**	46	115		78
sardine	34	93	**38**	**100**	42	108	46	115		
sea bass	n/a		**45**	**113**	48	118	50	122		5·175
skate	n/a		48	118	**52**	**126**	54	129		78
snapper	n/a		48	118	**50**	**122**	52	126		78
sole	n/a		**42**	**108**	45	113	50	122		319
sturgeon*	n/a		46	115	**50**	**122**	54	129		
trout	37	99	40	104	**46**	**115**	48	118		77
tuna loin*	38	100	**42**	**108**	45	113	48 / 54	118 / 129	if cooking to 54 °C / 129 °F, brine in 4% saline solution, refrigerated, for 3 h before cooking	
tuna belly*	38	100	**43**	**109**	48	118	50	122		
turbot	n/a		44	111	**49**	**120**	52	126		76

from page 3·102

*(Many stocks of these species are considered overharvested and are protected in several parts of the world. We recommend always checking the status of fish before purchasing. For updates and more details, see the Monterey Bay Aquarium Seafood Watch web site at www.seafoodwatch.org. Temperatures in **bold** are those that we prefer.)

LING COD WITH BERGAMOT-INFUSED MILK

ADAPTED FROM MARTÍN BERASATEGUI

Yields 700 g (four portions)

INGREDIENT	QUANTITY	SCALING	PROCEDURE
Verjuice (store-bought)	50 g	12.5%	① Vacuum seal together.
Golden raisins	30 g	7.5%	② Cook sous vide in 80 °C / 176 °F bath for 20 min.
			③ Cool completely.
			④ Drain plumped raisins, and reserve for garnish.
Milk	525 g	130%	⑤ Combine.
Heavy cream	25 g	6.25%	⑥ Bring to boil, and then remove from heat.
Bergamot zest, thinly sliced	60 g	15%	⑦ Add to hot milk.
			⑧ Steep, covered, for 10 min, and then strain.
Salt	to taste		⑨ Season infused milk, and reserve.
Ling cod fillet, skin on	400 g	100%	⑩ Divide evenly into four 100 g portions.
Extra-virgin olive oil	80 g	20%	⑪ Vacuum seal individually, with 20 g of oil each.
			⑫ Cook sous vide in 41 °C / 106 °F bath to core temperature of 40 °C / 104 °F, about 25 min.
Salt	to taste		⑬ Season fish.
			⑭ Arrange one portion in each of four bowls.
			⑮ Garnish with plumped raisins and infused milk.

from page 3·103

If fresh bergamot is unavailable, use bergamot essential oil, page 2·310.

ESCOLAR WITH RED WINE BUTTER ADAPTED FROM ERIC RIPERT

Yields 500 g (four portions)

INGREDIENT	QUANTITY	SCALING	PROCEDURE
Yukon Gold potatoes, peeled and sliced 1 mm / 1⁄32 in thick	150 g (one potato)	50%	① Deep-fry in 150 °C / 300 °F oil until crisp and golden brown.
Neutral oil	as needed		② Drain on paper towels.
Salt	to taste		③ Season chips.
			④ Reserve.
Red wine (dry)	100 g	33%	⑤ Combine.
Red wine vinegar	45 g	15%	⑥ Reduce to 30 g.
Shallot, minced	10 g	3.3%	
Tarragon	2 g	0.7%	
Black peppercorns	1 g	0.3%	
Thyme	0.5 g	0.17%	
Red wine reduction, from above	30 g	10%	⑦ Blend into reduction until fully emulsified.
Xanthan gum (Keltrol T, CP Kelco brand)	0.5 g	0.17% (1.7%)*	
Unsalted butter	40 g	13.3%	⑧ Blend into reduction.
Brown butter see page 4·213	30 g	10%	⑨ Strain red wine butter through fine sieve into small saucepan.
Salt	to taste		⑩ Season red wine butter.
			⑪ Reserve, keeping warm.
Escolar fillet	300 g	100%	⑫ Cut fillet into four 75 g portions.
Extra-virgin olive oil	80 g	27%	⑬ Vacuum seal individually with 20 g of olive oil each.
			⑭ Cook sous vide in 39 °C / 102 °F bath to core temperature of 38 °C / 100 °F, about 20 min.
Salt	to taste		⑮ Season fillets.
			⑯ Slice, and arrange in center of serving plates.
Shallot, minced	3 g	1%	⑰ Combine.
Tarragon leaves, thinly sliced	1 g	0.3%	⑱ Garnish center of fish slices.
Black pepper, coarsely ground	to taste		⑲ Drizzle warm red wine butter around plates.
Sea beans, cut into 5 cm / 2 in lengths	4–5 beans		⑳ Top fish slices with potato crisps and sea beans.

from page 3·104

*(% of total weight of red wine reduction)

MEAT AND SEAFOOD

TURBOT WITH ONION AND MARROW BROTH
ADAPTED FROM DAVID KINCH

Yields 800 g (four portions)

David Kinch recommends aging very fresh turbot or sole for three to four days to develop flavor and make the flesh more tender. Ask your fishmonger when the fish was caught to make the proper adjustment.

INGREDIENT	QUANTITY	SCALING	PROCEDURE
White onions, peeled and halved widthwise	1.5 kg	250%	① Place in bottom of deep rectangular baking pan, and cover with foil.
			② Bake in 230 °C / 450 °F oven for 1 h.
			③ Lower oven temperature to 90 °C / 200 °F, and bake for 8 h until most of the juice has rendered and collected in bottom of pan.
			④ Pass roasted onion juice through fine sieve.
			⑤ Measure 250 g.
			⑥ Reserve cold.
Veal marrow bones, cut into 7.5 cm / 3 in lengths	1.5 kg	250%	⑦ Bake in 175 °C / 350 °F oven for 30 min to render fat, or render another way (see page 3·145).
			⑧ Strain through fine sieve, and measure 50 g of rendered marrow fat.
Turbot, on bone	600 g	100%	⑨ Cut into four equal portions.
Unsalted butter	40 g	6.5%	⑩ Vacuum seal individually with 10 g of butter each.
			⑪ Cook sous vide in 50 °C / 122 °F bath to core temperature of 49 °C / 120 °F, about 25 min.
Roasted onion juice, from above	250 g	42%	⑫ Blend gums into onion jus until fully dispersed.
Propylene glycol alginate (FMC BioPolymer brand)	0.2 g	0.03% (*0.08%*)*	⑬ Bring to simmer.
Xanthan gum (Keltrol T, CP Kelco brand)	0.2 g	0.03% (*0.08%*)*	
Rendered veal marrow fat, from above	50 g	8.5%	⑭ Blend into warm onion jus until emulsified.
			⑮ Reserve warm.
Amaranth leaves	100 g	17%	⑯ Sauté leaves until just wilted.
Olive oil	10 g	1.5%	
Salt	to taste		⑰ Season jus, amaranth leaves, and turbot.
			⑱ Arrange equally in four shallow bowls.
from page 3·105		*(% of total weight of onion jus)	

BLACK COD

Yields 500 g

INGREDIENT	QUANTITY	SCALING	PROCEDURE
Black cod fillet	500 g	100%	① Cut fillet into four equal portions.
Salt	7 g	1.4%	② Combine with salt and sugar.
Sugar	3 g	0.6%	③ Vacuum seal portions individually, and refrigerate for 1 h to cure.
			④ Remove cured fish from bags.
			⑤ Rinse and pat dry.
Condrieu wine (optional)	as needed		⑥ To cook fish with Girardet method, place fish portions in shallow pan and pour wine around to submerge fish, leaving its skin exposed.
			⑦ Place fish under hot broiler and cook until wine reaches 55 °C / 131 °F, and skin has darkened and crisped, 6–10 min.
			⑧ Remove pan from under broiler and wait for core temperature of fish to reach 52 °C / 125 °F, about 5 min.
			⑨ Remove fish from pan and rest for 5 min at room temp.
			⑩ Alternatively, vacuum seal fish and cook sous vide in 53 °C / 127 °F bath to core temperature of 52 °C / 125 °F, about 25 min.
Condrieu butter see page 25	150 g	30%	⑪ Serve with warm butter.
from page 5·173			

STEELHEAD TROUT CONFIT WITH FENNEL SALAD

ADAPTED FROM TETSUYA WAKUDA

Yields 560 g (four portions)

INGREDIENT	QUANTITY	SCALING	PROCEDURE
Steelhead trout fillet	400 g	100%	① Remove skin.
			② Divide fillet into four 100 g portions, and reserve.
Garlic-infused olive oil see page 28	100 g	25%	③ Whisk together.
			④ Vacuum seal each fish portion individually with 15 g of oil.
Thyme essential oil	0.1 g	0.025%	⑤ Reserve remaining 40 g of garlic oil for garnish.
Rosemary essential oil	0.05 g	0.013%	⑥ Refrigerate portions for 2 h to marinate.
			⑦ Cook sous vide in 43 °C / 109 °F bath to core temperature of 42 °C / 108 °F, about 25 min.
Fennel bulb	80 g	20%	⑧ Shave very thin on mandoline.
Black pepper, finely crushed	to taste		⑨ Season fennel shavings.
Lemon juice	to taste		
Lemon-scented olive oil see page 28	to taste		
Salt	to taste		
Kombu chips, finely chopped (store-bought)	8 g	2%	⑩ Place portion of fish on each plate.
			⑪ Dress each portion with fennel salad and kombu chips.
Flaky salt	to taste		⑫ Season with flaky salt, and drizzle garlic oil around plates.
Steelhead trout caviar	30 g	7.5%	⑬ Garnish fish evenly, and serve.

from page 3·106

SOUS VIDE MONKFISH PAVÉ

Yields 450 g

INGREDIENT	QUANTITY	SCALING	PROCEDURE
Salt	28 g	7%	① Combine to make cure.
Lemon zest, grated	0.4 g	0.1%	
Monkfish fillet	400 g	100%	② Dust cure evenly over all surfaces of fillet.
			③ Vacuum seal, and refrigerate for 45 min.
			④ Rinse fillet, and pat dry.
Extra virgin olive oil	as needed		⑤ Cut cured monkfish into four squares of 100 g each.
			⑥ Brush top surface of each square with olive oil.
Baby zucchini, sliced 1 mm / 1/16 in thick	200 g	50%	⑦ Lay zucchini slices neatly and in overlapping fashion, on top surface of each square to resemble fish scales.
Extra virgin olive oil	80 g	20%	⑧ Vacuum seal each square individually with 20 g of olive oil.
			⑨ Cook monkfish sous vide in 48 °C / 119 °F bath to core temperature of 47 °C / 117 °F, about 25 min.
Spice mix emulsion see page 309	100 g	25%	⑩ Pour warm emulsion around fish.

from page 5·155

SOUS VIDE SNAPPER

Yields 350 g

INGREDIENT	QUANTITY	SCALING	PROCEDURE
Sambal badjak (store-bought)	70 g	28%	① Combine.
			② Pass through fine sieve, and reserve.
Kejap manis (store-bought)	15 g	6%	
Shaoxing wine	10 g	4%	
Snapper, filleted and skinned	250 g	100%	③ Cut snapper into four 60 g portions.
			④ Brush sieved mixture in layer 1 mm / 1/16 in thick, onto snapper portions.
Salt	to taste		⑤ Season.
			⑥ Cook snapper portions sous vide in 52 °C / 125 °F bath to core temperature of 51 °C / 123 °F, about 20 min.
Malaysian aromatic oil see page 30	25 g	10%	⑦ Garnish.
Crispy snapper skin see page 5·168	four pieces		

from page 5·169

SOUS VIDE SALMON

Yields 400 g

INGREDIENT	QUANTITY	SCALING	PROCEDURE
Water	150 g	37.5%	① Whisk together until sugar is fully dissolved to make brine.
Salt	5.5 g	1.35%	
Sugar	5 g	1.25%	
Salmon fillet (preferably wild king)	400 g	100%	② Cut fillet into four 100 g portions.
			③ Soak in brine for 24 h.
			④ Drain.
Extra virgin olive oil	120 g	30%	⑤ Vacuum seal each salmon portion with 30 g of oil.
			⑥ Refrigerate for 2 h for brine to permeate salmon.
			⑦ Cook salmon sous vide in 41 °C / 106 °F bath to core temperature of 40 °C / 104 °F, about 25 min.
Root vegetable jus, warmed see page 36	140 g	35%	⑧ Serve with warm jus.

from page 5·162

SKATE PAVÉ WITH BREAD CRUST

Yields 480 g

INGREDIENT	QUANTITY	SCALING	PROCEDURE
Skate wings	600 g (four 125 g wings)	100%	① Dust evenly with Activa, ensuring grain of all wings faces same direction.
			② Stack wings, alternating thick and thin ends, and vacuum seal.
Activa RM	as needed		③ Refrigerate for at least 6 h for proteins to bond.
			④ Remove from bag, and cut into 100 g squares.
			⑤ Vacuum seal individually, and refrigerate.
White bread, crustless and cut into four slices, 3 mm / 1/8 in thick	80 g	13%	⑥ Cut bread slices into squares slightly larger than skate squares, and reserve.
Clarified unsalted butter see page 4·213	as needed		⑦ Cook skate sous vide in 52 °C / 126 °F bath to core temperature of 51 °C / 124 °F, about 25 min.
			⑧ Remove skate portions from bags, pat dry on paper towels, and place slice of bread on each.
Salt	to taste		⑨ Sear, bread sides down, in clarified butter until bread is crisp and golden.
			⑩ Season.

from page 5·159

VARIATION: Cooking Shellfish Sous Vide

① Select an ingredient and target temperature from the table below.
② Prep as indicated, and then vacuum seal as in step 2 on page 74. Blanch cockles, clams, mussels, and razor clams by vacuum sealing them while in the shell and immersing the bag in boiling water for 2 min, and then shucking. Use a clean bag when vacuum sealing the shellfish again for cooking.
③ Follow steps 3–5 on page 74.

Best Bets for Cooking Tender Shellfish Sous Vide

		Barely cooked			Tender			Firm				
Ingredient	Prep	(°C)	(°F)	(min)	(°C)	(°F)	(min)	(°C)	(°F)	(min)	Note	See page
cockles or clams	blanched and shucked*	48	118	10	**56**	**133**	**8**	65	149	5	cook in its own juice	36, 5·229
langoustine	shelled	48	118	15	**56**	**133**	**12**	70	158	6	sear quickly after cooking	
lobster claws	shelled	**54**	**129**	**to core**	60	140	to core	65	149	to core	best cooked in butter	
lobster tails	shelled	**46**	**115**	**to core**	54	129	to core	59	138	to core	best cooked in butter	next, 81
					50	122	to core					
mussels	blanched and shucked*	**62**	**144**	**10**	65	149	10	68	154	7	cook in its own juice	below
oysters	shucked	**45**	**113**	**10**	48	118	10	52	126	7	cook in its own juice	81
razor clams	blanched and shucked*	**45**	**113**	**10**	60	140	10	65	149	5	siphon only	85, 171
scallops	whole	**42**	**108**	**to core**	50	122	to core	54	129	to core		
shrimp (prawns)	peeled	**48**	**118**	**to core**	60	140	7	80	176	4		next, 81
					54	129	to core					

from page 3·103   *(see note on page 74)   (temperatures in **bold** are those that we prefer)

SOUS VIDE MUSSELS

Yields 450 g

INGREDIENT	QUANTITY	SCALING	PROCEDURE
Live mussels, rinsed and beards removed	250 g	100%	① Vacuum seal. ② Cook in boiling water or steam for 3 min. ③ Chill in ice-water bath. ④ Shuck, reserving mussels and juice. ⑤ Strain juice, and reserve.
Shallots, thinly sliced	70 g	28%	⑥ Combine mussels with reserved juice and remaining ingredients.
Fennel, thinly sliced	50 g	20%	⑦ Vacuum seal.
White wine (dry)	50 g	20%	⑧ Cook mussels sous vide in 65 °C / 149 °F bath for 12 min.
Pastis (or Ouzo)	5 g	2%	⑨ Serve warm with toasted garlic bread.
Preserved lemon zest, minced see page 174	2 g	1%	
Bay leaf	0.5 g	0.2%	

from page 5·154

MEAT AND SEAFOOD

19TH-CENTURY-STYLE LOBSTER WITH SHERRY AND COCOA

ADAPTED FROM OLIVIER ROELLINGER

Yields 450 g (four portions)

INGREDIENT	QUANTITY	SCALING	PROCEDURE
Lobster shells and trimmings	50 g	17%	① Sauté together until golden, about 7 min.
Shallot, minced	50 g	17%	
Neutral oil	25 g	8.5%	
Shellfish stock see page 6	150 g	50%	② Deglaze pan with shells.
			③ Reduce stock mixture to 90 g, and remove from heat.
Amontillado sherry	75 g	25%	
Chervil tips	1 g	0.3%	④ Whisk into stock reduction.
Coriander seeds, toasted	0.8 g	0.25%	⑤ Cover, and steep for 10 min.
Annatto powder	0.5 g	0.15%	⑥ Strain.
Tarragon leaves	0.3 g	0.1%	
Vanilla seeds and pulp	0.2 g	0.05%	
Unsweetened cocoa powder	0.1 g	0.03%	
Unsalted butter, cubed	20 g	6.7%	⑦ Warm infused reduction, and blend butter in until fully emulsified.
Lime juice	to taste		⑧ Season sauce, and reserve warm.
Lime zest	to taste		
Salt	to taste		
Sherry vinegar	to taste		
Lobster tails, shelled	300 g (four 75 g tails)	100%	⑨ Vacuum seal individually with 20 g of butter each.
			⑩ Cook sous vide in 51 °C / 124 °F bath to core temperature of 50 °C / 122 °F, about 20 min.
Unsalted butter	80 g	27%	
Salt	to taste		⑪ Season.
Green mango, brunoise	80 g	27%	⑫ Garnish with mango and sauce.

from page 5·154

SHRIMP COCKTAIL INSPIRED BY GRANT ACHATZ

Yields 280 g (four portions)

INGREDIENT	QUANTITY	SCALING	PROCEDURE
Raspberry gazpacho see page 33	300 g	100%	① Disperse gelatin into 75 g of gazpacho.
			② Bring to boil to fully hydrate, and whisk into remainder of gazpacho base.
160 Bloom gelatin	6 g	2%	③ Cast onto nonstick baking sheet, 2 mm / 1/16 in thick.
			④ Freeze completely, and cut into 3.75 cm / 1½ in rectangles. Reserve frozen until use.
Spot prawn tails, peeled	200 g (about 8)	67%	⑤ Vacuum seal together, and cook in 60 °C / 140 °F bath for 7 min.
Extra-virgin olive oil	30 g	10%	⑥ Cool completely and remove from bag.
Garlic clove, crushed	3 g	1%	⑦ Reserve refrigerated until use.
Tarragon sprigs	2 g	0.7%	
Celery, peeled, brunoise	6 g	2%	⑧ Align two prawns down center of each plate.
Piquillo pepper, brunoise	6 g	2%	⑨ Season with salt, and garnish with celery, piquillo, olives, and horseradish as desired.
Green olives, thinly sliced	6 g	2%	⑩ Lay frozen sheet over prawns and garnish, and allow to thaw and drape over other components of dish, about 5 min, before serving.
Horseradish, finely grated	to taste		
Salt	to taste		

from page 3·107

OYSTER ESCABECHE

Yields 12 pieces

INGREDIENT	QUANTITY	SCALING	PROCEDURE
Virginica oysters, or similar	12 oysters		① Shuck and clean oysters well.
			② Vacuum seal oysters, and then poach sous vide in 45 °C / 113 °F bath for 10 min.
			③ Cool in ice-water bath, and refrigerate.
Extra virgin olive oil	45 g	100%	④ Combine to make escabeche.
Lime juice	24 g	53%	⑤ Marinate oysters in escabeche, refrigerated, for 45 min.
Sweet onions, finely minced	12 g	27%	
White wine vinegar	6 g	13%	
Bird's eye chili, thinly sliced	0.8 g	1.8%	
Bay leaf, julienne	0.2 g	0.4%	
Salt	to taste		

from page 5·206

STEAMED LIVE SPOT PRAWN

Yields 12 prawns

INGREDIENT	QUANTITY	SCALING	PROCEDURE
Live spot prawns	12 prawns		① Steam at 90 °C / 195 °F with 100% relative humidity for 3 min. Alternatively, vacuum seal in single even layer, and cook sous vide in 45 °C / 114 °F bath for 20 min.
			② Shock in ice-water bath.
			③ Peel and refrigerate until use.

from page 5·183

POACHED LOBSTER TAIL

Yields 240 g

INGREDIENT	QUANTITY	SCALING	PROCEDURE
Lobster tails	240 g (four tails)	100%	① Vacuum seal together.
Carotene butter or unsalted butter see page 40	100 g	42%	② Cook sous vide in 52 °C / 125 °F bath to core temperature of 51 °C / 123 °F, about 10 min.
			③ Rest cooked lobster for 2 min, and then sear each side for 10 s to tighten flesh.
			④ Cut each tail into three equal medallions, and season.
Salt	to taste		⑤ Season medallions, and serve with emulsion.
Coconut-lobster, emulsion, warmed see page 319	100 g	42%	

from page 5·187

TOUGH MEATS, POULTRY, AND SHELLFISH

Best Bets for Cooking Tough Poultry

Ingredient	Cook sous vide — Tender and juicy (°C)	(°F)	(h)	Cook sous vide — Flaky (°C)	(°F)	(h)	Pressure-cook at 1 bar / 15 psi (gauge) (min)	Note	See page
chicken leg and thigh	64	147	1½	68	154	3	15		119, 5·113
	62	144	15						
chicken wing	62	144	12	72	162	8			
duck leg	60	140	48	**62**	**144**	**18**	35	best cured before cooking	below, 105
	62	144	12	68	154	8			
duck tongue	88	190	5		n/a		25	make sure to debone while still hot	5·81
guinea hen leg	60	140	4		n/a			best marinated in yogurt or other tenderizing solution before cooking	next
pigeon leg	65	149	3	68	154	7		cure with confit mix 2 h before cooking	5·125, 72
quail leg	60	140	12	68	154	3			
turkey leg	62	144	8	65	149	2		inject with 10% by weight of 7% brine	3·174
turkey wing	58	136	12	**62**	**144**	**18**		brine before cooking	204, 103

from page 3·108   (*temperatures in **bold** are those that we prefer*)

SOUS VIDE DUCK CONFIT PAVÉ

Yields 850 g

INGREDIENT	QUANTITY	SCALING	PROCEDURE
Salt	200 g	24.5%	① Combine.
Allspice berries	10 g	1.2%	② Grind coarsely to form rub.
Thyme	8 g	1%	
Garlic, thinly sliced	5 g	0.6%	
Star anise	1.9 g	0.23%	
Rosemary	1 g	0.12%	
Bay leaves	0.9 g	0.11%	
Black pepper	0.8 g	0.1%	
Coriander seeds	0.8 g	0.1%	
Orange zest, grated	0.1 g	0.01%	
Duck legs, boneless	825 g	100%	③ Coat duck legs with rub.
			④ Cure in refrigerator for 6 h.
			⑤ Rinse legs, and pat dry on paper towel–lined tray.
Activa RM	8 g	1%	⑥ Dust meat side of cured duck legs with Activa.
			⑦ Pack together, with skin sides facing out, in mold, 10 cm by 20 cm / 4 in by 8 in, and 5 cm / 2 in deep.
			⑧ Vacuum seal.
			⑨ Cook sous vide in **60 °C / 140 °F** bath for 48 h.
			⑩ Panfry duck confit (or use griddle), skin sides only, until golden and crisp.
			⑪ Carve into slices 1.5 cm / ¾ in thick.

from page 5·82   *(% of total weight of cured duck legs)

SOUS VIDE GUINEA HEN

Yields 250 g

INGREDIENT	QUANTITY	SCALING	PROCEDURE
Live culture Greek-style strained yogurt	50 g	33%	① Combine.
Garlic, thinly sliced	25 g	16.5%	
Guinea hen breasts, boneless and skinless	150 g	100%	② Vacuum seal 25 g of yogurt mixture with breasts.
Guinea hen thighs, boneless and skinless	150 g	100%	③ Vacuum seal remaining 25 g of yogurt mixture with thighs.
			④ Marinate breasts and thighs, refrigerated, for 5 h.
			⑤ Cook thighs sous vide in 62 °C / 144 °F bath for 5 h.
			⑥ Cook breasts sous vide in 59 °C / 138 °F bath to core temperature of 58 °C / 136 °F, about 30 min. Hold breasts at temperature for 30 min to ensure proper pasteurization.
			⑦ Slice guinea hen into pieces 1 cm / ⅜ in thick.
Tagine base, warmed see page 39	100 g	67%	⑧ Serve with guinea hen.

from page 5·137

Best Bets for Cooking Tough Shellfish

	Cook sous vide								Pressure-cook at 1 bar / 15 psi (gauge)		
	Barely cooked			Firm			Tender braised				
Ingredient	(°C)	(°F)	(min)	(°C)	(°F)	(min)	(°C)	(°F)	(h)	(min)	Note	See page
abalone	45	113	15	88	190	8 h	**100**	**212**	**12**	35		next
octopus		n/a		80	176	3 h	**85**	**185**	**4**	25	freezing and thawing before cooking can increase tenderness	85
geoduck	50	122	30	65	149	7	**88**	**190**	**1½**	15	the siphon is quite firm; the belly meat is far more tender	314
snail		n/a		65	149	15	**68**	**154**	**5**	20		5·239
squid and cuttlefish	50	122	10	**65**	**149**	**5**	65	149	4	30	apply same temperatures for cooking sea cucumbers	next

from page 3·108 (*temperatures in **bold** are those that we prefer*)

The times and temperatures given for "barely cooked" will not pasteurize the food; other time-temperature combinations indicated will. See page 1·190 for more food safety information.

SOUS VIDE BRAISED SNAILS

Yields 550 g

INGREDIENT	QUANTITY	SCALING	PROCEDURE
White chicken stock see page 11	600 g	150%	① Vacuum seal together.
Burgundy snails (canned), cleaned	400 g	100%	② Cook sous vide in 68 °C / 154 °F bath for 5 h.
			③ Drain, and reserve juices.
Carrots, peeled and thinly sliced	200 g	50%	④ Pick out snail meat, and discard vegetables and aromatics.
			⑤ Vacuum seal snails with reserved juices, and refrigerate until use.
Sweet onions, thinly sliced	180 g	45%	⑥ To serve, reheat snails in 58 °C / 136 °F bath for about 20 min.
Salt	15 g	3.75%	
Thyme	1.5 g	0.4%	
Bay leaf	0.4 g	0.1%	
Montpellier butter (optional) see page 298	150 g	37.5%	⑦ Melt in pot over low heat and stir in snails.

from page 5·243

MEAT AND SEAFOOD

SQUID SICILIAN LIFEGUARD-STYLE INSPIRED BY MARIO BATALI

Yields 550 g

INGREDIENT	QUANTITY	SCALING	PROCEDURE
Garlic, thinly sliced	10 g	5%	① Combine to make cure.
Salt	4 g	2%	
Lemon zest	3 g	1.5%	
Squid tubes, cut vertically to make sheets and surface membranes peeled	200 g	100%	② Spread cure over surface of squid sheets.
			③ Vacuum seal, and refrigerate for 15 min.
			④ Brush off cure, and cut sheets into thin strips.
Extra-virgin olive oil	10 g	5%	⑤ Vacuum seal strips with oil, and reserve.
Tomato confit, pureed see page 179	75 g	37.5%	⑥ Combine, and heat until just warmed through.
			⑦ Reserve tomato confit mixture.
Israeli couscous, boiled in 2% brine until al dente, and then cooled	60 g	30%	⑧ Cook squid strips sous vide in 65 °C / 149 °F bath for 4 min.
Pine nuts, toasted	18 g	9%	
Dry currants	15 g	7.5%	
Caper berries, thinly sliced	10 g	5%	
Tomato water see page 40	150 g	75%	⑨ Season tomato water generously.
Red wine vinegar	to taste		
Salt	to taste		
Scallions, whites only, fine julienne	30 g	15%	⑩ Spoon reserved warm tomato confit mixture into bottom of bowls.
Chili oil see page 29	20 g	10%	⑪ Top with squid strips, and garnish with scallions and chili oil.
			⑫ Pour seasoned tomato water around each portion.

from page 3·113

ABALONE AND FOIE GRAS SHABU-SHABU WITH YUBA AND ENOKI

Yields 900 g

INGREDIENT	QUANTITY	SCALING	PROCEDURE
Abalone	120 g	100%	① Steam at 100 °C / 212 °F for 12 h. Alternatively, vacuum seal and cook sous vide in 90 °C / 194 °F bath for 16 h.
			② Reserve.
Raw foie gras	120 g	100%	③ Cut into slices 3 mm / ⅛ in thick.
			④ Refrigerate.
Soy yuba see page 249	120 g	100%	⑤ Measure and reserve.
Enoki mushroom	60 g	50%	⑥ Cut from stem into individual mushrooms.
Pea vines	80 g	66.6%	⑦ Select tender leaves and tips, and refrigerate.
Sweet onions, thinly sliced	300 g	250%	⑧ Sweat onions until very tender, about 30 min.
Rendered foie gras fat	70 g	58%	
Hon dashi see page 15	350 g	292%	⑨ Deglaze onions, and simmer for 30 min to make shabu shabu broth.
			⑩ Strain.
			⑪ Centrifuge at 27,500g for 1 h.
			⑫ Cool and refrigerate.
Soy sauce	120 g	100%	⑬ Combine to make tosazu (dipping sauce).
Mirin	50 g	41.7%	⑭ Refrigerate.
Agave syrup	24 g	20%	
Rice vinegar	20 g	17%	
Foie gras fat or unsalted butter	80 g	66.7%	⑮ Bring broth to boil, and maintain at simmer in shabu shabu pot over portable gas or electric stove.
			⑯ Warm tosazu (dipping sauce), and blend in foie gras fat to form loose emulsion.
			⑰ Serve emulsion on side, and invite guests to dip raw ingredients into warm broth for desired doneness and then briefly into tosazu.
			⑱ Broth is shared among diners after raw ingredients have been eaten.

from page 5·203

RAZOR CLAM WITH SAUCE VERTE   INSPIRED BY ALICE WATERS

Yields 550 g (eight portions)

INGREDIENT	QUANTITY	SCALING	PROCEDURE
Ramp bulbs (or scallion whites)	100 g	20%	① Vacuum seal.
			② Cook in boiling water until tender, about 5 min.
			③ Cool in sous vide bag placed in ice-water bath.
			④ Drain and reserve.
Ramp greens (or scallion greens)	150 g	30%	⑤ Blanch greens individually in boiling water until tender.
			⑥ Shock in ice water.
Chives	5 g	1%	⑦ Pat dry, and reserve.
Chervil	4 g	0.8%	
Basil	3.5 g	0.7%	
Mint	2.2 g	0.4%	
Caper berries	28 g	5.5%	⑧ Puree with bulbs and blanched greens until smooth, to make sauce verte.
Olive oil	25 g	5%	
Dijon mustard	10 g	2%	
White wine vinegar	10 g	2%	
Salt	to taste		⑨ Season sauce verte, and reserve in refrigerator.
Marcona almonds, toasted	50 g	10%	⑩ Pulse in food processor to crumb-size particles, and reserve.
Razor clams	500 g	100%	⑪ Vacuum seal together.
White wine (dry)	40 g	8%	⑫ Steam or boil at 100 °C / 212 °F for 3 min.
Borage blossoms (optional)	as needed		⑬ Chill, in bag, in ice-water bath.
			⑭ Remove from bag, and strain clam cooking juices through fine sieve lined with coffee filter, reserving juices.
			⑮ Remove clams from shells.
			⑯ Clean meat, and vacuum seal with reserved juices.
			⑰ Cook sous vide in 60 °C / 140 °F bath for 10 min.
			⑱ Chill sous vide bag in ice-water bath.
			⑲ To serve, drain, reserving clams and juice separately.
			⑳ Slice clams thinly.
			㉑ Whisk some reserved juice into sauce verte, to taste.
			㉒ Garnish clams with sauce verte and almond crumbs.

from page 3·112

SOUS VIDE OCTOPUS

Yields 450 g

INGREDIENT	QUANTITY	SCALING	PROCEDURE
Octopus legs	500 g (eight legs)	100%	① Blanch for 30 s to remove slime.
			② Cool in ice-water bath.
			③ Vacuum seal individually.
			④ Cook sous vide in 85 °C / 185 °F bath for 4 h.
			⑤ Cool in bag, in ice-water bath.
			⑥ Peel skin off four octopus legs, leaving skins on remaining four legs.
Extra virgin olive oil	50 g	10%	⑦ Vacuum seal peeled octopus legs with 25 g of oil.
			⑧ Reserve remaining 25 g of oil.
Salt	to taste		⑨ Warm peeled octopus in bag, in 60 °C / 140 °F bath, for 15 min.
			⑩ Brush reserved oil onto skins of unpeeled octopus legs.
			⑪ Grill unpeeled octopus legs on griddle or over coals until deeply charred, about 2 min. Season all legs with salt.

from page 5·194

MEAT AND SEAFOOD

COOKING TOUGH CUTS

① Select an ingredient and target temperature from the table below.
② If cooking sous vide, set a water bath to the temperature indicated for the desired texture. If pressure cooking, set the gauge pressure to 1 bar / 15 psi, and cook for the time indicated, and then skip to step 5.
③ Vacuum seal the food together with any flavorings, fats, or liquids.
④ Cook sous vide for the time indicated.
⑤ Serve immediately, or chill, and then refrigerate until needed. Reheat in a bath set to the cooking temperature.
⑥ Optionally, sear the food. See page 2·270 for searing methods.
⑦ Season as desired.

Best Bets for Cooking Tough Cuts

	Cook sous vide												Pressure-cook at 1 bar / 15 psi (gauge)		
	Firm, steak-like			Tender, yielding			Tender, flaky			Very flaky					
Ingredient	(°C)	(°F)	(h)	(°C)	(°F)	(h)	(°C)	(°F)	(h)	(°C)	(°F)	(h)	(min)	Note	See page
beef cheek	58	136	72	**62**		**72**	68	154	36	80	176	12	60	remove connective tissue	5·55
beef short rib, bone in	56	133	72	58	136	72	**60**		**72**	88	190	7	50	texture is best when carved just before serving	5·42
beef brisket	58	136	72	60	140	72	**63**		**72**	70	158	72		use the fattier, thick end of the brisket called the nose	88
beef flatiron	52	126	24	**55**	**131**	**12**	62	144	48	88	190	5		remove central muscle sheath, then apply Activa	5·49
							55	131	48						
flank steak	50	122	3	**55**	**131**	**12**	62	144	36	88	190	7			
beef hanger steak	50		2	55	131	12	62	144	36	88	190	6			
							55	131	48						
oxtail		n/a		**60**		**100**	65	149	48	70	158	24	70		5·49
lamb shank	58	136	48	**62**		**48**	85	185	5	88	190	5	**60**		5·89
lamb shoulder	56	133	48	62	144	48	65	149	24	85	185	5	40	coat meat with 5.0% olive oil and 0.1% thyme to prevent stronger lamb notes from developing	88
pork belly	60		72	65	149	36	70	158	18	88	190	8	50	for firm texture, cure with pink brine before cooking	5·101
pork shoulder or fresh ham	54	129	48	60	140	72	65	149	36	84	183	4	60	many individual muscles can be treated like tender cuts	89
pork cheek, fat cap on		n/a		65	149	38	68	154	48	85	185	5	35		122
pork ribs		n/a		60		48	65	149	48	75	167	7			88
pork trotter and hock		n/a			n/a			n/a		85	185	12	**120**		169
suckling pig shoulder and leg		n/a		60	140	36	**65**	**149**	**24**	80	176	8	60		
rabbit shoulder		n/a		60	140	4	**66**	**151**	**1**	85	185	1		hotter-than-core cooking may be required for younger animals	
veal breast	54	129	to core	62	144	5	68	154	24	85	185	6	75	for steak-like texture, use individual breast muscles; remove fat and sinew	3·216
veal shank		n/a		60	140	72	**62**		**72**	85	185	8	90	cook veal shanks whole	5·60

from page 3·109   (*temperatures in **bold** are those that we prefer*)

SUCKLING PIG SHOULDER WITH SHALLOT AND ORANGE SAUCE

Yields 750 g (four portions)

ADAPTED FROM JOAN ROCA

INGREDIENT	QUANTITY	SCALING	PROCEDURE
Suckling pig shoulders	500 g (one shoulder)	100%	① Vacuum seal individually.
			② Cook sous vide in 65 °C / 149 °F bath for 24 h.
Extra-virgin olive oil	60 g	12%	
Sugar	20 g	4%	③ Cook in small pot until dark caramel forms.
Brown pork stock see page 6	150 g	30%	④ Deglaze caramel.
			⑤ Reduce to 150 g.
Orange juice, freshly squeezed and strained	150 g	30%	
Shallots, peeled and halved	400 g (about eight small halves)	80%	⑥ Add to orange sauce.
			⑦ Simmer until tender, about 30 min.
Red wine vinegar	10 g	2%	⑧ Season orange sauce and shallots.
Cloves, finely ground	to taste		
Salt	to taste		
Frying oil	as needed		⑨ Debone warm pork shoulders, leaving skins on and keeping structures intact.
			⑩ Fry, skin side down only, in thin film of oil, until skin is crisp, about 4 min.
Elderflowers	eight small tufts		⑪ Cut each shoulder in half.
			⑫ Distribute among four plates.
			⑬ Garnish with shallots, orange sauce, and elderflower tufts.
Flaky sea salt	to taste		⑭ Season pork shoulder and shallots.

from page 3·110

CRISPY DUCK TONGUES

Yields 65 g

INGREDIENT	QUANTITY	SCALING	PROCEDURE
Water	250 g	167%	① Vacuum seal.
Duck tongues	150 g	100%	② Cook sous vide in 88 °C / 190 °F bath for 5 h.
Salt	5 g	3%	③ Remove from bag, and pull out central bone from each tongue while warm.
			④ Dehydrate tongues in 50 °C / 120 °F oven until completely dry, about 2 h.
Frying oil	as needed		⑤ Heat oil for duck tongues to 205 °C / 400 °F.
			⑥ Deep-fry duck tongues until crispy and puffed, about 1 min.
			⑦ Drain on paper towels, and season with salt.

from page 5·84

BEEF SHANK RILLETTE

Yields 365 g

INGREDIENT	QUANTITY	SCALING	PROCEDURE
Beef shank, boneless	200 g	100%	① Cook sous vide in 85 °C / 185 °F bath for 5 h.
			② Cool quickly in ice-water bath. Shred meat.
White beef stock, cold see page 6	125 g	62.5%	③ Disperse agar and gelatin into stock.
			④ Boil for 3 min to fully hydrate.
160 Bloom gelatin	1.5 g	0.75% (0.9%)*	⑤ Refrigerate until firmly set.
			⑥ Puree until fluid.
Agar	1.15 g	0.58% (0.7%)*	
Rendered beef suet	40 g	20%	⑦ Heat fat until liquid is warm, but not hot.
			⑧ Blend into stock fluid gel until fully emulsified.
			⑨ Fold in shredded meat.
Black pepper	to taste		⑩ Season meat mixture generously, and vacuum seal.
Salt	to taste		⑪ Reheat in 50 °C / 122 °F bath for 20 min, or refrigerate until use.

from page 5·52   *(% of total weight of beef stock and beef suet)

SOUS VIDE PORK BELLY

Yields 1.6 kg

INGREDIENT	QUANTITY	SCALING	PROCEDURE
Whole pork belly, on bone	2.4 kg	100%	① Inject brine in amount equal to 10% of pork belly weight.
Pink brine see page 101	240 g	10%	② Vacuum seal in remaining brine for 3 d. ③ Drain brine from bag, and reseal pork belly. ④ Refrigerate for 2 d before cooking to diffuse salt through meat. ⑤ Remove meat from bag, and drain.
Water	800 g	33%	⑥ Vacuum seal pork belly with water. ⑦ Cook sous vide in 62 °C / 144 °F bath for 40 h. ⑧ Chill in ice-water bath until firm. ⑨ Remove belly from bag, and discard gelled cooking juices. ⑩ Carve belly from ribs, and remove skin. Discard bones and skin. ⑪ Portion belly into square blocks of 150 g each. ⑫ Vacuum seal each portion individually. ⑬ Refrigerate.
Frying oil	as needed		⑭ To serve, reheat bagged pork belly portions in 62 °C / 144 °F bath, about 15 min. ⑮ Remove pork belly portions from bag, and sear, fat side only, until golden, about 2 min.

from page 5·102

BRAISED LAMB SHOULDER

Yields 500 g

INGREDIENT	QUANTITY	SCALING	PROCEDURE
Lamb shoulder, boneless	500 g	100%	① Vacuum seal.
Brown lamb stock see page 6	100 g	20%	② Cook sous vide in 56 °C / 133 °F bath for 48 h.
Rendered duck fat	50 g	10%	③ Slice or shred as desired, or cool bagged shoulder in ice-water bath and refrigerate until use.
Garlic, thinly sliced	9 g	1.8%	
Thyme	0.4 g	0.08%	
Salt	to taste		④ Season.

from page 5·83

BEEF BRISKET

Yields 500 g

INGREDIENT	QUANTITY	SCALING	PROCEDURE
Beef brisket	700 g	100%	① Smoke at 65 °C / 149 °F with 65% relative humidity (wet-bulb temperature should be 55 °C / 131 °F) for 7 h. ② Vacuum seal. ③ Cook sous vide in 63 °C / 146 °F bath for 72 h. ④ Trim off extra fat. ⑤ Slice meat to serve.
Kansas City barbecue sauce see page 220	100 g	14%	⑥ Brush on sliced meat.

from page 5·79

PORK RIBS

Yields 500 g

INGREDIENT	QUANTITY	SCALING	PROCEDURE
Pork spare ribs, membrane removed	1.2 kg	100%	① Smoke at 65 °C / 149 °F with 60% relative humidity (wet-bulb temperature 55 °C / 131 °F) for 7 h. ② Vacuum seal. ③ Cook sous vide in 60 °C / 140 °F bath for 48 h.
Dry rub, from above	30 g	2.5%	④ Rub onto ribs just before serving. ⑤ Flash with blowtorch, or brown lightly if desired.

from page 5·78

PULLED PORK SHOULDER
Yields 500 g

INGREDIENT	QUANTITY	SCALING	PROCEDURE
Pork shoulder, skin on, boneless	300 g	100%	① Smoke at 65 °C / 149 °F with 60% relative humidity (wet-bulb temperature at 55 °C / 131 °F) for 7 h.
			② Vacuum seal.
			③ Cook sous vide in 65 °C / 150 °F bath for 72 h.
			④ Pull meat apart with two forks, and discard pieces of fat.
Barbecue sauce, see page 4·49	300 g	100%	⑤ Mix into pulled meat.

from page 5·78

BRAISED VEAL FORESHANK
Yields 500 g

INGREDIENT	QUANTITY	SCALING	PROCEDURE
Veal foreshank	1 kg (one whole)	100%	① Vacuum seal together.
Water	125 g	12.5%	② Cook sous vide in 62 °C / 144 °F bath for 72 h.
			③ Remove foreshank from bag, and cool in ice-water bath for 30 min.
			④ Divide foreshank into four equal portions, reserving cooking juices and bones separately.
			⑤ Vacuum seal meat portions individually, and refrigerate.
			⑥ Refrigerate cooking juices for making glaze, and reserve bones for making custard.
Squash glaze, see page 39	100 g	12.5%	⑦ Reheat meat portions in 62 °C / 144 °F bath for 25 min.
Flaky sea salt	to taste		⑧ Brush with glaze, and season with sea salt.

from page 5·62

AMERICAN WAGYU BEEF CHEEK
Yields 450 g

INGREDIENT	QUANTITY	SCALING	PROCEDURE
Wagyu beef cheeks, trimmed of sinew and silverskin	500 g	100%	① Vacuum seal together.
Goulash broth, see page 19	75 g	15%	② Cook sous vide in 62 °C / 144 °F bath for 72 h.
Neutral oil	25 g	5%	
Goulash broth, see page 19	400 g	80%	③ Reduce to 75 g to make glaze, and reserve warm.
			④ Remove beef cheeks from bag and cut into slices 1 cm / ½ in thick.
			⑤ Brush slices with warm glaze.
Flaky salt	to taste		⑥ Season and serve.

from page 5·57

RARE FLATIRON STEAK
Yields 500 g

INGREDIENT	QUANTITY	SCALING	PROCEDURE
Flatiron steak	500 g	100%	① Butterfly steak to remove tendon.
Activa RM or GS	as needed		② Dust each piece evenly with thin layer of Activa.
			③ Fold steak closed.
			④ Vacuum seal together.
			⑤ Refrigerate for at least 6 h to ensure bonding.
			⑥ Cook sous vide in 55 °C / 131 °F bath for 12 h.
Neutral oil	as needed		⑦ Sear steak until just golden, about 30 s. Slice into portions 1 cm / ⅜ in thick, and season with salt.
Salt	to taste		

from page 5·50

BRAISED SHORT RIBS

Yields 1.2 kg

INGREDIENT	QUANTITY	SCALING	PROCEDURE
Short ribs, four-bone plate with ribs 10–12.5 cm / 4–5 in long	3 kg	100%	① Remove fat cap and silverskin covering ribs.
White beef stock see page 6	225 g	7.5%	② Vacuum seal ribs with beef stock.
			③ Cook sous vide at 60 °C / 140 °F, for 72 h.
			④ Chill vacuum-sealed ribs quickly in ice-water bath.
			⑤ Remove ribs from bag, strain juices, and reserve.
			⑥ Peel meat from bones, and set on plates.
			⑦ Trim gristle from meat, and cut meat into even block-shaped portions (about 10 blocks).
			⑧ Vacuum seal, and reheat braised short ribs in 60 °C / 140 °F bath for 30 min.
Salt	to taste		⑨ Remove short ribs from bags, and flash briefly with blowtorch to sear surface until golden, about 30 s.
			⑩ Season.

from page 5·44

SOUS VIDE VEAL TONGUE

Yields 250 g

INGREDIENT	QUANTITY	SCALING	PROCEDURE
Veal tongues	550 g	100%	① Blanch for 2 min.
			② Drain and cool.
Water	100 g	18%	③ Combine with tongues, and vacuum seal.
Cider vinegar	45 g	8%	④ Cook sous vide in 70 °C / 158 °F bath for 24 h.
Carrot, peeled and thinly sliced	20 g	4%	⑤ Remove tongues and cooking liquid from bag, reserving both.
Garlic, thinly sliced	10 g	2%	⑥ Peel tongues and slice thinly lengthwise.
Sweet onion, thinly sliced	10 g	2%	⑦ Reduce cooking liquid until syrupy, about 10 min.
			⑧ Strain.
Salt	7 g	1.3%	⑨ Add sliced tongues to pan and warm through.
			⑩ Season with additional salt to taste.

from page 5·50

BEEF SHORT RIBS

Yields 500 g

INGREDIENT	QUANTITY	SCALING	PROCEDURE
Beef short ribs	1.2 kg	100%	① Smoke at 65 °C / 149 °F with 65% relative humidity (wet-bulb temperature 55 °C / 131 °F) for 7 h.
			② Vacuum seal.
			③ Cook sous vide in 60 °C / 140 °F bath for 72 h.
			④ Slide bones out while meat is warm.
			⑤ Slice meat to serve.
East Texas barbecue sauce from above	100 g	8%	⑥ Brush on sliced meat.

from page 5·79

GLAZED OXTAIL

Yields 325 g

INGREDIENT	QUANTITY	SCALING	PROCEDURE
Oxtail, cut between joints	300 g	100%	① Vacuum seal.
Brown beef jus see page 34	75 g	25%	② Cook sous vide in 60 °C / 140 °F bath for 100 h.
			③ Remove oxtail and juices from bag.
			④ Dislodge pieces of meat from bones and gristle, and refrigerate meat.
			⑤ Strain cooking juices.
			⑥ Reduce juice to thick glaze. Glaze will thin when combined with oxtail pieces.
			⑦ Cool glaze.
			⑧ Vacuum seal oxtail pieces with glaze.
			⑨ Reheat in 50 °C / 122 °F bath for 20 min, or refrigerate until use.

from page 5·50

HOW TO PRESSURE-COOK TOUGH CUTS FOR QUICK RESULTS

① Add 0.5–1 cm / ¼–½ in of water to the pressure cooker.

② Add the meat and any seasonings.

③ Heat to a gauge pressure of 1 bar / 15 psi, and then lower heat slowly until hissing steam no longer leaves the pot.

④ Vent steam for 1–2 min.

⑤ Cook for 20 min to make the meat firm but tender; for as long as 60 min to make it flaky. Whole muscles or large portions will take longer to cook.

⑥ Cool the pressure cooker under cold running water.

⑦ Lift the meat from the jus. Reduce the cooking juices to serve alongside the meat or for later use.

SOUS VIDE AND PRESSURE-COOKED VEAL BREAST WITH BULBOUS VEGETABLES

Yields 1 kg

INSPIRED BY GRAY KUNZ

INGREDIENT	QUANTITY	SCALING	PROCEDURE
Veal breast, sinew and excess fat trimmed	1 kg	100%	① Rub veal with oil, and sear both sides in nonstick pan until golden.
Neutral oil	as needed		
White wine (dry)	475 g	47.5%	② Deglaze, and then transfer to pressure cooker.
Apple cider (fresh)	300 g	30%	
White peppercorns, crushed	9 g	0.9%	③ Add to veal-wine mixture.
			④ Pressure-cook at gauge pressure of 1 bar / 15 psi for 1¼ h.
Bay leaf	0.2 g	0.02%	⑤ Drain veal, and reserve in warm place with 50 g of cooking liquid.
Clove	0.2 g	0.02%	⑥ Reserve remaining cooking liquid for vegetables.
Cumin seeds	0.1 g	0.01%	
Veal breast, central muscle, fat and sinew removed	500 g	50%	⑦ Meanwhile, cook sous vide in 55 °C / 131 °F bath to core temperature of 54 °C / 129 °F, about 1½ h.
			⑧ Allow to rest for 10 min at room temperature.
White cabbage, quartered	475 g	47.5%	⑨ Cook vegetables in oil in bottom of pressure cooker until golden.
Sweet onions, quartered	275 g	27.5%	⑩ Deglaze with reserved cooking liquid.
Leeks, greens removed and halved	175 g	17.5%	⑪ Pressure-cook for 7 min.
			⑫ Remove vegetables, and strain cooking liquid to form sauce.
Shallots, skin on	135 g	13.5%	⑬ Peel skins from cooked vegetables, and reserve warm.
Garlic cloves, with skin	65 g	6.5%	⑭ Reduce strained sauce to glaze.
Vegetable oil	as needed		⑮ Season, and reserve warm.
Unsalted butter	20 g	2%	⑯ Briefly heat cooked vegetables with butter until glazed, about 2 min.
Neutral oil	as needed		⑰ Brown both pieces of veal over high heat for 30 s on each side.
Black pepper, finely ground	to taste		⑱ Season meat and vegetables.
			⑲ Slice meats as desired, and divide among plates.
Salt	to taste		⑳ Pour sauce around.

from page 3·111

PRESSURE-COOKED CARNITAS

Yields 800 g

INGREDIENT	QUANTITY	SCALING	PROCEDURE
Pork shoulder, boneless, cut into 2 cm / ¾ in cubes	1 kg	100%	① Remove all tendons and sinew.
			② Fill pressure cooker with 6 mm / ¼ in water. Add meat.
			③ Bring to pressure. When steam emerges, depress valve stem for 2 min to vent fully.
			④ Cook at gauge pressure of 1 bar / 15 psi for 20 min, for tender but firm texture; or 40 min, for flaky texture. Allow pressure cooker to cool for 10 min before lifting meat from cooking juices.
			⑤ Coarsely shred meat, if desired; set aside.
Pork cooking juices, from above	200 g	20%	⑥ Reduce cooking juices until slightly syrupy.
Achiote paste	15 g	1.5%	⑦ Combine, and stir into reduced juices to make sauce.
Ancho chili powder	5 g	0.5%	
Chipotle chili powder	5 g	0.5%	
Neutral frying oil	as needed		⑧ Deep-fry shredded meat in 180 °C / 355 °F oil until golden brown, about 1 min.
			⑨ Remove three-quarters of meat, straining out oil. Reserve.
			⑩ Continue to fry remaining meat until very dark and crisp, about 5 min.
			⑪ Combine all meat with sauce.
Lime juice	to taste		⑫ Season.
Salt	to taste		

from page 3·114

MICROWAVED TILAPIA WITH SCALLIONS AND GINGER ADAPTED FROM MRS. ZHU

Yields 550 g

INGREDIENT	QUANTITY	SCALING	PROCEDURE
Tilapia, cleaned and gutted	800 g (one whole)	100%	① Combine on microwave-safe plate.
Scallion whites, thinly sliced	150 g	19%	② Cover tightly with plastic wrap.
			③ Microwave at 600 W for 6 min.
Shaoxing rice wine	5 g	0.6%	④ Remove scallions and ginger.
Ginger, peeled and thinly sliced	2.5 g	0.3%	
Scallion greens, julienne	10 g	1.3%	⑤ Mound on top of cooked fish to garnish.
Ginger, peeled and julienne	3 g	0.38%	
Cilantro leaves	1 g	0.1%	
Peanut oil	50 g	6.3%	⑥ Heat to 190 °C / 375 °F.
			⑦ Drizzle hot oil over garnished fish.
Soy sauce	25 g	3%	⑧ Combine.
Toasted sesame oil	2 g	0.25%	⑨ Pour over fish evenly.
			⑩ Lift fillets from bones, and serve with sauce and garnish.

from page 3·115

HOW TO PUFF THE SKIN ON A PORK ROAST

① Remove the pork skin from the roast by cutting close to the meat.

② Cook the pork skin. Vacuum seal skin with water, and cook sous vide in a 95 °C / 203 °F bath for 12 h or pressure-cook for 60 min at a gauge pressure of 1.4 bar / 20.3 psi to complete the transition to a gelatin.

③ Lay the skin flat with the side toward the meat facing up, and gently scrape away the fat.

④ Dehydrate the prepared skin on a baking sheet in a 115 °C / 240 °F oven until the skin becomes rigid.

⑤ Use a food processor to chop the dried skin into small pieces. Use sieves to remove fragments much larger or smaller than 3 mm / ⅛ in across. Store the crumbled skin in an airtight container with a silica gel desiccant. Use the too-big or too-small pieces for other purposes.

⑥ Truss the meat, and cook it. Bind the frenched and trimmed pork loin with acetate to form a tight cylinder. Cook the roast sous vide to the preferred doneness; we recommend a core temperature of 60 °C / 140 °F.

⑦ Plunge the cooked meat in liquid nitrogen for 30 s to freeze a thin surface layer (optional). You can also ladle nitrogen over the meat. This step helps prevent the pork flesh from overcooking in the fryer.

⑧ Dip the meat in warm water for 3 s. The surface will become tacky.

⑨ Coat the meat with a pregelatinized starch such as Ultrasperse M. Shake off any excess.

⑩ Disperse the Methocel into boiling water. Cool Methocel solution completely, and whip to stiff peaks. Dip the roast in foam to evenly coat entire surface. For more on making this foam, see page 5·17.

⑪ Roll the roast in the crumbled, dried skin to form an even coating. Allow 1 min before frying to ensure the skin pieces stay adhered to surface of meat during frying.

⑫ Deep-fry the roast in 200 °C / 390 °F oil. Cook just long enough for the crumbled pork skin to puff into a golden, crispy crust, about 30 s.

⑬ Season, slice, and serve the meat.

Yields 800 g

INGREDIENT	QUANTITY	SCALING
Pork skin, from roast	1 kg	100%
Water	250 g	25%
Rack of pork, skinless, frenched	1 four-rib roast	
Ultra-Sperse M (or tapioca starch)	as needed	
Water	100 g	10%
Methocel K100M (Dow brand)	0.5 g	0.05%
Frying oil	as needed	
Salt	to taste	

from page 3·126

This approach works best for meats with a thick skin that otherwise would be too hard to eat.

ULTRACRISP CHICKEN CROWN

Yields 500 g

INGREDIENT	QUANTITY	SCALING	PROCEDURE
Whole chicken skin, removed in one piece	200 g	20%	① Lay flat, feather side down, on silicone mat.
Salt	2 g	0.2%	② Dust evenly over skin.
			③ Refrigerate uncovered for 12 h to dehydrate.
Chicken skin pieces, chopped	250 g	25%	④ Combine, pack tightly into Pacojet, and freeze.
Activa GS	5 g	0.5%	⑤ Process three times; pack firmly and freeze thoroughly after each cycle.
Salt	2.5 g	0.25%	⑥ Alternatively, puree in food processor, and pass through fine sieve.
			⑦ Spread onto dehydrated chicken skin in even layer 2.5 mm / ⅛ in thick.
Skin, from above	280 g	28%	⑧ Dust Activa GS around perimeter of skin.
Activa GS	3 g	0.3%	
Chicken crown	1 kg	100%	⑨ Place skin over chicken crown, and tuck in all edges. Vacuum seal.
			⑩ Refrigerate for 30 min to ensure all air pockets between skin and meat are removed.
			⑪ Refrigerate uncovered for at least 5 h before assembly.
Liquid nitrogen	as needed		⑫ Cook chicken crown in convection oven at 65 °C / 149 °F to core temperature of 60 °C / 140 °F, about 40 min.
Neutral frying oil	as needed		
			⑬ Lower temperature to 60 °C / 140 °F, and hold for 1 h.
			⑭ Heat oil to 200 °C / 390 °F.
			⑮ Dip cooked chicken crown in liquid nitrogen for 30 s, preferably with wire hook.
			⑯ Deep-fry in hot oil for 45 s.
			⑰ Repeat dipping in liquid nitrogen and deep-frying until crown is golden and very crispy, about three cycles.
Salt	to taste		⑱ Carve chicken from crown, and season with salt.

from page 3·134

PORK LOIN ROAST

Yields 900 g

INGREDIENT	QUANTITY	SCALING	PROCEDURE
Kosher salt	250 g	17%	① Mix together thoroughly.
Pain d'épices powder see page 51	100 g	7%	
Rack of pork loin (first eight ribs from shoulder) with fat cap and skin	1.5 kg	100%	② Roll pork loin in spiced salt without letting salt touch ends of loin. ③ Wrap in plastic wrap, and cure in refrigerator for 48 h. ④ Remove skin and fat, and refrigerate.
Gelatinized pork skin, dried and finely minced see page 93	300 g	20%	⑤ Measure and reserve individually.
Crisp Coat UC (National Starch brand)	60 g	4%	
Water	200 g	13%	⑥ Bring water to simmer, and mix in methylcellulose with hand blender.
Methocel E4M (Dow brand)	5 g	0.3%	⑦ Hold at simmer for 2 min while blending continuously. ⑧ Cool, and vacuum seal.
Liquid nitrogen (optional)	as needed		⑨ Refrigerate for 12 h to allow methylcellulose to hydrate. ⑩ Cook pork loin sous vide in 61 °C / 142 °F bath to core temperature of 60 °C / 140 °F, about 1½ h; longer for full pork loin. ⑪ Whip methylcellulose solution with electric whisk or mixer until stiff peaks form. ⑫ Transfer solution to container large enough to accommodate whole pork loin. ⑬ Dip cooked pork loin in liquid nitrogen for 30 s, and then in warm water for 5 s. (This step is optional. See page 3·126.) ⑭ Sift thin layer of starch over pork loin, and shake off excess. ⑮ Roll meat in whipped methylcellulose, and then in minced pork skin.
Frying oil	as needed		⑯ Deep-fry in 185 °C / 365 °F oil until just puffed and golden, about 30 s. ⑰ Rest meat for 3 min. ⑱ Slice roast between each bone and serve.

from page 5·23

PUFFED COCKSCOMB

Yields 100 g

INGREDIENT	QUANTITY	SCALING	PROCEDURE
Cockscombs	100 g	100%	① Vacuum seal together.
White chicken stock see page 11	50 g	50%	② Cook in 85 °C / 185 °F bath for 2 h to gelatinize skins. ③ Cool. ④ Remove from bag. ⑤ Dehydrate at 50 °C / 120 °F until cockscombs are half their original weight, about 2 h.
Frying oil	as needed		⑥ Deep-fry cockscombs in 190 °C / 375 °F oil until slightly puffed, very crispy, and no longer bubbling, about 5 min. ⑦ Drain on paper towels.
Salt	to taste		⑧ Season.

from page 3·133

MONKFISH WITH CONSTRUCTED SKIN ADAPTED FROM ANDONI LUIS ADURIZ

Yields 420 g

INGREDIENT	QUANTITY	SCALING	PROCEDURE
Cod skins, washed and desalted	1 kg	250%	① Cover with water, and bring to boil.
			② Simmer until reduced to one-quarter of original volume.
			③ Strain.
			④ Reduce broth by half, until it is very thick.
			⑤ Measure 150 g of reduction, and reserve.
Water	1.5 kg	375%	⑥ Hydrate gelatin in cold water for 5 min.
160 Bloom gelatin	2 g	0.5%	⑦ Squeeze out excess moisture in gelatin, and then mix into warm reduction until fully dissolved.
			⑧ Spread on nonstick surface in layer 1 mm / 1/32 in thick.
			⑨ Dry at room temperature until dry film has formed, about 1 d.
Vodka	2.5 g	0.63%	⑩ Mix together.
Edible silver powder	0.5 g	0.13%	⑪ Paint onto film with brush.
			⑫ Dry film at room temperature for 3 h.
			⑬ Cut into 5 cm / 2 in squares.
			⑭ Reserve in airtight container.
Monkfish fillet, trimmed and cut into 5 cm / 2 in cubes	400 g	100%	⑮ Vacuum seal together.
			⑯ Cook sous vide in 48 °C / 118 °F bath to core temperature of 47 °C / 117 °F, about 20 min.
Extra-virgin olive oil	30 g	7.5%	
Salt	15 g	4%	⑰ Season monkfish.
			⑱ Lay piece of film "skin" on top of each monkfish cube.

from page 3·132

PUFFED SALMON SKIN PILLOWS

Yields 35 g

INGREDIENT	QUANTITY	SCALING	PROCEDURE
Salmon skin (one intact piece)	25 g	100%	① Vacuum seal.
			② Cook sous vide in 85 °C / 185 °F bath for 3 h.
			③ Remove from bag to cool.
			④ Trim, and cut into at least 24 squares, each measuring 3.5 cm / 1½ in.
Activa GS	5 g	20%	⑤ Whisk together.
Water, 10–25 °C / 50–77 °F	5 g	20%	⑥ Brush mixture on 3 mm / ⅛ in edge of each salmon skin square.
			⑦ Sandwich two squares together to seal.
			⑧ Repeat to make total of at least 12 sandwiched squares.
			⑨ Vacuum seal without overlapping.
			⑩ Refrigerate for at least 6 h.
Frying oil	as needed		⑪ Deep-fry salmon skin pillows in 175 °C / 350 °F oil until golden and puffed, about 8 min.
Salt	to taste		⑫ Drain, and season with salt.

from page 5·163

PUFFED CHICKEN FEET

Yields 80 g

INGREDIENT	QUANTITY	SCALING	PROCEDURE
Chicken feet	500 g	100%	① Vacuum seal together.
Water	100 g	20%	② Cook sous vide in 90 °C / 194 °F bath for 12 h.
Salt	2 g	0.4%	③ Drain.
			④ Remove bones using scalpel and tweezers.
			⑤ Dehydrate at 115 °C / 240 °F for 3 h.
Frying oil	as needed		⑥ Deep-fry chicken feet in 190 °C / 375 °F oil until puffed, 30–45 s.
			⑦ Drain on paper towels.

Puffed chicken feet are the chicken equivalent of a puffed pork skin or puffed snack (see page 342). Feet work well because of their high gelatin content.

from page 3·133

MEAT AND SEAFOOD

OFFAL SOUS VIDE

① Prepare the meat. Many organ meats require an initial preparation step, such as blanching or soaking in water or a marinade.

② Vacuum seal. Most offal recipes require no other ingredients.

③ Cook sous vide to the desired doneness. The tables below list recommended temperatures; those printed in bold are our favorites.

Estimated cooking times are given in some cases; in others, "to core" indicates that cooking should continue until the core temperature of the food reaches the recommended temperature.

④ Sear (optional).

⑤ Chill and set (for meat served cold).

Best Bets for Cooking Tough Offal Sous Vide

	Tender, juicy			Braised texture			Note	See page
	(°C)	(°F)	(h)	(°C)	(°F)	(h)		
beef and veal tongue	68	**154**	**12**	67	153	48		5·49
duck tongue	70	158	8	**88**	**190**	**5**	remove central bone while still hot	87
chicken gizzard	n/a			**60**	**140**	**12**	cure before cooking	5·125
veal heart	n/a			**80**	**176**	**5**		
honeycomb tripe	n/a			**88**	**190**	**2**		
cockscomb	n/a			**85**	**185**	**2**	blanch and peel before cooking	94

from page 3·146   (*times in **bold** are those we prefer*)

Best Bets for Cooking Tender Organ Meats Sous Vide

	Medium rare			Pink			Medium			Note	See page
	(°C)	(°F)	(h)	(°C)	(°F)	(h)	(°C)	(°F)	(h)		
duck foie gras	50	122	to core*	**54**	**129**	**to core***	60	140	to core*		below, 98, 99
				56	133	to core*					
poultry liver	52	126	to core*	**56**	**133**	**to core***	60	140	to core*		
veal liver	58	136	to core*	**62**	**144**	**to core***	65	149	to core*	soak in milk or water for at least 8 h before serving	
lamb sweetbreads	n/a			**55**	**131**	**2**	65	149	1	soak in water for at least 5 h before serving	
veal sweetbreads	n/a			**60**	**140**	**1**	67	153	1		next page, 99, 100
cock's kidney	n/a			**70**	**158**	**20 min**	n/a			panfry briefly after cooking for best texture	98
kidney (mammal)	n/a			**56**	**133**	**to core***	60	140	1	pork kidney is ideal because it is often milder tasting than other types of kidneys	

from page 3·146   *(*If cooked just to these core temperatures, these meats may not meet food safety guidelines. To pasteurize, hold at the cooking temperature for the period of time given by the table on page 1·184. Times in **bold** are those we prefer.*)

SOUS VIDE FOIE GRAS

Yields 400 g

INGREDIENT	QUANTITY	SCALING	PROCEDURE
Flash-frozen foie gras, presliced, 2.5 cm / 1 in	400 g (four 100 g portions)	100%	① Vacuum seal portions individually. ② Reserve frozen until ready to serve. ③ Cook foie gras sous vide directly from freezer at 53 °C / 127 °F to core temperature of 52 °C / 126 °F, about 35 min.
Flaky salt	to taste		④ Cut each portion into slices 1 cm / ⅜ in thick. ⑤ Season.
Duck broth with vanilla and bay leaf, warmed see page 16	100 g	25%	⑥ Pour around foie gras portions.

from page 5·110

ANKIMO TORCHON

Yields 450 g

INGREDIENT	QUANTITY	SCALING	PROCEDURE
Monkfish liver (ankimo quality)	500 g	100%	① Remove main veins.
			② Cover in water, and soak refrigerated for 3 h, changing water every 30 min.
			③ Drain and reserve.
Water	200 g	40%	④ Whisk together to make brine.
Sake	50 g	10%	⑤ Vacuum seal monkfish livers with brine, and refrigerate for 24 h.
Salt	8.75 g	1.75% (3.5%)*	
			⑥ Drain.
Sugar	6.25 g	1.25% (2.5%)*	⑦ Roll livers together into tight cylinder by using plastic wrap.
			⑧ Vacuum seal.
			⑨ Cook sous vide in 63 °C / 145 °F bath to core temperature of 62 °C / 144 °F, about 35 min.
			⑩ Cool, and refrigerate overnight to allow flavors to mature.
Daikon, julienne	as desired		⑪ Slice monkfish liver, garnish with daikon, and serve with ponzu.
Sous vide ponzu see page 22	as desired		

from page 3·147   *(% of total combined weight of water and sake)

Many recipes for foie gras, liver, sweetbreads, and other offal include a soaking step before cooking. For kidneys, this step serves a very simple purpose: to remove any trace of the animal's bodily fluids. Recipes often call for soaking foie gras, liver, and sweetbreads in milk. It is often said that milk improves the taste, purges blood, lightens the color, or affects some other property of the meat. We were skeptical, so we tried several experiments. With a mild-flavored organ meat like foie gras, we could taste a difference, but, frankly, in our tests, we prefer the taste of water-soaked to milk-soaked foie gras. With stronger-flavored organ meats, there is even less of a difference than with foie gras. So our suggestion is to simply soak the meat in water.

SWEETBREADS WITH SOUR MANGO POWDER AND SHIITAKE

ADAPTED FROM JEAN-GEORGES VONGERICHTEN

Yields 650 g (four portions)

INGREDIENT	QUANTITY	SCALING	PROCEDURE
Veal sweetbreads	600 g	100%	① Peel off exterior membranes.
White vegetable stock see page 6	200 g	33%	② Vacuum seal with stock and salt.
			③ Cook sous vide in 67 °C / 153 °F bath for 1 h.
Salt	9 g	1.5%	
Carrot, finely minced	60 g	10%	④ Sweat until carrots and ginger are tender, about 5 min.
Unsalted butter	60 g	10%	
Ginger, finely minced	32 g	5.5%	
Shiitake, thinly sliced	120 g	20%	⑤ Add, and cook until tender, about 5 min.
Shallot, thinly sliced	80 g	13.5%	
Brown chicken stock see page 6	110 g	18.5%	⑥ Deglaze sauce base.
			⑦ Reduce until syrupy, about 5 min.
White port (dry)	40 g	6.5%	
Manzanilla sherry	25 g	4%	
Amchoor (sour mango powder)	34.5 g	6%	⑧ Whisk 4.5 g of amchoor and 1 g of licorice into sauce, and reserve.
Licorice powder	6 g	1%	
Freeze-dried carrot powder see page 340	30 g	5%	⑨ Combine with remaining amchoor and licorice powder.
			⑩ Dust powder over surfaces of cooked sweetbreads.
Clarified unsalted butter	70 g	11.5%	⑪ Fry sweetbreads in very hot butter until golden on both sides, about 1 min each.
Salt	to taste		⑫ Season sauce and sweetbreads.
Lemon juice	to taste		⑬ Slice sweetbreads into desired dimensions.
			⑭ Divide evenly among four plates, and garnish with sauce.

from page 3·151

FOIE GRAS AND BUTTON MUSHROOM TART

Yields 800 g

ADAPTED FROM PASCAL BARBOT

INGREDIENT	QUANTITY	SCALING	PROCEDURE
Verjuice (store-bought)	1 kg	140%	① Marinate foie gras in verjuice for 3 h.
Duck foie gras, Grade A	700 g	100%	② Cut carefully into slices 5 mm / 3/16 in thick, and reserve.
Button mushrooms	450 g (12 large mushrooms)	65%	③ Peel, and rub with lemon juice to prevent discoloration.
			④ Slice very thinly on mandoline, and reserve about 20 slices for garnish.
Lemon juice	16 g	2%	
Roasted-hazelnut oil	10 g	1.5%	⑤ Season remaining mushroom slices, and reserve.
Orange zest, finely grated	3 g	0.4%	
Black pepper	to taste		
Salt	to taste		
Maple syrup	40 g	5.5%	⑥ Whisk together to make maple butter.
Unsalted butter, melted	20 g	3%	
Brik pastry sheets	three pieces		⑦ Lay one sheet of pâte à brick on silicone mat.
			⑧ Brush carefully with maple butter.
			⑨ Repeat with other two sheets until three-layer pastry stack is formed.
			⑩ Punch out 12 cm / 4¾ in circles from stack, using pastry cutter; makes about 20 rounds.
			⑪ Place rounds on baking sheet between two silicone mats.
			⑫ Bake in 160 °C / 320 °F oven for 12 min.
Dried mushrooms, ground to fine powder	as needed		⑬ Arrange seasoned mushrooms on each pâte à brick round.
			⑭ Top with slices of marinated foie gras.
			⑮ Dust lightly with mushroom powder.
			⑯ Top with reserved, unseasoned mushroom slices.
			⑰ Dust with more mushroom powder.
Eggless citrus curd see page 307	70 g	10%	⑱ Slice rounds (tarts) into quarters.
			⑲ Serve with dab of curd on side.

from page 3·148

SOUS VIDE PIGEON OFFAL

Yields 300 g

INGREDIENT	QUANTITY	SCALING	PROCEDURE
Pigeon hearts	100 g (four hearts, 25 g each)	100%	① Measure and reserve individually.
Rendered duck fat	50 g	50%	
Cock's kidneys	100 g (four kidneys, 25 g each)	100%	② Vacuum seal.
			③ Cook sous vide in 70 °C / 158 °F bath for 20 min.
Pigeon gizzards, split and peeled	150 g	150%	④ Vacuum seal together.
			⑤ Cook sous vide in 60 °C / 140 °F bath for 12 h.
Rendered duck fat	50 g	50%	⑥ Reserve duck fat.
Neutral frying oil	as needed		⑦ Brown kidneys gently in oil to achieve golden crust.
Salt	to taste		⑧ Slice browned kidneys in half lengthwise and gizzards into thin pieces, and season with salt.
			⑨ Brown hearts on all sides in reserved duck fat for 2 min, and season with salt.
			⑩ Serve as garnish for ragout of grains; see page 156.

from page 5·130

FOIE GRAS SOUP WITH BOMBA RICE AND SEA LETTUCE
ADAPTED FROM ANDONI LUIS ADURIZ   Yields 800 g (four portions)

INGREDIENT	QUANTITY	SCALING	PROCEDURE
Foie gras lobe, Grade B	600 g	100%	① Cut into two or three large pieces, depending on size. If three pieces, cut off ends by about 1 cm / ½ in to facilitate removing blood.
Whole milk	1 kg	167%	② Whisk until salt has dissolved, and bring to 30 °C / 86 °F.
Water	1 kg	167%	
Table salt	10 g	1.7%	③ Add foie gras pieces; keep submerged for 3 h.
			④ Remove foie gras from milk brine, and pat dry.
Sunflower oil	50 g	8.3%	⑤ Sear brined foie gras until golden brown on all sides.
			⑥ Bake in 130 °C / 265 °F oven to core temperature of 58 °C / 136 °F.
			⑦ Remove, and place weighted sheet pan on top of foie gras to press out excess fat and blood.
			⑧ Rest in warm place for 5 min.
Extra-virgin olive oil	10 g	1.7%	⑨ Sweat until lightly golden, about 7 min.
Yellow onion, finely chopped	25 g	4.2%	
Bomba rice	50 g	8.3%	⑩ Add rice to onion, and toast for 5 min.
White vegetable stock, brought to a boil see page 6	500 g	83%	⑪ Pour in hot vegetable broth, and simmer for 15 min.
Sea lettuce (fresh)	50 g	8.3%	⑫ Add to rice, simmer for 5 min, and remove from heat.
			⑬ Cover pot, let stand for 15 min, and pass through fine sieve.
Salt	as needed		⑭ Season broth.
			⑮ Slice foie gras into four portions, each 4 cm / 1½ in thick, and place in center of four warm bowls.
			⑯ Finish with rice broth.

An alternative to baking foie gras in the oven is to seal raw foie gras in a sous vide bag and cook it at 58 °C / 136 °F. Remove the meat from the bag, place a weighted sheet pan on top of the foie gras to press out excess fat and blood, and then sear the meat. This procedure replaces steps 5–7 in the recipe at left.

from page 3·149

SOUS VIDE VEAL SWEETBREADS
Yields 500 g

INGREDIENT	QUANTITY	SCALING	PROCEDURE
Veal sweetbreads	500 g	100%	① Cover sweetbreads with water. Refrigerate for 4 h.
Water	as needed		② Drain, and then repeat process twice for total soaking time of 12 h.
			③ Discard liquid.
			④ Peel membrane off sweetbreads, and trim away fat and veins.
			⑤ Vacuum seal.
			⑥ Cook sous vide in 67 °C / 153 °F bath for 1 h.
White veal stock see page 6	300 g	60%	⑦ Meanwhile, combine, and reduce to 50 g.
			⑧ Bring reduction to boil, and remove from heat.
Fino sherry	150 g	30%	
Dried licorice root	2.5 g	0.5%	⑩ Add to hot reduction, and infuse for 7 min.
Fennel seeds	0.5 g	0.1%	⑪ Strain.
Star anise	0.5 g	0.1%	
Kaolin clay	2 g	0.4%	⑫ Whisk into infused reduction to create glaze.
Salt	to taste		⑬ Season clay glaze.
			⑭ Add sweetbreads to hot glaze, and baste until glaze has reduced and sweetbreads are well coated, about 1 min.
			⑮ Cut sweetbreads into portions 2.5 cm / 1 in thick.

from page 5·32

CRISPY SWEETBREADS ADAPTED FROM SCOTT ANDERSON

Yields 1.2 kg (six portions)

INGREDIENT	QUANTITY	SCALING	PROCEDURE
White soy sauce	140 g	23.5%	① Combine, and vacuum seal.
Extra-virgin olive oil	70 g	11.5%	② Cook sous vide in 93 °C / 199 °F bath for 10 min.
Garlic cloves, thinly sliced	60 g	10%	③ Cool, strain, and reserve.
Black pepper, coarsely ground	1.5 g	0.25%	
Veal sweetbreads	600 g	100%	④ Peel off exterior membranes.
			⑤ Separate along seams, using sharp knife, into 2.5 cm / 1 in pieces, and reserve.
			⑥ Vacuum seal sweetbreads with cooled infusion.
			⑦ Cook sous vide in 60 °C / 140 °F bath for 1 h.
			⑧ Cool quickly in ice-water bath.
Wondra flour	20 g	3.5%	⑨ Combine to make dredging powder, and reserve.
Pistachio powder	15 g	2.5%	
Salt	3 g	0.5%	
Dried orange zest powder	2 g	0.3%	
White asparagus stalks, chopped	130 g	22%	⑩ Sweat together until asparagus stalks are tender.
Spanish onion, thinly sliced	90 g	15%	
Extra-virgin olive oil	15 g	2.5%	
Soy milk	300 g	50%	⑪ Add to asparagus mixture, and simmer until very tender, about 15 min.
Macadamia nut butter	35 g	6%	⑫ Puree, and pass through fine sieve.
Salt	to taste		⑬ Season asparagus stalk puree, and reserve warm.
Asparagus tips, blanched and cut lengthwise	90 g	15%	⑭ Warm in small pot.
			⑮ Drain cooked sweetbread pieces, and coat with dredging powder.
			⑯ Fry in 190 °C / 375 °F oil until golden brown and just warmed through, about 45 s.
			⑰ Drain on paper towels.
Chickpeas, cooked and peeled	60 g	10%	⑱ Spoon asparagus puree into bowls.
			⑲ Top with crisp sweetbread pieces, asparagus tips, and chickpeas.
Black summer truffle, julienne	12 g	2%	⑳ Garnish plates.
Chive flowers	as needed		㉑ Dust with additional dredging powder.

from page 3·150

BRINES, CURES, AND DRY RUBS

① Select a brine, wet cure, or dry rub; the Best Bets tables below and on the next page suggest many good options.

② Combine the ingredients, stir fully to dissolve, and then refrigerate the solution. Quantities for rubs are given relative to the amount of salt. For example, to make a basic dry rub, use 10 g of sugar and 5 g of spices for every 100 g of salt. For convenience, quantities for brines and wet cures are given using two distinct kinds of baker's percentages. Quantities in the scaling 1 column are relative to the combined weight of the meat and water (excluding the weight of any bones), and are appropriate for the equilibrium brining method described on page 3·170. Quantities in the scaling 2 column are for use with the more traditional high-concentration approach described on page 3·171, and are explained there.

Best Bets for Brines

Recipe	Ingredients	(scaling 1)	(scaling 2)	Note	See page
basic brine	meat and water	100%		works well for most applications	5·113
	water	as needed	100%		
	salt	1%	7%		
	sugar	0.4%	3%		
basic seafood brine	meat and water	100%		higher sugar content balances this brine for delicate fish and shellfish	5·161
	water	as needed	100%		
	salt	1%	5%		
	sugar	0.6%	3.5%		
basic pink brine	meat and water	100%		has an effective nitrite concentration of 0.12%; works well with color-sensitive meats, such as pork belly or tongue	5·101
	water	as needed	100%		
	salt	10%	10%		
	Insta Cure No. 1	0.2%	2%		
basic phosphate brine	meat and water	100%		firms meat and maintains moisture; using more sodium tripolyphosphate than indicated here can produce a rubbery texture	
	water	as needed	100%		
	salt	1%	7%		
	sodium tripolyphosphate	0.007%	0.05%		
umami brine	meat and water	100%		saltiness varies with brand and type of soy sauce but is usually about 19%; usukuchi shoyu has an excellent flavor	
	water	as needed	100%		
	usukuchi shoyu	5.3%	100%		
	honey	1%	20%		
cola brine	meat and cola	100%		popular sweet brine in the American South; never add curing salts to cola brines because the mixture will release a lethal gas	
	cola (not diet cola)	as needed	100%		
	salt	1%	8%		
dairy brine	meat & cultured whey	100%		has a mild tenderizing effect; adds characteristic dairy sweetness; especially good with mild meats like chicken and fish	
	cultured whey	as needed	100%		
	salt	1%	6%		

from page 3·168

The resting step that follows brining works very much like the resting one does after cooking meat. The salt, just like the heat, continues to diffuse through the meat after it is removed from the source. Another way to judge when brining is complete is to calculate the final weight of the meat when it has reached the desired salinity, D (in percent), which typically ranges from lightly brined at 0.7% salinity to an intense cure of 2%. First, determine the salinity S of the brine from the weight of salt and water in grams by using the formula S = 100 × salt ÷ (salt + water). Next weigh the unbrined meat to obtain the starting weight M in grams. Then calculate the target weight of the meat T by using the formula T = M + (D × M ÷ S).

As the meat soaks in the brine, remove and weigh it periodically to check whether the weight has increased to the target weight. For example, if brining 1 kg pork chops in the basic brine recipe above, S = 100 × 7 ÷ (7 + 100) = 6.54; M = 1,000 g, the starting weight of the pork chops. To achieve a final salinity D = 0.7%, brine to a target weight of T = 1,000 + (0.7 × 1,000 ÷ 6.54) = 1,107 g. The pork chops will thus weigh about 1.107 kg when they have reached the desired degree of saltiness.

Sometimes cured meats and seafood are also smoked as part of the ripening process. We discuss the details of smoking food in chapter 7 on Traditional Cooking, page 2·2, and in chapter 11 on Meat and Seafood, page 3·208. We mention it here to point out that it can be an important step after curing. Sometimes, it is done early, often during the resting step, after the curing is complete. Other times, it's done at the end, after the product is fully mature. The choice to do it early or late comes down to whether or not you want a distinct smoky aroma. Over time, smoke aromas dissipate to the point that you would no longer describe the flavor as smoky.

Best Bets for Wet Cures

Recipe	Ingredients*	(scaling 1)	(scaling 2)	Effective salinity	Effective nitrite concentration	Note
basic wet cure	water and meat	100%		17%	0.1%	keep meats and seafoods submerged and refrigerated
	water	as needed	100%			
	salt	2%	20%			
	Insta Cure No. 1**	0.14%	1.40%			
basic sweet cure	water and meat	100%		17%	0.1%	sugar, corn syrup, honey, molasses, and treacle are all commonly used sweeteners
	water	as needed	100%			
	salt	2%	20%			
	sweetener	1.5%	15%			
	Insta Cure No. 1**	0.14%	1.4%			
Wiltshire tank cure	water and meat	100%		19%	0.10% nitrite 0.25% nitrate	traditionally used for bacon
	water	as needed	100%			
	salt	2%	20%			
	sodium nitrite	0.001%	0.01%			
	sodium nitrate	0.003%	0.03%			
corned beef cure	water and meat	100%		10%	0.1%	to make pickling spice mix, combine 10 g coriander seed, 8 g black peppercorns, 5 g yellow mustard seeds, 5 g dill seeds, 5 g star anise, 1 g mace, 1 g clove, and two fresh bay leaves for each 1 kg cure; combine cure ingredients and bring to boil; cool completely to infuse; inject 10% cure to weight of meat; submerge meat in remaining cure; refrigerate for 3–5 d; rinse
	water	as needed	100%			
	salt	2%	8%			
	brown sugar	1.7%	4.5%			
	Insta Cure No. 1	0.14%	1.4%			
	pickling spice mix	see note				

from page 3·169   *(allow sufficient cure to cover meat or seafood); **(optional)

Phosphates in brines or wet cures should be dissolved separately in a small amount of warm water and added to the main mixture only after fully dissolved.

For the herbs and spices in the dry rub recipes, use any spice mix, such as our Indies Spice Blend (page 48), Kansas and Memphis Rubs (page 49), Pastrami Spice Blend (see page 121), or various curry blends (see page 5·89).

Best Bets for Dry Rubs

Recipe	Ingredients*	(scaling)	Effective nitrite concentration	Note
basic dry rub	salt	100%	none	customizable to your own taste
	sugar (optional)	10%		
	herbs and spices (optional)	5%		
sweet dry rub	salt	100%	none	
	sugar	50%		
	herbs and spices (optional)	5%		
pink salt rub	salt	100%	less than 0.15%	only suitable for brief dry-curing or brining under refrigeration
	Insta Cure No. 1	16%		
	sugar (optional)	20%		
	herbs and spices (optional)	5%		
slow-curing rub	salt	100%	less than 0.15% for both nitrites and nitrates	recipe includes nitrates; must be used only for dry, long cures
	Morton Tender Quick	43%		
	sugar (optional)	30%		
	herbs and spices (optional)	5%		

from page 3·169   * (allow sufficient rub to cover meat or seafood)

Best Bets for Brining

Meat	Recommended brine	Thickness (cm)	(in)	Soak* (h)	Rinse (min)	Rest (h)	Note	See page
chicken breast, boneless and skinless	basic brine	3.2	1¼	4	n/a	2	extend soaking time if skin on or bone in	101
chicken legs, skin on, bone in	basic brine	3.8	1½	7	n/a	3		101
duck breast, skin on, boneless	basic phosphate brine	3.2	1¼	10	n/a	5		101
fish fillet, portion, skinless	basic seafood brine	3.8	1½	5	n/a	1		101
lobster tail, whole, shelled	basic seafood brine	3.2	1¼	3	n/a	1		101
shrimp, whole, shelled	basic seafood brine	1.25	½	2	n/a	½		101
pork belly, whole, skin on, bone in	basic pink brine	6.4	2½	72	2 h	24	adjust soaking time for preportioned cuts	101
pork chop, bone in	basic brine	2.5	1			see note	vacuum seal pork with brine until meat absorbs 10% of liquid	101
pork tenderloin, whole	juniper brine	3.8	1½	12	n/a	8		69
pork shoulder, whole, skin on	cola brine	23	9	72	2 h	n/a	inject with 7% brine, and immerse in remaining brine**	101
sweetbreads, membrane peeled	umami brine	3.8	1½	10	30	n/a		101
veal tongue	basic phosphate brine	7.6	3	24	2 h	n/a	inject with 14% brine, and immerse in remaining brine**	101, 90
whole chicken	basic brine	2.5 kg		24	n/a	24		
whole turkey	basic brine	5 kg		48	n/a	48		

from page 3·172

* *(tumbling or injecting the meat reduces the soaking time required);*
***(by weight of meat, which is about 60% of weight of whole poultry)*

Best Bets for Curing

Meat	Recommended rub or cure	Thickness (cm)	(in)	Cure time* (d)	Rinse (h)	Rest (h)	Example use	Note	See page
beef tenderloin, whole	basic dry rub	8.75	3½	2	n/a	24	cured beef		
brisket, whole	pastrami cure	7.5	3	7.5	n/a	n/a	corned beef pastrami	we prefer the meat from the nose end	88
duck breast, skin on	basic sweet cure, corned beef cure	2.5	1	1	wipe off cure	12	corned duck, duck ham	for corned duck, cook after curing; for duck ham, hang dry in refrigerator for 7 d	
duck leg, skin on	basic dry rub	3.2	1¼	6 h	wipe off cure	n/a	duck confit	can be cured for up to 12 h for a firmer texture	105
fish fillet, whole side, skin on	3% salt, 1% sugar to weight of fish	3.75	1½	24–28 h	wipe off cure	n/a	smoked salmon	vacuum sealing recommended	121
pork belly, whole, skin on, bone in	basic dry rub, Wiltshire tank cure	6.25	2½	5–7	n/a	7 d	bacon	omit resting if using Wiltshire tank cure	
pork leg, skin on, bone in (fresh ham)	basic wet cure, blackstrap molasses cure	17.5	7	12–15	8	8	honey baked ham, prosciutto	injection curing recommended	110
pork jowl, skin on	pink salt cure	3.75	1½	1	2	n/a	guanciale		
pork shank, skinless (ham hock)	sweet dry rub	7	2¾	5	quick rinse	12	smoked ham hock		

from page 3·172

**(cure time is approximate, but varies with the thickness of the meat)*

MEAT AND SEAFOOD

FOIE GRAS TORCHON

Yields 875 g

INGREDIENT	QUANTITY	SCALING	PROCEDURE
Raw duck foie gras, Grade A	800 g	100%	① Bring lobe of foie gras to room temperature.
Water, cold	as needed		② Butterfly lobe carefully to reveal network of blood vessels.
			③ Remove veins and any remaining blood by scraping away with spoon.
			④ Set aside foie gras.
White port (sweet)	16 g	2%	⑤ Blend to form cure.
Salt	14 g	1.75%	⑥ Rub onto foie gras; cover completely.
Cognac	4 g	0.5%	⑦ Vacuum seal foie gras.
Sugar	4 g	0.5%	⑧ Refrigerate for 12 h to cure.
Insta Cure No. 1	2 g	0.25%	⑨ Cook cured foie gras sous vide in 56 °C / 133 °F bath to core temperature of 55 °C / 131 °F, about 20 min.
			⑩ Remove from bag, and cool at room temperature for 10 min, or until fat begins to congeal.
			⑪ Reserve 50 g of fat.
Synthetic sausage casing, 5 cm / 2 in diameter, 20 cm / 8 in long	1 piece		⑫ Puree cooked foie gras.
			⑬ Pour into synthetic sausage casing.
			⑭ Tie ends of casing with butcher's twine.
			⑮ Refrigerate for at least 3 d to age.
Brioche loaf	300 g	37.5%	⑯ Cut into slices 2.5 cm / 1 in thick and 75 g each.
Foie gras fat, from above	50 g	6.25%	⑰ Brush brioche slices evenly with reserved foie gras fat.
Salt	3 g	0.4%	⑱ Toast slices in nonstick pan until edges are golden and centers are tender, about 3 min.
Yuzu and kumquat marmalade see page 181	40 g	5%	⑲ Serve slices of aged foie gras with marmalade and hot, toasted brioche.

from page 3·176

FOIE GRAS PARFAIT

Yields 600 g

INGREDIENT	QUANTITY	SCALING	PROCEDURE
Raw duck foie gras	425 g	100%	① Slice 1 cm / ⅜ in off each end of lobe.
Whole milk	as needed		② Cover foie gras with milk, soak for 5 h in refrigerator to drain blood, and then drain and vacuum seal.
			③ Cook sous vide in 57 °C / 135 °F bath to core temperature of 56 °C / 133 °F, about 20 min.
White duck stock warmed see page 6	170 g	40%	④ Whisk salts and sugar into stock until dissolved. Cool completely.
			⑤ Blend foie gras with stock.
Insta Cure No. 1	6 g	1.4%	⑥ Vacuum seal and refrigerate until use.
Salt	6 g	1.4%	
Sugar	3 g	0.7%	

from page 5·268

BACON CHIP

Yields 100 g

INGREDIENT	QUANTITY	SCALING	PROCEDURE
Maple syrup	50 g	20%	① Simmer together until dissolved.
Water	50 g	20%	② Cool syrup.
Glucose syrup DE 40	45 g	18%	
Isomalt	25 g	10%	
Sorbitol	1 g	0.4%	
Cured bacon, sliced 1 mm / ¹⁄₁₆ in thick store-bought or see page 107	250 g	100%	③ Soak bacon slices in syrup in refrigerator for 2 h.
			④ Dehydrate at 60 °C / 140 °F until crisp, 12–14 h.
			⑤ Store chips in cool, dry place.

from page 5·220

SHAVED FOIE GRAS ADAPTED FROM DAVID CHANG

Yields 1.2 kg (16 portions)

INGREDIENT	QUANTITY	SCALING	PROCEDURE
Lychees, drained (canned in syrup)	200 g	50%	① Quarter.
			② Refrigerate until use.
For Riesling gelée:			
160 Bloom gelatin	4 g (two sheets)	1%	③ Combine, and bring to simmer.
			④ Refrigerate in small mixing bowl for 6–8 h.
Riesling (dry)	250 g	62.5%	⑤ Stir, and thoroughly break up gelée once an hour with long-tined fork. This will give appearance of shattered glass.
Rice vinegar	4 g	1%	
			⑥ Cover gelée, and store refrigerated for no more than 1 wk.
For pine nut brittle:			
Sugar	100 g	25%	⑦ Cover baking sheet with parchment paper or silicone mat, and set aside for caramel.
Glucose	100 g	25%	⑧ Combine sugar, glucose, and isomalt in heavy-bottom saucepan.
Isomalt	100 g	25%	⑨ Cook over medium heat without disturbing until golden caramel forms, 12–15 min, and remove from heat.
Pine nuts	400 g	100%	⑩ Meanwhile, toast nuts in 150 °C / 300 °F oven until golden and fragrant, 6–7 min.
			⑪ Fold into caramel.
Unsalted butter, brought to room temperature	75 g	18.75%	⑫ Stir into caramel until fully incorporated, about 30 s.
			⑬ Pour caramel immediately onto prepared baking sheet in thin layer, and cool.
Kosher salt	to taste		⑭ Break brittle into small, bite-size pieces.
Foie gras torchon, frozen see previous page	400 g	100%	⑮ Place two tablespoons of quartered lychees in bottom of each of eight serving bowls.
			⑯ Top lychees with tablespoon of Riesling gelée.
			⑰ Top gelée with tablespoon of cracked brittle.
			⑱ Grate mound of frozen foie gras with Microplane onto each bowl, as generously as desired.

from page 3·177

DUCK LEG CONFIT WITH POMMES SARLADAISES
ADAPTED FROM PAULA WOLFERT

Yields 1.4 kg (four portions)

INGREDIENT	QUANTITY	SCALING	PROCEDURE
Moulard duck legs	1.6 kg (four legs)	100%	① Pack cure evenly onto duck legs.
			② Vacuum seal.
Confit cure mix see next page	288 g	18%	③ Refrigerate for 10 h.
			④ Rinse off cure, and blot legs until completely dry.
Rendered duck fat	80 g	5%	⑤ Vacuum seal legs individually with 20 g of fat each.
			⑥ Cook sous vide in 82 °C / 180 °F bath for 8 h.
			⑦ Cool quickly in ice-water bath, and refrigerate.
Waxy potato, sliced 5 mm / 3⁄16 in thick and cut into 3 cm / 1 3⁄16 in coins	160 g	10%	⑧ Vacuum seal together.
			⑨ Cook sous vide in 88 °C / 190 °F bath until just tender, 20–25 min.
Water	30 g	1.9%	⑩ Warm duck legs in 80 °C / 176 °F bath for 12 min.
Rendered duck fat	20 g	1.25%	⑪ Brown legs in skillet, skin side down, until skin is crisp, about 4 min.
Garlic, thinly sliced	5 g	0.3%	⑫ Garnish crisped legs with potatoes.
Salt	1.4 g	0.09%	
Thyme leaves	0.5 g	0.03%	

from page 3·178

CONFIT CURE MIX

Yields 1.1 kg

INGREDIENT	QUANTITY	SCALING	PROCEDURE
Kosher salt	1 kg	100%	① Combine, vacuum seal, and refrigerate until use.
Coriander seeds, toasted	100 g	10%	② Use to cure poultry and game.
Garlic cloves, mashed	11 g	1.1%	
Star anise, finely crushed	7 g	0.7%	
Orange zest, finely grated	5 g	0.5%	
Thyme leaves	2 g	0.2%	
Black peppercorns, coarsely crushed	0.8 g	0.08%	
Bay leaves, thinly sliced	0.4 g	0.04%	

from page 3·179

MISO-CURED BLACK COD   INSPIRED BY NOBU MATSUHISA

Yields 500 g

INGREDIENT	QUANTITY	SCALING	PROCEDURE
White miso	500 g	125%	① Combine to make cure.
Mirin	100 g	25%	
Sake	80 g	20%	
Shoyu	35 g	8.75%	
White soy sauce	25 g	6.25%	
Yuzu zest, finely grated	8 g	2%	
Lime zest, finely grated	5 g	1.25%	
Lemon zest, finely grated	3 g	0.75%	
Black cod fillet, skin on, 3.25 cm / 1¼ in thick	400 g	100%	② Cut into four 100 g portions. ③ Spread cure over all surfaces of fish. ④ Vacuum seal individually. ⑤ Refrigerate for 12 h. ⑥ Remove from bags, and wipe off excess cure.
Unsalted butter	60 g	15%	⑦ Vacuum seal each portion with 15 g of butter. ⑧ Cook sous vide in 49 °C / 120 °F bath to core temperature of 48 °C / 118 °F, about 20 min.
Toasted sesame seeds	15 g	3.75%	⑨ Blend in spice grinder to fine powder.
Ginger powder	4 g	1%	
N-Zorbit M (National Starch brand)	4 g	1%	
Clarified unsalted butter	80 g	20%	⑩ Dust cooked fish generously with sesame powder. ⑪ Brown in very hot butter until just golden, about 45 s.
Daikon, fine julienne	40 g	10%	⑫ Toss together.
Spring onion, fine julienne	40 g	10%	⑬ Garnish each fish portion.
Sesame oil	to taste		
White soy sauce	to taste		
Yuzu juice	to taste		

from page 3·179

GRAPEFRUIT-CURED SALMON

Yields 350 g

INGREDIENT	QUANTITY	SCALING	PROCEDURE
Salmon belly, 2.5 cm / 1 in thick	400 g	100%	① Trim, and remove skin.
			② Set salmon aside.
Salt	60 g	15%	③ Blend to form dry cure.
Sugar	40 g	10%	④ Rub cure onto salmon to completely cover.
Young Douglas fir buds	30 g	7.5%	⑤ Vacuum seal rubbed salmon.
Vodka	15 g	3.75%	⑥ Refrigerate salmon for 12 h to cure.
Pink grapefruit zest, finely grated	5 g	1.25%	⑦ Remove cured salmon from bag.
			⑧ Rinse cure off with water, and dry.
Juniper berries, crushed	4 g	1%	⑨ Vacuum seal, and refrigerate salmon to store.
Black peppercorns, finely ground	2 g	0.5%	
Douglas fir essential oil	0.1 g	0.025%	
Pink grapefruit essential oil	0.1 g	0.025%	

from page 3·180

Fir tree buds can be picked from early May through mid-June. You can omit them if they are not available—the taste will be subtly different but still good.

HOUSE-CURED BACON

Yields 3.5 kg

INGREDIENT	QUANTITY	SCALING	PROCEDURE
Salt	100 g	2.5%	① Mix to make cure.
Sugar	72 g	1.8%	
Insta Cure No. 1	24 g	0.6%	
Fermento	7 g	0.175%	
Black peppercorns, coarsely ground	4 g	0.1%	
Coriander seeds, toasted, finely ground	4 g	0.1%	
Mace, finely ground	4 g	0.1%	
Star anise, coarsely ground	4 g	0.1%	
Sodium erythorbate	2.2 g	0.055%	
Pork belly, bone in	4 kg	100%	② Rub cure thoroughly on surface of meat.
			③ Let sit 10 min so that spices adhere.
			④ Pack remaining cure around meat.
			⑤ Vacuum seal.
			⑥ Refrigerate for 1 wk, turning over once a day.
			⑦ Brush away cure from surface of meat.
			⑧ Hang cleaned meat on meat hook, and refrigerate uncovered for 1 wk in well-ventilated area so that cure can permeate all areas evenly.
			⑨ Smoke in 77 °C / 170 °F smoker with 60% relative humidity for 7 h (wet-bulb temperature: 65 °C / 150 °F).
			⑩ Chill for 12 h before using.

from page 3·182

Although we use Fermento culture for flavor, this is a cured, rather than a fermented, bacon.

MICROWAVED BEEF JERKY

Yields 300 g

INGREDIENT	QUANTITY	SCALING	PROCEDURE
Beef flank steak	500 g	100%	① Cut with grain into even, rectangular strips 5 mm / 3⁄16 in thick, and set aside.
Soy sauce	125 g	25%	② Combine.
Fish sauce	85 g	17%	③ Place meat strips in marinade.
Sugar	14 g	2.8%	④ Vacuum seal together, and refrigerate for 48 h.
Salt	5.3 g	1.06%	⑤ Drain.
			⑥ Place strips on paper towel–lined tray; pat strips dry.
			⑦ Lay three strips in center of microwavable plate.
			⑧ Microwave at 50% power for 1 min, and flip strips over. Repeat four more times for total cooking time of 5 min, and remove jerky.
			⑨ Repeat steps 7 and 8 with remaining strips, always working with batches of three.

from page 3·184

To dehydrate the jerky without a microwave, dry the marinated beef strips at 60 °C / 140 °F until leathery, 10–12 h.

CRISPY BEEF STRANDS

Yields 80 g

INGREDIENT	QUANTITY	SCALING	PROCEDURE
Beef flank steak	200 g	100%	① Cut with grain into even, rectangular strips, 5 mm / ¼ in thick, and reserve.
Soy sauce	50 g	25%	② Combine, and place meat strips in marinade.
Fish sauce	34 g	17%	③ Vacuum seal, and refrigerate for 48 h.
Sugar	5.5 g	2.8%	④ Drain.
Salt	2 g	1%	⑤ Microwave strips at full power (800 W) until dry, 3–5 min.
			⑥ Pull strips apart, strand by strand.
Canola oil	as needed		⑦ Fry strands in 180 °C / 355 °F oil until dry.
			⑧ Drain.
			⑨ Reserve in airtight container with silica packets.

from page 5·44

CRISPY BEEF AND SHALLOT SALAD

Yields 100 g

INGREDIENT	QUANTITY	SCALING	PROCEDURE
Red shallots, sliced 1 mm / 1⁄16 in thick	50 g	100%	① Deep-fry shallot slices in 170 °C / 340 °F oil until dry and golden.
Canola oil	as needed		② Drain on paper towels.
Salt	as needed		③ Season shallot slices.
			④ Reserve in airtight container with silica packets.
Sweet, sour, and savory glaze see page 5·44	100 g	200%	⑤ Warm together, stirring to dissolve sugar and reserve.
Palm sugar	18 g	36%	
Crispy beef strands, warmed see above	80 g	160%	⑥ Toss together with fried shallots.
			⑦ Fold warm glaze in carefully to taste.
Cilantro stems, cut into 1 cm / 3⁄8 in lengths	3 g	6%	
Scallion, fine julienne	2 g	4%	
Small cilantro leaves	2 g	4%	
Small mint leaves	2 g	4%	
Small Thai basil leaves	2 g	4%	
Lime zest, fine julienne	1.5 g	3%	
Bird's eye chili, seeded and sliced paper-thin	1 g	2%	
Lime juice	to taste		⑧ Season.
Salt	to taste		

from page 5·47

JUNIPER BRINE

Yields 600 g

INGREDIENT	QUANTITY	SCALING	PROCEDURE
Water	500 g	100%	① Combine.
Juniper berries, crushed	60 g	12%	② Bring to boil, to dissolve salt fully.
Salt	35 g	7%	③ Cool, and infuse refrigerated for 12 h.
Coriander seeds	12 g	2.4%	④ Strain.
Lemon zest, grated	4 g	0.8%	
Angelica root, sliced	3.2 g	0.64%	
Bitter orange zest, grated	2.5 g	0.5%	
Malt, roasted	2 g	0.4%	
Hops	0.8 g	0.16%	
Cinnamon stick	0.4 g	0.08%	
Ginger, minced	0.4 g	0.08%	
Allspice berry	0.25 g	0.05%	

from page 5·36

SOUS VIDE DUCK HAM ADAPTED FROM WYLIE DUFRESNE

Yields 750 g

INGREDIENT	QUANTITY	SCALING	PROCEDURE
Salt	18 g	1.2%	① Combine to make cure.
Insta Cure No. 1	7.5 g	0.5%	
Duck thighs, boneless and skinless	1.5 kg	100%	② Coat duck thighs with cure.
Water, warm	100 g	6.7%	③ Combine to prepare slurry.
Activa GS or RM see page 3·250	25 g	1.7% (25%)*	④ Brush cured duck thighs with slurry.
			⑤ Place duck thighs in terrine.
			⑥ Vacuum seal.
			⑦ Refrigerate terrine for 12 h.
			⑧ Cook sous vide in 69 °C / 156 °F bath for 6 h.
			⑨ Top bagged terrine with weight to flatten.
			⑩ Refrigerate until cool.
			⑪ Freeze and slice duck ham into sheets 1 mm / 1/16 in thick on meat slicer.

from page 5·87   *(% of total weight of water)

FOIE GRAS AND HAZELNUT GANACHE

Yields 650 g

INGREDIENT	QUANTITY	SCALING	PROCEDURE
Cognac	60 g	20%	① Reduce to 20 g and reserve.
Sauternes	30 g	10%	
Sweet onions, finely minced	100 g	33%	② Sweat until tender without coloring, about 10 min.
Rendered duck fat	15 g	5%	
Raw duck foie gras	300 g	100%	③ Combine alcohol reduction, onions and remaining ingredients, and puree until smooth.
Roasted hazelnut butter	100 g	33%	④ Pass through fine sieve.
Unsalted butter	50 g	16.7%	⑤ Freeze in Pacojet beaker, and reserve.
Roasted hazelnut oil	25 g	8.3%	⑥ To serve, Pacotize once and form into quenelles. Serve with toasted bread.
Salt	5 g	1.7% (1%)*	
Insta Cure No. 1	3.25 g	1.08% (0.7%)*	

from page 5·128   *(% of total weight of foie gras, hazelnut butter, unsalted butter, and hazelnut oil)

FLUKE CURED IN KOMBU ADAPTED FROM KYLE CONNAUGHTON

Yields 350 g

INGREDIENT	QUANTITY	SCALING	PROCEDURE
Dry kombu sheets, about 20 cm / 8 in long	eight sheets		① Soak in cold water until fully hydrated, about 20 min.
Fluke fillets, 1.5 cm / ¾ in thick, skinned and side fin muscle removed	400 g (four whole fillets)	100%	
Salt	40 g	10%	② Grind together to fine powder.
Kombu powder (store-bought)	8 g	2%	③ Dust evenly over one side of fillets.
			④ Lay fillets, seasoned side down, on kombu sheets.
Sugar	8 g	2%	⑤ Dust evenly with remaining salt, and cover with second sheet of kombu.
			⑥ Vacuum seal, and refrigerate for 1 h to cure surface.
			⑦ Remove fillets from cure, pat dry, and vacuum seal.
Sous vide ponzu see page 22			⑧ To serve, slice fluke thinly. Serve ponzu on side.

from page 3·181

BLACKSTRAP MOLASSES COUNTRY HAM
ADAPTED FROM MICHAEL RUHLMAN AND BRIAN POLCYN

Yields 6 kg

INGREDIENT	QUANTITY	SCALING	PROCEDURE
Kosher salt	1.3 kg	100%	① Combine.
Insta Cure No. 2 (or DQ Curing Salt)	340 g	26%	
Dark brown sugar	450 g	35%	② Add to salt blend, and stir together.
Blackstrap molasses	617 g	47%	
Dark rum	210 g	16%	
Ginger, grated or minced	10 g	0.8%	
Juniper berries, crushed	8 g	0.6%	
Cayenne pepper	3 g	0.2%	
Coriander seeds, black, toasted and ground	1 g	0.08%	
Fresh ham, skin on, aitchbone removed	7 kg	540%	③ Rub cure all over ham, applying more to area around exposed bone.
			④ Put in nonreactive container large enough for ham and for liquid that cure will draw out.
			⑤ Place 7 kg of weight on ham, using platter or board with weights on top.
			⑥ Refrigerate for 12–15 d (1 d per ½ kg). Turn ham; after 6 d, redistribute cure as necessary.
			⑦ Remove ham from refrigerator, and rinse off cure under cold water.
			⑧ Soak in cold water for 8 h to remove residual surface salt.
			⑨ Set ham on rack, and refrigerate uncovered for 8 h.
			⑩ Cold-smoke ham at 15 °C / 60 °F for 18 h.
			⑪ Hang ham to dry in cool, dark place, ideally at 15 °C / 60 °F with 65%–75% relative humidity, for 7 wk.

from page 3·183

CURED BEEF TENDERLOIN "BRESAOLA STYLE"

Yields 300 g

INGREDIENT	QUANTITY	SCALING	PROCEDURE
Beef tenderloin (or venison tenderloin), 5 cm / 2 in thick	1 kg	100%	① Remove silver skin, and trim tapered end for even curing. ② Set aside.
Espresso roast coffee, ground	50 g	5%	③ Grind together to medium coarse. ④ Pack all over surface of tenderloin, and vacuum seal.
Salt	40 g	4%	⑤ If making cured carpaccio, refrigerate for 1 wk. Flip bag every 2 d to ensure even curing.
Sugar	40 g	4%	⑥ Rinse, and pat dry.
Cocoa nibs	16 g	1.75%	⑦ Slice thinly, and pound to desired thickness; or freeze, and slice paper thin on meat slicer.
Black pepper	10 g	1%	⑧ If making true bresaola, cure for 3 wk.
Juniper berries	10 g	1%	⑨ Rinse, and pat dry.
Insta Cure No. 2	2 g	0.2%	⑩ Tie with butcher's twine, and hang for minimum of 1 wk and up to 1 mo in refrigerator. Hanging time determines dryness of final texture. ⑪ Slice thinly.
Fermented black garlic (store-bought)	80 g	8%	⑫ Blend until smooth, and pass through fine sieve. ⑬ Verify seasoning.
Extra-virgin olive oil	40 g	4%	
Lemon juice	15 g	1.5%	
White balsamic	13 g	1.3%	
Salt	to taste		
Wild arugula	50 g	5%	⑭ Spoon small amount of fermented garlic paste across each plate.
Wild blackberries, halved	30 g	3%	⑮ Arrange slices of cured carpaccio or bresaola on each plate.
Celery stalk, peeled and thinly sliced	25 g	2.5%	⑯ Garnish with celery slices, arugula, blackberries, and celery leaves. ⑰ Season with salt, olive oil, and lemon juice.
Celery leaves	10 g	1%	
Lemon juice	to taste		
Extra-virgin olive oil	to taste		
Flaky sea salt	to taste		

from page 3·185

SEA URCHIN BOTTARGA

Yields 150 g

INGREDIENT	QUANTITY	SCALING
Sea urchin tongues (gonads)	200 g	100%
Salt	500 g	250%
Beeswax	500 g	250%

from page 3·186

① Pass sea urchin tongues through fine sieve.

② Pipe into sous vide bag molded into shape of fish roe sac, which is a thin, tapered triangle.

③ Vacuum seal, and cook sous vide in 64 °C / 147 °F bath for 50 min. Leave in bag, and chill in ice-water bath until hardened, about 20 min.

④ Pack cooked sea urchin in salt. Ensure all sides are completely covered, and refrigerate for 12 h.

⑤ Remove from cure. Rinse, and pat dry on paper towels.

⑥ Wrap cured sea urchin in cheesecloth. Tie both ends of cheesecloth with butcher's twine. Hang in refrigerator for 2 mo to yield sliceable, fudge-like consistency, or for 3 mo to make dry enough to grate.

⑦ Melt beeswax, and dip dried sea urchin carefully into wax to coat completely.

⑧ Vacuum seal, and refrigerate until needed.

SALTED HALIBUT

Yields 1.2 kg

INGREDIENT	QUANTITY	SCALING	PROCEDURE
Salt	750 g	37.5%	① Mix together to form cure.
Sugar	150 g	7.5%	
Lemon zest, finely grated	15 g	0.75%	
Lime zest, finely grated	10 g	0.5%	
Halibut fillet, skin on, cut into strips 5 cm / 2 in thick	2 kg	100%	② Rub cure on strips to cover completely.
			③ Vacuum seal strips.
			④ Refrigerate for 48 h.
			⑤ Remove from bag, and rinse, discarding cure and rendered juices.
			⑥ Wrap single layer of cheesecloth around each cured strip.
			⑦ Tie both ends of cheesecloth with butcher's twine.
			⑧ Hang wrapped fish in refrigerator for 15 d to air-dry.
			⑨ Remove from cheesecloth.
			⑩ Vacuum seal, and refrigerate indefinitely until needed.
			⑪ To serve, soak in water or milk for 48 h, refrigerated, changing soaking liquid every 12 h.
			⑫ Use for making brandade or lutefisk.

For a recipe for brandade, see below.
For a lutefisk recipe, see page 114.

from page 3·187

HALIBUT BRANDADE

Yields 800 g

INGREDIENT	QUANTITY	SCALING	PROCEDURE
Whole milk	as needed		① Soak halibut in milk, refrigerated, for 12 h.
Salted halibut optional, see above	160 g	100%	② Drain fish, and discard milk.
			③ Repeat steps 1 and 2 three more times, for total soaking time of 48 h. Reserve 20 g of liquid from final soaking.
Garlic, sliced and blanched twice	25 g	16%	④ Vacuum seal halibut, reserved soaking liquid, and garlic together.
			⑤ Cook sous vide in 58 °C / 135 °F bath to core temperature of 57 °C / 133 °F, about 20 min. Hold at temperature for 15 min.
			⑥ Pulse in food processor until finely shredded.
Water	1 kg	625%	⑦ Vacuum seal potatoes with water in thin, even layer.
Yukon Gold or other waxy potatoes, thinly sliced	250 g	156%	⑧ Cook sous vide in 90 °C / 194 °F bath for 45 min.
			⑨ Drain potatoes, and pass through ricer.
Extra virgin olive oil	90 g	56%	⑩ Mix into potatoes.
			⑪ Pass through fine sieve.
			⑫ Fold sieved potatoes into shredded halibut mixture.
Salt	to taste		⑬ Warm brandade and season.
Italian basil, julienne	to taste		⑭ Garnish.
Roasted hazelnut oil	to taste		

from page 5·152

SEAFOOD PAPER ADAPTED FROM CARLO CRACCO

Yields 80 g

INGREDIENT	QUANTITY	SCALING	PROCEDURE
White fish (prawns, scallops, or squid may be substituted)	250 g	100%	① Blend to fine puree in food processor or Pacojet, if available.
			② Pass through fine sieve.
			③ Cast fish or shellfish puree paper-thin (1 mm / 1/32 in thick) onto silicone baking mat.
Squid ink (optional)	1.25 g	0.5%	④ Cover with another silicone baking mat.
			⑤ Roll out evenly to 0.5 mm / 1/64 in with rolling pin.
			⑥ Dehydrate at 70 °C / 158 °F until sheets are dry but still flexible, about 15 min.
			⑦ Remove top silicone mat, and return to dehydrator or oven until surface of sheet is leathery, about 3 min.
			⑧ Cut to desired dimensions, and reserve.

from page 3·188

BACON CHIPS WITH BUTTERSCOTCH, APPLE, AND THYME
ADAPTED FROM GRANT ACHATZ

Yields 160 g (four portions)

INGREDIENT	QUANTITY	SCALING	PROCEDURE
Cured bacon strips, 10 cm / 4 in long and 2 mm / 1/16 in thick	100 g	100%	① Place bacon on dehydrator tray.
			② Dehydrate at 80 °C / 175 °F for 3 h.
			③ Store dehydrated bacon chips in airtight container.
Granny Smith apples, halved and cored	400 g	400%	④ Place on tray lined with silicone mat.
			⑤ Roast in 190 °C / 375 °F oven for 30 min.
			⑥ Cool.
			⑦ Scoop out flesh from skins.
			⑧ Puree flesh in blender.
			⑨ Pass through chinois.
			⑩ Spray acetate sheet with nonstick cooking spray, and wipe off excess liquid.
			⑪ Spread puree with palette knife in layer 2 mm / 1/16 in thick.
			⑫ Dehydrate at 70 °C / 160 °F for 45 min.
			⑬ Cut resulting apple leather into strips, 3 mm by 10 cm / 1/8 in by 4 in.
			⑭ Reserve.
Sugar	250 g	250%	⑮ Whisk together in small pot, and cook to 190 °C / 375 °F to make caramel.
Light corn syrup	150 g	150%	
Heavy cream	375 g	375%	⑯ Whisk into caramel to make butterscotch.
			⑰ Heat to 115 °C / 240 °F.
			⑱ Pour onto silicone mat, and cool.
			⑲ Transfer to pastry bag.
			⑳ Pipe dots of butterscotch onto each bacon chip, starting 2.5 cm / 1 in from top of strip, and leaving 6 mm / 1/4 in between dots.
			㉑ Wind six apple leather strips around each bacon chip, using butterscotch as glue.
Black pepper	to taste		㉒ Season.
Thyme leaves	to taste		㉓ Attach to bacon chips using small amount of butterscotch.

from page 3·189

KALBI FLANK STEAK
Yields 1 kg

Instead of flank steak, thin slices of beef short ribs can be used.

The pH level of the marinade should be around 4.5.

Depending on how tender you like your flank steak, the cooking time can be increased to 24 hours.

INGREDIENT	QUANTITY	SCALING	PROCEDURE
Flank steak, trimmed	1 kg	333%	① Reserve.
Water	300 g	100%	② Combine, and stir until sugar is dissolved.
Sugar	175 g	58.5%	③ Vacuum seal steak with marinade.
Light soy sauce	150 g	50%	④ Marinate in refrigerator for 5 d.
Fish sauce	75 g	25%	⑤ Remove steak from marinade, and vacuum seal again.
Apple juice (fresh)	50 g	16.5%	⑥ Cook sous vide in 54 °C / 129 °F bath for 1 h.
Toasted sesame oil	30 g	10%	⑦ Cool.
Mirin	23 g	7.5%	⑧ Trim steak to desired size, and sear both sides quickly.
Scallions, thinly sliced	20 g	6.5%	
Garlic, crushed	10 g	3.5%	
Rice vinegar	10 g	3.5%	
Korean chili flakes	5 g	1.5%	
Black pepper, coarsely ground	3 g	1%	
Kimchi see page 175	as desired		⑨ Slice, and serve with kimchi, butter lettuce and shiso leaves, kochujang paste, and other banchan (Korean side dishes).

from page 3·199

Jaccarding the steak improves its tenderness directly and, if done before marinating, also makes the marinade work better. Vacuum tumbling for 30 minutes reduces marination time greatly. For more on Jaccarding, see page 3·50; for vacuum tumbling, see page 3·174.

LUTEFISK
Yields 800 g

INGREDIENT	QUANTITY	SCALING	PROCEDURE
Halibut	1 kg (one large piece)	100%	① Remove skin, and cut away thin ends.
Water	3.5 kg	350%	② Whisk water and sodium hydroxide together until dissolved to make brine.
Sodium hydroxide	25 g	2.5% *(0.7%)**	③ Place fish in brine, and refrigerate for 24 h.
Salt	25 g	2.5% *(0.7%)**	④ Drain fish, and discard brine.
			⑤ Vacuum seal, and refrigerate for 24 h to allow brine to equilibrate through fish.
			⑥ Remove from bag, cover in fresh water, and soak refrigerated for 48 h.
			⑦ Change water, and soak again for 48 h, refrigerated.
			⑧ Drain.
			⑨ Vacuum seal, and refrigerate to store indefinitely.
Unsalted butter	100 g	10%	⑩ To serve, vacuum seal with fish.
			⑪ Cook sous vide in 50 °C / 122 °F bath for 45 min.
Salt	to taste		⑫ Season.

from page 3·200   *(% of weight of water)

Lutefisk is an acquired taste and texture, but it has been a Scandinavian delicacy for many centuries.

The dimensions of the fish are important for a good final result. The fish should be uniform in size and at least 4 cm / 1 ½ in thick for the brining time to be accurate. Smaller pieces of fish require some experimentation with brining time. If making with salted halibut or cod, omit salt from brine.

YAKITORI

Yields 600 g (four portions)

INGREDIENT	QUANTITY	SCALING	PROCEDURE
Mirin	400 g	100%	① Whisk together, and bring soy sauce mixture to simmer.
Honey (clear)	220 g	55%	
Light soy sauce (no vinegar added)	200 g	50%	
Sake (dry)	200 g	50%	
Ginger juice (fresh)	10 g	2.5%	
Pineapple rind and flesh, cubed	550 g	137.5%	② Pour hot soy sauce mixture over pineapple cubes, and cool completely.
			③ Vacuum seal, and macerate 12 h, refrigerated.
Rice vinegar	50 g	12.5%	④ Strain yakitori sauce.
Salt	30 g	7.5%	⑤ Season with vinegar and salt, and reserve.
Chicken skin	200 g	50%	⑥ Cook sous vide in 88 °C / 190 °F bath for 12 h.
			⑦ Drain from cooking juices, pat dry, and cool.
			⑧ Cut cooked skin into strips 2.5 cm by 12.5 cm / 1 in by 5 in.
			⑨ Thread onto soaked bamboo skewers, and reserve.
Chicken oysters or thigh meat cut into 2.5 cm / 1 in pieces, skinless	200 g	50%	⑩ Combine in bottom of 1 l whipping siphon to pressure-marinate.
			⑪ Charge with two nitrous oxide cartridges, shake, and refrigerate for 20 min.
			⑫ Vent pressure, remove pieces from siphon, and skewer individually.
Yakitori sauce, from above	30 g	7.5%	
Chicken thigh meat, coarse ground	400 g	100%	⑬ Stir together until all components are evenly distributed.
			⑭ Make four meatballs 5 cm / 1 in. in diameter by using plastic wrap to shape tightly.
Tokyo negi (Japanese leek), finely minced	45 g	11.25%	⑮ Skewer meatballs individually.
Egg white	35 g	8.75%	⑯ Blanch in 190 °C / 375 °F oil for 5 s to set shape of meatball.
Yakitori sauce, from above	20 g	5%	⑰ Reserve.
Toasted sesame oil	10 g	2.5%	
Young ginger, finely minced	6 g	1.5%	
Salt	4 g	1%	
Sansho pepper, ground	1 g	0.25%	
Yakitori sauce, from above	200 g	50%	⑱ Reduce to 65 g (light syrup), about 15 min. Cool and reserve.
Japanese charcoal	as needed		⑲ Burn coals in bottom of hibachi or similar grill until coals are white.
			⑳ Set grill screen on top of hot coals, and grill marinated chicken oysters and meatballs for 2–3 min on each side.
			㉑ Remove from heat, and brush all pieces with thin layer of yakitori glaze.
			㉒ Deep-fry skewered chicken skin in 190 °C / 375 °F oil for 2 min until very crispy and lightly puffed.
			㉓ Drain from oil, and brush with thin layer of yakitori glaze.
			㉔ Grill glazed chicken oyster, meatball, and skin skewers for 1 min on each side.
			㉕ Remove from heat, brush meatball with final layer of glaze, and serve.

from page 3·201

For a step-by-step procedure for pressure-marinating, see page 3·207.

TUNA RIBBONS WITH GINGER MARINADE
ADAPTED FROM JEAN-GEORGES VONGERICHTEN

Yields 600 g (eight portions)

INGREDIENT	QUANTITY	SCALING	PROCEDURE
Lime juice	100 g	33%	① Vacuum seal together.
Sugar	80 g	27%	② Cook sous vide in 55 °C / 131 °F bath for 1½ h.
Makrud (kaffir) lime leaves, thinly sliced	20 g	6.5%	③ Cool lime syrup completely.
			④ Strain.
			⑤ Measure 40 g of syrup, and reserve.
Ginger, peeled, thinly sliced	60 g	20%	⑥ Sauté in dry pan until slightly charred, about 5 min.
Rice vinegar	50 g	17%	⑦ Blend with ginger and reserved lime syrup until smooth.
White soy sauce	40 g	13.5%	⑧ Reserve ginger marinade.
Shoyu	36 g	12%	
Grapeseed oil	30 g	10%	
Avocado, peeled and thinly sliced	100 g	33%	⑨ Season avocado slices, and arrange in serving bowls.
Lime juice	to taste		
Salt	to taste		
Tuna (sashimi-quality), cut into thin, spaghetti-like ribbons	300 g	100%	⑩ Gently combine tuna with radish slices, chili oil, and lime leaves.
			⑪ Top each avocado portion with spoonful of tuna mixture.
			⑫ Pour ginger marinade around bowls, and serve.
Breakfast radish, sliced very thinly on mandoline	50 g	17%	
Spiced chili oil see page 29	25 g	8.5%	
Makrud (kaffir) lime leaf, fine julienne	5 g	1.5%	

from page 3·202

FLUKE CEVICHE ADAPTED FROM ERIC RIPERT

Yields 500 g (four to eight portions)

INGREDIENT	QUANTITY	SCALING	PROCEDURE
Fluke fillet (sushi-quality)	400 g	100%	① Slice on bias into segments, 1.75 cm by 5 cm / 11/16 in by 2 in.
			② Lay slices in single layer on large plate.
			③ Cover with plastic wrap.
			④ Refrigerate.
Fluke fillet, diced	80 g	20%	⑤ Combine.
Lemon juice (fresh)	30 g	7.5%	⑥ Cover.
Lime juice (fresh)	30 g	7.5%	⑦ Refrigerate for 1 h to macerate.
Red onion, sliced	20 g (quarter of onion)	5%	⑧ Strain through fine sieve, and reserve 50 g of fluke juice.
Sugar	13 g	3.25%	
Fine sea salt	10.5 g	2.5%	
Rendered fluke juice, from above	50 g	12.5%	⑨ Combine in bowl to make marinade.
Red onion, julienne	16 g	4%	
Extra-virgin olive oil	12 g	3%	
Cilantro, julienne	10 g	2.5%	
Tomato, blanched, peeled, and finely diced	10 g	2.5%	
Jalapeño pepper, minced	4 g	1%	
Basil, julienne	2.5 g	0.5%	
Mint, julienne	1.2 g	0.3%	
Lemon-infused olive oil	to taste		
Espelette pepper	to taste		⑩ Season fluke slices.
Salt	to taste		⑪ Cover slices with marinade, and allow to stand for 2–5 min, depending on desired firmness.
			⑫ To serve, divide ceviche among four small bowls.
			⑬ Garnish with more pepper, and serve immediately.

from page 3·203

CHICKEN TIKKA MASALA

Yields 1 kg

INGREDIENT	QUANTITY	SCALING	PROCEDURE
Water	24 g	5%	① Pour hot water over saffron threads.
Saffron threads	0.5 g	0.1%	② Cover, steep for 10 min, and then strain water, and reserve.
Coriander seeds, toasted	5 g	1%	③ Toast spices in dry skillet or 170 °C / 340 °F oven until aromatic.
Cumin seeds, toasted	5 g	1%	
Cinnamon, toasted	1 g	0.2%	④ Cool.
Clove, toasted	1 g	0.2%	⑤ Grind spices to fine powder.
			⑥ Reserve.
Greek-style strained yogurt (plain, full fat)	250 g	50%	⑦ Blend together to fine paste.
Neutral oil	100 g	20%	⑧ Add spice powder and saffron-infused water to make marinade.
Shallots, thinly sliced	25 g	5%	⑨ Reserve 50 g for later use.
Ginger, fine paste	24 g	4.8%	
Garlic, fine paste	10 g	2%	
Kashmiri chili	10 g	2%	
Annatto seeds	8 g	1.5%	
Green Thai chili, finely chopped	5 g	1%	
Bay leaves, fine julienne	1 g	0.2%	
Chicken breast, skinned	500 g	100%	⑩ Clean, and trim off any excess fat.
Chicken thigh, boneless and skinned	500 g	100%	⑪ Cut thighs and breasts into total of eight pieces, 125 g each.
Marinade, from above	200 g	40%	⑫ Slice three cuts across thick side of each thigh for marinade to penetrate.
			⑬ Place all chicken pieces in 200 g of marinade, and toss to coat thoroughly.
			⑭ Vacuum seal, and refrigerate for 12 h.
Clarified unsalted butter	40 g	8%	⑮ Remove chicken from marinade.
			⑯ Vacuum seal breasts and thighs in two separate bags with 20 g each of clarified butter.
			⑰ Cook breasts sous vide in 60 °C / 140 °F bath for 2 h.
			⑱ Cook thighs sous vide in 65 °C / 149 °F bath for 1½ h.
Marinade, from above	50 g	10%	⑲ Simmer for 5 min.
			⑳ Cool at room temperature.
			㉑ Brush over cooked chicken.
Clarified butter	as needed		㉒ Heat thin film of clarified butter over high heat. Sear chicken pieces, skin side only, until crisp, about 90 s. Remove from pan.
Lime juice	100 g	20%	㉓ Combine, and season with salt.
Shallots, finely sliced	50 g	10%	
Green chili, finely sliced	15 g	3%	
Salt	to taste		
Cilantro, fine julienne	to taste		㉔ Garnish chicken with lime dressing, cilantro, and mint.
Mint, fine julienne	to taste		

from page 3·204

For better marinade penetration, use a Jaccard tenderizer after slathering the chicken with the marinade, but be careful not to break the blades on the chicken bones.

Kashmiri chili punctuates a dish with bright red color and is only mildly hot.

GONG BAO CHICKEN ADAPTED FROM FUCHSIA DUNLOP

Yields 500 g

INGREDIENT	QUANTITY	SCALING	PROCEDURE
Chicken breast, boneless	400 g	100%	① Cut into 1.5 cm / ⅝ in strips.
			② Cut strips into small cubes, and reserve.
Water	50 g	12.5%	③ Whisk together.
Light soy sauce	10 g	2.5%	④ Mix into chicken, taking care to coat all pieces evenly.
Potato starch	7 g	1.75%	⑤ Vacuum seal, and refrigerate for 12 h to marinate.
Shaoxing wine	5 g	1.25%	⑥ Remove chicken from marinade, and reserve.
Baking soda	1 g	0.25%	
White chicken stock see page 11	20 g	5%	⑦ Whisk together until everything is incorporated.
			⑧ Reserve resulting sauce.
Sugar	15 g	3.75%	
Chinkiang vinegar	12 g	3%	
Toasted sesame oil	5 g	1.25%	
Dark soy sauce	4 g	1%	
Light soy sauce	4 g	1%	
Potato starch	1 g	0.25%	
Neutral oil	5 g	1.25%	⑨ Heat wok, and add oil.
Dried red chili pepper	8 g	2%	⑩ Add chili and pepper when oil is about to smoke.
Sichuan peppercorns (whole)	8 g	2%	⑪ Stir-fry until crisp and fragrant.
			⑫ Add marinated chicken, and fry on high flame for about 5 min.
Scallions, whites only, thinly sliced	24 g	6%	⑬ Add to wok, and stir-fry until chicken is cooked, about 2 min.
Garlic, thinly sliced	18 g	4.5%	⑭ Add sauce, and cook until thick, about 45 s.
Ginger, thinly sliced	18 g	4.5%	
Peanuts, blanched and peeled	75 g	19%	⑮ Roast peanuts in 170 °C / 340 °F oven until colored golden brown, or use pressure-cooked fried peanuts (see page 5·65).
Salt	to taste		⑯ Add peanuts, and adjust seasoning.

from page 3·205

Known as kung pao chicken to millions of American fans of Chinese food, this is a classic dish. The alkaline marinade, which includes baking soda, tenderizes the chicken and also promotes the Maillard reaction when the chicken cooks.

The baking soda marinade technique works beautifully with other lean cuts of meats, such as pork and beef tenderloin.

BEET JUICE–FED OYSTERS ADAPTED FROM DAVE ARNOLD AND NILS NORÉN

Yields 12 oysters

INGREDIENT	QUANTITY	SCALING	PROCEDURE
Kusshi oysters	12 oysters		① Rinse oysters thoroughly to remove any grit.
			② Arrange, upright and evenly layered, in metal container.
Red beet juice	1.25 kg (from 2 kg of beets)	100%	③ Blend.
			④ Strain juice through fine (25 micron / #500) sieve.
			⑤ Pour over oysters to cover.
Aquarium salt	32.5 g	2.6%	⑥ Seal container tightly with lid.
			⑦ Refrigerate for 48 h. Do not disturb, or oysters will not feed on juice.

from page 3·206

Using a very fine sieve to strain the juice is essential to prevent the oysters from suffocating on larger particles.

HOT- AND COLD-SMOKED MEATS AND SEAFOOD

① Select a recipe from the table below, and prepare the meat as indicated. See the referenced pages for further instructions.

② Smoke. Suggested smoking temperatures, humidities, and times are listed in the table. Not all smokers permit humidity control, but an improvised wet-bulb thermometer will help (see page 3·211). Adjust the smoking time to impart more or less smoke flavor.

③ Cook sous vide or otherwise. Some smoked foods, such as hams or smoked salmon, are meant to be consumed raw after smoking.

④ Season and finish. Many barbecued items are seared briefly at high heat or glazed. Finish by adding spices, dry rubs, or sauces.

Best Bets for Smoking Meats

Ingredient	Prep Method	Prep See page	Smoke Dry-bulb temperature (°C)	(°F)	Smoke Wet-bulb temperature (°C)	(°F)	Relative humidity	Time (h)	Cook	See page
Cold-smoked										
pork, Boston butt	n/a		10	50	6.5	44	60%	24	yes	86
pork ribs	n/a		10	50	6.5	44	60%	24	yes	5·66
foie gras, torchon	cure	3·176	10	50	6.5	44	60%	24	optional	96
ham	cure	3·183	10	50	6.5	44	60%	24	optional	86
salmon (Scottish)	cure	3·256	10	50	6.5	44	70%	24	no	
pork cheek	brine	3·168	10	50	6.5	44	60%	24	yes	86, 5·35
pork chop	brine	3·168	10	50	6.5	44	60%	24	yes	68
sablefish, black cod	brine	76	10	50	6.5	44	60%	24	optional	5·170
whitefish	brine	3·168	10	50	6.5	44	60%	24	yes	74
beef fillet, raw	n/a		10	50	8	46	80%	24	yes	68
caviar and fish roe	n/a		10	50	8	46	80%	12	no	
oyster	n/a		10	50	8	46	80%	24	optional	5·205
foie gras, raw	n/a		25	77	18	64	50%	4	no	
salmon, Russian style	cure	3·168	25	77	18	64	50%	4	no	
chicken, whole	brine injected	3·168	25	77	18	64	50%	4	yes	3, 71
pork chop	brine	3·168	25	77	18	64	50%	4	yes	68
Hot-smoked										
beef fillet, cured	cure	3·185	52	126	48	118	80%	12	no	
beef cheek pastrami	brine	3·257	77	171	62	144	50%	4	yes	121
beef short ribs	n/a		77	171	66	151	60%	4	yes	90
brisket pastrami	brine	3·257	77	171	62	144	50%	7	yes	86
pork belly (for bacon)	cure	3·182	77	171	66	151	60%	7	optional	86
beef tongue	brine injected	3·168	77	171	66	151	60%	4	yes	86
chicken, whole	brine injected	3·168	77	171	66	151	60%	4	optional	71, 122
beef flatiron	n/a		60	140	55	131	77%	4	yes	86, 89
pork ribs	n/a		65	149	57	135	65%	7	yes	86, 88
pork butt	n/a		65	149	57	135	65%	7	yes	86, 5·66
sausage	n/a		52	126	48	118	80%	12	yes	128, 130

from page 3·210

RUSSIAN SMOKED SALMON

Yields 1.2 kg

INGREDIENT	QUANTITY	SCALING	PROCEDURE
Salt	225 g	15%	① Combine to make cure.
Sugar	120 g	8%	
Salmon fillet, whole side, skin on, pin bones removed	1.5 kg	100%	② Pack evenly onto both sides of fish.
			③ Vacuum seal, and refrigerate fish for 12 h to cure.
			④ Rinse off cure from surface of fish.
			⑤ Vacuum seal, and refrigerate for another 24 h to allow the salt to fully diffuse through the meat.
			⑥ Smoke at 25 °C / 77 °F with 60% relative humidity for 4 h.
			⑦ Vacuum seal.
			⑧ Refrigerate until use.

from page 3·212

For lox-style salmon, use a 3% salt and 1.5% sugar rub (with weights relative to the weight of the fish), and vacuum seal the fish refrigerated for 48 h.

For Scottish-style salmon, use a 3.5% salt rub, and vacuum seal refrigerated for 36 h. Follow the remaining steps described in the recipe for both styles.

BEEF CHEEK PASTRAMI

Yields 1 kg

INSPIRED BY JOHN PAUL CARMONA AND DAVID KINCH

INGREDIENT	QUANTITY	SCALING	PROCEDURE
Wagyu beef cheeks, cleaned	1 kg (about 4 cheeks)	100%	① Trim off any silverskin and excess fat.
Water	2.25 kg	225%	② Boil 500 g of water with sugar and salts to dissolve.
Brown sugar	145 g	14.5%	③ Remove brine from heat, add remaining water, and cool.
Salt	75 g	7.5%	
Insta Cure No. 1	15 g	1.5%	
Coriander seeds, toasted	3.5 g	0.35%	④ Combine aromatics with cooled brine.
Black peppercorns	2.5 g	0.25%	⑤ Vacuum seal beef cheeks with chilled brine.
Mustard powder	2.5 g	0.25%	⑥ Refrigerate for 72 h.
Pink peppercorns	2 g	0.2%	⑦ Remove cheeks from brine, and reserve brine.
Cinnamon stick, toasted and crushed	1 g	0.1%	⑧ Pat dry cheeks.
Fennel seeds	1 g	0.1%	⑨ Reserve.
Cloves (whole)	0.5 g	0.05%	
Red pepper flakes	0.25 g	0.025%	
Bay leaf	0.2 g	0.02%	
Juniper berries	75 g	7.5%	⑩ Grind together coarsely in coffee grinder to make spice rub.
Sugar	75 g	7.5%	
Black peppercorns	72 g	7.2%	⑪ Rub cheeks with 50 g (5% of their weight) of spice rub.
Coriander seeds, toasted	42 g	4.2%	⑫ Smoke for 4 h at 77 °C / 171 °F.
Garlic powder	10 g	1%	⑬ Boil reserved brine, and skim off surface foam.
Salt	10 g	1%	⑭ Strain and cool.
Chili flakes	6.5 g	0.65%	⑮ Vacuum seal smoked cheeks with 1 kg of cooled brine.
			⑯ Cook sous vide in 62 °C / 144 °F bath for 72 h.
			⑰ If serving immediately, rest for 15 min at room temperature, and slice. Otherwise, cool quickly in ice-water bath, and refrigerate.

from page 3·213

Food critic Jeffrey Steingarten (see page 1·65) likes to say that New York City has its own local barbecue tradition: the pastrami prepared by the city's many Jewish delicatessens. The most famous places for pastrami are Carnegie Deli in Midtown and Katz's Deli in the Lower East Side.

Pastrami might seem quite different than southern barbecue, but it certainly qualifies as part of that cuisine: cured and spiced meat that is smoked and then cooked low and slow.

This pastrami recipe also works well with other cuts of meat. Simply use the table below to adjust the brining time, and see page 86 for cooking times and temperatures.

Cut	Brine (d)
short rib, bone in	6
short rib, boneless	3
beef tongue	7
brisket, fatty end	7

HAY-SMOKED CHICKEN CROWN

Yields 1 kg

INGREDIENT	QUANTITY	SCALING	PROCEDURE
Whole chicken	1 kg	100%	① Remove legs and wings.
			② Cut through ribs to remove bone-in crown, and reserve crown.
			③ Optionally, reserve carcass, legs, and wings for sauce vin jaune (see page 308).
Water	400 g	40%	④ Combine to make brine.
Salt	28 g	2.8%	⑤ Immerse crown in brine.
Thyme	2 g	0.2%	⑥ Refrigerate for 12 h.
			⑦ Drain and rinse crown.
Yellow sweet meadow hay or straw	100 g	10%	⑧ Lay hay in bottom of hotel pan.
			⑨ Place crown in center of hay, and cover with more hay.
			⑩ Ignite hay with blowtorch until burning.
			⑪ Cover with another pan, and let smolder for 10 min.
			⑫ Remove crown from hay, and cool completely.
			⑬ Peel away skin, and discard.
			⑭ Cook chicken crown in 65 °C / 150 °F combi oven with 0% relative humidity until core temperature reaches 60 °C / 140 °F for about 2 h, depending on size of chicken. If using CVap oven, set browning level to 4 and doneness temperature as above.
			⑮ Optionally, to pasteurize, lower temperature to 60 °C / 140 °F, and hold for 1 h.

from page 5·114

SMOKED PORK CHEEK

Yields 240 g

Alternatively, smoke cheeks in a conventional smoker for 2 h. The taste will be different but still good.

INGREDIENT	QUANTITY	SCALING	PROCEDURE
Pork cheek, sinew removed	300 g (four cheeks)	100%	① Cold-smoke at 7 °C / 45 °F with 50% relative humidity for 24 h, which will produce wet-bulb temperature of 3 °C / 37 °F.
Alder wood chips	as needed		
Cherry wood chips	as needed		
Brown pork stock see page 6	150 g	50%	② Vacuum seal pork cheek with stock.
			③ Cook sous vide in 68 °C / 154 °F bath for 48 h.
			④ Slice and serve, or cool, in bag, in ice-water bath, and refrigerate.

from page 5·38

HEATHER-SMOKED STURGEON

Yields 450 g

INGREDIENT	QUANTITY	SCALING	PROCEDURE
Wild sturgeon fillet	500 g	100%	① Combine vodka, salt, sugar, and lemon zest to make cure. Coat fillet evenly with cure.
Vodka	35 g	7%	
Salt	20 g	4%	② Vacuum seal.
Sugar	7 g	1.4%	③ Cure in refrigerator for 8 h.
Lemon zest, finely grated	2 g	0.4%	④ Rinse, and pat dry with paper towels.
Cherry wood chips	750 g	150%	⑤ Smoke fillet with chips and blossoms at 52 °C / 125 °F with 50% relative humidity for 4 h.
Dried heather blossoms	100 g	20%	
			⑥ Serve, or cool and refrigerate until use.

from page 5·235

SMOKED OCTOPUS ADAPTED FROM JOAN ROCA

Yields 300 g (four portions)

INGREDIENT	QUANTITY	SCALING	PROCEDURE
Baby octopuses, heads removed and set aside for other use	150 g	100%	① Pat dry, and coat lightly with oil.
			② Sear on grill until just cooked through, about 4 min, turning once.
Frying oil	as needed		
Baked potato foam *see page 324*	150 g	100%	③ Vacuum seal.
			④ Warm in 70 °C / 158 °F bath.
Pistou basil leaves	to taste		⑤ Cover four glass bowls with layer of plastic wrap, pulling tightly on each until plastic is invisible.
Salt	to taste		
Sweet smoked paprika (Pimentón de la Vera, dulce)	to taste		⑥ Top plastic wrap with warmed potato foam.
			⑦ Top foam with octopuses.
			⑧ Season and reserve.
Oak wood sawdust, finely ground	15 g	10%	⑨ Place in smoke gun, and warm end of gun.
			⑩ Poke tip of gun into plastic wrap, and fill bowl with smoke. Repeat quickly for remaining three bowls.
			⑪ Serve immediately.

Although the heads are removed, the arms of each octopus should still be connected to its body.

from page 3·215

HAMBURGERS

① Choose a blend of well-marbled meat, and chill the meat deeply. The table Best Bets for Burgers lists several good options, each of which has a different flavor, texture, and cooking profile.

② Put ice cubes or liquid nitrogen in the grinder to chill it to just above 0 °C / 32 °F.

③ Cut. Cut away any large chunks of fat from the meat, and cut into cubes about 2 cm / ¾ in on a side. Chill the meat to −1 °C / 30 °F. Do not salt the meat.

④ Grind the cubes through a 3–4 mm / ⅛–³⁄₁₆ in plate. (For tender meat blends, chop by hand, and then shape into a loose patty 3 cm / 1¼ in thick, and skip to step 9.) When using a grinder, tighten the collar to prevent mashing and tearing. Don't force the meat through the grinder; let the auger pull it through.

⑤ Collect the extruded strands of ground meat in a cylindrical mold cut in half and lined with plastic wrap. (Select a mold slightly wider than the diameter desired for the patties.) Slowly pull the mold toward you as the meat exits the grinder so that the strands run straight along the mold. Build up layers of strands to fill the mold.

⑥ Repeat with a second mold, and then press the two molds together to form a complete cylinder of meat.

⑦ Use the surrounding plastic wrap to remove the meat from the mold. Tighten the wrap slightly to gently compress the cylinder—but take care not to overtighten and mash the meat together, which will make the patties less tender. The meat cylinder can be frozen at this point, but then it will have to be sawed into patties.

⑧ Use a sharp knife to cut hamburger discs of the desired thickness. Remove the plastic wrap from the cut patties, and refrigerate them until cooking.

⑨ Cook, season, and garnish. See the recipes for Mushroom Swiss Burger on page 5·11 and for Sous Vide Hamburger on page 3·86.

Best Bets for Burgers

Meat blend	Ingredients	(scaling)	Leanness (% fat)	Cook (°C)	(°F)
rare beef	filet mignon	100%	20	52	126
	rib eye cap	45%			
short rib	short-rib meat	100%	30	54	129
MC team favorite	short-rib meat	100%	25	56	133
	aged rib eye	100%			
	hangar	25%			
steak-house blend	chuck	100%	25	54	129
	sirloin	50%			
	flank	50%			

from page 3·234

When is the best time to add flavorful liquids and powdered seasonings to ground beef? Mixing them with the cubed meat before grinding is not the best approach because most additives bind the meat strands together. Seasonings containing salt, for example, extract the meat protein myosin, which forms a strong, elastic gel when cooked. That may be desirable in sausage making, but it produces a rubbery burger.

For the tenderest burgers, season the meat after you have cut it into patties. Avoid adding eggs, starches such as bread crumbs, or protein-laden liquids such as milk. During cooking, these ingredients gel and act like edible glue.

COARSE-GROUND SAUSAGES

① Choose a recipe and a binding strategy, which will determine the pregrinding treatment if any—see page 3·228. Depending on the strategy selected, add salt and any polyphosphates during this step. Add Activa, if needed, during step 3.

② Grind meat and fat separately (see page 3·228). Before grinding, freeze the meat partially, and freeze the fat fully. Optionally, prepare a fat gel with fatty tissue or a rendered fat or oil, as described on page 3·145.

③ Combine the ground meats and fats with liquid, spices, and fresh herbs, plus other ingredients in a kitchen stand mixer. The spices should be finely ground, and the herbs finely minced. If using Activa, add it now.

④ Mix at low speed with a paddle mixing blade. Keep mixture below 15 °C / 59 °F.

⑤ Perform a poach test (see page 3·225) to check that the sausage binds properly. If binding is insufficient, add polyphosphate or Activa (but not both)—each yields a somewhat different texture. If binding is too strong, add water (up to a few percent) or fillers such as bread crumbs.

⑥ Form, mold, or stuff, as discussed on page 3·240.

⑦ Cook in a water bath to the core temperature indicated in the table. Note that vacuum sealing the meat will affect the cooked texture.

Best Bets for Coarse-Ground Sausages

Sausage recipe	Meat	(scaling)	Fat	(scaling)	Liquid	(scaling)	Spice and herbs	(scaling)
sweet Italian	pork shoulder	100%	pork fatback	25%	water	14%	sweet paprika	1.7%
							oregano, fresh	1.7%
							basil, fresh	1.7%
							fennel seed, cracked	1.1%
							coriander seed, finely crushed	0.6%
							hot pepper flakes (optional)	0.2%
							black pepper, coarse-ground	0.1%
British banger, adapted from Heston Blumenthal	pork shoulder	100%	pork fatback	50%	water	30%	black pepper	0.4%
							white pepper	0.4%
							mace	0.3%
							nutmeg	0.3%
							ginger powder	0.1%
Kielbasa Kminkowa	pork shoulder	100%	pork fatback	30%	water	20%	marjoram	0.50%
	pork shoulder	(80%)*	pork fatback	35%			caraway, coarsely ground	0.35%
	beef chuck	(20%)*					white pepper	0.20%
breakfast-style	pork shoulder	100%	pork fatback	35%	water	16%	sage	0.70%
	duck breast, skinless	100%	whole duck skin	50%			black pepper	0.20%
							ground ginger	0.15%
cotechino	pork shoulder	100%	pork jowl fat	60%	water	5%	wild fennel seed	0.30%
							rosemary	0.20%
							lemon zest, finely grated	0.10%
merguez	lamb shoulder	100%	pork fatback	22.5%	water	6%	sweet paprika, smoked	0.80%
							oregano	0.80%
							hot pepper flakes	0.30%
							black pepper	0.25%
Thai chicken inspired by David Thompson	chicken thigh	100%	chicken skin and fat	20%	fish sauce	5%	lemongrass	1.1%
			pork fatback	20%	soy sauce	1%	cilantro	1.0%
							galangal	0.6%
							makrud lime leaves	0.6%
							dried Thai red chili	0.2%
							long pepper	0.1%
							cassia	0.1%

from page 3·236   *(set total weight of pork shoulder and beef chuck to 100%)*

Other ingredients	Salt (scaling)	(scaling)	Binder	(scaling)	Cook (°C)	(°F)	Note
sugar	2%	3.2%	**Activa** polyphosphate blend	**0.25%** 0.10%	58	136	
white bread, toasted grain mustard Tate & Lyle Golden Syrup	10% 4% 2%	3%	Activa **polyphosphate blend**	0.175% **0.070%**	58	136	Toast bread at 170 °C / 340 °F until dry and golden brown, about 30 min.
garlic, finely minced Insta Cure No. 1 sugar	0.50% 0.25% 0.45%	3%	Activa **polyphosphate blend**	0.175% **0.070%**	55	131	Grind using a 2 mm / 1/16 in plate. Dry sausages for 2 d at 2–6 °C / 35–42 °F and 85% relative humidity. Smoke for 1–2 d at 10 °C / 50 °F and 85% relative humidity.
maple syrup, smoked sweet onion, finely chopped	3% 2%	2.6%	**Activa** polyphosphate blend	**0.25%** 0.10%	59	138	
whole green lentils, cooked Parmesan, grated	40.0% 4.5%	3.8%	Activa **polyphosphate blend**	0.25% **0.10%**	57	135	
roasted red pepper, minced garlic, minced sugar	8.00% 1.40% 0.25%	2%	**Activa** polyphosphate blend	**0.25%** 0.10%	55	131	
shallot, finely minced fresh coconut, finely grated garlic, finely minced	3.0% 3.0% 1.0%	2.3%	**Activa** polyphosphate blend	**0.25%** 0.10%	60	140	Mix finely ground spices and herbs with shallot, coconut, and garlic to make a paste.

*(binder selections in **bold** are those we prefer)*

FARCE ROYALE

Yields 300 g

INGREDIENT	QUANTITY	SCALING	PROCEDURE
Pigeon leg meat, cold	150 g	100%	① Combine, puree until smooth, and reserve.
Rendered foie gras fat	10 g	6.7%	
Salt	3 g	2%	
Insta Cure No. 1	1.9 g	1.3%	
Nutrifos 088 (Astaris brand), dissolved in warm water	0.16 g	0.12%	
Brown pigeon stock see page 6	200 g	133%	② Reduce stock to 25 g to make glaze.
160 Bloom gelatin	3.25 g	2%	③ Bloom gelatin, and dissolve in glaze.
			④ Add meat puree, and cool over ice-water bath.
Pancetta, brunoise	40 g	27%	⑤ Fold into meat mixture until completely incorporated.
Hazelnuts, skinned and finely minced	35 g	23%	⑥ Place mixture between two silicone baking mats.
Porcini, finely minced	35 g	23%	⑦ Roll out with heavy rolling pin; use two dowels 5 mm / ¼ in each in diameter, for calibration, placing one on each side of stacked sheets.
Garlic, blanched and brunoise	7 g	4.7%	⑧ Refrigerate farce royale until set.
Nutrifos 088 (Astaris brand), dissolved in warm water	0.16 g	0.12%	

from page 5·132

TOULOUSAIN GARLIC SAUSAGE

Yields 750 g

INGREDIENT	QUANTITY	SCALING	PROCEDURE
Lean pork	735 g	100%	① Combine salt with lean pork, and refrigerate for 12 h.
Pork fatback, frozen	255 g	35%	② Grind meat and fatback through 5 mm / 3⁄16 in grinding plate.
Salt	18 g	2.4%	
Garlic confit see page 176	30 g	4.1%	③ Combine ground meat and fat, and spices in stand mixer.
Nutmeg, finely ground	1 g	0.14%	
Natural casings, 2.5 cm / 1 in diameter	as needed		④ Prepare, stuff, and link casings 10 cm / 4 in long.
			⑤ Hang sausages in refrigerator for 12 h.
			⑥ Cut into two long links, and vacuum seal without crushing.
			⑦ Cook garlic sausages sous vide in 59 °C / 138 °F bath to core temperature of 58 °C / 136 °F, about 35 min. Hold at temperature for 30 min to pasteurize.
			⑧ Cut sausages into slices 1 cm / ½ in thick.
			⑨ Sear on 220 °C / 425 °F griddle until all sides are golden.

Using polyphosphates can shorten presalting time. Alternatively, skip this step altogether by adding 0.25% Activa TI. For details, see page 3·250.

from page 5·82

GREEN GARLIC AND PORK SAUSAGE

Yields 300 g

INGREDIENT	QUANTITY	SCALING	PROCEDURE
Pork shoulder, boneless	250 g	100%	① Cut into cubes.
Fatback	80 g	32%	② Toss with meat and fat cubes, and refrigerate for 4 h.
Salt	4.5 g	1.8%	③ Grind all cubes through 5 mm / ¼ in grinding plate.
Nutrifos 088, dissolved in small amount of warm water	0.66 g	0.26% (0.2%)*	
Green garlic, blanched and finely minced	8 g	3.2%	④ Mix thoroughly with ground pork mixture.
			⑤ Form into sausages 3.75 cm / 1½ in. in diameter and 10 cm / 4 in long by using plastic wrap to mold meat mixture.
			⑥ Refrigerate links for 12 h to mature.
			⑦ Vacuum seal, and cook sous vide in 61 °C / 142 °F bath to core temperature of 60 °C / 140 °F, about 45 min.
			⑧ Cool in ice-water bath, and slice sausage on diagonal into slices 1 cm / ⅜ in thick.

from page 5·86

*(% of total weight of pork shoulder and fatback)

EMULSION-STYLE SAUSAGES

① Choose a recipe from the table of Best Bets below.
② Grind meat and fat separately, as described on page 3·228. Use a pretreatment for the meat, which will affect binding ingredients.
③ Puree ground meat in a food processor or bowl chopper. Keep the temperature below 15 °C / 59 °F. Add liquids chilled or frozen to keep meat cool. Optionally, sprinkle the meat with liquid nitrogen to chill it.
④ Add the fat, and continue to puree. Keep the mixture cold.
⑤ Chop or fold in the spices and fresh herbs, plus other ingredients. The spices should be finely ground, and the herbs finely minced.
⑥ Do a poach test (see page 3·225). Adjust the binder as needed.
⑦ Stuff or mold the sausage.
⑧ Smoke the sausage (optional). For best results, the wet-bulb temperature should not exceed 56 °C / 132 °F during smoking.

Best Bets for Emulsion-Style Sausages

Sausage variety	Meat	(scaling)	Fat	(scaling)	Liquid	(scaling)	Spices and herbs	(scaling)
blood sausage	n/a		pork fatback, small dice and blanched	42%	pork blood	100%	bay leaf, powdered	0.3%
					whole milk	20%		
			foie gras fat, rendered	16%	Calvados (or applejack)	8%		
bratwurst	pork shoulder	100%	pork fatback	52%	whole milk	9%	white pepper	0.5%
	veal shoulder	33%			heavy cream	9%	ginger powder	0.3%
							nutmeg	0.3%
boudin blanc, chicken	chicken thigh	100%	rendered chicken fat	33.0%	infused milk (see page 131)	107%	quatre épices (see page 48)	0.2%
			pistachio oil	8.5%	alcohol reduction (see note)	3.7%		
boudin blanc, veal or blend	veal shoulder (or chicken/veal mix)	100%	veal jowl fat	33.0%				
			pistachio oil	8.5%				
frankfurter, all beef	beef chuck	100%	beef fat	55%	water	40%	liquid smoke (optional)	1.50%
frankfurter	beef chuck	(65%)*					mustard powder	1.25%
	pork leg	(35%)*					onion powder	1.00%
							sweet paprika	1.00%
							white pepper	0.25%
							coriander seed	0.20%
							nutmeg	0.10%
ham and cheese	pork shoulder	100%	Gruyère cheese, grated	35%	water	35%	n/a	
mortadella	pork shoulder	100%	pork fatback, blanched (see note)	100%	water	60%	white pepper	0.35%
					white wine (dry)	7%	coriander seed	0.30%
							garlic powder	0.25%
							nutmeg	0.10%
							cinnamon	0.10%
shellfish	scallop, shrimp, or lobster	100%	n/a		heavy cream	55%	chervil	1.0%
					alcohol reduction (see note)	15%	chive	1.0%
							tarragon	1.0%
							white pepper	0.1%
							star anise	0.1%

from page 3·238   *(set total weight of beef chuck and pork leg to 100%)*

⑨ Cook sous vide or steam at temperature indicated. To pasteurize, hold at cooking temperature for time indicated on page 1·184. Plunge into cold water or use a cold-water shower.

⑩ Peel sausages if they are in removable casings.

Other ingredients	(scaling)	Salt (scaling)	Binder	(scaling)	Cook (°C)	(°F)	Note
onions, minced	100%	5.4%	Activa RM	0.6%	82	180	Combine flour, puree, milk, and half of the foie gras fat. Bring to boil. Chill. Emulsify blood into mixture, and reserve. Sweat apples and onions in remaining foie gras fat until very tender. Deglaze with Calvados. Chill. Combine apples and onions with fatback, breadcrumbs, Activa, and seasonings. Fold in blood, and mold. Before cooking, blanch in boiling water for 1 min.
chestnut puree (store-bought)	20%						
fine breadcrumbs	13%						
apple, small dice	10%						
chestnut flour	5%						
whole egg	8.5%	5%	n/a		55	130	
soy protein concentrate	7.0%						
egg white	16.2%	4.4%	n/a		61	142	For alcohol reduction, combine 14.7% cognac, 11% Madeira, and 3.7% white port, and reduce to one-eighth of starting volume.
egg yolk	4.4%						
Sicilian pistachios	11.0%						
black truffles, optional	7.0%						
glycerin monostearate	2.00%	4.5%	Activa or polyphosphate blend (not both)	0.22% 0.09%	60	140	For hot-smoked version, air-dry for 30 min after stuffing. Smoke for 90 min at 70 °C / 158 °F and 85% relative humidity. Poach at 70 °C / 158 °F to core temperature of 68 °C / 154 °F. Plunge in cold water for 2 min. Refrigerate until cold, and peel.
skim milk powder	1.85%						
Insta Cure No. 1	0.15%						
dextrose	0.20%						
sodium citrate	0.2%	4%	n/a		55	130	Add sodium citrate to boiling water, and blend in cheese until smooth. Cool. Blend with meat. Slice frozen bread very thinly. Wrap cooked, uncased sausage in bread slice, and fry in butter until crisp.
pullman loaf, frozen (see note)	as needed						
Sicilian pistachios, peeled	18%	4.6%	Activa	0.25%	55	130	Reserve 25% of pork fatback, and cut into 1 cm / ½ in cubes. Blanch in boiling water for 10 s, and then cool. Fold into the sausage mix along with the pistachios before stuffing.
microcrystalline cellulose (Avicel CG 200, FMC BioPolymer brand)	7%						
Insta Cure No. 1	0.55%						
whole egg	11.0%	2.5%	n/a		65	149	For alcohol reduction, reduce two parts dry sherry and one part cognac by half, and cool completely.
sodium caseinate	0.4%						

ITALIAN SAUSAGE

Yields 1.8 kg

INGREDIENT	QUANTITY	SCALING	PROCEDURE
Pork shoulder, cubed and chilled to -1 °C / 30 °F	1 kg	100%	① Chill coarse grinder die and extruder bowl.
Pork fatback, cubed and frozen	300 g	30%	② Grind pork shoulder and fatback separately through chilled die into chilled bowl. Keep forcemeat chilled.
			③ Fold ground meat and fat together, and reserve.
Ice water	140 g	14%	④ Finely mince fresh basil and oregano.
Salt	20 g	2%	⑤ Grind fennel seeds and toasted coriander seeds to fine powder.
Sugar	20 g	2%	
Basil	17 g	1.7%	⑥ Coarsely grind peppercorns.
Hungarian paprika	17 g	1.7%	⑦ Combine seasonings, and fold into forcemeat.
Oregano	17 g	1.7%	
Fennel seeds, toasted	11 g	1.1%	
Coriander seeds, toasted	6 g	0.6%	
Hot pepper flakes	2 g	0.2%	
Black peppercorns	1 g	0.1%	
Hog casings, 32–35 mm / 1¼–1⅜ in. in diameter	as needed		⑧ Stuff seasoned forcemeat into casing.
			⑨ Twist links to desired lengths.
			⑩ Refrigerate sausages for at least 1 h.
			⑪ Poach or steam sausages at 61 °C / 142 °F until core temperature reaches 60 °C / 140 °F, about 25 min.

from page 3·242

FRANKFURTER

Yields 2.2 kg

INGREDIENT	QUANTITY	SCALING	PROCEDURE
Beef chuck, cubed and chilled to -1 °C / 30 °F	1 kg	100%	① Chill fine die and extruder bowl.
			② Grind beef chuck and fat separately.
Beef fat, cubed and frozen	550 g	55%	③ Puree ground meat and ice until smooth.
Ice, crushed	400 g	40%	④ Add fat, and continue to puree until smooth.
			⑤ Reserve ground meat mixture chilled.
Salt	33 g	3.3%	⑥ Grind nutmeg, white pepper, and toasted coriander seeds to fine powder.
Skim milk powder	18.5 g	1.85%	
Mustard powder	12.5 g	1.25%	⑦ Fold spices and additives into cold ground-meat mixture.
Onion powder	10 g	1%	
Sweet paprika	10 g	1%	
Nutmeg	5 g	0.5%	
Insta Cure No. 1	3.3 g	0.33%	
White pepper	2.5 g	0.25%	
Glycerin monostearate (4mular brand)	2.2 g	0.22%	
Coriander seeds, toasted	2 g	0.2%	
Dextrose	2 g	0.2%	
Sheep casing, 2 cm / ¾ in. in diameter	as needed		⑧ Stuff forcemeat paste into casing.
			⑨ Twist links to desired lengths.
			⑩ Refrigerate sausages for at least 1 h.
			⑪ Poach or steam links at 61 °C / 142 °F to core temperature of 60 °C / 140 °F, about 25 min.

from page 3·242

The sausages can be cold-smoked at 10 °C / 50 °F for 24 h or hot-smoked at 52 °C / 125 °F for 12 h. See page 120 for details on smoking.

BOUDIN BLANC

Yields 2 kg

INGREDIENT	QUANTITY	SCALING	PROCEDURE
1% milk	750 g	103%	① Vacuum seal together.
Button mushrooms, thinly sliced	75 g	10%	② Cook sous vide in 85 °C / 185 °F bath for 1 h.
Clarified unsalted butter	50 g	7%	③ Strain.
Sweet onions, thinly sliced	50 g	7%	④ Measure 725 g of infused milk, and reserve refrigerated.
Dried morels, ground to powder	5 g	0.7%	
Bay leaf	0.75 g	0.1%	
Thyme	0.5 g	0.07%	
Cognac	100 g	14%	⑤ Combine, and reduce to 25 g.
Madeira wine	75 g	10.5%	⑥ Cool completely, and reserve.
White port	25 g	3.5%	
Infused milk, from above	725 g	100%	⑦ Puree until smooth, while keeping temperature below 7 °C / 45 °F.
Chicken thighs, finely ground	680 g	94%	⑧ Refrigerate for 10 min.
Egg whites, blended	110 g	15%	
Egg yolks, blended	30 g	4%	
Salt	30 g	4%	
Quatre épices see page 48	1.5 g	0.2%	
Rendered chicken fat	227 g	31.5%	⑨ Blend into chilled chicken puree until fully emulsified.
Pistachio oil	58 g	8%	⑩ Optionally, for aerated texture, transfer mixture to 1 l whipping siphon and charge with two cartridges of nitrous oxide. Omit added pistachios and truffles pieces in step 11.
Green Sicilian pistachios, quartered	75 g	10.5%	⑪ For regular boudins, fold into mixture to make forcemeat.
Black truffles, optional finely minced	50 g	7%	
Natural casings, 4 cm / 1½ in. in diameter	as needed		⑫ For aerated texture, shake siphon vigorously, and dispense forcemeat directly into casings.
			⑬ For regular boudins, stuff casings with forcemeat.
Frying oil	as needed		⑭ Poach or steam sausages (boudins) at 61 °C / 142 °F to core temperature of 60 °C / 140 °F, about 35 min.
			⑮ Puncture membrane of sausage with needle in several places to prevent explosion.
			⑯ Sear boudins in oil until evenly golden and slightly puffed.

from page 3·243

If not using a siphon, whip the egg whites separately. Fold the emulsified mixture into the whipped egg whites, and stuff.

FERMENTED SAUSAGE

① Select a sausage recipe and a fermentation approach. The table Best Bets for Fermented Sausages below lists several good options, and the Fermentation Methods table at right suggests cultures and parameters for slow, medium, and fast methods.

② Select a culture and a curing salt. We recommend Bactoferm F-LC culture, which works for all three approaches; for slow-fermented sausages, Bactoferm T-SPX produces a more traditional flavor. Follow manufacturer's instructions for rehydrating the culture before use. Use the curing salt indicated in the table on the next page.

③ Grind trimmed meat and fat separately. For details, see page 3·228. Recommended grinding plate dimensions are given in the table below.

④ Combine all ingredients. To avoid degrading the activity of the culture, mix the curing salt, carbohydrates, and seasonings into the meat thoroughly before adding the culture. Add the salt and fat last. Quantities in the recipes below are given relative to the principal meat used. For example, when making chorizo add 3 g salt, 0.3 g curing salt, 0.02 g culture, and 25 g fatback to every 100 g of pork shoulder. Use a stand mixer with a paddle mixing blade; run the mixer at low speed.

⑤ Stuff. Stuff the sausage mixture into casings of the dimensions indicated in the table.

⑥ Ferment by holding at the temperature, relative humidity (%RH), and time indicated in the table above.

⑦ Smoke, dry, or both (optional). Dry at the temperature and humidity shown in the table above until sausage has lost at least 25% of its original wet weight for semidried, or about 50% for dried sausage; approximate times are listed in the table above. To encourage a coating of mold to grow on the outside of the casing, dip the sausages into a solution of Christian Hansen M-EK-4 mold culture before drying. For more information about smoking meat, see page 3·208.

Best Bets for Fermented Sausages

Sausage	Meat	(scaling)	Fat	(scaling)	Grind (mm)	Grind (in)	Salt (scaling)	Curing salt (scaling)	Culture (scaling)
salami	pork shoulder beef, chuck	100% 40%	pork fatback	25%	5 2	3/16 1/16	4.2%	0.4%	0.03%
saucisson sec	pork shoulder	100%	pork fatback	35%	5	3/16	3.0%	0.3%	0.02%
pepperoni	pork shoulder beef chuck	100% 42.5%	pork fatback	40%	5	3/16	5.1%	0.4%	0.02%
chorizo	pork shoulder	100%	pork fatback	25%	8	5/16	3.0%	0.3%	0.02%
lap cheong	pork shoulder	100%	pork fatback	20%	10	3/8	3.0%	0.3%	0.02%

from page 3·246

Fermentation Methods

Method	Curing salt	Ferment (°C)	(°F)	(d)	(%RH)	Dry (°C)	(°F)	(%RH)	(d)
Slow, dried	Insta Cure No. 2	18	64	10	85	12	54	70	25–40
Medium, semidried	Insta Cure No. 1	24	75	3	85	15	59	70	10–25
Fast, fresh	Insta Cure No. 1	37	100	1	100	n/a	n/a	n/a	n/a

Fast fermentation lowers the pH of the sausage more quickly and further by using fast-acting cultures that work at higher temperatures, but require higher sugar content. And provided the food is refrigerated, you can skip the lengthy drying step.

VARIATION: Fermenting Sous Vide

Follow steps 1 to 5 on the previous page.

① Vacuum seal sausages together in a single row. Be careful not to squish the sausages when sealing them in the bag.

② Ferment sous vide in a water bath, combi oven, or water-vapor oven at the desired temperature—usually 37 °C / 100 °F—for 1 d.

③ Pasteurize at 55 °C / 130 °F for 2–3 h (optional).

④ Cool. The sausages must be refrigerated.

⑤ Vacuum dry, or dry conventionally at the temperature, humidity, and time indicated in the table above (optional, see page 2·433). Drying can simulate the texture of a sausage made with the traditional, slow-dried approach.

Carbohydrate	(scaling) (slow/medium/fast)	Seasonings		Casing (mm)	(in)
dextrose	0.35%/0.7%/1.1%	black pepper, coarsely ground	0.15%	75	3
		garlic, finely minced	0.10%		
dextrose	0.25%/0.5%/0.75%	hazelnuts, peeled, roasted, and coarsely chopped (optional)	9.0%	75	3
		black pepper, coarsely ground	0.7%		
		garlic, finely minced	0.1%		
dextrose	0.35%/0.7%/1.1%	red chili powder	1.25%	60	2 3/8
		hot paprika	1.10%		
		allspice	0.75%		
		cayenne (optional)	0.50%		
		black pepper	0.50%		
dextrose	0.25%/0.5%/0.75%	hot pimentón de la Vera	0.7%	33	1 5/16
		Ancho chili powder	0.7%		
		cayenne pepper	0.2%		
		garlic, finely minced	0.2%		
dextrose	0.25%/0.5%/0.75%	soy sauce	3.00%	20	3/4
		shaoxing wine	1.00%		
		monosodium glutamate	1.00%		
		cassia, finely ground	0.15%		

SAUCISSON SEC

Yields 1.5 kg

INGREDIENT	QUANTITY	SCALING	PROCEDURE
Pork shoulder, cubed and chilled to –1 °C / 30 °F	1 kg	100%	① Chill grinder extruder bowl, coarse die, and 3 mm / ⅛ in fine die.
Pork fatback, cubed and frozen	250 g	25%	② Grind pork shoulder and fatback separately through chilled coarse die into chilled bowl. ③ Grind both separately through chilled fine die into chilled bowl. ④ Fold ground meat and fat together, and reserve chilled.
Garlic	13 g	1.3%	⑤ Blanch once in boiling water, drain, and mince. Reserve.
Pork fatback	100 g	10%	⑥ Freeze, and cut into small dice. Reserve frozen.
Hazelnuts, roasted, peeled, and chopped	90 g	9%	⑦ Fold minced garlic, nuts, dextrose, pepper, and Insta Cure into chilled ground pork to make forcemeat.
Dextrose	10 g	1%	
Black pepper, coarsely ground	7 g	0.7%	
Insta Cure No. 2	2.5 g	0.25%	
Bactoferm F-RM 52 (Christian Hansen brand)	1.125 g	0.1% (0.07%)*	⑧ Whisk bacterial culture into water at 20 °C / 68 °F to make slurry. ⑨ Fold into forcemeat, and mix thoroughly to evenly distribute slurry.
Distilled water	35 g	3.5%	⑩ Fold in frozen fat and salt.
Salt	35 g	3.5%	
Synthetic casings, 3 cm by 61 cm / 1¼ in by 24 in	as needed		⑪ Stuff meat into casings, and then twist into 25 cm / 10 in links; tie ends with butcher's twine. ⑫ Dip sausages into distilled water to moisten surface, and immediately hang in fermentation chamber or other controlled-atmosphere chamber. ⑬ Ferment at 22 °C / 72 °F and 90% relative humidity for 3 days. A thin film of bacterial growth may form on surface of sausage casing. ⑭ Hang sausages in cool room at 12 °C / 54 °F to dry for 3–4 wk, until sausages have lost 25%–40% of their original weight. The more water weight sausages lose, the denser they become.

from page 3·247

*(% of total weight of meat and fat)

FERMENTED SHRIMP SHEETS INSPIRED BY WYLIE DUFRESNE

Yields 300 g

INGREDIENT	QUANTITY	SCALING	PROCEDURE
Raw shrimp, ground	200 g	100%	① Puree in food processor until smooth.
Coconut milk	100 g	50%	② Pass through fine sieve.
Shrimp paste (belacan)	15 g	7.5%	③ Spread on silicone mat in layer 1 mm / ¹⁄₁₆ in thick.
Activa TI (or Activa RM)	6 g	3%	④ Cover, and steam in combi oven at 55 °C / 131 °F for 4 min covered.
Salt	1.25 g	0.65%	⑤ Refrigerate for 1 h to set. ⑥ Steam at 100 °C / 212 °F for 1 min, or cook sous vide at same temperature and time. ⑦ Cool and refrigerate.

from page 5·168

FAST-CURED PEPPERONI

Yields 1.5 kg

INGREDIENT	QUANTITY	SCALING	PROCEDURE
Bactoferm F-LC	0.85 g	0.085% (0.05%)*	① Whisk bacterial culture into water at 20 °C / 68 °F to make slurry. Reserve.
Distilled water	10 g	1%	
Pork shoulder, cubed and chilled to −1 °C / 30 °F	1 kg	100%	② Chill grinder extruder bowl and 3 mm / ⅛ in fine die.
Beef chuck, cubed and frozen	425 g	42.5%	③ Dry-blend seasonings except salt.
			④ Toss cubed meat with seasoning powder.
Pork fatback, cubed and frozen	400 g	40%	⑤ Cover, and refrigerate for 3 h.
			⑥ Grind seasoned meat and fat separately into chilled bowl.
Salt	51 g	5.1%	⑦ Stir culture slurry into meat until evenly distributed, and fold in fat and salt.
Dextrose	17 g	1.7%	⑧ Vacuum seal mixture, and hold at 38 °C / 100 °F for 24 h.
Sugar	17 g	1.7%	⑨ Optionally, to make pepperoni sheets, add 0.25% Activa RM to weight of meat, and roll mixture in a sous vide bag into sheet 1 mm / 1/32 in thick (see page 2·208).
Red chili powder	12.5 g	1.25%	
Smoked paprika	11 g	1.1%	⑩ Cook sous vide in 55 °C / 131 °F bath for 10 min.
Lactic acid	8.5 g	0.85% (0.5%)*	⑪ To make quick-dried pepperoni stick, form forcemeat into 1 cm / ⅜ in diameter sticks.
			⑫ Cook sous vide in 55 °C / 131 °F bath for 25 min.
Allspice, powder	7.5 g	0.75%	⑬ Vacuum dry for 8–24 h (see page 2·433) or air dry, refrigerated, for 2–3 days until desired texture is achieved.
Black pepper, powder	5 g	0.5%	
Cayenne	5 g	0.5%	
Insta Cure No. 1	3.5 g	0.35% (0.2%)*	

from page 3·247

*(% of total weight of meat)

MODERNIST SAUSAGES

COARSE FAT-GEL SAUSAGE

Yields 420 g

INGREDIENT	QUANTITY	SCALING	PROCEDURE
Pork fatback	70 g	100%	① Cut into medium-size cubes.
			② Vacuum seal, and heat to 70 °C / 158 °F.
Sodium caseinate	5 g	7%	③ Disperse gellan and sodium caseinate in water, and blend.
Water	70 g	100%	
Low-acyl gellan (Kelcogel F, CP Kelco brand)	0.7 g	1%	④ Bring to simmer.
			⑤ Blend in warm fat cubes until fully emulsified.
			⑥ Continue blending for 3 min until mixture forms bright-white fat gel.
			⑦ Pour into container, cover, and refrigerate for 24 h.
Pork shoulder, chilled	280 g	400%	⑧ Cube pork, and mix with Nutrifos and salt.
Salt	8.4 g	12%	⑨ Mix with fat gel, and grind through coarse 5 mm / ¼ in die.
Nutrifos 088	0.28 g	0.4%	
			⑩ Stuff or shape, and cook in 63 °C / 145 °F bath to core temperature of 62 °C / 144 °F.

from page 3·248

You can add the spice mix for any coarse sausage to the recipe above as a flavoring, and similarly use any spice mix for emulsified sausage in the recipe below.

EMULSIFIED SAUSAGE WITH FAT GEL

Yields 600 g

INGREDIENT	QUANTITY	SCALING	PROCEDURE
Water	100 g	100%	① Disperse alginate in water, and blend until fully hydrated.
Sodium alginate (Manugel DMF, FMC BioPolymer brand)	10 g	10% (5%)*	
Rendered fat or oil (liquid)	100 g	100%	② Blend in until emulsified.
			③ Chill to 0 °C / 32 °F.
Meat	500 g	500%	④ Grind meat in fine 3 mm / ⅛ in die.
			⑤ Place all ingredients in food processor, and puree until emulsified.
			⑥ Form in mold, and cook in 62 °C / 144 °F bath to core temperature of 61 °C / 142 °F.
Salt	12 g	12%	

from page 3·248

*(% of total weight of water and fat)

LOW-FAT CHICKEN SAUSAGE

Yields 450 g

INGREDIENT	QUANTITY	SCALING	PROCEDURE
Water	138 g	46%	① Blend together until fully hydrated.
Xanthan gum	0.45 g	0.15%	
Guar gum	0.18 g	0.06%	
Salt	6.9 g	2.3%	
Rendered chicken fat or oil	4.5 g	1.5%	② Combine meat and fat, and blend with gum mixture, from above, until smooth.
			③ Form sausages, and cook in 74 °C / 165 °F bath to core temperature of 73 °C / 163 °F.
Chicken breast	300 g	100%	④ Chill. Reheat to serve.

from page 3·248

RARE BEEF SAUSAGE

Yields 1.8 kg

INGREDIENT	QUANTITY	SCALING	PROCEDURE
Beef chuck	1 kg	100%	① Cut meats into 12.5 mm / ½ in cubes, and combine.
Beef sirloin	500 g	50%	② Freeze meat until semifirm, −1 °C / 30 °F.
Beef short rib	300 g	30%	③ Chill grinder dies and parts, as well as extruder bowl.
			④ Grind beef mixture once through chilled 3 mm / ⅛ in die.
Activa RM	4.5 g	0.45% (0.25%)*	⑤ Dry blend.
Salt	36 g	3.6% (2%)*	⑥ Fold seasoning mixture into chilled ground beef mixture until evenly distributed.
Insta Cure No. 1	3.6 g	0.36% (0.2%)*	⑦ Roll in plastic wrap to form cylinder 4 cm / 1½ in thick, and tie ends tightly.
Nutrifos 088	1.8 g	0.18% (0.1%)*	⑧ Refrigerate for 3 h.
			⑨ Cook in 55 °C / 131 °F bath to core temperature of 54 °C / 129 °F, about 35 min.
N-Zorbit M (National Starch brand)	36 g	3.6% (2%)*	⑩ Slice to desired thickness.
Black pepper, coarsely ground	9 g	0.9%	
Flat leaf parsley, minced	36 g	3.6%	
Alsatian mustard, optional see page 176	as needed		⑪ Serve with mustard if desired.

from page 3·249

(% of total weight of meat)

The temperatures given here will cook the sausage beef to medium rare.

FRIED CHICKEN SAUSAGE

Yields 1.5 kg

INGREDIENT	QUANTITY	SCALING	PROCEDURE
Chicken thighs, skinless and boneless, cubed	1 kg	100%	① Chill grinder dies and parts, as well as extruder bowl.
Salt	26 g	2.6%	② Combine chicken pieces with salt and Nutrifos 088.
Nutrifos 088	2.5 g	0.25%	③ Grind chicken mixture once through chilled fine die.
Activa RM	2.5 g	0.25%	④ Fold in Activa.
Ice, crushed	200 g	20%	⑤ Combine with ground chicken in food processor, and puree until smooth and ice is melted.
			⑥ Reserve.
Pressure-rendered chicken fat see page 3·145	400 g	40%	⑦ Heat fat to 65 °C / 149 °F, and whisk in glyceride flakes until fully dissolved.
			⑧ Cool fat mixture to 40 °C / 104 °F.
Mono- and diglycerides (Glice, Texturas brand)	28 g	2.8% (7%)*	⑨ Slowly drizzle fat into running food processor until fully emulsified.
Synthetic casing, 4 cm / 1½ in. in diameter	as needed		⑩ Stuff forcemeat into casings to make 30 cm / 12 in lengths. Tie off ends.
			⑪ Poach in 60 °C / 140 °F bath for 1 h.
			⑫ Peel casing from cooked sausages, and cut into four 7.5 cm / 3 in portions.
			⑬ Reserve.
Chicken skin, frozen and finely ground	2 kg	200%	⑭ Wet-render over medium-low heat until all water has evaporated and skin pieces have fried in their own fat, about 30 min.
Water	400 g	40%	⑮ Remove from heat, and blend with immersion blender until all skin is finely ground.
			⑯ Drain skin, and reserve fat.
			⑰ Dry skin between paper towels in 93 °C / 200 °F oven, about 20 min.
Salt	as needed		⑱ Season powdered skin with 1% of its weight in salt.
			⑲ Roll sausage portions in seasoned powder just before serving.

from page 3·249

(% of total weight of fat)

MEAT AND SEAFOOD

FRUITS AND VEGETABLES SOUS VIDE

① Select and prep ingredients. Some of our favorites, along with prep steps, are listed in the tables on these two pages.
② Vacuum seal. See chapter 9 on Cooking Sous Vide, page 2·192, for details.
③ Cook. Recommended cooking temperatures and times appear in the tables, as do references to elsewhere in the book.

Best Bets for Cooking Fruits Sous Vide Until Tender

Ingredient	Prep	Cut to (cm)	Cut to (in)	Cook (°C)	Cook (°F)	Cook (min)	See page
apricots	peeled, pitted	halves		88	190	15	
apples	peeled, cored	halves		88	190	40	320
bananas	skin on	whole		88	190	12	280
cantaloupes	peeled, seeded, cubed	2.5	1	53	127	15	
cherries		whole		88	190	7	
cranberries		whole		88	190	45	
grapes		whole		83	181	10	
mangoes	peeled, pitted, cubed	2.5	1	75	167	10	
nectarines	peeled, pitted	halves		88	190	12	
peaches	peeled, pitted	halves		88	190	16	
pears	peeled, cored	whole		88	190	60	
persimmons, soft Hachiya	stemmed	quarters		88	190	20	
pineapples	peeled, cored, cubed	2.5	1	75	167	60	
plums	pitted	halves		75	167	20	

from page 3·288

SOUS VIDE BABY BEET SALAD

Yields 375 g

INGREDIENT	QUANTITY	SCALING	PROCEDURE
Baby beets, trimmed but not peeled	250 g	100%	① Vacuum seal together.
Extra virgin olive oil	75 g	30%	② Cook sous vide in 88 °C / 190 °F bath for 1 h.
Water	50 g	20%	③ Remove from bag, reserving juices, and rub off beet skins with clean kitchen towel.
Salt	3.5 g	1.4%	④ Vacuum seal beets and juices together.
			⑤ Refrigerate for at least 2 h before serving.
Passion fruit–white soy sauce vinaigrette see page 23	50 g	20%	⑥ Toss beets with vinaigrette and oil.
			⑦ Season with additional salt.
Toasted sesame oil	10 g	4%	

from page 5·183

SOUS VIDE GLAZED PEARL ONION

Yields 50 g

INGREDIENT	QUANTITY	SCALING	PROCEDURE
Pearl onions	50 g	100%	① Blanch for 1 min.
			② Shock in ice-water bath.
			③ Peel and reserve.
Water	20 g	40%	④ Combine.
Extra virgin olive oil	5 g	10%	⑤ Vacuum seal with onions.
Black pepper	to taste		⑥ Cook sous vide in 90 °C / 194 °F bath for 2½ h.
Salt	to taste		
Neutral oil	as needed		⑦ Drain, and season or refrigerate until use.
Black pepper	to taste		
Salt	to taste		

from page 5·221

Best Bets for Cooking Vegetables Sous Vide Until Tender

Ingredient	Peel	Cut to (cm)	Cut to (in)	Cook (°C)	Cook (°F)	Cook (min)	See page
asparagus, green or white	yes	15	6	85	185	15	5·147, 33
bamboo shoots, fresh	yes	2.5	1	80	176	6 h	5·247
beets, baby	no	whole		85	185	1 h	5·183
beets, large	optional	5	2	82	180	1 h	
carrots, large	yes	15	6	85	185	45	5·164
carrots, young	no	whole		85	185	40	25
celery roots	yes	5	2	85	185	1½ h	
chard stems		15	6	88	190	25	
corn, on cob		7.5	3	60	140	15	
daikon radishes	yes	5	2	85	185	25	
endives, Belgian		whole		88	190	50	
fennel bulbs		cut in half		85	185	30	
hearts of palm	yes	whole		85	185	1½ h	
kohlrabi	optional	5	2	88	190	1¼ h	
leeks	root removed	cut in half		85	185	50	
mushrooms (shiitake, crimini, oyster, shimeji, enoki, lobster, porcini)	no	whole		90	194	10	144
onions, cipolline	yes	whole		90	194	2 h	141
onions, pearl	yes	whole		85	185	50	140
onions, sweet	yes	cut in half		88	190	45	
rutabagas	yes	5	2	85	185	1 h	5·53
salsify	yes	5	2	88	190	15	5·205
shallots	yes	whole		85	185	1 h 25	
Jerusalem artichokes (sunchokes)	optional	5	2	85	185	1 h	
squash, summer (zucchini, yellow)	no	5	2	65	149	40	
squash, firm autumn varieties (Hokkaido, kabocha, kuri)	yes	5	2	90	194	15	
squash, tender autumn varieties (acorn, butternut, delicata)	yes	5	2	85	185	25	
turnips	yes	5	2	85	185	35	139

from page 3·289

SOUS VIDE TURNIP

Yields 200 g

INGREDIENT	QUANTITY	SCALING	PROCEDURE
Turnips	200 g	100%	① Cut turnips into slices 3 mm / ⅛ in thick.
			② Cut discs from each slice with 2.5 cm / 1 in pastry cutter.
Unsalted butter	25 g	12.5%	③ Vacuum seal discs in single even layer with butter, water, and salt.
Water	25 g	12.5%	④ Cook sous vide in 85 °C / 185 °F bath for 20 min.
Salt	2 g	1%	⑤ Season with additional salt to taste.

from page 5·33

GLAZED WHITE CARROT

Yields 300 g

INGREDIENT	QUANTITY	SCALING	PROCEDURE
Small white carrots, peeled	300 g	100%	① Vacuum seal together.
			② Cook sous vide in 85 °C / 185 °F bath for 45 min.
Water	50 g	17%	③ Pour cooking juices into pot, leaving carrots in bag.
Unsalted butter	45 g	15%	④ Reduce cooking juices until syrupy, about 8 min.
Fructose	6 g	2%	⑤ Stir in carrots until just warmed, and season with additional salt to taste.
Salt	3 g	1%	

from page 5·32

BRAISED TURNIPS WITH SAFFRON

Yields 200 g

INGREDIENT	QUANTITY	SCALING	PROCEDURE
Turnips, peeled and cut to slices 5 mm / ¼ in thick	250 g	100%	① Vacuum seal together. ② Cook sous vide in 85 °C / 185 °F bath for 35 min. ③ Serve, or refrigerate until use.
Water	100 g	40%	
Saffron threads	0.25 g	0.1%	
Salt	2 g	0.8%	

from page 5·123

GLAZED PEARL ONION

Yields 230 g

INGREDIENT	QUANTITY	SCALING	PROCEDURE
Pearl onions, blanched and peeled	100 g	111%	① Prepare onions as directed. ② Vacuum seal onions with other ingredients.
Water	90 g	100%	③ Cook sous vide in 85 °C / 185 °F bath for 1 h.
Champagne vinegar	30 g	33%	④ Cool in ice-water bath.
Honey	7 g	8%	⑤ Refrigerate until use.
Salt	3 g	3.5%	
Neutral oil	as needed		⑥ To serve, drain pearl onions, cut in half through stem ends, and pat dry. ⑦ Sear pearl onions in oil, cut sides only, until surfaces are golden and onions are just warmed, about 3 min.

from page 5·263

POTATO SALAD

Yields 600 g

INGREDIENT	QUANTITY	SCALING	PROCEDURE
Fingerling potatoes	400 g	100%	① Toss together.
Salt	5 g	1.25%	② Cook sous vide in 88 °C / 190 °F bath for about 30 min. (Cooking time will depend on size of potatoes.) ③ Cool in ice-water bath. ④ Cut into halves or quarters, depending on size, and reserve.
Crème fraîche	50 g	12.5%	⑤ Whisk together.
Muscat vinegar	20 g	5%	⑥ Mix gently with cut potatoes.
Walnut oil	15 g	3.75%	
French whole-grain mustard	4 g	1%	
Salt	2 g	0.5%	
Sugar	2 g	0.5%	
Egg yolk, cooked sous vide, at 68 °C / 154 °F for 35 min, cooled and quartered	80 g	20%	⑦ Fold gently into potato salad.
Pickled pearl onions, petals see page 182	48 g	12%	
Celery leaves, thinly sliced	3 g	0.75%	
Coriander seeds, toasted and crushed	2 g	0.5%	
Scallions, whites only	40 g (four pieces)	10%	⑧ Sauté scallions over medium heat until tender. ⑨ Arrange on potato salad.
Potato skins	200 g	50%	⑩ Toss potato skins with starch.
Potato starch	15 g	3.75%	⑪ Fry in 180 °C / 360 °F oil until golden and crisp, about 3 min.
Frying oil	as needed		⑫ Toss with salt.
Salt	to taste		⑬ Serve with potato salad.

from page 5·73

FRESH BEAN SALAD

Yields 100 g

INGREDIENT	QUANTITY	SCALING	PROCEDURE
Fava beans, shelled and peeled	25 g	100%*	① Vacuum seal peas and each type of bean individually.
English peas, shelled and peeled	20 g		② Cook sous vide in 88 °C / 190 °F bath for 20 min, or to desired doneness.
Romano beans, trimmed	15 g		③ Cool in ice-water bath.
Green beans, trimmed	14 g		④ Cut beans crosswise into 2.5 cm / 1 in pieces.
Yellow wax beans, trimmed	14 g		⑤ Combine.
			⑥ Refrigerate until use.
Purslane leaves	7 g	8%	⑦ Measure ingredients individually.
Roasted hazelnut oil	7 g	8%	⑧ Toss with cold beans and peas.
Vermouth vinegar (or other semisweet white vinegar)	5 g	5.7%	
Scallion, thinly sliced	4 g	4.5%	
Lime juice	3 g	3.4%	
Black pepper	to taste		⑨ Season salad.
Salt	to taste		

from page 5·87   *(100% is the total weight of all beans used)

SWEET-AND-SOUR CIPOLLINE ONION

Yields 80 g

INGREDIENT	QUANTITY	SCALING	PROCEDURE
Cipolline onion, peeled	100 g	100%	① Vacuum seal together.
White wine vinegar	55 g	55%	② Cook sous vide in 90 °C / 194 °F bath for 1 h 50 min.
Chestnut honey	29 g	29%	③ Remove from bag and drain.
Neutral oil	25 g	25%	
Water	10 g	10%	
Salt	1.5 g	1.5%	
Neutral oil	as needed		④ Cut onions in half horizontally, and sear until golden.

from page 5·19

CARROT AND DILL FRICASSEE

Yields 125 g

INGREDIENT	QUANTITY	SCALING	PROCEDURE
Carrots, peeled	110 g	100%	① Halve carrots lengthwise, and core.
Extra virgin olive oil	10 g	9%	② Cut into half-moons 5 mm / ¼ in thick.
			③ Vacuum seal with oil.
			④ Cook sous vide in 85 °C / 185 °F bath for 40 min.
Unsalted butter	10 g	9%	⑤ Combine remaining ingredients, and warm through in small pot.
Ajowan seeds	2 g	1.8%	⑥ Stir in cooked carrots and season.
Dill	2 g	1.8%	
Semisweet vinegar (honey or white balsamic)	2 g	1.8%	
Salt	to taste		

from page 5·164

SOUS VIDE LENTILS

Yields 650 g

INGREDIENT	QUANTITY	SCALING	PROCEDURE
Carrots, thinly sliced	120 g	34%	① Prepare vegetables as noted.
Sweet onions, thinly sliced	120 g	34%	② Place vegetables and aromatics together in sachet.
Shallots, thinly sliced	80 g	23%	
Leeks, thinly sliced	70 g	20%	
Celery, thinly sliced	50 g	14%	
Garlic, thinly sliced	25 g	7%	
Thyme sprig	3 g	0.8%	
Bay leaf	2 g	0.6%	
Black peppercorns	2 g	0.6%	
Distilled water	1 kg	286%	③ Combine, add sachet, and cook sous vide in 90 °C / 194 °F bath for 1 h 15 min.
French green lentils, soaked in cold water for 2 h	350 g	100%	④ Discard sachet, and rest lentils at room temperature for 30 min.
			⑤ Cool in ice-water bath, and refrigerate until use.
Salt	17 g	4.8%	
Cherry vinaigrette see page 5·270	5 g	1.5%	⑥ To serve, fold into cooked lentils.
Green hazelnuts, thinly sliced	90 g	26%	⑦ Garnish dressed lentils.
Black radish, small dice	15 g	4%	
Chervil tops	15 g	4%	
Frisée tops	15 g	4%	
Chamomile blossoms (fresh)	5 g	1.5%	

from page 5·271

SOUS VIDE GREEN ASPARAGUS

Yields 200 g

INGREDIENT	QUANTITY	SCALING	PROCEDURE
Green asparagus, stalks peeled (about 1.5 cm / ⅝ in thick)	200 g	100%	① Vacuum seal all ingredients together.
			② Cook sous vide in 85 °C / 185 °F bath for 15 min.
Water	20 g	10%	
Extra virgin olive oil	10 g	5%	
Salt	2 g	1%	

from page 5·149

SOUS VIDE ARTICHOKE

Yields 100 g

INGREDIENT	QUANTITY	SCALING	PROCEDURE
Water	200 g	200%	① Vacuum seal together.
Baby artichokes, peeled, and chokes and tough leaves discarded	100 g (four pieces)	100%	② Cook sous vide in 90 °C / 194 °F bath for 45 min.
			③ Slice artichokes and serve, or cool and refrigerate until use.
Yellow onion, thinly sliced	25 g	25%	
Carrot, peeled and thinly sliced	15 g	15%	
Lemon peel	5.5 g	5.5%	
Salt	2.5 g	2.5%	
Ascorbic acid	1 g	1%	
Thyme	1 g	1%	
Black coriander seeds	0.5 g	0.5%	
Black peppercorns	0.5 g	0.5%	
Bay leaf	0.2 g	0.2%	

from page 5·244

VARIATION: Cooking Vegetables Sous Vide with Fat

① Select and prep. See the table below for suggestions and prep steps.

② Add fat, and vacuum seal. The fat column in the table indicates the kind and quantity that work best. Proportions are relative to the weight of the vegetable. For example, add 20 g of olive oil to the sous vide bag for every 100 g of trimmed artichokes.

③ Cook. Recommended cooking temperatures and times appear in the table below.

Best Bets for Cooking Vegetables Sous Vide with Fat Until Tender

Ingredient	Cut to (cm)	Cut to (in)	Fat	(scaling)*	Cook (°C)	Cook (°F)	Cook (min)	See page
artichokes, baby		whole	olive oil	20%	85	185	1 h	142
artichokes, mature		half	olive oil	20%	85	185	1½ h	5·172
carrots, large	7.5	3	butter	30%	83	181	45	
chestnuts, peeled		whole	lard	15%	90	194	12 h	this page
crosnes (Chinese artichokes)		whole	clarified butter	20%	85	185	35	
Japanese yams	7.5	3	butter	20%	95	203	45	5·35
garlic		whole cloves	olive oil	40%	88	190	7 h	
potatoes	7.5	3	butter	30%	85	185	45	184
shallots		whole	neutral oil	15%	85	185	1 h 25 min	
squash, kabocha	7.5	3	olive oil	15%	90	194	1 h	
sweet potatoes	7.5	3	clarified butter	10%	90	194	40	
turnips	7.5	3	butter	10%	85	185	15	

from page 3·292

*(set weight of vegetable to 100%)

CHESTNUT CONFIT

Yields 200 g

INGREDIENT	QUANTITY	SCALING	PROCEDURE
Italian chestnuts	180 g	100%	① Cut X into stem side of each chestnut.
			② Blanch for 30 s.
			③ Peel off receded skins and shell carefully.
Rendered pork fat	90 g	50%	④ Vacuum seal chestnuts with fat and salt.
Salt	2 g	1%	⑤ Cook sous vide in 90 °C / 194 °F bath for 12 h.
			⑥ Serve, or cool to room temperature and refrigerate.

from page 5·18

SALSIFY FONDANT

Yields 100 g

INGREDIENT	QUANTITY	SCALING	PROCEDURE
Salsify, peeled and cut into 5 cm / 2 in lengths	100 g	100%	① Vacuum seal together.
			② Cook sous vide in 95 °C / 203 °F bath for 1 h.
Extra virgin olive oil	20 g	20%	③ Serve, or cool and refrigerate.
Water	15 g	15%	
Lime juice	1.5 g	1.5%	
Salt	1 g	1%	

from page 5·18

SWEET POTATO FONDANT

Yields 200 g

INGREDIENT	QUANTITY	SCALING	PROCEDURE
White sweet potatoes (satsuma imo), peeled	175 g	100%	① Use ring cutter to cut potatoes into tubes 4 cm / 1½ in thick and 6 cm / 2½ in. in diameter.
Water	125 g	71.4%	② Vacuum seal together with potatoes.
Unsalted butter, melted	27.5 g	15.7%	③ Cook sous vide in 95 °C / 203 °F bath for 45 min.
Salt	4.5 g	2.6%	④ Serve, or cool and refrigerate.

from page 5·39

LOBSTER MUSHROOM CONFIT

Yields 200 g

INGREDIENT	QUANTITY	SCALING	PROCEDURE
Lobster mushroom	200 g	100%	① Vacuum seal together.
Carotene butter (or unsalted butter)	100 g	50%	② Cook sous vide in 80 °C / 176 °F bath for 40 min.
			③ Serve, or refrigerate until use.
Salt	4 g	2%	

from page 5·187

VARIATION: Cooking Fruits or Vegetables Sous Vide for Puree

① Select and prep ingredients. See the table below for recommendations. Peel, stem, or pit the produce to remove coarse or bitter components and to simplify handling after cooking. Cut evenly.

② Vacuum seal. See chapter 9 on Cooking Sous Vide, page 2·192, for details.

③ Cook. Recommended cooking temperatures and times appear in the table below, along with references to recipes elsewhere in the book.

④ Puree until smooth. Use a blender or food processor, and then pass through a fine sieve, ricer, or food mill. See page 2·424 for more details.

Best Bets for Cooking Fruits or Vegetables Sous Vide for Purees

Ingredient	Cut to (cm)	Cut to (in)	Cook (°C)	Cook (°F)	Cook (h)	See page
apples, peeled	quarters, cored		88	190	2	next page
bananas, peel on	whole		88	190	12 min	41
blackberries	whole		65	149	1	
dates, pitted	whole		80	176	2	next page
garlic	cloves, peeled		88	190	1	
kohlrabi	7.5	3	88	190	1½	
mangoes	5	2	75	167	20 min	
mushrooms, dried	whole		90	194	1	
mushrooms, fresh	whole		90	194	2	
nettles	leaves		95	203	10 min	
onions and shallots	7.5	3	88	190	2	
pears, peeled	halves, cored		88	190	1½	
potatoes, peeled	7.5	3	100	212	35 min	148, 151
rhubarb	7.5	3	88	190	1	
rutabagas	7.5	3	85	185	2	
spinach	leaves		90	194	7 min	
squash, winter varieties (Hokkaido, kabocha, kuri)	7.5	3	90	194	45 min	39
tomatoes, peeled and seeded	quarters, cored		85	185	25 min	
turnips	7.5	3	85	185	30 min	
watercress	leaves		90	194	10 min	56

from page 3·290

SALTED CARAMEL APPLE PUREE

Yields 200 g

INGREDIENT	QUANTITY	SCALING	PROCEDURE
Sugar	40 g	27%	① Cook to dark caramel, about 4 min.
Apple cider (store-bought)	80 g	52%	② Deglaze caramel.
			③ Cool syrup to room temperature.
Apples (firm and tart), peeled, cored, and quartered	150 g	100%	④ Vacuum seal together with syrup.
			⑤ Cook sous vide in 90 °C / 194 °F bath for 2½ h.
			⑥ Transfer from vacuum bag to small pan.
Lemon juice	2.5 g	1.7%	⑦ Reduce juice, basting apple constantly, to thick syrup, about 5 min.
Clarified brown butter	2 g	1.3%	
Salt	1 g	0.7%	
Xanthan gum	0.3 g	0.2%	⑧ Puree with apples and syrup to smooth consistency.
			⑨ Pass through fine sieve.
			⑩ Refrigerate.

from page 5·20

TAMARIND PASTE

Yields 300 g

INGREDIENT	QUANTITY	SCALING	PROCEDURE
Tamarind, pulp with seeds and fibers	350 g	100%	① Vacuum seal together.
			② Cook sous vide in 80 °C / 170 °F bath for 30 min.
Water	125 g	36%	③ Press through fine sieve to form fine paste, and refrigerate until use.

from page 5·99

DATE PUREE

Yields 400 g

INGREDIENT	QUANTITY	SCALING	PROCEDURE
Dates, pitted	300 g	100%	① Vacuum seal together.
Water	90 g	30%	② Cook sous vide in 80 °C / 176 °F bath for 2 h.
Ginger juice	9 g	3%	③ Blend fully.
Salt	1.2 g	0.4%	④ Press through fine sieve.
Black pepper, finely ground	1 g	0.3%	⑤ Discard pulp, and refrigerate puree until use.
Cardamom pods	0.2 g	0.1%	

from page 5·122

VARIATION: Cooking Fruits or Vegetables Sous Vide in Sugar Syrup

① Make the syrup. Use equal amounts of water and sugar (sucrose or other, less sweet sugars such as isomalt or glucose syrup), or adjust the sweetness to accommodate your taste and the sweetness of the fruit. Fully dissolve the sugar in the water.

② Select and prep ingredients. The table below offers some good options. For easy handling after cooking, peel away tough skins, remove pits, and cut evenly.

③ Add syrup, and vacuum seal. The syrup column in the table below indicates the quantity to use relative to the weight of the fruit. For example, add 20 g of syrup to the sous vide bag for every 100 g of dried apricot.

④ Cook. Recommended cooking temperatures and times appear in the table below, along with references to recipes elsewhere in this book.

Best Bets for Cooking Fruits Sous Vide in Sugar Syrup Until Tender

Ingredient	Prep	Syrup (scaling)*	Cook (°C)	(°F)	(h)	See page
apples	peeled, halved, cored	50%	90	194	3	
apricots, dry	whole	20%	80	176	1	217
chestnuts	peeled, whole	100%	90	194	12	
citrus fruits	whole	100%	90	194	4	
(oranges, limes, lemons,	segments	30%	88	190	40 min	
mandarins, kumquats)	quarters	40%	88	190	12	
cranberries	whole	10%	88	190	45 min	
grapes	whole, peeled	10%	83	181	8 min	
grapefruits	peels with pith only	200%	90	194	5	this page
Buddha's hand lemons	cut into fingers	100%	75	167	2	
quinces	peeled, halved, cored	100%	95	203	8	

from page 3·291   *(set weight of fruit to 100%)

PINK GRAPEFRUIT CONFIT

Yields 250 g

INGREDIENT	QUANTITY	SCALING	PROCEDURE
Pink grapefruit peel with pith from one grapefruit, pulp reserved for garnish	200 g	100%	① Cut grapefruit peel into eight equal pieces. ② Blanch three times, starting from cold water each time.
Water	450 g	225%	③ Combine water and salt, and bring to boil.
Salt	60 g	30%	④ Add peel pieces, and simmer for 8 min. ⑤ Drain, rinse, and cool. ⑥ Reserve.
Fructose	210 g	105%	⑦ Stir together to make syrup.
Water	210 g	105%	⑧ Add blanched peel pieces to syrup.
Isomalt	92 g	46%	⑨ Cook sous vide in 90 °C / 194 °F bath for 4 h.
Citric acid	4.5 g	2.25%	⑩ Cool in ice-water bath, remove peel pieces from bag, and reserve syrup. ⑪ Dice chilled peel pieces finely, and return to syrup. ⑫ Vacuum seal, and refrigerate until use.

from page 5·226

VARIATION: Cooking Heat-Sensitive Vegetables Sous Vide

① Select and prep ingredients.
② Vacuum seal. See chapter 9 on Cooking Sous Vide, page 2·192, for details.
③ Cook. Recommended cooking temperatures and times appear in the table at right.

Best Bets for Warming Vegetables Sous Vide

Vegetable	Prep	Warm (°C)	(°F)	(min)	See page
asparagus	whole, stalks peeled	70	158	5	
corn	cobb	60	140	15	
		70	158	15	
fava beans	peeled	75	167	25	256
green chickpeas	whole	75	167	20	
kohlrabi	thinly sliced	75	167	20	
peas	peeled	70	158	18	256
spring turnips	quartered	70	158	15	
young carrots	whole, peeled	75	167	45	
zucchini	thinly sliced	75	167	20	

from page 3·292

RED WINE CABBAGE

Yields 375 g

INGREDIENT	QUANTITY	SCALING	PROCEDURE
Red cabbage leaves	100 g	100%	① Vacuum seal.
			② Blanch sous vide in 90 °C / 194 °F bath for 4 min.
			③ Cool in ice-water bath, and remove from bag immediately.
			④ Trim off and discard larger ribs; julienne leaves finely.
			⑤ Reserve.
Red wine (dry)	200 g	200%	⑥ Combine, and reduce to 200 g.
Red cabbage juice	180 g (from about 300 g cabbage)	180%	⑦ Add julienned cabbage leaves, and finish cooking through, about 1 min.
Pineapple juice (fresh)	65 g (from about 100 g pineapple)	65%	
Red wine vinegar	50 g	50%	
Red onion juice	40 g (from about 100 g onions)	40%	
Lime juice	1.2 g	1.2%	⑧ Season cabbage mixture.
Salt	to taste		
Unsalted butter	40 g	40%	⑨ Warm cabbage and fold in remaining ingredients.
Pineapple, small dice	35 g	35%	
Coriander seeds, toasted and coarsely crushed	2 g	2%	
Lime zest, finely grated	0.5 g	0.5%	

from page 5·105

Best Bets for Potato Purees

Recipe	Potato solid	(scaling)	Liquid	(scaling)	Fat	(scaling)	Other ingredients	(scaling)	See page
Robuchon pommes purée	Ratte or fingerling	100%	whole milk crème fraîche	25% 6%	unsalted butter	50%	salt	2.0%	
Blumenthal puree	Charlotte	100%	whole milk	20%	unsalted butter	30%	salt	2.0%	
fluffy mash	Russet	100%	whole milk	15%	unsalted butter	15%	salt	1.5%	
potato foam	Yukon Gold	100%	vegetable broth or milk heavy cream	60% 50%	olive oil	14%	salt	1.5%	324
pommes aligot	Belle de Fontenay or Yukon Gold	100%	crème fraîche	25%	Cantal or Gruyère cheese, grated unsalted butter	80% 10%	salt	1.5%	
roasted potato puree	Yukon Gold dried potato flakes	100% 10%	Yukon Gold potato juice	65%	unsalted butter	73%	salt Ultra-Sperse 3	2.5% 1.0%	5·5

from page 3·297

POTATO PUREE

Yields 700 g

INGREDIENT	QUANTITY	SCALING	PROCEDURE
Yukon Gold potatoes, peeled	375 g	250%	① Juice potatoes in vegetable juicer. ② Centrifuge juice at 27,500*g* for 1 h. ③ Decant juice through fine sieve. ④ Vacuum seal. ⑤ Cook sous vide in 90 °C / 194 °F bath for 20 min. ⑥ Pass through fine sieve, and reserve 150 g.
Potato juice, from above	150 g	100%	⑦ Warm butter over low heat.
Clarified unsalted butter	37.5 g	25%	⑧ Add potato flakes and toast, stirring constantly, until golden brown, about 7 min.
Instant potato flakes	37.5 g	25%	⑨ Add potato juice, bring to boil, and remove from heat.
Unsalted butter, melted	200 g	133%	⑩ Fold butter in gently until melted. ⑪ Reserve 425 g.
Yukon Gold potatoes	325 g	216%	⑫ Bake in 200 °C / 400 °F oven for 1 h. ⑬ Cut potatoes in half, and scoop out hot flesh. ⑭ Pass through fine-mesh drum sieve. ⑮ Reserve 280 g of sieved potatoes.
Potato juice–butter mixture, from above	425 g	283%	⑯ Whisk Ultra-Sperse into potato juice–butter mixture over low heat until warm. ⑰ Whisk in sieved, baked potatoes slowly.
Sieved potatoes, from above	280 g	186%	
Ultra-Sperse A (National Starch brand)	3.5 g	2.3%	
Grain mustard, optional	30 g	20%	⑱ Season and stir in mustard, if desired.
Salt	to taste		

from page 5·8

COOKING PLANT FOODS UNDER PRESSURE

Best Bets for Pressure-Cooking Plant Foods

Ingredient	Advantage	See page
Quince, pears	develops flavors and colors	280
Caramelized coconut milk, onion soup		214
Chickpeas, white beans, other legumes	browns	5·138
Steel-cut oatmeal, pearl barley, other grains	accelerates softening	3·304
Whole citrus fruits, fresh coconut, nuts, other tough plant foods	softens	
Seeds, including mustard, sesame, sunflower		151

from page 3·300

BAKED BEANS

Yields 700 g

INGREDIENT	QUANTITY	SCALING	PROCEDURE
Dry navy beans	200 g	100%	① Soak in water, refrigerated, for 8 h.
			② Rinse beans.
			③ Place in fresh water, and pressure-cook at gauge pressure of 1 bar / 15 psi for 25 min.
			④ Cool in cooking water.
Brown pork stock see page 6	300 g	150%	⑤ Combine to make sauce.
			⑥ Bring to boil.
Sweet onions, finely minced	65 g	32.5%	⑦ Skim, and reduce to 250 g, or 150 g for thicker sauce.
Grade B maple syrup	40 g	20%	⑧ Vacuum seal sauce with cooled beans.
Pomegranate molasses (store-bought)	30 g	15%	⑨ Cook sous vide in 80 °C / 176 °F bath for 1 h.
Tomato confit see page 179	30 g	15%	
Bourbon (Wild Turkey brand)	20 g	10%	
Worcestershire sauce	18 g	9%	
Dijon mustard	15 g	7.5%	
Smoked Hungarian pepper, hydrated, and sieved	8 g	4%	
Smoked ham hock meat, finely minced	60 g	30%	⑩ Add to cooked beans.
Salt	to taste		⑪ Season.
Sherry vinegar	to taste		

from page 5·77

PRESSURE-COOKED TARBAIS BEANS

Yields 200 g

INGREDIENT	QUANTITY	SCALING	PROCEDURE
Sweet onions, thinly sliced	40 g	27%	① Sweat together in pressure cooker until onions are translucent.
Bacon, thinly sliced	30 g	20%	
Rendered duck fat	10 g	7%	
Garlic, thinly sliced	5.5 g	3.7%	
Thyme	0.5 g	0.3%	
Black pepper, cracked	0.2 g	0.13%	
Brown pork stock see page 6	400 g	267%	② Deglaze pressure cooker.
Dry tarbais beans (or navy beans)	150 g	100%	③ Add to pressure cooker.
Calcium chloride	1 g	0.67%	④ Pressure-cook at gauge pressure of 1 bar / 15 psi for 45 min.
Salt	to taste		⑤ Season.

from page 5·83

CARAMELIZED CARROT SOUP

Yields 1 kg

INGREDIENT	QUANTITY	SCALING	PROCEDURE
Young carrots, peeled and cored	500 g	100%	① Cut into 1.5 cm / ⅝ in pieces.
Unsalted butter	80 g	16%	② Melt butter in pressure cooker.
Salt	7.5 g	1.5%	③ Add carrot slices, salt, and baking soda.
Baking soda	2.5 g	0.5%	④ Pressure-cook at gauge pressure of 1 bar / 15 psi for 20 min to caramelize.
			⑤ Pour cold water over cooker to depressurize quickly.
			⑥ Blend mixture to smooth puree, and press through fine sieve.
Carrot juice, brought to simmer and centrifuged see page 2·360	635 g (from 1.4 kg of carrots)	127%	⑦ Blend with puree, and bring to simmer.
Water	as needed		⑧ Blend into soup to achieve desired viscosity.
Carotene butter (or unsalted butter) optional, see page 40	60 g	12%	⑨ Blend into soup.
Young ginger, finely diced	4 g	0.8%	⑩ Remove from heat, and season with more salt, if desired.
Tarragon, finely minced	2.5 g	0.5%	⑪ Garnish.
Ajowain seed, lightly crushed	0.5 g	0.1%	
Licorice powder, optional	0.5 g	0.1%	

from page 3·301

AUTOCLAVED ONION SOUP

Yields 700 g

INGREDIENT	QUANTITY	SCALING	PROCEDURE
Sweet onions	1 kg	500%	① Juice 500 g of onions, and reserve 200 g of resulting juice.
			② Slice remaining 500 g of onions thinly.
			③ Pack sliced onions into two 475 ml / 1 pt canning jars, and reserve.
Onion juice, from above	200 g	100%	④ Combine.
Red port (dry)	40 g	20%	⑤ Pour mixture over packed onions, and seal jars. Do not overtighten, or jars may explode.
Unsalted butter, cubed	35 g	17.5%	
Sugar	12 g	6%	⑥ Cook in **130 °C / 265 °F** autoclave for 20 min. Alternatively, pressure-cook in canner or pressure cooker at gauge pressure of 1 bar / 15 psi for 40 min.
Baking soda	1.5 g	0.75%	
Black peppercorns (whole)	1 g	0.5%	
Thyme	0.5 g	0.25%	
Salt	to taste		⑦ Season soup.
Sherry vinegar	to taste		⑧ Portion evenly among four bowls.
Clarified unsalted butter, melted (or rendered veal marrow fat)	28 g	14%	⑨ Spoon thin layer of melted butter over each portion to prevent any cloudiness caused by cheese foam.
Cheese foam optional, see page 317	80 g	40%	⑩ Siphon onto soup.

from page 3·302

The combination of pressure-cooking and baking soda can also be applied to make a baked-potato consommé. Roast 100 g of russet potato skins until golden, combine with 400 g russet potato juice and 1.6 g of baking soda, and then pressure-cook as described in step 6.

CRISPY BOILED PEANUTS

Yields 120 g

INGREDIENT	QUANTITY	SCALING	PROCEDURE
Water	200 g	200%	① Combine, and pressure-cook at gauge pressure of 1 bar / 15 psi for 25 min.
Raw peanuts, shelled	100 g	100%	② Transfer boiled peanuts to dehydrator tray.
			③ Dehydrate at 60 °C / 140 °F for 12 h.
			④ Deep-fry in 190 °C / 375 °F oil for 1 min.
			⑤ Drain on paper towels, cool, and reserve.
Water	100 g	100%	⑥ Combine; let seaweed soak for 30 min at room temperature.
Dried laver (seaweed)	20 g	20%	⑦ Strain to remove excess liquid from seaweed.
Sugar	20 g	20%	⑧ Dehydrate seaweed at 60 °C / 140 °F for 12 h.
Salt	2 g	2%	⑨ Deep-fry in 190 °C / 375 °F oil for about 1 min.
Monosodium glutamate (MSG), optional	1 g	1%	⑩ Drain on paper towels, cool, and measure 25 g.
Demerara sugar	2 g	2%	⑪ Grind together.
Chili powder	1 g	1%	⑫ Toss with cooled peanuts and reserved seaweed.
Salt	0.5 g	0.5%	

from page 3·303

PRESSURE-COOKED SESAME SEEDS

Yields 125 g

INGREDIENT	QUANTITY	SCALING	PROCEDURE
Water	250 g	500%	① Boil seeds in water for 2 min to remove bitterness.
Raw sesame seeds	50 g	100%	② Place blanched seeds and water in pressure cooker.
			③ Pressure-cook at gauge pressure of 1 bar / 15 psi for 1½ h.
			④ Remove mixture from cooker, and cool at room temperature.
			⑤ Strain seeds, and reserve.
Toasted sesame oil	40 g	80%	⑥ Combine.
Salt	to taste		⑦ Toss oil with cooled seeds, and season.

The same procedure used to pressure-cook the sesame seeds can also be applied to cook mustard seeds. Simply replace the toasted sesame oil with good-quality olive oil or mustard-seed oil.

from page 3·303

POTATO PUREE

INSPIRED BY JOËL ROBUCHON, JEFFREY STEINGARTEN, AND HESTON BLUMENTHAL

Yields 1 kg

INGREDIENT	QUANTITY	SCALING
Yukon Gold potatoes, peeled and skins reserved	500 g	100%
Water	2 kg	400%
Sugar	20 g	4%
Unsalted butter, cubed	250 g	50%
Whole milk	125 g	25%
Crème fraîche	30 g	6%
Salt	to taste	

Flavors can be infused into the liquids prior to using them; for instructions, see page 2·310. You can also use meat or vegetable stocks as liquids. If using fat-free liquids, supplement with a fat such as butterfat (one of our favorites), rendered chicken fat, or olive oil.

from page 3·296

① Peel and cut potatoes evenly, saving peels, and then rinse the potatoes.

② Vacuum seal potatoes with peelings and water (and sugar, if any), and then cook sous vide in a 70 °C / 158 °F bath for 35 min. See the table on page 148 for recommended liquids and quantities, which are expressed as a percentage of the weight of the potatoes after cooking. You can substitute the liquid from the bag for liquids in the recipe.

③ Remove potatoes from bag, drain, and cool completely.

④ Optionally, sauté instant potato flakes in butter until golden. Puree them using a mortar and pestle, and reserve for use as a flavor enhancer.

⑤ Boil potatoes until tender. Cooking times vary with the variety of potatoes and thickness of cut, but 15–25 min is typical.

⑥ Drain, and then press potatoes through ricer or food mill directly over cubed butter. Then fold the potatoes with the butter.

⑦ Pass potatoes through a sieve for a smoother texture. Robuchon's silky potatoes recipe, for example, calls for three passes through the sieve. We find that one pass through a very fine sieve is enough. At this point, the puree can be refrigerated for later use.

⑧ Warm the liquid (including skin infusion, if prepared), and whisk into the potato mixture to the desired consistency. Add pureed potato flakes if made in step 4.

⑨ Season with salt, and gently fold in Ultra-Sperse 3 or any other starch called for in the recipe.

⑩ Optionally, add cheese, and stir until fully melted and incorporated.

⑪ Serve warm.

RISOTTOS

PARBOILING RISOTTO

① Freeze a sheet tray, and bring a pan of water to a boil.
② Parboil the grains. See the table below for recommended times.
③ Drain with a fine sieve.
④ Spread the grains evenly in a thin layer on the chilled tray to cool.
⑤ Cover tightly with plastic wrap or vacuum seal. Refrigerate until needed, but for no more than one week.
⑥ Finish cooking for the time recommended in the table. Follow steps 8–10 on page 153.
⑦ Season. If using a non-starchy grain you may need to thicken (see page 156).

VARIATION: PRESSURE-COOKING RISOTTO

① Freeze a sheet tray.
② Combine grains with twice their weight in water in pressure cooker. Parcook for time recommended in the table below.
③ Follow steps 3–7 at left.

VARIATION: COOKING RISOTTO SOUS VIDE

① Preheat the water bath to 90 °C / 194 °F.
② Vacuum seal the grains with twice their weight in liquid.
③ Parcook. See the cook sous vide column in the table below for recommended times.
④ Chill in an ice-water bath. Refrigerate in the bag until needed.
⑤ Follow steps 6 and 7 at left.

Best Bets for Risotto

Grain	Yield after cooking*	Boil (min)	Pressure-cook (min)	Cook sous vide (min)	For boiled (min)	For pressure-cooked (min)	For sous vide (min)	Sauce or finish	See page
amaranth, rinsed well	190%	13	4	17	1½	2	2	thicken	156
bomba rice	240%	8	4	n/a	4½	3	n/a	mantecato	next page
brown rice	225%	12	6	30	6	5	4	mantecato	
forbidden rice	150%	17	7	23	3	3	3	integral sauce	
pearl barley	185%	18	12	25	4	4	5	thicken	156
pine nuts	110%	9	7	25	1	½	2	thicken	155
quinoa	235%	7	2	10	2	3	2	mantecato	156
risotto rices (Arborio, carnaroli)	200%	6	3	n/a	3	3	n/a	mantecato	153
short-grain Japanese rice	210%	4	2½	n/a	3	2	n/a	thicken	
spelt, soaked overnight	150%	15	12	25	3	4	3	integral sauce	156
steel-cut oats, rinsed	185%	7	5	9	2½	2	2	thicken	154
wild rice	150%	30	25	45	2½	2	4	mantecato	

from page 3·305   *(final cooked weight of each grain—for example, every 100 g of dry bomba rice yields 240 g when cooked)

STEAMED STICKY RICE

Yields 150 g

INGREDIENT	QUANTITY	SCALING	PROCEDURE
White chicken stock or water see page 6	60 g	100%	① Hand-blend together. ② Reserve refrigerated.
Coconut milk	40 g	67%	
Clarified unsalted butter, warmed	12 g	20%	
Salt	2 g	3.5%	
Water	480 g	800%	③ Combine.
Sticky rice	60 g	100%	④ Refrigerate for 12 h to soak rice. ⑤ Drain rice. Spread on cheesecloth-lined perforated tray. ⑥ Steam rice for 30 min. Allow to rest, uncovered, for 5 min. ⑦ Warm reserved stock and coconut milk mixture, and fold into cooked rice.

from page 5·119

RISOTTO MILANESE INSPIRED BY GUALTIERO MARCHESI

Yields 250 g

① Freeze a sheet tray to use for cooling the rice.
② Bring stock to boil.
③ Sauté onions and shallots. When translucent, add rice, and continue sautéing until also translucent, about 5 min.
④ Deglaze pan with wine.
⑤ Ladle 100 g of stock into pan, and parcook over high heat. Add two more 100 g ladlefuls of stock, allowing each amount to be fully absorbed before adding another. Parcook for exactly 6 min.
⑥ Drain with a fine sieve, reserving any liquid.
⑦ Spread the risotto in a thin layer on the chilled tray, and cover tray tightly with plastic wrap. Refrigerate until needed. Up to this point, you can substitute other parcooking techniques such as sous vide or pressure cooking (see previous page).
⑧ To finish cooking, put cooled, parcooked risotto in pan, and add remaining stock. Cook for another 3 min for al dente or until desired texture is achieved.
⑨ Remove from heat, and fold in cheese, butter, saffron, and pepper. Season with salt.
⑩ Spoon one portion of risotto onto center of plate or bowl. Garnish with gold leaf.

INGREDIENT	QUANTITY	SCALING
Sous vide vegetable stock see page 13	400 g	267%
Olive oil	45 g	30%
Yellow onions, finely minced	50 g	33%
Shallots, finely minced	10 g	6.5%
Carnaroli rice	150 g	100%
Italian white wine (dry)	100 g	67%
Parmigiano Reggiano cheese, finely grated	57 g	38%
Unsalted butter, cubed	30 g	20%
Saffron threads	0.4 g	0.25%
Black pepper, finely ground	to taste	
Salt	to taste	
Gold leaf	four sheets	

from page 3·306

PAELLA RICE

Yields 350 g

INGREDIENT	QUANTITY	SCALING	PROCEDURE
Spanish onions, finely minced	25 g	20%	① Sauté together in pressure cooker until tender and translucent, about 7 min.
Olive oil	20 g	16%	
Piquillo pepper, finely minced	20 g	16%	
Sweet pimento pepper, finely minced	15 g	12%	
Smoked bomba rice (or regular bomba rice) see page 183	125 g	100%	② Add rice to onion mixture, and cook until translucent, about 2 min.
Paella stock see page 9	325 g	260%	③ Add wine and 150 g of stock to rice and onion mixture, and pressure-cook at gauge pressure of 1 bar / 15 psi for 3 min.
Spanish white wine (dry and fruity)	35 g	28%	④ Run cold water over sealed pressure cooker.
			⑤ Drain rice, discarding liquid.
			⑥ Spread rice on chilled baking sheet to speed cooling.
			⑦ Transfer to container, and refrigerate rice and remaining 175 g of paella stock separately until use.
Saffron threads	2 g	1.6%	⑧ Finish cooking paella rice by simmering, while adding remaining stock a little at a time, until rice is al dente, about 5 min.
Salt	to taste		⑨ Remove from heat, add saffron, and season with salt.

from page 5·241

SOUS VIDE CLAM AND OAT RISOTTO

Yields 585 g

INGREDIENT	QUANTITY	SCALING	PROCEDURE
Water	150 g	150%	① Vacuum seal together.
Steel-cut oats, rinsed with warm water to remove starch	100 g	100%	② Cook sous vide in 90 °C / 194 °F bath for 10 min.
			③ Strain, and reserve liquid.
			④ Cool oats, and reserve.
Mussel juice *see page 37*	50 g	50%	
Geoduck clams, belly meat only	100 g	100%	⑤ Vacuum seal.
			⑥ Cook sous vide in 50 °C / 122 °F bath for 30 min.
			⑦ Slice thinly, and reserve.
Montpellier butter *see page 298*	100 g	100%	⑧ Melt in pan and then add cooled oats.
			⑨ Stir until warmed through, and then add reserved cooking liquid as necessary to achieve desired consistency.
Salt	to taste		⑩ Season oats, and reserve warm.
Wild arugula	25 g	25%	⑪ Combine in small bowl, and toss to coat evenly.
Extra, virgin olive oil	15 g	15%	⑫ Spoon oats in thin layers in warmed bowls.
Leeks, whites only, fine julienne	15 g	15%	⑬ Top each portion with geoduck belly.
			⑭ Garnish with salad.
Radishes, fine julienne	15 g	15%	
Champagne vinegar	10 g	10%	
Young ginger, fine julienne	7.5 g	7.5%	

from page 3·308

PRESSURE-COOKED VEGETABLE RISOTTO

Yields 600 g

INGREDIENT	QUANTITY	SCALING	PROCEDURE
Shallots, minced	40 g	20%	① Sauté shallots in uncovered pressure cooker until translucent.
Vegetable oil	20 g	10%	
Carnaroli rice	200 g	100%	② Add to shallots, and sauté until slightly toasted and translucent, about 2 min.
White vegetable stock *see page 6*	180 g	90%	③ Stir liquids into rice mixture.
			④ Pressure-cook at gauge pressure of 1 bar / 15 psi for 5½ min.
Carrot juice	110 g	55%	⑤ Pour cold water over pressure cooker to quickly depressurize.
Celery juice	110 g	55%	
Vermouth	50 g	25%	
Aged Gouda cheese, finely grated	100 g	50%	⑥ Mix into hot risotto.
Unsalted butter, cubed	12 g	6%	
Salt	to taste		⑦ Season risotto.

from page 3·308

BRAISED PINE NUTS WITH WINTER SQUASH

Yields 500 g

INGREDIENT	QUANTITY	SCALING	PROCEDURE
White veal stock see page 6	250 g	250%	① Puree until smooth, and reserve.
Tomato confit see page 179	10 g	10%	
Kabocha squash juice	1 kg (from 4 kg squash)	1,000%	② Bring to simmer, and remove from heat. ③ Strain through fine sieve to clarify, and reserve.
White wine (dry)	75 g	75%	④ Reduce to 50 g, about 5 min, and reserve.
Olive oil	25 g	25%	⑤ Sauté until tender.
Shallots, finely minced	25 g	25%	
Pine nuts, lightly toasted	100 g	100%	⑥ Add to shallots, and deglaze with wine reduction. ⑦ Add stock mixture and kabocha squash juice. ⑧ Pressure-cook at gauge pressure of 1 bar / 15 psi for 7 min. ⑨ Cool. ⑩ Drain, reserving pine nuts and liquid separately. ⑪ Reduce liquid to form glaze. ⑫ Fold glaze into reserved pine nuts, and cool. ⑬ Vacuum seal, and refrigerate.
Kuri squash, peeled and cut into large dice	100 g	100%	⑭ Vacuum seal. ⑮ Cook sous vide in 90 °C / 194 °F bath for 1¼ h. ⑯ Pass through fine sieve.
Extra virgin olive oil	10 g	10%	
Salt	to taste		⑰ Season kuri squash puree, and measure 80 g.
Pickled butternut squash, drained, from above	100 g	100%	⑱ Reheat reserved pine nuts, and fold into kuri squash puree. ⑲ Fold in pickled butternut squash, olive oil, and cheese.
Extra virgin olive oil	15 g	15%	
Parmigiano-Reggiano cheese, grated	12 g	12%	
Saffron threads	0.1 g	0.1%	⑳ Season squash mixture.
Black pepper, freshly ground and sifted	to taste		
Orange zest, grated	to taste		
Salt	to taste		

from page 5·65

RAGOUT OF GRAINS

Yields 280 g

INGREDIENT	QUANTITY	SCALING	PROCEDURE
Button mushrooms, peeled	2 kg	2,000%	① Coat mushrooms in oil.
Grapeseed oil	100 g	100%	② Roast in 175 °C / 350 °F oven until golden, about 30 min.
Water	800 g	800%	③ Place with roasted mushrooms in pot, and simmer for 1 h.
			④ Strain.
			⑤ Measure and reserve 1 kg of mushroom stock, divided into four portions of 250 g each.
			⑥ Measure and reserve 25 g more of mushroom stock for use during finishing.
Spelt, soaked for 12 h	35 g	35%	⑦ Combine with 250 g mushroom stock and pressure-cook at gauge pressure of 1 bar / 15 psi for 12 min.
			⑧ Drain, cool, and refrigerate.
Pearl barley, rinsed	40 g	40%	⑨ Combine with 250 g mushroom stock and pressure-cook at gauge pressure of 1 bar / 15 psi for 12 min.
			⑩ Drain, cool, and refrigerate.
Quinoa	35 g	35%	⑪ Combine with 250 g mushroom stock and pressure-cook at gauge pressure of 1 bar / 15 psi for 2 min.
			⑫ Drain, cool, and refrigerate.
Sprouted brown rice	35 g	35%	⑬ Combine with 250 g mushroom stock and pressure-cook at gauge pressure of 1 bar / 15 psi for 6 min.
			⑭ Strain, cool, and reserve.
Raw foie gras, brought to room temperature	20 g	20%	⑮ Drain.
Unsalted butter, cubed, brought to room temperature	20 g	20%	⑯ Pass through fine sieve, and whisk with butter.
			⑰ Vacuum seal foie gras butter, and refrigerate.
Shiitake mushrooms, finely minced	100 g	100%	⑱ Sauté mushrooms in duck fat until light golden and tender, about 10 min.
			⑲ Add cooked grains, and warm through.
Shallots, finely minced	75 g	75%	⑳ Finish with reserved foie gras butter, brown chicken jus, and mushroom stock.
Seasonal wild mushrooms, finely minced	40 g	40%	
Rendered duck fat	45 g	45%	
Brown chicken jus see page 34	25 g	25%	
Mushroom stock, from above	25 g	25%	
Lemon juice	to taste		㉑ Season ragout.
Salt	to taste		

from page 5·129

ROOT VEGETABLE RISOTTO

Yields 450 g

INGREDIENT	QUANTITY	SCALING	PROCEDURE
Shallots, finely minced	60 g	50%	① Sauté shallots until tender.
Olive oil	48 g	40%	
White wine	160 g	133%	② Deglaze shallots, and reduce until dry.
Carrots, cut like rice	120 g	100%	③ Add to shallots.
Potatoes, cut like rice	120 g	100%	④ Cook together until vegetables are al dente, about 7 min.
Turnips, cut like rice	120 g	100%	
Vegetable stock see page 6	40 g	33%	⑤ Whisk together in bowl.
			⑥ Stir into cooked vegetables.
Ultra-Sperse 5 (National Starch brand)	2.4 g	2%	⑦ Bring mixture to simmer, and remove immediately from heat.
Squash puree, warmed see page 55	60 g	50%	⑧ Stir into risotto.
Unsalted butter, cubed	30 g	25%	⑨ Fold into risotto until creamy.
Parmesan cheese, finely grated	24 g	20%	
Salt	to taste		⑩ Season.

from page 3·309

MICROWAVED VEGETABLES

① Select a technique. The table below lists our recommendations.
② Prepare your ingredients in a uniform size.
③ Evenly arrange them on a microwave-safe dish, or seal as specified.
④ Microwave at the prescribed power level.

Best Bets for Microwaving Vegetables

Technique	Best Bets	Prep	Procedure	Time (min)	Power (W)
cooking root vegetables	baby beet, carrot, celery root, potato, turnip	whole	vacuum seal	3–7	800
cooking leafy greens	bok choy, broccoli, cabbage	whole	place in 2 mm / $\frac{1}{16}$ in of water in microwave-safe dish, and cover with plastic wrap	3–5	800
cooking bulbs and fibrous vegetables	artichoke, cardoon, celery, fennel, leek, onion, scallions	whole	vacuum seal	2–5	600
frying herbs	basil, carrot top, Italian parsley, sage	leaves	arrange on oiled plastic wrap	3–4	600
dehydrating raw vegetable purees into powders	beet, carrot, mushroom, parsnip, spinach	puree	spread raw puree thinly onto microwave-safe dish	12–20	200

from page 3·311

MICROWAVE-FRIED PARSLEY ADAPTED FROM HESTON BLUMENTHAL

Yields 8 g

INGREDIENT	QUANTITY	SCALING	PROCEDURE
Frying oil	as needed		① Stretch plastic wrap over microwave-safe plate, ensuring that it is flush with bottom of plate and adheres tightly to plate's edges.
			② Brush plastic wrap with thin film of oil.
Flat-leaf Italian parsley, leaves only	30 g	100%	③ Lay parsley across plastic wrap, leaving approximately 2 cm / ¾ in between leaves.
			④ Brush tops of leaves thinly with oil.
			⑤ Microwave at 600 W (75% power) for 4 min or until crisp, checking leaves every 1½ min to prevent burning.
Salt	to taste		⑥ Transfer fried parsley to paper towel–lined tray.
			⑦ Season.
			⑧ Reserve in airtight container, preferably lined with silica gel desiccant.

from page 3·312

TOMATO POWDER ADAPTED FROM THOMAS KELLER

Yields 15 g

INGREDIENT	QUANTITY	SCALING	PROCEDURE
Tomato pulp, peeled, seeded, and finely chopped	200 g	100%	① Squeeze tightly in towel to extract excess moisture.
			② Spread in thin, even layer on microwave tray lined with parchment paper.
			③ Microwave on low power for 30–40 min, or until pulp has dried completely but still retains its color.
			④ Cool to room temperature.
			⑤ Grind in coffee or spice grinder until as fine as possible.
			⑥ If some pieces do not break up during grinding, sift powder through fine mesh strainer while stirring with spoon.
			⑦ Store in covered plastic container.

Inexpensive PVC-based cling film should not be used for this technique because it poses health hazards. Use polyethylene-based films instead.

Microwave ovens can be used for dehydrating fruits, vegetables, and herbs in the same manner as this recipe. Of course, conventional methods of dehydration could also be used (see page 2·428).

from page 3·312

ARTICHOKE AND POTATO CHAAT

Yields 600 g (4 portions)

INGREDIENT	QUANTITY	SCALING	PROCEDURE
Artichoke hearts, cleaned	200 g	100%	① Combine and vacuum seal.
Water	100 g	50%	② Microwave at 800 W (full power) for 3 min, and then cool for 2 min in bag.
Extra, virgin olive oil	40 g	20%	③ Remove artichokes very carefully from bag (steam will escape), and cool completely.
Unsalted butter	32 g	16%	④ Cut into small dice, and reserve.
Fingerling potatoes (whole)	200 g	100%	⑤ Combine and vacuum seal.
			⑥ Microwave at 800 W for 3 min, and then cool for 2 min in bag.
Brown butter see page 4·213	40 g	20%	⑦ Remove potatoes very carefully from bag, and cool completely.
Water	25 g	12.5%	⑧ Cut into small dice, and reserve.
Saffron threads	0.1 g	0.05%	
Masala Sev (chickpea flour noodles), store-bought	30 g	15%	⑨ Toss with diced artichokes and potatoes.
Cashews, coarsely crushed	10 g	5%	
Cilantro leaves (small)	10 g	5%	
Dates, thinly sliced	10 g	5%	
Mint, fine julienne	5 g	2.5%	
Lime juice	to taste		⑩ Season chaat, and divide into equal portions.
Salt	to taste		
Yogurt foam see page 329	100 g	50%	⑪ Garnish chaat generously.
Tamarind paste see page 145	40 g	20%	
Chaat masala see page 50	to taste		

from page 3·313

SICHUAN BOK CHOY

Yields 350 g (4 portions)

INGREDIENT	QUANTITY	SCALING	PROCEDURE
Hoisin sauce (store-bought)	20 g	10%	① Combine, and bring to simmer.
			② Cool and reserve.
Fermented black bean and chili paste (store-bought)	15 g	7.5%	
Shaoxing wine	8 g	4%	
Soy sauce	5 g	2.5%	
Toasted-sesame oil	1 g	0.5%	
Shiitake mushroom caps (smallest possible)	100 g	50%	③ Blanch in boiling water for 2 min.
			④ Transfer to bowl, and reserve.
Rice wine vinegar	100 g	50%	⑤ Whisk together until fully dissolved.
Water	50 g	25%	⑥ Bring brine to simmer, and remove from heat.
Sugar	25 g	12.5%	⑦ Pour warm brine over blanched mushrooms.
Salt	3 g	1.5%	⑧ Cool completely to pickle mushrooms, and reserve.
Baby bok choy, cleaned and cut in half	200 g	100%	⑨ Vacuum seal together.
			⑩ Microwave at 800 W (full power) for 2 min, and then cool for 2 min in bag.
Water	50 g	25%	⑪ Remove bok choy from bag, and serve immediately.
Pressure-cooked sesame seeds see page 151	50 g	25%	⑫ Garnish bok choy with spicy sauce, pickled mushrooms, sesame seeds, and chili oil.
			⑬ Serve with steamed rice.
Dried chili oil see page 28	10 g	5%	

from page 3·313

Best Bets for Naked Frying

Ingredient	Prep (cm)	(in)	Deep-fry (min)
artichokes, baby	quartered		3
asparagus, green and white	whole		3
bok choy	quartered		4
broccoli, florets	2.5	1	3
Brussels sprouts	halved		5
cauliflower, florets	2.5	1	4
cucumber	2.5	1	4
daikon radish	1.25	0.5	8
eggplant	2.5	1	5
green beans	whole		3
scallions	whole		2
shiitake, fresh	whole		4
shiitake, dried	whole		2
squash, autumn	2.5	1	3
sunchoke	1.25	0.5	3
zucchini	1.25	0.5	1½

from page 3·320

① Prep. Preheat frying oil to 190 °C / 375 °F, and cut vegetables to dimensions indicated. The dried shiitake must be hydrated with warm water for at least 30 min before frying.
② Fry for the time indicated in the table. The vegetables typically turn very dark brown and look almost overcooked.
③ Drain, and transfer fried vegetables to a tray lined with paper towels. Season with salt.

TOASTED GARLIC CHIPS

Yields 24 pieces

INGREDIENT	QUANTITY	SCALING	PROCEDURE
Garlic cloves	50 g	100%	① Slice 1 mm / 1⁄16 in thick.
Milk, cold	as needed		② Cover garlic slices with milk, heat to 70 °C / 158 °F, and drain.
			③ Repeat two more times.
Frying oil	as needed		④ Deep-fry garlic slices in 160 °C / 320 °F oil until golden and crisp, about 5 min.
Salt	to taste		⑤ Season.
			⑥ Serve or store in cool, dry place.

from page 5·9

DEEP-FRIED BRUSSELS SPROUTS
ADAPTED FROM DAVID CHANG

Yields 350 g (four portions)

INGREDIENT	QUANTITY	SCALING	PROCEDURE
Fish sauce	130 g	26%	① Whisk together until sugar dissolves.
Lime juice	70 g	14%	② Reserve sauce.
Sugar	60 g	12%	
Water	55 g	11%	
Rice wine vinegar	25 g	5%	
Garlic clove, minced	5 g	1%	
Bird's eye chili, minced	3 g	0.6%	
Xanthan gum (Keltrol T, CP Kelco brand)	0.53 g	0.1% (0.15%)*	
Rice puffs	20 g	4%	③ Measure individually, and reserve for garnish.
Cilantro stems, 1 cm / 3⁄8 in long	10 g	2%	
Small mint leaves	4 g	0.8%	
Brussels sprouts	500 g	100%	④ Peel off tough outer leaves until only cores remain, about 2 cm / ¾ in each in diameter.
			⑤ Slice in half.
Frying oil	as needed		⑥ Deep-fry sprouts in 180 °C / 355 °F oil until tender and very dark, about 5 min.
			⑦ Drain on paper towels.
			⑧ Toss with sauce, arrange on plates, and garnish.

from page 3·321

*(% of total weight of first five ingredients)

POMMES PONT-NEUF INSPIRED BY HESTON BLUMENTHAL

Yields 350 g

INGREDIENT	QUANTITY	SCALING	PROCEDURE
Russet potatoes	500 g	100%	① Cut into batons 1.5 cm / ⅝ in thick by 1.5 cm / ⅝ in tall.
Water	500 g	100%	② Whisk sugar, salt, and baking soda into water.
Sugar	15 g	3%	③ Add potatoes and water mixture to pot, and boil for about 20 min until very tender and nearly falling apart.
Salt	7.5 g	1.5%	
Baking soda	0.75 g	0.15%	④ Drain, and place warm potatoes on wire rack in vacuum chamber.
			⑤ Pull vacuum until surfaces of chips are dry and chips feel cool, 3–4 min.
			⑥ Optionally, vacuum cool again, or air cool in single layer.
			⑦ Blanch in 150 °C / 300 °F oil until chips are mostly cooked but still pale, about 7 min.
			⑧ Deep-fry in 220 °C / 430 °F oil until crisp, about 2 min.
			⑨ Drain on paper towels.

from page 3·323

A vacuum treatment both cools and dries the exterior of the fries. Heston Blumenthal found that this process produces a thicker, crunchier crust. He does the vacuum cooling and drying step twice: first after boiling, and again after parcooking.

Air-cooling the chips after the boiling step yields a thinner, more delicate crust. To air-cool the fries, place them in a single layer on a wire rack. You can use a household fan to speed the process.

We find that vacuum cooling and drying after parfrying produces a chip that is too dry for our tastes. We prefer to vacuum cool after boiling, but to air cool after parfrying.

PECTINASE-STEEPED FRIES

ADAPTED FROM NILS NORÉN AND DAVE ARNOLD

Yields 350 g

INGREDIENT	QUANTITY	SCALING	PROCEDURE
Russet potatoes	500 g	100%	① Cut into batons 1.5 cm / ⅝ in thick by 1.5 cm / ⅝ in tall.
			② Rinse thoroughly to remove surface starch.
Water	500 g	100%	③ Combine with rinsed potatoes.
Pectinex Ultra SP-L (Novozymes brand)	2 g	0.4%	④ Soak for 1 h, and drain.
Water	500 g	100%	⑤ Vacuum seal with potatoes in one even layer.
Salt	10 g	2%	⑥ Steam at 100 °C / 212 °F for 20 min.
			⑦ Drain and cool.
			⑧ Blanch in 162 °C / 325 °F oil for 3 min, and cool.
			⑨ Deep-fry in 190 °C / 375 °F oil until crisp, about 3 min.
			⑩ Drain on paper towels.

from page 3·324

STIR-FRIED FIDDLEHEAD FERNS

Yields 155 g

INGREDIENT	QUANTITY	SCALING	PROCEDURE
Fiddlehead ferns	120 g	100%	① Stir-fry fiddleheads in very hot oil for 2 min, moving them constantly to ensure blistering without burning. Douse with stock or water, a little at a time, until cooked through.
White chicken stock or water see page 11	40 g	33%	
Frying oil	20 g	16.7%	
Alsatian bacon, small dice	20 g	16.7%	② Add garnishes and continue stir-frying for 20 s.
Scallions, fine julienne	10 g	8.3%	
Garlic, germ removed and finely minced	6 g	5%	
Black peppercorns, coarsely ground	2.5 g	2%	③ Season garnished fiddleheads, and arrange on plates.
Salt	to taste		

from page 5·119

STARCH-INFUSED FRIES

Yields 350 g

INGREDIENT	QUANTITY	SCALING	PROCEDURE
Russet potatoes	500 g	100%	① Cut into batons 1.5 cm / ⅝ in thick by 1.5 cm / ⅝ in tall, and rinse thoroughly to remove surface starch.
Water	100 g	20%	② Combine with rinsed potatoes.
Potato starch	50 g	10%	③ Vacuum seal.
			④ Refrigerate for 30 min, and drain.
Water	500 g	100%	⑤ Vacuum seal with potatoes in one even layer.
Salt	10 g	2%	⑥ Steam at 100 °C / 212 °F for 20 min.
			⑦ Drain.
			⑧ Place hot fries on wire rack in vacuum chamber.
			⑨ Pull vacuum until surfaces of fries are dry.
			⑩ Blanch in 162 °C / 325 °F oil for 3 min, and cool.
			⑪ Deep-fry in 190 °C / 375 °F oil until crisp, about 3 min.
			⑫ Drain on paper towels.

from page 3·325

ULTRASONIC FRIES

Yields 350 g

INGREDIENT	QUANTITY	SCALING	PROCEDURE
Russet potatoes	500 g	100%	① Cut into batons 1.5 cm / ⅝ in thick by 1.5 cm / ⅝ in tall, and rinse thoroughly to remove surface starch.
Water	500 g	100%	② Vacuum seal with potatoes in one even layer.
Salt	10 g	2%	③ Cook at 100 °C / 212 °F for 20 min.
			④ Transfer to ultrasonic bath, and cavitate for 45 min.
			⑤ Flip bag, and cavitate in ultrasonic bath for another 45 min.
			⑥ Drain.
			⑦ Place hot fries in single layer on wire rack.
			⑧ Cool at room temperature, with or without fan.
			⑨ Blanch in 162 °C / 325 °F oil for 3 min, and cool.
			⑩ Deep-fry in 190 °C / 375 °F oil until golden and very crisp, about 5 min.
			⑪ Drain on paper towels.

from page 3·325

STARCH-INFUSED ULTRASONIC FRIES

Yields 350 g

INGREDIENT	QUANTITY	SCALING	PROCEDURE
Russet potatoes	500 g	100%	① Cut into batons 1.5 cm / ⅝ in thick by 1.5 cm / ⅝ in tall, and rinse thoroughly to remove surface starch.
Water	500 g	100%	② Vacuum seal together with potatoes.
Salt	10 g	2%	③ Cook at 100 °C / 212 °F for 20 min.
			④ Drain. Cool, and reserve.
Water	100 g	20%	⑤ Whisk together.
Potato starch	50 g	10%	⑥ Vacuum seal carefully with cooked potatoes.
			⑦ Cavitate in ultrasonic bath for 45 min.
			⑧ Flip and cavitate in ultrasonic bath for another 45 min.
			⑨ Drain.
			⑩ Place hot fries on wire rack in vacuum chamber.
			⑪ Pull vacuum until surfaces of fries are dry.
			⑫ Blanch in 162 °C / 325 °F oil for 3 min, and cool.
			⑬ Deep-fry in 190 °C / 375 °F oil until crisp, for 3 min.
			⑭ Drain on paper towels.

from page 3·325

The chips must be cooled and dried both after the boiling step and after parfrying. Vacuum cooling and air cooling both work, but yield different textures—see page 3·322.

We use a 21 l / 5½ gal Branson 8510 ultrasonic bath set at a frequency of 40 kHz for making these fries.

FRUIT AND VEGETABLE CHIPS

Best Bets for Fried Fruit and Vegetable Chips

Ingredient	Slice (mm)	Slice (in)	Deep-fry (°C)	Deep-fry (°F)	(s)
apple	1	1/32	150	300	105
Asian pear	1	1/32	162	325	100
carrot	1	1/32	162	325	40
celery root	1–3	1/32–1/8	150	300	60
cucumber (and pickles)*	1–3	1/32–1/8	150	300	15–25
eggplant*	3	1/8	150	300	90
jalapeño*	3	1/8	150	300	15
lotus root	1–3	1/32–1/8	162	325	15–25
melon	1	1/32	150	300	105
pineapple	1	1/32	150	300	120
potato	1–3	1/32–1/8	162	325	35
strawberry*	3	1/8	150	300	40
tomato*	3	1/8	150	300	15
watermelon	1	1/32	150	300	105

from page 3·328 *(dehydrate at 60 °C / 140 °F for 1 h before frying)

① Slice evenly. See the table at left for suggested ingredients and thicknesses. Use a meat slicer, if available, to produce slices of uniform thickness.

② Mix Crisp Coat UC or potato starch with water to make a slurry. Optionally, add Methocel K100M to the slurry to reduce oil.

③ Dip slices in starch slurry, and arrange them in one layer in a sous vide bag. Vacuum seal. A full vacuum impregnates the slices with starch, yielding a texture similar to that of a thin potato chip.

④ Remove slices from bag, and pat dry.

⑤ Dehydrate (optional). For delicate fruits and vegetables such as tomatoes, cucumbers, and jalapeños, dehydrate the starch-coated slices at **50 °C / 122 °F** until completely dry, up to 2 h.

⑥ Deep-fry until crisp and golden. See the table for a recommended oil temperature and frying time.

⑦ Drain on absorbent paper towels, and season with salt.

WATERMELON CHIPS Yields 100 g

INGREDIENT	QUANTITY	SCALING
Seedless watermelon flesh, skin and pith removed	200 g (from one whole)	100%
Water	100 g	50%
Crisp Coat UC (National Starch brand) or raw potato starch	50 g	25%
Salt	to taste	
Neutral oil	as needed	

from page 3·328

Adding 0.5% of Methocel K100M by weight of slurry can reduce the oil uptake of the chips after frying by up to 20%. For regular potato chips, simply compress the potato slices with a stock solution of 100% water and 0.5% Methocel K100M before frying for similar results. The film-forming properties of methylcellulose prevent the vacuoles from absorbing as much oil upon cooling.

RESTRUCTURED POTATO CHIPS Yields 100 g

INGREDIENT	QUANTITY	SCALING
Water	200 g	400%
Instant potato flakes	50 g	100%
Raw potato starch (or Ultra-Crisp CS or Crisp Coat UC for puffed chips)	18.5 g	37%
Neutral oil	15 g	30%
Salt	1.5 g	3%

from page 3·330

To make puffed chips, use Ultra-Crisp CS or Crisp Coat UC rather than raw potato starch, and include step 5. For a great flavor addition, replace the water with cheese-infused water (see page 20).

① Combine all ingredients.

② Blend (optional). For puffed chips only, puree with hand blender or blender until smooth, about 1 min.

③ Cast mixture into circular template, 2 mm / 3/32 in thick and 7.5 cm / 3 in. in diameter.

④ Bake in **175 °C / 350 °F** oven on tray lined with silicone mat until golden and crisp, about 9 min.

⑤ Turn over (optional). For puffed chips only, flip and bake another 8–10 min to ensure they are completely baked through.

BATTER-FRYING

① Select a batter. Use the Batter Textures table at right to choose an option that yields the texture you desire.
② Mix flours or starches with seasonings. Ingredients and proportions are listed in the table below.
③ Blend liquid with rising agents.
④ Whisk liquid into dry mixture.
⑤ Pour batter into siphon (for siphoned batters only). Charge siphon with the gas listed in the scaling column.
⑥ Coat food with an adhesive (optional). Batters cling better to low-moisture foods if you first dip the food in milk, eggs, or another sticky substance.
⑦ Coat evenly in dry starch (see page 162). Shake off any excess.
⑧ Dispense batter into bowl, and coat the food evenly.
⑨ Fry. For recommended frying temperatures and times, see individual recipes.
⑩ Pat dry, and season. Salt is appropriate for most foods.

Batter Textures

	Crisp	Crunchy	Extra crispy
airy	tempura, whole egg		
lacy	yeast		crispy tempura
thin	cider		
rich		egg yolk	
dense	beignet	cornmeal	

from page 3·332

Best Bets for Batters

Batter	Flour or starch	(scaling)	Seasoning	(scaling)	Liquid	(scaling)	Rising agent	(scaling)	See page
tempura	flour	67%	n/a		sake	100%	baking powder	2%	5·197
	rice flour	67%			vodka	75%	siphon*	two charges of CO_2	
					malt syrup	8%			
whole egg	sweet-potato starch	37.5%	salt	2%	blonde ale	100%	dry yeast	0.6%	
	flour	37.5%			egg	15%	siphon*	two charges of N_2O	
yeast	Trisol (Texturas brand)	90%	salt	1%	water	100%	fresh yeast	2%	164
	flour	65%							
crispy tempura	flour	28.5%	salt	3%	water	100.0%	baking powder	0.5%	
	cornstarch	12.5%			vodka	12.5%	siphon*	two charges of N_2O	
	Ultra Crisp CS (National Starch brand)	10.0%							
cider	tapioca starch	35%	n/a		hard cider	100%	baking soda	0.75%	166
	flour	25%					siphon*	two charges of N_2O	
	xanthan gum	0.15%							
egg yolk	potato starch	50%	salt	2.5%	ice water	100%	thermal shock		
	flour	35%	Old Bay	1.0%	malt vinegar	30%			
	glutinous rice flour	15%	salt		egg yolk	8%			
beignet	flour	33.0%	salt	2%	carbonated water	100%	baking soda	1.5%	
	tapioca starch	33.0%			vodka	11%			
	trehalose	16.5%							
cornmeal	cornmeal	40.0%	salt	1.5%	buttermilk	100%	Methocel SGA 150	1.25%	
	flour	17.5%	cayenne pepper	0.5%			baking powder	0.60%	

from page 3·333   *(we use 1 l siphons; fill siphon at least half full, and adjust quantity of charges as needed)

SPOT PRAWN AND LOTUS ROOT TEMPURA WITH SMOKED WHITE SOY SAUCE

Yields 600 g

INGREDIENT	QUANTITY	SCALING	PROCEDURE
Shrimp meat	150 g	75%	① Combine, and blend to fine paste.
Lard	15 g	7.5%	
Japanese potato starch	10 g	5%	
Egg yolk	8 g	4%	
Egg white	7 g	3.5%	
Sake	7 g	3.5%	
White soy sauce	7 g	3.5%	
Ginger, mashed to paste	2 g	1%	
Salt	2 g	1%	
Young lotus roots, peeled and sliced 1 cm / ⅜ in thick	90 g	45%	② Fill cavities of lotus root slices with shrimp paste. ③ Refrigerate until firm, about 30 min.
Live spot prawns	200 g (four prawns)	100%	④ Peel. ⑤ Refrigerate.
Sake, cold	150 g	75%	⑥ Combine flour, rice flour, and baking powder for tempura batter.
Vodka	112 g	56%	⑦ Blend flour mixture with sake, vodka, and malt syrup until well incorporated.
All-purpose flour	100 g	50%	⑧ Transfer batter to siphon, and charge with two nitrous oxide cartridges. Siphon batter into bowl.
Rice flour	100 g	50%	
Malt syrup	12 g	6%	⑨ Dip lotus root slices into batter to coat evenly.
Baking powder	3 g	1.5%	⑩ Deep-fry lotus root slices and spot prawns in 190 °C / 375 °F oil until crisp and golden, about 2 min.
Smoked white soy sauce see page 183	100 g	50%	⑪ Arrange on plates, and serve with smoked white soy sauce for dipping.

from page 5·201

FRIED PICKLES

Yields 250 g

INGREDIENT	QUANTITY	SCALING	PROCEDURE
Water	200 g	80%	① Mix to make batter.
All-purpose flour	130 g	52%	② Allow to rest at room temperature for 30 min.
Trisol (Texturas brand)	180 g	72% (55%)*	
Yeast (fresh)	4 g	1.6% (0.8%)**	
Salt	2 g	0.8%	③ Season batter, and reserve.
Pickling cucumbers	250 g	100%	④ Cut into slices 6 mm / ¼ in thick, and reserve.
White wine vinegar	200 g	80 g	⑤ Combine to make brine, and let cool.
Water	150 g	60%	
Sugar	125 g	50%	
Salt	12.5 g	5%	
Garlic, thinly sliced	6.5 g	2.5%	
Celery seeds	0.5 g	0.3%	
Chili flakes	0.1 g	0.05%	
Dill	2 g	0.8%	⑥ Vacuum seal with cucumber slices and cooled brine. ⑦ Refrigerate for at least 12 h.
Frying oil	as needed		⑧ Dip pickle slices in batter. ⑨ Deep-fry in 200 °C / 390 °F oil for 2 min. ⑩ Drain on paper towels.

from page 5·75

*(% of total weight of water and flour used for batter)
**(% of total weight of first three ingredients)

CRISPY HALIBUT CHEEK ADAPTED FROM HESTON BLUMENTHAL Yields 800 g

INGREDIENT	QUANTITY	SCALING	PROCEDURE
All-purpose wheat flour	200 g	50%	① Sift together, and reserve.
Rice flour	200 g	50%	
Salt	4 g	1%	
Baking powder	3 g	0.75%	
Vodka	350 g	87.5%	② Blend.
Water	200 g	50%	③ Whisk into dry mixture until completely incorporated.
Malt syrup	12 g	3%	④ Pour into 1 l siphon, and charge with one cartridge of nitrous oxide.
			⑤ Shake vigorously and reserve siphon refrigerated.
Halibut cheeks, cleaned of connective tissue	400 g (four cheeks)	100%	⑥ Dust Trisol evenly over cheeks.
			⑦ Skewer each cheek.
Trisol (Texturas brand)	100 g	25%	⑧ Siphon batter into bowl.
			⑨ Coat cheeks evenly with foam batter.
Neutral oil	as needed		⑩ Fry in 200 °C / 400 °F oil.
			⑪ Lift extra batter from bowl with fork, and drizzle onto cheeks to build lacy surfaces. Make sure to flip cheeks in oil while drizzling batter, to build an even crust.
			⑫ Remove each cheek from oil when its core reaches 50 °C / 122 °F, about 6 min.
			⑬ Drain on paper towels.

from page 3·334

THE COLONEL'S FRIED CHICKEN INSPIRED BY COLONEL HARLAN SANDERS Yields 800 g

INGREDIENT	QUANTITY	SCALING	PROCEDURE
Chicken, drumsticks	800 g	100%	① Clean, pat dry on paper towels, and reserve.
Cake flour	200 g	25%	② Combine and reserve.
All-purpose bleached wheat flour	160 g	20%	
Whole wheat flour	32 g	4%	
Black peppercorns	10 g	1.25%	③ Grind spices and herbs finely.
White peppercorns	8 g	1%	④ Combine with flour mixture.
Paprika	4.5 g	0.56%	
Onion powder	4 g	0.5%	
Caraway seeds	2.5 g	0.31%	
Nutmeg	1.5 g	0.18%	
Sage, rubbed	0.7 g	0.08%	
Allspice, ground	0.5 g	0.06%	
Thyme	0.5 g	0.06%	
Cayenne pepper	0.3 g	0.03%	
Bay leaf	0.1 g	0.01%	
Salt	24 g	3%	⑤ Combine with seasoned flour mixture, and reserve.
Monosodium glutamate (MSG)	14 g	1.75%	
Whole milk	120 g	15%	⑥ Blend together until smooth.
Eggs	60 g	7.5%	⑦ Dip chicken pieces into egg mixture, and dredge in seasoned flour mixture.
			⑧ Pressure-fry coated chicken in 160 °C / 325 °F oil for 7 min. Alternatively, fry in 180 °C / 360 °F oil until golden and cooked through, about 12 min.

from page 3·336

MODERNIST FRIED CHICKEN

Yields 1 kg

INGREDIENT	QUANTITY	SCALING	PROCEDURE
Chicken legs with skin	1 kg (four legs)	100%	① Remove thigh bones from legs; leave lower leg bones in.
Water	500 g	50%	② Whisk together until salt dissolves to make brine.
Salt	35 g	3.5%	③ Vacuum seal with prepared chicken legs.
			④ Brine in refrigerator for 5 h, or vacuum tumble for 30 min (see page 3·152), and then drain.
Chicken skin, from whole chicken	20 g	2%	⑤ Cut pieces of skin to match dimensions of exposed thigh meat.
			⑥ Dust Activa over cut skin pieces and exposed, boneless thigh meat.
Activa RM	10 g	1%	⑦ Press matching skin pieces to meat so that no skin remains exposed.
			⑧ Wrap each leg tightly with plastic wrap, and refrigerate 12 h to let proteins bond.
Water	50 g	5%	⑨ Mix until baking soda dissolves.
Baking soda	5 g	0.5%	
Vodka	450 g	45%	⑩ Mix with baking soda solution to make brine.
			⑪ Unwrap chicken legs, and vacuum seal individually with equal portions of brine.
			⑫ Brine, refrigerated, for 3 h, or vacuum tumble for 30 min.
			⑬ Remove from bag, and pat dry.
			⑭ Vacuum seal dry chicken legs.
			⑮ Cook sous vide in 64 °C / 147 °F bath for 2 h.
			⑯ Blot dry.
Spray-dried buttermilk see page 59 or store-bought	15 g	1.5%	⑰ Whisk together spice mixture, and reserve.
Cayenne pepper	2 g	0.2%	
Bay leaf, powdered	1 g	0.1%	
Black pepper, coarsely ground	1 g	0.1%	
Frying oil	as needed		⑱ Fry thighs in 225 °C / 435 °F oil for 4 min.
			⑲ Drain on paper towels, and dust with spice mixture.

from page 3·337

OYSTER BEIGNET

Yields 12 beignets

INGREDIENT	QUANTITY	SCALING	PROCEDURE
Tapioca starch	85 g	35%	① Mix together.
All-purpose flour	60 g	25%	
Baking soda	2 g	0.85%	
Xanthan gum	0.4 g	0.17%	
Hard cider	240 g	100%	② Whisk into dry mixture to form batter.
			③ Transfer batter to 1 l whipping siphon.
			④ Charge batter-filled siphon with two nitrous oxide cartridges and shake vigorously.
Kumamoto oysters	12 oysters		⑤ Toss oysters in cornstarch and skewer them.
Cornstarch	as needed		⑥ Dispense batter into container, and dip oysters in batter to coat fully.
Salt	to taste		⑦ Deep-fry oysters briefly in 200 °C / 390 °F oil until crispy, golden, and just warmed through, about 2 min.
			⑧ Remove from skewers, dry on paper towels, and season with salt.

from page 5·28

BREADING

Breadings

Coating	Density	Texture	Oil absorption
bread crumbs	heavy	crispy	moderate
processed grain (cream of wheat, rolled oats, instant polenta, pressed rice flakes)	light	crunchy to crispy	moderate
freeze-dried vegetable flakes (carrot, corn, onion, potato)	light	very crispy	high
puffed snacks	varies	crunchy	low

Adhesives

Coating	Stickiness	Flavor
albumin powder	acceptable	egg
flour	good	raw flour
starch	good	varies, raw starch
modified starch	very good	neutral
Trisol (Texturas brand)	very good	neutral

① Prep the core ingredient, if required.
② Cut into even pieces. If the food pieces differ greatly in size, some will overcook while others don't cook enough.
③ Dust food evenly with an adhesive coating. The Adhesives table lists some that we recommend.
④ Dip in a liquid coating, and drain excess. See the Liquids table for suggestions.
⑤ Roll food in breading to cover. All of the options listed in the Breadings table can work well.
⑥ Refrigerate breaded food until crust is firm, at least 1 h.
⑦ Deep-fry until golden. We fried these in 190 °C / 375 °F oil for about 90 s. For other recommended temperatures and times, see individual recipes.
⑧ Drain on paper towels, and season.

Liquids

Coating	Film thickness	Film flavor
whole egg	thick	egg
egg yolk	medium	egg
egg white foam	medium	egg
slurry of 100% starch, 30% water	thin	neutral
methylcellulose K100M, slurry, or foam (100% water, 0.5% K100M)	thin	methylcellulose

from page 3·338–339

CRISPY OKRA

Yields 120 g

INGREDIENT	QUANTITY	SCALING	PROCEDURE
Okra, cut in half lengthwise	100 g	100%	① Combine, and let marinate for 5 min.
Lime juice	2 g	2%	② Drain.
Salt	2 g	2%	
Chili powder	1 g	1%	
Chickpea flour	35 g	35%	③ Coat okra in chickpea flour, and shake off excess.
Frying oil	as needed		④ Deep-fry okra until crispy and golden, about 3 min.
			⑤ Drain on paper towel-lined tray.

from page 3·338

CROMESQUIS INSPIRED BY MARC MENEAU

Yields 1.5 kg (50 cromesquis)

INGREDIENT	QUANTITY	SCALING	PROCEDURE
Red port, chilled	450 g	129%	① Disperse gelatin in port.
160 Bloom gelatin	50 g	14.3%	② Simmer until reduced to 200 g, and reserve warm.
Raw duck foie gras	350 g	100%	③ Cut foie gras into cubes.
			④ Sear until exteriors are golden but centers are still raw, about 1 min, and reserve warm.
Heavy cream	600 g	171%	⑤ Whisk together and season.
Black truffle juice (store-bought) or mushroom jus see page 37	50 g	14.3%	
Salt	15 g	4.3%	
Black pepper, ground	0.2 g	0.05%	
Ultra-Sperse 3 (National Starch brand)	6 g	1.7% (0.5%)*	⑥ Dry blend powders, and disperse into cold cream mixture.
			⑦ Bring to simmer while blending to hydrate fully.
Iota carrageenan	2.4 g	0.68% (0.2%)*	⑧ Blend in warm port reduction and foie gras until smooth.
Low-acyl gellan (Kelcogel F, CP Kelco brand)	1.8 g	0.51% (0.15%)*	
Black truffle, finely minced	30 g	8.5%	⑨ Fold into hot puree.
			⑩ Cast mixture in nonstick mold in layers 2 cm / ¾ in thick.
			⑪ Refrigerate until set, at least 4 h.
			⑫ Cut foie gras gel into 2.5 cm / 1 in cubes.
Trisol (Texturas brand)	as needed		⑬ Dredge cubes in Trisol.
Eggs	300 g	85%	⑭ Blend until smooth.
Egg yolks	75 g	21.4%	
Fine, dry bread crumbs	150 g	43%	⑮ Coat floured cubes in egg mixture, and then dredge in bread crumbs.
			⑯ Refrigerate cubes for 2 h to harden crusts.
Frying oil	as needed		⑰ Fry cubes in 190 °C / 375 °F oil until golden, about 2 min.
			⑱ Drain on paper towels.

from page 3·340

*(% of total weight of first five ingredients)

FRIED GREEN TOMATOES

Yields 250 g

INGREDIENT	QUANTITY	SCALING	PROCEDURE
Green tomatoes, cored	300 g	100%	① Blanch for 1 min.
			② Shock in ice-water bath.
			③ Peel off skins.
			④ Cut slices 8 mm / 5⁄16 in thick.
Cultured buttermilk	150 g	50%	⑤ Blend to make wash.
Eggs, blended	150 g	50%	
Cornmeal	100 g	35%	⑥ Mix to make cornmeal breading.
Panko	25 g	8.5%	⑦ Dredge tomato slices in wash.
Black pepper	0.8 g	0.25%	⑧ Coat slices with cornmeal breading.
Cayenne pepper	0.2 g	0.05%	
Canola oil	as needed		⑨ Deep-fry in 200 °C / 390 °F oil for 2 min.
			⑩ Drain on paper towels.
Salt	to taste		⑪ Season.

from page 5·74

CORN CROQUETTA INSPIRED BY DAVID KINCH

Yields 350 g (24 croquettas)

INGREDIENT	QUANTITY	SCALING	PROCEDURE
Frozen sweet corn, thawed	200 g	67%	① Combine, and puree until smooth.
Heavy cream	90 g	30%	② Strain through fine sieve, and reserve 300 g of corn puree.
Salt	5 g	1.7%	
Cayenne pepper	3 g	1%	
Vanilla seeds and pulp	1.5 g (from one vanilla bean)	0.5%	
Corn puree, from above	300 g	100%	③ Disperse gelatin in 100 g of reserved corn puree.
160 Bloom gelatin	9 g	3%	④ Warm mixture until gelatin is fully dissolved.
			⑤ Whisk in remaining reserved corn puree.
			⑥ Cast mixture in layer 2.5 cm / 1 in thick in nonstick mold.
			⑦ Refrigerate until set, at least 4 h.
Water	100 g	33%	⑧ Bring water to simmer.
Methylcellulose E4M	1.5 g	0.5%	⑨ Blend in methylcellulose until fully dissolved, 2–3 min.
			⑩ Refrigerate at least 4 h to hydrate.
Crisp Coat UC (National Starch brand)	5 g	1.7%	⑪ Cut gelled puree into 2.5 cm / 1 in cubes.
			⑫ Dust cubes evenly with Crisp Coat to coat.
			⑬ Whip hydrated methylcellulose with electric whisk to form stiff and foamy peaks.
			⑭ Coat cubes evenly with whisked methylcellulose, and reserve.
Corn powder, freeze-dried see page 188	50 g	16.7%	⑮ Mix to make breading.
			⑯ Dredge foam-covered cubes in breading mix.
Panko	50 g	16.7%	⑰ Refrigerate cubes to firm and bind crusts, about 30 min.
Frying oil	as needed		⑱ Fry cubes in 190 °C / 375 °F oil until golden, about 1½ min.
			⑲ Drain on paper towels.
Salt	to taste		⑳ Season.

from page 3·341

PORK TROTTER BEIGNET

Yields 400 g

INGREDIENT	QUANTITY	SCALING	PROCEDURE
Brown pork stock see page 6	600 g	120%	① Reduce to about 100 g, until glaze is achieved.
			② Cool and reserve.
Water	1 kg	200%	③ Pressure-cook together at gauge pressure of 1 bar / 15 psi for 2½ h.
Pork trotter	500 g	100%	④ Remove bones from trotter and snout, and separate skin and collagen from meat.
Pork snout	250 g	50%	⑤ Dice skin and meat finely, keeping them separate.
			⑥ Combine 120 g of meat and 30 g of skin, and reserve.
Shallots, minced	200 g	40%	⑦ Cook together until shallots and mushrooms are very tender, about 20 min.
Neutral oil	50 g	10%	
Black trumpet mushrooms, minced	40 g	8%	⑧ Remove from heat.
Cured ham, brunoise	40 g	8%	⑨ Fold with cooked pork into shallot mixture.
Grain mustard	10 g	2%	⑩ Whisk in reserved pork glaze.
Fine salt	2.2 g	0.44%	⑪ Cast onto silicone mat in layer 1.5 cm / ¾ in thick.
Black pepper, coarsely ground	0.2 g	0.04%	⑫ Refrigerate until set, at least 3 h.
			⑬ Cut into cubes.
Nutmeg, grated	0.1 g	0.02%	
Eggs, whisked	200 g	40%	⑭ Dredge each beignet cube in Methocel K100M until evenly coated.
Dried brioche crumbs	100 g	20%	⑮ Roll cubes in egg, and then coat with brioche crumbs.
Methocel K100M (Dow brand)	30 g	6%	⑯ Refrigerate for at least 1 h before frying, to firm crusts.
			⑰ Deep-fry cubes in 190 °C / 375 °F oil for 1 min, and then drain on paper towels.

from page 5·38

ONION RINGS

Yields 250 g (about 10 onion rings)

INGREDIENT	QUANTITY	SCALING	PROCEDURE
Onions, thinly sliced	750 g	375%	① Saute until light golden, about 10 min and cool.
Unsalted butter	100 g	50%	② Vacuum seal cooked onions with water.
Water	150 g	75%	③ Cook sous vide in 90 °C / 194 °F bath for 1 h.
Onion stock, cold *see page 11*	45 g	22.5%	④ Strain and cool onion stock. Measure 245 g for recipe.
			⑤ Bring onion stock to simmer, and disperse Methocel A15C and salt.
Methocel A15C (Dow brand)	4 g	2%	⑥ Refrigerate Methocel solution for at least 8 h to hydrate fully, and reserve cold.
Salt	1.5 g	0.75%	
Onion stock, cold, from above	200 g	100%	⑦ Combine and blend all ingredients in food processor to fine, smooth paste.
			⑧ Vacuum seal.
Tapioca starch	120 g	60%	⑨ Cook sous vide in 93 °C / 200 °F bath for 20 min.
Salt	3 g	1.5%	⑩ Cool completely until hardened, at least 12 h.
			⑪ Remove from bag, and grate with Microplane.
			⑫ Dehydrate at 70 °C / 160 °F until hardened, about 3 h.
			⑬ Reserve breading in airtight container.
Yellow onions, thinly sliced	500 g	250%	⑭ Brown onions over low heat.
			⑮ Deglaze with water as needed until very tender, about 40 min.
Neutral oil	50 g	25%	⑯ Drain excess oil, and blend to smooth puree.
			⑰ Cool completely, and measure 100 g.
			⑱ Blend 100 g of puree with Methocel solution, and transfer mixture to pastry bag.
			⑲ Pipe onion ring shapes onto silicone mat.
			⑳ Freeze.
Tapioca starch	100 g	50%	㉑ Dredge frozen onion rings in tapioca starch, and shake off excess.
Egg, blended	50 g	25%	㉒ Dip rings in egg.
Frying oil	as needed		㉓ Dredge rings in breading until evenly coated, and place on silicone mat.
			㉔ Deep-fry rings in 190 °C / 375 °F oil for 2 min, ensuring that puree stays inside coating.
			㉕ Drain on paper towels.

from page 3·342

RAZOR CLAM "TAKOYAKI"

Yields 250 g (10 balls)

INGREDIENT	QUANTITY	SCALING	PROCEDURE
Live razor clams	900 g	450%	① Vacuum seal together.
Ginger, thinly sliced	5 g	2.5%	② Steam at 100 °C / 212 °F for 6 min.
Scallions, thinly sliced	5 g	2.5%	③ Strain clam juice, and reserve 50 g.
Sake (dry)	30 g	15%	④ Shuck clams, reserving any additional juice.
			⑤ Mince clam meat, and reserve.
Tokyo negi (Japanese leek), finely minced	225 g	112.5%	⑥ Sweat until tender, about 3 min.
Unsalted butter, cubed	40 g	20%	
Heavy cream	150 g	75%	⑦ Add, and bring to simmer.
Clam juice, from above	50 g	25%	⑧ Strain, and measure 200 g of clam cream.
			⑨ Refrigerate until cold.
Clam cream, from above	200 g	100%	⑩ Whisk into cold clam cream, and bring to simmer to hydrate.
Salt	4 g	2%	⑪ Puree with immersion blender over ice-water bath to form fluid gel.
Ultra-Sperse 3 (National Starch brand)	1 g	0.5%	⑫ Fold in reserved minced clam meat.
Iota carrageenan	0.4 g	0.2%	⑬ Pipe mixture into spherical silicone molds 2 cm / ¾ in. in diameter.
Low-acyl gellan (Gellan F, CP Kelco brand)	0.3 g	0.15%	⑭ Freeze until gel balls are hardened, at least 45 min.
Water, boiling	50 g	25%	⑮ Disperse methylcellulose into boiling water, blending constantly.
Methocel K100M (Dow brand)	0.25 g	0.125%	⑯ Cool and reserve.
Batter Bind S (National Starch brand)	50 g	25%	⑰ Dust over balls.
			⑱ Whip methylcellulose mixture into stiff foam.
			⑲ Dip dusted balls into foam to fully cover surface.
Panko, finely ground	50 g	25%	⑳ Roll coated balls in panko.
			㉑ Dip breaded balls in methylcellulose foam and then panko once more.
			㉒ Refrigerate to firm crust, at least 2 h.
Mutsu apple, cut into batons	20 g	10%	㉓ To serve, deep-fry takoyaki balls in 190 °C / 375 °F oil until golden, about 1 min. Set in centers of small bowls.
Grey mullet bottarga	10 g	5%	㉔ Toss together apple and sea beans and place with takoyaki balls.
Sea beans, blanched	10 g	5%	㉕ Season bowls with lime juice and salt.
Frying oil	as needed		㉖ Garnish with shavings of bottarga.
Lime juice	to taste		
Salt	to taste		

from page 5·199

PLANT FOODS

CRISPY CORN PUDDING

Yields 780 g

INGREDIENT	QUANTITY	SCALING	PROCEDURE
For the popcorn puree:			
Whole milk	800 g	355%	① Bring milk to boil, and remove from heat.
Popped corn	140 g	62%	② Add corn, cover, and steep for 30 min.
			③ Puree mixture.
			④ Pass through fine sieve.
			⑤ Cool.
			⑥ Measure 350 g of popcorn puree, and reserve.
For the corn pudding:			
Frozen white corn, thawed	225 g	100%	⑦ Sauté until lightly golden.
Unsalted butter	20 g	9%	⑧ Cool and reserve.
Popcorn puree, cold, from above	350 g	155%	⑨ Disperse gelatin in popcorn puree.
			⑩ Bring to simmer to dissolve.
160 Bloom gelatin	20 g	9% (5.7%)*	⑪ Remove from heat, and cool.
Heavy cream	100 g	44.5%	⑫ Blend until smooth with sautéed white corn and gelled puree.
Egg yolks	36 g	16%	⑬ Pass through fine sieve.
Maple syrup (Grade B)	34 g	15%	⑭ Cast in mold in layer 2.5 cm / 1 in thick.
Salt	7 g	3%	⑮ Refrigerate until set, at least 4 h.
Cayenne pepper	3 g	1.5%	⑯ Cut into cubes.
Thyme essential oil	0.01 g	0.004%	
For the corn pudding crust:			
Freeze-dried corn see page 188	200 g	89%	⑰ Combine to make breading, and reserve.
Panko	200 g	89%	
All-purpose bleached flour	100 g	44.5%	⑱ Combine.
Ultra-Crisp (National Starch brand)	50 g	22%	⑲ Dredge corn cubes in starch blend until evenly coated.
Eggs, whisked	125 g	56%	⑳ Dip cubes in eggs, and finish by coating with reserved breading. Refrigerate until use.
Frying oil	as needed		㉑ Deep-fry corn pudding cubes in 190 °C / 375 °F oil until golden, about 1 min. Drain on paper towels.

from page 5·104

*(% of weight of popcorn puree)

SALTING, PICKLING, AND FERMENTING

① Select an ingredient and a preservation method. The Best Bets for Preservation table on page 182 suggests many good options.

② Mix brine or cure, and combine with aromatics. Use the table below to determine quantities. Note that weights are scaled in proportion to the vinegar for vinegar pickles and to the fruit or vegetable for other kinds of preserves.

③ Cook or ferment. For sour or sweet vinegar pickles, bring the brine and aromatics to a simmer, and pour over the prepared ingredients. For oil and sugar preserves, cook all ingredients over low heat until they are very tender and their surfaces are nearly dry. Keep fermented pickles or sauerkraut unsealed in a dark, cool place for at least two weeks; check that liquid exuded from the ingredients always covers the solids.

④ Refrigerate (nonfermented preserves only). After cooking, cover the ingredients completely with brine or cure, vacuum seal them or place them in an airtight container, and then refrigerate them to pickle or cure.

⑤ Keep brined and cured products refrigerated.

Formulas for Preserving Produce

Product	Ingredient	(scaling)	Aromatics	(scaling)	See page
sour vinegar pickles	vinegar	100%	garlic	1.5%	176
	water	40%	black peppercorns	0.5%	
	salt	4%	mustard seeds	0.5%	
	calcium lactate (optional, to firm)	1%	red chilies (optional)	0.2%	
sweet vinegar pickles	vinegar	100%	coriander seeds	1.00%	178
	water	70%	star anise	1.00%	
	sugar	40%	ginger	1.00%	
	salt	5%	lemon zest	0.40%	
	pectin methylesterase enzyme (NovoShape brand, optional, to firm)	0.4%	white peppercorns	0.25%	
salt pickles	fruit or vegetable	100%	n/a		
	salt	9%			
	sugar	9%			
fermented pickles	fruit or vegetable	100%	n/a		177
	salt	1.5%			
	lactic acid (optional, to enhance flavor)	0.2%			
sugar preserves	fruit or vegetable	100%	lemon zest	0.5%	180
	sugar	100%	vanilla pulp and seeds	0.1%	
	water	100%			

from page 3·348

Note that the table above does not include the preparation steps that should be taken to pasteurize the food. Store any unpasteurized foods in the refrigerator as you would fresh foods. Canning and heat preservation require more intense pasteurization; see Canning, page 2·75, for details.

PRESERVED PEAR IN MUSTARD OIL

Yields 300 g

INGREDIENT	QUANTITY	SCALING	PROCEDURE
Anjou pears	250 g	100%	① Peel and core.
			② Scoop 12 spheres with melon baller, and reserve.
Mustard oil	10 g	4%	③ Toast seeds and curry leaves in oil until golden, about 3 min, and reserve.
Yellow mustard seeds	10 g	4%	
Curry leaves	2 g	0.8%	
Water	100 g	40%	④ Combine remaining ingredients, and warm to make syrup.
White wine vinegar	75 g	30%	⑤ Add mustard oil mixture.
Glucose syrup DE 40	50 g	20%	⑥ Vacuum seal pear spheres with syrup.
Sugar	25 g	10%	⑦ Refrigerate for at least 2 h before using, and up to 24 h total, after which pear spheres will become too soft.

from page 5·283

PRESERVED LEMONS ADAPTED FROM BRADFORD THOMPSON

Yields 2 kg

INGREDIENT	QUANTITY	SCALING	PROCEDURE
Lemons (organic)	3 kg (about 25 large)	100%	① Cut off one slice, 2.5 cm / 1 in thick, from one end of each lemon.
			② Cut each lemon as if to quarter, but keep lemon intact by not fully cutting through its flesh and not cutting through its unsliced end.
			③ Reserve lemons in large bowl.
Salt	1.5 kg	50%	④ Combine.
Sugar	800 g	26.6%	⑤ Place five 1 l / 32 fl oz canning jars with lids in boiling water to sterilize.
Black peppercorns	50 g	1.6%	⑥ Air-dry sterilized jars and lids on rack.
Cinnamon sticks, crushed lightly	25 g	0.8%	⑦ Open up each lemon without breaking its unsliced end; lemon should resemble a bloomed flower.
Coriander seeds	25 g	0.8%	⑧ Sprinkle seasoned salt generously inside lemons.
Fennel seeds	20 g	0.6%	⑨ Pack lemons into canning jars, five per jar, covering each layer with remaining salt mixture.
Saffron threads	18 g	0.6%	⑩ Seal jars tightly and refrigerate. Preserved lemons can be used after 4 wk but are best after 3–4 mo. Store refrigerated for up to 1 y.
Star anise, crushed lightly	10 g	0.3%	
Black onion seeds	5 g	0.2%	

from page 3·350

PICKLED GARLIC

Yields 75 g

INGREDIENT	QUANTITY	SCALING	PROCEDURE
Garlic cloves	100 g	100%	① Blanch for 3 min.
			② Drain.
			③ Arrange in single layer in rigid container.
White wine vinegar	200 g	200%	④ Combine, and bring to boil.
Water	75 g	75%	⑤ Pour over garlic cloves.
Sugar	25 g	25%	⑥ Cool.
Thyme	5 g	5%	⑦ Refrigerate for at least 12 h before serving.
Salt	4 g	4%	

from page 5·26

PICKLED TAPIOCA PEARL

Yields 200 g

INGREDIENT	QUANTITY	SCALING	PROCEDURE
Water	200 g	200%	① Combine.
Tapioca pearls	100 g	100%	② Boil for 20 min, and simmer until tender and translucent, 30–35 min.
			③ Drain.
Rice wine vinegar	110 g	110%	④ Combine to make brine.
Oyster juice see page 81	40 g	40%	⑤ Mix together brine and cooked tapioca pearls.
			⑥ Vacuum seal, and refrigerate.
Sugar	15 g	15%	
Lime juice	10 g	10%	
Salt	3 g	3%	

from page 5·207

KIMCHI ADAPTED FROM DAVID CHANG

Yields 650 g

INGREDIENT	QUANTITY	SCALING	PROCEDURE
Sugar	75 g	9%	① Combine salt with 30 g of sugar.
Salt	22 g	2.6%	
Napa cabbage head with leaves attached	825 g	100%	② Rub mixture thoroughly into leaves while keeping cabbage head intact.
			③ Cover, and refrigerate for 12 h.
			④ Drain and reserve.
Garlic, finely minced	100 g	12%	⑤ Combine with remaining 45 g of sugar.
Fish sauce	65 g	8%	⑥ Rub mixture completely into leaves, keeping head intact.
Light soy sauce	62 g	7.5%	⑦ Cover, and store at 18–24 °C / 64–75 °F for 2–4 wk to ferment. Final pH should be less than 4.0.
Korean chili powder	48 g	6%	
Scallions, minced	37 g	4.5%	⑧ To serve, cut individual leaves away from core.
Ginger, finely minced	35 g	4%	
Carrot, julienne	30 g	4%	
Dried salted shrimp	7 g	1%	

from page 3·352

WATERMELON RIND KIMCHI

Yields 140 g

INGREDIENT	QUANTITY	SCALING	PROCEDURE
Water	500 g	250%	① Whisk together until salt and acid have fully dissolved, to make pickling brine.
Salt	35 g	17.5%	
Scallions, thinly sliced	30 g	15%	
Sugar	25 g	12.5%	
Ginger, minced	20 g	10%	
Garlic, minced	8 g	4%	
Lactic acid	6 g	3% (1.2%)*	
Dried shrimp, minced	5 g	2.5%	
Bird's eye chilies, minced	2 g	1%	
Watermelon rind, peeled and cut into strips 5 cm / 2 in wide	200 g	100%	② Vacuum seal rind pieces with brine.
			③ Refrigerate for 12 h.
			④ Drain.
			⑤ Refrigerate until use.

from page 5·286   *(% of total weight of water)

NUKAZUKE

Yields 350 g

INGREDIENT	QUANTITY	SCALING	PROCEDURE
Water	1 kg	100%	① Combine.
Salt	200 g	20%	② Stir until salt is completely dissolved.
Rice bran (nuka)	1 kg	100%	③ Combine.
Ginger, cut into chunks	20 g	2%	④ Add solution from above.
Cabbage leaves	15 g	1.5%	⑤ Cover, and leave at room temperature for 2 wk; stir once daily.
			⑥ Discard cabbage leaves and ginger; reserve rice bran mixture.
Carrots	200 g	20%	⑦ Rub surfaces of vegetables with salt.
Japanese cucumbers (or Persian)	200 g	20%	⑧ Place in deep crock with rice bran mixture; bury vegetables completely in mixture.
			⑨ Cover top of crock tightly with plastic wrap.
Radishes	100 g	10%	⑩ Store in dry place at room temperature until desired texture is achieved, 4–24 h.
Salt	as needed		⑪ To serve, remove vegetables from rice bran mixture, and rinse.
			⑫ Reserve rice bran mixture, refrigerated, for future pickling.

from page 3·354

SOUS VIDE CUCUMBER PICKLES

Yields 300 g

INGREDIENT	QUANTITY	SCALING	PROCEDURE
Small pickling cucumbers	300 g	100%	① Slice to 4 mm / ¼ in thick, and reserve.
White wine vinegar	350 g	117%	② Combine, and bring to boil.
Water	150 g	50%	③ Remove brine from heat, and cool.
Sugar	80 g	27%	④ Refrigerate to cool completely.
Salt	8 g	2.7%	
Black peppercorns	1 g	0.3%	
Caraway seeds	1 g	0.3%	
NovoShape PME enzyme (optional, Novozymes brand)	2 g	0.67% (0.4%)*	
Fresh dill sprigs	8 g	2.7%	⑤ Add dill and sliced cucumbers to chilled brine.
			⑥ Vacuum seal.
			⑦ Refrigerate for 1–2 d.

from page 3·353 *(% of total weight of vinegar and water)

GARLIC CONFIT

Yields 250 g

INGREDIENT	QUANTITY	SCALING	PROCEDURE
Olive oil	500 g	200%	① Place garlic cloves and aromatics in Mason jars, and cover with oil.
Garlic cloves, peeled	250 g (about 35 cloves)	100%	② Place Mason jars in pressure cooker, and pour water halfway up their sides.
Rosemary sprigs	3 g	1.2%	③ Pressure cook at 1 bar / 15 psi (gauge) for 2 h.
Thyme sprigs	3 g	1.2%	④ Alternatively, vacuum seal together, and cook sous vide in 88 °C / 190 °F bath for 7 h.
			⑤ Serve, or cool and refrigerate.

from page 3·354

Pressure-cooked garlic confit has a darker appearance and deeper flavor than sous vide garlic confit does. This recipe can also be made with other typical Provençal aromatics, such as fennel seed, bay leaf, lavender, and sage, instead of—or in addition to—rosemary and thyme.

AROMATIC ALSATIAN MUSTARD

Yields 245 g

INGREDIENT	QUANTITY	SCALING	PROCEDURE
Yellow mustard seeds	75 g	100%	① Blanch three times in scalding water, discarding water each time to remove bitterness.
Cider vinegar	190 g	253%	② Combine seeds with vinegar.
			③ Refrigerate for 12 h.
Fennel, brunoise	2.2 g	2.9%	④ Combine with soaked mustard seeds in food processor.
Tarragon, finely minced	1.5 g	2%	⑤ Puree for 1 min to coarse texture.
Coriander seeds, ground	1.2 g	1.6%	⑥ Vacuum seal mustard.
Salt	1 g	1.33%	⑦ Refrigerate for at least 7 d before use.
Black cardamom seeds, ground	0.8 g	1.1%	
Ground cinnamon	0.7 g	0.9%	
Ground cloves	0.7 g	0.9%	
Black pepper, ground	0.5 g	0.7%	
Bay leaf, finely minced	0.2 g	0.3%	

from page 5·37

SAUERKRAUT

Yields 600 g

INGREDIENT	QUANTITY	SCALING	PROCEDURE
Savoy cabbage (green cabbage, red cabbage, rutabaga, or turnips may be substituted)	2 kg	100%	① Remove leaves, and cut out and discard their central ribs. ② Slice leaves into fine ribbons.
Salt	30 g	1.5%	③ Toss with cut leaves. ④ Pack salted leaves in crock or other deep, opaque container. ⑤ Cover mouth of container with cheesecloth, and top with clean rock or other heavy, sanitized object. ⑥ Store at 18–24 °C / 64–75 °F for 2–4 wk, or until pH is below 4.0. Cabbage must become fully submerged in its own juices. This should occur by the third day; if not, add 1% salt brine to cover. ⑦ Vacuum seal, and refrigerate sauerkraut with brine until needed.

from page 3·351

BRAISED SAUERKRAUT

Yields 480 g

INGREDIENT	QUANTITY	SCALING	PROCEDURE
Sweet onions, thinly sliced	90 g	60%	① Sauté together, without allowing onions to color, until very tender, about 25 min.
Goose fat	75 g	50%	
Garlic, finely minced	30 g	20%	
Cabbage sauerkraut see recipe above	150 g	100%	② Add to onion mixture. ③ Cook until cabbage is very tender and liquid is reduced by half, about 30 min.
Vegetable stock see page 6 and page 13	150 g	100%	
Riesling (dry)	105 g	70%	
Rutabaga sauerkraut see recipe above	100 g	66.7%	
Muscat (dry)	50 g	33.3%	
Bay leaf	0.5 g	0.33%	④ Combine in sachet.
Black peppercorns	0.2 g	0.13%	⑤ Add sachet to onion and cabbage mixture, and continue to cook until most of liquid has evaporated, about 25 min.
Juniper berries	0.15 g	0.1%	
Cloves	0.1 g	0.07%	⑥ Remove sachet.
Coriander seeds	0.1 g	0.07%	
Salt	to taste		⑦ Season sauerkraut.

from page 5·39

PICKLED FIGS

Yields 400 g

INGREDIENT	QUANTITY	SCALING	PROCEDURE
Red wine vinegar	350 g	175%	① Vacuum seal together.
Dried black figs	200 g	100%	② Cook sous vide in 80 °C / 176 °F bath for 4 h.
Sugar	200 g	100%	③ Cool completely.
White balsamic vinegar	195 g	97.5%	④ Refrigerate until use.
Balsamic vinegar	125 g	62.5%	
Lemon, thinly sliced	20 g	10%	
Ginger, peeled and thinly sliced	4 g	2%	
Cinnamon stick	3.5 g	1.75%	
Star anise, crushed	1.5 g	0.75%	
Cardamom seeds, black	0.5 g	0.25%	
Black peppercorns	0.2 g	0.1%	

from page 5·137

COMPRESSED DILL-PICKLED VEGETABLES

Yields 300 g

INGREDIENT	QUANTITY	SCALING	PROCEDURE
Red bell peppers, seeded and peeled	100 g	33%	① Cut into fine julienne.
Cucumbers	175 g	58%	② Peel and slice on diagonal 1 mm / 1/16 in thick with mandoline. Yield is about 100 g.
Hon-shimeji mushrooms, caps only	100 g	33%	③ Bring water and salt to boil.
			④ Blanch mushrooms for 2 min.
Water	100 g	33%	⑤ Shock in ice-water bath.
Salt	2 g	0.67%	⑥ Drain and reserve.
Red pearl onions, peeled	150 g	50%	⑦ Cut in half lengthwise.
			⑧ Vacuum seal.
			⑨ Blanch in 95 °C / 200 °F bath for 4 min.
			⑩ Separate into petals, and reserve.
White wine vinegar	300 g	100%	⑪ Combine, and bring to boil to make pickling brine.
Distilled water	150 g	50%	⑫ Pour approximately 100 g of brine over each vegetable: bell peppers, cucumbers, mushrooms, and onions.
Sugar	50 g	16.7%	
Dill	8.5 g	2.8%	⑬ Cool vegetables completely.
Salt	7.5 g	2.5%	⑭ Serve, or vacuum seal separately and refrigerate.
Black peppercorns	1.5 g	0.5%	
Caraway seeds	1.5 g	0.5%	

from page 5·58

PICKLED JERUSALEM ARTICHOKES

Yields 280 g

INGREDIENT	QUANTITY	SCALING	PROCEDURE
Champagne vinegar	150 g	100%	① Combine to make pickling brine.
Sugar	30 g	20%	
Salt	5 g	3.3%	
Jerusalem artichokes, peeled and cut into 0.5 cm / 1/4 in cubes	100 g	67%	② Vacuum seal with brine, and refrigerate.

from page 5·131

PICKLED RAMPS

Yields 450 g

INGREDIENT	QUANTITY	SCALING	PROCEDURE
Water	200 g	100%	① Combine and bring to simmer.
White wine vinegar	200 g	100%	
Sugar	80 g	40%	
Salt	12 g	6%	
Yellow mustard seeds	3 g	1.5%	
Black peppercorns	2.5 g	1.25%	
Coriander seeds	1.5 g	0.75%	
Bay leaf	0.5 g	0.25%	
Ramp bulbs, cleaned	450 g	225%	② Pour warm brine over bulbs.
			③ Cool mixture.
			④ Vacuum seal.
			⑤ Refrigerate for at least 12 h.

from page 5·118

PICKLED LEMON

Yields 125 g

INGREDIENT	QUANTITY	SCALING	PROCEDURE
Lemons	100 g	100%	① Slice 1 mm / 1/16 in thick.
			② Place in rigid container and reserve.
Water	100 g	100%	③ Combine to make brine.
White wine vinegar	50 g	50%	④ Bring to simmer to dissolve sugar.
Sugar	25 g	25%	⑤ Pour warm brine over lemon slices.
			⑥ Cool.
			⑦ Vacuum seal, and refrigerate until use.

from page 5·275

PICKLED CELERY ROOT

Yields 350 g

INGREDIENT	QUANTITY	SCALING	PROCEDURE
Celery juice, clarified	125 g (from 250 g celery)	125%	① Combine to make brine.
White wine vinegar	100 g	100%	
Sugar	30 g	30%	
Salt	5 g	5%	
Celery root, peeled and thinly sliced	100 g	100%	② Vacuum seal with brine.
			③ Refrigerate until use.
Black peppercorns	1 g	1%	
Coriander seeds, toasted	0.5 g	0.5%	

from page 5·133

TOMATO CONFIT ADAPTED FROM HESTON BLUMENTHAL

Yields 150 g

INGREDIENT	QUANTITY	SCALING	PROCEDURE
Tomatoes	1 kg	100%	① Core tomatoes.
			② Cut small X in blossom end of each tomato.
			③ Blanch until skin begins to lift at X, about 10 s.
			④ Shock in ice-water bath for 2 min. Peel off skins.
			⑤ Cut in half vertically, and scoop out seeds.
			⑥ Pat dry.
			⑦ Place cut side down on baking sheet lined with silicone mat, and reserve.
Glycerol	20 g	2%	⑧ Combine.
Water	20 g	2%	⑨ Brush evenly on tomatoes.
Extra virgin olive oil	40 g	4%	⑩ Brush evenly on tomatoes.
Garlic, thinly sliced	15 g	1.5%	⑪ Sprinkle equally and evenly over tomatoes.
Thyme leaves	4 g	0.4%	
Bay leaves, finely sliced	1 g	0.1%	
Salt	2 g	0.2%	⑫ Season tomatoes evenly.
Sugar	2 g	0.2%	⑬ Dry in 110 °C / 225 °F oven for about 1 h.
			⑭ Turn tomatoes over, reduce heat to 95 °C / 200 °F, and dry until deep red and shriveled, 3–4 h. Cool.
			⑮ Discard dried herbs from tomatoes.
			⑯ Vacuum seal tomatoes with their cooking oils.
			⑰ Refrigerate until use.

from page 5·62

PICKLED BING CHERRY

Yields 650 g

INGREDIENT	QUANTITY	SCALING	PROCEDURE
Bing cherries	500 g	100%	① Arrange in single layer in rigid plastic container that fits in vacuum sealer chamber.
Red wine vinegar	265 g	53%	② Bring remaining ingredients to boil to make brine.
Sour cherry juice (store-bought)	150 g	30%	③ Pour brine over cherries, and cool at room temperature.
			④ Pull full vacuum three times on cooled cherries.
Sugar	130 g	26%	⑤ Vacuum seal and refrigerate until use. Both cherries and their pickling brine are delicious and versatile acidifiers for dressings and sauces.
Water	130 g	26%	

from page 5·268

GREEN PAPAYA PICKLE

Yields 350 g

INGREDIENT	QUANTITY	SCALING	PROCEDURE
Papaya (semiripe), peeled	225 g	90%	① Julienne and reserve.
Cane vinegar	250 g	100%	② Reserve 150 g of vinegar.
Red onions, finely minced	75 g	30%	③ Combine 100 g of vinegar with remaining ingredients, and grind to coarse paste.
Black mustard seeds	25 g	10%	
Garlic, finely minced	8 g	3%	
Ginger, finely minced	8 g	3%	
Bird's eye chili, finely minced	1.5 g	0.5%	
Neutral oil	20 g	8%	④ Fry paste over medium heat, stirring constantly, until aromatic but not colored, about 10 min.
Sugar	40 g	16%	⑤ Add to cooked paste with reserved 150 g of vinegar.
Green chili, minced	5 g	2%	⑥ Fold julienned papaya into warm paste.
Salt	5 g	2%	⑦ Simmer for 2 min.
Turmeric (fresh), grated	4.5 g	1.8%	⑧ Cool completely, vacuum seal, and refrigerate until use.

from page 5·97

PICKLED BUTTERNUT SQUASH

Yields 100 g

INGREDIENT	QUANTITY	SCALING	PROCEDURE
Black peppercorns	3 g	3%	① Combine in sachet.
Coriander seeds, toasted	3 g	3%	
Star anise, lightly crushed	3 g	3%	
Orange zest, grated	2.5 g	2.5%	
Dried bitter orange peel	1.5 g	1.5%	
Saffron threads	0.1 g	0.1%	
White wine vinegar	130 g	130%	② Combine, and bring to boil.
Water	80 g	80%	③ Remove from heat, and add sachet.
Sugar	30 g	30%	④ Infuse for 3 min, discard sachet.
Salt	1 g	1%	
Butternut squash, brunoise	100 g	100%	⑤ Place squash in container.
			⑥ Pour hot brine over squash.
			⑦ Place open container in vacuum chamber, and pull vacuum several times to infuse squash thoroughly.
			⑧ Vacuum seal and refrigerate until use.

from page 5·64

CRISPY DOSA

Yields 800 g (12 dosas)

INGREDIENT	QUANTITY	SCALING	PROCEDURE
Jasmine rice	400 g	100%	① Soak together in water at room temperature for about 3 h.
Whole black gram (urad dal)	200 g	50%	② Drain.
Flattened rice flakes (poha)	25 g	6.25%	
Water	850 g	212.5%	
Water	100 g	25%	③ Combine with soaked grains and soaking liquid, and grind until smooth and fluffy.
Coconut (fresh), grated	30 g	7.5%	④ Add up to 100 g more water, as necessary, to achieve thin pancake-batter consistency.
Salt	10 g	2.5%	⑤ Measure 500 g of batter, and ferment in covered container at room temperature for 2 h. Refrigerate remaining batter.
Lactic acid	2.5 g	0.63%	⑥ Add to batter, and continue to ferment for 30 min.
Ghee see page 4·213	as needed		⑦ Bring nonstick skillet or griddle to medium heat.
			⑧ Ladle batter onto skillet. Use an outward spiral motion to spread evenly.
			⑨ Drizzle 5 ml / 1 tsp of butter around edges of each dosa.
			⑩ Cook until crispy and golden on bottom.
Masala curry sauce see page 225	80 g	20%	⑪ Combine potatoes and masala sauce; warm through.
			⑫ Warm foam in 60 °C / 140 °F bath for 20 min.
Sous vide cooked potatoes, cubed	120 g	30%	⑬ Fill dosas with potatoes, foam, and puffed lentils; serve on side.
Coconut chutney foam see page 325	150 g	37.5%	
Puffed lentils see page 342	80 g	20%	

from page 3·355

YUZU AND KUMQUAT MARMALADE

Yields 475 g

INGREDIENT	QUANTITY	SCALING	PROCEDURE
Fructose	100 g	40%	① Dry blend.
High-methoxyl pectin (Brown Ribbon HV, Obipektin brand)	2.5 g	1%	
Salt	1.5 g	0.6%	
Yuzu juice (fresh or bottled)	55 g	22%	② Reserve 5 g of juice.
			③ Blend powder mixture with remaining 50 g.
			④ Bring juice to boil to make syrup.
			⑤ Remove from heat, and cool completely.
Kumquats, quartered	250 g	100%	⑥ Blanch once in boiling water, and cool completely.
			⑦ Combine with cooled yuzu syrup.
			⑧ Vacuum seal together.
			⑨ Cook sous vide in 80 °C / 176 °F bath until very tender, about 4 h.
			⑩ Remove from bag to cool completely, and reserve.
Mandarin juice, freeze-concentrated see page 2·337	70 g	28%	⑪ Combine, and hand-blend until gums are completely incorporated.
			⑫ Fold into cooled marmalade base.
Guar gum	0.28 g	0.11% (0.2%)*	
Xanthan gum	0.2 g	0.08% (0.16%)*	
Citric acid	2 g	0.8%	⑬ Whisk into marmalade.
Yuzu juice, from above	5 g	2%	⑭ Add to marmalade, and refrigerate.

from page 3·356 *(% of total weight of yuzu and mandarin juices)

ENZYME-TREATED PINK GRAPEFRUIT

Yields 250 g

INGREDIENT	QUANTITY	SCALING	PROCEDURE
Pink grapefruit, peeled	300 g	30%	① Separate carefully into segments, leaving membranes intact, and reserve.
Water	1 kg	100%	② Combine, and transfer to sanitized jar.
Pectinex Ultra SP-L (Novozymes brand)	2 g	0.2%	③ Add grapefruit segments.
			④ Seal jar.
Pectinex Smash XXL (Novozymes brand)	1 g	0.1%	⑤ Refrigerate for 12 h to soak.
			⑥ Remove treated segments from water.
			⑦ Brush away any undissolved grapefruit membrane.

from page 3·357

Best Bets for Preservation

Ingredient	Vinegar pickle	Salt pickle	Fermented pickle	Sugar preserve
apple	✓	✓	✓	✓
apricot	✓			✓
bean sprout	✓	✓	✓	
beet	✓			✓
bell pepper	✓		✓	✓
cabbage	✓	✓	✓	
carrot	✓	✓	✓	✓
cauliflower	✓	✓	✓	
cherry	✓	✓		✓
chili	✓	✓	✓	✓
citrus	✓	✓		✓
coconut, young	✓			✓
cucumber	✓	✓	✓	
eggplant	✓			✓
fig	✓			✓
garlic	✓	✓	✓	✓
grape	✓			✓
green bean	✓	✓	✓	
lychee	✓			✓
mango, green	✓			
melon	✓	✓	✓	✓
mustard seeds	✓	✓		✓
mushroom	✓	✓	✓	
okra	✓	✓		
olive	✓	✓		✓
onion	✓		✓	✓
papaya, green	✓	✓	✓	
peach	✓			✓
pear	✓			✓
pineapple	✓			✓
radish	✓	✓	✓	
rhubarb	✓	✓		✓
rutabaga	✓		✓	
seaweed	✓	✓	✓	
tomato	✓			✓
turnip	✓	✓	✓	
zucchini	✓			✓

from page 3·348

HEAT-TREATED FRUIT

① The table at right suggests a number of fruits for which this process works well. Make certain the water bath has reached the temperature indicated before you drop the fruits in whole.

② Stir gently and submerge the fruits if necessary. If you remove them after the time indicated and dry them thoroughly, you can expect their shelf life to increase by half or more, as noted in the table.

Best Bets for Heat-Treated Fruit

Fruit	Warm bath (°C)	(°F)	(min)	Shelf life, untreated	Shelf life after treatment
blueberry	60	140	½	7	20
citrus, segments	60	140	20	6	11
grape	55	131	½	5	25
melon	50	122	60	12	15
pear	45	113	40	10	15
strawberry	60	140	¼	9	12
tomato	60	140	½	7	10

from page 3·359

SMOKED PLANT FOODS

① Select and prepare the ingredient. The table below offers a number of good options.

② Load the wood mixture into the smoker. Do not soak the wood chips first, because that results in acidic smoke (see page 2·140).

③ Set the smoker temperature and relative humidity to the values indicated. For smokers without temperature or humidity controls, place a pan of water on the bottom rack of the smoker, and use a wet-bulb thermometer to monitor the wet-bulb temperature.

④ Smoke for the time indicated in the table.

Best Bets for Smoked Plant Foods

Ingredient	Wood	(scaling)	Dry-bulb temp. (°C)	(°F)	Wet-bulb temp. (°C)	(°F)	Relative humidity	Time (h)	Note or example use	See page
apple	apple	100%	65	149	46	114	40	24	serve plain, or in tarte tatin	
asparagus	cherry	100%	7	45	4	39	80	24	sauté quickly	
corn, on the cob	oak / maple	100% / 25%	10	50	3	37	60	24	cook sous vide, and baste with smoked butter and pimentón	
eggplant	hickory	100%	65	149	46	114	40	6	baba ghanouj, moussaka	
fresh pasta	oak / nectarine	100% / 33%	10	50	3	37	60	24	pasta carbonara	
olive oil (or other oils and fats)	oak / nectarine	100% / 33%	10	50	3	37	60	12	vinaigrette, brushed on grilled bread	
onion, cooked sous vide	oak / maple	100% / 25%	65	149	54	129	60	24	cook sous vide, and finish in a roasting pan with bacon-infused butter	139
pecan	apple	100%	65	149	46	114	40	6	briefly roast, and toss with pecan oil, salt	
pineapple	oak / maple	100% / 25%	10	50	3	37	60	24	briefly grill, and brush with lime and vanilla syrup	
pine nut	hickory	100%	30	86	21	70	60	4	pesto	
potato, cooked sous vide	oak / nectarine	100% / 33%	10	50	3	37	60	24	cook sous vide with 2 g (1% total weight of potatoes) of high-quality liquid smoke mixed into the butter	next, 5·193
rice	oak / nectarine	100% / 33%	10	50	3	37	60	24	paella valenciana	5·239
soy sauce, dark	oak / nectarine	100% / 33%	50	122	40	104	60	24	shiro dashi or miso soup	
soy sauce, white	oak / nectarine	100% / 33%	10	50	3	37	60	24	spot prawn tempura	164
watermelon	hickory	100%	65	149	46	114	40	2	dessert for a barbecue	

from page 3·362

SMOKED POTATOES WITH VIN JAUNE SABAYON
ADAPTED FROM ALAIN PASSARD

Yields 625 g (four portions)

INGREDIENT	QUANTITY	SCALING	PROCEDURE
Ratte fingerling potatoes, peeled	100 g	100%	① Vacuum seal together.
Baby Yukon gold potatoes, peeled	100 g	100%	② Cook sous vide in 90 °C / 194 °F bath for 1 h.
			③ Remove potatoes from bag.
			④ Cold-smoke cooked potatoes at 10 °C / 50 °F for 24 h, or hot-smoke in stove-top smoker for 30 min.
			⑤ Cool.
Unsalted butter, melted	50 g	50%	⑥ Vacuum seal potatoes with butter.
Vin jaune	75 g	75%	⑦ Combine vin jaune with shallots.
Shallots, finely minced	50 g	50%	⑧ Reduce to syrup.
			⑨ Strain, and measure 10 g of vin jaune reduction.
White vegetable stock see page 6 and page 13	200 g	200%	⑩ Blend together fully with vin jaune reduction.
Egg yolks	156 g	156%	⑪ Cook mixture sous vide in 70 °C / 158 °F bath for 35 min.
Heavy cream	40 g	40%	⑫ Transfer sabayon to 1 l siphon, and charge with two cartridges of nitrous oxide.
Lemon juice	5 g	5%	
Salt	to taste		⑬ Keep siphon warm in 62 °C / 144 °F bath until ready to use.
			⑭ Warm sealed potatoes in same bath used for sabayon for 10 min.
			⑮ Remove potatoes from bath and bag; divide equally among four bowls.
			⑯ Dispense warm sabayon around potatoes.
Roasted hazelnut oil	20 g	20%	⑰ Garnish potatoes.
Toasted hazelnuts, quartered	20 g	20%	
Ginger, finely diced	7 g	7%	
Chives, finely minced	to taste		
Salt	to taste		

from page 3·363

If smoking is not an option, vacuum seal raw potatoes with a mixture of water and good-quality liquid smoke in step 1. Use 2 g of liquid smoke for every 100 g of water, and include enough smoke-water mixture to equal the weight of the potatoes.

SMOKED POTATO CONFIT

Yields 250 g

INGREDIENT	QUANTITY	SCALING	PROCEDURE
Yukon Gold potatoes, hot-smoked see page 183	200 g (four potatoes)	100%	① Cut out 3 cm by 6 cm / 1¼ in by 2¼ in cylinders using ring cutter.
Extra virgin olive oil	100 g	50%	② Vacuum seal together.
Salt	1.5 g	0.75%	③ Heat potatoes in 70 °C / 158 °F bath.

from page 5·195

184 VOLUME 6 · KITCHEN MANUAL

DEHYDRATED FRUITS AND VEGETABLES

① Choose a product. Use the table below to select the dehydrated form you wish to make, cross-referenced with the kind of produce you are using.

② Select a texture. The table on the next page presents our recommendations for chips, papers, leathers, glasses, and wafers.

③ Prepare the fruit or vegetable as indicated in the table.

④ Combine slices, puree, juice, or foam with other ingredients. Assign a scaling value of 100% to the fruit or vegetable preparation, and weigh the other ingredients proportionally. For example, use 0.8 g agar and 2.5 g of glycerol for every 100 g of raspberry puree to make a flexible raspberry leather.

⑤ Dehydrate by using the temperature and time listed.

Best Bets for Dehydration

Ingredient	Chips (thin slices)	Papers (purees)	Leathers (purees)	Glasses (purees and juices)	Wafers (purees and juices)
apple	✓	✓	✓	✓	✓
apricot	✓	✓	✓	✓	✓
beet	✓	✓	✓	✓	✓
cabbage	✓				
cauliflower	✓				✓
citrus	✓		✓		
corn		✓		✓	✓
flower petals	✓				
leek	✓	✓			
mango	✓	✓	✓	✓	✓
mushroom	✓	✓			✓
onion	✓	✓	✓	✓	✓
passion fruit		✓	✓	✓	✓
pear	✓	✓	✓		
persimmon	✓	✓	✓	✓	✓
pineapple	✓			✓	✓
raspberry		✓	✓	✓	✓
spinach	✓	✓			
squash	✓	✓	✓	✓	✓
strawberry	✓	✓	✓	✓	✓

from page 3·366

GARLIC NOUGATINE

Yields 400 g

INGREDIENT	QUANTITY	SCALING	PROCEDURE
Glucose syrup DE 40	100 g	100%	① Mix together.
Isomalt powder	100 g	100%	② Spread onto silicone baking mat in one layer, 1 mm / 1⁄16 in thick.
Unsalted butter, softened	100 g	100%	③ Cover with second silicone baking mat.
All-purpose flour	50 g	50%	④ Bake in **200 °C / 390 °F** oven until golden and soft, about 5 min.
Garlic, brunoise and blanched	50 g	50%	⑤ Pass rolling pin several times over top baking mat, while nougatine is still hot, to make as thin as possible.
Marcona almonds, brunoise	50 g	50%	⑥ Warm in oven.
Salt	4.5 g	4.5%	⑦ Cut into desired dimensions while still hot.
			⑧ Store in airtight container, ideally with silica gel packet.

from page 5·29

Formulas for Dehydrating Produce

Product	Texture	Preparation	Ingredients	(scaling)*	Dehydrate (°C)	(°F)	(h)
chips	very crisp	dust over sliced fruit or vegetable	trehalose or isomalt, fine powder	100%	50	120	8
	crisp	make syrup and brush onto slices	isomalt water	100% 65%	50	120	12
	crisp	whisk until dissolved, rest at room temperature about 20 min, and brush mixture onto produce	egg white gum arabic	100% 50%	50	120	7
	crisp	soak slices for 20 min	water maltodextrin DE19	50% 100%	55	130	5
	chewy	soak slices for 2 h	glycerol water sugar or trehalose	30% 40% 100%	60	140	12
papers	moist, chewy	spread mixture into paper-thin layer	methylcellulose E4M (Dow brand)	1.5%	55	130	6
	dry, flexible		glucose syrup DE 40 low-acyl gellan (Kelcogel F, CP Kelco brand)	5.0% 0.7%	55	130	7
	dry, brittle		N-Zorbit M (National Starch brand)	20%	55	130	3
leathers	tender	spread mixture into layer 1 mm / 1/16 in thick	vegetable oil	5%	55	130	8
	chewy		Ultratex 8 (National Starch brand) xanthan gum	3.0% 0.3%	60	140	5
	chewy		agar glycerol	0.8% 2.5%	60	140	5
glasses	crisp	spread mixture into layer 1 mm / 1/16 in thick	glucose syrup DE40 isomalt icing sugar	2% 10% 18%	60	140	36
	brittle	simmer mixture for 4 min, and then spread into layer 1 mm / 1/16 in thick	Pure Cote B790	12.5%	60	140	15–18
wafers	crisp and airy	whip mixture into stiff foam, and then spread into layer 3 mm / 1/8 in thick	egg white xanthan gum	18% 1%	55	130	12
	crunchy and airy		xanthan gum 160 Bloom gelatin	0.50% 1.25%	55	130	12

from page 3·367

(set weight of fruit or vegetable to 100%)

GREEN PEA WAFER

Yields 250 g

INGREDIENT	QUANTITY	SCALING	PROCEDURE
Green pea puree see page 55	400 g (from 750 g of frozen sweet peas)	100%	① Blend to fine puree. ② Pass through fine sieve.
Egg whites	75 g	18.5%	③ Whisk together into puree until light and fluffy in texture.
Xanthan gum	4.75 g	1%	④ Cast puree evenly into nonstick mold in layer 0.5 cm / 1/4 in thick. ⑤ Dehydrate at 57 °C / 135 °F until crisp, 2 h or longer. ⑥ Cut into rectangles.

from page 3·371

CRYSTALLIZED ROSE PETALS

Yields 30 g

INGREDIENT	QUANTITY	SCALING	PROCEDURE
Rose petals (organic)	50 g	100%	① Separate petals, and reserve.
Egg whites	50 g	100%	② Whisk together until gum arabic is fully dissolved.
Gum arabic	25 g	50%	③ Rest at room temperature until bubbles have dissipated, about 20 min.
			④ Brush mixture onto each petal to coat completely.
Sugar, isomalt, or trehalose	100 g	200%	⑤ Dredge petals.
			⑥ Place on dehydrator tray or parchment paper-lined baking sheet.
			⑦ Dry at 45 °C / 115 °F until dry and crisp, for 8–12 h.

from page 3·368

SPINACH PAPER

Yields 70 g

INGREDIENT	QUANTITY	SCALING	PROCEDURE
Spinach puree see page 55 and page 144	100 g	100%	① Season puree.
Salt	to taste		
N-Zorbit M (National Starch brand)	20 g	20%	② Whisk into puree.
			③ Spread mixture thinly on silicone mat.
			④ Dehydrate at 60 °C / 145 °F until crisp, 25–45 min.

from page 3·369

N-Zorbit, a modified starch (see page 4·34), dries to create a crisp glassy film.

MANDARIN LEATHER

Yields 200 g

INGREDIENT	QUANTITY	SCALING	PROCEDURE
Mandarins, quartered and seeds removed	200 g	100%	① Combine in pressure cooker.
Water	150 g	75%	② Pressure-cook at gauge pressure of 1 bar / 15 psi for 45 min.
Sugar	75 g	37.5%	③ Blend fully to puree.
			④ Strain through fine sieve.
			⑤ Cool puree, and measure 300 g.
Lime juice	10 g	5%	⑥ Blend together fully with puree.
Kosher salt	0.5 g	0.25%	⑦ Spread seasoned puree in layer 3 mm / 1/8 in thick on cellulose acetate sheet, 15 cm by 30 cm / 6 in by 12 in.
Grapeseed oil or other neutral oil	9 g	4.5% (3%)*	⑧ Place sheet on dehydrator tray.
			⑨ Dehydrate puree at 35 °C / 95 °F until leathery, about 8 h.

from page 3·369   *(% of total mandarin puree weight)

The addition of oil provides tenderness to the leather. Our favorite texture uses a scaling of 3% of the total puree weight. You can go up to 4.5% for even more tenderness. This recipe can be adapted to any fruit or vegetable puree.

For more on freeze-dried ingredients, see page 2·444.

PINEAPPLE GLASS ADAPTED FROM GRANT ACHATZ

Yields 200 g

INGREDIENT	QUANTITY	SCALING	PROCEDURE
Pineapple, juiced see page 2·338	275 g	100%	① Strain through fine sieve.
Fructose	7 g	2.5%	② Combine with strained juice.
Malic acid	2 g	0.7%	③ Bring to boil over medium heat, and remove immediately.
Salt	2 g	0.7%	
Saffron threads	0.25 g	0.1%	④ Add to warm juice, cover, and steep for 5 min.
			⑤ Strain.
Pure-Cote B790 (GPC brand)	35.5 g	13%	⑥ Blend with juice mixture on high speed for about 2 min. Simmer for 15 min.
			⑦ Pour liquid onto center of cellulose acetate sheet.
			⑧ Form sheet into U shape, and allow liquid to coat sheet evenly.
			⑨ Lay sheet on flat surface, and rest at room temperature until dry, 12–15 h.
			⑩ Peel glass off in single piece.

from page 3·370

FREEZE-DRIED FRUITS AND VEGETABLES

① Prepare the ingredients. The table below lists our recommendations.
② Arrange in a single layer on a tray.
③ Freeze-dry for the time indicated. Temperature and pressure settings for primary and secondary drying are given in chapter 10 on The Modernist Kitchen on page 2·450.

Best Bets for Freeze-Drying Plant Foods

Ingredient	Preparation	Cut (mm)	Cut (in)	Dry (h)	Typical use	See page
apples	peeled	2	1/16	24	whole; grind into a fine powder, and use to enhance apple recipes	
bananas	peeled	3	1/8	48	whole; grind into a fine powder, and add to Thai spice mix or to mustard base	
butternut squash	peeled	2	1/16	36	grind into a fine powder, and add to fresh butternut squash puree to deepen the flavor and thicken	
carrots	peeled and sliced, then blanched for 30 s	1	1/32	12	instant ramen	61
chives, mint, and other herbs		whole leaves		12	grind into a fine powder for seasoning	
corn, kernels		whole		36	whole; grind into a fine powder and use in Modernist breading, add to corn bread recipes or broths	209
grapes	perforated with needle	whole		48	whole; pickled; add to pastry recipes; infuse into broths	
lettuce		whole leaves		24	caesar salad	189
mushrooms		1	1/32	12	infuse into stocks and broths; rehydrate to make a puree; grind into a fine powder for breading	5·14
onions	cooked until tender	2	1/16	12	grind into a fine powder, and add to savory pastry	189
piquillo peppers	blanched, peeled	quartered		36	grind into a fine powder, and add to spice blends	5·239
raspberries		whole		24	whole; grind into a powder, and add to pastry or infuse into vinegar	
strawberries		2	1/16	24	whole; grind into a fine powder for seasoning and breading	33
tomatoes	peeled, cored	thinly sliced		24	whole; infuse into oils; grind into a fine powder, and add to sauces and spice blends	49

from page 3·372

ONION SABLÉ

Yields 350 g

INGREDIENT	QUANTITY	SCALING	PROCEDURE
Unsalted butter	500 g	500%	① Simmer over low heat for 2 h to infuse butter with onion flavor, being careful not to brown onions.
Sweet onions, thinly sliced	200 g	200%	② Strain butter, and reserve onions for other use.
			③ Measure 100 g of onion broth for making dough.
All-purpose flour	112.5 g	112.5%	④ Mix to form dough, and rest dough for 20 min at room temp.
Onion butter, from above	100 g	100%	⑤ Roll out dough in layer 1 mm / 1/16 in thick.
Almond powder	50 g	50%	⑥ Place on nonstick baking sheet.
Isomalt	50 g	50%	⑦ Bake in 175 °C / 350 °F oven until lightly golden, for 11 min.
Egg yolk, cooked sous vide in 65 °C / 149 °F bath for 7 min	25 g	25%	⑧ Cut into 3 cm by 8 cm / 1¼ in by 3¼ in rectangles while still warm.
			⑨ Cool completely.
Cornstarch	12.5 g	12.5%	⑩ Reserve in cool, dry place.
Freeze-dried onion powder see page 189	8 g	8%	
Salt	4.5 g	4.5%	
Heavy cream	3.3 g	3.3%	
Baking powder	1.5 g	1.5%	

from page 5·263

SEARED STRAWBERRY

Yields 100 g

INGREDIENT	QUANTITY	SCALING	PROCEDURE
Strawberries, halved lengthwise	60 g (two berries)	100%	① Coat halved strawberries with thin dusting of strawberry powder, and then sear in oil over high heat until charred, about 45 s.
Freeze-dried strawberry powder see page 188	12 g	20%	
Grapeseed oil	as needed		
Oloroso sherry vinegar	5 g	8.5%	② Season.
Salt	to taste		

from page 5·279

CAESAR SALAD

Yields 200 g

INGREDIENT	QUANTITY	SCALING	PROCEDURE
Egg yolk powder, freeze-dried see page 5·250	12 g	24%	① Dry blend powders.
Acetic acid	7 g	14%	
Salt	7 g	14%	
Black peppercorns, finely ground	3 g	6%	
Anchovy powder, freeze-dried	2 g	4%	
N-Zorbit M (National Starch brand)	20 g	40% (50%)*	
Extra-virgin olive oil	40 g	80%	② Whisk into powder mixture until fully incorporated.
Romaine lettuce, freeze-dried	50 g	100%	③ Toss greens together with dressing.
			④ Arrange salad on plate.
Basil leaves (small), microwave-fried	8 g	16%	
Chives, cut into 1 cm / ⅜ in batons and freeze-dried	8 g	16%	
Parsley, microwave-fried see page 157	4 g	8%	
Parmesan nuggets see page 206	20 g	40%	⑤ Garnish salad.
Salt-cured anchovies, freeze-dried	16 g	32%	
Brioche, cut into 1 mm / 1/32 in slices and dehydrated	12 g	24%	

from page 3·373 *(% of weight of olive oil)

FREEZE-DRIED ONION POWDER

Yields 40 g

INGREDIENT	QUANTITY	SCALING	PROCEDURE
Sweet onions, thinly sliced	350 g	100%	① Sauté in nonstick pan over low heat until translucent and tender, about 15 min.
Neutral oil	as needed		
Water	100 g	28.5%	② Deglaze as needed to prevent any browning.
			③ Cool at room temperature.
			④ Freeze-dry for 12 h.
			⑤ Grind into powder.
			⑥ Store in cool, dry place.

from page 3·373

SHRIMP AND GRITS INSPIRED BY SEAN BROCK

Yields 750 g (four portions)

INGREDIENT	QUANTITY	SCALING	PROCEDURE
Bacon, thinly sliced	100 g	50%	① Vacuum seal together.
Water	100 g	50%	② Cook sous vide in 88 °C / 190 °F bath for 2 h.
			③ Strain bacon broth, and cool.
			④ Discard resulting layer of fat, and measure 100 g of broth.
Bacon broth, from above	100 g	50%	⑤ Blend sucrose esters and whey protein isolate into broth, and reserve.
Sucrose esters (Sucro, Texturas brand)	2.4 g	1.2%	
Whey protein isolate	1.5 g	0.75%	
Eggs	four large		⑥ Cook in shells in 65 °C / 149 °F bath for 35 min.
Dried corn kernels or hominy	200 g	100%	⑦ Dip dried corn in liquid nitrogen until frozen.
			⑧ Blend frozen corn on high power until coarse texture is achieved.
Liquid nitrogen	as needed		⑨ Pass through coarse sieve to remove any unground pieces.
Water, shellfish stock, or vegetable stock see page 6 and page 9	1 kg	500%	⑩ Combine with cornmeal from above, and cook over medium heat for about 40 min; stir constantly until mixture softens and forms grits.
Spot prawn or shrimp tails, peeled	150 g	75%	⑪ Dip prawns in liquid nitrogen until frozen.
			⑫ Blend frozen prawns on high power until fine powder is achieved.
Liquid nitrogen	as needed		⑬ Fold into warm grits.
			⑭ Warm bacon broth, and whip with foaming wand.
Mascarpone	80 g	40%	⑮ Fold into grits, and reheat to make sure grits are warm.
Salt	to taste		⑯ Season grits, and portion into four bowls.
			⑰ Place peeled, cooked egg in center of each bowl.
Red-eye gravy see page 225	80 g	40%	⑱ Pour gravy over eggs and grits.

from page 3·377

PASTA

① Mix dry ingredients, texturing agent, and salt.
② Whisk in liquids.
③ Knead, or blend until dough is elastic, 5–10 min.
④ Roll out, and cut to desired shape.
⑤ Dry (optional). See page 2·430 for dehydrating strategies.

To make sodium carbonate for the alkaline ramen recipe in the table below, place some sodium bicarbonate in a shallow pan, and bake it in a 150 °C / 300 °F oven for 1 h.

Best Bets for Pasta Doughs

Pasta	Dry ingredient	(scaling)	Texturing agent	(scaling)	Salt (scaling)	Liquid	(scaling)	Dry
wheat	00 wheat flour	100%	xanthan gum	1%	2.5%	water	9%	no
						egg yolk	56.7%	
						neutral or olive oil	10.7%	
buckwheat	buckwheat flour, sifted	100%	Activa RM	4%	1.75%	milk	75%	optional
	all-purpose unbleached wheat flour	50%				egg yolks	37.5%	
						olive oil	20%	
semolina	all-purpose bleached wheat flour	25%	albumin powder	2%	1.3%	water	35%	yes
	semolina flour	100%				white wine	7%	
cocoa tajarin	00 wheat flour	100%	vital gluten	4%	1.5%	egg yolks	117%	no
	semolina flour	65%				water	27%	
	cocoa powder	44%				olive oil	22.5%	
rice flour	rice flour	100%	konjac gum	10%	2.5%	water	160%	yes
	tapioca starch	50%						
	glutinous rice flour	50%						
alkaline ramen	bread flour	100%	sodium carbonate	0.9%	1.5%	water	37.5%	no
			potassium carbonate	0.1%				

from page 3·381

HERB-EMBEDDED PASTA VEIL

Yields 300 g

INGREDIENT	QUANTITY	SCALING	PROCEDURE
All-purpose unbleached wheat flour	210 g	100%	① Combine to form smooth dough.
Water	50 g	24%	② Knead for 12 min.
Egg yolks	28 g	13.5%	③ Vacuum seal, and refrigerate for 12 h.
Canola oil	7.2 g	3.5%	
Toasted sesame oil	7.2 g	3.5%	
Gluten flour	2.5 g	1.2% (*1%*)*	
Salt	1 g	0.5%	
Cilantro, dill or other small-leaved herbs	as desired		④ Roll dough to 1 mm / 1/16 in thick.
			⑤ Divide into two sheets of equal length and width.
			⑥ Lay herbs individually on first sheet, and cover with second sheet.
			⑦ Roll layered dough to 1 mm / 1/16 in thick.
			⑧ Transfer to flour-dusted, parchment paper–lined tray, and cover with damp cloth.
			⑨ Refrigerate until needed.

from page 3·383   *(% of total weight of all other ingredients)

SPAGHETTI CARBONARA INSPIRED BY JEAN-FRANÇOIS PIÈGE

Yields 1.5 kg (about 30 portions)

INGREDIENT	QUANTITY	SCALING	PROCEDURE
Whipping cream	200 g	200%	① Combine, and vacuum seal.
Bacon, thinly sliced	90 g	90%	② Cook sous vide in 88 °C / 190 °F bath for 2 h.
Parmesan, grated	20 g	20%	③ Strain cream, and reserve warm.
Garlic, thinly sliced and blanched	15 g	15%	
Water	1 kg	1,000%	④ Boil spaghetti in salted water until al dente, about 8 min.
Dry spaghetti	100 g	100%	⑤ Transfer spaghetti to bacon cream, stirring to coat evenly.
Salt	20 g	20%	⑥ Arrange pasta strands straight and pressed against each other on sheet of plastic wrap.
			⑦ Refrigerate coated strands until set, about 2 h.
Sodium citrate	2.3 g	2.3%	⑧ Dry blend.
Low-acyl gellan (Kelcogel F, CP Kelco brand)	0.6 g	0.6% (0.26%)*	
High-acyl gellan (Kelcogel LT 100, CP Kelco brand)	0.3 g	0.3% (0.13%)*	
Whole milk	100 g	100%	⑨ Disperse powder blend in milk and bring to simmer.
Parmesan cheese, finely grated	130 g	130%	⑩ Shear cheese into simmering milk.
			⑪ Cast into nonstick mold in layer 1 cm / ⅜ in thick.
			⑫ Cool, and refrigerate until set, about 5 min.
			⑬ Cut set gel in strips measuring 5 cm by 10 cm / 2 in by 4 in.
			⑭ Place strips over cold spaghetti ribbons.
			⑮ Roll spaghetti with cheese strips into tight parcels.
Egg yolks, blended	50 g	50%	⑯ Vacuum seal.
			⑰ Cook sous vide in 68 °C / 154 °F bath for 35 min to form fluid gel.
			⑱ Pass fluid yolk mixture through sieve.
			⑲ Transfer to squeeze bottle with 5 mm / ¼ in diameter tip.
Chives, finely minced	10 g	10%	⑳ Steam spaghetti parcels until warmed through, about 4 min.
			㉑ Pipe stripe of egg yolk fluid gel across each spaghetti parcel.
			㉒ Garnish parcels with chives.
			㉓ Serve carbonara with braised pork belly, or finish with fresh black truffles.

from page 3·384 *(% of total weight of whole milk and Parmesan cheese)

MAC AND CHEESE INSPIRED BY HAROLD MCGEE

Yields 400 g (four portions)

INGREDIENT	QUANTITY	SCALING	PROCEDURE
Water	100 g	50%	① Whisk together.
Wheat beer	75 g	37.5%	② Bring to simmer.
Sodium citrate	10 g	5%	
Salt	4.5 g	2.25%	
Iota carrageenan	1.25 g	0.63% (0.26%)*	
Aged Gouda cheese, grated	200 g	100%	③ Hand-blend slowly into hot liquid until cheese is completely emulsified.
			④ Transfer to shallow bowl, and cool to room temperature.
Sharp cheddar cheese, grated	85 g	42.5%	⑤ Refrigerate until set, about 30 min.
			⑥ Grate coarsely.
Water	300 g	150%	⑦ Boil together over high heat until pasta has absorbed most of water and is al dente, about 7 min. Do not drain.
Macaroni (store-bought)	100 g	50%	
Salt	2.4 g	1.2%	⑧ Whisk 160 g of cheese and remaining liquid into pasta until cheese is melted.

from page 3·387 *(% of total weight of first two ingredients and cheeses)

PAD THAI ADAPTED FROM PIM TECHAMUANVIVIT

Yields 500 g (four portions)

INGREDIENT	QUANTITY	SCALING	PROCEDURE
Palm sugar	56 g	18.5%	① Combine, and bring to simmer until fully dissolved.
Fish sauce	40 g	13.5%	② Remove sauce from heat, and reserve.
Tamarind paste see page 145	18 g	6%	
Rice vinegar	11 g	3.5%	
Dried baby shrimp	50 g	16.5%	③ Fry baby shrimp over medium heat until golden brown, about 10 min.
Neutral oil	as needed		④ Transfer to paper towel-lined tray.
			⑤ Cool.
			⑥ Mince finely, and reserve for garnish.
Rice stick noodles	300 g	100%	⑦ Cover with warm water, and soak at room temperature for 2 h.
Shrimp, peeled and deveined	12 shrimp		⑧ Fry over medium heat until half cooked, about 1 min.
Neutral oil	as needed		
Bean sprouts, cut into 3 cm / 1¼ in strips	40 g	13.5%	⑨ Add, and stir-fry until slightly wilted and shrimp are fully cooked, 1–2 min.
			⑩ Remove shrimp, bean sprouts, and garlic chives, leaving oil in pan.
Garlic chives, diced	24 g	8%	
Shallot, minced	20 g	7%	⑪ Add to pan, and increase heat to high. Cook until golden, about 45 s.
Garlic, minced	10 g	3%	⑫ Add soaked noodles, and stir-fry over high heat until translucent, 2–3 min.
Ginger, minced	10 g	3%	⑬ Remove from heat.
Egg, beaten	60 g	20%	⑭ Add to pan, stirring constantly until incorporated and cooked through, about 1 min.
			⑮ Add 40 g of reserved sauce.
			⑯ Cook over high heat for 1 min.
			⑰ Stir in cooked shrimp, bean sprouts, and garlic chives; remove from heat.
Lime juice	to taste		⑱ Season.
Salt	to taste		⑲ Add more sauce if necessary.
Pressure-cooked peanuts, finely ground see page 151	30 g	10%	⑳ Garnish with dried shrimp, peanuts, and chili powder.
Roasted chili powder	to taste		

from page 3·385

PASTA MARINARA INSPIRED BY H. ALEXANDER TALBOT AND AKI KAMOZAWA

Yields 450 g (four portions)

INGREDIENT	QUANTITY	SCALING	PROCEDURE
Tomato water see page 40	500 g	100%	① Combine, and vacuum seal.
			② Infuse refrigerated for 12 h.
Basil	5 g	1%	③ Strain tomato water.
Thyme leaves	2.5 g	0.5%	
Bay leaf, julienne	1 g	0.2%	
Salt	10 g	2%	④ Season tomato water.
Spaghetti or tagliatelle (store-bought)	140 g	28%	⑤ Soak spaghetti in tomato water for 1 h.
			⑥ Drain, reserving tomato water.
			⑦ Transfer tomato water and pasta to separate containers, and refrigerate. Pasta can be stored for up to 8 h.
			⑧ Bring tomato water to boil. Add soaked pasta, and cook for 1 min 10 s.
			⑨ Drain.
Tomato confit, thinly sliced see page 179	40 g	8%	⑩ Toss with pasta to finish.
Basil leaves, julienne	5 g	1%	
Extra-virgin olive oil	to taste		

from page 3·386

COCOA TAJARIN

Yields 400 g

INGREDIENT	QUANTITY	SCALING	PROCEDURE
00 wheat flour	127 g	100%	① Combine.
Semolina flour	85 g	67%	
Dutch processed cocoa powder	57 g	45%	
Vital wheat gluten	5 g	4%	
Salt	2 g	1.5%	
Egg yolks	153 g	120%	② Add to flour mixture, and knead for 10 min to make dough.
Water	35 g	28%	③ Vacuum seal. Refrigerate for 12 h.
Extra virgin olive oil	29 g	23%	④ Roll into sheets 1 mm / 1/16 in thick.
			⑤ Cut into noodles 2 mm / 1/16 in wide.
			⑥ Place on parchment paper, cover with damp towel, and refrigerate.
Deodorized cocoa butter (food-grade)	40 g	31.5%	⑦ Melt cocoa butter, and reserve.
			⑧ Cook noodles in boiling 3% salt water for 40 s.
			⑨ Drain, and toss with melted cocoa butter.
Sea urchin butter warmed	100 g	79%	⑩ Garnish tajarin.

from page 5·227

RAMEN NOODLES

Yields 14.5 g

INGREDIENT	QUANTITY	SCALING	PROCEDURE
All-purpose flour	78 g	100%	① Mix together.
Semolina flour	57 g	73%	② Form into mound.
Wheat gluten	2.5 g	3.2%	③ Make well in center.
Salt	1 g	1.3%	
Egg yolks, whisked	76.5 g	98%	④ Combine, and pour into well.
Water	17.5 g	22%	⑤ Mix slowly by hand until dough forms.
Neutral oil	14.5 g	18.5%	⑥ Vacuum seal.
			⑦ Rest at room temperature for at least 1 h.
			⑧ Roll with pasta roller into sheets 1 mm / 1/16 in thick.
			⑨ Cut sheets into noodles 2 mm / 1/16 in wide.
			⑩ Cook noodles in 3% salt solution for 30 s.
Ramen broth, warmed (not freeze-dried) see page 61	400 g	513%	⑪ Divide noodles and broth evenly among four bowls.
			⑫ Garnish with zest.
Yuzu zest, finely grated (fresh)	to taste		

from page 5·250

BUCKWHEAT DOUGH

Yields 525 g

INGREDIENT	QUANTITY	SCALING	PROCEDURE
Buckwheat flour	200 g	100%	① Sift.
All-purpose flour	100 g	50%	② Combine with sifted buckwheat flour in food processor.
Activa TI or RM	12 g	6% (4%)*	③ Process to mix thoroughly.
Salt	3.5 g	1.75%	
Whole milk	150 g	75%	④ Blend thoroughly into flour mixture.
Egg yolks	75 g	37.5%	⑤ Transfer dough to floured surface, and knead for 10 min.
Grapeseed oil	40 g	20%	⑥ Vacuum seal.
			⑦ Refrigerate for 12 h to allow enzyme to bind proteins.
			⑧ Roll dough with pasta roller into sheets 2 mm / 1/16 in thick.
			⑨ Cut sheets into noodles 0.5 cm / 1/8 in wide.
			⑩ Cook noodles in 3% salt solution for 1½ min.
Oyster butter emulsion, warmed see page 297	100 g	50%	⑪ Toss noodles in oyster butter and serve.

from page 5·234   *(% of total weight of both flours)

SEMOLINA PASTA

Yields 450 g

INGREDIENT	QUANTITY	SCALING
Semolina flour	400 g	100%
All-purpose bleached wheat flour	100 g	25%
Water	100 g	25%
White wine (dry)	28 g	7%
Albumin powder	8 g	2%
Salt	5.2 g	1.3%

from page 3·382

COMPRESSED AND IMPREGNATED FRUITS AND VEGETABLES

① Peel, and cut the ingredients into even-size pieces. Arrange the food in a single layer in a sous vide bag.

② Add liquid (optional). To impregnate the fruit or vegetable with a liquid, add it to the bag or container; see the table at right for suggestions.

③ Vacuum-seal by using full vacuum power. Rest the produce in the bag or container for at least 10 min after the vacuum is released.

Best Bets for Compressing or Impregnating Produce

Ingredient	Liquid	See page
apple	apple juice	2·338
apricot	chamomile tea	
asparagus	asparagus juice	
celery	blue-cheese water	
cucumber	pickling brine	182
dragon fruit	lychee juice	
eggplant	barbecue sauce diluted in water	
fig	port	
grape, peeled	verjuice (store-bought sour grape juice)	
kiwi	strawberry juice	
lettuce	smoked water	this page
melon	bacon water or prosciutto stock	
onion	pickling brine	178
peach	vanilla syrup	
pear	red wine syrup	
pineapple	coconut water (store-bought or fresh), rum	
plum	almond milk	
rhubarb	grenadine syrup	
strawberry	thin cream infused with basil	
tomato	ketchup diluted in water	
watermelon	green tea	

from page 3·390

SMOKED LETTUCE

Yields 90 g

INGREDIENT	QUANTITY	SCALING	PROCEDURE
Water	150 g	167%	① Mix together.
Hickory liquid smoke (Wright's brand)	0.8 g (three drops)	0.9%	
Iceberg lettuce, cut into slices 1 cm / ⅜ in thick	90 g	100%	② Pour smoky water over lettuce.
			③ Place container, uncovered, in vacuum chamber.
			④ Pull vacuum until water boils, and then turn off machine and allow lettuce to absorb smoky water in vacuum chamber for 20 min.
			⑤ Drain lettuce, and refrigerate.

from page 5·15

CURRY-IMPREGNATED APPLE Yields 1 kg

INGREDIENT	QUANTITY	SCALING
Apple juice see page 2·338	1 kg	100%
Turmeric, freshly grated	20 g	2%
Black peppercorns (whole)	3 g	0.3%
Coriander seeds	2 g	0.2%
Cinnamon stick, toasted	1.5 g	0.15%
Cardamom	1 g	0.1%
Cloves (whole)	1 g	0.1%
Star anise, toasted	1 g	0.1%
Saffron threads	0.2 g	0.02%
Apples, peeled and cored	900 g	90%

① Vacuum seal juice and spices.
② Refrigerate for 12 h to infuse.
③ Place apples in bowl, and cover with infused juice.
④ Place bowl in chamber sealer, and pull moderate vacuum. Release vacuum when liquid begins to boil, and then run vacuum cycle twice more to boil a total of three times.
⑤ Hold under vacuum for 15 min. After last cycle, turn machine off, and leave machine sealed. When apples have fully absorbed liquid, release vacuum, and remove food.

from page 3·393

COMPRESSED MUSCAT GRAPES Yields 100 g

INGREDIENT	QUANTITY	SCALING	PROCEDURE
Muscat grapes	100 g	100%	① Blanch in boiling water for 20–45 s, depending on ripeness. Riper grapes will require shorter time. ② Shock in ice-water bath, peel, and reserve.
Grape juice, clarified	100 g	100%	③ Combine.
Verjuice (store-bought)	60 g	60%	④ Taste for seasoning balance.
Fructose	12 g	12%	⑤ Vacuum seal with peeled grapes to compress.
Malic acid	1.3 g	1.3%	⑥ Refrigerate for no more than 3–4 h before serving or grapes will become too soft.
Salt	to taste		

from page 5·110

COMPRESSED MELON TERRINE ADAPTED FROM H. ALEXANDER TALBOT AND AKI KAMOZAWA Yields 675 g

INGREDIENT	QUANTITY	SCALING	PROCEDURE
For the calcium lactate solution:			
Cold water	500 g	167%	① Disperse calcium lactate in water, and stir until fully dissolved.
Calcium lactate	2.5 g	0.8% (0.5%)*	
Honeydew melon, cut into five planks, each 1 cm / ⅜ in thick, 5 cm by 10 cm / 2 in by 4 in	375 g	125%	② Vacuum seal planks in one even layer with calcium solution. ③ Refrigerate for 20 min. ④ Remove from bag, and pat dry.
Cantaloupe, cut into four planks, each 1 cm / ⅜ in thick, 5 cm by 10 cm / 2 in by 4 in	300 g	100%	
For the pectin solution:			
Cold water	500 g	167%	⑤ Mix pectin in water, and blend until fully dispersed.
LM pectin (Genupectin LM 104 AS, CP Kelco brand)	15 g	5% (3%)*	⑥ Bring solution to boil while shearing for 1 min to fully hydrate. ⑦ Cool. ⑧ Brush one calcium-infused cantaloupe plank with cooled pectin solution, and lay calcium-infused honeydew plank on top. ⑨ Repeat brushing and layering process with remaining six planks. ⑩ Vacuum seal each stack to compress. ⑪ Refrigerate until bonded, about 12 h. ⑫ Cut terrines into slices, and serve.

from page 3·392   *(% of total weight of water used in the individual solution)

WATERMELON MEAT INSPIRED BY ANDONI LUIS ADURIZ

Yields 250 g

INGREDIENT	QUANTITY	SCALING
Watermelon, peeled and white rind discarded	500 g	100%
Water	100 g	20%
Salt	5 g	1%

from page 3·394

① Cut into 2.5 cm / 1 in "steaks." Cut from surface, seedless part only, reserving all remaining watermelon flesh for another use. Leave small lip of white rind to mimic fat cap of steak, if desired.

② Whisk together water and salt to make brine.

③ Vacuum seal watermelon steaks with brine, and refrigerate for 2 h.

④ Drain brined watermelon, and pat dry.

⑤ Dehydrate slices at 55 °C / 130 °F until dry and leather-like, 8–12 h.

⑥ Brush slices with water, vacuum seal, and refrigerate. This will moisten them just enough to keep them tender.

⑦ Serve as fun replacement for meat. See the plated-dish recipe for Watermelon Bulgogi on page 5·285.

VEGETABLE COALS ADAPTED FROM MUGARITZ

Yields 250 g

INGREDIENT	QUANTITY	SCALING	PROCEDURE
Cassava roots, peeled	675 g	100%	① Cut into 4.5 cm / 1¾ in cubes.
White fish stock see page 12	350 g	52%	② Combine stock and ink.
			③ Mix with cassava cubes.
Squid ink	15 g	2.2%	④ Simmer together until tender, 35–40 min.
Salt	to taste		⑤ Drain ink-stained cubes.
			⑥ Season.

from page 3·395

PULLED MUSHROOM INSPIRED BY H. ALEXANDER TALBOT AND AKI KAMOZAWA

Yields 200 g

INGREDIENT	QUANTITY	SCALING	PROCEDURE
King Trumpet mushrooms, sliced in half lengthwise	250 g	100%	① Vacuum seal oil with mushrooms.
			② Cook sous vide in 90 °C / 194 °F bath for 4 h.
			③ Drain on tray lined with paper towels.
Neutral oil	50 g	20%	④ Pull mushrooms apart into individual fibers.
Barbecue sauce see page 220	to taste		⑤ Mix in, and serve.

from page 3·396

SQUID-INK BEAN-SPROUT RISOTTO
ADAPTED FROM FERRAN ADRIÀ

Yields 700 g (eight portions)

INGREDIENT	QUANTITY	SCALING	PROCEDURE
Bean sprouts	250 g	100%	① Cut off ends.
			② Cut into 1 cm / ⅜ in sticks to resemble rice, and reserve.
Squid stock (or water) see page 6	50 g	20%	③ Blend stock and ink, and reserve, refrigerated.
Squid ink	2.5 g	1%	
Squid stock (or water)	50 g	20%	④ Disperse agar in stock, and bring to boil.
Agar (Texturas brand)	0.3 g	0.12%	⑤ Simmer for 2 min, and remove from heat.
			⑥ Cast evenly into nonstick mold in layer 1 cm / ⅜ in thick.
			⑦ Refrigerate until set, about 10 min.
			⑧ Cut squid jelly into cubes, and reserve.
Egg yolks	30 g	12%	⑨ Blend.
Garlic, mashed	8 g	3.2%	
Extra-virgin olive oil	150 g	60%	⑩ Drizzle slowly into yolks, while blending, until emulsified and mayonnaise forms.
Salt	to taste		⑪ Season and reserve.
Squid legs	75 g	30%	⑫ Sauté legs for 20 s on each side until just cooked through.
Neutral oil	as needed		⑬ Season, remove from pan, and reserve.
Salt	as needed		
Squid ink stock, from above	50 g	20%	⑭ Sauté bean sprouts.
			⑮ Add squid ink stock to sautéed sprouts.
Neutral oil	as needed		⑯ Simmer together until risotto is just cooked through and still crunchy, about 2 min.
Lemon herb oil see page 27			⑰ Portion risotto into four bowls.
			⑱ Garnish with squid jelly, garlic mayonnaise, squid legs, and parsley oil.

from page 3·397

FROZEN WHITE "TRUFFLE" ADAPTED FROM QUIQUE DACOSTA

① Disperse gelatin in cold soy milk, and then stir over medium heat until dissolved and fully hydrated.
② Blend in cheese until melted and fully incorporated into the mixture.
③ Strain and chill.
④ Add white truffle oil, salt, and pepper, and then place in 1 l whipping siphon. Charge with two cartridges of nitrous oxide.
⑤ Melt mannitol in small saucepan, and bring to 200 °C / 390 °F. Add colored powders, and then hold at 180 °C / 355 °F.
⑥ Dispense foam onto offset spatula in desired shapes. Insert bamboo skewer into each "truffle."
⑦ Dip in liquid nitrogen. After dipping, baste with nitrogen to ensure even freezing.
⑧ Swirl frozen truffle in warm mannitol to coat evenly and soften rough edges.
⑨ Refreeze in nitrogen. A brief dip will set mannitol shell.
⑩ Thaw in refrigerator for 1 h. Parmesan cream will soften as it warms.
⑪ Garnish with porcini powder.

Yields 900 g

INGREDIENT	QUANTITY	SCALING
160 Bloom gelatin	6 g	2%
Soy milk	500 g	166%
Aged Parmesan cheese, grated	300 g	100%
White truffle oil	12 g	4%
Black pepper, finely ground	0.5 g	0.17%
Salt	6 g	2%
Mannitol	800 g	267%
Gold powder	2 g	0.7%
Bronze powder	0.2 g	0.07%
Dried porcini powder	60 g	20%

from page 3·400

CLAY POTATOES ADAPTED FROM ANDONI LUIS ADURIZ

Yields 200 g

INGREDIENT	QUANTITY	SCALING	PROCEDURE
Water	3 kg	1,500%	① Combine in pot.
Salt	24 g	12%	
Whole baby Yukon Gold potatoes, skins on	200 g	100%	② Simmer in salted water for 20 min, until cooked but still firm.
			③ Strain.
			④ Place on bamboo skewers, and reserve warm.
Water	40 g	20%	⑤ Combine.
Kaolin clay	30 g	15%	⑥ Dip warm skewered potatoes into clay mixture to coat.
Lactose	20 g	10%	⑦ Place two cooling racks in deep hotel pan, one on bottom and one on top.
Carbon black powder	1.5 g	0.75%	⑧ Thread skewers to stand upright in racks.
			⑨ Dry in 45 °C / 115 °F oven for 15 min.
			⑩ Transfer potatoes from skewers to serving plates.
Garlic confit see page 176	100 g	50%	⑪ Blend.
Egg yolks	40 g	20%	
Extra-virgin olive oil	250 g	125%	⑫ Blend into garlic and yolk mixture until emulsified and aioli forms.
Salt	to taste		⑬ Season aioli, and serve with warm potatoes.

from page 3·398

FOSSILIZED SALSIFY BRANCH ADAPTED FROM ANDONI LUIS ADURIZ

Yields 350 g (four portions)

INGREDIENT	QUANTITY	SCALING	PROCEDURE
Water	500 g	125%	① Whisk calcium hydroxide into water to make brine.
Calcium hydroxide	4.5 g	1.13% (0.9%)*	
Salsify root, scrubbed and peeled	400 g (four medium roots)	100%	② Soak in brine at room temperature for 3 h; stir every 30 min to ensure that calcium hydroxide is distributed evenly.
			③ Remove from brine, and rinse.
			④ Bake in 170 °C / 340 °F oven for 45 min, and reserve warm.
Salted cod roe or pollock roe	100 g	25%	⑤ Whisk and reserve.
Extra-virgin olive oil	16 g	4%	
Sea beans (Salicornia)	40 g	10%	⑥ Toss.
Extra-virgin olive oil	10 g	2.5%	⑦ Place salsify root in center of each warmed plate.
			⑧ Garnish evenly with fish roe and sea beans.

from page 3·399

*(% of weight of water used for brine)

TRADITIONAL STARCH THICKENERS

① Disperse by mixing the starch with whatever liquid you want to thicken until a slurry forms.

② Heat to at least 80 °C / 176 °F to hydrate. Use a water bath if available; if heating on a stove top, stir the mixture constantly. The starch solution will change from milky to clear when it is fully hydrated.

Best Bets for Thickening with Natural Starch

Starch	Texture	Translucency	Flavor	Application	(scaling)*	Heat-sensitive	Stable when thawed
arrowroot	creamy	clear	neutral	broths	1%	no	unstable
				jus, gravies	2%		
corn	creamy	opaque	strong	broths	1.50%	yes	unstable
				velouté, cream sauce	2.0%–2.5%		
				gravies	3%–4%		
				puddings	5.0%–6.5%		
				set gels	9%		
kudzu	gelatinous	clear	neutral	broths	2%	no	unstable
				glazes	5%–7%		
				dense puddings, tofu	12%		
potato	sticky	clear	subtle	broths	1%	yes	unstable
				jus, gravies	2%		
				stir-fry sauces	2.5%		
rice	sticky	opaque	subtle	glazes	3.0%–3.5%	yes	unstable
				soups	4%–5%		
				puddings, purees	7%–8%		
tapioca	sticky	clear	neutral	broths	1.5%–2.0%	somewhat	stable
				jus, gravies	2.5%–3.0%		
				fruit fillings	4%–5%		
waxy corn	creamy	opaque	subtle	broths	1%	no	stable
				low-fat salad dressings	2.50%		
				gravies	4%		
wheat	creamy	opaque	strong	velouté, cream sauce	2.5%	yes	stable
				gravies	3.0%–3.5%		
				béchamel	4%–5%		

from page 4·28

*(set weight of liquid to be thickened to 100%)

PREGELATINIZED STARCH PASTE

Yields 500 g

INGREDIENT	QUANTITY	SCALING	PROCEDURE
Water	50 g	12.5%	① Whisk starch into water until fully dispersed.
Tapioca starch	50 g	12.5%	② Vacuum seal mixture.
			③ Cook sous vide in 80 °C / 176 °F bath for 2 h.
Water, hot	400 g	100%	④ Blend in hot water until fully incorporated while the paste is still warm.
			⑤ Strain, cool, and store vacuum-sealed at room temperature.

from page 4·29

MODERN STARCH THICKENERS

① Select a thickening agent from the table below. Note that starches marked as unstable below may break down upon heating or upon thawing from a frozen state.

② Whisk the starch into the liquid to be thickened by hand. Do not use a blender, which can make the mixture gluey or stringy.

③ Heat to hydrate if necessary. Bring Pure Cote B790 and Wondra to a simmer to hydrate fully; heat Novation PRIMA 600 to 75 °C / 167 °F.

Best Bets for Thickening with Modified Starch

Product	Brand	Source	Scaling range*	Translucency	Texture	Stable when Heated	Stable when Thawed	Example use	(scaling)*	See page
N-Zorbit M	National Starch	tapioca	20%–100%	nearly opaque	swelled granules	unstable	unstable	oil powders	30%–40%	207
								oil pastes	85%–100%	206
								bulking gels, sauces	5%–20%	
Ultra-Sperse 3	National Starch	tapioca	0.2%–8%	nearly to fully opaque	smooth	stable	stable	meat gravies, jus	3%–4%	204
								puddings	6%–8%	
Flojel 60	National Starch	corn	1%–10%	opaque	smooth, stringy	stable	unstable	cream sauce	4%	
								puddings	7%	
Novation Prima 600	National Starch	corn	1%–7%	opaque	smooth	stable	stable	broths	2.0%–2.5%	
								purees	4%	
Ultra-Tex 8	National Starch	tapioca	1%–10%	nearly opaque	creamy	stable	unstable	cream sauce	3.0%–3.5%	
								meat gravies, jus	4%	
								purees	6%	
								puddings	8%	
Pure-Cote B790	GPC	corn	0.5%–20%	clear	smooth	stable	unstable	films	12%	229
								thickened juices	15%	
Maltrin	GPC	corn	1%–30%	clear	smooth	stable	stable	thin sauces	10%	
								purees	20%	
Wondra	General Mills	barley malt, wheat	1%–15%	opaque	smooth	stable	unstable	gravies, velouté	6%–7%	
								béchamel	8%–9%	

from page 4·30

(set weight of liquid to be thickened to 100%)

AVOCADO PUREE ADAPTED FROM WYLIE DUFRESNE

Yields 150 g

INGREDIENT	QUANTITY	SCALING	PROCEDURE
Hass avocado, peeled	140 g	100%	① Puree until smooth.
Ultra-Sperse 5 (National Starch brand)	5 g	3.6%	② Transfer to squeeze bottle.
Ascorbic acid	1.4 g	1%	③ Pipe dots of avocado puree onto plates. Char lightly with blowtorch.
Lime juice	1.4 g	1%	
Salt	to taste		

from page 5·207

MODERNIST BÉCHAMEL
INSPIRED BY AKI KAMOZAWA AND H. ALEXANDER TALBOT

Yields 215 g

INGREDIENT	QUANTITY	SCALING	PROCEDURE
All-purpose bleached flour	250 g	125%	① Combine, and divide mixture among three 500 ml / 1 pt Mason jars.
Unsalted butter, melted	250 g	125%	② Seal jars, and place them upright in pressure cooker.
			③ Fill pressure cooker with water to middle of jars.
			④ Pressure-cook fat at gauge pressure of 1 bar / 15 psi for 2 h.
			⑤ Cool resulting roux at room temperature; measure 15 g for recipe, and refrigerate remainder for later use.
Whole milk, warmed to 45 °C / 113 °F	200 g	100%	⑥ Whisk together with reserved roux until smooth to form béchamel.
Pressure-cooked roux, from above	15 g	7.5%	⑦ Warm béchamel to desired temperature.
Ultra-Sperse 3 (National Starch brand)	7 g	3.5%	
Lambda carrageenan (Texturas brand)	0.2 g	0.1%	
Nutmeg, freshly grated	to taste		⑧ Season.
Salt	to taste		

from page 4·31

The béchamel can also be made by using 1.25% (2.5 g) lambda carrageenan rather than the amount indicated above and substituting 1% (2 g) pregelatinized starch paste for the Ultra-Sperse 3. For more details, see page 200.

If pressure-cooked in a canning jar, the roux can be stored without refrigeration. It has effectively been canned (see page 2·88). Once opened, it must be refrigerated.

JERUSALEM ARTICHOKE PUDDING

Yields 160 g (four portions)

INGREDIENT	QUANTITY	SCALING	PROCEDURE
Jerusalem artichokes, thinly sliced	200 g	200%	① Combine in nonstick pan.
Neutral oil	20 g	20%	② Cook artichoke slices over medium heat until golden brown and very tender, about 20 min.
Whole milk	400 g	400%	③ Puree milk with cooked artichokes until smooth.
			④ Pass puree through fine sieve; reserve 100 g of artichoke puree for recipe.
Jerusalem artichoke puree, from above	100 g	100%	⑤ Blend with reserved puree to form pudding.
			⑥ Divide pudding equally among four small bowls.
Ultra-Sperse 3 (National Starch brand)	3 g	3%	⑦ Cover and refrigerate bowls of pudding.
Xanthan gum	0.2 g	0.2%	
Lambda carrageenan (Texturas brand)	0.1 g	0.1%	
Jerusalem artichokes, thinly sliced	25 g	25%	⑧ Heat oil to 190 °C / 375 °F.
Grapeseed oil	as needed		⑨ Add artichokes, and fry until golden brown, approximately 2 min.
			⑩ Transfer artichokes to tray lined with paper towels, and cool.
Roasted-hazelnut oil	8 g	8%	⑪ Drizzle oil evenly over each bowl of pudding.
Roasted hazelnuts, quartered	10 g	10%	⑫ Garnish puddings.
Pickled Jerusalem artichoke, fine julienne see page 178	6 g	6%	
Parmigiano-Reggiano, grated	5 g	5%	
Flaky salt	to taste		⑬ Season puddings.
			⑭ Top with fried artichokes.

from page 4·31

STEAMED COD WITH COD ROUTÉ VELOUTÉ
ADAPTED FROM MIGUEL SANCHEZ ROMERA

Yields four portions

INGREDIENT	QUANTITY	SCALING	PROCEDURE
White fish stock see page 6	50 g	100%	① Blend together.
Pregelatinized starch paste see page 200	20 g	40%	
Water	25 g	50%	② Combine warm, and stir until dissolved to make syrup.
Sugar	10 g	20%	③ Cool completely.
Lemon juice	10 g	20%	④ Add juice and zest to syrup.
Lemon zest	2.5 g	5%	⑤ Blend syrup with fish stock mixture to make velouté.
Cod fillet	300 g	600%	⑥ Cut loin into four portions of 75 g each.
			⑦ Vacuum seal portions individually.
			⑧ Cook sous vide in 43 °C / 109 °F bath to core temperature of 42 °C / 108 °F, about 25 min.
Salted cod roe (or tobiko)	30 g	60%	⑨ Warm velouté.
			⑩ Whisk in roe.
Salt	to taste		⑪ Season roe velouté.
Garlic oil see page 28	50 g	100%	⑫ Place one cooked loin portion in center of each of four bowls.
			⑬ Spoon roe velouté over loins.
			⑭ Drizzle oil on top.

from page 4·32

SMOKED PEPPER PUREE

Yields 250 g

INGREDIENT	QUANTITY	SCALING	PROCEDURE
Goulash broth, see page 19	185 g	100%	① Vacuum seal together.
Red bell pepper, thinly sliced	30 g	16%	② Cook sous vide in 85 °C / 185 °F bath for 2 h.
Red onion, thinly sliced	23 g	12.5%	③ Blend to fine puree.
Cured ham, thinly sliced	15 g	8%	④ Pass through fine sieve.
Smoked Hungarian paprika	8 g	4.5%	⑤ Measure 200 g.
Red wine vinegar	to taste		⑥ Season puree.
Salt	to taste		
Ultra-Sperse 5 (National Starch brand)	5.2 g	2.8% (2.6%)*	⑦ Whisk into puree.
			⑧ Reheat and serve, or refrigerate until use.

from page 4·5

*(% of total weight of pepper puree)

CARAMELIZED CRÈME FRAÎCHE

Yields 300 g

INGREDIENT	QUANTITY	SCALING	PROCEDURE
Crème fraîche	250 g	100%	① Combine.
Baking soda	2.5 g	1%	② Pressure-cook in Mason jars at gauge pressure of 1 bar / 15 psi for 2½ h.
			③ Cool.
Garlic confit, sieved see page 176	50 g	20%	④ Blend into crème fraîche.
Pregelatinized starch paste (or Ultra-Sperse 3) see page 200	3.75 g	1.5%	
Salt	to taste		⑤ Season.
			⑥ Serve, or refrigerate until use.

from page 4·5

Raising the pH level (by adding baking soda) and pressure-cooking temperature greatly accelerates the Maillard reaction that produces a brown color and distinct flavor.

POMEGRANATE AND GARUM JUS

Yields 550 g

INGREDIENT	QUANTITY	SCALING	PROCEDURE
Brown duck stock *see page 6*	200 g	100%	① Combine.
			② Bring to boil.
Pomegranate juice	34 g	17%	③ Cool.
Garum (or fish sauce)	20 g	10%	
Malt vinegar	as needed		④ Season jus with vinegar.
Ultra-Sperse 3 (National Starch brand)	4.8 g	2.4%	⑤ Blend in Ultra-Sperse 3 to thicken.
			⑥ Serve, or refrigerate until use.

from page 5·122

TURKEY WING

Yields 300 g (four portions)

INGREDIENT	QUANTITY	SCALING	PROCEDURE
Turkey wings, ends cut off	300 g	100%	① Mix salt and sugar and rub evenly onto wings.
Salt	9 g	3%	② Vacuum seal.
Sugar	3 g	1%	③ Refrigerate to cure for 24 h.
			④ Remove cured wings from bags; rinse off cure.
Clarified butter	15 g	5%	⑤ Vacuum seal wings with butter.
			⑥ Cook sous vide in 58 °C / 136 °F bath for 12 h.
			⑦ Remove wings from bag while still hot; carefully debone without rupturing meat.
			⑧ Refrigerate.
Potato starch	25 g	8.3%	⑨ Coat wings with starch.
Frying oil	as needed		⑩ Pour thin film of oil in nonstick pan.
Sage, leaves	as needed		⑪ Fry coated wings for 2 min on each side.
			⑫ Transfer to serving plates, and garnish with gravy and whole sage leaves.

from page 4·33

THANKSGIVING TURKEY GRAVY

Yields 245 g

INGREDIENT	QUANTITY	SCALING	PROCEDURE
Brown chicken or turkey stock *see page 6*	600 g	300%	① Reduce to 200 g, and reserve.
Reduced chicken or turkey stock, from above	200 g	100%	② Blend reduced stock and garlic confit together to make gravy.
Garlic confit, pureed *see page 176*	25 g	12.5%	③ Whisk in Ultra-Sperse 3.
			④ Warm gravy to 70 °C / 160 °F.
Ultra-Sperse 3	8 g	4%	
Dried cranberries, finely minced	10 g	5%	⑤ Whisk into warm gravy.
Sage, finely minced	2 g	1%	
Black peppercorns, coarsely ground	0.15 g	0.075%	
Salt	to taste		⑥ Season gravy.

from page 4·33

HEATHER-SMOKED STURGEON RILLETTES

Yields 200 g

INGREDIENT	QUANTITY	SCALING	PROCEDURE	
Shallots, finely minced	15 g	15%	① Marinate shallots at room temperature for 30 min.	
White balsamic vinegar	13 g	13%		
Heather-smoked sturgeon see page 122	100 g	100%	② Shred sturgeon. ③ Combine shallots, sturgeon, and remaining ingredients in stand mixer.	Store-bought sturgeon can be substituted in this recipe.
Basic mayonnaise see page 303	75 g	75%	④ Whip on medium-high speed until fluffy and all ingredients are well incorporated.	
Celery, finely minced	9 g	9%	⑤ Refrigerate until use.	
Chives, minced	5 g	5%		
Celery leaf, minced	1.5 g	1.5%		
Chervil, minced	1.5 g	1.5%		
Tarragon, minced	1.5 g	1.5%		
Smoked salt	1.2 g	1.2%		
Ultra-Sperse 3 (National Starch brand)	1.2 g	1.2%		
Lime zest, finely grated	1 g	1%		
Lemon juice	0.7 g	0.7%		

from page 5·235

CRISPY GOAT'S MILK RICOTTA DUMPLING

ADAPTED FROM WYLIE DUFRESNE

Yields 290 g

INGREDIENT	QUANTITY	SCALING	PROCEDURE
Goat milk ricotta or cow milk ricotta store-bought or see page 248	200 g	100%	① Blend together fully.
Heavy cream	80 g	40%	
Salt	2.8 g	1.4%	
Black pepper	0.5 g	0.25%	
Ultra-Tex 4 (National Starch brand)	8 g	4% (3%)*	② Fold into ricotta mixture. ③ Roll into logs 3 cm / 2¼ in. in diameter on nonstick surface, using your palms. ④ Cut logs crosswise into 3 cm / 2¼ in pieces. ⑤ Arrange pieces on nonstick baking sheet and refrigerate until use.
Frying oil	as needed		⑥ To serve, dehydrate dumplings in 45 °C / 115 °F oven for 45 min. ⑦ Deep-fry dumplings in 195 °C / 385 °F oil until crispy and golden, about 1 min, and drain on paper towels.

from page 5·274   *(% of total weight of goat's milk ricotta and heavy cream)

MARCONA ALMOND BUTTER PASTE

Yields 350 g

INGREDIENT	QUANTITY	SCALING	PROCEDURE
Raw Marcona almonds	500 g	143%	① Roast in 175 °C / 350 °F oven until golden, about 15 min. ② Process roasted nuts with colloid mill or food processor until smooth, and measure 350 g.
Marcona almond butter, from above	350 g	100%	③ Blend together to thicken.
Ultra-Sperse 5 (National Starch brand)	10.5 g	3%	
Salt	to taste		④ Season butter, and refrigerate until use. Before use, temper at room temperature for 15 min.

from page 5·282

THICKENERS

MALT VINEGAR POWDER

Yields 250 g

INGREDIENT	QUANTITY	SCALING	PROCEDURE
Spray-dried malt vinegar	200 g	100%	① Grind together, and sift through fine sieve.
Acetic acid	40 g	20%	② Season with salt to taste.
Salt	36 g	18%	③ Store in an airtight container in dark, cool place.
Sugar	12 g	6%	
N-Zorbit M (National Starch brand)	8 g	4%	

from page 4·34

BACON POWDER SQUARES ADAPTED FROM GRANT ACHATZ

Yields 250 g

INGREDIENT	QUANTITY	SCALING	PROCEDURE
Smoked bacon fat, rendered see page 3·145	100 g	100%	① Warm bacon fat just enough to liquefy it.
N-Zorbit M (National Starch brand)	80 g	80%	② Whisk bacon fat into N-Zorbit M a little at a time until fully incorporated with powder.
Salt	to taste		③ Season powder.
Black pepper, fine powder	to taste		④ Form powder into squares 13 mm / ½ in wide, and set aside.
Pineapple glass see page 187	70 g	70%	⑤ Cut glass into squares 5 cm / 2 in wide.
			⑥ Place one single bacon powder square in center of each glass square.
			⑦ Fold glass squares over bacon powder squares to form small packets.
			⑧ Serve immediately, or store packets in cool, dry environment.

from page 4·34

PARMESAN NUGGETS INSPIRED BY FERRAN ADRIÀ

Yields 35 g

INGREDIENT	QUANTITY	SCALING	PROCEDURE
Parmesan, grated	100 g	100%	① Microwave until oil separates from solids.
			② Strain; reserve 10 g of oil for recipe.
N-Zorbit M (National Starch brand)	25 g	25%	③ Whisk oil into N-Zorbit M a little at a time, until fully incorporated. Resulting powder may be used as seasoning.
			④ Spoon thin layer of resulting powder into nonstick pan.
			⑤ Sauté powder over low heat; swirl constantly until small spheres form and begin to dry.
			⑥ Serve at room temperature, or refrigerate.

from page 4·35

SPICED ASH

Yields 80 g

INGREDIENT	QUANTITY	SCALING	PROCEDURE
Pain d'épices powder see page 51	45 g	100%	① Whisk together.
Carbon color powder (MSK brand)	8.5 g	19%	
Kaolin clay powder (MeadowSweet Herbs and Oils brand)	7 g	15.5%	
Roasted hazelnut oil	12 g	27%	② Whisk oil slowly into N-Zorbit M.
N-Zorbit M (National Starch brand)	10 g	22%	③ Incorporate tinted spice blend thoroughly.

from page 5·22

VANILLA OLIVE OIL POWDER ADAPTED FROM GRANT ACHATZ

Yields 350 g

INGREDIENT	QUANTITY	SCALING	PROCEDURE
Confectioner's sugar	80 g	80%	① Dry blend.
N-Zorbit M (National Starch brand)	160 g	160%	
Vanilla pulp and seeds	14 g (from four beans)	14%	
Salt	4 g	4%	
Olive oil	100 g	100%	② Whisk into powder until fully incorporated.
			③ Press through fine tamis to remove clumps.
			④ Store in airtight container in cool, dry place.

from page 4·35

CASHEW HALVAH

Yields 130 g

INGREDIENT	QUANTITY	SCALING	PROCEDURE
Cashews, roasted	100 g	100%	① Combine.
N-Zorbit M (National Starch brand)	30 g	30%	② Grind to fine powder.
			③ Refrigerate until use.
Salt	1.5 g	1.5%	

from page 5·93

ALMOND POLENTA ADAPTED FROM WYLIE DUFRESNE

Yields 575 g

INGREDIENT	QUANTITY	SCALING	PROCEDURE
Marcona almonds, toasted and finely grated	250 g	100%	① Whisk together.
			② Set dry mixture aside.
N-Zorbit M (National Starch brand)	30 g	12% (5%)*	
Ultra-Sperse M (National Starch brand)	5 g	2% (0.9%)*	
Xanthan gum	0.4 g	0.16%	
White chicken stock see page 6 and page 11	250 g	100%	③ Pour stock into pot.
			④ Whisk in dry mixture from above.
			⑤ Cook over medium heat; stir until just thickened, about 3 min.
Sweet almond oil	40 g	16%	⑥ Whisk in.
Salt	to taste		⑦ Season.

from page 4·36 *(% of total weight of all ingredients)

EDIBLE EARTH INSPIRED BY RENÉ REDZEPI AND WYLIE DUFRESNE

Yields 475 g

INGREDIENT	QUANTITY	SCALING	PROCEDURE
Almond flour, toasted	200 g	100%	① Blend in food processor until resembles soil.
Black bread, thinly sliced and dehydrated at 135 °C / 275 °F	150 g	75%	
N-Zorbit M (National Starch brand)	20 g	10%	
Barley malt powder	18.5 g	9.25%	
Dried chicory root, coarsely ground	17 g	8.5%	
Dried porcini powder	15 g	7.5%	
Freeze-dried shiitake powder see page 188	14 g	7%	
Grapeseed oil	31 g	15.5%	② Drizzle into dry mixture while continuing to blend with food processor until oil is fully incorporated.
Toasted–pumpkin seed oil	9 g	4.5%	
Caramel color powder	as needed		③ Adjust color if necessary.
Salt	to taste		④ Season.
			⑤ Transfer to airtight container and store in cool, dry place.

from page 4·37

This is our homage to the edible landscapes of Michel Bras (*Le Gargouillou de Jeunes Légumes*), David Kinch (*Into the Vegetable Garden*), and the many modern chefs who have simulated the aesthetics of nature in their dishes, including Quique Dacosta, Ferran and Albert Adrià, Andoni Luis Aduriz, Yoshiaki Takazawa, and Sam Mason, among others.

CORN PEBBLES ADAPTED FROM WYLIE DUFRESNE

Yields 95 g

INGREDIENT	QUANTITY	SCALING	PROCEDURE
Corn, freeze-dried and ground into powder see page 188 or store-bought	30 g	100%	① Dry blend.
N-Zorbit M (National Starch brand)	15 g	50%	
Spray-dried buttermilk see page 59 or store-bought	15 g	50%	
Smoked-grapeseed oil (store-bought)	6 g	20%	② Combine oils.
Grapeseed oil	30 g	100%	③ Whisk into powder mixture until fully incorporated.
Salt	to taste		④ Season resulting corn pebble base.
			⑤ Form into 1 cm / ⅜ in diameter balls; wearing latex gloves will help.
			⑥ Bake in 135 °C / 275 °F oven until balls become lightly golden and begin to firm, about 6 min.
			⑦ Serve immediately, or store in airtight container in cool, dry place.

from page 4·36

THICKENED HOT AND COLD LIQUIDS

① Choose the amount of thickening desired and a corresponding formula. We recommend those listed in the tables that follow. Proportions are given relative to the weight of liquid used. For example, add 0.5 g of guar gum and 0.35 g of xanthan gum to every 100 g of carrot juice to make a thick, hot carrot sauce.

② Disperse the thickeners. Thickening agents listed as cold-soluble can be stirred directly into cold liquids; those listed as hot-soluble can be stirred into hot liquids. Otherwise, stir the agent into a small amount of cold liquid to dissolve it, and then add it to the remaining liquid, and finally whisk to disperse it.

③ Hydrate fully. Heat as directed in the hydration column of the tables. Temperatures indicated are the minimum required for proper hydration.

Best Bets for Thickening Hot Liquids

Amount of thickening	Thickeners	(scaling)*	Hydrate (°C)	(°F)	(min)	Heat stability	Note	Example use
very little	xanthan gum	0.2%	hot or cold			thins at high temp		light consommés and broths, flavored milks
	lambda carrageenan	0.1%	cold			yes	best used in dairy applications	
little	gum arabic	10%	60	140	5	yes	slightly opaque, not suited to clear liquids	constructed broths, light soups
	160 Bloom gelatin	3%						
	lambda carrageenan	0.25%	cold			yes	best used in dairy applications	
	xanthan gum	0.35%	hot or cold			thins at high temp		
moderate	propylene glycol alginate	0.65%	82	180	3			cream sauces, veloutés, soups
	microcrystalline cellulose	1.5%	cold			yes		
	gum tragacanth	0.35%						
	lambda carrageenan	0.4%	82	180	3	thickens at high temp	high-calcium solutions may become too thick	
	locust bean gum	0.2%						
great	guar gum	0.5%	hot or cold			thins at high temp	good for liquids with a high ratio of suspended solids, slightly opaque	soups and coating sauces, veloutés
	xanthan gum	0.35%						
	160 Bloom gelatin	9%	60	140	5	yes	sucrose, fructose or another, less sweet sugar solid may be substituted	meat glazes, constructed jus (see page 34)
	glucose syrup DE40	4%						
	cellulose gum LV	0.5%						
	lambda carrageenan	0.8%	cold			yes	best used in dairy applications	light puddings
very great	xanthan gum	0.3%	cold			yes		purees and spreads, thick glazes, savory puddings
	lambda carrageenan	0.7%						
	cellulose gum LV	1.2%	room temperature		30	thickens at high temp	shear for 5 min after dispersing to ensure konjac fully hydrates; best texture when fat concentration is above 12%	
	konjac gum	0.15%						
	xanthan gum	0.15%						

from page 4·46   *(set weight of liquid to be thickened to 100%)

Best Bets for Thickening Cold Liquids

Amount of thickening	Thickeners	(scaling)*	Hydrate (°C)	(°F)	(min)	Note	Example use
very little	guar gum	0.35%	hot or cold			opaque, not suited for clear liquids	flavored milks
	xanthan gum	0.15%	hot or cold				cold consommés
little	lambda carrageenan	0.15%	cold				broths, light soups
	xanthan gum	0.10%					
	xanthan gum	0.25%	hot or cold				broths, light soups
moderate	guar gum	0.25%	cold				cold cream sauces
	cellulose gum LV	0.50%					
	lambda carrageenan	0.25%	cold				light fruit and vegetable purees, soups
	xanthan gum	0.15%					
	xanthan gum	0.4%	hot or cold				light fruit and vegetable purees, soups
great	konjac gum	0.3%	82	180	3	shear for 5 min after dispersing to ensure that konjac hydrates fully	gazpachos and other cold soups
	locust bean gum	0.1%					
	cellulose gum LV	1.0%	cold			opaque, not suited for clear liquids	coating sauces
	lambda carrageenan	0.5%					
very great	gum tragacanth	0.5%	cold			best texture when fat concentration is above 12%	pastes, thick purees
	xanthan gum	0.2%					
	cellulose gum LV	2.25%	82	180	3	best texture when solids ratio is high	
	propylene glycol alginate	0.50%					

from page 4·46   *(set weight of liquid to be thickened to 100%)*

HAM CONSOMMÉ WITH MELON BEADS ADAPTED FROM FERRAN ADRIÀ

Yields 600 g (10 servings)

INGREDIENT	QUANTITY	SCALING	PROCEDURE
Water, cold	500 g	200%	① Combine, and simmer for 15 min.
Ibérico ham, excess fat removed, thinly sliced	250 g	100%	② Cool completely, and remove congealed fat from surface of broth.
			③ Pass broth through fine sieve, and reserve 250 g of consommé.
Ibérico ham consommé, from above	250 g	100%	④ Blend thoroughly with consommé.
			⑤ Refrigerate for later use.
Xanthan gum (Texturas brand)	0.6 g	0.24%	
Melon juice see page 2·336	500 g (from about 800 g of melon)	200%	⑥ Blend together until dissolved.
			⑦ Vacuum seal to remove any trapped air.
			⑧ Transfer to Texturas-style syringe.
Sodium alginate (Algin, Texturas brand)	2 g	0.8% (0.4%)*	
Water	500 g	200%	⑨ Blend together until fully dissolved.
Calcium chloride	2.5 g	1%	⑩ Expel juice from syringe, one droplet at a time, into calcium chloride bath.
			⑪ Remove resulting beads from bath after 3 min, and rinse beads in clean water bath.
			⑫ To serve, fill 10 champagne flutes with 50 g each of cold ham consommé.
			⑬ Spoon 10 g of melon juice beads into each flute; beads will remain suspended.
Black peppercorns, finely ground	to taste		⑭ Garnish.

from page 4·48   *(% of weight of melon juice)*

TOMATO WHEY BROTH

Yields 230 g

INGREDIENT	QUANTITY	SCALING	PROCEDURE
Tomato water see page 40	100 g	100%	① Whisk together.
Whey, from making goat milk ricotta see page 248	100 g	100%	
Lambda carrageenan (Texturas brand)	0.20 g	0.2% (0.1%)*	② Dry blend together. ③ Blend into tomato-whey mixture until fully hydrated.
Xanthan gum (Keltrol T, CP Kelco brand)	0.20 g	0.2% (0.1%)*	④ Refrigerate.
Salt	to taste		⑤ Season just before serving, or whey will curdle.
Tomato vinegar (optional) see page 315 or lemon juice	to taste		⑥ Serve cold with fresh mozzarella or on tomato salad.

from page 4·49

*(% of total weight of tomato water and whey)

TRUFFLE JUS INSPIRED BY MARC VEYRAT

Yields 250 g

INGREDIENT	QUANTITY	SCALING	PROCEDURE
Shallots, finely minced	30 g	30%	① Cook together over low heat until tender, about 5 min.
Clarified butter	15 g	15%	
Black peppercorns, ground	0.5 g	0.5%	
Red port (dry)	40 g	40%	② Add to pan of cooked shallots.
Red wine (dry)	40 g	40%	③ Simmer together for 2 min to cook off alcohol flavor. ④ Keep port base hot for later use.
Mushroom jus, cold see page 37	100 g	100%	⑤ Disperse gum into cold mushroom jus. ⑥ Whisk mushroom jus into hot port base.
Konjac gum (Ticagel Konjac HV, TIC Gums brand)	0.54 g	0.54% (0.3%)*	⑦ Bring to simmer, and blend continuously for 5 min to ensure konjac is fully dispersed.
Black truffles, vacuum-packed, frozen, thawed, then minced	35 g	35%	⑧ Whisk into warm mushroom jus and wine mixture.
Black truffle oil	7 g	7%	
Dark cocoa powder	4 g	4%	
Thyme essential oil	0.05 g	0.05%	
Salt	to taste		⑨ Remove jus from heat.
Sherry vinegar	to taste		⑩ Season.

from page 4·53

*(% of total weight of red port wine and mushroom jus)

BEEF TENDERLOIN WITH JUS DE ROTI

Yields 500 g (four portions)

INGREDIENT	QUANTITY	SCALING	PROCEDURE
Beef tenderloin	400 g	400%	① Vacuum seal together.
Rendered beef marrow or suet	40 g	40%	② Cook sous vide in 53 °C / 127 °F bath to core temperature of 52 °C / 126 °F.
Brown beef stock see page 10	100 g	100%	③ Combine. ④ Bring jus to low simmer to dissolve solids.
160 Bloom gelatin	9 g	9%	
Fructose	2.5 g	2.5%	
D-Ribose Powder (Solgar brand)	1.75 g	1.75%	
Cellulose gum (Cekol LVD, CP Kelco brand)	0.5 g	0.5%	
Koji-Aji (Ajinomoto brand)	0.4 g	0.4%	
Caramel coloring	0.2 g	0.2%	
Malic acid	to taste		⑤ Season jus, and serve with sliced beef tenderloin.
Salt	to taste		

from page 4·54

OLIVE OIL SPREAD

Yields 325 g

INGREDIENT	QUANTITY	SCALING	PROCEDURE
Deodorized cocoa butter	100 g	44%	① Heat to 40 °C / 104 °F to melt.
Olive oil	225 g	100%	② Blend with melted butter.
			③ Allow mixture to harden at room temperature.
			④ Blend again to silky consistency.
Black pepper, ground	1 g	0.4%	⑤ Whisk into spread.
Thyme essential oil (optional)	0.2 g	0.09%	
Rosemary essential oil (optional)	0.1 g	0.04%	
Fleur de sel	to taste		⑥ Season, and warm at room temperature for 20 min before serving.

from page 4·51

WHITE GRAPE SYRUP

Yields 430 g

INGREDIENT	QUANTITY	SCALING	PROCEDURE
Muscat grapes (or other white grapes)	2 kg	500%	① Juice with Champion juicer or similar appliance.
			② Clarify juice with pressure or vacuum filtration.
			③ Reserve 400 g.
Clarified grape juice, from above	400 g	100%	④ Blend.
			⑤ Adjust sweetness and acidity to taste.
Fructose	20 g	5%	
Malic acid	4.5 g	1.1%	
Cellulose gum (Cekol LVD, CP Kelco brand)	4 g	1%	⑥ Shear into juice mixture.
			⑦ Vacuum seal, and refrigerate syrup.
Xanthan gum (Keltrol T, CP Kelco brand)	1.2 g	0.3%	

from page 4·52

XO SAUCE

Yields 275 g

INGREDIENT	QUANTITY	SCALING	PROCEDURE
Brown pork stock see page 6	250 g	125%	① Combine, and vacuum seal.
			② Cook sous vide in 90 °C / 194 °F bath for 1 h.
Cured ham, finely minced	60 g	30%	③ Strain, and press solids to remove as much liquid as possible.
Ginger, peeled and thinly sliced	40 g	20%	④ Measure 200 g of infused stock, and cool.
Agave nectar (or honey)	10 g	5%	
Infused pork stock, from above	200 g	100%	⑤ Shear into reserved stock to hydrate.
Cellulose gum (Cekol LV, CP Kelco brand)	2 g	1%	
Xanthan gum (Keltrol T, CP Kelco brand)	0.5 g	0.25%	
Salted dried shrimp, minced	14 g	7%	⑥ Fry together until tender, about 2 min.
Ginger, minced	12 g	6%	⑦ Blot excess oil with paper towels.
Dried scallop, minced	7 g	3.5%	⑧ Fold mixture into thickened stock base.
Fermented black beans, minced	7 g	3.5%	⑨ Serve with Deep-Fried Custard (page 255), or cool and refrigerate.
Garlic, minced	7 g	3.5%	
Dried red chilies, seeded and minced	3 g	1.5%	
Frying oil	5 g	2.5%	

from page 4·52

THICKENERS

CARAMELIZED COCONUT CREAM

Yields 550 g

INGREDIENT	QUANTITY	SCALING	PROCEDURE
Coconut milk	350 g	350%	① Combine.
Palm sugar	50 g	50%	② Pressure-cook mixture at gauge pressure of 1 bar / 15 psi for 1¼ h.
Baking soda	1.5 g	1.5%	③ Cool completely; liquid may curdle as it cools, which is normal.
Coconut water (canned or fresh)	100 g	100%	④ Blend until PGA is completely dissolved.
			⑤ Combine with coconut milk mixture.
Propylene glycol alginate (Protanal Ester BV, FMC BioPolymer brand)	1.75 g	1.75% (0.35%)*	
Young coconut meat (frozen or fresh)	50 g	50%	⑥ Add to coconut milk mixture, and blend until smooth.
			⑦ Strain through fine sieve.
			⑧ Refrigerate.

from page 4·50   *(% of total weight of all ingredients)

PRESSURE-COOKED POLENTA WITH STRAWBERRY MARINARA

Yields 800 g (12 portions)

INGREDIENT	QUANTITY	SCALING	PROCEDURE
For the strawberry marinara:			
Strawberries, thinly sliced	220 g	88%	① Combine all ingredients in pot, and simmer until reduced and thickened, about 90 min.
Heirloom tomato, peeled	190 g	76%	
Strawberry juice, clarified	185 g	74%	
Sweet onion, finely minced	100 g	40%	
White wine (dry)	100 g	40%	
Garlic, thinly sliced and blanched	3 g	1.2%	
Basil leaves, torn	2 g	0.8%	
Tarragon leaves, crushed	2 g	0.8%	
Strawberry marinara, from above	250 g	100%	② Whisk gum into marinara base until fully dispersed.
Xanthan gum (Keltrol T, CP Kelco brand)	0.6 g	0.24%	
Salt	to taste		③ Season marinara, and reserve.
Lime juice	to taste		
For the corn husk consommé:			
Water	1 kg	400%	④ Line baking sheet with corn husks, and toast in 205 °C / 400 °F oven for 10 min.
Corn husks, fresh	125 g	50%	⑤ Flip husks, and toast for another 5 min until deep golden brown.
			⑥ Combine husks with water, and simmer for 30 min to infuse. Strain and reserve.
Cellulose gum (Cekol LVD, CP Kelco brand)	2 g	0.8% (0.2%)*	⑦ Blend gum into consommé base, and season.
Fructose	to taste	4%	
Salt	to taste		
For the polenta:			
Clarified butter	15 g	6%	⑧ Sauté polenta in butter until golden, 3–4 min.
Stone-ground polenta	100 g	40%	⑨ Cool completely.
Corn juice, clarified	300 g	120%	⑩ Combine with toasted polenta, and vacuum seal.
			⑪ Place in pressure cooker, and cover with water. Pressure-cook at gauge pressure of 1 bar / 15 psi for 8 min.
Mascarpone see page 226 or store-bought	20 g	8%	⑫ Remove cooked polenta from bag, and whisk in mascarpone and ricotta.
			⑬ Season with salt.
Ricotta salata, grated	15 g	6%	⑭ Divide among bowls, and garnish with strawberry marinara.
Salt	to taste		⑮ Pour some consommé over polenta at table.

from page 4·50   *(% of total weight of corn husk consommé)

CREAMED SPINACH

Yields 125 g

INGREDIENT	QUANTITY	SCALING	PROCEDURE
Baby spinach, cleaned	150 g	100%	① Sauté until wilted, about 1 min.
Olive oil	5 g	3.3%	② Season, and cool completely.
Salt	to taste		③ Transfer to colander, and press to remove excess liquid.
			④ Chop finely.
Garlic confit, mashed see page 176	6 g	4%	⑤ Sauté until shallots are translucent.
			⑥ Add spinach.
Olive oil	5 g	3.3%	⑦ Stir together, and cook for 3 min.
Shallots, finely minced	5 g	3.3%	⑧ Remove spinach from heat.
Mascarpone see page 226 or store-bought	27 g	18%	⑨ Stir into spinach until completely incorporated.
			⑩ Set spinach mixture aside.
Low-fat milk	20 g	13.3%	⑪ Dry blend Ultra-Sperse 3 and xanthan gum.
Ultra-Sperse 3 (National Starch brand)	0.5 g	0.3%	⑫ Whisk dry mixture into cold milk until fully hydrated.
Xanthan gum (Keltrol T, CP Kelco brand)	0.1 g	0.06%	⑬ Mix thickened milk into creamed spinach.
Comté cheese, finely grated	10 g	6.7%	⑭ To serve, fold Comté cheese into creamed spinach, and scatter some on top.
Lemon zest, finely grated	0.5 g	0.3%	⑮ Season with lemon zest and black pepper.
Black peppercorns, ground	0.2 g	0.1%	⑯ Serve warm or cold.

from page 4·55

WARM POTATO AND PISTACHIO PESTO SALAD

Yields 2 kg

INGREDIENT	QUANTITY	SCALING	PROCEDURE
Italian basil leaves	80 g	80%	① Blanch in boiling water individually until tender, about 2 min each.
Cilantro leaves	70 g	70%	② Cool in ice water, and squeeze to remove excess moisture.
Chives	70 g	70%	③ Reserve refrigerated.
Scallion greens	70 g	70%	
Garlic cloves, peeled	16 g	16%	④ Blanch in boiling water for 2 min. Drain and reserve.
Extra virgin olive oil	190 g	190%	⑤ Puree together with cooked herbs and blanched garlic until smooth.
Parmigiano Reggiano, finely grated	100 g	100%	⑥ Measure 900 g of pistachio pesto.
Pistachios, peeled and toasted	100 g	100%	
Roasted-pistachio oil	40 g	40%	
Spinach puree see page 144	30 g	30%	
Lemon juice	20 g	20%	
Pistachio pesto, from above	900 g	900%	⑦ Season.
Salt	to taste		
Microcrystalline cellulose (Avicel CG 200, FMC BioPolymer brand)	9 g	9% (1%)*	⑧ Blend into pistachio pesto to fully hydrate. ⑨ Vacuum seal, and refrigerate for at least 1 h to macerate.
Xanthan gum (Keltrol T, CP Kelco brand)	1.8 g	1.8% (0.2%)*	
Fingerling potatoes, skin on	1 kg	1,000%	⑩ Vacuum seal, and cook sous vide in 90 °C / 194 °F bath until tender, about 45 min.
Olive oil	100 g	100%	⑪ Remove from bag while still warm.
			⑫ Slice thinly.
			⑬ Toss with pesto as desired.

from page 4·53

*(% of weight of pistachio pesto)

THICKENERS

AGED RARE BEEF JUS

Yields 250 g

INGREDIENT	QUANTITY	SCALING	PROCEDURE
Aged beef chuck steak, cut into 2.5 cm / 1 in cubes	700 g	700%	① Vacuum seal.
Bromelain capsules, ground to fine powder (optional, NOW Foods brand)	1.4 g	1.4%	② Cook sous vide in 53 °C / 127 °F bath for 4 h. ③ Press against fine sieve to get juice, discarding meat. ④ Centrifuge juice at 27,500g for 30 min to yield about 100 g of aged beef jus, and reserve.
Water, cold	100 g	100%	⑤ Disperse gums in water.
Xanthan gum	0.3 g	0.3% (0.15%)*	
Guar gum	0.1 g	0.1% (0.05%)*	
Aged beef jus, from above	100 g	100%	⑥ Blend gum mixture into aged beef jus until completely fluid.
Monosodium glutamate (MSG)	2 g	2%	⑦ Season jus.
Salt	to taste		⑧ Cool, vacuum seal, and refrigerate until use. To serve, reheat if necessary, no higher than 52 °C / 125 °F, and serve.

from page 5·6   *(% of total weight of water and aged beef jus)

SHIITAKE MARMALADE

Yields 150 g

INGREDIENT	QUANTITY	SCALING	PROCEDURE
Shallots, finely minced	70 g	70%	① Sauté over low heat until tender, about 20 min.
Shiitake mushrooms, brunoise	26 g	26%	
Clarified unsalted butter	10 g	10%	
Garlic, brunoise	10 g	10%	
Rendered beef marrow	10 g	10%	
Tomato water see page 40	40 g	40%	② Add to shallot mixture, and reduce to 50 g to make marmalade base. ③ Reserve.
Sherry vinegar	20 g	20%	
Brown beef jus see page 34	100 g	100%	④ Disperse gelatin into beef jus. ⑤ Heat to fully dissolve gelatin.
160 Bloom gelatin	3 g	3%	
Xanthan gum	0.3 g	0.3%	⑥ Blend into beef jus. ⑦ Fold in reserved marmalade base.
Black pepper, coarsely ground	0.25 g	0.25%	⑧ Season marmalade.
Salt	to taste		⑨ Serve or cool, vacuum seal, and refrigerate until use.

from page 5·7

MAPLE VINEGAR GASTRIQUE

Yields 300 g

INGREDIENT	QUANTITY	SCALING	PROCEDURE
Maple syrup (Grade B)	175 g	175%	① Whisk together.
Sherry vinegar	100 g	100%	② Vacuum seal.
Cider vinegar	20 g	20%	③ Refrigerate until use.
Microcrystalline cellulose (Avicel CG-200, FMC Biopolymer brand)	3 g	3%	

We used Avicel CG200 microcrystalline cellulose, made by FMC Biopolymer.

from page 5·128

MUSHROOM KETCHUP

Yields 750 g

INGREDIENT	QUANTITY	SCALING	PROCEDURE
Yellow onions, thinly sliced	350 g	54%	① Sauté until translucent, about 7 min.
Olive oil	53 g	8%	
Garlic, thinly sliced	32 g	5%	② Add to onions, and cook for 1 min.
Ginger, thinly sliced	7 g	1%	
Crimini mushrooms, thinly sliced	650 g	100%	③ Combine with onion mixture and simmer, stirring frequently, until mushrooms are very tender and liquid has evaporated, about 35 min.
Malt vinegar	155 g	24%	④ Blend until smooth.
Dark ale	105 g	16%	⑤ Pass through fine sieve.
Mushroom broth, from above	70 g	11%	⑥ Adjust seasoning to taste.
Barley malt syrup	40 g	6%	⑦ Measure 800 g of ketchup.
Cane vinegar	40 g	6%	
Molasses	40 g	6%	
Fish sauce	34 g	5%	
Freeze-dried shiitake mushrooms (or dried shiitake powder)	30 g	4.5%	
Sea salt	15.5 g	2.5%	
Honey	10 g	1.5%	
Horseradish, freshly grated	7 g	1%	
Mace blades	4.2 g	0.6%	
Allspice berries	2.2 g (two berries)	0.3%	
Freeze-dried coffee powder see page 58	0.6 g	0.1%	
Ketchup, from above	800 g	123%	⑧ Blend together until smooth, and refrigerate.
Xanthan gum	1.6 g	0.25% *(0.2%)**	

from page 5·13   *(% of total weight of ketchup)

APRICOT AND JASMINE PUREE

Yields 250 g

INGREDIENT	QUANTITY	SCALING	PROCEDURE
Unripe apricot juice, fresh	315 g	100%	① Blend together to fine puree.
Dried apricots, chopped	100 g	32%	
Xanthan gum	0.5 g	0.15% *(0.11%)**	
Osmanthus vinegar	25 g	8%	② Whisk into apricot puree.
Jasmine essential oil	0.1 g (one drop)	0.03%	③ Refrigerate until use.

from page 5·173   *(% total weight of all other ingredients)

SEAWEED TAPENADE

Yields 525 g

INGREDIENT	QUANTITY	SCALING	PROCEDURE
Green olives, finely minced	200 g	100%	① Drain ingredients soaked in water.
Dulse seaweed, soaked in water for 1 h, finely minced	100 g	50%	② Reserve all ingredients separately.
Shallots, finely minced	75 g	37.5%	
Arame seaweed, soaked in water for 1 h, finely minced	50 g	25%	
Hijiki seaweed, soaked in water for 1 h, finely minced	50 g	25%	
Capers, finely minced	25 g	12.5%	
Anchovy paste	10 g	5%	③ Whisk together until smooth.
Dijon mustard	10 g	5%	④ Fold in reserved ingredients from above.
Lemon juice	7 g	3.5%	
Garlic, finely minced	5 g	2.5%	
Xanthan gum	0.2 g	0.1%	
Salt			⑤ Season tapenade.
			⑥ Serve, or refrigerate until use.

from page 5·27

TAMARIND PUREE

Yields 240 g

INGREDIENT	QUANTITY	SCALING	PROCEDURE
Tamarind paste see page 145	140 g	100%	① Vacuum seal together.
Sour Indian plum (alubukhara)	140 g	100%	② Cook sous vide in 90 °C / 194 °F bath for 1 h.
Water	50 g	36%	③ Pass through fine sieve, and measure 225 g of tamarind puree.
Coconut sugar (store-bought)	3.5 g	2.5%	④ Blend with tamarind paste and plum mixture.
Salt	1.5 g	1.1%	⑤ Pass through fine sieve.
Sherry vinegar	1 g	0.7%	⑥ Refrigerate until use.
Xanthan gum	0.45 g	0.32% (0.2%)*	

from page 5·282

*(% of total weight of cooked tamarind, plum, and water puree)

SOUTH CAROLINA BARBECUE SAUCE

Yields 380 g

INGREDIENT	QUANTITY	SCALING	PROCEDURE
Dijon mustard	300 g	100%	① Mix together in heavy-bottom pot.
Lager beer	125 g	42%	② Simmer, stirring frequently to prevent sticking, until reduced to 380 g, about 20 min.
Cider vinegar	30 g	10%	
Tomato puree	30 g	10%	
Brown sugar	15 g	5%	
Worcestershire sauce	10 g	3%	
Black pepper, ground	1.5 g	0.5%	
Garlic powder	1.5 g	0.5%	
Cayenne pepper	to taste		③ Season sauce, and refrigerate until use.
Cider vinegar	to taste		
Salt	to taste		

from page 5·70

KENTUCKY BARBECUE SAUCE

Yields 300 g

INGREDIENT	QUANTITY	SCALING	PROCEDURE
Ketchup (Heinz brand)	300 g	100%	① Mix together in heavy-bottom pot.
Cider vinegar	60 g	20%	② Simmer, stirring frequently to prevent sticking, until reduced to 300 g, about 15 min.
Brown sugar	50 g	17%	
Molasses	30 g	10%	
Pineapple juice (fresh)	30 g	10%	
Bourbon (Wild Turkey brand)	25 g	8.5%	
Bacon fat	8 g	2.7%	
Worcestershire sauce	5 g	1.7%	
Unsalted butter	8 g	2.7%	③ Blend into warm mixture until fully emulsified.
Bourbon (Wild Turkey brand)	20 g	6.7%	④ Season sauce, and refrigerate until use.
Lemon juice	to taste		
Salt	to taste		

from page 5·71

NORTH CAROLINA (LEXINGTON-STYLE) BARBECUE SAUCE

Yields 300 g

INGREDIENT	QUANTITY	SCALING	PROCEDURE
Cider vinegar	115 g	100%	① Mix together in heavy-bottom pot.
Distilled white vinegar	115 g	100%	② Simmer, stirring frequently to prevent sticking, until reduced to 300 g, about 10 min.
Ketchup (Heinz brand)	70 g	61%	
Maple syrup	30 g	26%	
Sugar	9.5 g	8.5%	
Chili flakes	7 g	6%	
Black pepper, ground	4.5 g	4%	
Salt	to taste		③ Season sauce, and refrigerate until use.

from page 5·71

HOUSE BARBECUE SAUCE

Yields 120 g

INGREDIENT	QUANTITY	SCALING	PROCEDURE
Malt vinegar	50 g	50%	① Combine in pot.
White beef stock see page 6	50 g	50%	② Cook mixture over low heat until reduced to about 100 g.
Maple syrup	25 g	25%	③ Puree until smooth.
Yellow onion, finely diced	15 g	15%	④ Pass sauce base through fine sieve.
Bourbon	13.5 g	13.5%	⑤ Cool.
Rendered bacon fat	12 g	12%	
Sherry vinegar	5 g	5%	
Smoked Hungarian paprika pepper (or other dried, smoked pepper), ground	5 g	5%	
Cayenne pepper, dried and ground	0.5 g	0.5%	
Yellow mustard powder	0.5 g	0.5%	
Liquid hickory smoke (Lazy Kettle brand)	0.1 g	0.1%	
Barbecue sauce, from above	100 g	100%	⑥ Shear into cold sauce base until evenly distributed and smooth.
Tomato powder, freeze-dried see page 157 (or store-bought)	20 g	20%	
Microcrystalline cellulose (Avicel CG 200, FMC BioPolymer brand)	1 g	1%	
Salt	to taste		⑦ Season sauce.
Red wine vinegar	to taste		

from page 4·49

KANSAS CITY BARBECUE SAUCE

Yields 250 g

INGREDIENT	QUANTITY	SCALING	PROCEDURE
Ketchup (Heinz brand)	225 g	100%	① Mix in heavy-bottom pot.
Tomato paste	40 g	17.8%	② Simmer, stirring frequently to prevent sticking, until reduced to 250 g, about 20 min.
Water	40 g	17.8%	
White wine vinegar	40 g	17.8%	
Brown sugar	35 g	15%	
Black pepper, ground	5 g	2.2%	
Chili powder (McCormick brand)	5 g	2.2%	
Mustard powder	4.5 g	2%	
Salt	4.5 g	2%	
Cayenne pepper	4 g	1.8%	
Green Thai chili, minced	4 g	1.8%	
Garlic powder	1 g	0.4%	
Onion powder	0.75 g	0.3%	
Ginger, peeled and finely minced	0.25 g	0.1%	
Cumin powder	0.1 g	0.05%	
Lemon juice	5.5 g	2.4%	③ Season sauce, and refrigerate until use.
Salt	to taste		

from page 5·68

MEMPHIS BARBECUE SAUCE

Yields 250 g

INGREDIENT	QUANTITY	SCALING	PROCEDURE
Canned tomatoes	300 g	100%	① Mix in heavy-bottom pot.
Cider vinegar	80 g	27%	② Simmer, stirring frequently to prevent sticking, until reduced to 250 g, about 20 min.
Lemon juice	40 g	13%	
Unsalted butter	40 g	13%	
Brown sugar	35 g	11.5%	
Worcestershire sauce	30 g	10%	
Chili powder (McCormick brand)	2.5 g	0.85%	
Black pepper, ground	1.5 g	0.5%	
Onion powder	1.5 g	0.5%	
Tabasco sauce	1 g	0.3%	
Mustard powder	0.75 g	0.25%	
Cayenne pepper	0.5 g	0.15%	
Salt	to taste		③ Season sauce, and refrigerate until use.
Lemon juice	to taste		

from page 5·70

NORTH CAROLINA (EASTERN REGION) BARBECUE SAUCE

Yields 250 g

INGREDIENT	QUANTITY	SCALING	PROCEDURE
Cider vinegar	200 g	100%	① Mix together in heavy-bottom pot.
Distilled white vinegar	200 g	100%	② Simmer, stirring frequently to prevent sticking, until reduced to 250 g, about 20 min.
Maple syrup	30 g	15%	
Chili flakes	10 g	5%	
Sugar	5 g	2.5%	
Black pepper, ground	3 g	1.5%	
Salt	to taste		③ Season sauce, and refrigerate until use.

from page 5·70

EAST TEXAS BARBECUE SAUCE

Yields 200 g

INGREDIENT	QUANTITY	SCALING	PROCEDURE
Yellow onions, finely minced	135 g	169%	① Sweat onions until translucent and tender in heavy-bottom pot, about 7 min.
Unsalted butter	40 g	50%	
Garlic, finely minced	7 g	9%	
Distilled vinegar	80 g	100%	② Combine.
Water	80 g	100%	③ Add to onion mixture.
Ketchup (Heinz brand)	50 g	62.5%	④ Simmer, stirring frequently to prevent sticking, until reduced to 200 g, about 20 min.
Ancho chili paste	40 g	50%	
Worcestershire sauce	4 g	5%	
Chili powder (McCormick brand)	2 g	2.5%	
Mustard powder	2 g	2.5%	
Bay leaf, crushed	0.15 g	0.19%	
Cayenne pepper	0.5 g	0.6%	
Lemon juice	13.5 g	17%	⑤ Season sauce, and refrigerate until use.
Sugar	2 g	2.5%	
Salt	to taste		

from page 5·69

MUGHAL CURRY SAUCE
Yields 450 g

Instead of soaking the nuts and seeds for 12 h, you can alternatively soften them in a pressure cooker at a gauge pressure of 1 bar / 15 psi for 45 min.

INGREDIENT	QUANTITY	SCALING	PROCEDURE
Raw almonds	160 g	80%	① Cover with water, and soak in refrigerator for 12 h.
Raw cashews	160 g	80%	② Drain, grind together to fine paste, and reserve.
Poppy seeds	8 g	4%	③ Cover with water, and soak in refrigerator for 12 h.
			④ Drain, grind to fine paste, and reserve.
Shallots, thinly sliced	200 g	100%	⑤ Sauté shallots until translucent and lightly golden.
Ghee	30 g	15%	
Garlic, grated	6 g	3%	⑥ Combine aromatics, and add to shallots.
Ginger, grated	6 g	3%	⑦ Sauté until golden, about 5 min, and reserve.
Green Thai chili, finely minced	5 g	2.5%	
Turmeric (fresh), grated	4 g	2%	
Nutmeg, grated	2 g	1%	
Bay leaf	0.25 g	0.13%	
Mace blade	1.6 g	0.8%	⑧ Toast spices together in 170 °C / 340 °F oven until aromatic and golden, 10–15 min.
Coriander seed	1 g	0.5%	
Black pepper	0.5 g	0.25%	⑨ Grind to fine powder in blender or coffee grinder.
Cinnamon stick	0.5 g	0.25%	⑩ Add to sautéed mixture.
Clove	0.5 g	0.25%	
Cumin seeds	0.5 g	0.25%	
Green cardamom seeds	0.1 g	0.05%	
Raisins	25 g	12.5%	⑪ Add raisins to sautéed mixture, and then add nut and poppy seed pastes.
Water	200 g	100%	
			⑫ Simmer for 25 min, and remove from heat.
Plain yogurt	8 g	4%	⑬ Add to sauce.
Lime juice	to taste		⑭ Season.
Salt	to taste		⑮ Cool and refrigerate until use.

from page 5·92

PEA VINE SALAD
Yields 200 g

INGREDIENT	QUANTITY	SCALING	PROCEDURE
Pea vines, tips only	120 g	100%	① Measure and reserve individually.
Pickled lemons, drained see page 179	36 g	30%	
Cinnamon basil leaves	15 small		
Lemon-infused olive oil	30 g	25%	② Whisk together to form vinaigrette.
Vermouth vinegar	10 g	8.3%	③ Toss vinaigrette with reserved salad components.
Lime juice	5 g	4.2%	
Microcrystalline cellulose (optional; Avicel CG200, FMC Biopolymer brand)	0.3 g	0.25% (0.67%)*	
Black pepper	to taste		④ Season salad.
Salt	to taste		

from page 5·275

*(% of total weight of first three ingredients for vinaigrette)

MUSLIM CURRY SAUCE

Yields 350 g

INGREDIENT	QUANTITY	SCALING	PROCEDURE
Sweet onions, thinly sliced	110 g	55%	① Sauté onions until translucent and lightly golden, about 10 min.
Ghee see page 4·213	40 g	20%	
Garlic, grated	7 g	3.5%	② Add to onions, and sauté until fragrant, about 5 min.
Ginger, grated	7 g	3.5%	
Black peppercorns, toasted and ground	2 g	1%	③ Toast in shallow pan in 170 °C / 340 °F oven until aromatic and golden, 10–15 min.
Cinnamon stick, toasted and ground	2 g	1%	④ Grind to fine powder in blender or coffee grinder.
Cumin seeds, toasted and ground	2 g	1%	
Green cardamom seeds, toasted and ground	2 g	1%	
Mace blade, toasted and ground	0.8 g	0.4%	
Cane sugar	4 g	2%	⑤ Mix with ground spices and sautéed onion mixture.
Nutmeg, grated	0.8 g	0.4%	
Heavy cream	200 g	100%	⑥ Add to spiced onion mixture.
Water	60 g	30%	⑦ Simmer for 30 min, and remove from heat.
Unsalted butter	16 g	8%	⑧ Whisk into sauce.
Lime juice	4 g	2%	
Saffron threads	0.8 g	0.4%	
Rose water	to taste		⑨ Season.
Salt	to taste		⑩ Cool and refrigerate until use.

These curry sauces have a traditional texture. They stick to meat better if you add 0.2% xanthan gum, relative to the total weight of the sauce. Use a blender or rotor-stator homogenizer to blend in the gum after the final step in the recipe.

from page 5·93

GREEN MANGO AND CASHEW SALAD

Yields 256 g

INGREDIENT	QUANTITY	SCALING	PROCEDURE
Green mango, fine julienne	100 g	100%	① Measure and reserve individually.
Cashews, roasted	30 g	30%	
Mint leaves, torn	8 g	8%	
Cilantro stems and leaves, thinly sliced	4 g	4%	
Coconut water (fresh or canned)	60 g	60%	② Blend together until smooth to make dressing, and reserve. ③ Toss green mango with reserved salad elements, and dress to taste.
Fish sauce	40 g	40%	
Distilled vinegar	19 g	19%	
Lime juice	13 g	13%	
Sugar	8 g	8%	
Salt	1 g	1%	
Xanthan gum	0.28 g	0.28% (0.2%)*	

from page 5·169

*(% total weight of six preceding ingredients)

GOAN CURRY SAUCE

Yields 200 g

INGREDIENT	QUANTITY	SCALING	PROCEDURE
Sweet onions, thinly sliced	120 g	100%	① Sauté onions until translucent and golden, about 10 min.
Ghee	35 g	29%	
Tomato puree *see page 144*	60 g	50%	② Add to onions.
			③ Sauté mixture for 5 min.
Garlic, finely grated	7 g	5.8%	
Ginger, finely grated	7 g	5.8%	
Black peppercorns	5 g	4%	④ Add to onion and tomato mixture, and sauté until fragrant, about 10 min.
Green cardamom seeds	4.2 g	3.5%	
Turmeric, grated	4 g	3.3%	⑤ Toast in shallow pan placed in 170 °C / 340 °F oven until golden and aromatic, 10–15 min.
Fennel seeds	3.4 g	2.8%	
Coriander seeds	2.4 g	2%	⑥ Grind to fine powder in blender or coffee grinder.
Cumin	2.4 g	2%	
Yellow mustard seeds	2 g	1.7%	
Water	250 g	208%	⑦ Combine with sauce.
Cane vinegar	40 g	33%	⑧ Simmer for 45 min.
Raw cane sugar	12 g	10%	
Bay leaf	0.5 g	0.4%	
Lime juice	to taste		⑨ Season sauce.
Salt	to taste		⑩ Cool and refrigerate until use.

from page 5·95

The traditional way to toast spices in Indian cuisine is in a dry skillet. We prefer an oven for more control, but even with this method, you need to watch that you don't burn your spices.

KERALA CURRY SAUCE

Yields 350 g

INGREDIENT	QUANTITY	SCALING	PROCEDURE
Shallots, finely minced	120 g	85%	① Sauté until shallots are translucent and golden, about 10 min.
Ghee	35 g	25%	
Green Thai chili, minced	12 g	8.5%	
Garlic, finely grated	10 g	7%	② Add to shallot mixture, sauté for 5 min, and reserve.
Ginger, finely grated	10 g	7%	
Curry leaves	5 g	3.5%	
Bay leaf	0.5 g	0.4%	
Black peppercorns	14 g	10%	③ Mix together thoroughly.
Cumin seeds	4 g	2.8%	④ Toast in shallow pan placed in 170 °C / 340 °F oven until golden and aromatic, 10–15 min.
Green cardamom seeds	3 g	2%	
Star anise	1.4 g	1%	⑤ Grind to fine powder in blender or coffee grinder.
Cinnamon stick	1 g	0.7%	⑥ Add to shallot mixture, and sauté until fragrant, about 3 min.
Cloves	1 g	0.7%	
Coconut milk	140 g	100%	⑦ Add to shallot mixture, and simmer for 45 min.
Salt	to taste		⑧ Season sauce.
			⑨ Cool and refrigerate until use.

from page 5·96

Curries are by no means exclusive to India. Southeast Asia has its yellow, green, and red curries; there are adaptations from Iran to Britain to Japan. But they all share the basics: meat, seafood, or just loads of flavorful vegetables in a fragrant, spicy sauce, usually served with rice.

MASALA CURRY SAUCE

Yields 300 g

INGREDIENT	QUANTITY	SCALING	PROCEDURE
Sweet onions, thinly sliced	200 g	80%	① Sauté onions until amber and translucent, about 25 min.
Ghee	30 g	12%	
Tomato puree see page 144	250 g	100%	② Add to onions, and sauté for 1 min. ③ Reserve warm.
Curry leaves	2.5 g	1%	
Coconut (fresh), grated	60 g	24%	④ Grind together to fine paste.
Garlic, finely grated	10 g	4%	⑤ Add to onion and tomato mixture, and sauté for 3 min.
Ginger, finely grated	10 g	4%	⑥ Reserve warm.
Dried bird's eye chili, crushed	3.5 g	1.4%	
Fenugreek seeds	2.4 g	1%	⑦ Toast in shallow pan placed in 170 °C / 340 °F oven until aromatic and golden, 10–15 min.
Coriander seeds	2 g	0.8%	⑧ Grind to fine powder in blender or coffee grinder.
Fennel seeds	2 g	0.8%	⑨ Stir into warm onion and tomato mixture. ⑩ Sauté until aromatic.
Water	160 g	64%	⑪ Add to mixture.
Tamarind paste see page 145	60 g	24%	⑫ Simmer for 45 min.
Turmeric (fresh), grated	9 g	3.6%	
Lime juice	to taste		⑬ Season sauce.
Salt	to taste		⑭ Cool and refrigerate until use.

from page 5·98

RED-EYE GRAVY

Yields 75 g

INGREDIENT	QUANTITY	SCALING	PROCEDURE
Sweet onions, thinly sliced	80 g	16%	① Sauté onions until tender and golden, about 15 min.
Rendered pork fat	30 g	6%	
Star anise	0.2 g	0.04%	② Add to onions. ③ Continue cooking over lower heat until onions are dark amber and star anise is fragrant.
Brown pork stock see page 6	500 g	100%	④ Deglaze. ⑤ Reduce to 75 g, and remove gravy from heat.
Maple syrup (Grade B)	15 g	3%	
Coffee beans	25 g	5%	⑥ Add to gravy, and cover. ⑦ Infuse for 5 min. ⑧ Strain, discarding coffee beans.
Microcrystalline cellulose (Avicel CC-200, FMC Biopolymer brand)	0.2 g	0.04% (0.27%)*	⑨ Blend into gravy to thicken.
Smoked salt	to taste		⑩ Season and serve, or refrigerate until use.

from page 5·102

*(% of total weight after reduction)

THICKENERS

MILKS AND CREAMS

① Select a recipe. Some of our favorites appear in the table below. Proportions are relative to the main liquid. For example, use 80 g of tigernuts for every 100 g of water to make chufa milk.

② Blend liquids with thickeners. Dissolve acidifiers or rennet in a small amount of water, milk, or cream before adding them to the liquid.

③ Hydrate the thickeners. Soak or heat as indicated in the Procedure column of the table.

④ Sieve if needed to remove lumps. Nut and legume milks should be sieved after steeping.

Best Bets for Making Milks and Creams

Recipe	Liquid	(scaling)	Thickeners	(scaling)	Procedure
almond milk	water	100%	almonds, finely ground	60%	soak 24 h, and sieve
	sweet almond oil	2%	sugar	1%	
clotted cream	whole milk*	100%	n/a		combine liquids, and pour in open container; steam or cook in 80 °C / 176 °F bath for 1 h undisturbed; refrigerate 24 h; skim clotted cream from surface
	heavy cream	50%			
chufa milk	water	100%	chufas (tigernuts)	80%	soak 12 h, and sieve
buttermilk	butter whey see page 4·286	100%	lactic acid	0.4%	season with salt to taste, and allow to rest overnight; adjust amount of heavy cream to taste
	heavy cream	20%	lambda carrageenan	0.2%	
skyr	low-fat milk	100%	live culture (Yogotherm brand)	1.0%	heat milk to 82 °C / 180 °F, and cool to 42 °C / 108 °F; add culture and acid, pour into sanitized containers, and incubate at 45 °C / 113 °F for 5 h; drain for 2 h
			lactic acid	0.2%	
yogurt	whole milk	100%	live culture (Yogotherm brand)	1%	heat milk to 82 °C / 180 °F, and cool to 42 °C / 108 °F; add culture, pour into sanitized containers, and incubate at 45 °C / 113 °F for 8 h; drain 12 h for thick, Greek-style texture; for firmer yogurt, scald milk at 85 °C / 125 °F for 25 min, and cool before adding culture
mascarpone	heavy cream	100%	ascorbic acid (or glucono delta-lactone)	0.2%	combine, heat cream to 90 °C / 190 °F, cool for 30 min, wrap in cheesecloth, and hang, refrigerated, for 12 h

from page 4·56   *(whole milk used in clotted cream should be unhomogenized for best results)*

LOW-FAT "CREAM"

Yields 200 g

INGREDIENT	QUANTITY	SCALING	PROCEDURE
Sweet whey powder	5 g	2.5%	① Dry blend.
Cellulose gum (Cekol LV, CP Kelco brand)	0.7 g	0.35%	
Lambda carrageenan (Texturas brand)	0.2 g	0.1%	
Skim milk	200 g	100%	② Shear powder mixture into milk until fully hydrated.
			③ Refrigerate.

from page 4·57

INSTANT CRÈME FRAÎCHE

Yields 400 g

INGREDIENT	QUANTITY	SCALING	PROCEDURE
Heavy cream (free of stabilizers or thickeners)	400 g	100%	① Heat heavy cream to 40 °C / 104 °F.
			② Blend in carrageenan to fully hydrate, and remove from heat.
Lambda carrageenan	1.6 g	0.4%	
Lactic acid	1.6 g	0.4%	③ Dissolve lactic acid in water.
Water	8 g	2%	④ Stir lactic acid solution into warm cream, and refrigerate for 10 min before using.
			⑤ Pass through fine sieve, and refrigerate until needed.

from page 4·57

HERBED CHEESE SPREAD

Yields 125 g

INGREDIENT	QUANTITY	SCALING	PROCEDURE	
Heavy cream (free of stabilizers or thickeners)	75 g	100%	① Dry blend locust bean gum and carrageenan.	
			② Disperse into cold milk and cream.	
Whole milk	25 g	33%	③ Bring mixture to boil while blending to hydrate.	Locust bean gum and lambda carrageenan are often combined to create commercial cream cheese in the United States.
Locust bean gum (POR/A2 Powder, TIC Gums brand)	1 g	1.3% *(1%)**	④ Remove from heat.	
			⑤ Strain and cool.	
Lambda carrageenan (Texturas brand)	0.2 g	0.27% *(0.2%)**		
Fresh goat cheese	30 g	40%	⑥ Add to heavy cream mixture.	
			⑦ Blend together until homogenized to make spread base.	
Garlic confit, pureed see page 176	10 g	13.3%	⑧ Fold into cheese spread.	
Chives, minced	3 g	4%		
Parsley, minced	2 g	2.7%		
Tarragon, thinly sliced	1 g	1.3%		
Lemon juice	to taste		⑨ Season, and refrigerate until use.	
Black pepper, cracked	to taste			
Salt	to taste			

from page 4·57   *(% of total weight of first two ingredients)*

SOY MILK

Yields 1 kg

INGREDIENT	QUANTITY	SCALING	PROCEDURE
Dried organic soybeans	250 g	100%	① Vacuum seal together.
Water	250 g	100%	② Soak, refrigerated, until beans absorb all water, about 14 h.
			③ Remove from bag.
Water, cold	750 g	300%	④ Puree soaked soybeans in food processor.
			⑤ Add cold water.
			⑥ Blend for 10 min until texture is creamy and grainy.
Water, boiling	425 g	170%	⑦ Pour into saucepan, and bring mixture to simmer.
			⑧ Add boiling water to soybeans; surface should start to foam.
			⑨ Stir until foam subsides, about 20 min.
			⑩ Strain mixture through fine sieve lined with cheesecloth, and collect soy milk.
			⑪ Wrap mixture in cheesecloth.
			⑫ Wring cloth tightly to extract all remaining soy milk.
			⑬ Vacuum seal soy milk, and refrigerate.

from page 4·58

THICKENERS

TOASTED RICE MILK

Yields 1.5 kg

INGREDIENT	QUANTITY	SCALING	PROCEDURE
Arborio rice	50 g	33%	① Arrange dry rice in thin, even layer on baking sheet.
			② Toast in 175 °C / 350 °F oven until evenly golden, about 45 min.
			③ Remove from oven.
Water	1.5 kg	1,000%	④ Combine all rice and 1 kg of water in pot.
Long grain rice	150 g	100%	⑤ Soak rice for 3 h at room temperature.
Fresh pandan leaves (optional)	30 g	20%	⑥ Add to rice and water, if using.
			⑦ Simmer mixture for 30 min.
			⑧ Remove from heat.
			⑨ Add reserved 500 g of water, and puree coarsely to release starch.
			⑩ Strain through cheesecloth-lined fine sieve to extract 1.5 kg, about 1 h. To avoid unwanted solids, do not press.
Sugar	60 g	40%	⑪ Whisk into rice milk until dissolved, and cool.

from page 4·59

TOASTED ALMOND MILK

Yields 650 g

INGREDIENT	QUANTITY	SCALING	PROCEDURE
Water	750 g	250%	① Blend into coarse puree.
Marcona almonds, toasted (or regular almonds, skinless)	300 g	100%	② Refrigerate for 24 h.
			③ Blend chilled puree until smooth.
Sugar	15 g	5%	④ Strain through fine sieve to extract almond milk.
Sweet almond oil	15 g	5%	
Salt	9 g	3%	
Almond extract (optional)	to taste		⑤ Add sparingly to milk.
			⑥ Vacuum seal almond milk, and refrigerate until needed.

from page 4·59

HORCHATA (CHUFA MILK)

Yields 200 g

INGREDIENT	QUANTITY	SCALING	PROCEDURE
Chufas (tigernuts)	450 g	100%	① Cover nuts with fresh water.
Water	as needed		② Soak in refrigerator for 12 h.
			③ Drain nuts, and discard water.
Water	250 g	56%	④ Combine with softened nuts.
Sugar	20 g	4.4%	⑤ Blend to fine, smooth texture.
Whey protein isolate (optional)	1.4 g	0.3%	⑥ Strain milk, pressing on solids to extract as much liquid as possible. Discard solids.
			⑦ Vacuum seal milk, and refrigerate until needed.

from page 4·59

LEMON STRIPS ADAPTED FROM HESTON BLUMENTHAL

Yields 50 g (50 strips)

INGREDIENT	QUANTITY	SCALING	PROCEDURE
Glycerin	3.75 g	1.67%	① Blend together to make lemon water, and reserve.
Lemon essential oil	2.55 g	1.13%	
Deionized water	225 g	100%	
Maltodextrin DE8	7.95 g	3.53%	② Dry blend.
Algin 400F (TIC Gums brand)	8.58 g	3.81%	③ Whisk slowly into lemon water until completely incorporated.
Viscarin TP 389 (FMC BioPolymer brand)	3.18 g	1.41%	④ Vacuum seal or refrigerate for 8 h to remove trapped air bubbles.
Aspartame	0.12 g	0.05%	⑤ Spread mixture onto acetate sheet using film applicator or improvised dowel with a spacer to form very thin and even coating.
			⑥ Dry at room temperature for about 24 h.
			⑦ Slice hardened film into 2 cm by 3 cm / ¾ in by 1¼ in strips.
			⑧ Peel off strips from sheet.
			⑨ Store in airtight container.

from page 4·61

EDIBLE FILMS

① Select a texture and a corresponding film formula. The Best Bets for Edible Films table below lists several good options that range from tender to brittle.

② Mix thickeners into cold liquid to create a slurry. Quantities in the table are given relative to the weight of the liquid. For example, if you are making a clear, brittle tomato water film, use 10 g of Pure-Cote B790 for every 100 g of tomato water.

③ Hydrate fully. Times and temperatures are indicated in the table below. For instructions, see page 4·26.

④ Cast into a film onto a flat, level surface. Keep the liquid cold, so that it is more viscous and coats the surface more easily. Films are typically cast in a layer 0.5–1 mm / 1/64–1/32 in thick; crisps and tuiles are usually thicker, 1.5–2 mm / 1/16–3/32 in. For more on making films, see the example recipes on the next two pages.

⑤ Dehydrate at the lowest humidity and temperature feasible. Dehydrating at 30 °C / 86 °F is ideal. Slow, low-temperature drying produces films that have an even texture; films often crack when dried too quickly and warp when exposed to humidity. The greater the degree of dehydration, the less flexible and more brittle the film becomes. For more information on dehydrating techniques, see page 2·428.

Best Bets for Edible Films

Texture	Clarity	Formula	(scaling)*	Hydrate (°C)	(°F)	(min)	Example use
tender	clear	Methocel SGA 150**	0.75%	refrigerated		8 h	edible wrappers, paper coating films
		160 Bloom gelatin	0.75%	60	140	5	
		sugar	15%	95	203	3	
		HM pectin	2%				
	opaque	agar	1.0%	95	203	3	
		glycerin	1.2%				
		xanthan gum	0.2%				
crisp	clear	low-acyl gellan	0.5%	95	203	3	flavored crisps, delicate tuiles
		propylene glycol alginate	0.5%	60	140	5	
		160 Bloom gelatin	0.3%				
		maltodextrin DE 8	15%	cold			
		sugar or isomalt	10%				
	opaque	Methocel E4M**	1.25%	refrigerated		8 h	crispy cream cheese (see below)
brittle	clear	Pure-Cote B790	10%	100	212	15	Grant Achatz's pineapple glass wrapper for bacon powder (see page 187)
	opaque	N-Zorbit M	20%	cold			seasoned glasses, fruit and vegetable glasses
		glucose powder	15.0%	95	203	3	
		LM pectin	1.5%				
		agar	0.6%				

from page 4·60   *(set weight of liquid to 100%); **(for dispersal instructions, see page 4·24)

CRISPY CREAM CHEESE ADAPTED FROM WYLIE DUFRESNE

Yields 100 g

INGREDIENT	QUANTITY	SCALING	PROCEDURE
Water	100 g	50%	① Bring water to boil.
Methylcellulose E4M (Dow brand)	6 g	3% (2%)*	② Shear in methylcellulose, and simmer until completely dispersed, at least 3 min.
Cream cheese, at room temperature	200 g	100%	③ Pour mixture onto cream cheese.
			④ Add salt, and blend.
Salt	1.5 g	0.75%	⑤ Cool cream cheese mixture to 10 °C / 50 °F.
			⑥ Spread onto silicone mat in layer 2 mm / 1/16 in thick.
			⑦ Dehydrate at 50 °C / 120 °F until crisp and brittle, 10–12 h.
			⑧ Allow to cool completely before using.

from page 4·63   *(% of total weight of water and cream cheese)

THICKENERS

SPICED HONEY GLASS

Yields 365 g

INGREDIENT	QUANTITY	SCALING	PROCEDURE
Honey, spray-dried (store-bought)	180 g	100%	① Combine and heat to 160 °C / 320 °F, stirring constantly.
Trehalose or sugar	180 g	100%	② Pour onto 27.5 cm by 40 cm / 11 in by 16 in silicone mat, and cool until hardened.
Water	45 g	25%	③ Break glass into shards, and grind to fine powder.
			④ Pass powder through fine sieve onto baking sheet lined with silicone mat, forming layer 1.5 mm / 1/16 in thick, and reserve.
Coriander seeds, toasted	4 g	2%	⑤ Crush spices together to make coarse powder.
Sichuan peppercorns	2.5 g	1.5%	⑥ Use fine sieve to remove fine particles.
Fennel seeds	2 g	1%	⑦ Sprinkle coarse particles evenly over tray of sugar powder.
Black pepper, coarsely ground	1.5 g	0.8%	⑧ Bake in 150 °C / 300 °F oven until completely melted, about 6 min.
			⑨ Cut into 2.5 cm by 7.5 cm / 1 in by 3 in pieces while still hot and pliable.
			⑩ Store in cool, dry place.

from page 5·123

DRIED CHERRY AND HAZELNUT NOUGATINE

Yields 240 g

INGREDIENT	QUANTITY	SCALING	PROCEDURE
Sugar	50 g	100%	① Heat together to 150 °C / 300 °F to make syrup.
Trehalose (or isomalt)	50 g	100%	
Glucose syrup DE 40	25 g	50%	
Water	20 g	40%	
Hazelnut butter	50 g	100%	② Whisk into syrup, and heat mixture to 170 °C / 340 °F.
Unsalted butter	10 g	20%	
Dried sour cherries, minced	20 g	40%	③ Fold remaining ingredients into mixture.
			④ Pour onto silicone mat. Cover with second silicone mat, and roll mixture out into layer 1 mm / 1/16 in thick.
Hazelnuts, peeled and minced	15 g	30%	⑤ Cool until brittle, break into irregular shards, and serve, or store in cool, dry place.
Salt	2.2 g	4.4%	
Baking powder	1.5 g	3%	

from page 5·270

EDIBLE WRAPPERS ADAPTED FROM HESTON BLUMENTHAL

Yields 130 g (65 wrappers)

INGREDIENT	QUANTITY	SCALING	PROCEDURE
Water	400 g	100%	① Combine to bloom gelatin.
200 Bloom gelatin	6 g	1.5%	② Heat solution; whisk constantly to dissolve gelatin.
Glycerin	0.2 g	0.05%	③ Transfer 6 g of solution to 9 cm / 3½ in diameter petri dish with pipette.
			④ Swirl solution to coat dish bottom evenly and eliminate air bubbles.
			⑤ Repeat with remaining solution in individual petri dishes, one for each wrapper.
			⑥ Rest in warm place until resulting films are completely dry, 20–24 h.
			⑦ Peel off wrappers, and store in airtight container.

from page 4·62

ONION ARLETTE

Yields 500 g

INGREDIENT	QUANTITY	SCALING	PROCEDURE
Sweet onion juice	300 g (from about 500 g onions)	100%	① Combine, and cook at 155 °C / 310 °F, until light golden caramel forms.
			② Pour hot onion syrup onto silicone mat.
			③ Cool and harden at room temperature, about 20 min.
Trehalose (or isomalt or sugar)	130 g	43.3%	④ Grind to fine powder, and reserve resulting onion sugar.
Glucose syrup DE 40	70 g	23.3%	
Puff pastry dough (store-bought or fresh-made)	500 g	167%	⑤ Roll out dough in rectangle 0.5 cm / ¼ in thick.
			⑥ Cut dough into five progressively smaller rectangles.
Clarified unsalted butter, melted	150 g	50%	⑦ Stack in layers, brushing with butter and dusting with thin coat of onion sugar between each layer.
			⑧ Fold and roll dough into cylinder, and then pinch top to give dough a bulb shape.
			⑨ Freeze until very hard, about 45 min.
			⑩ Cut dough with meat slicer into slices 1 mm / 1⁄16 in thick.
			⑪ Place slices between two silicone mats, and pass rolling pin over top until slices are nearly translucent; they should retain their shape.
			⑫ Dust flattened slices with more onion sugar to fully coat surfaces.
			⑬ Transfer to silicone mat–lined baking sheet.
			⑭ Bake in 170 °C / 340 °F oven for 7 min.
			⑮ Dust with additional onion sugar, and bake at same temperature for 2–3 min.
			⑯ Cool, and reserve in cool, dry place.

from page 5·262

BBQ CARAMELS

Yields 750 g

INGREDIENT	QUANTITY	SCALING	PROCEDURE
KC Masterpiece honey barbecue sauce	500 g	286%	① Reduce sauce over low heat to 250 g.
			② Reserve.
Sugar	175 g	100%	③ Blend.
Salt	10 g	5.7%	
HM pectin (Brown Ribbon HV, Obipektin brand)	4.7 g	2.7% (0.53%)*	
Glucose syrup DE40	175 g	100%	④ Combine with sugar mixture in pot.
Water	175 g	100%	⑤ Heat to 145 °C / 293 °F.
Unsalted butter, cubed	110 g	63%	⑥ Stir into reduced barbecue sauce to form caramel base.
			⑦ Heat to 135 °C / 275 °F, and remove from heat.
Liquid hickory smoke (Lazy Kettle brand)	5 g	3%	⑧ Stir into caramel base quickly while base is still hot.
			⑨ Pour into mold 1.5 cm / 5⁄8 in thick.
			⑩ Refrigerate until solidified.
			⑪ Cut caramel sheet with scissors into desired shapes.
Edible wrappers, from above	as needed		⑫ Wrap caramels individually.
			⑬ Store in cool, dry place.

from page 4·62

*(% of total weight of reduced honey barbecue sauce, sugar, glucose, water, and unsalted butter)

You can substitute our House Barbecue sauce (see page 220) or one of the regional sauces (see page 5·66).

For the texture of the caramel to be correct, the sugar content should be 88 °Brix as measured on a refractometer. Extend the cooking time as needed to reach the correct Brix level.

COOKED WHOLE EGGS

Best Bets for Cooking Whole Eggs

Recipe	Cook (°C)	Cook (°F)	Cook (min)	Equipment	See page
pasteurized egg	55	131	2 h	water bath	1·190
onsen egg (Japanese slow-cooked egg)	62–68	144–154	35	water bath	4·76
perfect soft-boiled egg	100	212	3	water baths and blowtorch	4·79
	64	147	35		
perfect hard-boiled egg	79	174	35	water bath	4·76
fast hot-spring egg adapted from Aki Kamozawa and H. Alexander Talbot	75	167	13	water bath	
fast hot-spring quail egg adapted from Ferran Adrià	70	158	7	water bath	
Arzak egg blossom	85	185	12	water bath	this page

from page 4·78

LIQUID CENTER DUCK EGG
Yields 340 g

INGREDIENT	QUANTITY	SCALING	PROCEDURE
Duck eggs (shelled)	320 g (four eggs)	100%	① Immerse eggs in boiling water for 4 min.
			② Cool in ice-water bath for 20 min.
			③ Cook in 62 °C / 143 °F bath for about 30 min.
			④ Cool again in ice-water bath.
			⑤ Crack eggshells gently all over with back of spoon, but do not remove shells.
			⑥ Reserve.
Red beet juice	800 g	250%	⑦ Combine, reduce to 750 g, and cool.
Red port wine	350 g	109%	⑧ Immerse eggs in reduction, and soak in refrigerator for 12 h.
			⑨ Drain, and then gently peel off eggshells.
			⑩ Reheat eggs in 62 °C / 143 °F bath for about 25 min.
Flaky sea salt	to taste		⑪ Season.
Constructed red wine glaze, warmed see page 24	65 g	20%	⑫ Garnish with glaze.

from page 5·220

The egg white needs more heat to coagulate than the yolk does, so first use boiling water to set the white firmly enough that it can be peeled later. Then use a low temperature water bath to cook the center. If substituting chicken eggs, which usually are smaller than duck eggs, you may need to reduce the initial boiling time to 3–3½ min.

EGG BLOSSOM INSPIRED BY JUAN MARI ARZAK
Yields four eggs

INGREDIENT	QUANTITY	SCALING	PROCEDURE
Whole eggs	four large		① Line small bowl with plastic wrap.
Duck fat	50 g	100%	② Combine fats, and brush center of plastic wrap.
Extra-virgin olive oil	25 g	50%	③ Break one egg in center of bowl.
Truffle oil	10 g	20%	④ Season with salt and additional fat.
Salt	to taste		⑤ Gather edges of plastic wrap together carefully.
			⑥ Twist wrapped mixture into ball, and tie off top of wrap.
			⑦ Repeat procedure with remaining eggs.
			⑧ Cook eggs in 85 °C / 185 °F water bath for 12 min.
			⑨ Cut away plastic wrap to serve.

from page 4·80

Add 2 min to the cooking time if using duck eggs.

This recipe uses a single step of 12 min in an 85 °C / 185 °F bath, but you could also cook the eggs in a two-stage manner (as when making soft-boiled eggs as described on the previous page): boil them for 1–3 min, and then cook in a 40–64 °C / 104–147 °F water bath.

DEVILED EGGS

Yields four portions

INGREDIENT	QUANTITY	SCALING	PROCEDURE
Whole eggs, in shell	200 g (four large)	100%	① Cook in 72 °C / 162 °F bath for 35 min. ② Plunge in ice water. ③ Peel, and separate yolks from whites. ④ Set yolks aside. ⑤ Retain whites for mayonnaise.
Reserved egg whites, from above	145 g	72.5%	⑥ Blend.
Champagne vinegar	25 g	12.5%	
Dijon mustard	10 g	5%	
Extra-virgin olive oil	100 g	50%	⑦ Drizzle slowly into egg white mixture while blending.
Walnut oil	20 g	10%	⑧ Emulsify fully to make mayonnaise.
Tarragon, thinly sliced	4 g	2%	⑨ Fold in.
Black pepper, coarsely ground	to taste		⑩ Season mayonnaise.
Cayenne pepper	to taste		⑪ Smear on each plate, and garnish each plate with one yolk.
Salt	to taste		
Bottarga di Muggine (store-bought)	20 g	10%	⑫ Grate finely over each plate.

from page 4·81

At 72 °C / 162 °F, the yolk sets hard enough that it remains spherical rather than flattening from its own weight—as it does at lower temperatures (see page 4·76). These yolk balls have a wonderful consistency. They can be used as a kind of dumpling in soups or other dishes.

CUSTARDS

The perfect custard temperature depends on three things: whether you use yolks or whole eggs; the proportion of egg to other liquid; and the final core temperature. Using the table below, you can achieve any result you want.

Note that "milk," "quiche," and other terms in the table below refer to the resulting texture, not to ingredients or a specific recipe.

Custard Textures

	Whole egg					Egg yolk				
Cook (°C) (°F)	70 158	75 167	80 176	83 181	88 190	70 158	75 167	80 176	83 181	88 190
Egg (scaling)*										
10%	milk	half-and-half	thin cream	heavy cream	thin crème anglaise	milk	thin cream	heavy cream	thin crème anglaise	crème anglaise
30%	milk	thin crème anglaise	crème anglaise	crème brûlée	flan	milk	thin crème anglaise	crème anglaise	thick crème anglaise	flan
50%	milk	crème anglaise	crème brûlée	flan	soft-scrambled	milk	thick crème anglaise	pudding	flan	firm flan
70%	milk	thick crème anglaise	flan	soft-scrambled	frittata	thin cream	crème brûlée	flan	firm flan	quiche
90%	half-and-half	crème brûlée	quiche	frittata	tender omelet	heavy cream	flan	firm flan	quiche	soft-scrambled
110%	thin cream	flan	frittata	tender omelet	omelet	thin crème anglaise	firm flan	quiche	soft-scrambled	frittata
130%	heavy cream	firm flan	tender omelet	omelet	firm omelet	crème anglaise	quiche	soft-scrambled	frittata	tender omelet
150%	thin crème anglaise	quiche	omelet	firm omelet	dry-scrambled	thick crème anglaise	soft-scrambled	frittata	tender omelet	firm omelet
200%	crème anglaise	soft-scrambled	firm omelet	dry-scrambled	chewy	soft-scrambled	frittata	tender omelet	firm omelet	dry-scrambled
250%	thick crème anglaise	frittata	dry-scrambled	chewy	rubbery	frittata	tender omelet	firm omelet	dry-scrambled	chewy

from page 4·84 *(set weight of liquid to 100%)*

PRESERVED AND PICKLED EGGS

① Select a recipe. See the table Best Bets for Pickled and Preserved Eggs below for suggestions.

② Make the brine or curing agent. Prepare enough to completely cover all eggs. Weights in the table are scaled to be proportional to the weight of the principal liquid. For example, to make a dozen century eggs, weigh out enough water to cover the eggs completely, and then add 9 g of salt and 4.2 g of sodium hydroxide for every 100 g of water.

③ Submerge very fresh whole eggs in brine or cure, and refrigerate for the time indicated. Note that all of the recipes here, except the vinegar-coagulated egg, require that the eggs remain in the shell when immersed in brine.

④ Cook (optional). For a more familiar texture, lightly cook the cured eggs, using the time and temperature indicated in the table.

Best Bets for Pickled and Preserved Eggs

Recipe	Coagulant	(scaling)	Brine/cure	(days)	Cook (°C)	(°F)	(min)	See page
century egg	water	100%	brine	20	68	154	35	below
	salt	9%	soak	2				
	sodium hydroxide (lye)	4.2%	dry	5				
salt-coagulated egg	water	100%	brine	28	68	154	35	
	salt	32%						
vinegar-coagulated egg	vinegar	100%	brine	½–1	62	144	20	below
miso-cured egg yolks	red miso	100%	cure	5	n/a			236
	sake	18.5%						
	sugar	16%						

from page 4·82

CENTURY EGG

Yields 400 g

INGREDIENT	QUANTITY	SCALING	PROCEDURE
Water	1 kg	100%	① Whisk together until fully dissolved to make brine.
Salt	90 g	9%	
Sodium hydroxide (lye)	42 g	4.2%	
Whole duck eggs, washed and checked for cracks	450 g (about six)	45%	② Vacuum seal eggs with brine.
			③ Refrigerate in bag for 20 d.
			④ Remove from bag, and soak in fresh water for 2 d.
			⑤ Air-dry at room temperature for 5 d.
			⑥ Optionally, cook in 68 °C / 154 °F bath for 35 min. Cool and peel.
			⑦ If desired, garnish with pickled mushrooms and seaweed vinegar.

from page 4·83

PICKLED QUAIL EGGS INSPIRED BY HERVÉ THIS

Yields 150 g

INGREDIENT	QUANTITY	SCALING	PROCEDURE
Quail eggs	200 g (about 10)	100%	① Crack open; reserve whole quail eggs individually.
Champagne vinegar	500 g	250%	② Combine to make brine, and bring to simmer.
Water	250 g	125%	
Sugar	135 g	67.5%	
Salt	8 g	4%	
Black peppercorns	1 g	0.5%	③ Combine.
White peppercorns	1 g	0.5%	④ Pour hot brine over spice mixture, and cool.
Pink peppercorns	0.5 g	0.25%	⑤ Strain cold brine into large sous vide bag.
Yellow mustard seeds	1 g	0.5%	⑥ Slide eggs gently, one by one, into brine-filled bag, while taking care to avoid collisions that could burst their yolks.
Celery seeds	1 g	0.5%	
Dill seeds	1 g	0.5%	⑦ Vacuum seal, and refrigerate for 12 h.
Aleppo pepper flakes	0.1 g	0.05%	⑧ Drain eggs, and cook in 62 °C / 144 °F bath for 15 min.

from page 4·83

SEPARATED EGG GELS

① Select a texture. The table below lists our recommendations.

② Measure the yolk, white, liquid, and salt. Scale the ingredients relative to the weight of the eggs (for example, use 2 g of salt for every 100 g of egg yolk in a sliceable yolk).

③ Blend eggs with liquid, and whisk in seasoning. Eggs for the two-stage fried egg should just be separated. For the two-stage baked eggs, blend the whites with the cream and keep the yolks whole.

④ Cook. Appropriate methods, times, and temperatures are indicated, along with references to example recipes.

Best Bets for Separated Egg Gels

Texture	Egg yolk (scaling)	Egg white (scaling)	Liquid	(scaling)	Salt (scaling)	Cook Method	(°C)	(°F)	(min)	See page
crème anglaise	100%	n/a	milk or cream	400%	5.5%	sous vide	80	176	12	below
egg yolk droplets	100%	n/a	n/a		1.1%	open container in sous vide bath	77	171	2	236
sliceable yolk	100%	n/a	n/a		2%	sous vide	70	158	1 h	238
crème brûlée	100%	n/a	cream / milk	200% / 175%	5%	steam oven	79	174	35	237
egg white custard	n/a	100%	cream / milk	110% / 110%	3.5%	steam oven	83	181	15	
egg white droplets	n/a	100%	n/a		1.1%	stove top	74	165	3	236
two-stage baked eggs	white / yolk	100% / 1 per serving	cream / n/a	35%	1.4% / to taste	steam oven	74 / 64	165 / 147	30 / 20	
Nathan's two-stage fried egg	white / yolk	1 per serving / 1 per serving	n/a		to taste	buttered ring mold, steam oven	79 / 63	174 / 145	15 / 25	2

from page 4·85

CAULIFLOWER CRÈME ANGLAISE

Yields 300 g

INGREDIENT	QUANTITY	SCALING	PROCEDURE
Cauliflower, thinly sliced	400 g	160%	① Roast in 160 °C / 320 °F oven until deep amber, about 25–30 min. Alternatively, deep-fry in 190 °C / 375 °F oil for 5–6 min.
			② Cool completely.
Whole milk	500 g	200%	③ Vacuum seal with roasted cauliflower.
			④ Cook in 85 °C / 185 °F bath for 1 h to infuse milk.
			⑤ Remove from bag, and strain.
			⑥ Measure 250 g of cauliflower milk.
			⑦ Cool milk to room temperature.
Cauliflower milk, from above	250 g	100%	⑧ Blend together until smooth, and vacuum seal.
Egg yolks	63 g	25%	⑨ Cook sous vide in 80 °C / 176 °F bath for 35 min.
			⑩ Remove from bag, and cool.
			⑪ Add additional cauliflower milk or heavy cream to achieve desired viscosity.
			⑫ Vacuum seal and refrigerate.
Nutmeg, freshly grated	to taste		⑬ To serve, reheat crème anglaise in 70 °C / 158 °F bath for 10 min.
Salt	to taste		⑭ Pour into serving container.
			⑮ Season.

from page 4·89

EGGS BENEDICT INSPIRED BY PEDRO SUBIJANA AND GRANT ACHATZ

Yields 610 g

INGREDIENT	QUANTITY	SCALING	PROCEDURE
Egg yolks	150 g	100%	① Whisk yolks together with salt, and strain through fine sieve.
Salt	3 g	2%	② Transfer to squeeze bottle.
Egg whites	150 g	100%	③ Whisk whites together with salt, and strain through fine sieve.
Salt	3 g	2%	④ Transfer to second squeeze bottle.
Clarified butter see page 4·213	750 g	500%	⑤ Divide butter evenly among two small pots. ⑥ Heat one pot to 72 °C / 162 °F and second pot to 90 °C / 194 °F. ⑦ Squeeze droplets of yolk mixture into 72 °C / 162 °F bath; keep drops separated. ⑧ Cook for 1 min. ⑨ Lift drops slightly from pot bottom with small spatula to help them float. ⑩ Remove droplets when they begin to float, reserving butter. Reserve warm. ⑪ Repeat procedure to make egg white droplets in 90 °C / 194 °F bath. ⑫ Reserve warm.
English muffins, ground	100 g	67%	⑬ Combine in nonstick pan.
Neutral oil	20 g	13.4%	⑭ Fry until golden, about 5 min, and drain.
Salt	to taste		⑮ Season toasted crumbs.
Sous vide instant hollandaise see page 305	150 g	100%	⑯ Heat in 62 °C / 144 °F bath for at least 10 min.
Canadian bacon, finely diced	45 g	30%	⑰ Warm with spoonful of reserved butter. ⑱ Fold into egg yolk droplets, egg white droplets, and toasted crumbs. ⑲ Portion egg, bacon, and crumb combination in small bowls. ⑳ Garnish with small amount of hollandaise.

from page 4·86

MISO-CURED EGG SHEETS

Yields 60 g

INGREDIENT	QUANTITY	SCALING	PROCEDURE
Red miso	75 g	75%	① Combine.
Sake	14 g	14%	② Line small bowl with cheesecloth, or use silicone hemispherical mold.
Sugar	12 g	12%	③ Spread mixture in prepared bowl or mold to form well shape.
Egg yolks, whole	100 g	100%	④ Place yolks, individually and intact, in center of well, and cover with remaining miso mixture. ⑤ Refrigerate for 48 h to cure. Flip yolks over, and refrigerate again for 72 h. ⑥ Remove yolks from cure. ⑦ Roll between two thin silicone mats or two pieces of plastic wrap to form sheets 1 mm / 1/32 in thick. ⑧ Dry at room temperature for 15 min to firm. ⑨ Use egg sheets for ravioli, or cut into noodles and dress with bonito flakes and olive oil.

Cure the yolks for 48 h on each side (96 h total) for a softer, more pliable texture.

The cured egg yolk sheets can be cooked in a 70 °C / 158 °F bath for a more flexible texture.

from page 4·87

PARMESAN CRÈME BRÛLÉE

Yields 450 g (about eight portions)

INGREDIENT	QUANTITY	SCALING	PROCEDURE
Heavy cream	350 g	140%	① Bring cream and cheese to simmer.
Parmesan, finely grated	80 g	32%	② Strain, and reserve 250 g of infused cream.
Cheese-infused cream, from above	250 g	100%	③ Blend together.
			④ Divide mixture evenly among individual ramekins.
Egg yolks	67.5 g	27%	⑤ Cover ramekins with plastic wrap.
Salt	1.32 g	0.5%	⑥ Cook in 78 °C / 172 °F bath or steam oven to core temperature of 77 °C / 171 °F, about 35 min.
			⑦ Refrigerate until cool, about 45 min.
Muscat grape syrup or onion sugar see page 213 or page 231	40 g	16%	⑧ Pour syrup over each crème brûlée to serve. Alternatively, dust onion sugar over surface of custards, and flash with blowtorch until caramelized.

from page 4·88

Sweet crème brûlée can be made with the same basic recipe. Omit the cheese, add 15%–20% sugar, and cook in a 82 °C / 180 °F bath to a core temperature of 81 °C / 178 °F.

For a lighter custard, substitute milk for part of the heavy cream. A typical ratio would be half milk, half cream.

SAUCE ALLEMANDE

Yields 370 g

INGREDIENT	QUANTITY	SCALING	PROCEDURE
White chicken stock see page 6	120 g	200%	① Blend until smooth.
			② Pass through fine sieve.
Heavy cream	100 g	167%	③ Vacuum seal.
Egg yolks, blended and sieved	60 g	100% (20%)*	④ Cook sous vide in 79 °C / 174 °F bath for 35 min.
			⑤ Blend until smooth once more.
Mushroom jus see page 37	50 g	83%	
Unsalted butter, melted	40 g	67%	
Nutmeg, freshly grated	to taste		⑥ Season.
Salt	to taste		⑦ Serve with poached artichokes (see page 3·292) and braised chicken thighs (see page 3·99).
White pepper	to taste		

from page 4·88

*(% of total weight of all other ingredients)

This is a slightly Modernist version of a French haute cuisine classic perfected by Auguste Escoffier in the early 20th century. We think he would approve. The savory custard base can be flavored with other stocks or juices.

EGG SALAD SANDWICH INSPIRED BY WYLIE DUFRESNE

Yields 700 g

INGREDIENT	QUANTITY	SCALING	PROCEDURE
Egg yolks, blended	200 g	100%	① Make sleeves measuring 2.5 cm by 30.5 cm / 1 in by 12 in from sous vide bags by using sealing strips of vacuum sealer.
			② Pipe yolks into sleeves, and tie tops of sleeves tightly to make tube shapes.
			③ Clip tubes to top of bath.
			④ Cook in 70 °C / 158 °F bath for 1 h.
			⑤ Remove yolks from sleeves, and cool completely.
			⑥ Cut yolks into slices 2 mm / 1/16 in thick.
			⑦ Cover with plastic wrap, and refrigerate.
Egg yolks	50 g	25%	⑧ Blend until smooth.
Lemon juice	15 g	7.5%	
Champagne vinegar	1 g	0.5%	
Neutral oil	200 g	100%	⑨ Drizzle slowly into yolk mixture, while blending, until fully emulsified.
			⑩ Set aside mayonnaise.
Salted pollock roe (store-bought)	30 g	15%	⑪ Combine.
			⑫ Fold into mayonnaise.
Cornichons, minced	10 g	5%	⑬ Set mixture aside.
Salt	3 g	1.5%	
Chives, finely minced	2 g	1%	
Sriracha sauce	1 g	0.5%	
Pain de mie or white bread, crusts removed and sliced 5 mm / 3/16 in thick	150 g	75%	⑭ Cut bread into sandwich-size slices.
			⑮ Brush outside of slices with clarified butter.
			⑯ Toast carefully in pan until golden, about 1 min on each side.
Clarified butter, melted see page 4·213	as needed		⑰ Spread inside of each slice with mayonnaise.
			⑱ Arrange egg yolks on one slice of bread.
Black pepper	to taste		⑲ Season each yolk-covered slice.
Flaky sea salt	to taste		
Watercress leaves	40 g	20%	⑳ Garnish with leaves.
			㉑ Top each with second slice of toasted bread to complete sandwich.

from page 4·90

Wylie Dufresne came up with these molded egg yolk tubes to serve with his version of Eggs Benedict, which also involves Deep-Fried Hollandaise (see page 305) and crispy Canadian bacon. We've used them to make this delicious egg sandwich to show how versatile a preparation they can be.

BLENDED EGG GEL

① Measure yolks, whites, liquid ingredients, and seasonings. Use the weight of egg whites as 100%, and measure other ingredients proportionally—for instance, use 60 g of yolk and 10 g of cream for each 100 g of white in an omelet, and so on.

② Blend all ingredients thoroughly.

③ Vacuum seal if cooking sous vide (optional).

④ Cook. See the table below for recommended final core temperatures. The time required will vary depending on the thickness of the layer of egg mixture and of the cooking vessel.

Best Bets for Blended Egg Gels

Recipe	Egg yolk (scaling)	Egg white (scaling)	Liquid	(scaling)	Other ingredients	(scaling)	Cook Method	(°C)	(°F)	See page
American scrambled eggs	70%	100%	whole milk	10%	salt	1.8%	water bath	70	158	
French scrambled eggs	110%	100%	whole milk	45%	salt	3%	water bath	72	162	next
			unsalted butter, melted	45%						
omelet	60%	100%	heavy cream	10%	salt	2%	steam oven	82	180	next
savory flan (crème caramel)	50%	100%	whole milk	300%	salt	2%	steam oven or water bath	83	181	244
chawanmushi (savory Japanese custard)	50%	100%	mirin	3%	salt	2%	steam oven or water bath	82	180	242
			hon dashi see page 15	210%	Activa RM	1%				
royale custard	400%	100%	whole milk	600%	flavorful puree, juice, or stock	800%	steam oven or water bath	80	176	241
			heavy cream	300%						
frittata*	50%	100%	whole milk	50%	Taleggio cheese, grated	25%	steam oven	80	176	
			olive oil	15%	salt	3%				
quiche filling*	50%	100%	bacon-infused heavy cream see page 2·310	190%	salt	3%	steam oven	80	176	

from page 4·92 *(many different flavors can be adapted to these recipes)*

BOUDIN NOIR CUSTARD

Yields 950 g

INGREDIENT	QUANTITY	SCALING	PROCEDURE
Yellow onions, thinly sliced	100 g	22%	① Sauté onions until translucent.
			② Cool.
Rendered bacon fat	20 g	4.4%	
Whole milk, cold	200 g	44%	③ Disperse gelatin into milk.
160 Bloom gelatin	19 g	4.2%	④ Warm until gelatin is fully dissolved.
Heavy cream	450 g	100%	⑤ Combine with onions and milk.
Egg yolks	80 g	18%	⑥ Blend until smooth.
Pigeon blood (fresh)	60 g	13%	⑦ Strain through fine sieve.
Salt	14 g	3%	⑧ Vacuum seal.
Dutch-processed cocoa powder	4 g	0.9%	⑨ Cook sous vide in 70 °C / 158 °F bath for 1 h.
			⑩ Cool in ice-water bath.
Quatre épices see page 48	4 g	0.9%	⑪ Refrigerate.

For more on the steps involved in proper dispersion and hydration of gelatin, see page 4·124. For more on strategies for clarifying juice, see page 2·352.

from page 5·127

FRENCH SCRAMBLED EGGS

Yields 520 g

INGREDIENT	QUANTITY	SCALING	PROCEDURE
Egg yolks	150 g (from about eight large)	100%	① Combine, and blend until smooth.
			② Vacuum seal.
Egg whites	130 g (from about four large)	87%	③ Cook in 72 °C / 162 °F bath until thick, about 35 min.
			④ Optionally, transfer eggs to whipping siphon, and charge with two nitrous oxide cartridges for light, foamy texture.
Unsalted butter, melted	60 g	40%	
Whole milk	60 g	40%	⑤ Reserve warm.
Salt	4 g	2.7%	
Beech mushrooms (hon-shimeji), washed thoroughly	120 g	80%	⑥ Sauté until cooked through, about 4 min.
Unsalted butter	30 g	20%	
Pancetta, thinly sliced	45 g	30%	⑦ Add to mushrooms, and cook for 2 min.
Mushroom jus see page 37	45 g	30%	⑧ Add to mushrooms, and reduce until syrupy, about 3 min.
Crème fraîche	30 g	20%	⑨ Whisk into mushroom mixture.
Scallions, thinly sliced	15 g	10%	
Salt	to taste		⑩ Season.
			⑪ Portion scrambled eggs into four bowls, and garnish with mushroom mixture.

from page 4·93

This recipe, and its more formal cousin in volume 5 (see page 5·215), are among our favorites.

Daniel Patterson of Coi in San Francisco published a recipe for poached scrambled eggs in 2007. He carefully drops blended eggs into seasoned simmering water, while stirring, as if making traditional poached eggs. He then drains the eggs and serves them with olive oil and salt. They are extremely fluffy.

HAM AND CHEESE OMELET

Yields four omelets, about 75 g each

INGREDIENT	QUANTITY	SCALING	PROCEDURE
Whole eggs	145 g (about three)	100%	① Blend thoroughly.
			② Spread in layer 20 cm by 20 cm / 8 in by 8 in and 2 mm / 1⁄16 in thick on nonstick tray.
Heavy cream	15 g	10%	③ Steam at 80 °C / 176 °F until set, about 10 min.
Egg yolk	12 g	8%	④ Cool completely, and cut into four square portions, 5 cm by 5 cm / 2 in by 2 in.
Salt	2.5 g	1.7%	⑤ Set aside.
Cooked French ham, brunoise	75 g	52%	⑥ Combine.
Gruyère cheese, thinly spread (or brunoise) see page 299	60 g	41%	⑦ Fill each omelet evenly.
			⑧ Fold omelets over.
Basil, minced	0.35 g	0.24%	
Chervil, picked	0.35 g	0.24%	
Chives, minced	0.35 g	0.24%	
Tarragon, minced	0.35 g	0.24%	
Clarified brown butter see page 4·213	as needed		⑨ Brush onto omelet.
			⑩ Steam at 80 °C / 176 °F until cheese has melted, about 4 min.

from page 4·95

By using a combi oven or a low-temperature steamer (see page 2·162), perfectly done omelets can be made simultaneously for dozens or even hundreds of people.

This omelet can also be made in a conventional oven, but doing so requires great vigilance. Pour a thin layer of omelet base in a nonstick pan, wrap tightly with cling film or cover with a lid, and bake in a 120 °C / 250 °F oven until just set, 7–10 min depending on the wet-bulb temperature.

A dramatic mushroom omelet—a more complex version of the omelet recipe above—can be found on page 5·215. We use a pastry comb to create flavorful stripes of mushroom puree thickened with albumin and egg yolk powder.

ASPARAGUS ROYALE INSPIRED BY ALAIN DUCASSE   Yields 550 g (about eight royales)

INGREDIENT	QUANTITY	SCALING	PROCEDURE
Asparagus puree or juice see page 33 or page 55	200 g	100%	① Blend until smooth.
			② Press mixture through fine sieve.
Whole milk	150 g	75%	③ Pour layer 2.5 cm / 1 in thick into individual bowls.
Egg yolk	105 g	52.5% (24%)*	④ Cover bowls with plastic wrap.
Heavy cream	75 g	37.5%	⑤ Cook in 80 °C / 176 °F bath or steam oven to core temperature of 79 °C / 174 °F, about 30 min.
Egg white	25 g	12.5% (5.8%)*	⑥ Reserve royales warm, or refrigerate.
Salt	6.5 g	3.25%	
Roasted-hazelnut oil	5 g	2.5%	
Porcini oil (store-bought)	5 g	2.5%	
Brown chicken jus see page 34	80 g	40%	⑦ Combine.
			⑧ Whisk over low heat until just warm, about 2 min.
Black truffle concentrate see page 57	20 g	10%	
Unsalted butter	20 g	10%	
Lemon juice	to taste		⑨ Season warm truffle mixture.
Salt	to taste		⑩ Divide equally among royales.

from page 4·94   *(% of total weight of all other ingredients in royales)

Royales are savory custards, either served as is or cut into designs and floated on the surface of a consommé. We think even Antonin Carême would approve of this recipe, which uses Modernist temperature control to achieve the perfect texture.

DASHIMAKI TAMAGO   Yields 295 g

INGREDIENT	QUANTITY	SCALING	PROCEDURE
Egg whites	125 g	167%	① Combine, blending completely.
Egg yolks	75 g	100%	② Vacuum seal to remove bubbles.
Hon dashi see page 15	40 g	53%	③ Remove from bag, and cast into nonstick mold in layer 4 cm / 1½ in thick.
N-Zorbit M (National Starch brand)	30 g	40%	④ Steam, covered, at 79 °C / 174 °F until set, about 25 min.
			⑤ Refrigerate to cool completely, about 30 min.
Agave syrup	20 g	27%	⑥ Remove from mold.
White soy sauce	7 g	9.3%	⑦ Slice tamago into desired dimensions.
Sugar	5 g	6.7%	
Salt	1 g	1.3%	
Frying oil	as needed		⑧ Heat thin film of oil over medium heat. Sear each tamago on one side until evenly browned.
			⑨ Serve tamago while crust is warm and center is still cold for pleasant temperature contrast.

from page 4·94

PRESSURE-COOKED EGG TOAST ADAPTED FROM NILS NORÉN AND DAVE ARNOLD   Yields 180 g (about six toasts)

INGREDIENT	QUANTITY	SCALING	PROCEDURE
Egg yolks	200 g (about 11 yolks)	100%	① Blend until smooth.
			② Vacuum seal to remove excess air.
Baking powder	9 g	4.5%	③ Transfer egg mixture to small greased ramekins; fill each halfway full.
Salt	2 g	1%	④ Add enough water to pressure cooker to reach halfway up ramekin sides.
			⑤ Pressure-cook at gauge pressure of 1 bar / 15 psi for 40 min to form cooked, muffin-like eggs.
			⑥ Cool quickly by running cold water over cooker.
Clarified butter, unsalted	as needed		⑦ Cut egg rounds in half horizontally, and brush with butter.
			⑧ Fry rounds, cut side down, until golden.
Chives, finely minced	10 g	5%	⑨ Garnish.
Sturgeon caviar	as desired		

from page 4·97

GELS

CHAWANMUSHI

Yields 850 g (about eight chawanmushi)

INGREDIENT	QUANTITY	SCALING	PROCEDURE
Scallop stock or chicken stock *see page 6 or page 11*	350 g	350%	① Blend.
			② Vacuum seal.
Diver scallops, pureed and sieved	65 g	65%	③ Cook sous vide in 45 °C / 113 °F bath for 10 min to activate enzyme.
			④ Pour chawanmushi base into porcelain bowls to depth of 2.5 cm / 1 in.
White soy sauce	18 g	18%	⑤ Wrap bowls tightly with plastic wrap.
Whole eggs, blended	100 g (about two)	100% (23%)*	⑥ Cook in 82 °C / 180 °F water bath or steam oven to core temperature of 81 °C / 178 °F, about 40 min.
Activa RM	8 g	8% (1.5%)**	
Scallop stock or chicken stock *see page 6 or page 11*	100 g	100%	⑦ Simmer stock and sake together for 3 min.
Sake	75 g	75%	
Xanthan gum	0.3 g	0.3%	⑧ Blend into stock mixture.
Unsalted butter, cubed	50 g	50%	⑨ Blend into stock mixture until fully emulsified.
Salt	to taste		⑩ Season sauce.
Prosciutto crudo, finely diced	30 g	30%	⑪ Whisk into sauce.
			⑫ Garnish each chawanmushi evenly.
Dates, finely diced	25 g	25%	
Scallions, thinly sliced	20 g	20%	
Lemon verbena, thinly sliced	3 g	3%	

from page 4·96

*(% of total weight of first three ingredients)
**(% of total weight of first four ingredients)

BOUDIN NOIR BREAD PUDDING

Yields 1 kg

INGREDIENT	QUANTITY	SCALING	PROCEDURE
Day-old brioche, crust removed	500 g	100%	① Cut into slices 2.5 cm / 1 in thick.
			② Place slices in bottom of deep hotel pan.
Boudin noir custard, warmed *see page 239*	500 g	100%	③ Pour custard over brioche, and place pan quickly in vacuum chamber. Warm custard will penetrate better than cold.
			④ Pull full vacuum twice, turn brioche slices over, and pull vacuum three more times, or as many times as necessary for bread to fully absorb custard.
			⑤ Refrigerate until set, at least 4 h.
			⑥ Cut gelled brioche slices into 3.75 cm / 1½ in by 5 cm / 2 in rectangles.
Frying oil	as needed		⑦ Dust brioche rectangles with trehalose on all sides.
Trehalose	as needed		⑧ Deep-fry in 175 °C / 350 °F oil for 3 min.
Glucose syrup DE 40	as needed		⑨ While frying rectangles, heat glucose syrup in nonstick sauté pan over medium high.
Salt	as needed		⑩ Remove rectangles from oil, and pat dry with paper towels. Transfer immediately to sauté pan, and coat with hot glucose syrup.
			⑪ Cook, flipping constantly, until golden shell forms on all sides, about 3 min.
			⑫ Transfer to nonstick surface, season with salt, and cool at room temperature until shells harden, about 1 min.

from page 5·127

CHORIZO FRENCH TOAST

Yields 250 g (four slices)

INGREDIENT	QUANTITY	SCALING
Whole milk	600 g	300%
Spanish chorizo, ground	150 g	75%
Chorizo milk, from above	600 g	300%
Whole eggs, blended	245 g	122.5% (41%)*
Salt	9 g	4.5%
Brioche, cut into 5 cm / 2 in rounds	200 g	100%
Quail eggs	four eggs	
Frying oil	as needed	

from page 4·98   *(% of weight of chorizo milk)

① Combine milk and chorizo.
② Vacuum seal, and cook sous vide in 85 °C / 185 °F bath for 1 h.
③ Cool completely. Strain, and reserve 600 g.
④ Blend reserved chorizo milk with eggs and salt until smooth.
⑤ Place brioche rounds in container, and pour custard over brioche.
⑥ Place container in vacuum chamber, and pull vacuum until custard boils.
⑦ Release vacuum; custard will be fully absorbed by brioche.
⑧ Sauté brioche rounds until golden on both sides. (This step can be reversed with step 10 if desired.)
⑨ Cook in 150 °C / 300 °F oven to core temperature of 80 °C / 176 °F, about 7 min. Alternatively, vacuum seal under weak vacuum, and cook sous vide in 80 °C / 176 °F bath or steam oven for 10 min.
⑩ Fry quail eggs in nonstick pan until whites are cooked through but yolks are still runny. If making large quantities, consider using the two-stage "fried" egg approach—see page 2 and page 235.
⑪ Top toast rounds with fried eggs. Serve with olive marmalade (recipe below). We garnish our chorizo French toast with thyme, but there are many other possibilities.

French toast is good when made with many savory flavors, such as aged cheese, foie gras, sweet peas, corn—even savory nut milks.

To make a foie gras version of this recipe, simply blend 400 g of milk with 200 g of raw foie gras, and use this mixture instead of the chorizo-infused milk. We also had great success with a blend of 300 g of milk and 300 g of toasted almond milk (see page 228).

OLIVE MARMALADE

Yields 100 g

INGREDIENT	QUANTITY	SCALING	PROCEDURE
Fennel, finely minced	30 g	100%	① Sauté over low heat until tender, about 12 min.
			② Cool completely.
Olive oil	30 g	100%	③ Fold into fennel.
Shallots, minced	10 g	33%	
Picholine olives, minced	30 g	100%	
Candied orange rind, minced	15 g	50%	
Niçoise olives, minced	10 g	33%	
Thyme, leaves	0.1 g	0.33%	④ Season.
Salt	to taste		

from page 4·99

Stripes of mushroom puree make for a visually stunning omelet in the recipe below, but skipping this step greatly simplifies the recipe and saves nearly an hour of effort. Also, omitting the stripes does not take away from what makes this omelet special: the remarkable texture. Truffle concentrate (see page 57) is a decadent substitute for the mushroom puree.

OMELET BASE

Yields 300 g (about four omelets)

INGREDIENT	QUANTITY	SCALING	PROCEDURE
Eggs	145 g	100%	① Blend thoroughly to create egg base, and reserve.
Heavy cream	15 g	10.3%	
Egg yolks	12 g	8.3%	
Salt	2.5 g	1.7%	
Mushroom puree see page 55	100 g	69%	② Combine, and spread onto silicone mat in layer 20 cm / 8 in square and 2 mm / 1/16 in thick.
Egg yolk powder	15.5 g	10.7%	③ Pull pastry comb with 3 mm / 1/8 in teeth through mushroom puree mixture to create even lines. If pastry comb is unavailable, proceed to step 4.
Heavy cream	10.3 g	7.1%	④ Pour egg base evenly over mushroom puree mixture, between lines if pastry comb was used, in layer 2 mm / 1/16 in thick.
Albumin powder (store-bought)	8.8 g	6%	⑤ Steam in 82 °C / 180 °F combi oven with 100% relative humidity, or CVap oven with same settings, until set, about 10 min.
Salt	1.7 g	1.1%	⑥ Cut into four 5 cm / 2 in squares.
			⑦ Reheat omelet squares in 82 °C / 180 °F combi oven with 100% relative humidity, or CVap oven at same temperature with browning level set to 0, for 3 min.
Scrambled egg foam, warmed see page 5·216	200 g	138%	⑧ Dispense straight line of scrambled egg foam down centers of omelet squares.
			⑨ Spoon marmalade in straight lines next to scrambled egg foam lines.
Mushroom marmalade, warmed see page 5·217	80 g	55%	

from page 5·217

GELS

SMOKED EGGS AND DAIRY PRODUCTS

① Select the ingredient. The table below lists several good options.
② Preheat and prehumidify the smoker to the temperature and relative humidity indicated in the table. Some smokers allow you to set the temperature and relative humidity directly; otherwise, place a pan of water on the bottom rack of the smoker, and use gauges to monitor the heat and humidity.
③ Smoke for the time indicated.
④ Use immediately, or chill quickly and thoroughly.

Best Bets for Smoking Dairy and Eggs

Ingredient	Dry-bulb temperature (°C)	(°F)	Wet-bulb temperature (°C)	(°F)	Relative humidity	(h)	Example use	See page
cold-smoked eggs, shelled	60	140	48	118	50%	7	flan, crème anglaise, mayonnaise	below
cream	7	45	5	42	75%	4½	cream sauce, cream cheese	
butter, hot-smoked	30	85	22	72	50%	4	spread for toast	
butter, cold-smoked	10	50	6	43	55%	24	poached salmon with smoked beurre blanc	5·161
cheese (mozzarella, Parmesan, cheddar)	10	50	6	43	55%	24	pizza, cheese plate	

from page 4·100

SMOKED EGG CRÈME CARAMEL

Yields 200 g

If cold smoking the eggs is not an option, use fresh eggs, and add 0.75 g (0.5% of the total weight of infused milk and eggs) of good quality liquid smoke instead.

INGREDIENT	QUANTITY	SCALING	PROCEDURE
Whole milk	150 g	150%	① Vacuum seal together, and cook sous vide in 90 °C / 194 °F bath for 1½ h.
Bacon, minced	100 g	100%	
Shallots, finely minced	30 g	30%	② Remove from bag, and strain; reserve 100 g of milk.
			③ Cool milk.
Bacon-infused milk, from above	100 g	100%	④ Blend together until smooth.
Cold-smoked eggs, shelled see above	50 g	50%	⑤ Vacuum seal to remove any trapped air bubbles.
Salt	2.3 g	2.3%	
Sugar	40 g	40%	⑥ Combine in pan. Cook over medium heat until sugar becomes dark caramel, about 7 min.
Water	20 g	20%	
Black pepper, coarsely ground	0.1 g	0.1%	⑦ Pour caramel into four ramekins, and cool.
			⑧ Spoon 2.5 cm / 1 in thick layer of custard over caramel.
			⑨ Steam ramekins at 83 °C / 181 °F for 15 min, and cool completely.
			⑩ To serve, invert onto plates.

from page 4·101

PECORINO WITH TRUFFLE HONEY ON CEDAR ADAPTED FROM SCOTT CARSBERG

Yields 300 g

INGREDIENT	QUANTITY	SCALING	PROCEDURE
Smoked Tuscan Pecorino cheese, aged 18 months	250 g	100%	① Cut cheese into four triangular chunks, each 1.25 cm / ½ in thick. Set aside at room temperature.
Black truffles, finely chopped	50 g	20%	② Combine.
Acacia honey	10 g	4%	③ Set aside at room temperature.
Cedar plank			④ To serve, preheat oven to 260 °C / 500 °F.
			⑤ Place cheese chunks on plank, and bake until bubbling and very soft, about 5 min.
			⑥ Remove plank from oven. Ignite edges of plank with blowtorch to create smoke.
Candied chestnuts (store-bought), cut into small cubes	25 g	10%	⑦ Garnish bubbling cheese with truffle honey and candied chestnuts (marrons glacé).
			⑧ Serve on smoking plank to imbue room with smoked-wood aroma.

from page 4·101

PROTEIN CURDS

① Select a curd recipe and texture. The table presents good options that use a variety of coagulants with different flavors and textures.

② Adjust soluble solids concentration, if using soy milk, to 10–14 °Brix. Use a refractometer or a float that measures the density (see page 2·313). You may need to reduce fresh soy milk to achieve this concentration; the higher the density, the richer, firmer, and less elastic the tofu will be.

③ Measure liquid. Scale ingredients relative to the weight of the liquid; in ricotta, for example, use 0.3 g of lactic acid for every 100 g of milk.

④ Preheat the liquid to the cooking temperature. Use a water bath, if available. Do not preheat if making silken tofu or ricotta.

⑤ Dissolve the coagulant in a small amount of water, and then stir the mixture into the milk or cream. The amounts of lactic acid, citric acid, and glucono delta-lactone indicated were selected to achieve the pH shown. If curd texture is too firm (pH too high) or too loose (pH too low), adjust the coagulant quantity accordingly (see page 2·316).

⑥ Heat at temperature indicated for the time shown.

⑦ Remove from heat, and allow to curdle. Approximate setting times are given in the table.

⑧ Season (optional). See example recipes on the pages indicated.

⑨ Cut, drain, and press evenly (for firm-textured curds only). Press both dairy and soy curds while they are still warm (65–75 °C / 149–167 °F) to ensure proper bonding and a good final texture.

Best Bets for Protein Curds

Recipe	Liquid	(scaling)	Texture	Coagulant*	(scaling)	Heat (°C)	(°F)	(min)	Set (min)	Note	pH	See page
basic milk curd	raw milk or unhomogenized, pasteurized milk	100%	tender, brittle	rennet	0.35%	38	100	1	7	set in serving container; for firmer curds, cut curds, and heat at 47 °C / 116 °F for ½–1 h, and then drain, and cut again	8.2	247
ricotta	whole milk / heavy cream	100% / 10%	tender, brittle	lactic acid	0.3%	85	185	1	35	for salted and aged ricotta, fold in 0.7% salt, press refrigerated for 1–3 d, drain, and hang for 1–3 wk	5.4	248
fresh cottage cheese	whole milk	100%	tender, brittle	rennet	1%	38 / 38	100 / 100	1 / 1 h	7	whisk to break apart curd, hold at 38 °C / 100 °F for 1 h, and drain whey; fold in cream to taste	8.2	
paneer	whole milk / cultured yogurt	100% / 1%	firm, elastic	lactic acid	0.35%	82	180	5	20	press while warm, and refrigerate for 24 h	5.8	
tofu	soy milk see page 227	100%	silken	glucono delta-lactone	0.2%	80	176	1	15	milk density affects tofu texture; let silken tofu set in serving container, and then steam undisturbed at 80 °C / 176 °F	6.3	246
			medium firm	nigari granules	0.35%	85	185	1	30		n/a	
			firm	calcium sulfate	0.4%	80	176	3	20		n/a	248
farmer's cheese	whole milk / heavy cream	100% / 5%	firm, brittle	rennet / buttermilk	0.4% / 0.4%	23 / 36	73 / 97	1 / 1¼ h	n/a	heat milk for 1 min at 23 °C / 73 °F, and then add other ingredients, and hold for 1¼ h at 36 °C / 97 °F; press while warm, and refrigerate for 12–24 h	8.1	
posset	heavy cream (stabilizer-free)	100%	tender, smooth	citric acid	0.7%	88	190	1	4 h	add 15%–25% sugar to make a posset dessert	6.7	

from page 4·104   *(BioRen rennet tablets were used for all of our recipes; other brands may alter the formulations slightly)

GELS

COCOA NIB CURD INSPIRED BY MICHEL TROISGROS

Yields 1 kg (10 portions)

INGREDIENT	QUANTITY	SCALING	PROCEDURE
Whole milk, unhomogenized	1 kg	100%	① Vacuum seal together, and refrigerate for 12 h to infuse.
Cocoa nibs	50 g	5%	② Remove from bag, and strain.
			③ Heat milk to 38 °C / 100 °F.
Rennet tablet (BioRen brand)	3.5 g	0.35%	④ Dissolve rennet tablet in water.
Water	10 g	1%	⑤ Stir in warm milk.
			⑥ Stir for 10 s.
			⑦ Leave mixture in pot, or pour quickly into small bowls to depth of 2.5 cm / 1 in.
			⑧ Let stand at room temperature until set, about 7 min.
Cocoa nibs, toasted	to taste		⑨ Garnish as desired, and season evenly.
Fleur de sel	to taste		
Grapefruit zest, finely grated	to taste		
Maple syrup	to taste		
Olive oil	to taste		
Shiso leaves, fine julienne	to taste		

from page 4·105

You can use glucono delta-lactone in place of the rennet and still achieve the same texture. Dissolve the GDL in cold milk, pour the mixture into molds or bowls, and then steam at 80 °C / 176 °F for 20 min.

GOAT CHEESE DUMPLINGS ADAPTED FROM H. ALEXANDER TALBOT AND AKI KAMOZAWA

Yields 550 g

INGREDIENT	QUANTITY	SCALING	PROCEDURE
Goat cheese, fresh	300 g	100%	① Blend completely.
Ricotta, fresh	200 g	67%	② Transfer mixture to pastry bag.
Egg yolk	36 g	12%	③ Pipe into silicone sphere molds measuring 2.5 cm / 1 in. in diameter (see page 4·135).
Activa YG	5.4 g	1.8% (1%)*	④ Tap molding sheet on counter to eliminate bubbles.
			⑤ Refrigerate, covered, for 12 h to set.
Salt	3.5 g	1.2%	⑥ To serve, warm spheres gently in simmering water. When hot, serve with desired sauce or glaze.
Cayenne pepper	0.25 g	0.08%	

from page 4·105   *(% of total weight of first three ingredients)

SILKEN TOFU

Yields 585 g

INGREDIENT	QUANTITY	SCALING	PROCEDURE
Soy milk see page 227	400 g	100%	① Check density of soy milk, and dilute or reduce as needed to reach 12 °Brix.
Glucono delta-lactone (GDL)	0.8 g	0.2%	② Dissolve GDL in small amount of soy milk, and then whisk solution into remaining milk for 10 s to distribute evenly.
			③ Pour into small bowls or mold to depth of 2.5 cm / 1 in.
			④ Steam in 80 °C / 176 °F combi oven or water-vapor oven until set, 30–40 min.
			⑤ Transfer to molds, and cool at room temperature until slightly firmed, about 15 min, and then refrigerate.
Tomato water see page 40	100 g	25%	⑥ Combine to make dressing.
White soy sauce	10 g	2.5%	⑦ Check seasoning; add salt if necessary.
Rice vinegar	8 g	2%	⑧ Set aside.
Salmon roe	60 g	15%	⑨ Garnish tofu.
Basil, leaves	8 g	2%	
Extra-virgin olive oil	as needed		⑩ Season, and pour dressing at table.
Black pepper, coarsely ground	to taste		

from page 4·113

FRESH CHEESE CURDS

Yields 800 g

INGREDIENT	QUANTITY	SCALING	PROCEDURE
Whole milk	4 kg	100%	① Verify that pH of milk is 8–9.
			② Heat to 30 °C / 86 °F, and hold at that temperature in warm bath.
Mesophilic starter (Mesophile Type II)	1 g	n/a*	③ Sprinkle over surface of warm milk, and let sit 5 min.
			④ Stir in until evenly distributed.
Thermophilic starter (Thermophile Type II)	1 g	n/a*	⑤ Sprinkle over surface of warm milk, and let sit 5 min.
			⑥ Stir in until evenly distributed.
Water	40 g	1%	⑦ Dissolve rennet in water.
Rennet tablet (BioRen brand)	0.5 g	0.01%	⑧ Stir mixture into warm milk, and wait for milk to set into one large curd, 15–30 min.
			⑨ Remove from heat, and cut into 2 cm / ¾ in cubes.
			⑩ Heat cut curds in 40 °C / 104 °F bath, removing whey from surface every 10–20 min until texture resembles elastic egg white, 1–1½ h.
			⑪ Check that pH is 5–5.2. If it is not, hold curd at 40 °C / 104 °F until pH reaches target range.
			⑫ Drain curd, and cut to desired size.
			⑬ Refrigerate for 2 h.
			⑭ Serve or use within 24 h; cultures cause curd to start to sour after 1 d.

from page 4·106

*(these are live cultures; follow directions on manufacturer's packaging when scaling quantities)

To make squeaky curds, follow the recipe above, but in step 10 heat the curds to 47 °C / 117 °F, and hold there for 1 h. Drain, cut, and season. Serve, or cool quickly and store, refrigerated, for up to 2 d.

To make curds without rennet or cultures, heat them in a pressure canner or autoclave to at least 128 °C / 262 °F for 30–40 min. The curds will turn light brown and develop a flavor reminiscent of crème caramel. Add 0.3% of sodium hexametaphosphate to yield a more cohesive, firm puck.

To make feta, use the recipe above with at least 70% sheep's milk. At step 12, press curds lightly into a basket to drain, and rest for 24 h at about 20 °C / 68 °F. The pH should drop to 4.7–4.8. Soak, refrigerated, in a brine containing 3% salt and 0.07% calcium chloride for 1 wk. For drier curds, cure briefly with dry salt at room temperature, and rinse.

To make fresh mozzarella, follow the recipe above through step 11, and then drain curds, and cut into 1.25 cm / ½ in cubes. Heat reserved whey to 85 °C / 185 °F, and ladle over cubes to just cover. Let rest 4 min until softened, and then drain. Repeat process three times, covering curds with hot whey until they begin to melt together. Mold curds by hand into teardrop shapes, or pour into a mold. The mozzarella becomes stretchier and firmer with handling. Hold formed balls in a bowl of cold water. Season, and serve warm or soak in a brine containing 4% salt and 0.07% calcium chloride for 12–24 h.

MODERNIST BURRATA

Yields 700 g

INGREDIENT	QUANTITY	SCALING	PROCEDURE
For the filling:			
Fresh cheese curds see above	300 g	100%	① Puree 100 g curds, and shred remaining 200 g.
Heavy cream	300 g	100%	② Mix cream and salt into curds to make cream-curd filling.
Salt	6 g	2%	③ Refrigerate.
For the skin:			
Whole milk	300 g	100%	④ Mix milk, cream, salt, and gelatin.
Heavy cream	100 g	33%	⑤ Bring to 65 °C / 149 °F to dissolve gelatin.
Salt	4 g	1.3%	⑥ Cool to 50 °C / 122 °F.
Activa YG	6 g	2%	⑦ Add Activa.
160 Bloom gelatin	8 g	2.7%	⑧ Cast onto level, nonstick surface.
			⑨ Rest at room temperature for 1 h, and then refrigerate overnight.
			⑩ Cut to desired size, and lay over plated cream-curd filling.
Extra-virgin olive oil	to taste		⑪ Garnish and season.
Salt	to taste		
Seasonal herbs, leaves	to taste		

from page 4·109

GOAT MILK RICOTTA

Yields 850 g

INGREDIENT	QUANTITY	SCALING	PROCEDURE
For ricotta:			
Lactic acid	4 g	0.2%	① Dissolve acid into water, and stir acid solution into cold milk.
Water	25 g	1.4%	② Heat milk to 85 °C / 185 °F, stirring gently. As soon as milk starts coagulating, stop stirring.
Goat milk	1.8 kg	100%	③ Continue to heat as needed until milk reaches 85 °C / 185 °F.
			④ Remove from heat, and allow to curdle at room temperature for 30 min.
			⑤ Strain curds through cheesecloth, and then drain curds, refrigerated, for 3 h for wet ricotta or for up to 12 h for drier cheese. Discard liquid.
Heavy cream	250 g	14%	⑥ Fold into drained curds. Refrigerate if not serving immediately.
For frozen honey powder (optional):			
Water	200 g	11%	⑦ Whisk together.
Buckwheat honey	80 g	4.4%	⑧ Pour into Pacojet beaker.
			⑨ Freeze to –20 °C / –4 °F or below.
			⑩ To serve, Pacotize once to make fine powder.
			⑪ Spoon around ricotta.
Thyme (several varieties such as lemon, English, caraway, silver)	to taste		⑫ Garnish as desired.
Extra-virgin olive oil	to taste		
Black pepper, coarsely ground	to taste		

from page 4·108

For tender, coarse ricotta, stop stirring as soon as coagulation begins, regardless of the temperature of the milk. For ricotta with a finer, more traditional grain, keep stirring until the target temperature is reached.

FIRM TOFU

Yields 250 g

These tofu recipes use fresh, homemade soy milk (see page 227). Store-bought soy milk often will not work with these recipes because it contains various additives.

A quick alternative for making instant firm tofu is to hydrate 0.2% low-acyl gellan and 0.15% high-acyl gellan in soy milk at 85 °C / 185 °F. The mixture will set as it cools.

The amount of calcium sulfate or other coagulant required depends on the amount of protein available in the mixture. Soy beans vary in their protein content, so always test a small amount of soy milk before making each batch. When the proper amount of coagulant is used, the whey becomes transparent. A yellow hue to the whey and a coarse curd texture signal overcoagulation; a cloudy whey is a sign of undercoagulation.

INGREDIENT	QUANTITY	SCALING	PROCEDURE
Calcium sulfate	2 g	0.4%	① Dissolve calcium sulfate in cold water.
Water	20 g	4%	② Set aside.
Soy milk (12 °Brix) see page 227	500 g	100%	③ Check solid content of soy milk, and dilute or reduce as needed to reach 12–14 °Brix.
Salt	3 g	0.6%	④ Add salt, and bring to 80 °C / 176 °F while stirring constantly.
			⑤ Add calcium sulfate water to hot milk, and remove from heat.
			⑥ Coagulate at room temperature for 3–4 min.
			⑦ Line mold for tofu with cheesecloth.
			⑧ Ladle coagulated soy milk into mold.
			⑨ Seal mold quickly while curds are warm (68–70 °C / 154–156 °F), and put heavy weight on lid.
			⑩ Press at room temperature for 25 min, and then remove from mold, and refrigerate until firm.
Scallions, thinly sliced	50 g	10%	⑪ Cut to desired dimensions, and garnish.
Daikon radishes, finely grated	40 g	8%	
Fresh ginger, fine julienne	40 g	8%	
Bonito flakes (katsobushi)	20 g	4%	
White soy sauce	50 g	10%	⑫ Combine to make sauce.
Dark soy sauce	30 g	6%	⑬ Garnish tofu with sauce as desired.
Mirin	15 g	3%	
Rice vinegar	7 g	1.4%	

from page 4·112

MOZZARELLA BALLOONS INSPIRED BY GRANT ACHATZ

Yields 700 g

INGREDIENT	QUANTITY	SCALING	PROCEDURE
Fresh cheese curds see page 247	800 g	100%	① Cut into 2 cm / ¾ in cubes. ② Reserve 150 g of curds for cream filling. ③ Reserve 650 g of curds in large bowl to make balloon skins.
Whole milk	180 g	22.5%	④ Blend thoroughly to form cream filling.
Fresh cheese curds, from above	150 g	18.8%	⑤ Pour into 1 l siphon.
Heavy cream	30 g	3.75%	⑥ Charge with one cartridge of nitrous oxide.
Salt	2.75 g	0.34%	⑦ Refrigerate.
Xanthan gum (Keltrol T, CP kelco brand)	0.1 g	0.01%	
Water	5 kg	625%	⑧ Heat water to 75 °C / 167 °F.
Fresh cheese curds, from above	650 g	81%	⑨ Ladle water into bowl to cover curds. ⑩ Let curds sit undisturbed for 3 min. ⑪ Pour out first covering of water. ⑫ Ladle in second covering of water. ⑬ Let curds sit undisturbed again for 3 min. ⑭ Pour out second covering of water. ⑮ Ladle in third covering of water. ⑯ Touch curds. If they begin to stretch and shine, they are ready. If not, let sit longer, and cover with fresh hot water every 3–5 min. ⑰ Pick up lime-size ball of curd. Knead surface to develop smooth and shiny skin. Reserve remaining curds in warm water. ⑱ Shake siphon vigorously. ⑲ Place ball of curd over tip of inverted siphon. ⑳ Fill curd ball quickly with cream filling; try to keep out excess air. Complete filling process within 20 s. ㉑ Once desired size is reached, pinch each balloon closed. ㉒ Repeat steps 17–21 to fill remaining curds. ㉓ If curds will not be served immediately, reserve in cold water bath.
Tomato whey broth or tomato water see page 212 or page 40	200 g	25%	㉔ To serve, place balloons in bowls, and pour seasoned broth or tomato water around balloons. ㉕ Garnish with basil and, optionally, with basil oil (see page 27).
Cinnamon basil, leaves	to taste		

from page 4·110

GREEN PEA YUBA INSPIRED BY TAKASHI SUGIMOTO

Yields 150 g

INGREDIENT	QUANTITY	SCALING	PROCEDURE
Soy milk see page 227	950 g	100%	① Reserve 50 g of soy milk for later use.
Green pea puree see page 55	400 g (from 500 g of frozen peas)	42%	② Blend pea puree with 900 g soy milk until smooth. ③ Strain pea milk through fine sieve, and transfer to pot. ④ Bring to 80 °C / 176 °F over medium heat. ⑤ Lower heat. Yuba will form on surface of pea milk mixture in about 3 min. ⑥ Line baking sheet with plastic wrap, and brush sheet with reserved soy milk. ⑦ Lift yuba carefully from pot, and transfer to milk-brushed sheet. Cover with plastic wrap. ⑧ Refrigerate for 1 h until firm.
Chervil, leaves	as needed		⑨ Arrange several yuba sheets on each plate.
Flaky sea salt	to taste		⑩ Garnish.
Ginger oil	to taste		
Fresh horseradish, finely grated	to taste		

from page 4·115

MILK SKIN WITH GRILLED SALSIFY AND TRUFFLE PUREE
ADAPTED FROM RENÉ REDZEPI

Yields 600 g (four portions)

INGREDIENT	QUANTITY	SCALING	PROCEDURE
Raw or nonhomogenized whole milk	1 kg	100%	① Blend.
			② Pour into pot whose diameter is desired size of milk skin.
Skim milk powder	30 g	3%	③ Cut parchment paper circles to match diameter of pot. Parchment paper will help transfer and store milk skins.
			④ Bring milk to boil, and hold at 80 °C / 176 °F until skin forms, about 7 min.
			⑤ Discard first skin, which is too tender to work with.
			⑥ Place parchment circle on top of second skin, and delicately peel skin off.
			⑦ Rest skin on parchment circle at room temperature.
			⑧ Repeat process to make four skin sheets. (Although 1 kg of milk will make many more than four sheets, it can be difficult to work with very small quantities of milk.)
Salsify roots, peeled and cut into tubes 10 cm / 4 in long	400 g	40%	⑨ Sauté salsify in thin film of oil in nonstick pan, while basting constantly with oil, until tubes are golden on all sides, about 4 min.
Neutral oil	as needed		⑩ Drain, and pat dry.
Salt	to taste		⑪ Season salsify.
			⑫ Cool to room temperature.
			⑬ Divide salsify into four portions, and place each one on center of plate.
			⑭ Remove each milk skin from parchment, and cover salsify portion.
Black trumpet mushroom puree see page 2·424	50 g	5%	⑮ Blend together mushroom and truffle purees until smooth.
			⑯ Garnish plates evenly.
Black truffle concentrate see page 57	10 g	1%	
Extra-virgin canola (rapeseed) oil	30 g	3%	
Wild watercress leaves (or regular watercress)	20 g	2%	

from page 4·114

TRANSGLUTAMINASE GELS

① Select a recipe. The table below gives some examples.

② Blend Activa into the liquid or puree. Quantities in the table are given as a proportion of the main fluid. For example, to make a flourless gnocchi, use 1.3 g of Activa GS, 3 g of 160 Bloom gelatin, and 6.6 g of heavy cream for every 100 g of potato puree.

③ Refrigerate 12–24 hours to set. If the base is heat-tolerant, you can reduce the setting time to 1 h in the refrigerator by first warming the mixture to 40–45 °C / 104–113 °F for 10 min, or 55 °C / 130 °F for 5 min. Warming it above 60 °C / 140 °F destroys the enzyme activity.

Best Bets for Gelling with Transglutaminase (Activa)

Application	Type	Components	Typical concentration (scaling)*	Example recipe	Base
dairy gels	Activa YG	transglutaminase, lactose, yeast extract, maltodextrin	0.05%–3.0%	yogurt	low-fat yogurt
				mozzarella noodle adapted from Aki Kamozawa and H. Alexander Talbot	mozzarella
					ricotta
				heat-stable milk skin	milk
					160 Bloom gelatin
				ricotta gnocchi	ricotta
				sour cream spaetzle	sour cream
					ricotta
					water
					whey protein isolate
					160 Bloom gelatin
egg gels and soy gels	Activa RM	transglutaminase, sodium caseinate, maltodextrin	0.1%–2.0%	chawanmushi	whole egg
					pureed scallop
					flavorful liquids
gelatin gels	Activa GS	transglutaminase, gelatin, trisodium phosphate, maltodextrin	0.05%–1.8%	flourless potato gnocchi	potato puree
					heavy cream
					160 Bloom gelatin

from page 4·116

Activa is made by Ajinomoto, the same Japanese company that commercialized monosodium glutamate in 1909 (see page 1·213).

Avoid inhaling Activa or any other enzyme or powder.

For more on the origin of transglutaminase and how this enzyme works, see page 3·250.

SOUR CREAM SPAETZLE   Yields 150 g

INGREDIENT	QUANTITY	SCALING
160 Bloom gelatin	6 g	3.3%
Water	40 g	22.2%
Sour cream	180 g	100%
Ricotta	180 g	100%
Whey protein isolate	65 g	36%
Activa YG	4 g	2.2% (0.9%)*
Salt	3 g	2%
Clarified butter	50 g	27.8%
Salt	to taste	

from page 4·117

*(% of total weight of all ingredients except butter and salt)

① Disperse gelatin into cold water, and heat to dissolve. Allow to cool.
② Blend sour cream with gelatin mixture, and rest at room temperature for 5 min.
③ Set spaetzle maker or perforated pan over an ice-water bath, and grate spaetzle base to form individual dumplings.
④ Transfer in one layer to sheet lined with plastic wrap.
⑤ Refrigerate for at least 4 h to set protein.
⑥ Drain spaetzle, and fry in clarified butter until golden, about 3 min.
⑦ Season to taste.

(scaling)	Activa (scaling)	Prep	Set (°C)	(°F)	(h)	See page
100%	0.15%	stir in	55	131	5 min	
100% 34%	1.3% (1%)*	puree until smooth with Pacojet or food processor; cast onto acetate 1 mm / 1/32 in thick	refrigerated		18	
100% 1%	1%	cast onto acetate 1 mm / 1/32 in thick	45	113	10 min	247
100%	0.7%	shape logs for cutting gnocchi before setting	refrigerated		12	
100% 100% 40% 36%	2.2% (0.9%)*	see above	refrigerated		12	below
100% 65% 368%	8% (1.5%)*	cast onto acetate 1 mm / 1/32 in thick	45	113	10 min	242
100% 6.6% 3%	1.3% (1%)*	stir into cold puree; shape logs for cutting gnocchi before setting	refrigerated		12	254

*(% of total weight of base ingredients)

SALMON CUSTARD

Yields 120 g

INGREDIENT	QUANTITY	SCALING	PROCEDURE
Salmon belly, skinless	700 g	700%	① Combine in food processor, and blend to smooth paste.
White fish stock see page 6	450 g	450%	② Vacuum seal.
Salt	7 g	7%	③ Cook in 40 °C / 104 °F bath for 1 h.
Nutrifos 088 (ICL Performance Products brand)	2 g	2%	④ Centrifuge at 12,000g for 1 h. ⑤ Separate salmon liquid and rendered salmon fat, and reserve. Discard solids.
Salmon liquid, from above	100 g	100%	⑥ Disperse PGA into salmon liquid.
Propylene glycol alginate (Protanal Ester BV 4830, FMC BioPolymer brand)	0.5 g	0.5% (0.42%)*	⑦ Heat gently to 50 °C / 122 °F to hydrate fully.
Rendered salmon fat, from above	20 g	20%	⑧ Slowly drizzle into warm salmon liquid while homogenizing.
Activa RM	0.9 g	0.9% (0.75%)*	⑨ Add to mixture, and blend until smooth. ⑩ Transfer to molds, and chill.
Xanthan gum (Keltrol T, CP Kelco brand)	0.1 g	0.1%	⑪ To serve, cook custard in 53 °C / 127 °F bath or steam oven to core temperature of 52 °C / 126 °F, about 25 min.

from page 4·119

*(% of total weight of salmon liquid and fat)

EDAMAME SHEETS, KING CRAB, CINNAMON DASHI   ADAPTED FROM WYLIE DUFRESNE   Yields 300 g

INGREDIENT	QUANTITY	SCALING	PROCEDURE
Fresh edamame (or defrosted frozen edamame)	250 g	125%	① Blend to fine puree.
			② Pass through fine sieve.
Water	100 g	50%	③ Reserve 200 g for later use.
160 Bloom gelatin	13.75 g	6.8%	④ Disperse gelatin in cold water.
Water	50 g	25%	⑤ Heat until melted.
Edamame puree, from above	200 g	100%	⑥ Combine with gelatin mixture.
Water	25 g	12.5%	⑦ Blend until completely smooth.
Activa RM	3.5 g	1.75% (1.2%)*	⑧ Cast onto silicone mat, and spread into even layer 0.5 mm / 1/64 in thick.
Activa GS	2 g	1% (0.69%)*	⑨ Refrigerate until set, at least 6 h, and cut into squares 7.5 cm / 3 in wide.
Hon dashi see page 15	200 g	100%	⑩ Combine and warm. Add more cinnamon extract to taste. If the broth coagulates, strain through fine sieve.
Cinnamon extract see page 27	2.5 g	1.25%	
Salt	to taste		⑪ Season cinnamon dashi.
			⑫ Add edamame sheets to stack, warming them.
			⑬ Set aside.
King crab tails or claws	160 g (about four pieces)	80%	⑭ Sear until just cooked through, about 1 min per side.
Clarified butter	50 g	25%	
Salt	to taste		⑮ Season crab pieces.
Seasonal herbs	as needed		⑯ Place one piece on each plate.
			⑰ Drape warmed edamame sheet over each piece.
			⑱ Pour cinnamon dashi over edamame, and sprinkle with seasonal herbs. Serve immediately.

from page 4·118   *(% of total weight of gelatin mixture, edamame puree, and water)

FLOURLESS GNOCCHI   Yields 650 g

INGREDIENT	QUANTITY	SCALING	PROCEDURE
Russet potatoes, washed	900 g (about four large)	150%	① Cook sous vide in 92 °C / 198 °F bath for 2 h.
			② Cut potatoes in half, and scoop out hot potato flesh.
			③ Press, while still hot, through ricer or food mill.
			④ Cool.
			⑤ Reserve 600 g of puree.
160 Bloom gelatin	19.2 g	3.2% (3%)*	⑥ Bloom gelatin in cold cream.
			⑦ Warm cream mixture until gelatin is dissolved.
Heavy cream	40 g	6.6%	⑧ Cool.
Activa GS	6.4 g	1.07% (1%)*	⑨ Whisk into cream.
Potato puree, from above	600 g	100%	⑩ Fold cream into potato mixture to form dough.
Salt	to taste		⑪ Season dough.
			⑫ Gently roll into log 2 cm / ¾ in. in diameter.
			⑬ Cut into desired size gnocchi.
			⑭ Transfer to parchment paper-lined tray.
			⑮ Refrigerate until firm, about 12 h.
			⑯ Bring gnocchi to room temperature, about 20 min.
Unsalted butter, cut into cubes	120 g	20%	⑰ Cook butter in sauté pan until solids begin to brown, about 3 min.
			⑱ Add gnocchi, gently stirring until warmed through, about 2 min.
			⑲ Remove from heat.
Sage, thinly sliced	6 g	1%	⑳ Fold in.

from page 4·119   *(% of total weight of potatoes and cream)

STARCH GELS

DEEP-FRIED CUSTARD

Yields 450 g

INGREDIENT	QUANTITY	SCALING	PROCEDURE
All-purpose flour	32 g	12.8%	① Whisk together.
White chicken stock see page 6 or page 11	250 g	100%	② Bring to boil, and cook for 5 min.
Egg yolks, blended	25 g	10%	③ Whisk together into smooth paste.
Cornstarch	9 g	3.6%	④ Temper hot stock into egg mixture.
			⑤ Return to pan, and cook over low heat until mixture thickens, about 2 min.
Unsalted butter, cubed	10 g	4%	⑥ Stir butter into cooked custard until melted.
			⑦ Quickly cast hot mixture into silicone mold in 2.5 cm / 1 in thick layer.
			⑧ Refrigerate until set, about 3 h.
Potato starch	as needed		⑨ Cut custard into cubes or desired shapes, and dredge in potato starch; shake off excess.
Frying oil	as needed		⑩ Deep-fry cubes in 190 °C / 375 °F oil until golden, about 2 min.
Salt	to taste		⑪ Drain and season.
XO sauce see page 213	100 g	40%	⑫ Pour over fried cubes generously just before serving.

from page 4·120

The starch in the custard, and dusted on its exterior, allows us to deep-fry it without a batter. This recipe is essentially a deep-fried savory pastry cream. For a sweet version of the recipe, replace the chicken stock with whole milk, and add 26 g of sugar (8% of the overall weight).

BURMESE CHICKPEA TOFU LAKSA

Yields 1.4 kg

INGREDIENT	QUANTITY	SCALING	PROCEDURE
Water	1 kg	100%	① Blend until completely homogenized.
Chickpea flour	350 g	35%	② Line fine sieve with three layers of cheesecloth.
			③ Strain chickpea mixture through fine sieve into pot.
			④ Bring to boil.
			⑤ Remove from heat.
Salt	14 g	1.4%	⑥ Whisk into hot chickpea mixture.
Turmeric powder	0.5 g	0.05%	⑦ Divide mixture evenly among molds 5 cm / 2 in thick.
			⑧ Refrigerate for 4 h until firmly set.
			⑨ Cut into cubes.
Kumamoto or Olympia oysters	12 pieces		⑩ Shuck, reserving juices separately.
Laksa broth see page 17	200 g	20%	⑪ Warm broth.
			⑫ Add oyster juice to taste.
Oyster juice, from above	to taste		⑬ Add half of tofu cubes and oysters to broth, and warm through.
Frying oil	as needed		⑭ Deep-fry remaining cubes in 190 °C / 375 °F oil until golden, about 3 min.
Mint, leaves	as needed		⑮ Garnish.
Cucumber, peeled, seeded, and sliced	as needed		

from page 4·121

The particles in the chickpea mixture must be very fine to yield an elastic, homogenized gel instead of one with a grainy, brittle texture. Sieving with a fine sieve or through cheesecloth is crucial to achieve a good result.

The chickpea tofu is delicious when deep-fried and served with a sweet-and-sour glaze or a spicy paste.

This so-called tofu is really a starch gel that plays a big role in the traditional cuisine of Myanmar (formerly Burma).

CORN BREAD

Yields 1 kg

INGREDIENT	QUANTITY	SCALING	PROCEDURE
Corn kernels (fresh-cut)	560 g (from about six ears)	100%	① Sauté until browned, about 12 min.
Unsalted butter	150 g	27%	
Lard	100 g	18%	
Eggs, blended	100 g	18%	② Combine in blender with cooked corn, and puree until smooth.
Heavy cream	100 g	18%	
Whole milk	50 g	10%	
Flour	150 g	27%	③ Mix together.
Isomalt	140 g	25%	④ Fold into corn cream mixture.
Cornmeal	100 g	18%	⑤ Transfer to floured and grease loaf mold, filling half full.
Sugar	50 g	10%	
Baking powder	3.2 g	0.5%	⑥ Bake in 175 °C / 350 °F oven for 10 min, and then reduce oven temperature to 130 °C / 265 °F and bake to core temperature of 88 °C / 190 °F, about 20 min.
Baking soda	1.75 g	0.3%	
Thyme leaves, chopped	to taste		
			⑦ Rest at room temperature for 5 min.
			⑧ Unmold, and slice to desired thickness.
			⑨ Serve warm or toasted with bacon jam (see page 304).

from page 5·76

There are many styles of corn bread across the United States. This version is nontraditional but has an amazing flavor and texture. Sieving out the kernel skins is a nice, but optional, refinement.

CORN CUSTARD INSPIRED BY DAVID KINCH

Yields 340 g (four portions)

INGREDIENT	QUANTITY	SCALING	PROCEDURE
Frozen organic sweet yellow corn, thawed	500 g	500%	① Juice corn, preferably with Champion-style juicer (see page 2·332), reserving 100 g juice.
Corn juice, from above	100 g	100%	② Blend starch and salt into cold juice to distribute evenly.
Cornstarch	4 g	4%	
Salt	1.7 g	1.7%	
			③ Pour 25 g of juice in layer 1 cm / ⅜ in deep into each of four molds.
			④ Steam at 88 °C / 190 °F until custards are just set, about 30 min.
			⑤ Cool completely.
Fava beans, peeled	50 g	50%	⑥ Vacuum seal in one even layer.
Olive oil	8 g	8%	⑦ Cook sous vide in 75 °C / 167 °F bath for 25 min.
			⑧ Remove from bag.
Fresh sweet peas, shucked	50 g	50%	⑨ Vacuum seal in one even layer.
Olive oil	8 g	8%	⑩ Cook sous vide in 70 °C / 158 °F bath for 18 min.
			⑪ Remove from bag.
Sous vide vegetable jus see page 36	70 g	70%	⑫ Combine while bringing to simmer.
Tomato water see page 40	30 g	30%	
Unsalted butter, cubed (use olive oil if serving cold)	35 g	35%	⑬ Blend into simmering liquid until fully emulsified.
			⑭ Remove from heat.
Anise hyssop, fine julienne	5 g	5%	⑮ Whisk into warm butter sauce.
			⑯ Steep for 3 min, and strain.
Lime juice	to taste		⑰ Season sauce.
Salt	to taste		⑱ Fold in warm beans and peas.
			⑲ Reheat custards, and garnish with sauce.
			⑳ Finish with hyssop blossoms, if available.

from page 4·122

For a tender starch custard, a 9% ratio of cornstarch to liquid seems to be ideal. The percentage of starch in fresh corn varies dramatically—this recipe assumes that the corn juice itself contains 5% starch. You can test the recipe using a small amount of your corn juice, and adjust the quantity of cornstarch to achieve the texture you prefer.

In this interpretation of David Kinch's Corn Pudding, we have presented the typical flavors of a late summer succotash. The accompaniments can be varied seasonally, but the custard can be made year-round with good quality frozen corn.

PEANUT "TOFU" INSPIRED BY YOSHIHIRO MURATA

Yields 550 g

INGREDIENT	QUANTITY	SCALING	PROCEDURE
Water	400 g	100%	① Combine in pot.
Coconut milk	50 g	12.5%	② Stir until palm sugar is completely dissolved.
Fish sauce	25 g	6.25%	
Palm sugar	10 g	2.5%	
Peanut butter (smooth)	50 g	12.5%	③ Blend into mixture.
Kuzu starch	42.5 g	10.6% (8%)*	④ Add to mixture, blending until starch is completely dispersed.
			⑤ Pass through fine sieve.
			⑥ Simmer for 20 min until thick.
Salt	to taste		⑦ Season mixture.
			⑧ Pour quickly into silicone molds.
			⑨ Refrigerate until set, about 12 h.
Tom yum broth *see page 18*	200 g	50%	⑩ Bring broth to simmer.
Scallions, shredded	as needed		⑪ Transfer tofu to bowl, and garnish with scallions and warm broth.

from page 4·122

*(% of total weight of first five ingredients)

This recipe makes a typical Asian peanut sauce, which is then set into a gel by using Kuzu starch. The result isn't true tofu, but it has a tofu-like texture.

IDIAZÁBAL GNOCCHI ADAPTED FROM ANDONI LUIS ADURIZ

Yields 500 g

INGREDIENT	QUANTITY	SCALING	PROCEDURE
Cheese water (made with Idiazábal) see page 20	130 g	100%	① Blend together.
			② Vacuum seal.
Kuzu root starch	32 g	25% (18%)*	③ Cook in 95 °C / 203 °F bath for 1½ h to create starch base.
Idiazábal cheese (or other semifirm cheese such as Pecorino), grated	50 g	38%	④ Blend into starch base over medium heat until fully incorporated.
			⑤ Transfer dough to piping bag.
Salt	2.5 g	2%	⑥ Extrude directly into ice water; cut equally sized dumplings with scissors as dough is extruded.
Ham broth see page 16	260 g	200%	⑦ Heat broth.
			⑧ Stir in gnocchi to warm through.
Extra-virgin olive oil	to taste		⑨ Garnish.
Perilla (red and green), leaves	as needed		
Lemon balm, leaves	as needed		
Micro scallion greens	as needed		

from page 4·123

*(% of total weight of water and cheese)

EVERYTHING BAGEL BROTH

Yields 200 g

INGREDIENT	QUANTITY	SCALING	PROCEDURE	
Tomato juice	200 g	100%	① Combine juices.	
Cucumber juice	50 g	25%		
Red onion juice	30 g	15%		
Bagels, toasted until golden and finely ground	50 g	25%	② Combine with juice mixture.	This broth and the squid ink on the previous page are both examples of fluid gels (see page 285).
			③ Vacuum seal.	
Toasted sesame seeds	7 g	3.5%	④ Infuse in refrigerator for 24 h.	
Dried onion flakes	5 g	2.5%	⑤ Centrifuge at 27,500g for 1 h.	
Black poppy seeds	3 g	1.5%	⑥ Measure 200 g of clear broth.	
Sodium hexametaphosphate	0.6 g	0.3%	⑦ Dry blend together.	
Low-acyl gellan (Kelcogel F, CP Kelco brand)	0.2 g	0.1%		
Infused bagel broth, from above	200 g	100%	⑧ Bring broth to room temperature.	
			⑨ Add gellan mixture to broth, and shear until gellan is fully dispersed.	
Red wine vinegar	to taste		⑩ Season broth, and refrigerate.	
Salt	to taste			

from page 4·130

DILL SPHERES

Yields 300 g

INGREDIENT	QUANTITY	SCALING	PROCEDURE
Low-acyl gellan (Kelcogel F, CP Kelco brand)	1.6 g	0.64% (0.48%)*	① Dry blend.
Sodium hexametaphosphate	0.4 g	0.16% (0.12%)*	
Dill sprigs	130 g	52%	② Blanch dill sprigs in boiling water until tender, about 2 min.
Deionized water	150 g	60%	③ Cool quickly, drain, and puree until smooth with deionized water.
			④ Pass mixture through fine sieve, and measure 85 g for recipe.
Water	250 g	100%	⑤ Disperse gellan blend in dill puree. Bring to simmer while shearing, and cool completely.
Dill puree, from above	85 g	34%	⑥ Transfer mixture to squeeze bottle with 0.4 mm / 1/8 in tip.
			⑦ Pipe small droplets into liquid nitrogen to freeze.
			⑧ Drain frozen spheres, and reserve.
Celery juice, clarified	500 g	200%	⑨ Whisk together until fully dissolved to make setting bath.
Calcium gluconate	30 g	12% (6%)**	⑩ Drop frozen spheres into setting bath, and allow skin to form for 2 min.
			⑪ Drain set spheres, and transfer to fresh water bath to rinse.
Citric acid	0.4 g	0.16% (0.08%)**	⑫ Drain once more, and hold in fresh water bath until ready to serve.

from page 4·130

*(% of total weight of water and dill puree)
**(% of total weight of celery juice)

SQUID INK FLUID GEL

Yields 140 g (400 g with other components)

INGREDIENT	QUANTITY	SCALING	PROCEDURE
Water	100 g	100%	① Blend until smooth.
Capers, brined	15 g	15%	
Squid ink	10 g	10%	
Champagne vinegar	to taste		② Season squid ink mixture.
Salt	to taste		
Low-acyl gellan (Kelcogel F, CP Kelco brand)	0.5 g	0.5% (0.4%)*	③ Dry blend, and disperse in squid ink mixture.
			④ Boil mixture for 1 min to fully hydrate.
Sodium hexametaphosphate	0.125 g	0.125% (0.1%)*	⑤ Pour into desired container, and refrigerate until set, about 5 min.
			⑥ Puree squid ink gel to fluid gel, transfer to squeeze bottle, and reserve.
Olive oil	10 g	10%	⑦ Whisk to make black pepper oil.
Black pepper essential oil	1 g	1%	
Brominated vegetable oil (weighting agent)	0.1 g	0.1% (1%)**	
Bagel broth see previous page	200 g	200%	⑧ Divide cold broth evenly among four bowls.
Dill spheres see above	100 g	100%	⑨ Spoon individually into each bowl.
Tobiko roe, washed in aquavit	50 g	50%	
Chives, minced	as desired		
Dill tips	as desired		
Squid ink fluid gel, from above	40 g	40%	⑩ Stir contents gently to evenly distribute roe, spheres, and herbs. Drip some squid ink fluid gel and black pepper oil into consommé, and stir once, gently, to create suspended black streaks and oil droplets.

from page 4·131

*(% of total weight of first three ingredients)
**(% of total weight of olive oil)

COLD GELS

① Select a texture and firmness. Possibilities range from brittle to rubbery, and from very tender to very firm.

② Choose the gelling agents. The table below offers at least two options for each texture. Many of the formulas use a mixture of two or more gelling agents.

③ Measure the gelling agents. Quantities are given relative to the weight of the liquid, which is set to 100%. For example, use 8.5 g of 160 Bloom gelatin for every 1 kg of wine to make a tender, elastic wine gel.

④ Dry blend the gelling agents, and disperse them into the cold flavorful liquid.

⑤ Hydrate fully. Blend while heating to ensure the gelling agents are evenly distributed during hydration. The table lists appropriate hydration times and temperatures.

⑥ Cast the gel into a mold. For detailed instructions, see page 4·132.

Best Bets for Cold Gels

Texture	Firmness	Gelling agents	(scaling)*	Hydrate (min)	(°C)	(°F)	Cast or mold
elastic	very tender	160 Bloom gelatin	0.75%	5	60	140	cast directly into serving vessel
		kappa carrageenan	0.1%	3	85	185	
		iota carrageenan	0.1%				
		high-acyl gellan	0.20%	3	95	203	
		kappa carrageenan	0.05%				
	tender	160 Bloom gelatin	0.85%	25	60	140	pour directly into serving vessel and mold; cutting not recommended
		iota carrageenan	0.20%	3	85	185	
		kappa carrageenan	0.15%				
	firm	locust bean gum	0.15%	3	95	203	best molded; cut with care
		agar	0.10%				
		xanthan gum	0.20%				
		160 Bloom gelatin	1%	25	60	140	
		LM pectin	2%	3	100	212	
		calcium gluconate	1%				
		iota carrageenan	0.25%	3	85	185	
		kappa carrageenan	0.25%				
	very firm	160 Bloom gelatin	1.5%	25	60	140	best suited for cutting and shaping
		sucrose	65%	1	110	230	
		HM pectin	1.75%				
		citric or tartaric acid	1.5%				
brittle	firm	low-acyl gellan	0.25%	3	95	203	
		high-acyl gellan	0.15%				
		agar	0.35%	3	95	203	
		locust bean gum	0.4%	3	85	185	
		kappa carrageenan	0.2%				
	very firm	agar	0.5%	3	95	203	
		low-acyl gellan	0.35%	3	95	203	

from page 4·140   *(% of total weight of all liquids)

SALT GEL

Yields 450 g

INGREDIENT	QUANTITY	SCALING	PROCEDURE
Distilled water, cold	400 g	100%	① Disperse salt and agar in water.
Salt	40 g	10%	② Bring to boil, and hold for 2 min while stirring to hydrate.
Agar	12 g	3%	③ Cast in desired mold.
			④ Refrigerate until set, about 10 min. Grate over food as seasoning.

The salt gel can be grated and used to season any dish in which you want salt crystals that will not dissolve.

from page 5·9

Note	Example use	See page
keep cold; softens rapidly at room temperature	coating gelées, layered tender jellies	
highly stable when used with dairy liquids	set yogurt	
opaque; not suitable for consommé gels	eggless crème brûlée	
firmness of gel increases for 24 h	cauliflower panna cotta	263
works well with dairy liquids	eggless custard/flan	
texture very similar to that of gelatin but doesn't melt in the mouth as gelatin does	chili pearls	265
tenderize by tempering at room temperature	firm panna cotta	
firm texture develops when made with liquid of 18 °Brix	savory pâte de fruit	
highly stable when used with dairy liquids	cold terrines	
tenderize by tempering at room temperature	firm aspics, suspended solids	
firm texture develops when made with liquid of 75 °Brix	pâte de fruit	
highly stable	firm aspics, suspended solids	
works well with all liquids but tends to weep over time		
highly stable when used with dairy liquids	sunny-side up egg	268
works well with all liquids but tends to weep over time	Parmesan spaghetti	next
	gel noodles	

GELS

TWO-METER PARMESAN SPAGHETTO ADAPTED FROM FERRAN ADRIÀ

Yields 300 g (about 15 spaghetto strands)

INGREDIENT	QUANTITY	SCALING	PROCEDURE
Parmesan cheese, finely grated	450 g	150%	① Combine, and bring to boil.
Water	450 g	150%	② Remove from heat, and infuse for 1 min at room temperature.
			③ Strain through fine sieve lined with cheesecloth, and cool.
			④ Measure 300 g of Parmesan water.
Parmesan water, from above	300 g	100%	⑤ Dry blend agar and locust bean gum, and disperse into cold Parmesan water.
Agar (Texturas brand)	2.1 g	0.7%	⑥ Bring to boil, and hold for 2 min to fully hydrate. Skim any surface scum that appears.
Locust bean gum (POR/A2 Powder, TIC Gums brand)	0.45 g	0.15%	⑦ Fill Texturas-style syringe immediately with Parmesan water.
			⑧ Pipe quickly into coiled PVC tubes measuring 2 m / 6½ ft long and 0.5 cm / ¼ in. in diameter; hold opposite end of each tube shut with one hand to prevent Parmesan water from shooting out.
			⑨ Seal tubes.
			⑩ Submerge filled tubes in ice-water bath until set, about 2 min.
			⑪ Shoot air from soda siphon into one end of each tube to extrude noodles.
Black pepper, coarsely ground	to taste		⑫ Season.
Flaky sea salt	to taste		
Lemon zest, finely grated	to taste		
Warm Parmesan oil (or olive oil) see page 206	to taste		

Instead of topping pasta with a cheese sauce or grated cheese, this recipe makes a "pasta" out of the cheese itself.

from page 4·143

LONG ISLAND ICED TEA GEL SHOT

Yields 435 g

INGREDIENT	QUANTITY	SCALING	PROCEDURE
Water	50 g	42%	① Disperse gelatin into cold water.
160 Bloom gelatin	6.75 g	5.6% (*1.6%*)*	② Heat until fully dissolved.
			③ Remove mixture from heat, and let cool.
Cola	120 g	100%	④ Combine, and whisk in gelatin mixture.
Lemon juice	60 g	50%	⑤ Pour into serving containers.
Gin	40 g	33%	⑥ Refrigerate until fully set, about 5 h.
Rum	40 g	33%	
Tequila	40 g	33%	
Triple Sec	40 g	33%	
Vodka	40 g	33%	

from page 4·141

*(% of total weight of all liquids)

SPICED WALNUT VINEGAR GEL

Yields 200 g

INGREDIENT	QUANTITY	SCALING	PROCEDURE
White duck stock, cold see page 11	200 g	100%	① Disperse agar in stock.
Agar	6 g	3%	
Salt	6 g	3%	② Whisk into stock until dissolved.
Ascorbic acid	1 g	0.5%	
Sugar	1 g	0.5%	
Black peppercorns, toasted and cracked	3 g	1.5%	③ Add to stock.
			④ Boil for 3 min to hydrate agar.
Coriander seeds, toasted and crushed	2 g	1%	⑤ Strain through fine sieve directly into hemisphere nonstick mold.
Sichuan peppercorns, toasted and crushed	1.5 g	0.75%	⑥ Refrigerate until set. Grate over sous vide foie gras or other poultry as seasoning.

from page 5·111

CAULIFLOWER PANNA COTTA ADAPTED FROM THOMAS KELLER

Yields 850 g (about 16 panna cottas)

INGREDIENT	QUANTITY	SCALING	PROCEDURE
For the panna cotta:			
Water	500 g	200%	① Simmer over low heat for 1 h.
Cauliflower trimmings, thinly sliced	300 g	120%	② Strain through fine sieve.
			③ Cool stock at room temperature, and reserve 400 g for later use.
Cauliflower stock, from above	350 g	140%	④ Combine in pot.
Cauliflower florets, thinly sliced	250 g	100%	⑤ Simmer for 35 min or until florets are very tender.
Heavy cream	215 g	86%	⑥ Puree until smooth.
Unsalted butter	30 g	12%	⑦ Strain puree through fine sieve.
Salt	to taste		⑧ Season.
			⑨ Measure 400 g of puree, and reserve.
Cauliflower stock, from above	50 g	20%	⑩ Bloom gelatin in cooled stock.
160 Bloom gelatin	3.8 g	1.52% (*0.85%*)*	
Cauliflower puree, from above	400 g	160%	⑪ Stir stock into warm puree until gelatin has dissolved, 3–5 min.
			⑫ Spoon into 16 small serving bowls or cups.
			⑬ Refrigerate panna cotta for at least 4 h to set.
For the oyster juice gelée:			
Water	28 g	11.2%	⑭ Bloom gelatin in cold water in small, stainless steel bowl.
160 Bloom gelatin	0.2 g	0.08% (*0.28%*)**	⑮ Warm until dissolved.
Oyster juice (from shucked oysters)	42 g	17%	⑯ Combine with gelatin mixture.
Black peppercorns, finely ground	to taste		⑰ Season mixture.
			⑱ Refrigerate gelée for 30 min.
			⑲ Strain.
			⑳ Add about 6 g of oyster juice gelée to top of each panna cotta portion to coat.
			㉑ Refrigerate until completely set, about 4 h.
Sturgeon caviar	as needed		㉒ Garnish.
from page 4·142		*(*% of total weight of cauliflower stock and cauliflower puree used in panna cotta*)	
		**(*% of total weight of water and oyster juice used in oyster juice gelée*)	

KNOT FOIE ADAPTED FROM WYLIE DUFRESNE

Yields 300 g (four portions)

INGREDIENT	QUANTITY	SCALING	PROCEDURE
Foie gras torchon see page 104	225 g	100%	① Microwave or otherwise heat to 82 °C / 180 °F. Torchon fat will melt, and terrine will split.
Konjac gum (Ticagel Konjac HV-D, TIC Gums brand)	1.05 g	0.47%	② Dry blend.
			③ Blend with warm foie gras.
Agar (Telephone brand)	0.6 g	0.27%	
Xanthan gum	0.45 g	0.2%	
Water	75 g	33.3%	④ Heat water to 80 °C / 176 °F.
Egg yolk	10 g	4.4%	⑤ Blend in egg yolk.
			⑥ Blend in foie gras mixture until fully incorporated.
			⑦ Pour into nonstick mold in layer 1.5 cm / ⅝ in thick.
			⑧ Refrigerate foie gras until set, about 3 h.
Kimchi	250 g	111%	⑨ Puree until smooth.
Xanthan gum	0.4 g	0.18%	⑩ Transfer to squeeze bottle.
White raisins	200 g	88%	⑪ Combine.
Water	125 g	55.6%	⑫ Refrigerate for 3 h to steep.
Xanthan gum (Keltrol T, CP Kelco brand)	0.4 g	0.17%	⑬ Shear with raisins to form puree.
Salt	to taste		⑭ Season raisin puree.
			⑮ Transfer to second squeeze bottle.
Cilantro Delfino springs or cilantro stems, cut into 1 cm / ⅜ in batons	30 g	13.3%	⑯ Cut set foie gras into strips 8 mm by 12.5 cm / ¼ in by 5 in.
			⑰ Tie strips carefully into knots without breaking them.
Japanese puffed rice	50 g	22.2%	⑱ Divide knotted foie gras among four plates.
			⑲ Garnish with cilantro and puffed rice.
			⑳ Dot plates with reserved kimchi and raisin purees.

from page 4·144

MADEIRA GELÉE

Yields 350 g

INGREDIENT	QUANTITY	SCALING	PROCEDURE
Madeira wine (dry)	200 g	100%	① Combine.
White chicken stock see page 6	150 g	75%	② Bring to simmer.
			③ Remove from heat.
Cassia bark, toasted and crushed	2 g	1%	④ Add to hot stock, and infuse for 5 min.
			⑤ Strain and cool.
Salt	4 g	2%	⑥ Season cooled liquid.
Low-acyl gellan (Kelcogel F, CP Kelco brand)	2.1 g	1.05% (0.6%)*	⑦ Blend into cooled liquid.
			⑧ Heat to 95 °C / 203 °F, and hold at temperature for at least 3 min to fully hydrate.
Sodium citrate	0.7 g	0.35% (0.2%)*	⑨ Pour layer 0.5 cm / ¼ in thick into nonstick mold.
			⑩ Refrigerate until set, about 5 min.
High-acyl gellan (Kelcogel LT100, CP Kelco brand)	0.55 g	0.27% (0.15%)*	⑪ Cut into cubes, and refrigerate until use. Use as seasoning for salads or hearty stews.

from page 5·131

*(% of total weight of Madeira and chicken consommé)

CHILI PEARLS INSPIRED BY MICHAEL LAISKONIS

Yields 350 g

INGREDIENT	QUANTITY	SCALING	PROCEDURE
For chili oil:			
Grapeseed oil	250 g	250%	① Combine.
Aleppo pepper flakes	30 g	30%	② Vacuum seal, and cook sous vide in 70 °C / 158 °F bath for 12 h.
Cayenne	10 g	10%	③ Strain through fine sieve, and cool.
Chili flakes	7 g	7%	④ Reserve 250 g of oil in bowl over ice.
For chili pearls:			
Piquillo peppers, roasted and peeled (store-bought)	260 g	260%	⑤ Blend.
			⑥ Press through sieve.
Salt	6 g	6%	⑦ Measure 250 g of puree; keep hot.
Fresh red Thai chili peppers	2.5 g	2.5%	
Xanthan gum (Keltrol T, CP Kelco brand)	0.3 g	0.3%	
Red pepper puree, from above	250 g	250%	⑧ Combine to form chili pearl base.
Water	100 g	100%	
Salt	3 g	3%	⑨ Blend.
Agar (Texturas brand)	1 g	1% *(0.18%)**	⑩ Disperse into chili pearl base.
			⑪ Bring base to boil.
Locust bean gum (POR/A2 Powder, TIC Gums brand)	0.4 g	0.4% *(0.07%)**	⑫ Simmer for 2 min.
			⑬ Transfer hot mixture quickly to syringe or fine-tipped squeeze bottle.
Chili oil, from above	250 g	250%	⑭ Expel chili pearl base one drop at a time while still hot onto surface of cold chili oil. Beads will set almost instantly.
			⑮ Serve immediately, or store beads in chili oil, refrigerated.

from page 4·145

*(% of total weight of first six ingredients in chili pearls)

GUINNESS "PÂTE DE FRUIT"

Yields 400 g

INGREDIENT	QUANTITY	SCALING	PROCEDURE
Sugar	150 g	150%	① Mix together in pot.
Isomalt	100 g	100%	
HM pectin (Brown Ribbon HV, Obipektin brand)	10 g	10% *(1.7%)**	
Guinness beer	300 g	300%	② Combine with sugar and isomalt mixture, and cook to 110 °C / 230 °F.
Glucose syrup DE 40	50 g	50%	③ Use refractometer to check soluble solids concentration, and cook until reduced to 75 °Brix.
Tartaric acid	10 g	10%	
			④ Cast hot mixture into mold.
			⑤ Cool at room temperature for 4 h to set gel.
			⑥ Chill in freezer for 5 min to simplify cutting.
			⑦ Cut into 2 cm / ¾ in squares.
Pretzels, ground	50 g	50%	⑧ Blend together to fine powder.
Isomalt	20 g	20%	⑨ Dust over cut pâte de fruit.
N-Zorbit M (National Starch brand)	10 g	10%	⑩ Serve, or reserve dusted squares on nonstick sheets at room temperature.

from page 4·145

*(% of total weight of sugar, isomalt, beer, and glucose)

OLIVE OIL NOODLES INSPIRED BY JORDI CRUZ

Yields 350 g

INGREDIENT	QUANTITY	SCALING	PROCEDURE
Tapioca starch	100 g	62.5%	① Vacuum seal, and cook sous vide in 80 °C / 176 °F bath for 2 h.
Water	100 g	62.5%	② Measure 80 g of pregelatinized starch paste, and reserve warm.
Olive oil	160 g	100%	③ Heat to 30 °C / 85 °F.
			④ Hold warm.
Salt	5 g	3.1%	⑤ Dry blend to make gel powder.
300 Bloom gelatin	4 g	2.5%	
LM pectin (Genupectin LM 104 AS, CP Kelco brand)	2 g	1.25%	
Agar (Texturas brand)	0.7 g	0.44%	
Mineral water	120 g	75%	⑥ Whisk gel powder into water.
			⑦ Bring mixture to boil.
Pregelatinized starch paste, from above	80 g	50%	⑧ Blend starch paste into warm gel solution.
			⑨ Remove from heat, and blend by hand over ice until completely cool and fluid.
			⑩ Slowly blend in warmed olive oil until fully emulsified to form olive oil noodle base.
Olive oil, chilled but still fluid	as needed		⑪ Transfer noodle base to pastry bag.
			⑫ Extrude noodles 3 mm / ⅛ in thick into chilled olive oil bath.
			⑬ Refrigerate, and allow to set for at least for 4 h before serving.
			⑭ Garnish with flaky salt and herbs as desired.

from page 4·146

SEA URCHIN TOFU, TOKYO NEGI, SESAME, PONZU
INSPIRED BY YOSHIHIRO MURATA

Yields 400 g (about 8 servings)

INGREDIENT	QUANTITY	SCALING	PROCEDURE
Hon dashi, cold see page 15	200 g	100%	① Disperse gelatin and agar in dashi.
			② Boil for 3 min to fully hydrate agar.
160 Bloom gelatin	3.6 g	1.8% *(0.9%)	
Agar	0.4 g	0.2% *(0.1%)	
Sea urchin tongues	200 g	100%	③ Blend into hot dashi.
			④ Cast immediately into eight small individual bowls to create layer 3 cm / 1¼ in thick.
			⑤ Refrigerate until tofu is fully set, at least 5 h, before serving.
Tokyo negi, thinly sliced	40 g	20%	⑥ Toss negi with yuzu juice and toasted sesame oil, and arrange on top of tofu.
Sous vide ponzu see page 22	80 g	40%	⑦ Pour ponzu around tofu.
Yuzu juice	8 g	4%	
Toasted sesame oil	5 g	2.5	

from page 5·202

*(% of total weight of hon dashi and sea urchin tongues)

OLIVE OIL GUMMY WORMS

Yields 445 g

INGREDIENT	QUANTITY	SCALING	PROCEDURE
200 Bloom gelatin	20 g	27%	① Disperse gelatin into cold water.
Water	40 g	53%	② Vacuum seal gelatin mixture.
			③ Hydrate in 60 °C / 140 °F bath for 30 min.
			④ Set aside gelatin mixture.
Water	110 g	147%	⑤ Combine.
Isomalt	100 g	133%	⑥ Bring to boil.
Clear honey	55 g	73%	⑦ Whisk in gelatin mixture.
Glucose syrup DE 40	25 g	33%	
Gum arabic	20 g	27%	
Olive oil	75 g	100%	⑧ Whisk in; emulsify fully to form gummy worm base.
Vanilla seeds and pulp	1 g	1.3%	⑨ Whisk into gummy worm base.
Thyme essential oil	0.1 g	0.13%	⑩ Cast base into worm-shaped molds.
			⑪ Cool.
			⑫ Refrigerate for at least 4 h to set.
			⑬ Remove from molds.

from page 4·147

SHERRY GEL CUBE

Yields 215 g

INGREDIENT	QUANTITY	SCALING	PROCEDURE
Water	50 g	33%	① Steep blossoms in 70 °C / 158 °F water for 10 min.
Chamomile blossoms	15 g	10%	② Strain and cool.
Agar	2 g	1.3%	③ Disperse agar in cooled chamomile tea.
Sherry vinegar	150 g	100%	④ Mix into chamomile tea, and bring to boil.
			⑤ Pour quickly through fine sieve into desired mold, and set at room temperature for 5 min.
			⑥ Cut into 3 mm / ⅛ in cubes, and refrigerate until use. Use as seasoning for cold cuts and salad.

from page 5·270

SUNNY-SIDE UP "EGGS" ADAPTED FROM WYLIE DUFRESNE

Yields 800 g (about 25 "eggs")

INGREDIENT	QUANTITY	SCALING	PROCEDURE
For the egg whites:			
Coconut milk	500 g	100%	① Combine.
Sugar	20 g	4%	② Steep milk mixture for 20 min in refrigerator.
Cardamom, cracked	9 g	1.8%	③ Strain.
Guar gum (8/22A Powder, TIC Gums brand)	0.8 g	0.16%	④ Blend to fully incorporate into milk mixture.
			⑤ Heat to 80 °C / 176 °F.
Locust bean gum (POR/A2 Powder, TIC Gums brand)	0.8 g	0.16%	⑥ Pour 20 g of mixture directly from pot onto each of 25 plates to create egg white shapes. Work quickly; gel mixture sets rapidly.
Xanthan gum (Keltrol T)	0.8 g	0.16%	⑦ Refrigerate "egg" whites.
For the egg yolks:			
Carrot juice	250 g (from about 500 g of carrots)	50%	⑧ Blend until fully incorporated.
Glucose syrup DE 40	25 g	5%	
Xanthan gum (Keltrol T)	1.5 g	0.3%	
Smoked maple syrup	to taste		⑨ Season juice mixture.
Salt	to taste		⑩ Pour into silicone hemisphere molds 5 cm / 2 in. in diameter.
			⑪ Freeze completely, about 2 h, to form yolks.
For assembly:			
Water	250 g	50%	⑫ Blend in pot.
Kappa carrageenan (Genugel CHP2, CP Kelco brand)	1 g	0.2%	⑬ Heat gum mixture to 80 °C / 180 °F.
			⑭ Cool to 45 °C / 113 °F, and hold at temperature.
Locust bean gum (POR/A2 Powder, TIC Gums brand)	1 g	0.2%	⑮ Remove frozen yolks from molds with toothpick or skewer.
			⑯ Dip yolks into cooled gum mixture.
Potassium chloride	0.12 g	0.024%	⑰ Place one coated yolk in center of each "egg" white.
			⑱ Allow yolks to thaw at least 30 min before serving.
Black pepper, coarsely ground	to taste		⑲ Season.
Coarse salt	to taste		
Olive oil	to taste		

from page 4·148

COATING GELS

① Select a temperature and texture. If the food will be coated hot, fewer options are available, but the table Best Bets for Firm Coating Gels below presents good formulas that yield textures ranging from elastic and tender to brittle and firm.
② Choose the gelling agent. We give several options for hot and cold coating gels in the table of formulas. Some options use a mixture of two or more gelling agents.
③ Measure and mix the gelling agents. Set the weight of the liquid to 100%. For example, to make a smooth licorice coating gel for cold food, use 0.7 g of low-acyl gellan and 0.2 g of high-acyl gellan for every 100 g of licorice infusion.
④ Disperse the gelling agents in the liquid.
⑤ Hydrate fully. Hydration times and temperatures are indicated in the table.
⑥ Apply the coating. Control the temperature of the gel to maintain a barely liquid consistency while dipping the food or brushing on the coating.

Best Bets for Firm Coating Gels

Temperature	Texture	Firmness	Gelling agent	(scaling)*	Hydrate (°C)	(°F)	(min)	Coat	Example use	See page
cold	elastic	tender	160 Bloom gelatin	2.3%	60	140	5	cool over ice until syrupy, about 15 min, before applying to food	traditional chaudfroid, sous vide chicken breast with truffle jus coating, cured salmon loin with watercress juice coating	
			xanthan gum	0.2%						
		firm	160 Bloom gelatin	3%	60	140	5			
	brittle	tender	iota carrageenan	0.45%	75	167	3	keep gel base warm while applying coating; the gel sets quickly	crimini in amber	271
			kappa carrageenan	0.35%						
hot or cold	elastic	tender	sorbitol	3.00%	95	203	3	chill food with liquid nitrogen before coating to get a thin covering	modern chaud-chaud, warm oysters with seaweed vinegar gelée	
			agar	0.60%						
			xanthan gum	0.25%						
			low-acyl gellan	0.35%	95	203	3			
			xanthan gum	0.20%						
		firm	sorbitol	2%	95	203	3	prechill food with liquid nitrogen to coat thinly	foie gras torchon with beet and hibiscus glaze	272
			160 Bloom gelatin	1%						
			agar	1%						
	brittle	firm	low-acyl gellan	0.7%	95	203	3	dip food in bath of gel solution to coat evenly	salmon with licorice	272
			high-acyl gellan	0.2%						

from page 4·151   *(set weight of liquid to 100%)

One problem with coating gels is their tendency to slip off the surface rather than coating it. A way to avoid this problem is to prepare the surface by scoring or pricking it (see page 4·158). Another method to help adherence is to get the surface very cold. Dousing it in liquid nitrogen helps with this.

FOIE GRAS PARFAIT SPHERES

Yields 600 g

INGREDIENT	QUANTITY	SCALING	PROCEDURE
Raw duck foie gras	425 g	100%	① Cook sous vide in 57 °C / 135 °F bath to core temperature of 56 °C / 133 °F, about 20 min.
White duck stock, see page 6	170 g	40%	② Disperse gelatin in small amount of cold stock, and heat until fully dissolved.
160 Bloom gelatin	10 g	2.4%	③ Whisk gelatin mixture into remaining stock.
Insta Cure No. 1	6 g	1.4%	④ Blend warm foie gras with gelatin mixture and remaining ingredients.
Salt	6 g	1.4%	⑤ Pipe 12 g of mixture into each of 36 silicone hemisphere molds, each 2.5 cm / 1 in. in diameter.
Sugar	3 g	0.7%	⑥ Refrigerate for at least 4 h to set.
			⑦ If using kernel "pit," scoop 1 cm / ⅜ in hemisphere from center of molded foie gras.
Hazelnuts or apricot kernels, roasted and peeled (optional)	18 whole		⑧ Melt flat surface of each hemisphere with blowtorch, and press kernel into center divot.
			⑨ Join pairs of hemispheres to form spheres.
			⑩ Insert 10 cm / 4 in skewer into each foie gras sphere, and freeze.
			⑪ Using metal skewer dipped in very hot water, indent top of each sphere to mimic dimple that holds stem, and sculpt side of sphere to mimic natural crevasse of cherry.
			⑫ Dip sphere into hot water and then into liquid nitrogen. Refrigerate until cool.

from page 4·152

FOIE GRAS CHERRIES

Yields 18 cherries

INGREDIENT	QUANTITY	SCALING	PROCEDURE
Sour cherry juice	150 g	100%	① Disperse gellan into juice, and bring to boil.
Low-acyl gellan (Kelcogel F, CP Kelco brand)	1.5 g	1% (0.26%)*	② Pour liquid into beaker set in ice-water bath.
			③ Blend mixture with immersion blender as it sets to form sour cherry fluid gel.
Cherry pickling brine, see page 180	85 g	57%	④ Disperse gelatin in small amount of brine.
160 Bloom gelatin	14 g	9.3% (2.4%)*	⑤ Heat mixture until gelatin is fully dissolved.
			⑥ Blend in remaining ingredients.
Black cherry puree	200 g	133%	⑦ Whisk in sour cherry fluid gel.
Amarena cherry syrup	150 g	100%	⑧ Vacuum seal to remove accumulated air bubbles.
Xanthan gum (Keltrol T, CP Kelco brand)	0.6 g	0.4% (0.1%)*	
Foie gras parfait spheres, see above	18 spheres		⑨ Dip frozen foie gras spheres into cherry liquid, coating evenly.
			⑩ Refrigerate until set, about 1 h. To serve, temper at room temperature for 10 min.

from page 4·153   *(% of total weight of all other ingredients except foie gras)

HALIBUT CHEEK GEL BASE

Yields 180 g

INGREDIENT	QUANTITY	SCALING	PROCEDURE
White fish stock, see page 6	400 g	100%	① Reduce stock to 150 g.
Malt vinegar	30 g	7.5%	② Mix with reduced stock.
Salt	4 g	1%	③ Cool stock completely.
Fish stock mixture, from above	150 g	37.5%	④ Disperse gellans and sodium citrate in cold stock.
Low-acyl gellan (Kelcogel F, CP Kelco brand)	0.75 g	0.19% (0.5%)*	⑤ Heat to 95 °C / 203 °F, and hold at temperature for 3 min to fully hydrate.
High-acyl gellan (Kelcogel LT100, CP Kelco brand)	0.36 g	0.1% (0.25%)*	⑥ Keep gel mixture above 65 °C / 149 °F to prevent it from gelling prematurely.
Sodium citrate	0.36 g	0.1% (0.25%)*	
Halibut cheeks, from above	400 g	100%	⑦ Dip skewered cheeks into hot gelled stock three times, allowing gel to set between dips.
			⑧ Place coated cheeks on silicone baking mat.
			⑨ Refrigerate for 1 h to cool and set.
			⑩ Vacuum seal and cook sous vide in 49 °C / 120 °F bath to core temperature of 48 °C / 118 °F, about 35 min.

from page 5·144   *(% of total weight of reduced fish stock)

CRIMINI IN AMBER INSPIRED BY FERRAN ADRIÀ

Yields 200 g

INGREDIENT	QUANTITY	SCALING	PROCEDURE
Crimini mushrooms, stem on, peeled	50 g	100%	① Clean. ② Cut into at least 20 slices 1 mm / $\frac{1}{32}$ in thick. ③ Cover with damp paper towel, and refrigerate.
Dried porcini	30 g	60%	④ Rinse. ⑤ Soak for 5 min. ⑥ Strain.
Water	400 g	800%	⑦ Add to rinsed and soaked porcinis. ⑧ Simmer for 10 min.
Salt	7.5 g	15%	⑨ Mix into porcini mixture.
Kombu	5 g	10%	⑩ Simmer for 10 min.
Koji-Aji (Ajinomoto brand)	2 g	4%	
Bonito flakes	1 g	2%	⑪ Add to porcini mixture. ⑫ Remove from heat. ⑬ Infuse for 1 min. ⑭ Strain; measure 200 g of stock.
Iota carrageenan (Texturas brand)	0.9 g	1.8% *(0.45%)**	⑮ Combine with reserved porcini stock. ⑯ Bring to boil to dissolve completely.
Kappa carrageenan (Texturas brand)	0.7 g	1.4% *(0.35%)**	⑰ Remove from heat. ⑱ Skim off any accumulated foam. ⑲ Dip chilled crimini slices in hot gel mixture; coat slices completely. ⑳ Transfer to nonstick baking sheet or lightly oiled plastic wrap; ensure slices remain coated.
Aged Parmesan, small dice	20 pieces		㉑ Garnish gel-encased crimini slices.
Breakfast radish, small dice	20 pieces		
Pickled dried fig, small dice see page 177	20 pieces		
Pressure-cooked sesame seeds see page 151	30 g	60%	㉒ Dab evenly on finished crimini.
from page 4·154		*(% of total weight of reserved porcini stock)*	

SALMON POACHED IN LICORICE ADAPTED FROM HESTON BLUMENTHAL

Yields 280 g

INGREDIENT	QUANTITY	SCALING	PROCEDURE
Distilled water	2.4 kg	150%	① Combine while bringing to simmer.
Hard, glassy black licorice sticks (store-bought), crushed into small pieces	125 g	7.8%	② Cool for 5 min.
			③ Process mixture in food processor for 5 min or until licorice is fully dissolved.
			④ Strain licorice stock through fine sieve.
			⑤ Reserve 1.6 kg of stock, refrigerated.
Low-acyl gellan (Kelcogel F, CP Kelco brand)	11.2 g	0.7% (0.46%)*	⑥ Dry blend.
High-acyl gellan (Kelcogel LT 100, CP Kelco brand)	3.2 g	0.2% (0.13%)*	
Licorice stock, from above	1.6 kg	100%	⑦ Disperse gellan gum mixture into cold stock.
			⑧ Heat mixture to 95 °C / 203 °F until gellans are hydrated, about 2 min.
			⑨ Skim any foam from surface using small sieve.
Salmon fillet, skinned and cut evenly into squares	200 g (four squares, 50 g each)	12.5%	⑩ Insert wooden skewer into side of each fish square and, holding skewer, dip squares individually into stock.
			⑪ Place coated salmon on plates to cool until set, about 5 min.
			⑫ Dip fish into stock again to apply second coat.
			⑬ Transfer fish to chilled tray lined with silicone mat.
			⑭ Set at room temperature, about 5 min.
			⑮ Wrap each coated square tightly in plastic wrap.
			⑯ Vacuum seal individually, and cook sous vide in 44 °C / 111 °F bath to core temperature of 43 °C / 109 °F, about 25 min.

from page 4·155

*(% of total weight of licorice stock)

FOIE GRAS TORCHON WITH BEET AND HIBISCUS GLAZE
ADAPTED FROM PAUL LIEBRANDT

Yields 600 g

INGREDIENT	QUANTITY	SCALING	PROCEDURE
Beet juice see page 2·336	800 g (from 1 kg of beets, about five large)	320%	① Reduce over medium heat until syrupy, about 30 min.
			② Cool at room temperature.
			③ Measure 250 g of reduced juice.
Reduced beet juice, from above	250 g	100%	④ Bring juice to boil, and remove from heat. Add hibiscus and orange peel, and steep at room temperature for 15 min.
Dried hibiscus flowers	20 g	8%	
Dried orange peel	5 g	2%	⑤ Strain, and cool completely.
Sorbitol	12.5 g	5%	⑥ Combine, and disperse in infused juice.
160 Bloom gelatin	5 g	2%	⑦ Boil for 2 min to fully hydrate, and keep warm.
Agar (Texturas brand)	2 g	0.8%	
Salt	to taste		⑧ Season.
			⑨ Cool mixture to 65 °C / 149 °F, and hold at temperature.
Foie gras torchon see page 104	500 g	200%	⑩ Center foie gras terrine on cooling rack.
			⑪ Prick evenly across surface with fine skewer so that gel will adhere more easily.
Liquid nitrogen	as needed		⑫ Ladle over liquid nitrogen to freeze terrine surface.
			⑬ Pour warm glaze directly from pot over terrine in one fluid motion to coat evenly; repeat.
			⑭ Refrigerate glazed terrine for at least 8 h before serving. Pigment from glaze will permeate terrine.

from page 4·158

This elegant preparation is a Modernist version of the classic foie gras terrine in aspic. Here, the hibiscus adds both flavor and color, some of which penetrates the foie gras.

HALIBUT IN VERBENA BUBBLE INSPIRED BY MARC VEYRAT

Yields 180 g (four portions)

INGREDIENT	QUANTITY	SCALING	PROCEDURE
Halibut fillet, skinless	100 g	100%	① Cut into four equal rectangles.
			② Set aside.
Coconut cream (store-bought)	100 g	100%	③ Combine.
240 Bloom gelatin	2 g	2%	④ Heat to dissolve gelatin.
Xanthan gum (Keltrol T, CP Kelco brand)	0.5 g	0.5%	⑤ Pour in layer 1 mm / 1/32 in thick into rectangular mold on baking sheet lined with plastic wrap.
			⑥ Refrigerate for 2 h to set.
			⑦ Place halibut rectangle on coconut gel; align width of rectangle with edge of gel sheet.
			⑧ Cut long rectangle of gel equal in width to halibut rectangle and long enough to wrap completely around fish.
			⑨ Roll halibut tightly in long gel rectangle.
			⑩ Cut and roll gel around remaining halibut portions.
For lemon verbena encasement:			
Water	400 g	400%	⑪ Blanch mint leaves for 2 min in boiling water.
Lemongrass, thinly sliced	40 g	40%	⑫ Cool quickly in ice water.
Mint leaves	20 g	20%	⑬ Blend blanched mint with remaining ingredients until smooth.
Lemon verbena essential oil	0.2 g	0.2%	⑭ Strain.
Agar (Texturas brand)	10 g	10% (2.5%)*	⑮ Disperse in mint mixture.
			⑯ Heat to 95 °C / 203 °F for 3 min to hydrate.
Sorbitol	2 g	2% (0.5%)*	⑰ Remove from heat, and pour enough gel mixture to make layer 2 mm / 1/16 in thick in bottom of four deep rectangular molds that are larger than halibut rectangles.
			⑱ Let gel set in molds for 2 min.
			⑲ Place rolled halibut on top of gel in each mold.
			⑳ Pour remaining gel mixture quickly over each rolled halibut to form airtight seal around fish.
			㉑ Refrigerate until set, about 10 min.
For fish sauce condiment:			
Fish sauce	30 g	30%	㉒ Blend together until dissolved, and reserve.
Honey	20 g	20%	㉓ Remove encased halibut portions from molds.
Lime juice	20 g	20%	㉔ Vacuum seal portions together.
Rice vinegar	10 g	10%	㉕ Cook sous vide in 48 °C / 118 °F bath or steam oven to core temperature of 47 °C / 117 °F, about 25 min.
Xanthan gum (Keltrol T, CP Kelco brand)	0.15 g	0.15%	㉖ Transfer portions from bag to plates.
			㉗ To serve, break verbena gel casing at table to reveal steamed fish and liquefied coconut gel. Remove verbena gel casing, and discard.
			㉘ Serve with fish sauce condiment.

from page 4·156

*(% of total weight of water in verbena bubble encasement)

The verbena gel encasement is intended only as an aromatic cooking vessel for the fish; it should not be consumed. It imbues the fish with the scent of the essential oil and makes for a dramatic presentation.

Marc Veyrat used a hot gel casing as a cooking vessel, in the same way that parchment, salt, clay, and pig bladders have been used in the past. The original version of this dish was a piece of turbot encased in lemongrass with white chocolate. Veyrat's insight presents a huge range of possibilities, both aesthetic and aromatic, for the Modernist chef. Imagine a steamed pigeon encased with suspended rose petals in a clear, rose-scented gel. Or a black gel that is broken open at the table to reveal a suspended whole egg.

The coconut cream is solidified with gelatin for assembly but melts into a liquid when served hot.

Be sure to work quickly with the hot gel because it begins to set below 45 °C / 113 °F. Warming the ladle will prevent the gel from setting on the surface of the ladle.

HOT GELS

① Select a texture. Possibilities range from tender to firm and from elastic to brittle.

② Choose the gelling agents. The table Best Bets for Hot Gels below gives at least two options for each texture. Most formulas use a mixture of two or more gelling agents.

③ Scale and mix the gelling agents. All quantities indicated in the table are proportional to the weight of the puree or juice. For example, to make a brittle, firm gel with consommé, use 0.5 g of agar for every 100 g of consommé.

④ Dry blend the gelling agents, and disperse them in the flavorful liquid.

⑤ Hydrate fully. Blend while heating to ensure that the gelling agents are evenly distributed during hydration. Usually 2–3 min at 95 °C / 203 °F is sufficient to hydrate the gelling agents.

⑥ Cast. See the table for casting directions and references to example recipes. See page 4·132 for illustrated, step-by-step instructions.

Most hot gels can also be served cold. Methycellulose gels are the one exception: they set when hot and melt when cold—see page 4·170.

Best Bets for Hot Gels

Texture	Gelling agents	(scaling)*	Hydrate (°C)	(°F)	Cast or mold	Note	Example	See page
tender, very elastic	xanthan gum	0.25%	95	203	cast directly into serving vessel	bone marrow-like texture	warm aspic	277
	low-acyl gellan	0.10%						
	sorbitol	5.00%	95	203	cast directly into serving vessel	opaque, so not suited to clear gels	warm panna cotta, eggless crème brûlée	
	high-acyl gellan	0.20%						
	agar	0.10%						
	high-acyl gellan	0.20%	95	203	cast directly into serving vessel	creamy mouthfeel	warm panna cotta, eggless crème brûlée	
	xanthan gum	0.15%						
	low-acyl gellan	0.10%						
tender, elastic	xanthan gum	0.15%	95	203	cast into serving vessel or mold			
	locust bean gum	0.15%						
	low-acyl gellan	0.10%						
	high-acyl gellan	0.20%	95	203	cast into serving vessel or mold		eggless flan, custard	
	low-acyl gellan	0.10%						
firm, elastic	locust bean gum	0.25%	85	185	best molded; cut with care	best with nondairy gels; add 5% sorbitol for tender texture	gel noodles	
	agar	0.20%						
	high-acyl gellan	0.25%	85	185	best molded; cut with care	pâte de fruit-like texture	hot eggless flan	
	low-acyl gellan	0.20%						
	xanthan gum	0.10%						
firm, semibrittle	agar	0.4%	85	185	best suited for cutting and shaping		hot terrine	
	guar gum	0.2%						
	high-acyl gellan	0.40%	95	203	best suited for cutting and shaping			
	agar	0.25%						
very firm, brittle	agar	0.5%	85	185	best suited for cutting and shaping	tends to weep over time	gel seasoning cubes	5·267
	low-acyl gellan	0.30%	95	203	best suited for cutting and shaping		gel seasoning cubes	
	high-acyl gellan	0.15%						

from page 4·160   *(set weight of liquid to 100%)

AGAR CARBONARA ADAPTED FROM FERRAN ADRIÀ

Yields 1 kg (about 20 portions)

INGREDIENT	QUANTITY	SCALING	PROCEDURE
Consommé madrilène see page 42	500 g	100%	① Blend, and bring to boil.
Agar (Texturas brand)	3 g	0.6%	② Cast onto tray measuring 60 cm by 40 cm / 24 in by 16 in to form layer 1 mm / 1/32 in thick.
Locust bean gum (POR/A2 Powder, TIC Gums brand)	1.25 g	0.25%	③ Refrigerate for 2 h.
			④ Cut into noodles 2 mm / 1/16 in wide.
			⑤ Arrange in even layer on silicone mat.
Unsalted butter, cut into small cubes	100 g	20%	⑥ Vacuum seal.
Bacon scraps	50 g	10%	⑦ Cook sous vide in 70 °C / 158 °F bath for 2 h.
			⑧ Strain, and reserve butter.
Heavy cream	250 g	50%	⑨ Reduce cream by half over medium heat.
			⑩ Reserve in squeeze bottle.
Egg yolks, pasteurized see page 4·78	40 g	8%	⑪ Strain.
			⑫ Reserve in squeeze bottle.
Smoked bacon, cut into 5 mm / ¼ in cubes	80 g	16%	⑬ Heat noodles in 200 °C / 390 °F oven until just warmed through, about 4 min.
			⑭ Warm bacon cubes in reserved bacon-infused butter over medium heat, about 4 min.
			⑮ Divide noodles equally among eight plates.
Parmigiano Reggiano, cut into 5 mm / ¼ in cubes	100 g	20%	⑯ Garnish each serving with bacon and Parmesan cubes, reduced cream, egg yolks, and truffle oil.
Truffle oil	10 g	2%	

from page 4·161

GRUYÈRE CUSTARD

Yields 670 g

INGREDIENT	QUANTITY	SCALING	PROCEDURE
Whole milk	250 g	250%	① Combine.
Heavy cream	75 g	75%	② Bring to simmer.
Sodium citrate	4.7 g	4.7% (0.7%)*	
Gruyère cheese, grated	100 g	100%	③ Blend into milk mixture, stirring until melted and smooth.
			④ Reserve.
Sweet onions, thinly sliced	50 g	50%	⑤ Sauté onions until tender, about 30 min.
Unsalted butter	20 g	20%	⑥ Cool.
			⑦ Hand-blend into reserved cheese mixture.
			⑧ Pass through fine sieve.
			⑨ Cool completely.
Onion stock, cold see page 11	175 g	175%	⑩ Disperse carrageenans into stock.
			⑪ Blend with cooled cheese mixture.
Iota carrageenan	3.35 g	3.35% (0.5%)*	⑫ Heat to 95 °C / 203 °F for 3 min to fully hydrate.
Kappa carrageenan	1.35 g	1.35% (0.2%)*	
Salt	to taste		⑬ Season warmed custard base.
			⑭ Cast evenly into mold to create layer 2.5 cm / 1 in thick.
			⑮ Refrigerate until set, about 10 min.
			⑯ Cut into 2.5 cm / 1 in cubes, and refrigerate until use.
			⑰ To serve, heat custard cubes in 70 °C / 160 °F oven until just warmed through, about 8 min.

from page 5·264

*(% of total weight of all other ingredients)

SHELLFISH CUSTARD HOMAGE TO JOËL ROBUCHON

Yields 1.2 kg

INGREDIENT	QUANTITY	SCALING	PROCEDURE
Heavy cream	300 g	100%	① Combine in pot.
Whole milk	140 g	47%	② Simmer for 5 min.
Mushroom jus see page 37	90 g	30%	③ Remove from heat.
Salt	5 g	1.7%	
Chervil, leaves	30 g	10%	④ Add to warm milk, and infuse for 20 min at room temperature.
Tarragon, leaves	6 g	2%	⑤ Strain and cool.
Shellfish stock see page 6	280 g	93%	⑥ Combine with cold milk mixture.
High-acyl gellan (Kelcogel LT 100, CP Kelco brand)	1.6 g	0.53% (0.2%)*	⑦ Dry blend, and disperse into shellfish stock mixture. ⑧ Heat to 90 °C / 194 °F, and hold at temperature for 3 min.
Xanthan gum (Keltrol T, CP Kelco brand)	1.2 g	0.4% (0.15%)*	⑨ Remove from heat. ⑩ Cast into desired molds to make custards of about 80 g each.
Low-acyl gellan (Kelcogel F, CP Kelco brand)	0.57 g	0.2% (0.07%)*	
Sodium hexametaphosphate	0.4 g	0.14% (0.05%)*	
Cauliflower fluid gel foam base see page 326	300 g	100%	⑪ To serve, transfer cauliflower foam base to 1 l siphon. ⑫ Charge with one cartridge of nitrous oxide. ⑬ Reheat custards, and warm siphon to 80 °C / 176 °F.
Sea urchin	100 g (24 tongues)	33%	⑭ Garnish each custard with three tongues. ⑮ Shake warmed siphon vigorously, and top each custard with cauliflower foam.
Coffee butter, melted see page 350	40 g	13.3%	⑯ Drizzle over custards.

from page 4·162

*(% of total weight of first four liquid ingredients)

BONE MARROW CUSTARD

Yields 650 g

Joël Robuchon is one of the world's most influential chefs. His original version of this dish consisted of a spoonful of oscietra caviar topped with layers of delicate shellfish gelée, cauliflower cream, and chlorophyl puree. It inspired many interpretations, from Ferran Adrià's hot version of the original to Thomas Keller's Cauliflower Panna Cotta (see page 263). We created this dish in homage to Robuchon and to the creative lineage that has followed it.

It can be hard to hydrate gellan in a liquid that contains calcium. Fortunately, the calcium in milk and cream is naturally sequestered. It poses no problem as long as sufficient heat is used during hydration. When using gellan with other liquids that contain calcium, a sequestrant may be necessary (see page 4·129).

INGREDIENT	QUANTITY	SCALING	PROCEDURE
Veal marrowbone (optional)	one foreshank bone		① Cut into four equal pieces, and reserve for casting custard. If not using bones, reserve other molds.
Water	500 g	400%	② Soak marrow in water for 12 h to remove blood.
Veal marrow	125 g	100%	③ Drain.
Whole milk, cold	125 g	100%	④ Disperse gelatin in milk.
160 Bloom gelatin	3.5 g	2.8% (0.9%)*	⑤ Vacuum seal with coffee beans. ⑥ Cook sous vide in 75 °C / 167 °F bath for 10 min.
Coffee beans	1.5 g	1.2%	⑦ Strain coffee-infused milk, and reserve.
Salt	3 g	2.4%	⑧ Combine.
High-acyl gellan (Kelcogel LT 100, CP Kelco brand)	0.55 g	0.44% (0.15%)*	
Low-acyl gellan (Kelcogel F, CP Kelco brand)	0.375 g	0.3% (0.1%)*	
White veal stock, warmed slightly see page 6	250 g	200%	⑨ Disperse gel mixture into stock. ⑩ Blend stock with veal marrow, coffee-infused milk, and garlic confit.
Garlic confit, pureed see page 176	15 g	12%	⑪ Bring mixture to boil, and simmer for 3 min. ⑫ Pour quickly into marrowbones or other molds. ⑬ Cool until set, about 5 min. ⑭ Reheat bone marrow custard in 75 °C / 165 °F combi oven with 100% relative humidity for 8 min. If combi oven is unavailable, reheat in steamer for 5 min.

from page 5·63

*(% of total weight of whole milk and white veal stock)

BOEUF EN GELÉE INSPIRED BY DANIEL BOULUD

Yields 1.5 kg (eight portions)

INGREDIENT	QUANTITY	SCALING	PROCEDURE
Carrots, brunoise	50 g	5%	① Sauté together until tender, about 5 min.
Parsnips, brunoise	50 g	5%	② Cool.
Shallots, brunoise	50 g	5%	
Neutral oil	15 g	1.5%	
Oxtail meat, cooked sous vide and shredded see page 90	300 g	30%	③ Fold into vegetable mixture.
Tomato confit, finely minced	40 g	4%	
Grain mustard	to taste		④ Season meat and vegetable mixture.
Salt	to taste		⑤ Divide into 50 g servings, and spoon evenly into bottom of eight small bowls.
Xanthan gum (Keltrol T, CP Kelco brand)	2.5 g	0.25%	⑥ Blend.
Low-acyl gellan (Kelcogel F, CP Kelco brand)	1.25 g	0.13%	
Oxtail consommé see page 46	1 kg	100%	⑦ Disperse gum mixture into cold consommé.
			⑧ Heat to 95 °C / 203 °F, and hold for 3 min.
			⑨ Pour hot gel into bowls of meat and vegetables until mixture is submerged 2.5 cm / 1 in below surface of gel.
			⑩ Refrigerate bowls.
Horseradish foam see page 327	120 g	12%	⑪ To serve, reheat bowls in 70 °C / 158 °F bath or steam oven until just warmed through, about 10 min.
Fresh wasabi, peeled	20 g	2%	⑫ Garnish evenly with horseradish foam and grated fresh wasabi as desired.

from page 4·163

HOT FRUIT AND VEGETABLE GELS

① Prepare and puree the fruit or vegetable. The gels can also be made with juice, but that approach yields a very different gel texture.

② Find the acidity of the puree or juice. Use the table of fruit and vegetable acidities, or measure the pH directly by using a pH meter.

③ Select a texture. Possibilities range from brittle to very elastic and soft.

④ Choose the gelling agent. We give two options for each texture in the table Best Bets for Hot Fruit Gels on the next page. Some options use more than one agent.

⑤ Mix the gelling agents. Set the weight of the puree or juice to 100%, and measure each gelling agent proportionally. The amount of sodium hexa-metaphosphate, if any, varies according to the pH of the food. Dissolve it in the juice before adding the gelling agent or agents.

⑥ Disperse the gelling agents into the cold juice or puree, and hydrate fully. A few minutes at 90 °C / 194 °F is usually sufficient to hydrate the gelling agents. Use a high-shear mixer, such as a blender, immersion blender, or rotor-stator homogenizer. You may need to add calcium when using low-acyl gellan. While still hot, shear in calcium lactate or another calcium salt after hydration, stirring well until dissolved. For more details on calcium salts, see page 4·129.

⑦ Cast into a mold, and then cut to size when set. Allow 5–10 min at room temperature, or 2–4 min in the refrigerator, for the gel to set to moderate firmness. The locust bean/xanthan gum formula will set after being frozen and thawed. A methocellulose/gelatin gel will set when heated to 90 °C / 194 °F.

Fruit and Vegetable Acidities

Low acidity (pH ≥ 4.6)	(pH)		(pH)	Medium acidity (pH 3–4.6)	(pH)	High acidity (pH ≤ 3)	(pH)
artichoke	6	peas	6	apple	4.0	cherry	3
asparagus	6	persimmon	6	apricot	3.7	cranberry	3
avocado	7	pumpkin	7	blackberry	3.5	gooseberry	3
banana	5	radish	7	black currant	3.3	lemon	2
beans	6	red cabbage	6	blueberry	3.7	lime	3
beets	6	red onion	6	elderberry	3.8		
bell pepper	5	russet potato	6	grape	3.8		
broccoli	7	rutabaga	6	grapefruit	3.7		
Brussels sprout	6	mushroom	7	greengage	3.4		
button mushroom	7	spaghetti squash	6	guava	4.1		
carrot	6	spinach	7	kiwi	3.6		
cauliflower	7	spring onion	6	mango	4.0		
celery	6	sweet onion	6	mulberry	3.5		
cucumber	6	sweet potato	7	nectarine	3.0		
eggplant	6	taro	6	orange	3.9		
fennel	6	tomato	5	passion fruit	3.5		
fig	6	turnip	6	peach	3.7		
jicama	7	watermelon	5	pineapple	3.5		
leek	6	yellow squash	6	plum	3.6		
lettuce	7	zucchini	7	pomegranate	4.0		
lychee	6			quince	3.7		
melon	5			raspberry	3.3		
napa cabbage	6			red currant	3.1		
papaya	6			rhubarb	3.4		
parsnip	6			strawberry	3.8		
pear	5			tangerine	4.1		

from page 4·164

The acidity found in fruits and vegetables is the primary issue with making gels with them. Calcium content can also be an issue, which is why, in general, we recommend using sodium hexametaphosphate as a sequestrant if gellan is in the gel mixture. In some cases, however, you may need to add extra calcium to gel (see page 4·129).

We took pains to measure and calculate the average pHs of these various fruits and vegetables because this information is useful for far more than making hot fruit gels. Whether you are seasoning broths and sauces, creating brines and marinades, or making preserves, pH plays a huge role in the final qualities of these preparations. Note that the pH can vary with ripeness and variety, so you may want to use a pH meter to measure it yourself.

For more on the role of pH in fruit and vegetables see page 3·274.

For more on how to measure pH, see page 2·316.

Best Bets for Hot Fruit Gels

Texture	Gelling agent	Low acidity (scaling)*	Medium acidity (scaling)*	High acidity (scaling)*
brittle	high-acyl gellan	0.30%	0.3%	0.3%
	sodium hexametaphosphate	0.05%	0.1%	0.2%
	agar	0.5%	0.5%	0.5%
semibrittle	high-acyl gellan	0.20%	0.2%	0.2%
	low-acyl gellan	0.10%	0.1%	0.1%
	sodium hexametaphosphate	0.05%	0.1%	0.2%
	agar	0.4%	0.4%	0.4%
	locust bean gum	0.3%	0.3%	0.3%
elastic	high-acyl gellan	0.20%	0.20%	0.20%
	low-acyl gellan	0.10%	0.10%	0.10%
	xanthan gum	0.15%	0.15%	0.15%
	sodium hexametaphosphate	0.05%	0.10%	0.20%
	locust bean gum	0.8%	0.8%	0.8%
	xanthan gum	0.2%	0.2%	0.2%
very elastic	methylcellulose E4M	1.5%	1.5%	1.5%
	160 Bloom gelatin	3.0%	3.0%	3.0%
	agar	0.4%	0.4%	0.4%
	locust bean gum	0.3%	0.3%	0.3%
	sorbitol	5.0%	5.0%	5.0%

from page 4·165   *(set weight of fruit or vegetable to 100%)*

For details on how to disperse and hydrate methylcellulose, see page 4·170.

HOT ORANGE GEL

Yields 300 g

INGREDIENT	QUANTITY	SCALING	PROCEDURE
Water	75 g	60%	① Mix to dissolve, and warm to make syrup.
Fructose	75 g	60%	② Vacuum seal with syrup, cook sous vide in 88 °C / 190 °F bath for 4 h.
Orange zest, blanched three times	50 g	40%	③ Puree, pass through fine sieve, measure 175 g of puree, and reserve.
Citric acid	2 g	1.6%	④ Dry blend powders.
Agar (Texturas brand)	1.2 g	0.96%	
Locust bean gum (TIC Gums brand)	0.9 g	0.72%	
Orange juice, sieved	125 g	100%	⑤ Mix 50 g (40%) of orange juice into puree.
			⑥ Disperse powder blend into cold mixture.
			⑦ Boil until fully hydrated, about 2 min.
Sorbitol	15 g	12%	⑧ Combine with remaining 75 g (60%) of juice, and blend into hot puree.
			⑨ Cast immediately into mold, and allow to set.

from page 4·167

HOT BANANA GEL

Yields 300 g

INGREDIENT	QUANTITY	SCALING	PROCEDURE
Banana, unpeeled	100 g	100%	① Cook sous vide in 88 °C / 190 °F bath for 12 min.
			② Peel.
			③ Sieve.
Water	175 g	175%	④ Blend all ingredients with banana flesh, and bring to simmer to hydrate locust bean gum.
Fructose	25 g	25%	⑤ Cast into mold, and cool.
Locust bean gum (POR/A2 Powder, TIC Gums brand)	2.2 g	2.2%	⑥ Freeze completely, and store until needed.
			⑦ Thaw gel to serve.
Xanthan gum (Keltrol T, CP Kelco brand)	0.55 g	0.55%	

from page 4·166

HOT GREEN APPLE GEL

Yields 300 g

INGREDIENT	QUANTITY	SCALING	PROCEDURE
Green apple, peeled and thinly sliced	100 g	100%	① Cook sous vide in 90 °C / 194 °F bath for 30 min.
			② Puree until smooth, and reserve.
Malic acid	4 g	4%	③ Dissolve acid into fresh juice to preserve juice color.
Green apple juice (or water)	175 g	175%	
Fructose	25 g	25%	④ Dry blend powders.
Calcium gluconate	1.25 g	1.25%	⑤ Disperse into juice mixture.
Low-acyl gellan (Kelcogel F, CP Kelco brand)	0.55 g	0.55%	⑥ Blend with reserved puree.
			⑦ Heat to at least 85 °C / 185 °F to hydrate.
Xanthan gum (Keltrol T)	0.42 g	0.42%	⑧ Cast into mold, and refrigerate until set, about 5 min.
High-acyl gellan (Kelcogel LT 100, CP Kelco brand)	0.275 g	0.275%	
Sodium hexametaphosphate	0.2 g	0.2%	

from page 4·166

HOT QUINCE GEL

Yields 300 g

INGREDIENT	QUANTITY	SCALING	PROCEDURE
Fragrant quince, halved, cored, and peeled, peels reserved	100 g	100%	① Pressure-cook (including reserved peels) at gauge pressure of 1 bar / 15 psi for 45 min. Discard skins.
			② Puree cooked quince and cooking liquid.
Water	127 g	127%	③ Cool completely.
Sugar	63 g	63%	
Citric acid	1.8 g	1.8%	④ Dry blend powders.
Calcium gluconate	0.82 g	0.82%	⑤ Disperse into cold puree.
Sodium hexametaphosphate	0.2 g	0.2%	⑥ Mix into puree.
High-acyl gellan (Kelcogel LT 100, CP Kelco brand)	0.3 g	0.3%	
Low-acyl gellan (Kelcogel F)	0.6 g	0.6%	
Malic acid	as needed		⑦ Add acid as needed to pH 4.5 or to taste.
			⑧ Heat to at least 85 °C / 185 °F.
			⑨ Cast into mold, and allow to set.

from page 4·167

QUINOA AND IDIAZÁBAL WITH BONITO STOCK VEIL
ADAPTED FROM ANDONI LUIS ADURIZ　　　　　　　　　　　　　　　　　　　　　　　　　Yields 800 g (eight portions)

INGREDIENT	QUANTITY	SCALING	PROCEDURE
White vegetable stock see page 6	700 g	233%	① Blend together.
			② Heat to 70 °C / 158 °F.
Idiazábal cheese, finely grated	300 g	100%	③ Rest for 10 min.
			④ Strain; reserve 700 g of cheese-infused stock.
Quinoa	200 g	67%	⑤ Combine with reserved stock.
			⑥ Simmer until quinoa is just cooked through, about 30 min.
			⑦ Cool completely.
Salt	to taste		⑧ Season quinoa, and reserve 470 g, refrigerated.
White vegetable stock see page 6	375 g	125%	⑨ Heat to 70 °C / 158 °F.
Bonito flakes	60 g	20%	⑩ Stir into vegetable stock.
			⑪ Remove from heat, and cover pot tightly with plastic wrap.
			⑫ Rest for 30 min.
			⑬ Strain.
			⑭ Cool completely, and reserve 300 g of bonito stock.
Bonito stock, from above	300 g	100%	⑮ Disperse into reserved bonito stock while cold.
160 Bloom gelatin	3 g	1%	⑯ Bring stock to boil, and simmer for 2 min.
Agar (Texturas brand)	1.2 g	0.4%	⑰ Cast onto tray lined with plastic wrap to form layer 1 mm / 1/32 in thick.
			⑱ Refrigerate until fully set, about 4 h.
			⑲ Cut circles 7.5 cm / 3 in. in diameter from bonito gel.
			⑳ Spoon quinoa into mounds on center of eight plates slightly smaller in diameter than gel circles.
			㉑ Cover each quinoa mound with gel circle.
			㉒ Heat plates in 80 °C / 175 °F oven for about 8 min.
Rosemary blossoms	32 blossoms		㉓ Garnish at table.
Creamed honey	to taste		

from page 4·168

DUNGENESS CRAB AND APPLE ROULADE　INSPIRED BY SCOTT CARSBERG　　　　　　　　　　　　Yields 500 g

INGREDIENT	QUANTITY	SCALING	PROCEDURE
Apple juice	200 g	100%	① Season juice.
Malic acid	to taste		
Fructose	to taste		
Agar (Texturas brand)	0.8 g	0.4%	② Disperse into juice.
High-acyl gellan (Kelcogel LT 100, CP Kelco brand)	0.6 g	0.3%	③ Bring juice to boil, and simmer for 2 min.
			④ Cast onto nonstick baking sheet to form layer 1 mm / 1/32 in thick.
			⑤ Refrigerate until set, about 5 min.
			⑥ Cut into circles 7 cm / 3 in. in diameter.
Dungeness crab meat	300 g	150%	⑦ Fold together to make crab salad.
Basic mayonnaise see page 303 or store-bought	50 g	25%	
Scallions, fine julienne	30 g	15%	
Sweet almond oil	24 g	12%	
Lemon balm, fine julienne	3 g	1.5%	
Vanilla seeds and pulp	1.5 g (from half a bean)	0.75%	
Lime juice	to taste		⑧ Season crab salad.
Salt	to taste		⑨ Place apple gel circle flat across large flat plate or cutting board.
Seasonal herbs	to taste		⑩ Spoon salad thinly and evenly across surface of each circle.
			⑪ Roll each circle to form tight roulade.
			⑫ Garnish with seasonal herbs.

from page 4·168

CELLULOSE GUM GELS

① Select a texture. Several options are listed in the table Best Bets for Methylcellulose Gels below.

② Make a methylcellulose stock solution. Measure the methylcellulose, and whisk it into hot water equal to about one-third of the weight of the fluid you want to gel. Avoid using cold water because it causes the powder to hydrate too quickly and clump. Quantities in the table are given as a percentage of the water used. For example, mix in 1.2 g of SGA 150 for every 100 g of water to produce a stock solution for firm, custard-like gels.

③ Hydrate fully in the refrigerator for 6–12 h. The mixture will become a clear liquid.

④ Add to the product to be set. The table suggests a number of uses. In general, add one part methylcellulose stock solution to every two parts flavored fluid. For example, to make 300 g of apple jelly, add 100 g of methylcellulose stock to 200 g of concentrated apple juice.

⑤ Cast the product into a container, and heat it to set. Heat it at least to the gelling temperature given in the table, and hold it above the melting temperature until ready to serve.

Best Bets for Methylcellulose Gels

Texture	Firmness	Gelling agent	Quantity (scaling)*	Gels (°C)	Gels (°F)	Melts (°C)	Melts (°F)	Example use	See page
very elastic	tender	K100M	1.5%	90	194	50	122	tender pudding, instant crème brûlée	
elastic	tender	A15C	1.5%	55	131	25	77	gel sheets, instant noodles	next
elastic	firm	E4M	1.5%	64	147	50	122	gel pancakes	
		F450	2.5%	68	154	35	95	dumplings, gnocchi	
semibrittle	firm	SGA 150	1.2%	44	111	15	59	firm custard, scrambled corn	
brittle	firm	SGA 7C	1.0%	44	111	15	59	hot sliceable terrine	

from page 4·171 *(set weight of liquid to 100%)

Properties and Applications of Cellulose Gums

Gel firmness	Category	Gelling agent	Viscosity (mPa·s)	Quantity (scaling)*	Hydrate (°C)	Hydrate (°F)	Gels (°C)	Gels (°F)	Melts (°C)	Melts (°F)	Example uses
soft	HPMC	K99	80–120	0.4%–4%	<30	<86	70–90	158–194	<50	<122	formation of films, fried products, tender gels
		K4M	2,700–5,040								
		K100	75,000–140,000								
semifirm	HPMC	E15	12–18	1.0%–3%	<25	<77	58–64	136–147	<50	<122	custards, noodles
		E50	40–60								
		E4M	2,700–5,040								
	HPMC	F50	40–60	0.2%–2.5%	<25	<77	62–68	144–154	<35	<95	foams, whipped toppings, puddings
		F450	360–540								
		F4M	2,700–5,040								
firm	MC	A15	12–18	0.1%–2%	<13	<55	50–55	122–131	<25	<77	baked goods, set foams, formation of films
		A4M	2,700–5,600								
		A40M	7,500–14,000								
very firm	Super MC	SGA 150	150–450	1.0%–3.5%	<10	<50	38–44	100–111	<15	<59	liquid coatings, firm-set gels
		SGA A7C	700–980								
		SGA A50M	50,000–120,000								

from page 4·170 *(set weight of liquid to 100%)

The gelling agents listed in the tables above refer to Dow brand products. For the names of comparable products made by other manufacturers, see the Hydrocolloid Product Guide on page II at the end of volume 5.

INSTANT TOFU NOODLES ADAPTED FROM WYLIE DUFRESNE

Yields 1.5 kg

INGREDIENT	QUANTITY	SCALING	PROCEDURE
Water	150 g	44%	① Disperse.
Methocel A 15C (Dow brand)	7.5 g	2.2% (1.5%)*	② Bring to boil.
Tofu, firm	340 g	100%	③ Blend into boiling water to form puree.
Salt	to taste		④ Season tofu puree.
Toasted sesame oil	to taste		⑤ Cool to 50 °C / 122 °F.
			⑥ Refrigerate until hydrated, at least 6 h.
			⑦ Transfer to squeeze bottle with tip 5 mm / 3/16 in. in diameter.
			⑧ Set aside.
Hon dashi see page 15	900 g	265%	⑨ Blend dashi with miso.
Aka miso	25 g	7.4%	⑩ Centrifuge at 27,500g for 1 h to make consommé.
Shiro miso	20 g	6%	
Salt	to taste		⑪ Season miso consommé.
			⑫ Bring to boil, and ladle into bowls.
Golden enoki mushrooms, tops only	50 g	15%	⑬ Garnish soup.
Fresh sea lettuce, thick julienne	17 g	5%	⑭ Extrude tofu puree into hot soup to form instant noodles.
Scallions, green parts only, thinly sliced	7 g	2%	

from page 4·172   *(% of total weight of tofu and water)

POTATO BEIGNETS WITH CAVIAR

Yields 700 g (about 25 beignets)

INGREDIENT	QUANTITY	SCALING	PROCEDURE
Baked potato stock see page 19	100 g	80%	① Bring water to boil.
Methocel E4M (Dow brand)	5.5 g	4.4% (0.4%)*	② Shear Methocel into boiling stock.
			③ Simmer for 3 min.
			④ Place pot in ice-water bath, and stir until cold and thickened.
			⑤ Vacuum seal, and refrigerate Methocel mixture for at least 8 h to hydrate.
Baked potato stock see page 19	125 g	100%	⑥ Blend together until smooth.
Cultured buttermilk (stabilizer-free)	125 g	100%	
Eggs	50 g	40%	
Crème fraîche	90 g	72%	
Methocel mixture, from above	45 g	36%	
All-purpose flour	120 g	96%	⑦ Dry-blend, and sift together.
Instant potato flakes (store-bought)	30 g	24%	⑧ Pour wet mixture in, and stir until completely incorporated. Do not overwork the batter.
Salt	5 g	4%	
Baking powder	5 g	4%	
Baking soda	2.5 g	2%	
Clarified butter	20 g	16%	⑨ Drizzle into batter while stirring; mix to distribute evenly.
Neutral oil	as needed		⑩ Roll 30 ml / 2 T portions gently in gloved hands until round and smooth. Do not completely deflate mixture.
			⑪ Drop balls into 190 °C / 375 °F oil until golden brown and slightly puffed, about 3 min.
			⑫ Drain on paper towels.
Caviar (best quality available)	as desired		⑬ Serve with warm beignets.
Crème fraîche	as desired		

from page 4·174   *(% of total weight of all other batter ingredients, excluding Methocel mixture)

GELS

SWEET PEA CLUSTERS INSPIRED BY FERRAN ADRIÀ AND ANDONI LUIS ADURIZ

Yields 375 g (four portions)

INGREDIENT	QUANTITY	SCALING	PROCEDURE
Pea juice (or vegetable stock) see page 41 or page 6	200 g	100%	① Bring juice to boil.
Methocel E4M (Dow brand)	4 g	2%	② Disperse methylcellulose into boiling juice.
			③ Simmer for 3 min.
			④ Refrigerate until hydrated, at least 6 h.
			⑤ Measure 20 g of E4M solution to coat peas.
Sweet peas, shelled	130 g	65%	⑥ Blend xanthan gum into methocel solution.
E4M solution, from above	20 g	10%	⑦ Mix peas with reserved solution; stir to coat peas evenly.
Xanthan gum	0.03 g	0.015%	⑧ Form 16 clusters of 9 g each.
			⑨ Arrange clusters, well separated, on baking sheet lined with plastic wrap, and refrigerate.
Water	1 kg	500%	⑩ To serve, transfer clusters carefully to salted 90 °C / 194 °F bath.
Salt	20 g	10%	⑪ Remove from bath when gel on clusters has fully set, about 1 min.
Ham broth see page 16	200 g	100%	⑫ Bring broth to simmer, and check seasoning.
			⑬ Divide broth equally among four bowls.
			⑭ Place two pea clusters in each bowl.
Walnut oil	20 g	10%	⑮ Season broth.
Mint leaves	8 g	4%	

from page 4·173

MACKEREL WITH SPICY TOMATO SKIN
INSPIRED BY HESTON BLUMENTHAL

Yields 800 g (four portions)

INGREDIENT	QUANTITY	SCALING	PROCEDURE
Water	225 g	100%	① Puree until smooth.
Tomato confit see page 179	150 g	67%	② Pass through fine sieve.
Red bell pepper, roasted and peeled	75 g	33%	
Cayenne pepper	2 g	0.9%	
Salt	to taste		③ Season puree.
160 Bloom gelatin	4.5 g	2% (1%)*	④ Disperse into puree.
			⑤ Heat to 90 °C / 194 °F.
Methocel F50 (Dow brand)	5.7 g	2.5% (1.27%)*	⑥ Blend into hot puree until fully dispersed, and continue blending for 1 min.
			⑦ Vacuum seal, and refrigerate until fully hydrated, at least 6 h.
			⑧ Spread puree on tray lined with plastic wrap to form layer 1 mm / 1/32 in thick.
			⑨ Dehydrate in oven at 110 °C / 230 °F for 15 min.
			⑩ Cool resulting tomato skin to room temperature.
Mackerel fillets, cleaned, pin bones and skin removed	320 g (four fillets)	142%	⑪ Cut tomato skin to match dimensions of each fillet.
			⑫ Press cut tomato skins onto fillets.
Olive oil	40 g	18%	⑬ Vacuum seal fillets individually.
			⑭ Refrigerate until set, at least 30 min.
			⑮ Remove fillets and skins from bags, and vacuum seal again individually with 10 g of olive oil in each bag.
			⑯ Cook fillets sous vide in 46 °C / 115 °F bath to core temperature of 45 °C / 113 °F, about 15 min.
			⑰ Remove fillets from bags.
Bouillabaisse broth see page 17	300 g	133%	⑱ Warm, and adjust seasoning.
Blood orange segments	40 g	18%	⑲ Toss together to make salad.
Fennel, thinly shaved	40 g	18%	⑳ Season salad.
Radish, thinly shaved	20 g	9%	㉑ Place each fillet covered in tomato skin in individual serving dish.
Thai basil leaves	5 g	2%	㉒ Garnish with salad.
Olive oil	to taste		㉓ Pour bouillabaisse broth around fillets at table.
Salt	to taste		

from page 4·175   *(% of total weight of first three ingredients)

FLUID GELS

① Select the temperature and desired viscosity. The table Best Bets for Fluid Gels below lists several options for both hot and cold gels.
② For egg fluid gels, cook eggs. The table suggests cooking times and temperatures.
③ For hydrocolloid fluid gels, scale and mix the gelling agents. The table offers two or more options for each combination of service temperature and viscosity. Quantities in the table are scaled relative to the weight of the principal liquid. For example, to make a thick, hot onion gel, use 0.8 g of low-acyl gellan for every 100 g of onion puree.
④ Disperse the gelling agents into the liquid. A sequestrant may be necessary if using gellan (see page 4·129).
⑤ Hydrate fully. Hydration times and temperatures are indicated in the table. If you use a sequestrant, or if the food has low calcium content, then you may need to add calcium after hydration (see page 4·129).
⑥ Cast the gel, and let it set.
⑦ Puree the gel to the preferred consistency. Additional liquid may be added as needed to thin the gel.
⑧ Sieve the fluid gel to produce a gel having a finer consistency (optional).

VARIATION: QUICK-SETTING A FLUID GEL

① Follow steps 1–5 above.
⑥ Set the gel in a beaker immersed in ice water.
⑦ Puree the gel with a hand blender as the gel sets.

Best Bets for Fluid Gels

Temperature	Viscosity	Gelling agents	(scaling)**	Hydrate or cook (min)	(°C)	(°F)	Note	Example use	See page
cold	thin	160 Bloom gelatin	0.8%	2–5	60	140	stir or sieve before serving; gel will continue to set	thickened consommé, broth	
		egg yolk	250%	35	65	149	select quantity to obtain amount of egg flavor desired	savory crème anglaise, lemon egg yolk sauce	287
			84%	35	69	156			
			25%	35	80	176			
		iota carrageenan	0.1%	3	75	167	higher viscosity with dairy	light cream sauce	
	medium-thick	160 Bloom gelatin	1.5%	2–5	60	140	stir or sieve before serving; gel will continue to heal	passion fruit jelly, coating gel for terrines	287
		egg yolk	150%	35	80	176		mustard sauce for cold cuts, smooth salad dressing	
		whole egg	100%	35	78	172			
		kappa carrageenan	0.4%	3	95	203	higher viscosity with dairy	light pudding	
	thick	160 Bloom gelatin	2.5%	2–5	60	140	stir or sieve before serving; gel will continue to set	vegetable or fruit juice puree, dense pudding	
		whole egg	250%	35	78	172		low-fat mayonnaise, aioli	
		iota carrageenan	0.35%	3	75	167	higher viscosity if used with dairy	traditional pudding	
		kappa carrageenan	0.20%						
hot	thin	agar	0.25%	3	95	203	slightly cloudy	broth	
		low-acyl gellan*	0.1%	3	95	203	acidic liquids may require a sequestrant to hydrate	consommé	
	medium-thick	egg yolk	80%	35	69	156	do not reheat above cooking temperature	rich egg-yolk sauce	
		agar	0.40%	3	95	203		gravy, cream-style sauce	
		xanthan gum	0.15%						
		low-acyl gellan*	0.5%	3	95	203	acidic liquids may require a sequestrant to hydrate	gravy, cream-style sauce	
	thick	agar	0.9%	3	95	203		fluid gel puree	
		xanthan gum	0.2%						
		egg yolk	150%	35	69	156		egg-only mayonnaise	
		low-acyl gellan*	0.8%	3	95	203	acidic liquids may require a sequestrant to hydrate	fizzy grape fluid gel	289

from page 4·177   *(add 0.15% calcium lactate for low calcium solutions; allow 3 h to fully set); **(set weight of liquid to 100%)

PASSION FRUIT BROWN BUTTER FLUID GEL

Yields 450 g

INGREDIENT	QUANTITY	SCALING	PROCEDURE
Passion fruit juice	250 g	100%	① Combine, and bring to boil.
Agar	1.35 g	0.54% (0.45%)*	② Pour liquid into beaker set in ice-water bath.
			③ Blend with immersion blender as gel sets, until cooled and fluid.
			④ Blend into fluid gel.
			⑤ Strain.
Horseradish, grated	7.5 g	3%	⑥ Blend into fluid gel.
			⑦ Adjust to taste.
Brown butter, melted	50 g	20%	⑧ Whisk in.
Malic acid	4.5 g	1.8%	⑨ Season, and refrigerate until use.
Salt	to taste		

from page 5·182   *(% of total weight of all other ingredients)

The earthy aroma of beet comes from a compound called geosmin. We think that it complements the bright acidity and pungency of passion fruit.

HOT AND COLD TEA ADAPTED FROM HESTON BLUMENTHAL

Yields 1.73 kg

INGREDIENT	QUANTITY	SCALING	PROCEDURE
Distilled water	1.8 kg	209%	① Stir together.
Earl Grey tea leaves	40 g	4.6%	② Vacuum seal, and infuse at room temperature for 1 h.
			③ Strain tea through fine sieve, and measure 1.73 kg.
			④ Divide reserved tea into two 865 g portions.
For cold tea:			
Earl Grey tea, from above	860 g	100%	⑤ Dry blend, and whisk into 865 g of reserved tea.
Unrefined caster sugar	80 g	9.3%	⑥ Bring mixture to simmer.
Low-acyl gellan (Kelcogel F, CP Kelco brand)	0.6 g	0.07%	⑦ Blend until completely dissolved.
			⑧ Cool over ice-water bath, and then refrigerate for 24 h.
Sodium citrate	0.6 g	0.07%	⑨ Pass tea mixture through fine sieve.
Malic acid	1 g	0.12%	⑩ Refrigerate until needed.
Calcium chloride	0.25 g	0.03%	
For hot tea:			
Earl Grey tea, from above	860 g	100%	⑪ Follow steps 5–10 above.
Unrefined caster sugar	80 g	9.3%	⑫ Warm fluid gel in 72 °C / 162 °F bath.
Low-acyl gellan (Kelcogel F, CP Kelco brand)	0.6 g	0.07%	⑬ Place tight-fitting vertical dividers down centers of four small glasses, aligning dividers perpendicular to handles.
Sodium citrate	0.6 g	0.07%	⑭ Remove cold tea gel from refrigerator.
Malic acid	3.5 g	0.4%	⑮ Pour hot tea and cold tea gels individually into separate halves of each glass, filling both sections to same height.
Calcium chloride	0.25 g	0.03%	
			⑯ Remove divider, and serve immediately without jostling or tipping. Align dividing lines with lips of drinkers so that they experience hot and cold teas simultaneously.

from page 4·182

PASSION FRUIT JELLY ADAPTED FROM HESTON BLUMENTHAL

Yields 580 g

INGREDIENT	QUANTITY	SCALING	PROCEDURE
Passion fruit puree (Boiron brand)	150 g	40%	① Disperse gelatin in cold water.
Fructose	45 g	12%	② Whisk together puree and fructose.
			③ Warm sweetened puree until fructose is completely dissolved.
160 Bloom gelatin	10.5 g	2.8% (2%)*	④ Add hydrated gelatin to warm puree, and stir together until dissolved.
Fresh oyster juice	375 g	100%	⑤ Whisk into warm liquid mixture.
			⑥ Refrigerate for 1 h to set.
			⑦ Press set gel through sieve to make it fluid.
			⑧ Spoon onto fresh oysters in cleaned shells, and serve immediately.

from page 4·180   *(% of total weight of passion fruit puree and oyster juice)

POPCORN PUDDING ADAPTED FROM WYLIE DUFRESNE

Yields 450 g

INGREDIENT	QUANTITY	SCALING	PROCEDURE
Organic microwavable popcorn	75 g (one bag)	19%	① Microwave popcorn.
Whole milk	2.5 kg	625%	② Blend with popped popcorn.
Freeze-dried corn see page 188 (or store-bought)	200 g	50%	③ Pass corn milk through fine sieve twice; measure 400 g of corn milk.
Corn milk (from above)	400 g	100%	④ Combine corn milk and water.
Water	45 g	11%	⑤ Disperse gums into liquid.
Iota carrageenan (Genuvisco J, CP Kelco brand)	2.7 g	0.68% (0.6%)*	⑥ Bring mixture to boil, and remove from heat.
			⑦ Cool until set.
Kappa carrageenan (Genugel CHP2, CP Kelco brand)	1.8 g	0.45% (0.4%)*	⑧ Blend to fine puree.
			⑨ Pass pudding through fine sieve.
Salt	to taste		⑩ Season.

from page 4·181   *(% of total weight of corn milk and water)

LEMON EGG-YOLK FLUID GEL

Yields 200 g of fluid gel

INGREDIENT	QUANTITY	SCALING	PROCEDURE
Strip steak	one steak		① Vacuum seal, and cook sous vide in 55 °C / 131 °F bath to core temperature of 54 °C / 129 °F, about 40 min.
Egg yolks	120 g	100% (84%)*	② Blend egg yolks, and vacuum seal.
			③ Cook sous vide in 69 °C / 156 °F bath for 35 min. Yolks will solidify.
			④ Remove from bag.
White beef stock see page 6	130 g	108%	⑤ Blend cold stock and lemon juice with yolk mixture until completely fluid.
			⑥ Pass through fine sieve.
Lemon juice	12 g	10%	
Salt	to taste		⑦ Season, and reheat to 60 °C / 140 °F. Keep temperature below 69 °C / 156 °F, otherwise sauce will thicken.

from page 4·180   *(% of total weight of stock and juice)

PARMESAN "POLENTA" INSPIRED BY DAVE ARNOLD AND NILS NORÉN

Yields 400 g

INGREDIENT	QUANTITY	SCALING	PROCEDURE
White chicken stock, see page 11	100 g	100%	① Shear powders into cold stock with immersion blender.
Parmesan water, see page 20	100 g	100%	② Bring mixture to boil.
Corn juice, see page 2·336	100 g	100%	③ Place mixture in pan, and place over ice-cold water bath to set.
Low-acyl gellan (Kelcogel F, CP Kelco brand)	3 g	3% (1%)*	④ Pulse set gel with hand blender—or press through potato ricer—to create an irregular, coarse-grained mixture.
			⑤ Refrigerate until use.
Unsalted butter, cubed	50 g	50%	⑥ To serve, reheat polenta, and whisk in butter until melted.
Parmesan, finely grated	50 g	50%	⑦ Whisk in Parmesan.
Salt	to taste		⑧ Season.

from page 4·181 *(% of total weight of chicken stock and corn juice)

ONION FLUID GEL ADAPTED FROM HESTON BLUMENTHAL

Yields 400 g

INGREDIENT	QUANTITY	SCALING	PROCEDURE
Onions, thinly sliced	250 g	62.5%	① Combine in pot.
Unsalted butter	30 g	7.5%	② Sauté onions until soft and translucent.
Thyme, sprig	1 g	0.25%	
Low-fat milk	200 g	50%	③ Add to cooked onions, and simmer mixture for 5 min.
White chicken stock, see page 6 and page 11	150 g	37.5%	④ Remove from heat, and discard thyme.
Heavy cream	95 g	23.8%	⑤ Blend mixture fully.
			⑥ Press through fine sieve, and reserve 400 g of infused milk.
Salt	to taste		⑦ Season infused milk, and let cool.
Infused onion milk, from above	400 g	100%	⑧ Disperse into cold infused milk.
			⑨ Bring milk to 93 °C / 199 °F, and hold for 3 min to fully hydrate gellan.
Low-acyl gellan (Kelcogel F, CP Kelco brand)	2.7 g	0.68%	⑩ Transfer to container, and cool over ice-water bath.
			⑪ Blend by hand until cold and completely fluid.
			⑫ Pass through fine sieve, and refrigerate.

from page 4·183

CONFIT EGG YOLK PUREE

Yields 110 g

INGREDIENT	QUANTITY	SCALING	PROCEDURE
Egg yolks, blended	100 g	100%	① Vacuum seal.
			② Cook sous vide in 69 °C / 156 °F bath for 45 min.
Champagne vinegar	8 g	8%	③ Puree with egg yolks.
Glucose syrup DE 40	4 g	4%	
Salt	to taste		④ Season puree, and refrigerate until use.

from page 5·148

UMAMI SEASONING FLUID GEL INSPIRED BY GRANT ACHATZ   Yields 625 g

INGREDIENT	QUANTITY	SCALING	PROCEDURE
Brown beef stock or water see page 10	300 g	100%	① Blend liquids, and disperse agar into cold mixture.
Tomato ketchup (Heinz brand)	80 g	26.7%	② Bring mixture to 95 °C / 203 °F, and hold for 3 min to hydrate fully.
Clear honey	60 g	20%	③ Remove from heat, and cast into mold.
Fish sauce	30 g	10%	④ Refrigerate until set, about 5 min.
Sherry vinegar	20 g	6.7%	⑤ Break gel into small pieces for easier blending.
Agar (Texturas brand)	6 g	2%	
Dark soy sauce	150 g	50%	⑥ Puree soy sauce with set gel until very smooth, and pass through fine sieve.
			⑦ Serve as seasoning for grilled mushrooms with shaved jalapeño peppers and avocado.

from page 4·183

FIZZY GRAPE FLUID GEL ADAPTED FROM HESTON BLUMENTHAL   Yields 800 g

INGREDIENT	QUANTITY	SCALING	PROCEDURE
White grape juice	720 g	100%	① Blend in pot.
Low-acyl gellan (Kelcogel F, CP Kelco brand)	6.4 g	0.89% *(0.8%)*	② Heat to 95 °C / 203 °F to fully hydrate, and hold for 3 min.
			③ Remove from heat, and strain through fine sieve.
			④ Cool over ice-water bath, blending continuously, until gel mixture is chilled and completely fluid.
Muscat wine (dry)	80 g	11%	⑤ Add to fluid gel, and blend.
			⑥ Pass through fine sieve, and cool.
Champagne	15 g	2%	⑦ Fold gently into fluid gel, and pour fluid gel into 1 l whipping siphon.
			⑧ Vent head space with one cartridge of carbon dioxide (see page 2·468). Charge with two cartridges of carbon dioxide, and shake siphon vigorously.
			⑨ Refrigerate for at least 2 h to carbonate.

from page 4·183   *(% of total weight of white grape juice, muscat wine, and Champagne)

SPHERIFICATION

① Select a spherification method from the table Best Bets for Spherification below. To gel a liquid that naturally contains calcium, we recommend using reverse spherification, described in the variation below.

② Scale and mix the gelling agents. Weigh the ingredients relative to the amount of liquid you will be gelling. For example, when making cranberry gel spheres, add 2 g of iota carrageenan for every 100 g of cranberry juice.

③ Disperse the gelling solution. Add sequestrants as needed (see page 4·129).

④ Hydrate fully. See the table of hydrocolloid properties on page 4·42 for hydration times and temperatures.

⑤ Vacuum seal (optional), and chill for 2 h. Vacuum sealing removes air from the solution and helps prevent bubbles from altering the shape and texture of the spheres as they form.

⑥ Prepare the setting bath. Stir the setting agent into clean water, and allow 1 h for it to dissolve fully. Optionally, add sugar syrup (up to 22% sugar concentration) or corn syrup to the bath so that its density matches that of the liquid to be gelled. This prevents the droplets from falling to the bottom of the setting bath.

⑦ Introduce drops of gelling solution into the bath. A common technique when making large spheres is to slide tablespoonfuls of gelling fluid gently into the bath water. A peristaltic pump (see page 4·139) can be set up to drip the droplets continuously. If you are making small spheres, use a syringe to dispense the solution. Allow the skin to form for 1–3 min; beads will grow increasingly firm as they soak.

⑧ Rinse the spheres with clear water. Rinsing slows the gelling process and washes away any lingering flavors from the setting solution. Rinse the spheres at least twice. Remove with a perforated spoon. Optionally, heat to 85 °C / 185 °F for 10 min to stop further solidification. Store the spheres in water or oil until needed.

Best Bets for Spherification

Method	For the sphere base	(scaling)*	For the setting bath	(scaling)*	Note	See page
alginate (direct)	sodium alginate	1%	calcium chloride	0.5%	xanthan gum thickens liquid and yields more even orbs	next
	xanthan gum (optional)	0.2%–0.5%				
	sodium alginate	1%	calcium gluconate	2.5%	see note above	
	xanthan gum (optional)	0.2%–0.5%				
alginate (reverse)	calcium lactate	3%	sodium alginate	0.5%	see note above	next
	xanthan gum (optional)	0.2%–0.5%	sodium citrate (optional)	1.2%	use sodium citrate when liquid is acidic or high in calcium	
carrageenan (direct)	iota carrageenan	2%	potassium phosphate	5%	hydrate carrageenan cold for at least 5 h; can also be made reverse	
gellan (direct)	low-acyl gellan	0.2%	calcium gluconate	6%	best made with low acid, moderate calcium liquids; make frozen hemispheres and set in 80 °C / 176 °F calcium bath; can also be made reverse	
	sodium hexametaphosphate	0.1%	lactic acid	0.1%		
LM pectin (reverse)	calcium lactate	5%	LM pectin	2%	can also be made direct	293

from page 4·187   *(set weight of liquid to 100%)*

VARIATION: SUSPENDING A SOLID IN A GELLED SPHERE

① Follow steps 1–6 above. If you are using reverse spherification, see the variation at right.

⑦ Add a solid to the center of the liquid or puree. The solid must be fully encased in the solution; if any part protrudes, an intact membrane will not form around the sphere. Continue with step 7 above for direct spherification, or see at right for reverse spherification.

VARIATION: REVERSE SPHERIFICATION

① In reverse spherification, the edible liquid is mixed with calcium lactate or another salt, and the gelling agent (such as alginate) is dispersed into the bath.

② When the edible liquid enters the bath, a skin of gel forms around it, encapsulating the liquid. Unlike direct spherification, the edible liquid itself does not set, although the skin does grow increasingly firm the longer the bead remains in the bath. Adding xanthan gum to the liquid thickens it and yields smoother spheres. Because the bath contains no salts, it is not necessary to rinse the beads.

CARBONATED MOJITO SPHERES ADAPTED FROM JOSÉ ANDRÉS

Yields 480 g (about 40 spheres)

INGREDIENT	QUANTITY	SCALING	PROCEDURE
Water, distilled	450 g	129%	① Blend until completely dissolved.
Lime juice	120 g	34.5%	
Sugar	120 g	34.5%	
Mint leaves, julienne	80 g	23%	② Blend into juice mixture.
Lime zest, grated	12 g	3.4%	③ Steep, refrigerated, for 1 h.
			④ Strain, and reserve 350 g of juice solution to make spheres. Reserve remainder to store spheres.
Lime juice mixture, from above	350 g	100%	⑤ Blend with reserved juice solution until incorporated.
White rum	130 g	37%	
Calcium lactate	6.7 g	1.9%	
Xanthan gum (Keltrol T, CP Kelco brand)	1.7 g	0.5%	
Ascorbic acid	0.3 g	0.08%	
Sodium alginate (Algin, Texturas brand)	5 g	1.43%	⑥ Blend water and sodium alginate until completely dissolved.
			⑦ Refrigerate bath for 1 h.
Water	1 kg	286%	⑧ Fill two whipping siphons with 100 g each of reserved juice mixture.
			⑨ Fill tablespoon with mixture, tip gently into alginate bath, and release contents.
			⑩ Set for 7 min; skin will form.
			⑪ Remove from bath with perforated spoon, and rinse sphere twice in fresh water.
			⑫ Place sphere gently into whipping siphon containing juice mixture.
			⑬ Repeat procedure with remaining mixture; fill each siphon only half full with spheres.
			⑭ Vent head space with one cartridge of carbon dioxide, and then charge each siphon with two cartridges of carbon dioxide at least 5 h before serving. Refrigerate siphons to carbonate spheres.
Lime zest, finely grated	to taste		⑮ Remove spheres from whipping siphons with perforated spoon, and place in cocktails.
			⑯ Garnish.

from page 4·188

MELON CAVIAR ADAPTED FROM FERRAN ADRIÀ

Yields 250 g

INGREDIENT	QUANTITY	SCALING	PROCEDURE
Sodium alginate (Algin, Texturas brand)	2 g	0.8%	① Combine sodium alginate with 50 g of melon juice.
			② Blend until dissolved.
Melon juice see page 2·336	250 g	100%	③ Mix in remaining melon juice.
			④ Strain.
			⑤ Vacuum seal; remove excess air.
Water	500 g	200%	⑥ Blend calcium chloride in water until dissolved.
Calcium chloride	2.5 g	1%	⑦ Set up three baths: one filled with calcium chloride solution to set spheres, two filled with cold water to rinse spheres.
			⑧ Fill syringes or droplet maker with melon juice mixture.
			⑨ Expel droplets one at a time into calcium chloride bath.
			⑩ Remove each droplet from bath after 1 min.
			⑪ Strain melon caviar.
			⑫ Rinse caviar twice in cold water baths.

from page 4·189

"POACHED" EGG

Yields five "eggs"

INGREDIENT	QUANTITY	SCALING	PROCEDURE
For the setting bath:			
Water	2 kg	333%	① Whisk together.
Sodium alginate (TICA-algin 400 Powder, TIC Gums brand)	10 g	1.7%	② Vacuum seal to remove excess air, and refrigerate for 2 h.
For the egg-yolk base:			
Calcium lactate	4 g	0.7%	③ Sift together.
Sugar	3 g	0.5%	
Salt	2 g	0.3%	
Egg yolks, pasteurized see page 232	150 g	25%	④ Blend into calcium lactate mixture, taking care to incorporate as little air as possible.
Rendered bacon fat	50 g	8.5%	⑤ Dispense with sauce gun into 2 cm / ¾ in hemisphere molds. Freeze.
			⑥ Heat sodium alginate solution until fluid is 60–65 °C / 140–149 °F.
			⑦ Remove from heat, and carefully drop in frozen hemispheres.
			⑧ Leave for 2 min, turn spheres over, and leave for 1 min longer.
			⑨ Fill three bowls with water: heat two to 75–80 °C / 167–176 °F; fill the third with cold water.
			⑩ Transfer spheres with slotted spoon to first bowl of warm water to rinse for 1 min.
			⑪ Rinse spheres again in second bowl of warm water, and reserve in cold water.
For the "cooked" egg-white base:			
Gruyère water see page 20	600 g	100%	⑫ Mix, and bring to boil.
Heavy cream	100 g	16.5%	⑬ Pour into sauce gun, and rest at room temperature until about 60 °C / 140 °F.
Iota carrageenan (Texturas brand)	4.2 g	0.7%	⑭ Dispense "egg" white into one half of plastic eggshell.
			⑮ Place yolk sphere in center of white, and cap with top half of plastic shell.
Locust bean gum (POR/A2 Powder, TIC Gums brand)	0.44 g	0.07%	⑯ Dispense remaining white into sealed shell through drilled hole until overflowing.
			⑰ Chill over ice.

from page 4·195

TOMATO SPHERES WITH BASIL OIL

Yields 300 g (about 12 spheres)

INGREDIENT	QUANTITY	SCALING	PROCEDURE
Tomato water see page 40	250 g	50%	① Blend until homogenized.
			② Press through fine sieve, and reserve refrigerated.
Sodium alginate (Algin, Texturas brand)	2 g	0.4%	
Grapeseed oil	200 g	40%	③ Puree in blender for 3 min.
Basil, blanched and shocked	100 g	20%	④ Press through fine sieve.
			⑤ Decant basil oil, and reserve in syringe.
Water	500 g	100%	⑥ Blend to dissolve completely.
Calcium lactate	2.5 g	0.5%	⑦ Set up four baths: fill one with calcium lactate solution, and fill three with cold water.
			⑧ Fill tablespoon with reserved tomato water solution.
			⑨ Tip spoon into calcium lactate bath to gently release contents.
			⑩ Set in bath until membrane has fully formed around tomato sphere, about 30 s.
			⑪ Inject approximately 3 ml / 0.1 oz of basil oil into submerged sphere.
			⑫ Remove syringe; wait for membrane puncture to heal and sphere to reshape, about 15 s.
			⑬ Remove sphere from bath with perforated spoon.
			⑭ Repeat procedures with remaining tomato water solution and basil oil.
			⑮ Rinse spheres in each of three cold water baths.
			⑯ Refrigerate until needed.

from page 4·192

GRUYÈRE SPHERES ADAPTED FROM WYLIE DUFRESNE   Yields 2 kg (about 24 spheres)

INGREDIENT	QUANTITY	SCALING	PROCEDURE
Gruyère cheese, finely grated	250 g	100%	① Spread on tray lined with silicone mat.
			② Bake in 175 °C / 350 °F oven until golden, about 12 min.
Whole milk	1 kg	400%	③ Blend with cheese until fully incorporated.
Propylene glycol alginate (Protanal Ester BV, FMC BioPolymer brand)	7.5 g	3%	④ Refrigerate overnight.
			⑤ Strain through fine sieve.
Salt	to taste		⑥ Season, and pipe into silicone hemisphere molds 3 cm / 1¼ in. in diameter.
			⑦ Freeze completely, about 2 h.
Water, room temperature	500 g	200%	⑧ Blend until completely dissolved.
LM pectin (Genupectin LM 104 AS, CP Kelco brand)	20 g	8%	⑨ Remove frozen cheese hemispheres from molds, and drop into pectin bath.
			⑩ Soak until coated with pectin, about 1½ min.
Water, room temperature	500 g	200%	⑪ Blend until completely dissolved to make setting bath.
Calcium lactate	2.5 g	1%	⑫ Drop pectin-coated spheres into setting bath.
			⑬ Allow membrane to form, at least 90 s, and then remove from bath; hold in cold water.
Yellow onions, thinly sliced	200 g	80%	⑭ Sauté onions until very tender and deep golden, about 35 min.
Unsalted butter	50 g	20%	⑮ Puree.
Xanthan gum (Keltrol T, CP Kelco brand)	0.8 g	0.32%	⑯ Blend into onion puree.
Salt	to taste		⑰ Season onion puree.
Rye bread, frozen, crusts removed	100 g	40%	⑱ Cut into slices 3 mm / ⅛ in thick with meat slicer.
			⑲ Roll slices through pasta machine to compress.
			⑳ Bake slices at 95 °C / 205 °F between two silicone mats for 45 min.
Oxtail consommé see page 46	500 g	200%	㉑ Combine, and bring to simmer.
			㉒ Season soup.
Salt	to taste		㉓ Drop cheese spheres into soup, and warm through.
Sherry vinegar	to taste		㉔ Serve spheres in hot consommé with rye bread slice smeared with onion puree.
Lemon thyme leaves	10 g	4%	㉕ Garnish.

from page 4·190

CAPER DROPLETS   Yields 100 g

INGREDIENT	QUANTITY	SCALING	PROCEDURE
Capers	90 g	100%	① Blend to fine puree.
White wine vinegar	6 g	6.7%	② Pass through fine sieve.
Caper brine	5 g	5.5%	
Calcium lactate	3 g	3.3% (3%)*	③ Whisk into caper puree.
Water	500 g	555%	④ Disperse alginate in cold water until fully dissolved, to make setting bath.
Sodium alginate (Algin, Texturas brand)	2.5 g	2.8% (0.5%)**	⑤ Fill squeeze bottle with caper puree.
			⑥ Expel droplets into bath, and leave for 30 s.
			⑦ Drain droplets, and rinse in fresh water.
Neutral oil	as needed		⑧ Reserve droplets in oil.

from page 5·159

*(% of total weight of capers, white wine vinegar, and caper brine)
**(% of total weight of water)

MUSSELS IN MUSSEL JUICE SPHERES ADAPTED FROM FERRAN ADRIÀ

Yields 200 g (about 20 spheres)

INGREDIENT	QUANTITY	SCALING	PROCEDURE
Mussel jus see page 34	100 g	100%	① Blend until completely dissolved.
Calcium gluconate	2.5 g	2.5%	② Vacuum seal solution to remove excess air.
Xanthan gum (Texturas brand)	0.5 g	0.5%	③ Refrigerate until needed.
Rock mussels	20 mussels		④ Steam for 3 min until just opened.
			⑤ Shuck.
			⑥ Refrigerate to cool quickly.
Water	1 kg	1,000%	⑦ Blend to dissolve completely.
Sodium alginate (Algin, Texturas brand)	5 g	5%	⑧ Vacuum seal to remove excess air.
			⑨ Set up three baths: fill one with sodium alginate solution, and fill two with cold water.
			⑩ Place one mussel at a time onto spoon 2.5 cm / 1 in. in diameter.
			⑪ Pour 4 g of reserved mussel juice solution onto mussel.
			⑫ Tip spoon carefully into sodium alginate bath to gently release contents.
			⑬ Set in bath until membrane has fully formed, about 5 min.
			⑭ Remove sphere from bath with perforated spoon.
			⑮ Repeat procedure with remaining mussels and mussel juice solution.
			⑯ Rinse spheres in two cold water baths.
Salt	7 g	7%	⑰ Dissolve salt in water to make brine.
Water	400 g	400%	⑱ Immerse mussel spheres in brine.
			⑲ Refrigerate until needed.
			⑳ To serve, warm spheres in 60 °C / 140 °F bath for 3 min.

from page 4·191

LIQUID PIMENTO OLIVE ADAPTED FROM FERRAN ADRIÀ

Yields 480 g

INGREDIENT	QUANTITY	SCALING	PROCEDURE
Extra-virgin olive oil	500 g	100%	① Combine to make aromatic olive oil.
Thyme	20 g	4%	② Reserve for later use.
Orange peel, julienne	15 g	3%	
Green olives, pitted	500 g	100%	③ Blend in food processor to fine paste.
Olive brine, from olives	200 g	40%	④ Press through fine sieve, and reserve 450 g of olive puree.
Calcium lactate	13.5 g	2.7% (3%)*	⑤ Blend by hand with olive puree until completely dissolved.
Xanthan gum (Texturas brand)	1.6 g	0.32% (0.36%)*	⑥ Blend gradually with olive puree.
			⑦ Cast into hemisphere molds.
Piquillo pepper, cut in thin strips (store-bought)	15 g	3%	⑧ Place pepper strip on top, and carefully push into each hemisphere.
			⑨ Freeze.
Sodium alginate (Algin, Texturas brand)	5 g	1%	⑩ Disperse with hand blender, and refrigerate until needed.
			⑪ Before use, blend until sodium alginate is completely incorporated.
Water	1 kg	200%	⑫ Vacuum seal to remove accumulated bubbles.
			⑬ Pour into bowl to make bath for setting olives.
			⑭ Bring bath to simmer.
			⑮ Remove each frozen hemisphere from mold, place on spoon, and tip gently into bath.
			⑯ Set in bath for 3 min. Hemispheres will thaw into spheres, and skin will form.
			⑰ Remove olive sphere from bath with perforated spoon.
			⑱ Rinse sphere twice in cold water.
			⑲ Repeat with remaining olive hemispheres.
			⑳ Store spherified olives, refrigerated, in reserved aromatic olive oil.

from page 4·193

*(% of weight of reserved olive puree)

PROSCIUTTO AND MELON "RAW EGG"

Yields five eggs

INGREDIENT	QUANTITY	SCALING	PROCEDURE
For the setting bath:			
Water	2 kg	400%	① Whisk together.
Sodium alginate (TICA-algin 400 Powder, TIC Gums brand)	10 g	2%	② Vacuum seal to remove excess air, and refrigerate for 2 h.
For the egg-yolk base:			
Sugar	20 g	4%	③ Sift together.
Calcium lactate	9 g	1.8%	
Xanthan gum	2.5 g	0.5%	
Salt	1.7 g	0.3%	
Malic acid	1.1 g	0.2%	
Melon juice	500 g (from about 900 g of melon)	100%	④ Blend juice into calcium lactate mixture, taking care to incorporate as little air as possible. ⑤ Dispense with sauce gun into 2 cm / ¾ in hemisphere molds. ⑥ Freeze. ⑦ Heat sodium alginate solution until fluid is 60–65 °C / 140–149 °F. ⑧ Remove from heat, and carefully drop in frozen hemispheres. ⑨ Leave for 2 min, turn spheres over, and leave for 1 min longer. ⑩ Fill three bowls with water: heat two to 75–80 °C / 167–176 °F; fill third with cold water. ⑪ Transfer spheres with slotted spoon to first bowl of warm water to rinse for 1 min. ⑫ Rinse spheres again in second bowl of warm water, and reserve in cold water.
For the "raw" egg-white base:			
Ham broth, gelatin-clarified see page 14 and page 16	500 g	100%	⑬ Mix, and bring to boil. ⑭ Pour into sauce gun, and rest at room temperature until about 60 °C / 140 °F. ⑮ Dispense "egg" white into one half of plastic eggshell. ⑯ Place yolk sphere in center of white, and cap with other half of plastic shell. ⑰ Dispense remaining white into sealed shell through drilled hole until overflowing. ⑱ Chill over ice.
Xanthan gum	1.25 g	0.25%	
Locust bean gum (POR/A2 Powder, TIC Gums brand)	0.032 g	0.006%	

from page 4·194

DAIRY EMULSIONS

ULTRASTABLE BEURRE BLANC

Yields 220 g

INGREDIENT	QUANTITY	SCALING	PROCEDURE
Water, stock, or heavy cream	100 g	100%	① Dry blend agar and propylene glycol alginate, and disperse in cold liquid.
Agar	0.5 g	0.5%	② Heat to 95 °C / 203 °F. Cool until fully set, about 10 min.
Propylene glycol alginate (Protanal Ester BV 4830, FMC BioPolymer brand)	0.5 g	0.5%	③ Puree to fluid gel. ④ Reserve.
White wine (dry)	100 g	100%	⑤ Reduce until almost syrupy, and strain.
Champagne vinegar	30 g	30%	⑥ Measure 20 g of reduction, and reserve.
Shallots, finely minced	30 g	30%	
Unsalted butter, small cubed	100 g	100%	⑦ Melt butter.
Liquid soy lecithin	1 g	1%	⑧ Whisk into warm butter.
Wine reduction, from above	20 g	20%	⑨ Blend reserved wine reduction with fluid gel.
Salt	to taste		⑩ Slowly pour in warm butter mixture while blending with rotor-stator homogenizer or other high-shear appliance until fully emulsified.
Lemon juice	to taste		⑪ Season, and serve hot with poached lobster (below), or cool and refrigerate.

from page 4·219

POACHED LOBSTER

Yields 300 g

INGREDIENT	QUANTITY	SCALING	PROCEDURE
Lobster tails, shelled	300 g (four tails)	100%	① Vacuum seal, and cook sous vide in 55 °C / 131 °F bath to core temperature of 54 °C / 129 °F, about 25 min.
Beurre blanc, from above	220 g	73%	② Warm beurre blanc in 90 °C / 194 °F bath or in small pot over medium heat.
Salt	to taste		③ Slice and season lobster, and serve with warm beurre blanc.

from page 4·219

BEET FLEXICURD ADAPTED FROM JOHNNY IUZZINI

Yields 900 g

INGREDIENT	QUANTITY	SCALING	PROCEDURE
Isomalt (or sugar)	100 g	25%	① Dry blend.
Salt	11 g	2.75%	
LM Pectin 104 AS (Genu pectin, CP Kelco brand)	8 g	2% (1%)*	
Malic acid	4 g	1%	
Agar (Texturas brand)	3.4 g	0.85% (0.425%)*	
High-acyl gellan (Kelcogel LT 100, CP Kelco brand)	2.6 g	0.65% (0.325%)*	
Kappa carrageenan (Texturas brand)	1 g	0.25% (0.125%)*	
Beet juice see page 2·336	300 g	75%	② Disperse isomalt mixture into cold juice. ③ Heat to 95 °C / 203 °F, and hold at that temperature.
Unsalted butter, melted	100 g	25%	④ Blend slowly into hot mixture until emulsified.
Beet puree, brought to simmer see page 55	400 g	100%	⑤ Add hot puree, and hold at simmer for 1 min. ⑥ Pour mixture into plastic-wrap-lined quarter sheet, and allow to set, about 3 min. ⑦ Cover with plastic wrap, and refrigerate. ⑧ Cut into desired shapes, and serve hot or cold.

from page 4·219   *(% of total weight of final three ingredients)

SEA URCHIN BUTTER

Yields 200 g

INGREDIENT	QUANTITY	SCALING	PROCEDURE
Sake (dry)	200 g	100%	① Combine in pot, and reduce to 150 g, about 10 min.
Vermouth (dry)	150 g	75%	② Strain.
Shallots, finely minced	50 g	25%	
Champagne vinegar	25 g	12.5%	
Tarragon leaves, minced	1 g	0.5%	
Black peppercorns, coarsely ground	0.25 g	0.13%	
Sea urchin tongues	40 g	20%	③ Heat reduction to simmer, and then blend in sea urchin tongues and butter until fully emulsified.
Unsalted butter, cubed	30 g	15%	
Pink grapefruit confit syrup see page 146	30 g	15%	④ Season butter.
Lime juice	to taste		
Salt	to taste		

from page 5·227

OYSTER BUTTER EMULSION

Yields 225 g

INGREDIENT	QUANTITY	SCALING	PROCEDURE
Shallots, finely minced	75 g	150%	① Sweat together until tender, about 10 min.
Clarified unsalted butter see page 4·213	50 g	100%	
Celery, peeled and finely minced	35 g	70%	
Oyster trimmings, from shucked and cleaned oysters	35 g	70%	② Add to shallot mixture. ③ Sweat for 2 min.
White vermouth	200 g	400%	④ Add to shallot mixture.
White fish stock see page 6	150 g	300%	⑤ Simmer until reduced to 150 g.
Oyster juice, see page 5·236	50 g	100%	
Darjeeling tea leaves	7 g	14%	⑥ Steep in reduction for 3 min. ⑦ Strain. ⑧ Cool, and refrigerate until use.
Unsalted butter	50 g	100%	⑨ To serve, warm reduction. Blend in butter and crème fraîche to form emulsion.
Crème fraîche	25 g	50%	
White wine vinegar	5 g	10%	⑩ Season.
Salt	to taste		

from page 5·236

BLACK BUTTER EMULSION

Yields 300 g

INGREDIENT	QUANTITY	SCALING	PROCEDURE
Brown fish stock see page 6	400 g	200%	① Reduce to 200 g.
Fish stock reduction, from above	200 g	100%	② Blend black butter, soy sauce, and ink into reduced stock.
Black butter, warmed see page 4·213	25 g	12.5%	
White soy sauce	20 g	10%	
Squid ink	2.7 g	1.35%	
Unsalted butter, cold	40 g	20%	③ Heat black butter emulsion base to low simmer.
White miso	20 g	10%	④ Blend in butter until fully emulsified, and then blend in miso.
Lemon juice	as needed		⑤ Season with lemon juice.

from page 5·158

BROILED TUNA BELLY WITH MONTPELLIER BUTTER

Yields 850 g of butter, 500 g of tuna with butter (four portions)

INGREDIENT	QUANTITY	SCALING	PROCEDURE
Egg yolks, blended	100 g	22%	① Vacuum seal, and cook sous vide in 67 °C / 153 °F bath for 30 min.
			② Strain through fine sieve.
Unsalted butter, melted	450 g	100%	③ Heat to 65 °C / 150 °F, stirring until flakes have dissolved, and remove from heat.
Mono- and diglycerides (Glice, Texturas brand)	54 g	12%	
160 Bloom gelatin	18 g	4%	④ Hand blend into warm butter mixture.
Sodium caseinate	1.8 g	0.4%	⑤ Blend in cooked egg yolks until smooth.
Garlic chives, pureed see page 55	125 g	28%	⑥ Combine, and fold into butter mixture until all components are evenly distributed.
Garlic confit see page 176	90 g	20%	⑦ Cast onto sheet in one layer 1.5 cm / ⅝ in thick to form Montpellier butter.
			⑧ Freeze, and cut into cubes.
Anchovy paste	30 g	6.7%	
Pickled ramp bulb, brunoise see page 178	25 g	5.5%	
Spinach, pureed see page 55	25 g	5.5%	
Chives, finely minced	15 g	3.3%	
Parsley, finely minced	15 g	3.3%	
Young ginger, finely diced	10 g	2.2%	
Salt	9 g	2%	
Lemon zest	2.5 g	0.6%	
Cayenne pepper	2 g	0.4%	
Lime juice	2 g	0.4%	
Black pepper	1.2 g	0.3%	
Star anise, finely ground	0.7 g	0.2%	
Tuna belly, sliced 5 mm / ¼ in thick	400 g	89%	⑨ Arrange five slices of tuna on each of four ovenproof plates.
			⑩ Dot with cubes of Montpellier butter, and place under broiler for 1 min until butter is melted, surface is golden, and fish is just warmed through.
Salt	to taste		⑪ Season.

The great advantage of this recipe is that it allows the butter to stay emulsified when hot. So when it melts into a fluid, it doesn't break into an oily slick the way that traditional compound butters do.

from page 4·220

BLOOD PUDDING CUSTARD   ADAPTED FROM HESTON BLUMENTHAL

Yields 450 g

INGREDIENT	QUANTITY	SCALING	PROCEDURE
Star anise	1.3 g	0.19%	① Combine.
Dried ginger	0.5 g	0.07%	② Toast on baking tray at 150 °C / 300 °F until fragrant, about 10 min.
Cinnamon stick	0.3 g	0.04%	③ Cool.
Sichuan peppercorns	0.3 g	0.04%	④ Crush lightly.
Cardamom seeds, black	0.15 g	0.02%	⑤ Place spice blend on cheesecloth.
			⑥ Bundle, and tie cloth at top to form sachet.
Heavy cream, stabilized with hydrocolloids (or processed at ultrahigh temperature)	690 g	100%	⑦ Heat to 70 °C / 160 °F.
			⑧ Add spice sachet.
			⑨ Refrigerate to cool.
			⑩ Discard sachet once infused cream is fully cooled.
Fresh pig's blood	160 g	23%	⑪ Combine with infused cream.
			⑫ Transfer to Thermomix fitted with butterfly whisk attachment or to beaker set on magnetic heating plate with overhead paddle-stirring attachment.
			⑬ Cook in 70 °C / 160 °F Thermomix or beaker just until pudding has thickened to custard, about 4 h. Emulsion will split if over-reduced.
Salt	8 g	1.2%	⑭ Season.
Sugar	5 g	0.7%	⑮ Vacuum seal.
			⑯ Refrigerate until needed.
			⑰ To serve, reheat sous vide in 60 °C / 140 °F bath.

from page 4·221

CONSTRUCTED CHEESES

① Combine the liquids and other ingredients (except cheese and milk powder), and bring to a simmer.

② Gradually whisk in the cheese. Also add milk powder, if called for. Whisk and melt until the cheese is completely incorporated.

③ Simmer for 2 min. This step is crucial in forming a smooth emulsion rather than a grainy, broken liquid.

④ Puree with an immersion blender until very smooth and silky. Do not puree fondue; the stringy strands are usually considered desirable.

⑤ Check pH. A target final pH is listed in the table. If the emulsion is not stable, and the pH reading is higher than listed, it may be necessary to add more emulsifying salts (sodium citrate or one of the phosphates).

⑥ Season the cheese with salt, and serve warm. Or pour it into a lightly oiled mold, and chill for later use.

⑦ Refrigerate. Cover the cheese surface tightly to prevent a skin from forming.

Best Bets for Constructed Cheeses

Recipe	Liquid	(scaling)	Other ingredients	(scaling)	Cheese	(scaling)	Final pH	Note
fondue (hot cheese dip)	water	80%	sodium citrate	4.4%	Gruyère or young Fontina, grated	100%	5.8	keep hot when serving; thickens slightly if reheated
	Fino sherry or dry white wine	40%	Joha SDS2 sodium phosphate (Fibrisol brand)	1.2%				
			lambda carrageenan	0.5%				
thin cheese spread, hot or cold	water	100%	sodium citrate	2.0%	Swiss cheese, grated	100%	5.9	very silky texture; very good either hot or cold
			whey protein concentrate	1.0%				
			Joha SDS2 sodium phosphate (Fibrisol brand)	1.2%				
thick cheese sauce/spread, hot or cold	water	100%	sodium citrate	2.0%	Swiss cheese, grated	100%	6.1	best choice for use in macaroni and cheese, and cheese omelet
			whey protein concentrate	1.0%				
cheese soup, hot	water	160%	sodium citrate	5.2%	Gruyère	100%	6.1	good pairings: beer and cheddar; dry Riesling and Gouda; port and Stilton
			whey protein concentrate	1.3%				
cheeseburger cheese slice	water	67%	sodium citrate	6.7%	Emmental, grated	100%	6.0	cast into mold quickly after combining, or mixture will set
	wheat ale	50%	iota carrageenan	3.0%	Comté, grated	90%		
			kappa carrageenan	1.0%				
cheese slice for baking (raclette analogue)	water	32%	sodium citrate	2.0%	Gruyère, grated	100%	5.8	best cut into slices and baked until melted
			disodium phosphate (BK Giulini brand)	0.8%	skim milk powder	4%		

from page 4·223

CONSTRUCTED VEAL CREAM

Yields 360 g

INGREDIENT	QUANTITY	SCALING	PROCEDURE
Tapioca starch	11.2 g	4.5%	① Combine to make emulsifying blend.
Salt	6 g	2.4%	
Whey protein isolate	6 g	2.4%	
Iota carrageenan	1 g	0.4%	
Acetic acid	0.5 g	0.2%	
Polysorbate 80	0.4 g	0.16%	
Xanthan gum	0.16 g	0.064%	
White veal stock, cold see page 6	250 g	100%	② Add emulsifying blend to stock, and homogenize thoroughly.
			③ Warm mixture to 85 °C / 185 °F, and reserve at same temperature.
Rendered veal marrow	80 g	32%	④ Warm fat to 85 °C / 185 °F.
			⑤ Drizzle into hot stock mixture while blending until fully emulsified.
			⑥ Serve with blanquette de veau in place of traditional cream sauce.

from page 5·33

THE AMERICAN CHEESE SLICE

Yields 635 g

INGREDIENT	QUANTITY	SCALING	PROCEDURE
Water	230 g	115%	① Mix dry ingredients, and disperse into water.
Salt	5 g	2.5%	② Bring to simmer to hydrate.
Sodium citrate	14 g	7% (2.3%)*	
Iota carrageenan (Texturas brand)	6 g	3% (0.98%)*	
Kappa carrageenan (Texturas brand)	2 g	1% (0.33%)*	
Swiss cheese, grated	200 g	100%	③ Add cheese gradually to simmering water mixture, blending constantly with hand blender.
White cheddar, grated	180 g	90%	
			④ Continue blending until texture is fluid and smooth.
			⑤ Pour cheese mixture into greased cylindrical mold 7 cm / 2¾ in. in diameter and at least 18 cm / 7 in long. Complete the transfer very quickly.
			⑥ Refrigerate for at least 2 h to set.
			⑦ Remove cheese from mold, and slice to desired thickness.
			⑧ Store refrigerated between sheets of plastic wrap or wax paper.

from page 4·224   *(% of total combined weight of water and cheeses)

CHEESE IN A TUBE

Yields 215 g

INGREDIENT	QUANTITY	SCALING	PROCEDURE
Sodium citrate	2 g	2%	① Combine, and bring to simmer.
Whey protein concentrate	1 g	1%	
Sodium phosphate (Joha SDS2, Fibrisol brand)	1.2 g	1.2%	
Water	100 g	100%	
Aged Gouda, finely grated	50 g	50%	② Gradually whisk cheese into hot liquid until fully incorporated. Simmer for 2 min.
Monterey jack, finely grated	50 g	50%	③ Puree with hand blender until smooth.
Jalapeño, finely minced	10 g	10%	④ Fold into warm cheese mixture.
Cayenne pepper powder	2 g	2%	
Salt	to taste		⑤ Adjust seasoning.
			⑥ Transfer to squeeze bottle, and pipe into unused empty paint tubes. Reserve chilled.

from page 4·225

CHEESY WHIP

Yields 480 g

INGREDIENT	QUANTITY	SCALING	PROCEDURE
Sodium citrate	4 g	2%	① Dry blend powders.
Whey protein concentrate	2 g	1%	
Sodium phosphate (Joha SDS2, Fibrisol brand)	2.4 g	1.2%	
Water	200 g	100%	② Disperse powder mixture in cold water, and bring to simmer.
Gruyère, finely grated	200 g	100%	③ Gradually whisk cheese into hot liquid until fully incorporated. Simmer for 2 min.
			④ Puree with hand blender until completely smooth.
Whole milk	80 g	40%	⑤ Blend into cheese mixture. Cool completely.
Salt	to taste		⑥ Season generously to compensate for aeration, and pour into 1 l whipping siphon.
			⑦ Charge with two cartridges of nitrous oxide.
			⑧ Shake vigorously, and dispense to serve.

from page 4·225

CHEDDAR SOUP

Yields 300 g

INGREDIENT	QUANTITY	SCALING	PROCEDURE
Brown butter see page 4·213	20 g	20%	① Melt butter in pot, and add shallots, garlic, and bay leaf.
			② Cook over medium heat until translucent, about 7 min.
Garlic cloves, thinly sliced	15 g	15%	
Shallots, thinly sliced	100 g	100%	
Wheat beer (Hefeweizen-style)	160 g	160%	③ Deglaze pot with beer, and reduce until pan is dry.
Sodium citrate	5 g	5%	④ Dissolve sodium citrate and whey protein in water, and add to pot.
Whey protein concentrate	1.3 g	1.3%	⑤ Bring to simmer.
Distilled water	160 g	160%	
Aged cheddar, finely grated	100 g	100%	⑥ Gradually whisk into simmering liquid until completely incorporated.
			⑦ Puree with hand blender until smooth. Pass through fine sieve.
Salt	to taste		⑧ Season and serve, or chill over ice and refrigerate until use.

from page 4·225

EMULSIONS

EGG EMULSIONS

RÉMOULADE SAUCE

Yields 200 g

INGREDIENT	QUANTITY	SCALING	PROCEDURE
Mayonnaise store-bought or see page 303	90 g	100%	① Combine. ② Refrigerate.
Lemon juice	55 g	60%	
Whole-grain mustard	31 g	35%	
Dijon mustard	17 g	20%	
Garlic clove, crushed	4 g	4.5%	
Green bird's eye chili (fresh), minced	3.5 g	4%	
Worcestershire sauce	2.5 g	2.5%	
Hot sauce	2 g	2%	
Hungarian sweet paprika	0.5 g	0.5%	
Celery, peeled and finely minced	30 g	35%	③ Fold into mayonnaise mixture just before serving.
Flat-leaf parsley, minced	4 g	4.5%	
Celery leaf, minced	2 g	2%	
Chives, minced	2 g	2%	
Black pepper, coarsely crushed	0.5 g	0.5%	
Salt	to taste		④ Season rémoulade.

from page 5·75

WHITE COLESLAW

Yields 300 g

INGREDIENT	QUANTITY	SCALING	PROCEDURE
Buttermilk	60 g	40%	① Blend thoroughly to make dressing; use rotor-stator homogenizer, if available, for richer texture.
Grapeseed oil	29 g	19%	
White balsamic vinegar	20 g	13.5%	
Egg yolk, cooked sous vide, at 65 °C / 149 °F for 35 min	19 g	12.5%	
Rendered bacon fat	9 g	6%	
Dijon mustard	7 g	5%	
Sugar	3 g	2%	② Season dressing, and reserve.
Salt	to taste		
Savoy cabbage, fine julienne	150 g	100%	③ Toss cabbage in salt. ④ Let soften for 1 min.
Salt	1 g	0.5%	⑤ Toss with dressing.
Green apple, small dice	120 g	80%	⑥ Arrange on coleslaw, and serve immediately.
Horseradish root, finely grated	2 g	1.5%	
Celery seeds, lightly toasted	1.5 g	1%	

from page 5·72

SEA URCHIN TARTAR SAUCE

Yields 300 g

INGREDIENT	QUANTITY	SCALING	PROCEDURE
Eggs (shelled)	60 g	71%	① Vacuum seal.
			② Cook sous vide in 65 °C / 149 °F bath for 30 min.
			③ Chill in ice-water bath.
			④ Peel.
Lime juice	7 g	8.5%	⑤ Blend with cooked eggs.
Dijon mustard	5 g	6%	
Grapeseed oil	85 g	100%	⑥ Drizzle into egg mixture while blending, until fully emulsified.
			⑦ Reserve.
Sea urchin tongues	75 g	88%	⑧ Pass through fine sieve.
			⑨ Blend into egg emulsion.
Cornichons, finely minced	28 g	33%	⑩ Fold into sauce.
Scallions, finely minced	20 g	24%	
Garlic chives, fine brunoise	7.5 g	9%	
Parsley, finely minced	7 g	8.5%	
Chervil, finely minced	4.7 g	5.5%	
Tarragon, finely minced	1.8 g	2%	
Salt	1.5 g	2%	⑪ Season sauce.
Black pepper	0.5 g	0.6%	⑫ Refrigerate until use.
Cayenne pepper	0.3 g	0.4%	

from page 5·145

BASIC MAYONNAISE

Yields 470 g

INGREDIENT	QUANTITY	SCALING	PROCEDURE
Egg yolks, blended	45 g	15%	① Vacuum seal, and cook sous vide in 67 °C / 153 °F bath for 30 min.
Water	75 g	25%	② Whisk together, and puree with cooked egg yolks until smooth.
Dijon mustard	21 g	7%	
Xanthan gum (Keltrol T, CP Kelco brand)	0.7 g	0.23% (0.15%)*	
Grapeseed oil	300 g	100%	③ Drizzle slowly into egg mixture while blending until mixture is fully emulsified.
Lemon juice	15 g	5%	④ Season.
White wine vinegar	10 g	3.3%	⑤ Refrigerate.
Salt	to taste		

from page 4·226 *(% of total combined weight of all other ingredients)*

HOT EGG MAYONNAISE ADAPTED FROM FERRAN ADRIÀ

Yields 490 g

INGREDIENT	QUANTITY	SCALING	PROCEDURE
Whole eggs	130 g	65%	① Blend until smooth.
Egg yolks	60 g	30%	② Vacuum seal, and cook in 65 °C / 149 °F bath for 35 min.
Dijon mustard	35 g	17.5%	
Sunflower oil (or other neutral oil)	200 g	100%	③ Combine.
			④ Blend with warm egg mixture until emulsified.
Extra-virgin olive oil	50 g	25%	
Salt	to taste		⑤ Season.
Sherry vinegar	to taste		⑥ Pour contents into 1 l whipping siphon, and charge with one cartridge of nitrous oxide.
			⑦ Hold filled siphon in 62 °C / 144 °F bath until ready to serve.
			⑧ Dispense mayonnaise from siphon, and serve with grilled asparagus or poached fish.

from page 4·227

SOFT-BOILED EGG AND GARLIC EMULSION INSPIRED BY MICHEL BRAS

Yields 400 g

INGREDIENT	QUANTITY	SCALING	PROCEDURE
Garlic confit, pressure cooked see page 176	30 g	30%	① Puree until smooth.
			② Pass through fine sieve.
White wine vinegar	25 g	25%	
Whole eggs	100 g (about two large)	100%	③ Vacuum seal, and cook sous vide in 67 °C / 153 °F bath for 35 min.
			④ Blend with garlic puree until smooth.
Grapeseed oil	100 g	100%	⑤ Drizzle in slowly while blending into egg-garlic mixture until fully emulsified.
Olive oil	100 g	100%	
Walnut oil	50 g	50%	
Salt	to taste		⑥ Season.
Green onions, very thinly sliced	30 g	30%	⑦ Fold in, and refrigerate.

from page 4·227

SOUS VIDE LEMON CURD

Yields 850 g

INGREDIENT	QUANTITY	SCALING	PROCEDURE
Egg yolks	120 g	30%	① Vacuum seal, and cook in 65 °C / 149 °F bath for 35 min.
			② Cool and reserve.
Sugar	300 g	75%	③ Bring to boil to dissolve sugar and acid.
Water	120 g	30%	④ Cool to room temperature.
Citric acid	8 g	2%	
Unsalted butter, room temperature	400 g	100%	⑤ Blend butter with egg yolks and sugar syrup until smooth.
			⑥ Add more essential oil to taste. Other oils besides lemon may be used.
Lemon essential oil (optional)	1 g	0.25%	⑦ Vacuum seal.
Salt	0.4 g	0.1%	⑧ Refrigerate until firm, 4–24 h.

from page 4·227

BACON JAM

Yields 375 g

INGREDIENT	QUANTITY	SCALING	PROCEDURE
Isomalt	50 g	50%	① Combine, and heat to 90 °C / 195 °F until fully dissolved.
Sugar	40 g	40%	② Cool and reserve.
Water	30 g	30%	
Maple syrup (Grade B)	30 g	30%	
Egg yolks	75 g	75%	③ Vacuum seal, and cook in 66 °C / 151 °F bath for 30 min.
			④ Strain through fine sieve.
			⑤ Blend into cooled syrup.
Rendered bacon fat, warm	100 g	100%	⑥ Drizzle slowly into egg syrup while blending constantly until fully emulsified.
			⑦ Refrigerate.
Bacon strips, finely diced	120 g	120%	⑧ Fry or bake in 175 °C / 350 °F oven until crisp, about 25 min.
			⑨ Drain on absorbent paper towels. Cool, and store in dry, cool place.
Salt	to taste		⑩ Season jam with salt.
Liquid caramel coloring (optional)	as needed		⑪ Add coloring to achieve desired shade.
			⑫ Fold in 50 g of bacon bits, and serve with warm biscuits (see page 5·77).
			⑬ If mixture has been refrigerated, it should be tempered for about 20 min before use.

from page 4·229

DEEP-FRIED HOLLANDAISE ADAPTED FROM WYLIE DUFRESNE

Yields 1.2 kg (40 pieces)

INGREDIENT	QUANTITY	SCALING	PROCEDURE
Unsalted butter, melted	640 g	640%	① Soften gelatin leaves in cold water.
160 Bloom gelatin sheet	60 g	60%	② Drain, and dissolve gelatin in butter.
			③ Reserve warm.
Low-acyl gellan (Kelcogel F, CP Kelco brand)	3.5 g	3.5%	④ Dry blend.
Sodium hexametaphosphate	2 g	2%	
Citric acid	0.6 g	0.6%	
Water	170 g	170%	⑤ Add blended powders to pot of water.
			⑥ Bring to boil, and remove from heat.
			⑦ Pour into container.
			⑧ Refrigerate until set, about 5 min.
Egg yolks, blended	100 g	100%	⑨ Puree gel with yolks until fluid, and reserve.
Water	110 g	110%	⑩ Whisk to combine.
Ultra-Sperse M (National Starch brand)	10 g	10%	⑪ Blend into yolk gel mixture until smooth.
			⑫ Drizzle in reserved warm butter while continuously blending to make hollandaise.
Lemon juice	to taste		⑬ Season hollandaise.
Salt	to taste		⑭ Cast into mold 2.5 cm / 1 in thick.
			⑮ Refrigerate until set, about 1 h.
			⑯ Cut set gel into cubes.
All-purpose wheat flour	100 g	100%	⑰ Dredge cubes evenly in flour, and shake off excess.
Eggs, blended	100 g	100%	⑱ Coat cubes evenly with blended eggs.
English muffins, dried and ground into powder	200 g (four muffins)	200%	⑲ Roll cubes in bread crumbs. Shake off any excess. Repeat breading procedure once.
			⑳ Freeze for 30 min to harden crusts.
Frying oil	as needed		㉑ Deep-fry cubes in 190 °C / 375 °F oil until golden, about 1½ min.
			㉒ Drain on paper towels.

from page 4·228

SOUS VIDE INSTANT HOLLANDAISE INSPIRED BY DANIEL HUMM

Yields 345 g

INGREDIENT	QUANTITY	SCALING	PROCEDURE
White wine (dry)	100 g	133%	① Combine.
Shallots, finely minced	50 g	67%	② Reduce to syrup-like consistency.
White vinegar	35 g	47%	③ Strain.
			④ Measure 20 g of wine reduction.
Egg yolks	75 g (four large)	100% (28%)*	⑤ Blend thoroughly with wine reduction.
			⑥ Vacuum seal.
Stock or water	20 g	27%	⑦ Cook in 65 °C / 149 °F bath for 30 min.
Unsalted butter, melted	225 g	300%	⑧ Remove cooked egg yolk mixture from bag, and blend in butter mixture until fully emulsified.
Salt	4 g	5.3%	⑨ Season.
Malic acid	1 g	1.3%	⑩ Transfer to 1 l siphon.
			⑪ Charge with two cartridges of nitrous oxide, and shake vigorously.
			⑫ Hold siphon in 60 °C / 140 °F bath.
Two-stage fried egg see page 2	four eggs		⑬ Garnish eggs with hollandaise.

from page 4·228

*(% of total weight of wine reduction, stock, and unsalted butter)

If you choose to use stock rather than water, consider the ingredient for which the hollandaise is being prepared: use fish stock for fish, poultry stock for poultry, and so on. For stock recipes, see page 2·296.

Alternatively, the hollandaise base can be cooked sous vide in a 63 °C / 145 °F bath to produce a lighter foam, or in a slightly warmer 67 °C / 153 °F bath for a denser foam.

OTHER EMULSIONS

BLACK OLIVE PUREE ADAPTED FROM FERRAN ADRIÀ

Yields 100 g

INGREDIENT	QUANTITY	SCALING	PROCEDURE
160 Bloom gelatin sheet	2 g	4%	① Soften gelatin in cold water.
			② Drain, and set aside.
Black olive juice	50 g (from 150 g pitted Kalamata olives)	100%	③ Heat 10 g of olive juice.
			④ Melt softened gelatin in warm juice.
			⑤ Add remaining 40 g of juice, and mix.
Sucrose esters (Sucro, Texturas brand)	0.5 g	1%	⑥ Blend into juice mixture.
			⑦ Set aside.
Olive oil	50 g	100%	⑧ Warm oil to 65 °C / 149 °F.
Mono- and diglycerides (Glice, Texturas brand)	0.5 g	1%	⑨ Dissolve Glice flakes in oil.
			⑩ Add oil mixture slowly to juice until it emulsifies and forms puree.
			⑪ Refrigerate puree until thickened, about 2 h.

from page 4·230

THICKENED OIL ADAPTED FROM FERRAN ADRIÀ

Yields 100 g

INGREDIENT	QUANTITY	SCALING	PROCEDURE
Extra-virgin olive oil (or other oil)	100 g	100%	① Heat to 65 °C / 149 °F in saucepan.
Mono- and diglycerides (Glice, Texturas brand)	7 g	7%	② Add, and stir to dissolve.
			③ Cool oil to room temperature.
			④ Transfer to bowl held in ice-water bath.
			⑤ Whisk until cold, opaque, and thickened to consistency of mayonnaise.
			⑥ Serve as spread, or use as garnish.
			⑦ Thickened oil can also be transferred to 1 l whipping siphon, charged with two cartridges of nitrous oxide, and dispensed to form thick oil foam.

from page 4·230

INVINCIBLE VINAIGRETTE

Yields 325 g

INGREDIENT	QUANTITY	SCALING	PROCEDURE
Champagne vinegar	80 g	80%	① Combine, and heat to 60 °C / 140 °F.
Quince vinegar	35 g	35%	② Blend over heat until ingredients are completely incorporated.
Pear juice	20 g	20%	
Dijon mustard	5 g	5%	
Propylene glycol alginate (Protanal Ester BV 4830, FMC BioPolymer brand)	0.98 g	0.98% (0.3%)*	
Extra-virgin olive oil	100 g	100%	③ Combine oils.
Pistachio oil	55 g	55%	④ Drizzle slowly into vinegar mixture while blending; process until emulsified.
Walnut oil	30 g	30%	
Liquid soy lecithin (NOW brand)	1.85 g	1.85% (1%)**	
Salt	to taste		⑤ Season.

from page 4·231   *(% of total weight of all ingredients); **(% of total weight of oils)

Use the above recipe as a template for any basic vinaigrette. Different oils and acids can be used to create a variety of effects. The vinaigrette is completely heat stable, so it can be made with animal fats or dairy fat for use in warm salads, eggs, and cooked meats.

For a low-fat version of this vinaigrette, replace 100 g of oil with 100 g of flavorful liquid, 1 g of Ultra-Sperse 5, and 0.2 g of xanthan gum. The overall flavor will be more acidic, so the liquid used should be quite flavorful or the quantity of vinegar used should be reduced.

SPOT PRAWNS WITH FOIE GRAS NAGE INSPIRED BY THIERRY RAUTUREAU   Yields 1.2 kg (four portions)

INGREDIENT	QUANTITY	SCALING	PROCEDURE
Brown vegetable stock see page 6	250 g	100%	① Dry blend propylene glycol alginate and salt.
Salt	3 g	1.2%	② Disperse powder blend into cold stock.
Propylene glycol alginate (Protanal Ester BV 4830, FMC BioPolymer brand)	0.2 g	0.08%	③ Heat to 60 °C / 140 °F to hydrate.
Raw foie gras, cubed	40 g	16%	④ Blend with warm stock until fully emulsified.
White miso paste	15 g	6%	
Chervil, chopped	8 g	3.2%	⑤ Add, and steep nage for 1 min.
			⑥ Strain.
Lime juice	to taste		⑦ Season nage, and reserve warm.
Salt	to taste		
Spot prawns	12 prawns (about 720 g)	about 290%	⑧ Steam in combi oven at 60 °C / 140 °F and 100% relative humidity for 12 min; or vacuum seal, and cook in 60 °C / 140 °F bath for 12 min.
Fresh lychees, peeled and seeded (or canned)	60 g	24%	⑨ Divide prawns among four bowls.
			⑩ Garnish.
Pink Lady apples, peeled and finely shaved with mandoline	60 g	24%	⑪ Pour warm nage around each portion.
Peanuts, roasted and crushed	10 g	4%	
Anise hyssop, small leaves	3 g	1.2%	

from page 4·233

EGGLESS CITRUS CURD INSPIRED BY PASCAL BARBOT   Yields 600 g

INGREDIENT	QUANTITY	SCALING	PROCEDURE
Lemons, washed, whole	300 g	230%	① Vacuum seal in retort pouch, or place in large Mason jar.
			② Place pouch or jar in pressure cooker filled with 2.5 cm / 1 in of water.
			③ Pressure-cook for 30 min at gauge pressure of 1 bar / 15 psi, and cool.
			④ Remove lemons from pouch or jar, and puree.
			⑤ Pass through fine sieve, and measure 130 g of puree.
Lemon puree, from above	130 g	100%	⑥ Mix together, and reserve.
Grapefruit juice	100 g	77%	
Lime juice	60 g	46%	
Lemon juice	50 g	38%	
Lemon zest, finely grated	14 g	11%	
Grapefruit zest, finely grated	6 g	4.6%	
Lime zest, finely grated	2 g	1.5%	
Water	130 g	100%	⑦ Combine, and boil for 3 min.
Honey	35 g	27%	⑧ Stir in citrus puree.
Sugar	30 g	23%	⑨ Bring mixture to simmer.
Propylene glycol alginate (Protanal Ester BV 4830, FMC BioPolymer brand)	5 g	3.8%	
Salt	5 g	3.8%	
Unsalted butter, cubed	200 g	154%	⑩ Blend or whisk butter cubes into hot citrus mixture in small batches until fully emulsified.
			⑪ Strain through fine sieve, and refrigerate for at least 3 h.

from page 4·234

MUSTARD VINAIGRETTE

Yields 700 g

INGREDIENT	QUANTITY	SCALING	PROCEDURE
Sous vide vegetable stock (or other flavorful liquid) see page 13	300 g	100%	① Whisk together.
Sherry vinegar	60 g	20%	
Polysorbate 80	1.5 g	0.5%	② Combine.
Xanthan gum	1.5 g	0.5%	③ Disperse in stock mixture, and blend until fully hydrated.
Extra-virgin olive oil	150 g	50%	④ Slowly blend into stock mixture until emulsified.
Walnut oil	130 g	43%	
Grain mustard	60 g	20%	⑤ Fold in.
Black peppercorns, finely crushed	to taste		⑥ Season.
Salt	to taste		

from page 4·231

SAUCE VIN JAUNE

Yields 200 g

INGREDIENT	QUANTITY	SCALING*	PROCEDURE
Chicken legs and wings, from above, cut into 3 cm / 1¼ in pieces	400 g	200%	① Sauté chicken pieces in pressure cooker until golden. ② Drain and reserve.
Clarified unsalted butter	75 g	37.5%	
Leeks, whites only, thinly sliced	100 g	50%	③ Cook together until vegetables are tender, about 30 min.
Carrot, peeled and thinly sliced	50 g	25%	
Chicken carcass, chopped and blanched	50 g	25%	
Shallot, thinly sliced	50 g	25%	
Brown chicken stock see page 6	450 g	225%	④ Combine with browned wings and cooked vegetable mixture in pressure cooker. ⑤ Cook at gauge pressure of 1 bar / 15 psi for 1½ h.
Thyme	5 g	2.5%	⑥ Cool.
Bay leaf	2 g	1%	⑦ Strain stock through fine sieve, and reserve.
Vin jaune du Jura (or Fino sherry)	120 g	60%	⑧ Reduce to 30 g, about 12 min. ⑨ Add reserved stock. ⑩ Reduce mixture to 200 g. ⑪ Cool.
Chicken stock reduction, from above	200 g	100%	⑫ Disperse PGA into stock reduction. ⑬ Bring to simmer to fully hydrate.
Propylene glycol alginate (Protanal Ester BV4830, FMC Biopolymer brand)	0.4 g	0.2%	⑭ Blend chicken fat into stock reduction until fully emulsified.
Rendered chicken fat	40 g	20%	
Lemon juice	to taste		⑮ Season and serve, or cool and refrigerate until use.
Salt	to taste		

from page 5·116 *(% of total weight of stock reduction)

EGGLESS MAYONNAISE

Yields 400 g

INGREDIENT	QUANTITY	SCALING	PROCEDURE
Water	200 g	100%	① Disperse agar in water.
Agar (Texturas brand)	1.2 g	0.6%	② Bring to boil, and hold for 1 min to fully hydrate.
			③ Cool completely until set, about 5 min.
Sucrose esters (Sucro, Texturas brand)	2 g	1%	④ Puree with set gel until smooth.
Olive oil	200 g	100%	⑤ Dissolve Glice flakes in oil heated to 50 °C / 122 °F.
Mono- and diglycerides (Glice, Texturas brand)	2 g	1%	⑥ Gradually blend oil into cold agar mixture until emulsified.
			⑦ Cool at room temperature.
Salt	to taste		⑧ Refrigerate for 2 h before serving.

from page 4·232

SPICE MIX EMULSION

Yields 250 g

INGREDIENT	QUANTITY	SCALING	PROCEDURE
Unsalted butter	24 g	20%	① Prepare ingredients as noted.
Garlic, finely minced	12 g	10%	② Sauté together over medium heat until fragrant.
Ginger, finely minced	6 g	5%	
Anchovy fillets, finely minced	5 g	4%	
Mussel juice see page 37	120 g	100%	③ Deglaze pan, and reduce mixture to 100 g.
Manzanilla sherry	48 g	40%	
Xanthan gum	0.2 g	0.17% (0.15%)*	④ Blend into reduction.
Extra virgin olive oil	30 g	25%	⑤ Blend into reduction until emulsified.
Fish spice mix see page 51	20 g	17%	⑥ Season emulsion, and serve or refrigerate until use.
Champagne vinegar	to taste		

from page 5·155   *(% of total weight of mussel–sherry reduction and olive oil)

OLIVE OIL "MARGARINE"

Yields 420 g

INGREDIENT	QUANTITY	SCALING	PROCEDURE
Water	80 g	31%	① Dry blend agar and propylene glycol alginate.
Propylene glycol alginate (Protanal Ester BV 4830, FMC BioPolymer brand)	1.85 g	0.7% (0.44%)*	② Disperse powder mixture into cold water.
			③ Bring mixture to boil to hydrate.
			④ Cool at room temperature until set.
Agar (Texturas brand)	1 g	0.4% (0.24%)*	⑤ Puree gel until smooth to form fluid gel.
Pregelatinized starch paste see page 200	80 g	31%	⑥ Blend into fluid gel.
Olive oil	260 g	100%	⑦ Warm to 30 °C / 85 °F.
			⑧ Blend oil gradually into fluid gel slowly until emulsified.
Salt	to taste		⑨ Season and chill.

from page 4·235   *(% of total weight of other ingredients)

EMULSIONS

CONSTRUCTED CREAMS

PISTACHIO GELATO
Yields 1.1 kg

INGREDIENT	QUANTITY	SCALING	PROCEDURE
Water	680 g	100%	① Blend until smooth.
Pistachio butter see page 54	210 g	30.9%	
Sugar	155 g	22.8%	
Pistachio oil	102 g	15%	
Salt	7 g	1%	
Locust bean gum (POR/A2 Powder, TIC Gums brand)	3 g	0.44%	② Dry blend, and disperse in pistachio mixture.
			③ Warm to 60 °C / 140 °F.
Lambda carrageenan (Texturas brand)	2 g	0.3%	④ Homogenize until very smooth, and cool.
			⑤ Season with more salt, if desired.
Polysorbate 80	0.8 g	0.12%	⑥ Churn, and reserve in freezer; or freeze in Pacojet container, and pacotize to serve.
Glycerol monostearate	0.15 g	0.02%	

If using a Pacojet in step 6, omit the locust bean gum.

from page 4·236

HAZELNUT "CREAM"
Yields 350 g

INGREDIENT	QUANTITY	SCALING	PROCEDURE
Water	250 g	100%	① Dry blend hydrocolloids other than polysorbate.
Tapioca starch	11.2 g	4.48%	② Disperse in cold water, and blend in polysorbate.
Whey protein isolate	6 g	2.4%	③ Homogenize thoroughly with commercial blender or rotor-stator homogenizer, if available.
Polysorbate 80	0.4 g	0.16%	
Xanthan gum (Keltrol T, CP Kelco brand)	0.16 g	0.06%	④ Warm to 85 °C / 185 °F, and hold mixture at that temperature.
Roasted-hazelnut oil see page 41 (or store-bought)	80 g	32%	⑤ Warm oil to 85 °C / 185 °F.
			⑥ Drizzle into mixture while shearing at full speed until fully emulsified, and then cool.
Salt	to taste		⑦ Season cream, and vacuum seal.
			⑧ Store refrigerated; serve hot or cold.

from page 4·236

JUS GRAS
Yields 280 g

INGREDIENT	QUANTITY	SCALING	PROCEDURE
Shallots, minced	80 g	40%	① Sauté shallots until golden, about 5 min.
Neutral oil	20 g	10%	
Fino sherry	100 g	50%	② Add to pan of sautéed shallots.
White port (dry)	50 g	25%	③ Reduce mixture to glaze.
Brown chicken stock see page 6	450 g	225%	④ Combine with glaze in pot.
			⑤ Reduce until syrupy, to about one-third of original weight.
Sous vide chicken juice see page 34	200 g	100%	⑥ Strain, and measure 200 g of reduced jus base.
Reduced jus base, from above	200 g	100%	⑦ Disperse emulsifiers into reduced jus base.
Propylene glycol alginate (Protanal Ester BV 4830, FMC BioPolymer brand)	0.6 g	0.3%	⑧ Warm to hydrate PGA, and blend in commercial blender or rotor-stator homogenizer until very smooth.
Liquid soy lecithin (NOW brand)	0.4 g	0.2%	
Xanthan gum (Keltrol T, CP Kelco brand)	0.4 g	0.2%	
Rendered chicken fat, or butter, melted see page 3·145	80 g	40%	⑨ Drizzle slowly into warm jus, blending constantly until fully emulsified.
Salt	to taste		⑩ Season and serve. Or cool, vacuum seal, and refrigerate until use.
Lemon juice	to taste		

from page 4·237

NANOEMULSIONS

CHILLED CHICKEN-NOODLE SOUP

Yields 1.2 kg (four portions)

INGREDIENT	QUANTITY	SCALING	PROCEDURE
Chicken thigh meat, ground	600 g	200%	① Puree until smooth.
White chicken stock see page 6 and page 11	300 g	100%	② Pass through fine sieve.
			③ Divide into 100 g portions.
Salt	10 g	3.3%	④ Vacuum seal each portion separately, and roll evenly into layer 1.5 mm / $\frac{1}{16}$ in thick.
Activa RM	8 g	2.7%	⑤ Cook sous vide in 62 °C / 144 °F bath for 12 min.
Sodium tripolyphosphate (Nutrifos 088, ICL Performance Products brand)	0.15 g	0.05%	⑥ Refrigerate sheets for 3 h. ⑦ Remove from sous vide bags, and cut chilled sheets into noodles 3 mm / $\frac{1}{8}$ in thick, yielding about 100 g per portion. Reserve.
Gum arabic	30 g	10%	⑧ Homogenize until smooth.
Bay essential oil	15 g	5%	
Thyme essential oil	15 g	5%	
Consommé madrilène see page 42	300 g	100%	⑩ Blend 1.2 g of gum-oil mixture into cold consommé. Liquid will remain clear.
Salt	to taste		⑪ Season consommé.
Tarragon leaves (small)	to taste		⑫ Divide noodles among four bowls, forming nest in each.
Thyme leaves	to taste		⑬ Pour consommé over noodles. Garnish chilled soup with leaves.

from page 4·238

GINGER COLA

Yields 340 g

INGREDIENT	QUANTITY	SCALING	PROCEDURE
Distilled water, cold	200 g	100%	① Combine, and steep at room temperature for 20 min.
Ginger, peeled and grated	35 g	17.5%	
			② Strain, and reserve 125 g of ginger water.
Ginger, thinly sliced and blanched three times in boiling water to remove bitterness	300 g	150%	③ Combine, and simmer until sugar is dissolved. ④ Remove from heat, and steep at room temperature for 20 min.
Distilled water	200 g	100%	⑤ Cool completely, and reserve 200 g of ginger syrup.
Sugar	120 g	60%	
Gum arabic	20 g	10%	⑥ Blend to form smooth essential oil base.
Brominated vegetable oil	5 g	2.5%	
Lemon essential oil	5 g	2.5%	
Sweet orange essential oil	5 g	2.5%	
Vanilla extract	2.5 g	1.25%	
Ginger syrup, from above	200 g	100%	⑦ Blend together until combined.
Ginger water, from above	125 g	62.5%	⑧ Pour mixture into soda siphon.
Lime juice	16.5 g	8.25 g	⑨ Vent with one cartridge of carbon dioxide, and then charge with two cartridges.
Liquid caramel color	1.25 g	0.62%	
Essential oil base, from above	0.33 g	0.16% *(0.1%)**	⑩ Refrigerate siphon on ice for at least 3 h before serving.

from page 4·239

*(% of total weight of ginger water and ginger syrup)

Other sodas can be made in a similar way by using a nanoemulsion with essential oils. Stock or an infusion can be used in place of the water.

"OpenCola" is a commercial drink with a published recipe (available on the Internet) said to be inspired by Coca-Cola. You can use that recipe with the techniques described here to make your own cola or to experiment with other ingredients. Ferran Adrià, Marc Veyrat, Jean-Georges Vongerichten, and a number of other chefs have featured homemade sodas in their restaurants.

FROTHS, AIRS, AND BUBBLES

① Select a texture, and choose your foaming agents. See the table below for our recommendations.

② Combine the foaming agents and the liquid. Many flavorful liquids, including fruit juices and vinegars, foam well. The proportions given are relative to the weight of the liquid (for example, whip in 1.25 g of soy lecithin for every 100 g of apple juice to make a dry, coarse apple air).

③ Process, using the tool suggested in the table, until the desired texture appears. All foams are heat stable unless otherwise noted.

Best Bets for Airs, Bubbles, and Froths

Texture	Foaming agents	(scaling)*	Equipment	Notes	Example	See page
dry, coarse airs	de-oiled soy lecithin powder	1.25%	handheld milk whipper	drain for 4 min	mignonette air	next
	Sucro (Texturas brand)	1.2%	electric whisk		milk foams	
	160 Bloom gelatin	2%	electric whisk	disperse cold, then heat for 10 min at 40 °C / 104 °F	dairy foams	
	Activa RM	1%				
wet, coarse bubbles	glucose syrup DE 40	10%	fish tank bubbler	use liquids with a pH of at least 4.5	honey bubbles	314
	albumin powder	2%				
	xanthan gum	0.1%				
wet, coarse froths	de-oiled soy lecithin	1%	hand blender	allow liquid to drain for 2 min before serving	citrus air	below
	xanthan gum	0.2%				
	glucose syrup DE 40	8%	handheld milk whipper	light sweetness from glucose	fruit and vegetable juice foams	
	de-oiled soy lecithin powder	0.7%				
	butter, melted	10%–20%	hand blender		foamy butter sauce	
	Sucro (Texturas brand)	1.2%				
	whey protein isolate	2%	handheld milk whipper	heat-stable up to 85 °C / 185 °F	foamy broths, light soups	
	sodium caseinate	0.5%				
	sodium caseinate	1%	handheld milk whipper	heat-stable up to 85 °C / 185 °F	light, beer-like foams	
	de-oiled soy lecithin	1%				
	Sucro (Texturas brand)	1.2%	handheld milk whipper	heat-stable up to 85 °C / 185 °F	latte style foams, light milk shake foams	315
	whey protein isolate	1%				

from page 4·264   *(set weight of liquid to 100%)

CITRUS AIR INSPIRED BY MARC VEYRAT

Yields 80 g

INGREDIENT	QUANTITY	SCALING	PROCEDURE
Lime juice	120 g	100%	① Combine and blend until sugar, lecithin, and xanthan are dissolved.
Lemon juice	80 g	67%	
Sugar	8 g	6.7%	② Whip with handheld foaming wand or hand blender until sufficient foam is formed.
Salt	2 g	1.7%	
De-oiled soy lecithin powder (Lecite, Texturas brand)	2 g	1.7% (1%)*	③ Allow to drain for 2 min for foam to stabilize.
Xanthan gum (Keltrol T, CP Kelco brand)	0.4 g	0.3% (0.2%)*	

from page 4·265   *(% of total weight of lime and lemon juices)

Marc Veyrat found that increasing the viscosity of lecithin foams prevents them from losing so much water and therefore gives them a better final texture and appearance. This can be done either with a hydrocolloid thickener such as xanthan gum or with dissolved solids such as sugar.

OYSTERS WITH MIGNONETTE AIR INSPIRED BY FERRAN ADRIÀ Yields 100 g

INGREDIENT	QUANTITY	SCALING	PROCEDURE
Water	200 g	50%	① Blend.
Sherry vinegar	150 g	37.5%	② Refrigerate for 1 h to macerate.
Seaweed vinegar *see page 23*	50 g	12.5%	③ Strain, yielding 400 g of vinegar mixture.
Shallots, thinly sliced	50 g	12.5%	
White balsamic vinegar	50 g	12.5%	
Black pepper, coarsely ground	5 g	1.25%	
Salt	to taste		
Vinegar mixture, from above	400 g	100%	④ Blend until lecithin powder is fully dissolved.
De-oiled soy lecithin powder (Lecite, Texturas brand)	5 g	1.25%	⑤ Whip with hand blender or handheld whipping wand until thick and coarse foam forms.
			⑥ Allow foam to drain for 2 min to stabilize.
Kumamoto oysters	four oysters		⑦ Garnish with foam.

from page 4·265

Soy lecithin-based "airs" are considered dry foams because most of the water that is used to create the foam drains away very quickly. Once the water drains away, there is very little left but a coarse matrix of bubbles. These types of foams should always be made with very intense flavors for their impact to be more than simply aesthetic.

PARSLEY FOAM Yields 265 g

INGREDIENT	QUANTITY	SCALING	PROCEDURE
Parsley juice	265 g (from about 500 g parsley)	100%	① Blend together until powder is thoroughly incorporated.
Deoiled soy lecithin powder	4 g	1.5%	
Salt	1 g	0.4%	② Season juice.
			③ Foam juice with immersion blender or handheld wand mixer (see page 4·252 for step by step).

from page 5·231

KANPACHI SASHIMI WITH CITRUS FOAM INSPIRED BY QUIQUE DACOSTA Yields 320 g (four portions)

INGREDIENT	QUANTITY	SCALING	PROCEDURE
White fish stock *see page 6*	500 g	100%	① Combine.
Lemongrass, finely chopped	30 g	6%	② Heat stock to 60 °C / 140 °F, and hold for 12 min.
Lemon verbena (fresh)	7 g	1.4%	③ Strain infused stock into open container.
Makrud (kaffir) lime leaves	5 g	1%	④ Cool completely.
Lemon zest	3.5 g	0.7%	
White peppercorns, crushed	0.75 g	0.15%	
Sucrose esters (Sucro, Texturas brand)	1.5 g	0.3%	⑤ Blend into cold, infused stock.
Salt	to taste		⑥ Season stock generously.
Lemon juice	to taste		⑦ Foam citrus-seasoned stock with fish tank bubbler.
Kanpachi (raw), thinly sliced	200 g	40%	⑧ Arrange fish on center of four plates, 50 g on each plate.
Kumquats, thinly sliced	40 g	8%	⑨ Garnish.
Mint leaves, torn	4 g	0.8%	
Sous vide ponzu *see page 22*	50 g	10%	⑩ Pour around fish.
			⑪ Garnish each portion with citrus foam.

from page 4·269

GEODUCK WITH SEAWATER FOAM

Yields 300 g

INGREDIENT	QUANTITY	SCALING	PROCEDURE
Geoduck juice, reserved from shucking	200 g	100%	① Blend with hand blender until powders are fully incorporated.
Water	50 g	25%	② Whip with handheld whipping wand until stiff seawater foam forms at liquid's surface.
White soy sauce	35 g	17.5%	
Sodium caseinate	2.5 g	1.25% (1%)*	
Deoiled soy lecithin powder (Texturas brand)	2.5 g	1.25% (1%)*	
Geoduck siphon, cleaned, peeled, and trimmed see page 5·200	200 g	25%	③ Slice thinly.
			④ Divide equally, and arrange on center of each plate.
Ficoïde glaciale (ice plant)	40 g	5%	⑤ Garnish.
Pickled ramps, thinly sliced see page 178	40 g	5%	⑥ Spoon some seawater foam on top of each portion.

from page 4·266   *(% of total weight of water and geoduck juice)

EDIBLE SOAP BAR WITH HONEY BUBBLES ADAPTED FROM ANDONI LUIS ADURIZ

Yields 400 g

INGREDIENT	QUANTITY	SCALING	PROCEDURE
Water	1 kg	100%	① Blend fully with hand blender.
Wildflower honey	150 g	15%	② Strain.
Albumin powder	20 g	2%	③ Vacuum seal to remove accumulated bubbles.
Xanthan gum (Keltrol T, CP Kelco brand)	1 g	0.1%	④ Refrigerate honey bubble base.
Salt	0.5 g	0.05%	
All-purpose flour, sifted	110 g	11%	⑤ Arrange in thin, even layer on baking sheet.
			⑥ Bake at 170 °C / 340 °F until golden brown, about 20 min.
Hazelnut flour	40 g	4%	⑦ Combine, and whisk into warm, browned all-purpose flour.
Sugar	30 g	3%	
Salt	3 g	0.3%	
Rendered ham fat, melted	40 g	4%	⑧ Combine.
Cocoa butter, melted	30 g	3%	⑨ Fold into flour mixture.
Olive oil	30 g	3%	⑩ Pour into small rectangular silicone molds that resemble bars of soap.
			⑪ Freeze "soap" bars completely, about 30 min.
			⑫ To serve, transfer honey bubble base to open container.
			⑬ Place aquarium bubbler tube at bottom of container.
			⑭ Turn on bubbler, and leave until desired amount of bubbles have accumulated, about 5 min.
			⑮ Arrange soap bar in center of each plate, and garnish with bubbles.

from page 4·267

SAFFRON HONEY FOAM

Yields 150 g

INGREDIENT	QUANTITY	SCALING	PROCEDURE
Water, warm	100 g	100%	① Combine.
Saffron threads	0.4 g	0.4%	② Infuse for 10 min at room temperature.
Honey	36 g	36%	③ Combine with saffron water.
Deoiled soy lecithin powder	1.4 g	1.4%	④ Blend until completely incorporated.
Whey protein isolate	0.2 g	0.2%	
Salt	to taste		⑤ Season generously to compensate for aeration.
			⑥ Whip with handheld whipping wand until abundant foam forms on surface.
			⑦ Allow to drain for 1 min before using.

from page 5·94

LYCHEE AND LIME SODA

INSPIRED BY SANG-HOON DEGEIMBRE

Yields 200 g (four servings)

INGREDIENT	QUANTITY	SCALING	PROCEDURE
Lychee juice, clarified	200 g	500%	① Season lychee juice.
Fructose	to taste		② Reserve refrigerated.
Malic acid	to taste		
Dextrose	40 g	100%	③ Combine to form lime base.
Baking soda	15 g	37.5%	④ Grind into fine powder with mortar and pestle.
Citric acid	15 g	37.5%	
Lime essential oil	0.05 g	0.1%	
Water	7 g	17.5%	⑤ Add slowly to lime base, incorporating small amount at a time; make sure mixture does not foam.
			⑥ Pack into circular molds (2.5 cm / 1 in. in diameter and 2.5 mm / 1 in high). This will produce 3 g tablets. Store in cool, dry place.
Lime tablets, from above	four tablets		⑦ To serve, pour 50 g of lychee juice into each of four serving glasses.
			⑧ Add one lime tablet to each glass; tablet fizzes as it dissolves.
			⑨ Allow to dissolve completely before consuming soda.

You can use store-bought lychee juice if you wish, but we prefer fresh. For methods of clarifying fresh fruit juice, see page 2·351.

This dish makes tablets reminiscent of Alka-Seltzer, which produces a fizzy drink when dissolved in water.

from page 4·268

TOMATO VINEGAR FOAM

Yields 125 g

INGREDIENT	QUANTITY	SCALING	PROCEDURE
Tomato water see page 40	1 kg	100%	① Reduce to 125 g.
White wine vinegar	150 g	15%	② Add to reduced tomato water.
Salt	2.5 g	0.25%	③ Cool.
Saffron threads	1 g	0.1%	④ Vacuum seal.
			⑤ Refrigerate for 12 h to infuse.
Whey protein isolate	2 g	0.2%	⑥ Whisk into infused tomato water until dissolved.
Deoiled soy lecithin	1 g	0.1%	⑦ Heat mixture to 35 °C / 95 °F.
			⑧ Whip mixture with handheld wand mixer until thick foam forms.
			⑨ Allow foam to drain for 1 min before using.

from page 5·65

CAPPUCCINO FOAM INSPIRED BY FERRAN ADRIÀ

Yields 100 g

INGREDIENT	QUANTITY	SCALING	PROCEDURE
2% milk	500 g	125%	① Combine.
Coffee beans, coarsely crushed	100 g	25%	② Vacuum seal.
			③ Refrigerate for 12 h to infuse.
Sugar	40 g	10%	④ Strain coffee milk, discarding coffee beans and cardamom seeds, and measure 350 g for recipe.
Glucose syrup DE 40	10 g	2.5%	
Black cardamom seeds	1 g	0.25%	
Infused milk, from above	400 g	100%	⑤ Dry blend powders, and disperse in infused milk.
Sucrose esters (Sucro, Texturas brand)	4.8 g	1.2%	⑥ Place in beaker of milk shake whipper; process until very frothy.
Whey protein isolate	4 g	1%	

from page 4·266

LIGHT FOAMS

① Select the recipe that matches the temperature and bubble size you want.
② Measure the ingredients carefully, and combine the foaming agents with the liquid. Set the weight of the liquid to 100%. For example, to make a hot, coarse foam, add 0.35 g of xanthan gum and 0.20 g of guar gum for every 100 g of liquid.
③ Hydrate, using the temperature and time given. This is not required for cold-soluble foaming agents.
④ Chill or heat the liquid to serving temperature.
⑤ To serve, aerate the mixture with a whisk or mixer. Alternatively, pour the liquid into a 1 l whipping siphon, pressurize by using the number of nitrous oxide cartridges suggested in the table, and dispense.

Best Bets for Light Foams

Serving temperature	Bubble size	Foaming agents	(scaling)*	Hydrate (°C)	(°F)	(min)	Foaming method	Nitrous oxide charges	Example	See page
cold	fine	160 Bloom gelatin	1%	60	140	5	siphon	2	blood orange foam	next
		160 Bloom gelatin	0.90%	60	140	5	siphon	2–3	corn foam	318
		xanthan gum	0.27%							
		albumin powder	10%	cold			electric whisk or siphon	3	light coating foam	
	coarse	xanthan gum	0.7%	cold			siphon	3	lemon verbena and peach froth	318
		xanthan gum	0.20%	95	203	3	siphon	2	cava foam	327
		agar**	0.25%							
hot and cold	fine	low-acyl gellan**	0.3%	95	203	3	siphon	2	eggless sabayon, warm, beer-like foam	
		agar**	0.4%	95	203	3	siphon	2		
		egg yolk**	29.0%	70	158	30	siphon	3	bergamot sabayon	319
		Maltrin M100	5.5%							
	coarse	xanthan gum	0.25%	cold			siphon	3	dairy-free milk shake	
		guar gum	0.15%							

from page 4·270   *(set weight of liquid to 100%); **(make fluid gel before filling siphon)

HORCHATA FOAM

Yields 200 g

INGREDIENT	QUANTITY	SCALING	PROCEDURE
Chufa nuts	450 g	225%	① Cover nuts with water.
			② Soak in refrigerator for 12 h.
			③ Drain.
Water	250 g	125%	④ Combine with soaked nuts.
Sugar	16 g	8%	⑤ Blend to smooth, fine texture.
			⑥ Pass through fine sieve to extract chufa milk.
			⑦ Vacuum seal, and refrigerate until cold.
Chufa milk, cold, from above	200 g	100%	⑧ Disperse soy lecithin and whey protein isolates in milk.
			⑨ Blend thoroughly.
Deoiled soy lecithin	6 g	3%	
Whey protein isolate	1.4 g	0.7%	
Salt	as needed		⑩ Season chufa milk.
			⑪ Vacuum seal, and refrigerate until use.
			⑫ To serve, foam horchata with handheld foaming wand or immersion blender until thick foam layer forms.

from page 5·244

WHIPPED CHEESE INSPIRED BY ALEX STUPAK

Yields 500 g

INGREDIENT	QUANTITY	SCALING	PROCEDURE
Gruyère water see page 20	500 g	100%	① Season cheese water.
Salt	to taste		② Reserve.
Maltrin M100 (GPC brand)	20 g	4%	③ Dry blend powders.
Iota carrageenan (Genuvisco J, CP Kelco brand)	1.25 g	0.25%	
Lambda carrageenan (Texturas brand)	0.75 g	0.15%	
Cheese-infused milk, from above	500 g	100%	④ Disperse powder mixture in cold milk.
			⑤ Bring to simmer, and remove from heat.
			⑥ While still warm, pour into standing mixer, and whip at high speed until stiff foam forms and becomes cold.
			⑦ Spoon into piping bag, and pipe to order.

Alex Stupak aerates a carrageenan fluid gel as it is setting. This process is quite versatile and can be adapted to make various aerated textures that are not dependent on a whipping siphon.

from page 4·272

BLOOD ORANGE FOAM ADAPTED FROM FERRAN ADRIÀ

Yields 250 g

INGREDIENT	QUANTITY	SCALING	PROCEDURE
160 Bloom gelatin	2.5 g	1%	① Disperse into 50 g of cold juice and heat until gelatin is fully dissolved.
Blood orange juice	250 g	100%	② Combine with remaining cold juice. Strain.
			③ Transfer to siphon, and charge with one nitrous oxide cartridge.
			④ Refrigerate siphon for at least 2 h before use.

This basic formula can be used for any cold foam.

from page 4·272

MILK FOAM

Yields 500 g

INGREDIENT	QUANTITY	SCALING	PROCEDURE
Skim milk	500 g	100%	① Vacuum seal together.
Leeks, whites only, thinly sliced	75 g	15%	② Cook sous vide in 85 °C / 185 °F bath for 1 h.
Button mushrooms, gills and skin removed, thinly sliced	50 g	10%	③ Strain.
			④ Reserve hot.
Turnip, peeled and thinly sliced	35 g	7%	
Sweet onions, thinly sliced	25 g	5%	
Garlic, thinly sliced	7 g	1.5%	
Thyme	0.75 g	0.15%	
Sucrose esters (Sucro, Texturas brand)	3.5 g	0.7%	⑤ Blend together.
			⑥ Shear into strained hot milk mixture.
Methocel F50 (Dow brand)	1.75 g	0.35%	⑦ Cool, and vacuum seal.
			⑧ Refrigerate milk foam for 12 h to hydrate.
			⑨ Warm infused milk to room temperature, and foam with handheld milk frother until abundant amount of foam forms on surface of milk, about 2 min. Allow to drain for 1 min, and then use as garnish.

from page 5·33

LEMON VERBENA AND PEACH FROTH ADAPTED FROM QUIQUE DACOSTA

Yields 700 g

INGREDIENT	QUANTITY	SCALING	PROCEDURE
Water	800 g	114%	① Combine.
Dried peaches	200 g	28.5%	② Bring to boil.
			③ Cool to 60 °C / 140 °F, and hold.
Lemon verbena (fresh)	50 g	7%	④ Add.
			⑤ Cover, and steep at 60 °C / 140 °F for 3 min.
			⑥ Strain through fine sieve, measuring 700 g of peach infusion.
			⑦ Cool completely.
Peach infusion, from above	700 g	100%	⑧ Blend until mixture thickens.
			⑨ Transfer to 1 l whipping siphon, and charge with three cartridges of nitrous oxide.
Xanthan gum (Keltrol T, CP Kelco brand)	5 g	0.7%	⑩ Shake vigorously, and dispense in desired amounts.
Seasonal herbs and blossoms	as needed		⑪ Garnish.

from page 4·273

CORN FOAM ADAPTED FROM FERRAN ADRIÀ

Yields 150 g

INGREDIENT	QUANTITY	SCALING	PROCEDURE
Corn juice	110 g (from 250 g corn kernels)	100%	① Combine xanthan gum with 55 g of corn juice.
Xanthan gum (Keltrol T, CP Kelco brand)	0.4 g	0.4% (0.27%)*	
160 Bloom gelatin	1 g	0.9% (0.7%)*	② Disperse gelatin into remaining 55 g of corn juice.
			③ Heat until fully dissolved.
Heavy cream	40 g	36%	④ Combine cream with corn juice and gelatin mixtures.
			⑤ Strain.
Salt	to taste		⑥ Season corn cream.
			⑦ Transfer to 1 l whipping siphon, and charge with one cartridge of nitrous oxide.
			⑧ Refrigerate for at least 3 h before use.

from page 4·273

*(% of total weight of other ingredients)

BLOOD ORANGE SABAYON

Yields 350 g

The spray-dried blood orange juice can be purchased from Obipektin, or see page 2·443 for a recipe.

INGREDIENT	QUANTITY	SCALING	PROCEDURE
Shallots, finely minced	75 g	29%	① Sweat until tender, about 7 min.
Clarified unsalted butter	50 g	19%	
White wine (dry)	450 g	173%	② Add to shallots, and reduce to 120 g.
White wine vinegar	20 g	7.7%	③ Reserve.
Blood orange juice	260 g	100%	④ Reduce orange juice to 30 g.
Unsalted butter, melted	62 g	24%	⑤ Combine with shallot and orange juice reductions to make sabayon base.
Egg yolk, cooked in 69 °C / 156 °F bath for 35 min	48 g	18.5%	⑥ Transfer to 1 l whipping siphon.
Spray-dried blood orange juice	40 g	15%	⑦ Warm sabayon-filled siphon in 65 °C / 150 °F bath for at least 20 min.
Heavy cream	38 g	14.6%	⑧ Charge siphon with two nitrous oxide cartridges.
Lemon juice	15 g	5.8%	⑨ Shake vigorously and dispense to serve.
Salt	4 g	1.5%	
Xanthan gum	0.2 g	0.08% (0.06%)*	

from page 5·148

*(% of total weight of shallot and orange juice reductions and other base ingredients)

SOUS VIDE SOLE WITH BERGAMOT SABAYON

Yields 900 g (four portions)

INGREDIENT	QUANTITY	SCALING	PROCEDURE
Vermouth (dry)	100 g	40%	① Combine.
Champagne vinegar	50 g	20%	② Reduce to syrup.
Shallots, finely minced	50 g	20%	③ Strain, discarding shallot bits.
			④ Measure 25 g of wine reduction, and set aside.
Egg yolks, blended	208 g	83.2% (65%)*	⑤ Cook sous vide in 70 °C / 158 °F bath for 35 min, and reserve.
Cream sherry	30 g	12%	⑥ Vacuum seal together.
Fino sherry	25 g	10%	⑦ Infuse in 85 °C / 185 °F bath for 6 min.
Earl Grey tea leaves	7.5 g	3%	⑧ Strain, reserving tea infusion.
White fish stock see page 6	250 g	100%	⑨ Combine.
			⑩ Blend with cooked egg yolks until smooth to make sabayon base.
Tea infusion, from above	45 g	18%	
Wine reduction, from above	25 g	10%	
Maltrin M100 (GPC brand)	15 g	6%	
Bergamot essential oil	0.1 g	0.04%	⑪ Season sabayon base generously.
Cayenne pepper	to taste		⑫ Transfer to 1 l whipping siphon, and charge with two cartridges of nitrous oxide.
Lemon juice	to taste		⑬ Hold filled siphon in 62 °C / 144 °F bath to reserve.
Salt	to taste		
Black mussels, live	250 g (24 small)	100%	⑭ Vacuum seal in one even layer.
			⑮ Submerge in boiling water for 3 min.
			⑯ Shock in ice water, and remove from bag.
			⑰ Shuck, reserving juices in bag and shells.
			⑱ Strain juice over shucked mussels.
			⑲ Refrigerate mussels.
Rex sole, skin removed	four whole (small)	varies	⑳ Vacuum seal each sole individually with 10 g of butter.
			㉑ Cook sole packets sous vide in 47 °C / 117 °F bath to core temperature of 46 °C / 115 °F, about 30 min.
Clarified unsalted butter see page 4·213	40 g	16%	
			㉒ Remove from packets, and place one fish on each serving plate.
			㉓ Warm mussels in small pot.
Salt	to taste		㉔ Season sole.
			㉕ Garnish with sabayon and mussels.
Bergamot (fresh)	one whole		㉖ Grate zest finely over sole to finish. Serve with crispy potatoes or potato puree.

from page 4·274   *(% of total weight of stock, tea infusion, and wine reduction)

COCONUT-LOBSTER EMULSION

Yields 600 g

INGREDIENT	QUANTITY	SCALING	PROCEDURE
Spiced shellfish stock see page 9	600 g	100%	① Reduce to 90 g.
			② Cool.
Coconut cream powder (store-bought)	25 g	4.2%	③ Whisk into reduced stock.
White soy sauce	to taste		④ Season stock.
Locust bean gum (TIC Gums brand)	0.86 g	0.15% (0.75%)*	⑤ Disperse into cold stock.
			⑥ Bring to boil to hydrate, and remove from heat.
Whey protein isolate	2.3 g	0.4% (2%)*	⑦ Whisk into stock until dissolved.
			⑧ Foam coconut-lobster emulsion with steam wand of espresso machine (see page 4·390), or heat while whipping with handheld milk frother until dense, wet foam forms.

from page 5·187   *(% of total weight of shellfish stock reduction and coconut cream powder)

MUSHROOM AND BACON CAPPUCCINO INSPIRED BY MARC VEYRAT

Yields 550 g

INGREDIENT	QUANTITY	SCALING	PROCEDURE
Smoked bacon, thinly sliced	100 g	50%	① Fry in dry nonstick pan until golden, about 10 min.
Heavy cream	60 g	30%	② Add to bacon, and simmer for 20 min.
Water	20 g	10%	③ Strain cream through fine sieve.
			④ Cool.
			⑤ Measure 75 g of bacon cream.
White pork stock, cold see page 6	200 g	100%	⑥ Whisk together, and season generously to compensate for aeration.
Bacon cream, from above	75 g	37.5%	
Whole milk, cold	15 g	7.5%	
Salt	to taste		
Agar (Texturas brand)	2 g	1% (0.7%)*	⑦ Disperse in cold stock and cream mixture.
			⑧ Heat to 95 °C / 203 °F, and hold for 3 min to fully hydrate.
			⑨ Pour into container, and allow to set, about 5 min.
			⑩ Puree to fluid gel, and transfer to 1 l whipping siphon.
			⑪ Charge with two cartridges of nitrous oxide.
			⑫ Heat siphon in 50 °C / 122 °F bath for 15 min to make bacon foam.
Mushroom jus see page 37	200 g	100%	⑬ Combine, and simmer for 2 min.
Madeira	15 g	7.5%	
Dry shiitake, thinly sliced	5 g	2.5%	
Star anise	1 g	0.5%	
Coffee butter see page 350	10 g	5%	⑭ Blend into hot mushroom jus mixture.
			⑮ Pour into cups or bowls.
			⑯ Garnish with bacon foam.

from page 4·275   *(% of total weight of cold stock and cream mixture)

POACHED APPLE WITH PECORINO FOAM

Yields 450 g (four portions)

INGREDIENT	QUANTITY	SCALING	PROCEDURE
Whole milk	650 g	163%	① Combine, and vacuum seal.
Pecorino Romano, grated	350 g	88%	② Infuse, refrigerated, for 12 h.
			③ Strain through fine sieve, and measure 400 g infused milk.
Cheese infused milk, from above	400 g	100%	④ Blend until smooth.
Heavy cream	100 g	25%	
Lambda carrageenan	1 g	0.25%	
Salt	to taste		⑤ Season cheese mixture.
			⑥ Transfer to 1 l whipping siphon, and charge with one cartridge of nitrous oxide.
Pink Lady apples, peeled, cored, and halved	200 g (two medium)	50%	⑦ Vacuum seal each apple half individually with equal quantities of cider, butter, bay leaf, and vanilla seeds.
Hard apple cider	50 g	12.5%	⑧ Cook sous vide in 80 °C / 176 °F bath for 2 h.
Unsalted butter	50 g	12.5%	⑨ Strain apples over small pot to catch cooking juices.
Bay leaf, thinly sliced	0.1 g	0.025%	⑩ Reduce juices to glaze.
Vanilla seeds and pulp, scraped from pod	0.1 g	0.025%	⑪ Serve warm apples with warm apple glaze, cool Pecorino Romano foam, and toasted brioche.

from page 4·276

GRAPEFRUIT AND BLACK PEPPER ADAPTED FROM DANIEL PATTERSON

Yields 1.1 kg (12 servings)

INGREDIENT	QUANTITY	SCALING	PROCEDURE
For grapefruit–black pepper sorbet:			
Sugar	60 g	12%	① Dry blend.
Pectin LM-104 (CP Kelco brand)	6 g	1.2%	
Glucose	30 g	6%	② Combine 100 g of grapefruit juice with the glucose, sorbitol, and sugar-pectin mixture.
Sorbitol	30 g	6%	③ Bring to boil to form syrup, strain through fine chinois, and chill over ice.
Grapefruit juice (fresh)	500 g	100%	
Salt	to taste		④ Combine remaining 400 g of grapefruit juice with chilled syrup, and season.
Lemon juice	to taste		⑤ Strain through fine sieve, and freeze in Pacojet beaker to make grapefruit sorbet.
For grapefruit mousse:			
Grapefruit juice	415 g	83%	⑥ Combine juices.
Lemon juice	30 g	6%	⑦ Mix in essential oils.
Ginger essential oil	one drop		
Black pepper essential oil	three drops		
Grapefruit essential oil	four drops		
160 Bloom gelatin	14 g	2.8%	⑧ Disperse in cold water.
Honey	15 g	3%	⑨ Combine in pot, and add enough juice mixture to cover.
Sugar	50 g	10%	⑩ Gently warm; add gelatin, stirring until dissolved.
			⑪ Combine with remaining juice mixture, and chill over ice.
			⑫ When completely set, puree in blender until fluid, and pass through fine sieve.
			⑬ Transfer to 1 l siphon, and charge with two cartridges of nitrous oxide. Refrigerate.
Pink grapefruit	one whole		⑭ Cut into supremes. Slice sections on bias in 1 cm / ½ in segments.
Tarragon, fine julienne	as needed		⑮ To serve, season grapefruit segments.
Simple syrup	to taste		⑯ Pacotize sorbet once more.
Cognac	to taste		⑰ Place spoonful of segments in bottom of each bowl.
Lemon juice	to taste		⑱ Top with quenelle of sorbet, and cover with mousse.

from page 4·276

THICK FOAMS

① Select a serving temperature and foaming agents. The table below suggests multiple formulations for creating cold and hot foams, both with and without fat.

② Measure the ingredients carefully, and combine the foaming agent with the liquid. Set the weight of the liquid to 100%. For example, to make whipped caramel, add 1 g of Versawhip and 0.15 g of xanthan gum for every 100 g of caramel.

③ Disperse and heat the liquid (not required for cold-soluble solutions). See the table for appropriate times and temperatures.

④ Heat or cool the liquid to serving temperature.

⑤ To serve, aerate the mixture with an electric whisk or mixer or use a siphon to expand it. Siphoning does not work well with very thick liquids; the upper limit is about the thickness of mayonnaise.

Best Bets for Thick, Fine-Textured Foams

Service temperature	Foaming agents	(scaling)**	Hydrate (°C)	(°F)	(min)	Foaming method	Nitrous oxide charges	Example
cold	160 Bloom gelatin	1.5%	60	140	5	siphon	2–3	thick fruit and vegetable juice foams
	Versawhip	1.00%	cold			electric whisk	n/a	shaving cream-like foam, whipped caramel
	xanthan gum	0.15%						
	albumin powder	14%	room temp.		20	siphon	2	savory and sweet mousses
	isomalt or sugar	10%						
	pregelatinized starch paste	5%	60	140	5	siphon	2	whipped puddings
	160 Bloom gelatin	1.2%						
hot and cold	low-acyl gellan*	0.8%	95	203	3	siphon	2–3	coconut chutney foam, hot whipped cream
	agar*	1.0%	95	203	3	siphon	3	thick, hot whipped cream; hot whipped topping
	xanthan gum	0.2%						
	methylcellulose F50	1.00%	100	212	5	electric whisk	n/a	eggless sabayon
	xanthan gum	0.15%						
	Ultra-Sperse 5	4.0%	80	176	10	siphon	3	potato and other starch foams
	iota carrageenan*	0.4%						
	albumin powder	7.0%	room temp.		20	siphon	1–2	hot whipped cream
	xanthan gum	0.2%						

from page 4·278 *(make fluid gel before foaming); **(set weight of liquid to 100%)

CHOCOLATE CHANTILLY ADAPTED FROM HERVÉ THIS Yields 500 g

INGREDIENT	QUANTITY	SCALING	PROCEDURE
Semisweet chocolate (50% cocoa), chopped into small chunks	300 g	100%	① Vacuum seal. ② Warm sous vide in 50 °C / 122 °F bath until completely melted; reserve.
Water	200 g	67%	③ Pour into bowl set over ice-water bath. ④ Incorporate chocolate into water gradually with electric whisk. ⑤ Whip at high speed to form dense foam, about 5 min. ⑥ Refrigerate foam until ready to serve.

from page 4·281

The same procedure used here can also be used to make chantilly-style foams of camembert, foie gras, or butter. For foie gras, use 200 g of melted foie gras for every 100 g of water or flavorful liquid. For butter, use 100 g of butter and 4 g of gelatin for every 20 g of water.

Note	See page
allow gelatin to set for at least 3 h before serving	
do not use with liquids containing fat	327
	200
make fluid gel before foaming; needs source of calcium for best results; if gellan does not hydrate, see page 4·129	325
see page 4·170 for the hydration procedure for methylcellulose	
reheating base will increase viscosity considerably	
do not heat above 60 °C / 140 °F	

INSTANT SWISS MERINGUE

Yields 150 g

INGREDIENT	QUANTITY	SCALING	PROCEDURE
Egg whites	100 g	100%	① Beat whites into sugar.
Sugar	100 g	100%	② Vacuum seal mixture.
			③ Cook sous vide in 74 °C / 165 °F bath for 30 min.
			④ Transfer to 1 l whipping siphon, and charge with four cartridges of nitrous oxide.
			⑤ Dispense for use as soft meringues.
			⑥ To set meringues, dispense on silicone mat, and bake in 150 °C / 300 °F oven for 1½ h.

from page 4·284

EGGPLANT FOAM ADAPTED FROM JOAN ROCA

Yields 950 g

INGREDIENT	QUANTITY	SCALING	PROCEDURE
Italian eggplant	1 kg (about two eggplants)	200%	① Roast whole at 190 °C / 375 °F until charred and thoroughly cooked, about 1½ h.
			② Cut open, and scoop out flesh while still hot. Discard seeds and skin.
			③ Puree flesh, and pass through fine sieve. Measure 500 g of puree.
Charred eggplant puree, from above	500 g	100%	④ Blend.
			⑤ Strain through fine sieve.
Heavy cream	250 g	50%	⑥ Pour into 1 l whipping siphon.
Albumin powder	25 g	5% (3.3%)*	⑦ Warm siphon in 50 °C / 122 °F bath for 15 min.
Xanthan gum (Keltrol T, CP Kelco brand)	1.5 g	0.3% (0.2%)*	
Salt	to taste		
Fresh sardines, cleaned and gutted	200 g (four fish)	40%	⑧ Grill for 2 min on each side until just cooked through, and season.
Sumac	10 g	2%	⑨ Garnish grilled sardines with foam and remaining ingredients.
Mint leaves	5 g	1%	
Olive oil	to taste		

from page 4·280

*(% of total weight of heavy cream and eggplant puree)

BAKED POTATO FOAM

Yields 400 g

Baked potato foam is a lighter alternative to potato puree. In this version, we use a broth made with baking soda to enhance the baked flavor, but a potato skin infusion could be used instead (see page 19). We use olive oil as a fat in this recipe, but melted butter could be substituted.

Hot potato foams were first made by Ferran Adrià, who made them with just potato and water. We find that adding some thickness with xanthan and a fluid gel improves the texture. In this recipe, we use iota carrageenan, but agar or gellan would also work here.

INGREDIENT	QUANTITY	SCALING	PROCEDURE
Yukon Gold potatoes, peeled and thinly sliced	500 g	200%	① Simmer until tender.
			② Press through fine tamis.
			③ Measure 250 g of puree, and keep warm.
Baked potato broth, cold see page 19	150 g	60%	④ Disperse iota carrageenan and xanthan gum into broth.
Iota carrageenan (Genuvisco J, CP Kelco brand)	1.25 g	0.5% (0.2%)*	⑤ Heat mixture to 95 °C / 203 °F, and hold for 3 min to fully hydrate.
Xanthan gum (Keltrol T, CP Kelco brand)	1 g	0.4% (0.16%)*	⑥ Remove from heat.
Heavy cream	125 g	50%	⑦ Blend into warm broth.
Olive oil	35 g	14%	
Yukon Gold potato puree, from above	250 g	100%	⑧ Fold in cream and broth mixture.
Salt	to taste		⑨ Season.
			⑩ Transfer to 1 l whipping siphon, and charge with one cartridge of nitrous oxide.
			⑪ Hold in 60 °C / 140 °F bath until needed.

from page 4·281

*(% of total weight of baked potato broth, heavy cream, olive oil, and prepared potato puree)

HOT BUTTER FOAM ADAPTED FROM FERRAN ADRIÀ

Yields 250 g

INGREDIENT	QUANTITY	SCALING	PROCEDURE
Egg whites	45 g (about one large white)	18%	① Blend until smooth, and strain.
			② Vacuum seal, and cook sous vide in 70 °C / 158 °F bath for 30 min.
Egg yolks	35 g (about two yolks)	14%	
Unsalted butter, melted	250 g	100%	③ Blend into egg mixture.
Salt	to taste		④ Season.
			⑤ Transfer to 1 l whipping siphon, and charge with two cartridges of nitrous oxide.
			⑥ To serve, warm siphon in 60 °C / 140 °F bath, and dispense foam. Serve with grilled bread or steamed potatoes.

from page 4·283

COCONUT CHUTNEY FOAM

Yields 400 g

INGREDIENT	QUANTITY	SCALING	PROCEDURE
Cilantro leaves	8 g	4%	① Puree herbs in food processor to fine paste.
Mint leaves	4 g	2%	② Pass through fine sieve.
Green chili (fresh), thinly sliced	2 g	1%	③ Measure 10 g of herb puree.
Coconut cream	200 g	100%	④ Blend.
Coconut milk (stabilizer free)	200 g	100%	
Herb puree, from above	20 g	10%	
Salt	to taste		⑤ Season coconut herb cream.
Low-acyl gellan (Kelcogel F, CP Kelco brand)	3.4 g	1.7% (0.8%)*	⑥ Combine.
Sodium citrate	0.6 g	0.3%	
Water, cold	20 g	10%	⑦ Disperse gellan mixture in water.
			⑧ Whisk gellan water into herb cream to form foam base.
			⑨ Bring to simmer while blending to fully hydrate.
			⑩ Remove from heat, and pour foam base into mold.
			⑪ Refrigerate until fully set, about 10 min.
			⑫ Blend set gel to fine puree.
			⑬ Place in siphon, and charge with one cartridge of nitrous oxide.
			⑭ Warm siphon in 60 °C / 140 °F bath for 15 min, and serve.

from page 4·282

*(% of total weight of coconut milk, coconut cream, herb puree, and water)

SUET MOUSSELINE (THICK)

Yields 300 g

INGREDIENT	QUANTITY	SCALING	PROCEDURE
White beef stock see page 6	350 g	100%	① Combine, and reduce to 100 g.
White wine (dry)	250 g	71%	② Strain.
Shallot, finely minced	55 g	16%	③ Cool.
White wine vinegar	35 g	10%	④ Measure 75 g.
Black pepper	0.7 g	0.2%	
Wine reduction, from above	75 g	21%	⑤ Disperse gellan in cream.
			⑥ Blend thickened cream with wine reduction.
Heavy cream, cold	50 g	14.5%	⑦ Vacuum seal.
Low-acyl gellan (Kelcogel F brand)	1.2 g	0.34% (0.29%)*	⑧ Hydrate in 85 °C / 185 °F bath for 5 min.
			⑨ Cool until set. Puree to fluid gel.
Egg yolks, cooked sous vide in 62 °C / 144 °F bath for 35 min	90 g	26%	⑩ Blend with fluid gel.
Rendered beef suet, vacuum-sealed	200 g	57%	⑪ Warm fluid gel mixture and suet separately in 62 °C / 144 °F bath.
			⑫ Blend warm suet into fluid gel until fully emulsified.
Lemon juice	to taste		⑬ Season mixture generously.
Salt	to taste		⑭ Pour into 1 l siphon, and charge with two nitrous oxide cartridges.
			⑮ Hold in 62 °C / 144 °F bath until use.

from page 5·8

*(% of total weight of heavy cream, wine reduction, egg yolks, and beef suet)

DAIRY-FREE WHIPPED CREAM

Yields 400 g

INGREDIENT	QUANTITY	SCALING	PROCEDURE
Water, or flavorful liquid	200 g	100%	① Dry blend powders, and disperse in cold water.
Cellulose gum (Cekol LVD, CP Kelco brand)	1 g	0.5%	② Bring to boil for 1 min to fully hydrate.
Propylene glycol alginate (Protanal Ester BV 4104, FMC BioPolymer brand)	0.8 g	0.4%	③ Remove from heat, and blend over ice until set.
Agar (Texturas brand)	0.4 g	0.2%	④ Puree until smooth to make fluid gel.
Neutral oil, or any flavored oil or fat	60 g	30%	⑤ Combine, and heat to 65 °C / 105 °F to dissolve flakes.
Glice (Texturas brand) or glycerin flakes (Terraspice brand)	4.2 g	2.1%	⑥ Slowly drizzle warm oil mixture into fluid gel, blending constantly, until fully emulsified.
			⑦ Cool completely, and pour mixture into 1 l whipping siphon.
			⑧ Simmer for 2 min, and remove from heat. Cool.
			⑨ Charge with two cartridges of nitrous oxide, and refrigerate until use.

from page 4·283

CAULIFLOWER FOAM

Yields 450 g

INGREDIENT	QUANTITY	SCALING	PROCEDURE
Whole milk	375 g	94%	① Simmer together for 20 min.
Cauliflower trimmings	300 g	75%	② Remove from heat, and infuse at room temperature for 45 min.
Water	175 g	44%	③ Strain.
			④ Measure 400 g of cauliflower milk, and refrigerate.
Cauliflower, thinly sliced	500 g	125%	⑤ Brown cauliflower slices in butters until very dark and nutty aroma is released.
Clarified brown butter	20 g	5%	⑥ Puree, and pass through fine sieve.
Cocoa butter (food grade)	15 g	4%	⑦ Measure 50 g of puree, and reserve.
Cauliflower milk, cold from above	400 g	100%	⑧ Disperse gums in cauliflower milk.
Low-acyl gellan (Kelcogel F, CP Kelco brand)	1 g	0.25%	⑨ Heat to 95 °C / 203 °F, and hold at temperature for 3 min to fully hydrate.
Locust bean gum (TIC Gums brand)	0.4 g	0.1%	⑩ Refrigerate until gel is set, about 5 min.
Browned cauliflower puree, from above	25 g	6.3%	⑪ Puree with gelled cauliflower milk until smooth.
Salt	to taste		⑫ Season pureed mixture.
			⑬ Load mixture into siphon, and warm in 70 °C / 158 °F water bath for 15 min.
			⑭ Charge with two nitrous oxide cartridges, shake vigorously, and dispense to serve.

from page 5·283

FRIED EGG FOAM

Yields 220 g

INGREDIENT	QUANTITY	SCALING	PROCEDURE
Egg whites	60 g	100%	① Fry egg whites until golden brown.
Grapeseed oil	30 g	50%	② Drain oil, pat dry, and reserve.
Heavy cream, cold	130 g	217%	③ Disperse gelatin in cream.
160 Bloom gelatin	2.4 g	4%	④ Bring to simmer to dissolve gelatin fully.
			⑤ Blend in fried egg whites.
Black pepper, ground to fine powder	to taste		⑥ Season egg and cream mixture.
Salt	to taste		⑦ Press through fine sieve, and transfer to 1 l whipping siphon.
			⑧ Charge egg-cream-filled siphon with two nitrous oxide cartridges.
			⑨ Warm siphon in 62 °C / 144 °F bath, about 15 min.
			⑩ Shake siphon thoroughly, and dispense to serve.

from page 5·212

HORSERADISH FOAM INSPIRED BY WYLIE DUFRESNE

Yields 400 g

INGREDIENT	QUANTITY	SCALING	PROCEDURE
Water	400 g	100%	① Blend.
Fresh horseradish, finely grated	150 g	37.5%	② Strain.
Horseradish water, from above	400 g	100%	③ Bring water to boil.
			④ Disperse methylcellulose and xanthan gum in boiling water.
Methylcellulose F50 (Dow brand)	4 g	1%	⑤ Simmer for 2 min, and remove from heat. Cool.
Xanthan gum (Keltrol T, CP Kelco brand)	0.6 g	0.15%	⑥ Vacuum seal. Refrigerate for at least 6 h to fully hydrate.
			⑦ Transfer to metal bowl.
Salt	to taste		⑧ Season, and set bowl over pot of simmering water.
			⑨ Whip foam base with electric whisk until soft peaks form.
			⑩ Serve with rib roast or Boeuf en Gelée.

from page 4·284

OYSTERS WITH CAVA FOAM ADAPTED FROM JOAN ROCA

Yields 700 g (four portions)

INGREDIENT	QUANTITY	SCALING	PROCEDURE
Cava or other sparkling dry white wine	400 g	100%	① Shear gum into wine.
			② Transfer to 1 l whipping siphon.
Xanthan gum (Keltrol T, CP Kelco brand)	1.6 g	0.4%	③ Charge siphon with one cartridge of carbon dioxide, and seal.
			④ Refrigerate.
Apple juice	100 g	25%	⑤ Disperse agar in juice.
Agar (Texturas brand)	1 g	0.25% (1%)*	⑥ Bring juice to boil.
			⑦ Remove from heat, and cool until gelled.
			⑧ Puree gel until completely fluid.
Kusshi oysters	20 oysters		⑨ Shuck and rinse.
			⑩ Divide equally among four bowls.
Candied lemon peel (store-bought)	four cubes		⑪ Garnish each bowl with dab of apple fluid gel, one cube of lemon peel, two pieces of ginger dice, and two pieces of pineapple dice.
Crystallized ginger, brunoise	eight pieces		
Fresh pineapple, brunoise	eight pieces		
Cumin seeds, ground fine	0.4 g	0.1%	⑫ Season.
Pain d'épices spice powder see page 51	0.4 g	0.1%	⑬ Dispense cava foam at table.

from page 4·277   *(% of weight of apple juice)

BARBECUED EEL WITH WHIPPED CARAMEL

Yields 450 g

ADAPTED FROM WYLIE DUFRESNE

INGREDIENT	QUANTITY	SCALING	PROCEDURE
Water	100 g	100%	① Cook together to 143 °C / 290 °F.
Sugar	100 g	100%	
Water	300 g	300%	② Deglaze caramel, and stir to dissolve. Reserve 300 g of caramel water, and chill.
Versawhip 600 (Kerry Bioscience brand)	3 g	3%	③ Disperse powders into reserved cold caramel water, and blend until fully incorporated.
			④ Whip with electric whisk until stiff, beer-head-like foam is achieved.
Xanthan gum (Keltrol T, CP Kelco brand)	0.45 g	0.45%	
Barbecued eel (store-bought)	200 g	200%	⑤ Broil for 2 min, skin side down.
			⑥ Arrange on plates, and garnish with whipped caramel.

from page 4·283

UNI WITH WHIPPED TOFU AND TAPIOCA ADAPTED FROM DAVID CHANG

Yields 3.85 kg (20 portions)

INGREDIENT	QUANTITY	SCALING	PROCEDURE
Soft tofu	1.25 kg	313%	① Puree together until smooth.
Water	450 g	113%	② Pass through fine sieve.
Yuzu juice	80 g	20%	
Sugar	20 g	5%	
Yuzu kosho	15 g	4%	
Salt	10 g	2.5%	
Xanthan gum (Keltrol T, CP Kelco brand)	9 g	2.25% (0.5%)*	③ Blend into tofu base until fully dispersed.
			④ Pour mixture into 1 l whipping siphon.
			⑤ Charge with two cartridges of nitrous oxide.
			⑥ Reserve refrigerated.
Bonito flakes (katsuobushi)	20 g	5%	⑦ Toss together to make furikake (Japanese mixed seasoning).
Egg yolk powder	20 g	5%	
Nori powder	20 g	5%	
Puffed rice	20 g	5%	
Shrimp cracker puffs, crumbled	20 g	5%	
Toasted sesame seeds	20 g	5%	
Black tapioca pearls	1.25 kg	313%	⑧ Combine, and bring to simmer.
Apple juice (Mott's)	150 g	37.5%	⑨ Cool.
Elderflower syrup	100 g	25%	⑩ Place spoonful of tapioca pearls in bottom of each bowl.
			⑪ Dispense large spoonful of whipped tofu onto each portion.
Santa Barbara sea urchin (uni) tongues	400 g	100%	⑫ Add three tongues to each bowl.
			⑬ Garnish with furikake.

from page 4·285

*(% of total weight of first six ingredients)

CHESTNUT CREAM

Yields 300 g

INGREDIENT	QUANTITY	SCALING	PROCEDURE
Whole milk, cold	150 g	150%	① Disperse iota carrageenan and gum over milk.
Iota carrageenan	0.6 g	0.6% (0.2%)*	
Konjac gum (TIC Gums brand)	0.3 g	0.3% (0.1%)*	
Chestnut puree (store-bought)	100 g	100%	② Blend with milk solution.
			③ Vacuum seal.
Heavy cream	25 g	25%	④ Place in 80 °C / 175 °F bath, and hold for 5 min to hydrate iota carrageenan.
Roasted hazelnut oil	15 g	15%	
Sugar	15 g	15%	⑤ Pour into mold, and refrigerate until set, about 10 min.
Water	10 g	10%	⑥ Puree gel until fluid.
Salt	2 g	2%	⑦ Fill 1 l siphon with fluid gel.
			⑧ Charge chestnut-cream-filled siphon with two nitrous oxide cartridges, and reheat in 70 °C / 158 °F bath for 15 min.

from page 5·21

*(% of total weight of all ingredients)

WHIPPED BUTTER

Yields 1 kg

INGREDIENT	QUANTITY	SCALING	PROCEDURE
Heavy cream (without stabilizers)	4 kg	400%	① Transfer to bowl of electric mixer.
			② Whisk on high until fat is totally separated from liquid and small granules of butter begin to form, about 10 min.
			③ Strain mixture through cheesecloth, discarding liquid.
			④ Wring cheesecloth tightly to remove any remaining moisture from butter.
			⑤ Measure 1 kg of sweet butter.
Sweet butter, from above or store-bought	1 kg	100%	⑥ Whisk into soft butter.
			⑦ Vacuum seal, and refrigerate for 24 h to mature butter flavor.
Lactic acid	1.5 g	0.15%	⑧ To serve, warm butter to 40 °C / 104 °F until fluid but not broken.
Delta decalactone (SAFC brand)	0.1 g	0.01%	⑨ Pour into 1 l whipping siphon, and charge with two cartridges of nitrous oxide.
			⑩ Dispense to serve.
Salt	15 g	1.5%	

from page 4·286

Whether you make your own butter or use store-bought butter, this incredible butter foam provides the essential taste of butter in a much lighter context. It may be held at 40 °C / 104 °F and foamed to order.

YOGURT FOAM AND SWEET POTATO CHIPS
(HOMAGE TO AMERICAN SCULPTOR RICHARD SERRA)
ADAPTED FROM JOSÉ ANDRÉS

Yields 500 g

INGREDIENT	QUANTITY	SCALING	PROCEDURE
160 Bloom gelatin	4 g	1.1%	① Bloom in cold water.
Heavy cream	150 g	43%	② Heat 50 g of cream.
			③ Add gelatin to dissolve.
Full-fat Greek-style strained yogurt	350 g	100%	④ Blend with gelatin mixture and 100 g of remaining cream.
			⑤ Transfer to 1 l whipping siphon, and charge with two cartridges of nitrous oxide.
			⑥ Refrigerate for at least 4 h.
Sweet potatoes, peeled	200 g	57%	⑦ Slice potatoes into sheets 1 mm / ¹⁄₃₂ in thick on Japanese rotary slicer.
Frying oil	as needed		⑧ Deep-fry in 190 °C / 375 °F oil until crisp and golden, about 3 min.
Salt	to taste		⑨ Season chips, and reserve.
Tamarind paste see page 145	100 g	28.5%	⑩ Blend well to form syrup, and transfer to squeeze bottle.
			⑪ Dispense yogurt foam into serving bowls.
Clear honey	40 g	11.5%	⑫ Drizzle syrup over foam, and serve with sweet potato chips on side.
Star anise powder	0.2 g	0.05%	

from page 4·287

SET FOAMS

① Select bubble size and foam temperature. The table Best Bets for Set Foams below offers multiple options for foams to be served cold or hot, with or without fat.

② Measure ingredients carefully, and disperse the foaming agents in the liquid. Set the weight of the liquid to 100%. For example, to make passion fruit marshmallows, add 4 g of 160 Bloom gelatin and 10 g of albumin powder for every 100 g of passion fruit base.

③ Hydrate, using the time and temperature given (not required for cold-soluble foaming agents).

④ Cool liquid completely.

⑤ Aerate with an electric whisk or mixture, or expand by using a 1 l whipping siphon, as indicated.

⑥ Heat or chill the foam to set its structure. Setting methods, temperatures, and times are listed in the table.

Best Bets for Set Foams

Serving temperature and bubble size	Foaming agents	(scaling)*	Hydrate (°C)	(°F)	(min)	Foaming method	Set Method	(°C)	(°F)	(h)
cold, fine	160 Bloom gelatin	3.00%	60	140	5	electric whisk	refrigerator			1
	xanthan gum	0.25%								
	160 Bloom gelatin	4.0%	60	140	5	stand mixer	refrigerator			3
	albumin powder	10%								
	heavy cream	200%	60	140	5	siphon with two cartridges of nitrous oxide	refrigerator			4
	egg yolk at 65 °C / 148 °F	30%								
	albumin powder	5%								
	160 Bloom gelatin	3%								
	xanthan gum	0.25%								
	albumin powder	18.0%	cold-soluble			stand mixer	vacuum oven	60	140	2
	glucose, syrup DE 40	16.5%								
	maltodextrin DE 19	5.0%								
	xanthan gum	0.3%								
hot and cold, fine	egg white	100.0%	n/a			electric whisk	steam oven	75	167	14 min
	lemon juice	10%								
	salt	1.3%								
	albumin powder	14.0%	cold-soluble			electric whisk	steam oven	78	172	16 min
	Maltrin M100	17.5%								
	egg yolk	27.0%								
	tartaric acid	0.2%								
hot and cold, coarse	egg white	104.0%	cold-soluble			siphon with two cartridges of nitrous oxide into perforated paper cup	microwave	full power		1 min
	nut butter	100.0%								
	egg yolk	67.0%								
	sugar or isomalt	67.0%								
	all-purpose flour	16.7%								
	160 Bloom gelatin	2.8%	100	212	5	electric whisk	blowtorch or broiler	high heat		1 min
	methylcellulose F50	1.4%								

from page 4·288   *(set weight of liquid to 100%)

Examples	Note	See page
gelatin sponges, soy sauce cloud	keep liquid very cold when whipping	339
delicate marshmallow, passion fruit marshmallow	cool before whisking with albumin powder	next
savory parfaits and mousses	best cast directly in serving vessel	
very light savory meringues, green olive meringue	vacuum at 19 mbar / 0.28 psi; meringue base can also be dehydrated or baked	339
blancmange	ideal pH around 8.7; add more acid to older egg whites	335
light soufflés	whip albumin and water with tartaric acid, and then fold in remaining ingredients	338
pistachio sponge cake	allow batter to rest for 1 h, refrigerated, before using; the container in which the sponge is cooked must have bottom ventilation	333
hot apricot marshmallow	best used with fruit or vegetable purees; use same day; see page 4·170 for details on methylcellulose	334

PASSION FRUIT MARSHMALLOW WITH CHORIZO POWDER

Yields 300 g

INGREDIENT	QUANTITY	SCALING	PROCEDURE
Chorizo (dry cured), very thinly sliced	300 g	150%	① Place in even layer on dehydrator tray.
			② Dehydrate at 55 °C / 131 °F for 12 h.
			③ Pat off any excess oil.
N-Zorbit M (National Starch brand)	50 g	25% (*16.7%*)*	④ Add to dried chorizo, and grind to fine powder.
160 Bloom gelatin	8 g	4%	⑤ Disperse gelatin into juice.
Passion fruit juice	200 g	100%	⑥ Heat juice and sugar to 60 °C / 140 °F until gelatin and sugar dissolve.
Fructose	75 g	37.5%	⑦ Remove from heat.
			⑧ Cool completely.
Albumin powder	20 g	10%	⑨ Whisk into cooled passion fruit juice mixture.
			⑩ Whip until stiff peaks form, about 10 min.
			⑪ Cast in 2.5 cm / 1 in layer on nonstick mold.
			⑫ Refrigerate until fully set, about 4 h.
			⑬ Cut resulting marshmallow into 2.5 cm / 1 in cubes.
			⑭ Toss cubes in chorizo powder to serve.

from page 4·290

*(% of total weight of chorizo)

CRYOPOACHED GREEN TEA SOUR ADAPTED FROM HESTON BLUMENTHAL

Yields 1 kg

INGREDIENT	QUANTITY	SCALING	PROCEDURE
Sugar	124 g	17.5%	① Combine.
HM pectin (Brown Ribbon HV, Obipektin brand)	11 g	1.5%	② Pass through tamis.
			③ Reserve sugar mixture.
Water	710 g	100%	④ Combine, and add sugar mixture.
Lime juice	133 g	19%	⑤ Hand-blend until sugar is completely incorporated.
			⑥ Bring to boil while whisking.
			⑦ Pass through chinois.
			⑧ Chill over ice to 4 °C / 39 °F.
Gunpowder tea	21 g	3%	⑨ Add to chilled mixture.
			⑩ Refrigerate infusion for 2 h.
			⑪ Pass through chinois lined with double layer of cheesecloth or 70 micron sieve.
Matcha green tea powder	1.5 g	0.2%	⑫ Blend into tea infusion.
			⑬ Pass through chinois to remove any lumps.
Egg whites	100 g	14%	⑭ Whisk into infusion to make meringue base.
Vodka	50 g	7%	⑮ Transfer meringue base to 1 l whipping siphon, and charge with two cartridges of nitrous dioxide. Store refrigerated.
			⑯ To serve, dispense small ball of meringue base onto spoon; transfer to Dewar flask filled with liquid nitrogen.
			⑰ Poach, turning meringue constantly until frozen on outside but still soft inside, about 30 s.
Matcha green tea powder	as needed		⑱ Dust over frozen meringue, and serve immediately.

from page 4·291

WHIPPED YOGURT CRISPS ADAPTED FROM AKI KAMOZAWA AND H. ALEXANDER TALBOT   Yields 600 g

INGREDIENT	QUANTITY	SCALING	PROCEDURE
Full-fat Greek-style strained yogurt	480 g	100%	① Whisk together until yogurt is completely incorporated.
Water	270 g	56.25%	② Set aside yogurt base.
Water	300 g	62.5%	③ Bring water to simmer.
Isomalt	50 g	10.4%	④ Stir in isomalt, Maltrin M100, and salt until dissolved.
Maltrin M100 (GPC brand)	25 g	5.2%	
Salt	5 g	1%	
Methocel K100 (Dow brand)	11.3 g	2.35% (1.08%)*	⑤ Whisk into water until fully incorporated.
			⑥ Remove from heat, and add to yogurt base, from above.
Xanthan gum (Keltrol T, CP Kelco brand)	2.26 g	0.47% (0.22%)*	⑦ Cool in bowl set over ice-water bath.
			⑧ Place bowl over hot water bath, and whip cooled mixture until consistency resembles whipped egg white meringue.
			⑨ Transfer to pastry bag.
			⑩ Pipe desired sizes onto tray lined with silicone mat.
			⑪ Dehydrate in 95 °C / 205 °F oven until crisp, about 1 h.

from page 4·292   *(% of total weight of first three ingredients)

GREEN TEA CAKE ADAPTED FROM JOHNNY IUZZINI   Yields 600 g

INGREDIENT	QUANTITY	SCALING	PROCEDURE
Sugar or isomalt, powdered	150 g	100%	① Blend until creamy.
Unsalted butter	85 g	57%	
Eggs, blended	150 g	100%	② Whisk into sugar mixture until smooth.
Vanilla seeds and pulp, scraped from pod	1 g	0.67%	③ Add.
Water	155 g	103%	④ Combine water and milk powder.
Skim milk powder	20 g	13.3%	⑤ Heat to boiling while whisking constantly.
			⑥ Pour hot milk into blender.
Methocel SGA 7C (Dow brand)	3.5 g	2.3% (2%)*	⑦ Blend into hot milk.
			⑧ Chill milk over ice-water bath.
			⑨ Add milk to blended sugar, butter, eggs, and vanilla seeds.
Cake flour	150 g	100%	⑩ Combine, and sift together.
Matcha green tea powder	8 g	5.3%	⑪ Fold into liquid ingredients to form batter, and rest, refrigerated, for 2 h.
Salt	4.5 g	3%	⑫ Load batter into 1 l whipping siphon, and charge with three cartridges of nitrous oxide.
			⑬ Dispense into perforated paper cups.
			⑭ Microwave on high for 1 min to cook through.
			⑮ Unmold and serve.

from page 4·292   *(% of total weight of water and milk powder)

MICROWAVED PISTACHIO SPONGE CAKE ADAPTED FROM FERRAN ADRIÀ   Yields 800 g

INGREDIENT	QUANTITY	SCALING	PROCEDURE
Egg whites	250 g	104%	① Blend until smooth.
Green pistachio butter see page 54	240 g	100%	② Refrigerate for 2 h to rest.
			③ Strain.
Egg yolks	160 g	67%	④ Transfer cake base to 1 l whipping siphon, and charge with one cartridge of nitrous oxide.
Sugar or isomalt	160 g	67%	⑤ Perforate bottoms of 10 paper cups to allow for air circulation.
All-purpose flour	40 g	16.7%	⑥ Dispense cake base into cups, filling each about half full.
			⑦ Microwave each cup separately at 900 W for 50 s.

from page 4·294

HOT APRICOT MARSHMALLOW INSPIRED BY FERRAN ADRIÀ

Yields: 250 g

INGREDIENT	QUANTITY	SCALING	PROCEDURE
Apricot puree see page 217	250 g	100%	① Combine methylcellulose with 200 g of apricot puree. Set aside remaining 50 g puree.
Methocel F50 (Dow brand)	3.5 g	1.4%	② Bring to boil, and hold for 2 min to fully disperse.
			③ Cool completely.
			④ Vacuum seal.
			⑤ Refrigerate for 12 h to hydrate methylcellulose.
160 Bloom gelatin	7 g	2.8%	⑥ Disperse gelatin in remaining 50 g of apricot puree.
			⑦ Simmer to dissolve.
			⑧ Combine with Methocel mixture.
			⑨ Whip with electric whisk for 7 min, until light and airy.
			⑩ Transfer to pastry bag.
			⑪ Pipe small mounds onto center of ovenproof plates.
			⑫ Cover plates with plastic wrap.
			⑬ Refrigerate until set, about 4 h.
			⑭ Remove plastic wrap.
Olive oil	100 g	40%	⑮ Combine.
Jasmine essential oil	1 g	0.4%	
Dried apricots, finely diced	40 g	16%	⑯ Bake apricot marshmallows at 120 °C / 250 °F for 3 min.
			⑰ Garnish.
Marcona almonds, finely chopped	20 g	8%	⑱ Drizzle a little infused olive oil over each meringue, and serve.
Chives, finely minced	5 g	2%	
Lemon balm leaves	5 g	2%	

from page 4·293

HAMBURGER BUN

Yields 12 buns

INGREDIENT	QUANTITY	SCALING	PROCEDURE
For the sponge:			
White Lily bread flour	310 g	65%	① Dissolve yeast in 89 g of water, and mix remaining 100 g with flour.
Water (5 °C / 41 °F)	189 g	40%	② Mix together on low speed, using paddle attachment, for 8 min.
Yeast (fresh)	2 g	0.4%	③ Cover tightly, and refrigerate for 24–48 h.
For the dough:			
White Lily bread flour	480 g	100%	④ Mix together flour and water on low speed for 4 min.
Water (30 °C / 86 °F)	270 g	56%	⑤ Stop mixer, and cover bowl with hot, wet cloth for 45 min.
Yeast (fresh)	9.5 g	2%	⑥ Mix into flour mixture.
Sponge, from above	120 g	25%	⑦ Add to flour mixture, and mix on medium speed for 4 min.
Sugar	72 g	15%	⑧ Ferment dough, covered, at room temperature for 1 h.
Egg yolks	50 g	10%	⑨ Form into twelve 90 g balls.
Vegetable shortening	25 g	5%	⑩ Arrange balls into 11 cm / 4¼ in ring molds.
Salt	9.5 g	2%	⑪ Proof in 40 °C / 104 °F combi oven with 85% relative humidity until dough has expanded to fill ring, about 1½ h. If proofing cabinet is unavailable, cover with oiled plastic wrap and keep in warm place until proofed, at least 1½ h.
Vanilla extract	0.5 g (two drops)	0.1%	
Lemon essential oil	0.2 g (one drop)	0.04%	⑫ Press gently on proofed buns to flatten.
L-cysteine	0.04 g	0.01%	
Whole milk	as needed		⑬ Brush bun tops lightly.
Black onion seeds	as needed		⑭ Combine, and sprinkle on bun tops.
Black poppy seeds, toasted	as needed		⑮ Bake in 260 °C / 500 °F oven for 6 min, and cool to room temperature.
Black sesame seeds, toasted	as needed		
Rendered beef suet	40 g	8.5%	⑯ Cut buns in half, and fry in suet until crisp and golden.

from page 5·12

BEET MERINGUE ADAPTED FROM FERRAN ADRIÀ

Yields 100 g

INGREDIENT	QUANTITY	SCALING	PROCEDURE
Beet juice see page 2·336	120 g (from about 250 g of beets)	100%	① Bring to simmer, and remove from heat. ② Skim top. ③ Cool completely.
Isomalt	24 g	20%	④ Blend first three ingredients into cooled juice.
Albumin powder	15 g	12.5%	⑤ Season with salt.
Ascorbic acid	1.2 g	1%	⑥ Refrigerate for 12 h to rehydrate.
Salt	to taste		⑦ Whip rehydrated meringue base until stiff. ⑧ Pipe meringue base into mold, 5 cm / 2 in high. ⑨ Dehydrate in 90 °C / 195 °F oven for 2 h. ⑩ Cut into desired shapes. ⑪ Reserve in cool, dry place.
Spray-dried yogurt powder see page 2·438, or store-bought	15 g	12.5%	⑫ Combine. ⑬ Dust over meringues before serving.
Citric acid	1 g	0.8%	

from page 4·295

STEAMED BLANCMANGE ADAPTED FROM JEAN-FRANÇOIS PIÈGE

Yields 200 g (four portions)

INGREDIENT	QUANTITY	SCALING	PROCEDURE
Egg whites	120 g	100%	① Whip together until stiff peaks form.
Lemon juice	12 g	10%	
Salt	2 g	1.7%	
Chives, finely minced	4 g	3.3%	② Fold in gently.
Black pepper, crushed	0.8 g	0.67%	③ Transfer to pastry bag.
Unsalted butter, room temperature	as needed		④ Grease four 10 cm / 4 in metal ring molds lightly. ⑤ Pipe egg white mixture into molds, filling each halfway full. ⑥ Press down in center of molds with back of wet spoon, making small depressions.
Egg yolks, whole	four whole		⑦ Add one yolk to center of each mold. ⑧ Fill molds with remaining egg white mixture, covering yolks. ⑨ Scrape off tops of each blancmange with offset spatula to flatten. ⑩ Flash sides lightly with blowtorch to tighten structure. ⑪ Brush plastic wrap with butter, and cover each blancmange. ⑫ Steam in 75 °C / 165 °F combi oven for 14 min. ⑬ Let rest in molds at room temperature for 2 min. ⑭ Transfer to serving plates.
Sauce vin jaune see page 308	120 g	100%	⑮ Warm sauce and pour over each blancmange at table.

from page 4·296

CHESTNUT PUFFS

Yields 430 g

INGREDIENT	QUANTITY	SCALING	PROCEDURE
Whole milk	160 g	160%	① Disperse gelatin over cold milk.
300 Bloom gelatin	10 g	10%	
Unsalted butter	45 g	45%	② Add to milk.
Rendered bacon fat	10 g	10%	③ Bring to boil.
Salt	2.5 g	2.5%	
All-purpose flour	100 g	100%	④ Add to boiling liquid all at once.
			⑤ Stir over medium heat until dough forms into ball and film develops on the inside of pot, about 2 min.
			⑥ Transfer to stand mixer.
Eggs	150 g	150%	⑦ Incorporate eggs, one at a time, followed by puree.
Chestnut puree (store-bought)	30 g	30%	⑧ Cast into mold in layer 1.5 cm / ⅝ in thick.
			⑨ Set for at least 3 h.
			⑩ Cut into 1.5 cm / ⅝ in cubes.
			⑪ Bake cubes in 200 °C / 390 °F oven for 10 min.
Frying oil	as needed		⑫ Deep-fry chestnut puffs in 185 °C / 365 °F oil for 4 min.
			⑬ Transfer to paper towel-lined baking sheet.
Chestnut cream, warmed see page 328	30 g	30%	⑭ Fill each puff with chestnut cream by using an injection attachment on a siphon to pierce puff.
Pain d'épices powder see page 51	as needed		⑮ Dust each puff with pain d'épices powder.

from page 5·20

BUTTERMILK BISCUITS

Yields 500 g

White Lily brand flour is milled from soft wheat. If unavailable, substitute another soft wheat flour or a pastry flour. If you use all-purpose flour, you may need to increase the amount of liquid slightly.

INGREDIENT	QUANTITY	SCALING	PROCEDURE
White Lily biscuit flour	300 g	100%	① Mix together.
Baking powder	13.5 g	4.5%	② Sift and reserve.
Sugar	12 g	4%	
Salt	3 g	1%	
Unsalted butter	115 g	38%	③ Freeze butter, or optionally, use liquid nitrogen.
Liquid nitrogen (optional)	as needed		④ Pulse frozen butter in food processor until round balls form, 3 mm / ⅛ in. in diameter.
			⑤ Toss balls into sifted flour, and reserve.
Heavy cream	115 g	38%	⑥ Mix together.
Crème fraîche	70 g	25%	⑦ Drizzle over reserved flour mixture.
Egg, blended	30 g	10%	⑧ Mix very lightly until wet dough forms.
			⑨ Place dough on plastic wrap.
			⑩ Roll into log 8 cm / 3¼ in. in diameter, and then wrap in plastic.
			⑪ Freeze partially.
			⑫ Cut into round slices 2 cm / ¾ in. thick.
			⑬ Place slices on baking sheet lined with floured silicone mat.
			⑭ Bake in 200 °C / 390 °F oven until golden on top, about 5 min.
			⑮ Serve warm with caramelized creme fraîche (see page 203).

from page 5·77

RYE BREAD ADAPTED FROM HORST BANDEL

Yields 1.25 kg

INGREDIENT	QUANTITY	SCALING	PROCEDURE
For the old rye bread soaker:			
Water, hot	870 g	483%	① Combine and cool to room temperature.
Day-old rye bread loaf (homemade or store-bought)	450 g	250%	② Vacuum seal. ③ Refrigerate for 12 h. ④ Squeeze out water. ⑤ Reserve for rye dough.
For the sourdough starter:			
Bread flour	200 g	111%	⑥ Mix together.
Water, 18 °C / 65 °F	100 g	56%	⑦ Ripen at 21 °C / 70 °F for 10–12 h.
Rye flour	75 g	42%	⑧ Measure 20 g of starter for rye dough.
Barley malt	10 g	5.5%	
Yeast (fresh)	5 g	2.8%	
For the cooked rye berries:			
Water	1 kg	555%	⑨ Vacuum seal together.
Rye berries, soaked for 12 h	250 g	139%	⑩ Cook sous vide in 90 °C / 194 °F bath for 5 h. ⑪ Drain. ⑫ Measure 180 g of cooked rye berries.
For the rye molasses meal:			
Old rye bread soaker, from above	180 g	100%	⑬ Combine in bowl.
Blackstrap molasses	36 g	20%	⑭ Mix on medium speed with paddle attachment until mealy, about 2 min.
Sourdough starter, from above	20 g	11%	⑮ Reserve rye molasses meal.
Water	360 g	200%	⑯ Combine in bowl.
Yeast (fresh)	6 g	3.3%	
Rye molasses meal, from above	236 g	131%	⑰ Mix on low speed with paddle attachment for 10 min. Mixture should look sticky but not wet.
			⑱ Ferment for 30 min at 25–30 °C / 77–86 °F.
High-gluten flour	224 g	125%	⑲ Transfer dough to cast-iron mold.
Rye chops (chopped rye berries)	224 g	125%	⑳ Ferment for 1 h at 25–30 °C / 77–86 °F.
Cooked rye berries, from above	180 g	100%	
Salt	12.2 g	6.8%	
Sesame seeds	as needed		㉑ Sprinkle seeds over fermented dough in mold.
Sprouted flaxseeds	as needed		㉒ Place uncovered mold on center rack of 220 °C / 425 °F oven, and bake for 10 min.
Sunflower seeds	as needed		㉓ Cover mold, and bake to core temperature of 99 °C / 210 °F, about 30 min.
			㉔ Remove cover, and let rest in mold at room temperature for at least 2 h.
Rendered beef marrow	90 g	50%	㉕ Cut bread into 3.5 cm / 1½ in wedges.
			㉖ Toast wedges in beef marrow fat in nonstick frying pan until golden and crisp, about 2 min on first side and 1½ min on second side.

from page 5·59

MOROCCAN BATBOUT FLATBREAD

Yields 725 g

INGREDIENT	QUANTITY	SCALING	PROCEDURE
Water, lukewarm	320 g	107%	① Sprinkle yeast over water, and stir to dissolve.
Active dry yeast	7 g	2.3%	② Let rest for 5 min.
All-purpose flour	300 g	100%	③ Mix with yeast mixture.
Fine semolina flour	100 g	33%	④ Knead dough for 10 min.
Salt	8 g	2.7%	⑤ Divide into three equal portions.
Turmeric, peeled and finely grated	4 g	1.3%	⑥ Let rise at room temperature until doubled in volume, about 1 h.
			⑦ Flatten portions into discs 1 cm / ⅜ in thick.
Golden oregano, finely minced	1.5 g	0.5%	⑧ Garnish with herbs.
			⑨ Refrigerate for up to 4 h.
Frying oil	as needed		⑩ Panfry discs on lightly oiled griddle or pan until cooked through and golden, about 2 min on each side.

from page 5·139

SIPHONED SOUFFLÉ À LA LORRAINE

Yields 200 g (four individual soufflés)

For a cheese version of the souffle, add 54 g (54%) of grated Gruyère cheese, and dissolve it with 0.4% sodium citrate in the warm milk. Cool completely, and proceed with the remaining instructions. Use only 1.8 g (1.8%) of salt.

For a chocolate version of the soufflé, replace corn starch with 7 g (7%) tapioca starch, whisk 39 g (39%) of grated semisweet chocolate into the warm milk, and omit the Maltrin, PGA, and 1.8 g of the salt. Cool completely, and proceed with instructions.

Sous vide cooking time of eggs will vary according to the size of the batch.

INGREDIENT	QUANTITY	SCALING	PROCEDURE
Whole milk	150 g	150%	① Vacuum seal together, and cook sous vide in 90 °C / 194 °F bath for 1½ h.
Bacon, rendered and drained	100 g	100%	② Remove from bag, and strain; measure 78 g of milk, and cool.
Sweet onions, thinly sliced	40 g	40%	③ Combine with infused milk, and blend until smooth.
			④ Cook sous vide in 78 °C / 172 °F bath for 30 min.
Egg whites	100 g	100%	⑤ Dust sugar over egg yolks, and let stand for 20 min at room temperature.
Infused milk, from above	78 g	78%	⑥ Blend whites, salt, butter and infused milk with sugar dusted egg yolks until smooth, and cook sous vide in 78 °C / 172 °F bath for 30 min to make egg base.
Egg yolks	20 g	20%	
Unsalted butter, melted	14 g	14%	
Salt	3.6 g	3.6%	
Sugar	1.1 g	1.1%	
Corn starch	13.5 g	13.5%	⑦ Dry blend, and whisk into cooked egg base until dispersed evenly.
Propylene glycol alginate (Propanal Ester BV, FMC BioPolymer brand)	0.31 g	0.31%	⑧ Pour into 1 l whipping siphon, and hold in 55 °C / 131 °F bath until ready to bake.
Maltrin M100 (GPC brand)	3.1 g	3.1%	⑨ To bake, charge with two cartridges of nitrous oxide and shake well.
Cream of tartar	0.7 g	0.7%	⑩ Line the sides of four ramekins with parchment collars.
			⑪ Brush inside of ramekins with oil or melted butter, and dust with flour.
			⑫ Dispense soufflé base two-thirds up sides of ramekins.
			⑬ Put in oven pan, and fill pan with enough water to cover bottom halves of ramekins.
			⑭ Bake in 190 °C / 375 °F oven for 20 min.

from page 4·297

GREEN OLIVE MERINGUE INSPIRED BY PIERRE GAGNAIRE

Yields 500 g

INGREDIENT	QUANTITY	SCALING	PROCEDURE
Green olives, pitted, bulk	900 g	300%	① Blend to fine puree.
Water	500 g	167%	② Strain through cheesecloth to extract juice.
			③ Measure 300 g of juice.
Green olive juice, from above	300 g	100%	④ Whisk together.
Albumin powder	54 g	18%	
Glucose syrup DE 40	50 g	16.5%	
Maltrin M100 (GPC brand)	15 g	5% (3.7%)*	⑤ Fold into olive juice mixture.
			⑥ Whip in stand mixer until dense foam forms, about 5 min.
Xanthan gum (Keltrol T, CP Kelco brand)	0.9 g	0.3% (0.2%)*	⑦ Pipe 5 cm / 2 in spheres of green olive meringue onto silicone baking mat.
			⑧ If available, bake in 60 °C / 140 °F vacuum oven at 19 mbar / 0.275 psi for 2 h.
			⑨ Otherwise, bake in 77 °C / 170 °F oven for 8 h, or 150 °C / 300 °F oven for 1½ h.
Green olives, pitted	100 g	33%	⑩ Dehydrate at 55 °C / 131 °F for 12 h.
			⑪ Grind to fine powder in food processor.
N-Zorbit M (National Starch brand)	40 g	13.3%	⑫ Whisk into powder.
Salt	to taste		⑬ Season.
Extra-virgin olive oil	30 g	10%	⑭ Whisk slowly into powder until fully incorporated.
			⑮ Dust over meringues to serve.

from page 4·298   *(% of total weight of green olive juice, albumin powder, and glucose)

SOY SAUCE CLOUD ADAPTED FROM FERRAN ADRIÀ

Yields 200 g

INGREDIENT	QUANTITY	SCALING	PROCEDURE
Water, cold	100 g	100%	① Place empty stand mixer bowl or stainless steel bowl in freezer for 25 min.
160 Bloom gelatin	6 g	6% (3%)*	② Hydrate gelatin in water.
			③ Bring water to simmer until gelatin is just dissolved.
			④ Cool quickly. Do not allow gelatin to set.
Soy sauce	100 g	100%	⑤ Combine, and whisk into gelatin mixture.
Xanthan gum (Xantana, Texturas brand)	0.5 g	0.5% (0.25%)*	⑥ Place in freezer-chilled bowl.
			⑦ Whip with electric whisk attachment or handheld automatic whisk until liquid becomes very dense and forms tight foam, about 15 min.
			⑧ Cast foam into nonstick mold, 1.5 cm / ⅝ in thick.
			⑨ Freeze mold for 2 min to firm.
			⑩ Transfer to refrigerator, and chill at least 2 h before using.
			⑪ Cut into desired shapes, and serve as garnish for foie gras or monkfish liver terrine.

from page 4·299   *(% of total weight of water and soy sauce)

FREEZE-DRIED CARROT FOAM ADAPTED FROM FERRAN ADRIÀ

Yields 200 g

INGREDIENT	QUANTITY	SCALING	PROCEDURE
160 Bloom gelatin	15 g	3%	① Bloom gelatin in cold water.
Carrot juice see page 2·336	500 g (from 800 g carrots)	100%	② Warm 250 g of juice. ③ Dissolve gelatin in warmed juice.
Xanthan gum (Keltrol T, CP Kelco brand)	1 g	0.2%	④ Blend with remaining 250 g of juice. ⑤ Combine with gelatin mixture. ⑥ Cool. ⑦ Transfer to 1 l whipping siphon, and charge with three cartridges of nitrous oxide. ⑧ Refrigerate for at least 3 h. ⑨ Dispense foam in 2.5 cm / 1 in thick layer into desired mold. ⑩ Freeze-dry for 48 h to create carrot meringue.
Honey	200 g	40%	⑪ Combine.
Sugar	180 g	36%	⑫ Heat to 170 °C / 338 °F.
Unsalted butter	50 g	10%	⑬ Pour hot mixture onto silicone mat. ⑭ Leave at room temperature to harden completely. ⑮ Break honey caramel into pieces, and measure 210 g.
Honey caramel, from above	210 g	42%	⑯ Grind together in food processor to fine powder.
N-Zorbit M (National Starch brand)	65 g	13% (31%)*	
Freeze-dried mint powder see page 188	5 g	1%	⑰ Break carrot meringue into large pieces. ⑱ Garnish with honey caramel and mint powders.

from page 4·300   *(% of total weight of honey caramel used)

GRUYÈRE SOUFFLÉ

Yields 500 g

INGREDIENT	QUANTITY	SCALING	PROCEDURE
Water	250 g	111%	① Combine, and bring to simmer.
Sodium citrate	8 g	3.5%	
Salt	2.5 g	1%	
Gruyère cheese, finely grated	150 g	67%	② Blend in hot water until completely melted. ③ Centrifuge at 27,500g or higher for 1 h. ④ Strain, and measure 225 g of cheese water.
Gruyère water, from above see page 20	225 g	100%	⑤ Blend until powder dissolves, and allow to hydrate, refrigerated, for at least 6 h.
Albumin powder	32 g	14%	
Tartaric acid	0.4 g	0.18%	⑥ Add, and whip to stiff peaks.
Egg yolks, blended	60 g	27%	⑦ Add and rewhip.
Corn maltodextrin (Maltrin M100, GPC brand)	40 g	17.5%	⑧ Cast into desired mold. ⑨ Steam at 77 °C / 170 °F until fully set. Cool cheese soufflé.
Gruyère, finely grated	120 g	53%	⑩ Spread on silicone mat. ⑪ Bake in 190 °C / 375 °F oven for 15 min, until crisp and golden. ⑫ Cool completely.
N-Zorbit M (National Starch brand)	8 g	3.5%	⑬ Combine with cooled cheese. ⑭ Grind in food processor to fine cheese powder.
Cauliflower crème anglaise see page 235	100 g	44%	⑮ Warm vacuum-sealed crème anglaise at 70 °C / 158 °F for 15 min. ⑯ Toss cold cheese soufflé in cheese powder until evenly coated. ⑰ Reheat in oven at 250 °C / 480 °F until outside is crisp, about 2 min. ⑱ Serve with warmed crème anglaise.

from page 4·301

This recipe is incredibly versatile. Any cheese can be used for this preparation. But, more importantly, the soufflé base can be molded and cut into any shape and reheated for service, thereby allowing you to make a square soufflé with a hollowed center that can accommodate a custard filling.

ZUCCHINI BLOSSOM BEIGNETS

Yields 650 g

INGREDIENT	QUANTITY	SCALING	PROCEDURE
Halibut brandade, see page 112	150 g	100%	① Fold together and reserve. This mixture can be deep-fried as it is similar to very aerated Portuguese bacalao fritters and French accras.
Pâte à choux, see below	250 g	166%	
Carbonated water, refrigerated	180 g	120%	② Combine to make batter.
All-purpose flour	60 g	40%	③ Transfer to 1 l whipping siphon.
Tapioca starch	60 g	40%	④ Charge with three cartridges of nitrous oxide, and shake vigorously.
Trehalose or isomalt	30 g	20%	
Vodka	20 g	13.5%	
Egg whites	45 g	30%	⑤ Whip to stiff peaks.
			⑥ Fold into brandade and pâte à choux mixture.
			⑦ Transfer to piping bag.
Zucchini blossoms	75 g (about eight blossoms)	50%	⑧ Pipe mixture into zucchini blossoms.
Frying oil	as needed		⑨ To serve, dispense batter into open container.
			⑩ Dip stuffed blossoms to coat fully.
			⑪ Deep-fry in 195 °C / 380 °F oil until golden brown, about 3 min.
			⑫ Drain on paper towel-lined tray.
Salt	as needed		⑬ Season beignets.

from page 5·153

PÂTE À CHOUX

Yields 725 g

INGREDIENT	QUANTITY	SCALING	PROCEDURE
Whole milk, heated to 90 °C / 194 °F	250 g	100%	① Disperse Methocel over hot milk, shearing constantly with immersion blender, for 3 min.
Methocel SGA 150 (Dow brand)	3.2 g	1.3% (0.5%)*	② Vacuum seal.
			③ Refrigerate for 12 h to hydrate.
Unsalted butter, melted	70 g	28%	④ Blend with milk, and bring to boil.
Extra virgin olive oil	40 g	16%	
Salt	5 g	2%	
Sugar	5 g	2%	
All-purpose flour, sifted	120 g	48%	⑤ Add to hot milk mixture all at once.
			⑥ Cook, stirring constantly, until mixture forms ball and pot is coated with shiny film of residual dough, about 5 min.
Eggs	250 g	100%	⑦ Transfer ball of dough to stand mixer.
			⑧ Add eggs, one at a time, mixing on low speed with paddle attachment until incorporated.
			⑨ Refrigerate until use.

from page 5·152   *(% of total weight of milk, butter, olive oil, and eggs)

PUFFED SNACKS

① Select a food that puffs well. The table Best Bets for Puffed Snacks below lists our recommendations and any prep steps.

② Parcook (optional). Most foods puff better if first dehydrated by parcooking. See the table for methods, times, and temperatures.

③ Dehydrate. Dry the food until it is 11%–15% water by weight as measured by a moisture analyzer. Dehydration times in the table are given as a guide and will vary. Whole grains do not need a dehydration step because they are already dehydrated.

④ Fry or microwave at 100% power.

Best Bets for Puffed Snacks

ingredient	Preparation	Parcook Method	(°C)	(°F)	(min)	Dehydrate (°C)	(°F)	(h)	Deep-fry (°C)	(°F)	(s)	Microwave at 800 W (s)	See page
legumes (chickpeas, lentils, and mung beans work best)	whole	cover with water and pressure-cook	1 bar / 15 psi		15	50	120	50 min	190	375	40	60 (in paper bag)	344
floury potatoes (for pommes soufflées)	sliced to 2 mm / 1/16 in thick	blanch in oil	157	315			n/a		195	380	30	n/a	below
pregelatinized starch cracker	roll to 1–2 mm / 1/32–1/16 in thick		n/a			65	150	1	200	390	15	35	344
processed grains (white rice and pearl barley work best)	whole	boil until tender	100	212	25	55	130	10	205	400	45	30	next page
rice crisp (white rice)	spread in a layer 2 mm thick after cooking	boil to a porridge (falling apart)	100	212	1 h	50	120	3	200	390	12	40	next page
tapioca starch cracker	roll before cooking or slice after cooking to 1–2 mm / 1/32–1/16 in thick	steam	100	212	70 (for loaf) 30 (for prerolled)	50	120	1	205	400	12	45	next page
dried wheat pasta	whole	boil	100	212	35	55	130	10	205	400	45	2 min	
whole grains (corn, wild rice, and barley with husk work best)	whole		n/a				n/a		200	390	15	90 (in paper bag)	344

from page 4·302

POMMES SOUFFLÉES

Yields 325 g

INGREDIENT	QUANTITY	SCALING
Russet potatoes, peeled and sliced into ovals or rectangles 3 mm / 1/8 in thick to 3.5 mm / 3/32 in thick	400 g	100%
Frying oil	as needed	
Salt	to taste	

from page 4·306

① Preheat two fryers or pots of oil. Bring oil in first pot to 145 °C / 290 °F and oil in second pot to 195 °C / 390 °F.

② Soak potatoes in ice water for 30 min.

③ Dry slices after they have firmed.

④ Blanch in 145 °C / 290 °F oil. Slices will blister in 7–8 min; cook them for another 60 s, and then drain, and pat dry. Rest for at least 5 min and for up to 4 h before puffing.

⑤ Puff in 195 °C / 390 °F oil for 1–3 min, moving potatoes constantly. Do not overcrowd pot. Remove each slice as soon as it has fully puffed and turned evenly brown.

⑥ Drain gently on paper towels. Season with salt.

TAPIOCA STARCH CRACKER

Yields 125 g

INGREDIENT	QUANTITY	SCALING
Warm water (or flavorful liquid)	120 g	60%
Tapioca starch	200 g	100%
Ground meat or shellfish (optional)	65 g	32.5%
Salt	5 g	2.5%
Frying oil	as needed	

from page 4·303

Use only polyethylene-based plastic wrap for this recipe. Films based on polyvinyl chloride (PVC) could leach into the food when used this way.

① Blend all ingredients to make very fluid, thixotropic dough. Use food processor, if available, or wet hands and flexible spatula.
② Roll dough in plastic wrap into tight cylinder, and tie ends firmly.
③ Steam 40–50 min until dough turns gray and slightly translucent.
④ Chill for at least 5 h. Dough will harden as it cools.
⑤ Cut into slices 1–2.5 mm / 1/32–1/8 in thick, using meat slicer, if available. Thin chips will be light and crisp. Thicker chips will be firm, with Styrofoam-like crunch similar to the prawn crackers that Vietnamese restaurants often serve.
⑥ Dehydrate at 50 °C / 122 °F until chips attain dry, yet flexible, plastic-like texture, about 3 h. Their residual moisture content should be 11–14%. To preserve for later use, vacuum seal under light pressure.
⑦ Deep-fry in 198 °C / 390 °F oil until fully puffed, 20–30 s. Remove from oil, and drain on paper towels.

BLACK SESAME RICE CRISPS INSPIRED BY FERRAN ADRIÀ

Yields 300 g

INGREDIENT	QUANTITY	SCALING	PROCEDURE
White long-grain rice	320 g	100%	① Boil until rice is overcooked and achieves porridge-like texture, about 1 h.
Water	1 kg	313%	② Puree with hand blender until nearly smooth but with small fragments throughout.
Black sesame seeds	75 g	23%	③ Mix into rice.
			④ Spread in layer 1.5 mm / 1/16 thick on silicone mat.
			⑤ Dehydrate at 50 °C / 120 °F until dry but still pliable, about 3 h.
			⑥ Break into large fragments, and reserve in dry environment.
Frying oil	as needed		⑦ Heat oil to 190 °C / 375 °F.
			⑧ Deep-fry rice crisps until crisp and slightly puffed, about 12 s.
			⑨ Drain on paper towels.
Salt	to taste		⑩ Season.

from page 4·304

RICE CRISP

Yields 350 g

INGREDIENT	QUANTITY	SCALING	PROCEDURE
Water	1 kg	500%	① Combine rice with 800 g of water. Reserve remaining 200 g of water.
Sushi rice	200 g	100%	② Cook until consistency of porridge, about 1 h.
Glutinous rice flour	120 g	60%	③ Make slurry with 200 g of water, and simmer for 2 min.
			④ Combine with cooked sushi rice, and puree until mostly smooth, but with small fragments throughout.
			⑤ Pour onto silicone mat in layer 1.5 mm / 1/16 in thick.
			⑥ Dehydrate in 50 °C / 122 °F oven until fully desiccated, about 3 h.
			⑦ Break into large fragments.
			⑧ Store in airtight container in cool, dry place.
Frying oil	as needed		⑨ Deep-fry rice crisps in 190 °C / 375 °F oil until very crispy and dry, about 45 s.
Fine salt	as needed		⑩ Drain on paper towels, and season with salt.

from page 5·32

PUFFED CHICKPEAS

Yields 200 g

This process can also be applied to puff whole grains such as forbidden rice and barley (both pictured above before and after puffing) or others such as wild rice, amaranth, and corn. Simply omit the cooking step and deep-fry in 200 °C / 390 °F oil until they puff, about 15 s — or instead coat them with oil and microwave them at 800 W for 90 s in a sealed paper bag.

① Cover chickpeas with twice their volume in cold water. Soak, refrigerated, for 12 h. Drain.
② Combine soaked chickpeas with water in pressure cooker, and cook at a gauge pressure of 1 bar / 15 psi for 15 min. Rest chickpeas for 5 min, and then drain and cool.
③ Spread cooked chickpeas evenly on dehydrator tray, and dehydrate at 50 °C / 120 °F for 50 min.
④ Deep-fry dried chickpeas in 190 °C / 375 °F oil until puffed and golden, about 40 s. Season.

INGREDIENT	QUANTITY	SCALING
Water	500 g	200%
Dry chickpeas	250 g	100%
Frying oil	as needed	
Salt	to taste	

from page 4·307

PUFFED CRAB CRACKER

Yields 125 g

INGREDIENT	QUANTITY	SCALING	PROCEDURE
Shellfish stock see page 6	400 g	100%	① Reduce to 55 g. ② Cool.
Tapioca starch	150 g	37.5%	③ Whisk together with reduced stock to form dough.
Water, warmed	55 g	14%	
Raw crabmeat or prawn meat, ground	55 g	14%	④ Blend with dough in food processor. ⑤ Spread paste on plastic wrap, and roll into cylinder 5 cm / 2 in. in diameter.
Salt	7 g	2%	⑥ Steam for 1 h 10 min. ⑦ Cool, and then refrigerate until rigid, at least 5 h. ⑧ Cut into slices 1 mm / 1/32 in thick, using meat slicer if available. ⑨ Dehydrate slices at 50 °C / 120 °F until brittle, about 1 h. ⑩ Store in airtight container at room temperature.
Frying oil	as needed		⑪ Deep-fry crab crackers in 190 °C / 375 °F oil until puffed, 5–10 s. Dry on absorbent paper towels.

from page 5·190

CHEESE PUFFS INSPIRED BY WYLIE DUFRESNE

Yields 170 g

INGREDIENT	QUANTITY	SCALING	PROCEDURE
N-Zorbit M (National Starch brand)	50 g	16.7%	① Blend until smooth paste. ② Spread thinly on nonstick sheet.
Thin cheddar cheese sauce see page 299	25 g	8.4%	③ Dehydrate at 50 °C / 122 °F for 8–12 h until completely dry. ④ Grind to make cheese powder.
Crisp Coat UC (National Starch brand)	66 g	22%	⑤ Dry blend powders.
Ultra-Sperse M (National Starch brand)	16.5 g	5.5%	
Salt	4 g	1.3%	
Cheddar cheese water see page 20	300 g	100%	⑥ Whisk cheese water into powder mixture to form paste. ⑦ Spread onto silicone mats in one layer, 3 mm / 1/8 in thick. ⑧ Dry in 65 °C / 150 °F oven for 1 h. ⑨ Break into desired shapes.
Frying oil	as needed		⑩ Fry shapes for 10–15 s at 200 °C / 390 °F. ⑪ Drain on paper towels. ⑫ Dust cheese powder over puffs.

from page 4·305

SOCARRAT TUILE

Yields 170 g (about 24 discs)

INGREDIENT	QUANTITY	SCALING	PROCEDURE
Water	160 g	160%	① Vacuum seal together.
Bomba rice	100 g	100%	② Cook sous vide in 90 °C / 194 °F bath until very tender, about 45 min.
Olive oil	5 g	5%	③ Puree with cooked rice mixture until smooth.
Salt	2 g	2%	④ Spread puree evenly on silicone baking mat.
Puffed wild rice see page 342	50 g	50%	⑤ Sprinkle puree evenly with puffed rice.
			⑥ Bake in 150 °C / 302 °F oven until crisp, about 10 min.
Freeze-dried piquillo pepper powder (or sweet paprika) see page 188	1 g	1%	⑦ Dust rice crisp, while still warm, with piquillo pepper powder.
			⑧ Break into desired shapes.
			⑨ Serve, or reserve in airtight container.

from page 5·245

CANDIED PUFFED OATS

Yields 200 g

INGREDIENT	QUANTITY	SCALING	PROCEDURE
Honey	100 g	100%	① Combine.
Trehalose	40 g	40%	② Heat to 185 °C / 365 °F.
Water	20 g	20%	
Baking soda	0.7 g	0.7%	③ Stir into hot sugar mixture.
Puffed oats see page 342	40 g	40%	④ Fold into hot sugar mixture.
			⑤ Pour onto silicone baking mat, and set at room temperature.
Cocoa nibs	9 g	9%	
Salt	1 g	1%	⑥ Break into small chunks, and reserve in airtight container in cool, dry place.
Quatre épices see page 48	0.2 g	0.2%	

from page 5·128

SCALLOP MOCHI

Yields 60 g

INGREDIENT	QUANTITY	SCALING
Water	100 g	200%
Dried scallops (store-bought)	20 g	40%
Mochi flour	50 g	100%
Scallop infusion, from above	50 g	100%
Glucose syrup DE 40	25 g	50%
Salt	1.2 g	2.4%
Frying oil	as needed	
Freeze-dried scallops, ground to fine powder see page 58	5 g	10%

from page 4·308

① Vacuum seal dried scallops with water.

② Cook in 90 °C / 194 °F bath for 1½ h.

③ Remove from bag, and strain. Measure 50 g of scallop infusion, and cool.

④ Mix mochi flour, scallop infusion, glucose, and salt into smooth paste.

⑤ Microwave dough for 2½ min on full power. The dough will turn opaque and become very elastic.

⑥ Roll out mochi dough to 2 mm / 3⁄16 in thick. Place dough between two silicone mats and use rolling pin.

⑦ Remove top mat, and dehydrate dough on bottom mat in a 107 °C / 225 °F oven for 10 min.

⑧ Flip dough over, and dehydrate for 10 min more.

⑨ Run dough through pasta machine to 1 mm / 1⁄32 in thickness.

⑩ Cut with round cutter into scallop shapes.

⑪ Lay each pair of cut shapes on top of each other, and laminate by running them together through pasta roller.

⑫ Repeat lamination process with remaining dough.

⑬ Dehydrate mochi discs at 60 °C / 140 °F until leathery and pliable, about 30 min, to make light puffs. Dehydrate at same temperature for up to 5 h until very dry to make very crispy, denser puffs.

⑭ Deep-fry dehydrated discs in 200 °C / 390 °F oil until fully puffed and golden brown, about 1½ min.

⑮ Dust with scallop powder.

GREMOLATA CRISP

Yields 135 g

INGREDIENT	QUANTITY	SCALING	PROCEDURE
Parsley leaves	245 g	100%	① Blanch until tender and shock, about 2 min.
Water	10 g	4%	② Blend with parsley to make fine puree.
			③ Pass through fine sieve, and measure 85 g.
Water	120 g	49%	④ Cook rice until completely soft and mixture has consistency of porridge, about 35 min.
Long-grain white rice	50 g	20%	⑤ Puree in food processor, leaving small grain specks visible.
			⑥ Cool, and measure 100 g.
Rice puree, from above	100 g	41%	⑦ Combine.
Parsley puree, from above	85 g	35%	⑧ Place crisp base in siphon, and charge with two nitrous oxide cartridges.
			⑨ Dispense onto silicone mat, and spread evenly in thin layer.
Egg whites	75 g	30.5%	⑩ Microwave at medium power (400 W) for 50–60 s to dehydrate. Sheet should be very crunchy.
Vodka	26 g	10.5%	⑪ Break into uneven pieces.
Baking powder	5.2 g	2.1%	⑫ Store crisps in airtight container at room temperature.
Salt	2.2 g	0.9%	
Garlic powder	2 g	0.8%	
Lemon zest, grated	1.3 g	0.5%	
Lemon juice	0.5 g	0.2%	
Black pepper, coarsely cracked	0.4 g	0.16%	
Ascorbic acid	0.35 g	0.14%	
Lemon essential oil	0.1 g (two drops)	0.04%	

from page 5·64

VACUUM-SET FOAMS

AERATED MANGO SORBET

Yields 700 g (17 portions)

INGREDIENT	QUANTITY	SCALING	PROCEDURE
Sugar	280 g	56%	① Whisk together in pot, and cook to 102 °C / 216 °F; syrup density should reach 75 °Brix.
Water	120 g	24%	② Measure and reserve 208 g of syrup.
Mango flesh, frozen	500 g	100%	③ Puree until very smooth and slightly foamy.
Syrup, from above	208 g	41%	④ Place in bowl set over salted ice water, and stir until very cold and viscous.
Citric acid	10.4 g	2%	⑤ Pour 40 g of mango base into 1 pt Mason jars; repeat until all base is used (up to 17 jars).
			⑥ Attach lids and rings, and close until just snug.
			⑦ Place in vacuum chamber, and pull vacuum until sorbet reaches top of jar.
			⑧ Freeze for at least 5 h.
			⑨ Remove from freezer, and open while frozen solid.
			⑩ Replace lid, and allow sorbet to soften slightly at room temperature for 5 min before serving.

from page 4·311

EDIBLE PRUNE COALS

Yields 300 g

INGREDIENT	QUANTITY	SCALING
Dried prunes	200 g	100%
Prune juice	100 g	50%
Armagnac (or cognac)	60 g	30%
Salt	1 g	0.5%
Water	20 g	10%
Gum arabic	10 g	5%
Sugar	75 g	37.5%
Trehalose	75 g	37.5%
Glucose, syrup DE 40	40 g	20%
Water	30 g	15%
Carbon black powder (natural food coloring)	5 g	2.5%
Baking soda, sieved	10 g	5%
Spiced ash see page 206	20 g	10%

from page 4·314

① Boil the dried prunes, with prune juice, Armagnac, and salt. After the prune mixture has come to a boil, remove it from the heat, and let cool.

② Vacuum seal the prunes and liquids together. This is an excellent way to marinate prunes and store them easily until needed. Refrigerate the bag for 12 h, and then remove the prunes from the marinade.

③ Arrange the prunes on a nonstick baking sheet, and brush them evenly with gum arabic solution. Gum arabic acts as a moisture barrier and prevents the black syrup coating (in a later step) from becoming sticky.

④ Dry the prunes in a 190 °C / 375 °F oven for 6 min, turning them every 1½ min to ensure even drying. As a quicker alternative, use a blowtorch to lightly flash each prune's surface. Hold a low flame 10 cm / 4 in away from each prune. Roll the prune while flashing until its surface is uniformly leathery.

⑤ Whisk the sugars and water together to create the black coating syrup. Caramelize it by heating it in a pan to 170 °C / 338 °F. Remove the mixture immediately from the heat, and then whisk in the baking soda and carbon black powder. Be careful—the hot syrup will bubble violently.

⑥ Skewer the dried prunes, and dip them immediately into the hot, black, foamy syrup. Coat all surfaces evenly, and place the coated prunes on a silicone-lined baking sheet. Then place the sheet immediately in a vacuum chamber.

⑦ Pull a vacuum for 20 s. As pressure in the vacuum chamber decreases, the higher pressure of the carbon dioxide inside the bubbles causes them to swell. A sugar coating will form. Turn off the machine, and maintain the pressure. Allow the sugar foam to harden for 10 min before opening the machine. The sugar should transform into a rigid glass that resists collapse when the vacuum is released. Store the prunes in a dry chamber, for no more than 8 h.

⑧ To serve, dust edible ash over the prepared prunes. Dusting the prune coals with ash made from pain d'épices powder blended with food coloring provides a final touch of realism.

AERATED FOIE GRAS ADAPTED FROM WYLIE DUFRESNE

Yields 425 g

INGREDIENT	QUANTITY	SCALING	PROCEDURE
Simplesse (CP Kelco brand)	5.5 g	1.7% (1.25%)*	① Dry blend powders.
Agar	1.7 g	0.5% (0.4%)*	
Konjac gum (TIC Gums brand)	0.7 g	0.2% (0.16%)*	
Xanthan gum (Keltrol T, CP Kelco brand)	0.3 g	0.1% (0.07%)*	
Foie gras torchon see page 104	315 g	100%	② Microwave in bowl until melted, about 2 min. ③ Add gum mixture, blending until completely incorporated.
Water	105 g	33.3%	④ Heat water in microwave for 1½ min.
Egg yolk	20 g (one large)	6.3%	⑤ Combine hot water slowly with yolk to temper, using hand blender. ⑥ Mix in gum and terrine mixture, emulsifying fully. ⑦ Blend emulsion with hand blender to whip in air as mixture cools. ⑧ Cool mixture to 36 °C / 97 °F. ⑨ Transfer to one-sixth-size hotel pan. ⑩ Place in vacuum chamber, and pull vacuum until mixture rises to top of pan. ⑪ Place pan over ice-water bath, and allow foie gras to set for 2 h. ⑫ Break into uneven pieces, and serve.

from page 4·311

*(% of total weight of last three ingredients)

AERATED GRUYÈRE

Yields 360 g

INSPIRED BY H. ALEXANDER TALBOT AND AKI KAMOZAWA

INGREDIENT	QUANTITY	SCALING	PROCEDURE
Skim milk	180 g	100%	① Blend until powders are incorporated.
160 Bloom gelatin	3.6 g	2% (1%)*	② Bring to boil over medium heat. ③ Remove from heat.
Agar (Texturas brand)	1 g	0.55% (0.28%)*	
Locust bean gum (POR/A2 Powder, TIC Gums brand)	0.1 g	0.05% (0.03%)*	
Gruyère cheese, grated	180 g	100%	④ Add to hot milk mixture, and stir until cheese has melted.
Salt	3 g	1.6%	⑤ Pour into blender, and process until completely homogenous.
Cayenne pepper powder	0.2 g	0.1%	⑥ Transfer to 1 l whipping siphon, and charge with two cartridges of nitrous oxide. ⑦ Dispense into four 235 ml / 8 fl oz Mason jars. ⑧ Seal with lids immediately. ⑨ Refrigerate for at least 5 h before opening.

from page 4·312

*(% of total weight of cheese and skim milk)

AERATED COFFEE ICE CREAM ADAPTED FROM ALEX STUPAK

Yields 300 g

INGREDIENT	QUANTITY	SCALING	PROCEDURE
Whole milk	500 g	100%	① Combine, and vacuum seal. Infuse, refrigerated, for 24 h.
Coffee beans	50 g	10%	
			② Strain.
Sugar	122 g	24.4%	③ Whisk into warm milk until dissolved.
Dextrose	97.5 g	19.5%	
Egg yolks	24.5 g (from two eggs)	4.9%	④ Pour warm milk over yolks, and whisk to temper.
Propylene glycol alginate (Protanal Ester BV 4830, FMC BioPolymer brand)	4.9 g	1% (0.5%)*	⑤ Transfer mixture to blender, and mix in PGA on low speed.
			⑥ Increase to high speed, and blend for 1 min.
Cream cheese	80.5 g	16.1%	⑦ Add to blender, and continue blending until smooth.
Unsalted butter	73 g	14.6%	⑧ Cool completely over ice water.
Salt	1.95 g	0.4%	⑨ Churn in ice cream machine according to manufacturer's instructions, or freeze in Pacojet beaker and pacotize.
			⑩ Transfer ice cream to piping bag, and pipe layer 1 cm / ½ in thick into bottom of Food Saver canister; or pipe into Mason jars, and cover with lids.
			⑪ Place container or jars in vacuum machine, and pull vacuum until foaming ice cream reaches top of container.
			⑫ Remove from machine, and freeze for at least 8 h before opening and serving.

from page 4·312   *(% of total weight of milk, sugar, dextrose, yolk, cream cheese, and butter)

Ice cream is a foam. Air bubbles, called overrun for ice cream, typically make up 33%–50% of ice cream by volume. Alex Stupak increases that percentage by using a vacuum to expand the foam.

AERATED CHOCOLATE ADAPTED FROM HESTON BLUMENTHAL

Yields 500 g

INGREDIENT	QUANTITY	SCALING	PROCEDURE
Milk chocolate (33% cocoa solids)	500 g	100%	① Combine, and vacuum seal.
			② Melt sous vide in 53 °C / 127 °F bath for 12 h.
Mycryo spray-dried cocoa butter (Callebaut brand)	10 g	2%	③ Place sheet of aluminum foil on bottom of 5 cm by 20 cm by 30.5cm / 2 in by 8 in by 12 in mold. Set mold in vacuum chamber.
			④ Transfer melted chocolate mixture to metal or glass bowl.
Mandarin essential oil (optional)	5 g	1%	⑤ Stir constantly until cooled to 28 °C / 82 °F.
Polyglycerol polyricinoleate (PGPR)	1 g	0.2%	⑥ Place bowl of chocolate over simmering water, and stir constantly until chocolate reaches 32 °C / 90 °F.
			⑦ Transfer to warmed 1 l whipping siphon, and charge with two cartridges of nitrous dioxide.
			⑧ Dispense quickly into foil-lined mold.
			⑨ Pull vacuum, and allow foam to rise to top of mold.
			⑩ Turn off vacuum machine, but hold foam under vacuum for 1 h to set.
			⑪ Remove aerated chocolate from chamber, and store in cool, dry environment.

from page 4·313

The British Aero candy bar was the original inspiration for Heston Blumenthal's aerated chocolate, which we have adapted for this book.

COFFEE BUTTER

Yields 125 g

INGREDIENT	QUANTITY	SCALING	PROCEDURE
Roasted coffee beans	175 g	100%	① Seal together in Mason jar.
Unsalted butter	125 g	71%	② Boil for 4 h. Or, vacuum seal mixture, and cook sous vide in 90 °C / 194 °F bath for 4 h.
			③ Refrigerate.

from page 4·371

Cold extraction is our favorite way to make coffee for use as an ingredient in cooking. A different approach to incorporating coffee flavor in food is to use commercial instant espresso powder. It can even be used dry, in a spice rub for a steak, for example.

For more on extracting flavors using butter and other fats, see page 2·328. You might think that extraction in this coffee butter would be more effective if the coffee were ground. It would be, but unfortunately, that makes the flavor unbalanced, so we prefer whole beans here.

STABLE LATTE FOAM

Yields 200 g

INGREDIENT	QUANTITY	SCALING	PROCEDURE
Skim milk	400 g	100%	① Dry blend powders, and disperse in cold milk.
Whey protein isolate	4 g	1%	② Blend until fully dissolved.
Sucrose esters (Sucro, Texturas brand)	4.8 g	1.2%	③ Steam with steam wand, or whip with an Aerolatte wand until stiff head of foam forms, 2–3 min.
			④ Stir to moisten with milk.
			⑤ Foam remains stable for up to 30 min.

from page 4·392

NOTES

REFERENCE TABLES

Converting Temperature

To convert temperatures from Celsius to Fahrenheit, multiply by 1.8, then add 32 to the product.

To convert from Fahrenheit to Celsius, subtract 32, then multiply the result by ⅝ (0.56).

Celsius to Fahrenheit		Fahrenheit to Celsius	
(°C)	(°F)	(°F)	(°C)
−196.0	−320.8	−200.0	−128.9
−78.5	−109.3	−80.0	−62.2
−60.0	−76.0	−60.0	−51.1
−40.0	−40.0	−40.0	−40.0
−20.0	−4.0	−20.0	−28.9
0	32.0	0	−17.8
1	33.8	1	−17.2
2	35.6	2	−16.7
3	37.4	3	−16.1
4	39.2	4	−15.6
5	41.0	5	−15.0
6	42.8	6	−14.4
7	44.6	7	−13.9
8	46.4	8	−13.3
9	48.2	9	−12.8
10	50.0	10	−12.2
11	51.8	11	−11.7
12	53.6	12	−11.1
13	55.4	13	−10.6
14	57.2	14	−10.0
15	59.0	15	−9.4
16	60.8	16	−8.9
17	62.6	17	−8.3
18	64.4	18	−7.8
19	66.2	19	−7.2
20	68.0	20	−6.7
21	69.8	21	−6.1
22	71.6	22	−5.6
23	73.4	23	−5.0
24	75.2	24	−4.4
25	77.0	25	−3.9
26	78.8	26	−3.3

Converting Temperature

Celsius to Fahrenheit		Fahrenheit to Celsius	
(°C)	(°F)	(°F)	(°C)
27	80.6	27	−2.8
28	82.4	28	−2.2
29	84.2	29	−1.7
30	86.0	30	−1.1
31	87.8	31	−0.6
32	89.6	32	0.0
33	91.4	33	0.6
34	93.2	34	1.1
35	95.0	35	1.7
36	96.8	36	2.2
37	98.6	37	2.8
38	100.4	38	3.3
39	102.2	39	3.9
40	104.0	40	4.4
41	105.8	41	5.0
42	107.6	42	5.6
43	109.4	43	6.1
44	111.2	44	6.7
45	113.0	45	7.2
46	114.8	46	7.8
47	116.6	47	8.3
48	118.4	48	8.9
49	120.2	49	9.4
50	122.0	50	10.0
51	123.8	51	10.6
52	125.6	52	11.1
53	127.4	53	11.7
54	129.2	54	12.2
55	131.0	55	12.8
56	132.8	56	13.3
57	134.6	57	13.9
58	136.4	58	14.4
59	138.2	59	15.0
60	140.0	60	15.6
61	141.8	61	16.1
62	143.6	62	16.7
63	145.4	63	17.2
64	147.2	64	17.8
65	149.0	65	18.3
66	150.8	66	18.9

Converting Temperature

Celsius to Fahrenheit		Fahrenheit to Celsius	
(°C)	(°F)	(°F)	(°C)
67	152.6	67	19.4
68	154.4	68	20.0
69	156.2	69	20.6
70	158.0	70	21.1
71	159.8	71	21.7
72	161.6	72	22.2
73	163.4	73	22.8
74	165.2	74	23.3
75	167.0	75	23.9
76	168.8	76	24.4
77	170.6	77	25.0
78	172.4	78	25.6
79	174.2	79	26.1
80	176.0	80	26.7
81	177.8	81	27.2
82	179.6	82	27.8
83	181.4	83	28.3
84	183.2	84	28.9
85	185.0	85	29.4
86	186.8	86	30.0
87	188.6	87	30.6
88	190.4	88	31.1
89	192.2	89	31.7
90	194.0	90	32.2
91	195.8	91	32.8
92	197.6	92	33.3
93	199.4	93	33.9
94	201.2	94	34.4
95	203.0	95	35.0
96	204.8	96	35.6
97	206.6	97	36.1
98	208.4	98	36.7
99	210.2	99	37.2
100	212	100	37.8
105	221	105	40.6
110	230	110	43.3
115	239	115	46.1
120	248	120	48.9
125	257	125	51.7
130	266	130	54.4

Converting Temperature

Celsius to Fahrenheit		Fahrenheit to Celsius	
(°C)	(°F)	(°F)	(°C)
135	275	135	57.2
140	284	140	60.0
145	293	145	62.8
150	302	150	65.6
155	311	155	68.3
160	320	160	71.1
165	329	165	73.9
170	338	170	76.7
175	347	175	79.4
180	356	180	82.2
185	365	185	85.0
190	374	190	87.8
195	383	195	90.6
200	392	200	93.3
205	401	205	96.1
210	410	210	98.9
215	419	215	101.7
220	428	220	104.4
225	437	225	107.2
230	446	230	110.0
235	455	235	112.8
240	464	240	115.6
245	473	245	118.3
250	482	250	121.1
255	491	255	123.9
260	500	260	126.7
265	509	265	129.4
270	518	270	132.2
275	527	275	135.0
280	536	280	137.8
285	545	285	140.6
290	554	290	143.3
295	563	295	146.1
300	572	300	148.9

USEFUL TEMPERATURES

Boiling point of liquid nitrogen:
−196 °C / **−321** °F

Sublimation temperature of dry ice:
−78.5 °C / **−109.3** °F

Freezing point of water:
0 °C / **32** °F

Boiling point of water at sea level:
100 °C / **212** °F

REFERENCE TABLES

Converting Grams to Volume for Common Ingredients

To convert the weights given in our recipes to volumetric measurements, divide the number of grams by the conversion factor below.

	1 ml	1 tsp	1 Tbsp	½ cup	1 cup
PANTRY ITEMS					
Flours and Starches					
00 flour	0.68	3.3	10.0	80	160
all-purpose flour	0.68	3.3	10.0	80	160
almond flour	0.57	2.8	8.4	68	135
buckwheat flour, sifted	0.55	2.7	8.1	65	130
cake flour	0.49	2.4	7.3	59	117
chickpea flour, sifted	0.56	2.8	8.3	66	132
cornmeal	0.67	3.3	9.9	79	158
cornstarch	0.03	0.2	0.5	4	8
durum flour	0.63	3.1	9.4	75	150
gluten flour	0.04	0.2	0.6	5	10
rice flour, glutinous	0.49	2.4	7.3	59	117
rice flour, sweet	0.63	3.1	9.4	75	150
semolina	0.79	3.9	11.7	94	187
tapioca	0.72	3.5	10.6	85	170
Grains and Legumes					
barley	0.70	3.5	10.4	83	166
brown rice crisp	0.15	0.8	2.3	18	36
chickpeas	0.85	4.2	12.5	100	200
lentils, black (urad dal)	0.85	4.2	12.5	100	200
lentils, green	0.87	4.3	12.9	104	207
oats, rolled	0.42	2.1	6.3	50	100
oats, steel-cut	0.75	3.7	11.1	89	178
oats, toasted	0.42	2.1	6.3	50	100
peas, black-eyed	0.85	4.2	12.5	100	200
quinoa	0.75	3.7	11.1	89	178
rice, Arborio	0.89	4.4	13.1	105	210
rice, basmati	0.79	3.9	11.8	94	188
rice, jasmine	0.83	4.1	12.3	98	196
rice, paella	0.80	4.0	11.9	95	190
rice, sushi	0.90	4.4	13.3	106	212
rice, wild	0.74	3.6	10.9	88	175
rye, berries	0.78	3.9	11.6	93	185
rye, cracked	0.68	3.3	10.0	80	160
soy beans	0.40	2.0	5.9	48	95
tapioca, small pearl	0.75	3.7	11.1	89	178

Converting Weights

To convert weights from grams to ounces, divide by 28.35. To convert from ounces to grams, multiply by 28.35.

Grams to ounces		Ounces to grams	
(g)	(oz)	(oz)	(g)
0.1	0.004	0.1	2.8
0.2	0.007	0.2	5.7
0.3	0.011	0.3	8.5
0.4	0.014	0.4	11.3
0.5	0.018	0.5	14.2
0.6	0.021	0.6	17.0
0.7	0.025	0.7	19.8
0.8	0.028	0.8	22.7
0.9	0.032	0.9	25.5
1	0.035	1	28.4
2	0.071	2	56.7
3	0.106	3	85.1
4	0.141	4	113.4
5	0.176	5	141.8
6	0.212	6	170.1
7	0.247	7	198.5
8	0.282	8	226.8
9	0.317	9	255.2
10	0.353	10	283.5
11	0.388	11	311.9
12	0.423	12	340.2
13	0.459	13	368.6
14	0.494	14	396.9
15	0.529	15	425.3
16	0.564	16	453.6
17	0.600	17	482.0
18	0.635	18	510.3
19	0.670	19	538.7
20	0.705	20	567.0
21	0.741	21	595.4
22	0.776	22	623.7
23	0.811	23	652.1
24	0.847	24	680.4
25	0.882	25	708.8
30	1.058	30	850.5
35	1.235	35	992.3
40	1.411	40	1,134.0

Converting Weights

Grams to ounces		Ounces to grams	
(g)	(oz)	(oz)	(g)
45	1.587	45	1,275.8
50	1.764	50	1,417.5
55	1.940	55	1,559.3
60	2.116	60	1,701.0
65	2.293	65	1,842.8
70	2.469	70	1,984.5
75	2.646	75	2,126.3
80	2.822	80	2,268.0
85	2.998	85	2,409.8
90	3.175	90	2,551.5
95	3.351	95	2,693.3
100	3.527	100	2,835.0
110	3.880	110	3,118.5
120	4.233	120	3,402.0
130	4.586	130	3,685.5
140	4.938	140	3,969.0
150	5.291	150	4,252.5
160	5.644	160	4,536.0
170	5.996	170	4,819.5
180	6.349	180	5,103.0
190	6.702	190	5,386.5
200	7.055	200	5,670.0
250	8.818	250	7,087.5
300	10.582	300	8,505.0
350	12.346	350	9,922.5
400	14.109	400	11,340.0
450	15.873	450	12,757.5
500	17.637	500	14,175.0
550	19.400	550	15,592.5
600	21.164	600	17,010.0
650	22.928	650	18,427.5
700	24.691	700	19,845.0
750	26.455	750	21,262.5
800	28.219	800	22,680.0
850	29.982	850	24,097.5
900	31.746	900	25,515.0
950	33.510	950	26,932.5
1,000	35.273	1,000	28,350.0

1 pound = 453.59 g = 16 oz
1 kg = 2.2 lb

Converting Grams to Volume for Common Ingredients

	1 ml	1 tsp	1 Tbsp	½ cup	1 cup
Liquids					
cocoa butter	0.58	2.9	8.6	69	138
cream, whipping	0.91	4.5	13.4	108	215
crème fraîche	0.96	4.8	14.3	114	228
milk, 1% fat	0.98	4.8	14.5	116	232
milk, 2% fat	0.93	4.6	13.7	110	219
milk, skim	0.98	4.8	14.5	116	232
milk, soy	0.97	4.8	14.4	115	230
milk, whole	0.97	4.8	14.4	115	230
oils	0.78	3.9	11.6	93	185
vinegars	0.86	4.3	12.8	102	204
vodka	0.80	4.0	11.9	95	190
water	0.97	4.8	14.4	115	230
wine	0.89	4.4	13.1	105	210
Nuts					
almonds, blanched	0.61	3.0	9.1	73	145
almonds, marcona, roasted	0.55	2.7	8.1	65	130
cashews, roasted	0.72	3.5	10.6	85	170
hazelnuts, peeled and roasted	0.64	3.2	9.5	76	152
macadamia nuts, roasted	1.14	5.6	16.9	135	270
pine nuts, roasted	0.61	3.0	9.1	73	145
pistachios, peeled and roasted	0.51	2.5	7.5	60	120
walnuts, roasted	0.38	1.9	5.6	45	90
Sauces and Syrups					
barley malt	1.69	8.3	25.0	200	400
ketchup	1.19	5.9	17.6	141	282
maple syrup	1.45	7.2	21.5	172	344
molasses	1.45	7.2	21.5	172	344
soy sauce, brown	1.08	5.3	16.0	128	256
soy sauce, white	1.08	5.3	16.0	128	256
tomato paste	1.12	5.5	16.6	133	265
Worcestershire sauce	1.19	5.9	17.6	141	282
Sugars					
agave nectar	1.45	7.2	21.5	172	344
fructose	0.82	4.1	12.2	98	195
glucose	1.45	7.2	21.5	172	344
honey	1.45	7.2	21.5	172	344
isomalt	0.95	4.7	14.1	113	225
sugar, brown	0.72	3.5	10.6	85	170
sugar, Demerara	0.70	3.5	10.4	83	166

Converting Grams to Volume for Common Ingredients

	1 ml	1 tsp	1 Tbsp	½ cup	1 cup
sugar, granulated	0.87	4.3	12.8	103	205
sugar, muscovado	1.08	5.3	15.9	128	255
sugar, palm	0.82	4.1	12.2	98	195
sugar, powdered	0.49	2.4	7.2	58	115
sugar, raw cane	0.98	4.8	14.5	116	232
SEASONINGS					
Chilies, Dry					
Aleppo peppers, crushed	0.50	2.5	7.4	59	118
black peppercorns, ground	0.32	1.6	4.8	38	77
black peppercorns, whole	0.61	3.0	9.0	72	144
cayenne, powder	0.41	2.0	6.0	48	96
Hungarian paprika, powder	0.37	1.8	5.5	44	88
pimentón de la Vera, powder	0.41	2.0	6.0	48	96
pink peppercorns, whole	0.44	2.3	6.5	52	104
red chili, powder	0.51	2.5	7.5	60	120
Sichuan pepper, crushed	0.47	2.3	7.0	56	112
Thai chili, flakes	0.37	1.8	5.5	44	88
white peppercorns, whole	0.68	3.3	10.0	80	160
Herbs and Aromatics, Fresh, Minced					
basil	0.39	1.9	5.8	47	93
chamomile, dry blossoms, powder	0.20	1.0	3.0	24	48
chamomile, dry blossoms, whole	0.10	0.5	1.5	12	24
cilantro	0.51	2.5	7.5	60	120
elderberry, dry	0.47	2.3	7.0	56	112
garlic	1.15	5.7	17.0	136	272
hawthorne berries	0.61	3.0	9.0	72	144
heather tips	0.17	0.8	2.5	20	40
juniper berries	0.47	2.3	7.0	56	112
lavender	0.14	0.7	2.0	16	32
lemon zest, grated	0.64	3.2	9.5	76	152
lemongrass, minced	0.47	2.3	7.0	56	112
licorice root, chunks	0.41	2.0	6.0	48	96
lime zest, grated	0.64	3.2	9.5	76	152
mint	0.20	1.0	3.0	24	48
orange zest	0.64	3.2	9.5	76	152
oregano	0.39	1.9	5.8	47	93
parsley	0.51	2.5	7.5	60	120
rosemary	0.39	1.9	5.8	47	93
shallots	0.49	2.4	7.3	59	117

Common Conversion Factors

To convert from:	To:	Multiply by:
ml	tsp	0.203
tsp	ml	4.93
ml	Tbsp	0.068
Tbsp	ml	14.787
ml	cup	0.004
cup	ml	236.59
tsp	cup	0.021
cup	tsp	48
Tbsp	cup	0.063
cup	Tbsp	16
ml	oz	0.034
oz	ml	29.574
pint	qt	0.5
qt	pint	2
qt	gal	0.25
gal	qt	4
qt	l	0.946
l	qt	1.057
l	gal	0.264
gal	l	3.785
oz	lb	0.063
lb	oz	16
g	oz	0.035
oz	g	28.35
g	lb	0.002
lb	g	453.592
oz	kg	0.028
kg	oz	35.274
lb	kg	0.454
kg	lb	2.2
mm	in	0.394
in	mm	25.4
cm	in	0.394
in	cm	2.54
m	ft	3.3
ft	m	0.305
s	min	0.017
J	BTU	0.001
BTU	J	1,055.10
kcal	BTU	3.966
BTU	kcal	0.252

Common Conversion Factors

To convert from:	To:	Multiply by:
kcal	J	4,184
J	kcal	0.000
W	BTU/h	0.001
BTU/h	W	1,055.04
W	hp	0.001
hp	W	745.7
g/cm³	oz/in³	0.578
oz/in³	g/cm³	1.73
N	lb force	0.225
lb force	N	4.482
mbar	torr	0.75
torr	mbar	1.333
mbar	psi	0.015
psi	mbar	68.95
bar	psi	14.5
psi	bar	0.069
Pa	mbar	0.01
mbar	Pa	100
bar	atm	0.987
atm	bar	1.013

Converting Volume Measures

Metric	U.S.	Imperial	
(ml)		(pint)	(fl oz)
5	1 tsp		⅖
15	1 Tbsp		½
30	2 Tbsp		1
60	¼ cup	⅛	2
90	⅓ cup	⅓	3
120	½ cup	⅕	4
150	⅔ cup	¼	5
180	¾ cup	⅓	6
240	1 cup	⅖	8
300	1¼ cups	½	10
480	2 cups	⅔	16
600	2½ cups	1	20
1,000	1 quart	2	32

Converting Grams to Volume for Common Ingredients

	1 ml	1 tsp	1 Tbsp	½ cup	1 cup
tarragon	0.34	1.7	5.0	40	80
Thai chili, minced	0.41	2.0	6.0	48	96
winter greens, dry	0.24	1.2	3.5	28	56
Herbs, Dry					
oregano	0.17	0.8	2.5	20	40
rosemary	0.20	1.0	3.0	24	48
savory	0.20	1.0	3.0	24	48
Salts					
salt, Bali pyramid	0.81	4.0	12.0	96	192
salt, black	0.68	3.3	10.0	80	160
salt, fine sea	1.14	6.2	18.5	135	270
salt, kosher	1.06	5.8	17.6	125	250
salt, Maldon	0.81	4.0	12.0	96	192
salt, sea	0.74	3.7	11.0	88	176
salt, sumac	0.81	4.0	12.0	96	192
Spices, Dry					
ajowan seed, powder	0.56	2.8	8.3	66	132
ajowan seed, whole	0.56	2.8	8.3	67	133
angelica seed, whole	0.09	0.5	1.4	11	22
barley malt vinegar, powder	0.57	2.8	8.5	68	136
caraway seed	0.52	2.6	7.8	62	124
cardamom seed, green	0.57	2.8	8.5	68	136
cassia, chunks	0.64	3.2	9.5	76	152
celery seed	0.47	3.0	7.0	56	112
chaat masala	0.64	3.2	9.5	76	152
chicory	0.44	2.2	6.5	52	104
cinnamon, powder	0.46	2.3	6.8	55	109
clove, powder	0.47	2.3	7.0	56	112
clove, whole	0.44	2.2	6.5	52	104
cocoa nib	0.54	2.7	8.0	64	128
cocoa powder	0.57	2.8	8.4	68	135
coconut cream, powder	0.37	1.8	5.5	44	88
coriander seed	0.34	1.7	5.0	40	80
cumin, black	0.46	2.3	6.8	55	109
cumin, powder	0.54	2.7	8.0	64	128
cumin, whole	0.23	1.1	3.4	27	54
fennel seed, powder	0.44	2.2	6.5	52	104
fennel seed, whole	0.79	3.9	11.7	94	187
fenugreek seed	0.95	4.7	14.0	112	224
four-spice, powder	0.41	2.0	6.0	48	96

REFERENCE TABLES

Converting Grams to Volume for Common Ingredients

	1 ml	1 tsp	1 Tbsp	½ cup	1 cup
garum masala, powder	0.54	2.7	8.0	64	128
ginger, powder	0.37	1.8	5.5	44	88
grains of paradise, whole	0.68	3.3	10.0	80	160
licorice, powder	0.51	2.5	7.5	60	120
mace, powder	0.34	1.7	5.0	40	80
mace, whole	0.41	2.0	6.0	48	96
mustard seed, black, whole	0.74	3.7	11.0	88	176
mustard seed, yellow, whole	0.74	3.7	11.0	88	176
nigella seed, whole	0.78	3.8	11.5	92	184
nutmeg, powder	0.44	2.2	6.5	52	104
pomegranate seed, whole	0.81	4.0	12.0	96	192
poppy seed, black	0.57	2.8	8.5	68	136
poppy seed, black or white	0.54	2.7	8.0	64	128
porcini mushroom, powder	0.51	2.5	7.5	60	120
saffron, threads	0.20	1.0	3.0	24	48
scallop, freeze-dried, powder	0.37	1.8	5.5	44	88
sesame seed, black	0.54	2.7	8.0	64	128
sesame seed, roasted	0.54	2.7	8.0	64	128
star anise, powder	0.44	2.2	6.5	52	104
tamarind, powder	0.47	2.3	7.0	56	112
tomato, freeze-dried, powder	0.61	3.0	9.0	72	144
turmeric, powder	0.51	2.5	7.5	60	120
Dairy					
butter	0.95	4.7	14.1	113	225
cream cheese	0.89	4.4	13.1	105	210
crème fraîche	0.95	4.7	14.1	113	225
Gruyère, grated	0.38	1.9	5.6	45	90
mascarpone	0.95	4.7	14.1	113	225
Parmesan, grated	0.30	1.5	4.4	35	70
ricotta	1.04	5.1	15.4	124	247
Eggs					
chicken egg, blended	0.98	5.8	17.5	116	232
chicken egg, large, white	0.91	4.5	13.4	108	215
chicken egg, large, yolk	0.85	4.2	12.5	100	200
Fish					
fish, ground	0.97	4.8	14.4	115	230
roe, steelhead trout	1.50	7.5	22.3	178	357
shrimp, ground	0.96	4.7	14.1	113	226

Water Content of Typical Foods

Food	Water content (%)
Animal Foods	
beef, eye of round, raw	73
beef, ground, 73% lean, raw	56
beef, ground, 85% lean, raw	64
beef, whole brisket, raw	71
butter or margarine	20
cheese, American	37
chicken fryer, whole, raw	66
chicken, dark meat, with skin, raw	66
chicken, white meat, with skin, raw	69
eggs, raw, whole	74
ham, cooked	54
milk, cow	87
pork, chops, broiled	45
turkey, roasted	62
veal, broiled	60
Fruits	
apple, raw	84
apricot, raw	86
banana, raw	75
blackberry, raw	86
blueberry, raw	85
cantaloupe, raw	90
cherry, raw	80
cranberry, raw	87
fruit cocktail, canned	80
grape, raw	82
grapefruit, raw	90
mango, raw	82
melon, honeydew, raw	90
orange, raw	87
papaya, raw	89
peach, raw	88
pear, raw	84
pineapple, raw	85

Water Content of Typical Foods

Food	Water content (%)
plum, raw	85
raspberry, raw	81
strawberry, raw	92
watermelon, raw	93
Grains, Legumes, Nuts, and Seeds	
almonds, raw	7
bread, whole wheat	35
coconut, dried	7
grains/legumes/seeds, dry	≤10
lentils, cooked	67
macaroni or spaghetti, cooked	70
pecans, raw	7
rice, bleached	68
walnuts, raw	4
Herbs	
cilantro, raw	92
parsley, raw	86
Sweeteners	
honey	15
jam/preserves	30
molasses	25
Vegetables	
asparagus, raw	92
bean sprout, raw	92
bean, green, raw	90
beet, raw	87
bok choy, raw	95
broccoli, raw	91
Brussels sprout, raw	86
cabbage, raw	92
carrot, raw	88
cassava, raw	60
cauliflower, raw	92
celery, raw	95
corn, sweet, fresh, raw	74
cucumber, raw	96

Water Content of Typical Foods

Food	Water content (%)
eggplant, raw	92
greens, beet, raw	92
greens, collard, raw	91
greens, dandelion, raw	86
greens, turnip	91
kale, raw	87
lettuce, iceberg, raw	96
lettuce, loose leaf, raw	94
lettuce, romaine, raw	95
mushroom, raw	92
okra, boiled or raw	90
olives	80
onions, raw	89
parsnip, raw	80
peas, green, raw	80
peppers, bell	92
pickle, cucumber	93
potato, raw	85
pumpkin, canned	90
pumpkin, raw	92
radish, raw	95
rutabaga, boiled	90
sauerkraut, canned	93
spinach, raw	92
squash, acorn, raw	88
squash, boiled	96
squash, butternut	94
squash, kabocha, raw	94
squash, spaghetti	94
squash, yellow	94
sweet potato, boiled in skin	71
sweet potato, raw	73
Swiss chard	94
tomato, raw	93
watercress, raw	90
zucchini	95

Converting Grams to Volume for Ingredients

	1 ml	1 tsp	1 Tbsp	½ cup	1 cup
Fish					
fish, ground	0.97	4.8	14.4	115	230
roe, steelhead trout	1.50	7.5	22.3	178	357
shrimp, ground	0.96	4.7	14.1	113	226
tobiko	0.80	3.9	11.8	94	189
Meat, Ground					
beef	1.27	6.3	18.8	150	300
chicken, breast	1.06	5.2	15.6	125	250
chicken, thigh	1.06	5.2	15.6	125	250
pork	1.27	6.3	18.8	150	300
Vegetables and Fruits					
apple, thinly sliced	0.49	2.4	7.2	58	115
avocado, puree	0.91	4.5	13.4	108	215
butternut squash, brunoise	0.05	0.2	0.7	6	11
butternut squash, thinly sliced	0.66	3.2	9.7	78	155
cabbage, red, thinly sliced	0.42	2.1	6.3	50	100
cabbage, white, thinly sliced	0.42	2.1	6.3	50	100
cantaloupe, thinly sliced	0.91	4.5	13.4	108	215
carrot, thinly sliced	0.42	2.1	6.3	50	100
cauliflower, thinly sliced	0.51	2.5	7.5	60	120
celery, thinly sliced	0.42	2.1	6.3	50	100
corn, kernels	0.76	3.8	11.3	90	180
fennel, thinly sliced	0.38	1.9	5.6	45	90
honeydew melon, thinly sliced	0.91	4.5	13.4	108	215
leek, thinly sliced	0.38	1.9	5.6	45	90
mushroom, button, thinly sliced	0.36	1.8	5.3	43	85
onion, thinly sliced	0.44	2.2	6.6	53	105
pea, green, shelled	0.68	3.3	10.0	80	160
pear, thinly sliced	0.72	3.5	10.6	85	170
pineapple, brunoise	0.08	0.4	1.2	9	18
pineapple, thinly sliced	0.82	4.1	12.2	98	195
scallion, thinly sliced (green part)	0.30	1.5	4.4	35	70
scallion, thinly sliced (white part)	0.41	2.0	6.1	49	98
shiitake mushroom, thinly sliced	0.27	1.4	4.1	33	65
tomatoes concassé	0.91	4.5	13.4	108	215

Fat Content of Typical Foods

Typical Food	Fat Content (%)
Eggs, Dairy, and Oils	
butter	87
cheese, aged, firm	25–31
cheese, aged, soft	23–35
cheese, Camembert	23
cheese, cheddar	31
cheese, cottage	4
cheese, cream	20
cheese, fresh	2–18
cheese, mozzarella	19
cheese, Parmesan	24–26
cheese, ricotta	13
cream, double	>38
cream, half-and-half	11–17
cream, heavy	38
cream, light whipping	32–36
cream, sour	12
crème fraîche	28
egg white	0.2
egg yolk	26
milk, cow	3.5
milk, goat	4.5
milk, grey seal	53
milk, low fat	2
milk, reindeer	17
milk, sheep	7
milk, skim	0
milk, water buffalo	9.5
milk, whole	3.5–4
oil, refined	99
oil, unrefined	96–99
Meats, Raw	
bacon	50–70
bacon, Canadian	1–4
bone marrow	75
brain	8
foie gras	45–52
heart	3
kidneys	20

Fat Content of Typical Foods

Typical Food	Fat Content (%)
liver, chicken	4
liver, veal	7
pork, backfat	80
pork, fatty	30
pork, lean	1.5–2
red meat, lean	4
red meat, marbled	10
red poultry (duck, goose, pigeon), breast meat, skinless	1–1.5
red poultry, leg meat	12
sweetbreads	15–18
tongue	15
veal, lean	3
white poultry (chicken, turkey), dark meat	6.5
white poultry, white meat	1–1.5
Fish and Shellfish	
cod	1
mackerel	5
rockfish	3
salmon	5–10
sardine	5
shellfish	1
tuna, belly	12–15
tuna, lean	1
whitefish	1–3
Nuts and Seeds	
almonds	55
cashews	44
coconut	57
hazelnuts	64
kukui nuts (candlenuts)	64
macadamia nuts	74
olives	3
peanuts	44
pecans	70

Fat Content of Typical Foods

Typical Food	Fat Content (%)
pistachios	55
sesame seeds	48
sunflower seeds	50
walnuts	61
Other Plant Foods	
avocado	14
bread, whole wheat	4.2
chickpeas, cooked	2
corn	2.7–8
fruit	<1
grains	0.15
lentils, boiled	0.5
vegetables	<1

Volumetric Equivalents for Amounts of Typical Foods

Typical food	Weight or amount	Equivalent (approximate)
asparagus spears, fresh	1 lb	16 to 20 spears
bananas, fresh	1 lb	3-4 fruits; 2 cups sliced; or 1½ cups mashed
beans, green, fresh	1 lb	3 cups
beans, kidney, dried	1 lb	2½ cups
beans, navy, dried	1 lb	2⅓ cups; 5⅓ cups, cooked
beans, soy, dried	1 lb	2 cups
bread crumbs, dry	4 oz	¾ cup
bread crumbs, fresh	4 oz	2 cups
broccoli, fresh	1 lb	2 cups, chopped
carrots/root vegetables, pureed	1 lb	1⅓ cups
carrots/root vegetables, sliced	1 lb	3 cups
cheese	3½ oz	1 cup
coffee, ground	1 lb	80 Tbsp
corn, fresh	2 medium ears	1 cup of kernels
eggs, whole, extra large	1 dozen	3 cups
eggs, whole, large	1 dozen	2⅓ cups
eggs, whole, medium	1 dozen	2 cups
eggs, whole, small	1 dozen	1¾ cups
egg whites, extra large	1 dozen	1¾ cups
egg whites, large	1 dozen	1½ cups
egg whites, medium	1 dozen	1⅓ cups
egg whites, small	1 dozen	1¼ cups
egg yolks, extra large	1 dozen	1 cup
egg yolks, large	1 dozen	⅞ cup
egg yolks, medium	1 dozen	¾ cup
egg yolks, small	1 dozen	⅔ cup
fats, solid (butter, shortening, etc.)	¼ lb; 4 oz	½ cup; 8 Tbsp; 1 stick
flours	1 lb	3½ cups, sifted
fruit, dried, pitted, plumped	1 lb	2⅔ cups
fruit, dried, pitted, cooked, pureed	1 lb	2⅓ cups
fruit, fresh, cooked and chopped	1 lb	2⅓ cups
fruit, fresh, pureed	1 lb	1¼ cups
fruit, fresh, raw and sliced	1 lb	3 cups
gelatin, unflavored	1 oz	¼ cup; 4 Tbsp, granulated
greens, leafy	1 lb	1½ cups
herbs, fresh, chopped	½ oz	1 Tbsp
honey	1 lb	1⅓ cups

Volumetric Equivalents for Amounts of Typical Foods

Typical food	Weight or amount	Equivalent (approximate)
maple syrup	16 fl oz	2 cups
meat, cooked and finely chopped	8 oz	1 cup
nuts, chopped	4 oz	¾ cup
nuts, ground	4 oz	1 cup, loosely packed
oil, vegetable	1 qt	4 cups
onions, white, fresh	1 lb	4 medium; 2-3 cups, chopped
peas, green, fresh, in pod	1 lb	1 cup, shelled
pecans	1 lb	4 cups, halved; 3¾ cups, chopped
pistachios	1 lb	3¼-4 cups
potatoes, raw, sliced or chopped	1 lb	3 cups
rice, raw	7½ oz	1 cup
spinach, fresh, cooked	1¼ lb, raw	1 cup, cooked, squeezed dry, chopped
sugar, brown	1 lb	1½ cups
sugar, confectioner's	1 lb	4 cups
sugar, granulated	7 oz	1 cup
tomatoes, fresh	¾-1 lb, whole	1 cup, peeled and seeded
vegetables (e.g., carrots, celery), raw, chopped fine	8 oz	1 cup

All conversions are approximate. Weights have been rounded to the nearest useful measure. Weights and measures of specific ingredients may vary with altitude, humidity, variations in preparation methods, and other factors.